THE PUBLIC CITY

THE PUBLIC CITY

The political construction of urban life in San Francisco, 1850–1900

PHILIP J. ETHINGTON

University of Southern California

UNIVERSITY OF CALIFORNIA PRESS

Berkeley · Los Angeles · London

University of California Press
Berkeley and Los Angeles, California

University of California Press, Ltd.
London, England

© Cambridge University Press 1994

First Paperback Printing 2001

Library of Congress Cataloging-in-Publication Data
Ethington, Philip J.

Library of Congress Cataloging-in-Publication Data
Ethington, Philip J.
    The public city : the political construction of urban life in San Francisco,
1850–1900 / Philip J. Ethington.
        p.   cm.
    Originally published: New York : Cambridge University Press, 1994.
    Includes bibliographical references and index.
    ISBN 0-520-23001-9 (alk. paper)
        1. Political culture—California—San Francisco—History—
19th century.   2. Political participation—California—San Francisco—
History—19th century.   3. San Francisco (Calif.)—Politics and
government.   4. San Francisco (Calif.)—Social conditions.   I. Title.
JS1437 .E84 2001
320.9794'61'09034—dc21   00-048893

Printed in the United States of America

08   07   06   05   04   03   02   01   00
        9   8   7   6   5   4   3   2   1

The paper used in this publication meets the minimum requirements
of ANSI/ NISO Z39.48-1992 (R 1997) (*Permanence of Paper*). ∞

This book is dedicated to
Carol M. Mangione, M.D.

Contents

List of illustrations and tables		*page* xi
Preface		xiii

Introduction: The public city: American political culture in
nineteenth-century San Francisco 1
From republican liberalism to pluralist liberalism 2
The public city 14
The public city and urban political history 24
The political community 29
Subject matter and methods 35
Outline of the analytical narrative 38

1   The agony of authority: People, public, party, and power,
1849–1859 43
The people of San Francisco in the 1850s 47
Social class: Some preliminary observations 50
The antebellum public sphere 58
The agony of organization and participation 65
The agony of authority 77
Preliminary conclusions 83

2   Republican terror: The origins of Vigilante movements of
1851 and 1856 86
A brief outline of the San Francisco vigilance committees .. 88
Interpretations 90
Composition of the two committees 92
"Down in front!": Crime and the popularity of executions ... 97
The popular origins of the Committee of 1851 105
The case of the nonnativist Know-Nothings 112
Violating the ballot box; or, "A crime of the darkest dye" . 117
Conclusion 124

3 Though the heavens fall: The Vigilante movement culture of
   1856   128
   Patterns of the committee: Ninety-nine days   130
   Disgrace of the elected officials   137
   Disciplinary authority   143
   Symbols and sword rituals   145
   Scenes of political-cultural change   149
   Mutualism for San Francisco   155
   The uses of cultural authority   157
   "A people's party for local purposes"   161
   Conclusion   167

4 Race and reaction: Civil War political mobilization   170
   Outline of party conflicts   171
   David C. Broderick in defense of white freedom   173
   A funeral oration and partisan realignment   177
   Race and freedom: The Republicans and civil rights   184
   Race and reaction: The conversion of Henry Haight   188
   Emancipation and the reversal of party fortunes   194
   The political origins of racial mobilization   200
   Conclusion   206

5 The postwar reconstruction of the urban public sphere   208
   Women as orators, lawyers, politicians: Natural rights versus the
      masculine public sphere   209
   Election law: The partisan struggle to reshape the political community   218
   The shape of the urban electorate during the third party system   230
   The origins of mass communication at the dawn of an interest-group
      discourse   236

6 A language of politics in a politics of class: The Workingmen's
   Party of California   242
   Party competition and the origins of a politics of class   248
   Estimating class mobilization   260
   A language of politics   265
   The self-destruction of the Republican paradigm   276
   Conclusion: On the survival of the "mainstream parties"   282

7 The institutional preconditions of progressivism   287
   "A species of force": The contradictions of
      organizational party politics in the 1880s   288
   Origins of interest-group lobbies   299
   From communications business to political-culture industry   308
   The reorganization of group identities   320

The politicization of women   327
Political entrepreneurs and the Reform Ballot Act of 1891   336

8 Progressivism as the politics of needs: The mobilization of
   group identities   345
   Intellectuals and the city   347
   Charlotte Perkins Gilman and the political mobilization of women   355
   The home and the state   363
   Progressives and silurians: The reform matrix of 1891–1896   370
   The mind of an urban progressive reformer: James Duval Phelan   377
   The politics of municipal charter reform   387
   The woman suffrage amendment   398
   Conclusions   401

Conclusion:
A new public sphere and a new government   408

Appendix: Statistical sources, methods, and supplementary tables   419
Bibliography   427
Index   454

Illustrations and tables

PLATES

1	San Francisco in 1853.	3
2	San Francisco in 1891.	4
1.1	"The Plaza," or Portsmouth Square, 1850s.	60
2.1	The execution of José Forni, 1852.	103
3.1	The "execution" (lynching) of James P. Casey and Charles Cora by the Vigilance Committee of 1856.	146
3.2	Silver medallion of the Vigilance Committee of 1856.	147
4.1	San Francisco police defending newspaper offices, April 1865.	199
5.1	"The Glass Ballot Box."	220
5.2	The Chronicle Building in the 1880s.	238
6.1	San Francisco seen from the South-of-Market neighborhood.	258
6.2	Thanksgiving Day Parade, 1877, led by Denis Kearney and the officers of the Workingmen's Party of California (WPC).	269
7.1	The Hearst Building and the Spreckels Building, 1905.	318
8.1	Charlotte Perkins Stetson [Gilman], 1894 or 1895.	357

TABLES

2.1	Occupational distribution and relative risk estimate of joining the Vigilance Committee of 1856	94
5.1	Occupational composition of the San Francisco registered electorate, 1867, compared to census of 1870	232
5.2	Native composition of the San Francisco registered electorate, 1867, compared to census of 1870	233
5.3	Occupational composition of the San Francisco registered electorate, 1880, compared to census of 1880	235
6.1	Linear regression estimates of class and ethnic voting for Democratic and Workingmen's Party candidates and issues: 1867–1882	262

8.1 Multiple linear regression analysis of voting on the 1896
city charter   392

8.2 Multiple linear regression analysis of voting on the 1898
city charter   397

A.1 Population and rates of increase: San Francisco, 1848–1900   425

A.2 Percentages of population by sex and nativity in San
Francisco, 1852–1900   425

A.3 Native origins at eligible voters in San Francisco, 1860–1900   426

A.4 Occupations of eligible voters in San Francisco, 1852–1900   426

FIGURE

3.1 Frequency of membership applications per day to the 1856
Committee of Vigilance   133

Preface

This book is about the changing relationship between state and society in the United States during the second half of the nineteenth century, exemplified through a case study of San Francisco. It is a study of the changing institutions, practices, and meaning of democratic participation at the urban level of analysis. It began with the question "Who participated in nineteenth-century urban politics and why?" When I began this project I was rather surprised to find that, despite the accumulation of generations of scholarship on urban political history, we still did not have a satisfactory answer to this question. Despite the fact that nineteenth-century American cities were the sites of developments central to scholarship – class formation, race and ethnic conflict, industrialization, political organization and innovation, to name only a few – the interested reader could find only scattered looks at the nature, extent, and meaning of political participation in American cities. The great majority of works merely assume that most white males of all classes at least voted, that they belonged to political parties, and that a very wide range participated more broadly. There certainly had been no dearth of talented historians nor shortage of archival labor. Something more fundamental had prevented the conduct of detailed studies of urban participation. Most historians, it seems, thought the story was so obvious that no one needed to research it. A familiar story was repeated so many times that many assumed it had been proven long ago. That story goes like this: "The rise of mass political parties and the elimination of property requirements for the franchise during the Jacksonian era opened wide the doors of the American political system. As industrialization produced the great cities during the second half of the nineteenth century, masses of immigrants and workers pushed aside the middle and upper classes to enjoy the benefits of urban machine politics. Colorful 'bosses' traded patronage rewards to these needy urban masses in exchange for votes. The cost of such inclusive democracy, however, was corruption, waste, and inefficiency. That colorful old system first came under attack during the Progressive Era, and was eventually supplanted by the weak-party politics and welfare-state policies of the New Deal and Great Society." For reasons that are explored at length in this book, scholars working at the level of policy analysis first showed that this folkloric wisdom was deeply problematic. A picture of noninclusive, fiscally conservative, relatively professional city governments emerged that simply did not conform with the received portrait of broadly based democratic machines. We lacked a realistic sense of what the urban constituency looked like in the nineteenth century.

To answer that simple question, of who participated and why, I had to embark on a project of finding out who was "who" in the first place. What were the sailient divisions in society? How did participation vary across those divisions? And how can we assess the "why" part of the question? What, from the perspective of contemporaries, constituted a sufficient reason to participate in urban politics in 1850, 1870, or 1900? In addition, I needed to determine the influence of institutions other than the government, especially parties, the press, and voluntary associations. Researching answers to these questions eventually led me to understand where the folklore of American urban political history had originated: in the profound changes that took place in American political culture in the 1890s. And those changes were the product of an extraordinary course of political development that began in the decade of the Civil War. Most importantly, my researches led me to an institutional sphere that was neither "state" nor "society," but the arena of collective action that linked those two domains: the *public*. It was on the terrain of the public sphere that the most important transformations in American political culture were contested and completed. The most succinct statement of the findings of this entire study is as follows: In 1850 American political culture was characterized by a political conception of society; by 1900 it was characterized by a social conception of politics. The pages of this book explicate that transformation.

This book may be read as a narrative history, replete with coups d'état, political executions, duels, suicides, an apparent working-class political rebellion, "bosses," feminist leaders, sensational journalists, and millionaire reformers. I hope to have restored some amount of the excitement and sheer drama of the political life of an American city during the last half of the nineteenth century. But this is also a social-scientific study of political and social development through the historical interaction of three variables: institutions (including those of the state and those of civil society); participants (including masses and elites); and ideologies (from unself-conscious "discourse" to strategically crafted party platforms). In each chapter I attempt to show how the relationship between "state" and "society" was structured by these three variables, and how elite and mass participants gradually altered that relationship over fifty years, so that by 1900 a completely new political culture had emerged.

ACKNOWLEDGMENTS

Since I first conceived this study as a dissertation in 1986, I have accumulated so many intellectual and empirical debts that I fear for the day these creditors come knocking at my door. My thanks go first to my advisors Estelle Freedman and Barton Bernstein at Stanford University. It was their example, most of all, and their careful attention that made me believe in the value of historical scholarship. To my brilliant colleague Valerie Kivelson goes special thanks for helping me to hammer out idea after idea since the first day I approached this study. John Smail and Patty Seleski are also holding enough intellectual credits to ruin me if they want to. Over the years two scholars in particular have had more than ordinary influence on my thought. J. Mills Thornton III, a true Romantic genius, inspired me long ago and has continued to supply me generously with his incomparable insights. It was the highly original work of Terrence McDonald that first led me to ask the research questions that guide this book. His critical theoretical and empirical work on American urban political history has opened up the field for fresh research in many directions. I am also grateful to him for reading the entire manuscript, for invaluable criticism, and for warning me away from several serious pitfalls.

Teaching at San Francisco State University, Brandeis University, Boston University and the University of Southern California, I have learned valuable lessons from hundreds of students, to whom I owe a general debt. I hope to have done justice to the generosity of the many colleagues who have taken the time to read my drafts of chapters and then spend hours telling me how to improve them. William Issel, Michael Kazin, Barbara Babcock, Robin Einhorn, and Kevin Mullen gave me especially useful advice on the earlier chapters. Robert Chandler both generously shared his work with me and provided a valuable critique of Chapter 4. David Thelen provided an extraordinary critique of the sixth chapter. James Kloppenberg, Eileen McDonagh, James Connolly, Adonica Lui, and Mary Odem greatly improved my arguments in the last chapters. Emily Rader helped me to clarify the meaning of my prose throughout. I am also grateful to Bernard Bailyn and Susan Hunt for a very profitable year at the Charles Warren Center for Studies in American History at Harvard, which enabled me to finish the last chapters of this book. Many thanks also to Diane Glass, Amy Greenberg, Brett Flehinger, and Leslie Harris for their valuable assistance.

Without the assistance of archivists and librarians at several great libraries this book would have been impossible to write. I want especially to thank Jim Knox of the Green Library at Stanford, and Bonnie Hardwick of the magnificent Bancroft Library at Berkeley. The professional staffs at the Huntington Library in San Marino, the California Historical Society Library, the Department of Special Collections at Stanford, the Doe Library of University of California at Berkeley, and the Widener Library of Harvard have all kept me supplied with the only resources that count for a historian.

I owe a special thanks to my Cambridge editors, Frank Smith and Camilla T. K. Palmer, for their patience and enthusiasm.

To my family, Donna, Paul, Bradley, and Russell Ethington, I owe boundless thanks for their immeasurable support through the years.

And finally, I can only say to Carol Mangione that my personal and intellectual debt to her is too great ever to be repaid.

The public city: American political culture in nineteenth-century San Francisco

Several Spanish soldiers and their families, under the leadership of the Franciscan Father Francisco Palóu, founded the town we know as San Francisco in 1776 on a site inhabited for several centuries by ancestors of the Costanoan people.[1] San Francisco, inhabited by only a few hundred persons for many decades, became part of the Federal Republic of Mexico when the Mexicans won their independence from Spain in 1821. The Mexicans of California, known as Californios, lost this independence when, under the orders of Commodore John D. Sloat, Captain John Montgomery raised the U.S. flag over an undefended San Francisco in July 1846. Californios in Los Angeles fought until January of 1847 before formally surrendering their territory to the United States.[2]

California at that moment was inhabited by perhaps one hundred thousand free native people, five thousand former Mexican citizens, and several thousand native people who worked in the status of debt peonage for a handful of Californio rancheros.[3] American expansionism, culminating in the conquest of the Mexican territories, would certainly have resulted in the gradual settlement of the nascent state by Anglo-Americans, but the accidental discovery of gold at Sutter's mill in January 1848, just days before the Treaty of

---

[1] Technically speaking, the bayshore site of the present city was a pueblo called Yerba Buena, and the first American alcalde of the town changed the name to San Francisco in 1846. "San Francisco," however, had been the name of the presidio (military fort) and the mission church (San Francisco de Asis) as well as the name of the Bay since the first Spanish settlement, and the name was commonly used to designate the entire settlement. John Walton Caughey, *California*, 2d ed. (Englewood Cliffs, N.J.: Prentice-Hall, 1953), 131–2; Andrew Rolle, *California: A History*, 4th ed. (Arlington Heights: Harlan Davidson, 1987), 49–54.

[2] Rolle, *California: A History*, 149–63.

[3] Edward D. Castillo, "The Impact of Euro-American Exploration and Settlement," in William C. Sturtevant, ed., *Handbook of North American Indians*, vol. 8 (Washington, D.C.: Smithsonian Institution, 1978–), 99–127.

Guadalupe Hidalgo ended the United States – Mexican War, triggered a global human onslaught that catapulted San Francisco to the status of a major American city in less than five years. These people came primarily from New York City and Boston, but also from Western Europe, China, Eastern Europe, Central and South America, and Australia.[4]

San Francisco's population rose very rapidly. At the news of gold in 1848, the town numbered about 1,000. In 1849 alone 39,000 people disembarked at San Francisco. Annual arrivals, mostly bound for the interior, averaged more than 30,000 for the next twenty years.[5] The first surviving census, taken in 1852, reports 36,000 inhabitants; by 1860 there were 57,000. Compared with the size of New York City or even of Boston, which numbered 814,000 and 178,000 respectively on the eve of the Civil War, San Francisco was not a very large city.[6] But its rapid growth never ceased during the nineteenth century, and it remained the largest, most important American city west of the Mississippi until 1920, when Los Angeles finally surpassed it. During the Civil War decade, which saw the completion of the transcontinental railroad, the city's population nearly doubled, to 149,500 in 1870. By 1880 the city had almost reached the quarter-million mark, and by the beginning of the twentieth century San Francisco officially numbered 342,782 persons, the ninth largest city in the United States.[7] Maps of the city in 1853 and 1891 illustrate the geographical space inhabited by this growing population (see Plates 1 and 2).

FROM REPUBLICAN LIBERALISM TO PLURALIST LIBERALISM

In the midst of the European revolutions of 1848 and the triumph of liberal political economy throughout the transatlantic world, news of gold in the Sierra foothills attracted men and some women from every continent and race to participate in a frenzy of primitive capital accumulation. Horace Greeley in New York told young men to

---

[4] Doris Marion Wright, "The Making of Cosmopolitan California: An Analysis of Immigration, 1848–1870," [two parts] *California Historical Society Quarterly* 19:4 (December 1940): 323–43; 20:1 (March 1941): 65–79; Bradford Luckingham, "Immigrant Life in Emergent San Francisco," *Journal of the West* 12:4 (October 1973): 600–17.

[5] Wright, "The Making of Cosmopolitan California," 341.

[6] U.S., Department of the Interior, *Statistics of the United States (Including Mortality, Property, & c.) in 1860* (Washington, D.C.: Government Printing Office, 1866), xviii.

[7] For all San Francisco population statistics see Appendix.

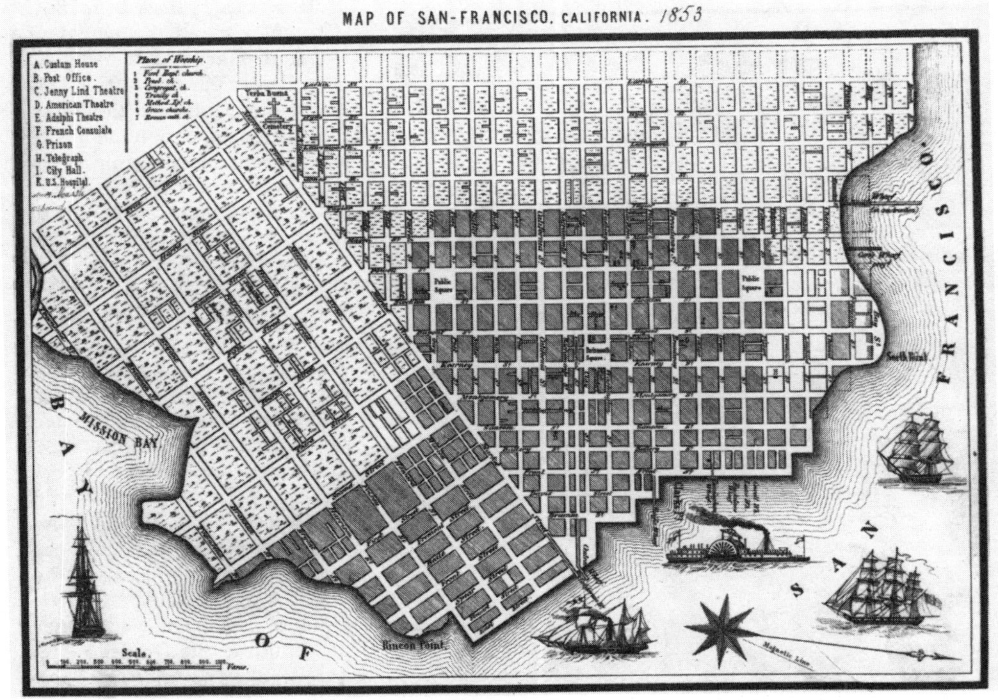

MAP OF SAN-FRANCISCO. CALIFORNIA. *1853.*

Plate 1. San Francisco in 1853. The map reproduced here illustrates the extent of the settled area (only the darkened blocks have been improved). With a population of about forty thousand and an area of about two square miles, this was undoubtedly a "walking city." The central public space, Portsmouth Square, known by its Spanish name, "the Plaza," marked the center of the new city. The Plaza was the address of the city's leading theaters, City Hall, the post office, and meeting halls. Courtesy of Bancroft Library.

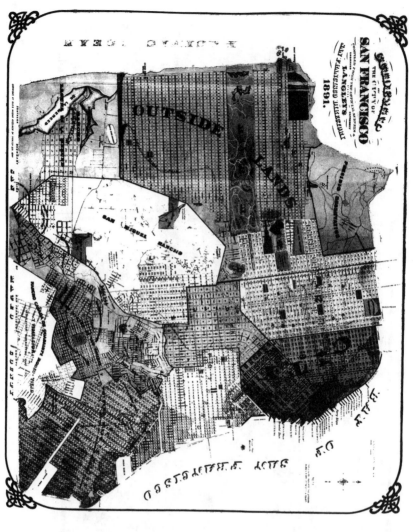

Plate 2. San Francisco in 1891.
This map shows the extent of
the settled area of the city by
1891, when the population was
about three hundred thousand.
The darkened area in the northwest corner of the peninsula is
the entire area covered by the
1853 map in Plate 1. The city of
today, far beyond that central
district, is clearly recognizable.
Golden Gate Park had just been
completed and substantial numbers of residences – primarily
single-family dwellings – had
been constructed in the newest
"suburban" districts (designated
as "outside lands" in this map).
These new neighborhoods began to replace stretches of wild
sand dunes: the "Richmond," lying north of the park, and the
sprawling "Sunset" lying to the
south of the park. At the west-
ernmost edge of the city, near
the mouth of the Golden Gate,
were the city's most popular
excursion sites, Ocean Beach,
the Cliff House restaraunt, and
Adoph Sutro's gardens and
baths, constructed in the 1890s.
Courtesy of Bancroft Library.

"go west"; labor recruiters in China's Guangdong Province (Canton) convinced young men to go east, to "Jiujinshan" (for San Francisco, meaning "Old Gold Mountain.") Leading the adventurers of small means were merchants from New York City to Hong Kong, who made San Francisco a world capital of commerce overnight.[8]

One might think that tens of thousands of actors had set about to dramatize the vivid phrases of Marx and Engels in their 1848 indictment of liberal capitalism, drafted at the very moment news of California's gold began to spread. Leaving "no other nexus between man and man than naked self-interest," these Argonauts seemingly plunged into "the icy water of egotistical calculation ... resolved personal worth into exchange values, and in place of the numberless indefeasible chartered freedoms ... set up that single, unconscionable freedom – Free Trade."[9] Naked, brutal exploitation of people and nature was unquestionably a central feature of San Francisco's first years, presenting an example of American liberalism in the purest form imaginable. The marketplace of San Francisco was for several years one of breathtaking, devastating competition, so fierce that even the ruthless scourge of the South, William Tecumseh Sherman, could not withstand the pressure of doing business there. A banker in San Francisco from 1853 through 1856, Sherman abandoned California, defeated by its economy and by the political rebellion of the Vigilance Committee of 1856, during which he commanded the state militia. His wife Ellen remembered their "entire stay in San Francisco" as a "terrible nightmare." "I can handle a hundred thousand men in battle, and take the 'City of the Sun,'" Sherman wrote in 1864, after the capture of Atlanta, "but am afraid to manage a lot in the swamp of San Francisco."[10] The real estate and commodities markets of San Francisco – not the

---

8   Sucheng Chan, *Asian Americans: An Interpretive History* (Boston: Twayne Publishers, 1991), 28; Peter R. Decker, *Fortunes and Failures: White Collar Mobility in Nineteenth Century San Francisco* (Cambridge: Harvard University Press, 1978); Roger Lotchin, *San Francisco, 1846–1856: From Hamlet to City* (New York: Oxford University Press, 1974).

9   Karl Marx and Friedrich Engels, "Manifesto of the Communist Party," in Robert C. Tucker, ed. *The Marx-Engels Reader* (New York: Norton, 1972), 337.

10 William T. Sherman was stationed in California from 1847 through 1849 before returning as a banker in 1853. Dwight L. Clarke, *William Tecumseh Sherman: Gold Rush Banker* (San Francisco: California Historical Society, 1969); Charles Royster, *The Destructive War: William Tecumseh Sherman, Stonewall Jackson, and the Americans* (New York: Alfred A. Knopf, 1991), 128–39. Quotations from pp. 133–4.

fabled Sierra gold mines – generated the great fortunes of the Gold Rush. For every fortune made, many thousands were lost.[11]

The radical liberalism evident in early San Francisco represented the extreme tendencies of late Jacksonian America. Yet this radical economic liberalism was enabled by an extraordinary political culture of republicanism.[12] Even this ferocious example of free trade did not drown every "nexus between man and man" in the "icy water of egotistical calculation." The settlers imported wholesale, like they did the shovels and stoves arriving in the holds of their clipper ships, the institutional and ideological cement that bound individuals together in civil and political society. The U.S. citizens who founded the political culture of San Francisco in the 1850s did so in public deliberation, by standards established during more than a half century of self-rule. Those standards elaborated the public context within which liberalism had to operate. Men competed in public to articulate a universal good that transcended individual gain and yet enabled it. Not just liberalism, but republicanism – that ideology of civic virtue, corruption, and tyranny, that great grandchild of the Florentine Renaissance, of James Harrington's *Commonwealth of Oceana*, and of Montesquieu's *L'Esprit des lois* and child of the American Revolution – framed the meaning of public life of early San Francisco.

Scholars have sharply debated whether republicanism, characterized by a "civic virtue" in the pursuit of the common good, or liberalism, characterized by "individualism" in the pursuit of self-interest, best typified political culture in the United States in the nineteenth century.[13] This book takes the position that American

---

[11] Peter R. Decker, *Fortunes and Failures: White Collar Mobility in Nineteenth Century San Francisco.* (Cambridge: Harvard University Press, 1978), 32–146.

[12] The concept of a "political culture" was first developed in Gabriel Almond and Sidney Verba, *The Civic Culture: Political Attitudes and Democracy in Five Nations* (Princeton: Princeton University Press, 1963). My usage of the term in this book takes the term more generally. See Carole Pateman, "The Civic Culture: A Philosophic Critique," in *The Civic Culture Revisited: an Analytic Study* Gabriel A. Almond, and Sidney Verba, eds, (Boston: Little, Brown, 1980): 57–102, and note 32 below.

[13] The literature on republicanism is now very large, constituting what Daniel T. Rodgers describes as a genuine "paradigm" (in Thomas Kuhn's sense) for the writing of American history. Daniel T. Rodgers, "Republicanism: The Career of a Concept," *Journal of American History* 79:1 (June 1992): 11–38; Rodgers's essay is the most recent in two decades of critical synthetic surveys of the the concept, beginning with Robert E. Shalhope, "Toward a Republican Synthesis: The Emergence of an Understanding of Republicanism in American Historiography," *William and Mary Quarterly* 29:1 (January 1972): 49–80; and idem, "Republicanism and Early American Historiography," *William and Mary*

political culture at mid-nineteenth century was *both* liberal *and* republican. I label this amalgam *republican liberalism* and explicate its content in detail through the early chapters. On the one hand, it would be absurd to ignore the rampant, self-interested greed that fueled the migration to San Francisco and the conduct of its economy; on the other hand, it would do violence to historical reality to ignore the powerful hold on contemporaries of criteria such as "virtue," "character," and "honor," whose meanings were at once romantic, neoclassical, masculine, Christian, and bourgeois.[14]

The coexistence of liberalism and republicanism is best introduced by Alexis de Tocqueville, who, like contemporary Americans, thought simultaneously as a liberal and a republican. He coined the term "individualism,"[15] but also carried Montesquieu's *L'Esprit des lois* with him as a model during his American tour. Tocqueville predicted in *Democracy in America* (1840) that "it must therefore be expected that personal interest will become more than ever the principal if not the sole spring of men's actions; *but it remains to be seen how each man will understand his personal interest.*"[16] To Tocqueville the site where "each man" came to *understand* his personal interest was the public sphere, identified by him as the various institutions of public life: voluntary associations, parties, the press, "public opinion," and local political office. Castigating "individualism" as a "feeling" that "proceeds from erroneous judgement" and "deficiencies of mind," Tocqueville argued that equality threatened to

Quarterly 39:2 (April 1982): 334–56. Statements contesting the "republican synthesis" with a defense of the view that liberalism best typifies American political culture include, most prominently, Joyce Appleby, *Capitalism and a New Social Order: The Republican Vision of the 1790s* (New York, 1984); idem, "Republicanism and Ideology," *American Quarterly* 37:4 (Fall 1985): 461–73, John Patrick Diggins, *The Lost Soul of American Politics: Virtue, Self-Interest, and the Foundations of Liberalism* (New York, 1984); idem, "Comrades and Citizens: New Mythologies in American Historiography," *American Historical Review* 90 (June 1985): 614–38, 644–9. I explore variations on the themes of republicanism and liberalism throughout this book; references to prominent works in these genres will be found in the notes to those sections.

14   My position is indebted to the portrait of a middle ground mapped out by Drew R. McCoy, *The Elusive Republic: Political Economy in Jeffersonian America* (Chapel Hill: University of North Carolina Press, 1980); and James T. Kloppenberg, "The Virtues of Liberalism: Christianity, Republicanism, and Ethics in Early American Political Discourse," *Journal of American History* 74:1 (June 1987): 9–33. Republican liberalism is merely introduced here; it is elaborated in following chapters.

15   For the early history and usage of the term "individualism," see J. R. Pole, *American Individualism and the Promise of Progress* (Oxford: Clarendon Press, 1980).

16   Alexis de Tocqueville, *Democracy in America*, abridged with an introduction by Thomas Bender (New York: Modern Library, 1981), 417. Emphasis added.

erase a consciousness of the commonweal in democratic societies. But the very processes of joining and participating in institutions, Tocqueville concluded, "remind every citizen, and in a thousand ways, that he lives in society."[17] Tocqueville understood that the ethical values operative in civil or in private life are shaped (or constructed) by the institutions of public and political life: "Thus political life makes the love and practice of association more general; it imparts a desire of union and teaches the means of combination to numbers of men who would otherwise have always lived apart."[18] Tocqueville brilliantly resolved the apparent contradiction between the pursuit of self-interest and the pursuit of the common interest. The promotion of the common good while holding public power was all the more important when everyone seemed to be pursuing the main chance.[19] To construct a liberal economy, Americans had to assemble participatory institutions of organization and communication, including parties and the press. Individuals acting through these institutions, in turn, constructed the meaning of the common activity of the polity.

This book traces the changing institutions and meaning of urban life from a period in which liberalism was modified by – indeed, framed within – republicanism, to one in which liberalism was modified by a consciousness of plural group interests. This latter formation I shall call *pluralist liberalism*. Pluralist liberalism describes the social understanding of politics familiar to twentieth-century Americans. It is a politics about social groups and their needs.[20] Whereas republican liberalism hinged ultimately on belief in a single, identifiable public good, one grounded in the ethics of political leaders, pluralist liberalism accepted the existence of multiple, or plural,

[17] *Democracy in America*, 295, 402.

[18] "Civil associations, therefore, facilitate political association; for, on the other hand, political association singularly strengthens and improves associations for civil purposes. In civil life every man may, strictly speaking, fancy that he can provide for his own wants; in politics he can fancy no such thing." *Democracy in America*, 412.

[19] Rowland Berthoff, "Independence and Attachment, Virtue and Interest: From Republican Citizen to Free Enterpriser, 1787–1837," in Richard L. Bushman et al., eds., *Uprooted Americans: Essays to Honor Oscar Handlin* (Boston: Little, Brown and Co., 1979), 106.

[20] On the politics of needs, see Daniel Bell, "The Public Household: On 'Fiscal Sociology' and the Liberal Society," *The Public Interest* 37 (Fall 1974): 29–68; and Nancy Fraser, "Struggle Over Needs: Outline of a Socialist-Feminist Critical Theory of Late Capitalist Political Culture," in *Unruly Practices: Power, Discourse, and Gender in Contemporary Social Theory* (Minneapolis: University of Minnesota Press, 1989), 161–190.

public goods, each grounded in the interests of competing groups in society. In the San Francisco of 1900 urban politics was no longer characterized by the public striving of private men for the honor and authority to define a single public good. Decades of political mobilization in the public sphere had hammered the social identities of race, class, ethnicity, and gender into the basic building blocks of society and politics. Politics was now activity practiced by men and women who cast themselves as leaders of class, racial, ethnic, and gender groups. The republican discourse about a unitary public good was no longer possible because truth itself had been pluralized as group interests became legitimate demands in the public sphere.[21]

Pluralist liberalism refers to a specific discourse about the relations between state and society that became dominant around 1900; it must not be confused with the theory of "liberal pluralism" that became dominant in American political science in the 1950s. Liberal pluralism, best exemplifed in the work of Robert Dahl, can in fact be understood as a logical extension of pluralist liberalism; it can be seen as the nether end of the spectrum that begins in this book with republican liberalism. In republican political understanding, there can be only one public good; in pluralist-liberal political understanding, there are many definitions of the public good, but there still remained the goal – typical among "progressives," – of identifying and promoting that overall general good. Liberal pluralists, writing in the shadow of the Second World War and totalitarian regimes, gave up on the search for a general public interest altogether and celebrated the ways in which a multitiude of interest groups canceled out one another's conceptions of the public good, resulting in a nonideological, pragmatic political economy free from radical excesses. Liberal pluralists claimed to explain the

---

21 Until "truth" itself was made relative and pluralistic by the end of the nineteenth century, "good" could be little else but singular. The classic statement is William James, *Pragmatism and the Meaning of Truth* (1907; Cambridge: Harvard University Press, 1975). For the connections between the philosophic and political transformations, see James T. Kloppenberg, *Uncertain Victory: Social Democracy and Progressivism in European and American Thought, 1870–1920* (New York: Oxford University Press, 1986). Although the term was not yet applied to politics by contemporaries, my use of the term "pluralist" is not anachronistic. John Dewey credited William James with giving the term *pluralism* currency, especially in the latter's *Will to Believe and Other Essays in Popular Philosophy* (New York: Longman Green, 1896); John Dewey, "Pluralism," in *Dictionary of Philosophy and Psychology*, 3 vols. (New York: Macmillan, 1902), 2:306.

American polity in terms of the *groups* that composed civil society and the *process* of resource allocation among those groups.[22]

Although it is beyond the scope of this book to trace the course of American political culture after the turn of the century, to place the findings of this study in the longer-term story of American political development it helps to observe that the liberal pluralist political science of the 1950s and 1960s was derived from the triumph of "group theory" in the 1890 to 1920 period, a triumph that occurred among both the general participants in the public sphere and the intellectuals creating the new social science disciplines. Foremost among these individuals was Arthur F. Bentley, who insisted in his *Process of Government* (1908) that "when the groups are adequately stated, everything is stated."[23] Bentley, representative of hundreds of contemporary intellectuals, activists, and politicians, merely articulated in an especially clear way an assumption that had become nearly universal by 1900. This pluralization of the common welfare by the Progressive generation is not only quite distinctive but also quite ironic because "progressives" of many stripes thought that their most important task was to heal the rifts that had appeared in American society as a result of industrial urban modernity. "It is the business of government," Woodrow Wilson would insist, "to orga-

22 In general, see John A. Hall *Liberalism: Politics, Ideology and the Market* (Chapel Hill: University of North Carolina Press, 1987). A founding statement of the modern theory of liberal pluralism is Robert A. Dahl, *Who Governs?: Democracy and Power in an American City* (New Haven: Yale University Press, 1961). For a critique of liberal pluralism as a normative, antidemocratic model of political science, see Michael P. Rogin, *The Intellectuals and McCarthy: The Radical Specter* (Cambridge: MIT Press, 1967); for a critique of the liberal-pluralist model in American urban historiography, see Terrence J. McDonald, "The Problem of the Political in Recent American Urban History: Liberal Pluralism and the Rise of Functionalism," *Social History* 10:3 (October 1985): 323–45; and for a general discussion see Stephen D. Krasner, "Approaches to the State: Alternative Conceptions and Historical Dynamics," *Comparative Politics* (January 1984): 223–46.

23 A founding text for sociology is Charles Horton Cooley, *Social Organization: A Study of the Larger Mind* (New York: Charles Scribner's Sons, 1909); for political science, Bentley, *The Process of Government* (Evanston, Ill.: Principia Press of Illinois, 1908), 209. An imporant treatment of Bentley as one of several group theorists is R. Jeffrey Lustig, *Corporate Liberalism: The Origins of Modern American Political Theory, 1890–1920* (Berkeley: University of California Press, 1982), 109–49. As Paul F. Kress shows, however, Bentley's thought went far beyond the articulation of a theory of "groups." He also sought to establish the theoretical framework of government as process. Kress, *Social Science and the Idea of Process: The Ambiguous Legacy of Arthur F. Bentley* (Urbana: University of Illinois Press, 1970); Bentley's framework reappeared in a simplified, empirical form, emphasizing the *group* theory over the *process* theory, in the postwar era with David Truman's *The Governmental Process* (New York, 1951). For a careful critique, see Michael Paul Rogin, "Nonpartisanship and the Group Interest," in Rogin, *Ronald Reagan, the Movie: and Other Episodes in Political Demonology* (Berkeley: University of California Press, 1987), 115–33.

nize the common interest against the special interests."[24] Indeed, leading studies of the Progressive Era from a wide variety of theoretical perspectives agree that a central problem of that period was the overcoming, or the integrating, or the advancement of group interests.[25] And it was in this period, Richard McCormick observes, that the "long-standing unwillingness to enact 'class legislation' recognizing the competing needs of different groups" finally broke down.[26]

The reification of social groups as legitimate political actors, and as the natural source of political action, reached its paradigmatic expression in Jane Addams's essay "Why the Ward Boss Rules," published in 1898. Addams argued that the notorious urban ward boss ruled not simply because he was corrupt, but because he faithfully represented the interests of his constituency:

> And if we discover that men of low ideals and corrupt practice are forming popular political standards simply because such men stand by and for and with the people, then nothing remains but to obtain a like sense of identification before we can hope to modify ethical standards.[27]

It was not the *discovery* of groups in society that marked the breakthrough of the 1890s, but the *legitimation* of groups in a pluralist ethics. James Madison, of course helped design the U.S. Constitution to contain group interests. Madison, however, did not approve of interest groups; he merely thought them a necessary evil, "sown in the nature of man." The noun that Madison used for a political group was "faction," which he defined as a group of citizens "united and actuated by some common impulse of passion, or of interest, adverse to the rights of other citizens, or to the permanent and

---

24 Wilson quoted in Richard Hofstadter, *The American Political Tradition and the Men Who Made It* (New York: Vintage, 1973), 330.

25 See, for example, Robert Wiebe, *The Search for Order 1877–1920* (New York: Hill and Wang, 1967); Morton Keller, *Regulating a New Economy: Public and Economic Change in America* (Cambridge: Harvard University Press, 1990); Thomas Pegram, *Partisans and Progressives* (Chicago: University of Illinois Press, 1992).

26 Richard L. McCormick, *The Party Period and Public Policy: American Politics from the Age of Jackson to the Progressive Era* (New York: Oxford University Press, 1986), 276.

27 Jane Addams, "Why the Ward Boss Rules," *Outlook* 58 (2 April 1898): 879–82, reprinted in Christopher Lasch, ed. *The Social Thought of Jane Addams* (Indianapolis: Bobbs Merrill, 1965). Quotation is from p. 133 in the Lasch edition; originally published in a longer form as "Ethical Survivals in Municipal Corruption," *International Journal of Ethics* 3 (1898): 273–91. The same argument, in much the same form, appears as the last chapter of Addams's influential *Democracy and Social Ethics* (New York: Macmillan, 1902).

aggregate interests of the community."[28] This last phrase neatly summarizes a central belief of the republican political discourse within which Madison and his generation operated, that there was such a thing as "the permanent and aggregate interests of the community."

This book begins with the Madisonian belief in a unitary common interest fully intact. Lincoln's "House-Divided" metaphor aptly characterizes the political culture of the 1850s. The United States could not "endure, permanently half *slave* and half *free*" because, Lincoln assumed, a polity that could not identify a common public interest was simply not viable. "I do not expect the Union to be dissolved," Lincoln told the Republican convention in Springfield that fateful day in June 1858, "but I *do* expect that it will cease to be divided. It will become *all* one thing, or *all* the other."[29]

This book ends with the belief in a unitary public interest in disarray. I have chosen to characterize the formation that emerged by 1900 as "pluralist liberalism" largely because of my focus on the ways constituencies have been organized in the public sphere. Some scholars have characterized the key innovation of the Progressive Era as the creation of "corporate liberalism," a phrase coined in the 1960s to describe the legitimation of corporate industrial political power. According to James Weinstein and others, corporate leaders at the turn of the century helped to reconstruct the American polity, including municipal charters, along the lines of the modern business corporation, stressing the values of organization, efficiency, and expertise over those of democratic participation. The theory of corporate liberalism does capture part of the new political culture that had taken hold by 1900, but it was only a part of the pluralist liberalism that made such theories necessary. Others included the Deweyan social-democratic strain in American

---

[28] Alexander Hamilton, John Jay, and James Madison, *The Federalist*, introduction by Edward Mead Earle (New York: Modern Library, n.d.), 54. John Patrick Diggins's argument that the framers of the Constitution "legitimated" factions rests on a misreading of the Federalist papers. Madison *recognized* factions in order to guard against their baneful effects. This is very different from *legitimating* factions, or interests, as the progressives would do a century later. See Diggins, *The Lost Soul of American Politics: Virtue, Self-Interest, and the Foundations of Liberalism* (New York: Basic Books, 1984), 9.

[29] Emphasis is Lincoln's. Roy P. Basler, ed., *The Collected Works of Abraham Lincoln*, 9 vols. (New Brunswick, N.J.: Rutgers University Press, 1953–5): 2:461. For a full explication of the political circumstances of Lincoln's speech, see Don E. Fehrenbacher, "The Origins and Purpose of Lincoln's 'House-Divided' Speech," *Mississippi Valley Historical Review* 46:4 (March 1960): 615–43.

thought, recovered for the Progressive Era by James Kloppenberg and
Robert Westbrook, and the "maternalist" strain among women activists, recovered for that period by Robyn Muncy and Theda Skocpol.[30]

The triumph of pluralist liberalism in the political public sphere
provided the background for the creation of what I call in this study
the "social-group paradigm" for understanding political development. In order to understand the lives of "the people" of the city
and to aid in the formulation of social legislation, Jane Addams
and many other social settlement activists produced their richly detailed "social surveys," empirical studies that marked an important
advance in the formation of the modern social sciences. These social
surveys in turn became the model for American "social history," the
historical study of ordinary people. Oscar Handlin's widely read
studies of urban immigration gave this tradition a liberal pluralist
casting in the 1950s. In the 1960s the "new social history" revived
the tradition and within this revival the great bulk of urban history
was researched and written. Political development in most of that
literature is treated, as it was by Addams and her founding generation, as the outcome of social-group processes. In reconstructing
the origins of the social-group paradigm in the emergence of pluralist liberalism, then, I am also carrying on an implicit critique of
scholarship written within that paradigm in recent years.

The transformation of the San Francisco of 1850 into that of 1900,
from a republican-liberal political culture to a pluralist-liberal one,
paralleled the transformation of the United States from a republic
to an empire. The neoclassical models for antebellum San Francisco were drawn from the Roman Republic; those for turn-of-
the-century San Francisco were drawn from the Roman Empire.
Symbolically speaking, the Romantic resonance of historic models
had been gradually drained from the city's political culture by the
1890s. Neoclassical references having devolved to the status of
superficial rhetorical dressing, they no longer carried the prescrip-
tive force they once had. Nevertheless, it presents a striking contrast
that public leaders in antebellum San Francisco treated their city

---

[30] Kloppenberg, *Uncertain Victory: Social Democracy and Progressivism in European and American
Thought, 1870–1920* (New York: Oxford University Press, 1986); Westbrook, *John Dewey
and American Democracy* (Ithaca: Cornell University Press, 1991); Muncy, *Creating a Female
Dominion for American Reform. 1890–1935* (New York: Oxford University Press, 1991). Skoc-
pol, *Protecting Soldiers and Mothers: The Political Origins of Social Policy in the United States*
(Cambridge: Harvard University Press, 1992).

like a polis, whereas those of 1900 treated it as an imperial city, promoting it as the Pacific metropolis for America's emerging global commercial and military reach. The European states that had defeated the republican revolutions of 1848 were now engaged with the United States in the nationalist contests that would culminate in the First World War. The Asian nations that had undergone merchant colonial invasions in the 1850s were now highly incorporated into the international systems of the European and American states. The pluralist-liberal political culture, at once relativist and evolutionary, legitimated and operationalized this international conquest.

Just fifty years after Captain Montgomery planted the U.S. flag in Portsmouth Square to signify the conquest of San Francisco, Vice-President Theodore Roosevelt broke the earth several blocks away, in Union Square, for the construction of a triumphal column to commemorate the sinking of the Spanish fleet and the conquest of the Philippines.[31] It took five conflict-ridden decades to bring about the transformation of San Francisco from its republican-liberal political culture to its pluralist-liberal political culture. The process was gradual, uneven, and very inefficient. The transformation from republican liberalism to pluralist liberalism characterized the whole of American political culture, but this book examines its unfolding in San Francisco. By focusing on San Francisco I do not claim that American political culture originated there, but that tendencies throughout the nation are as easily studied there as elsewhere, adjusting, of course, for regional variations on the dominant theme.

THE PUBLIC CITY

A central argument of this book is that American political development cannot be reduced to, or explained by, historical changes in civil society. Indeed, to a considerable extent the reverse has been the case: Social-group formation in San Francisco was largely the result of actions and institutions of the political public sphere. Developments such as the Vigilance Committee of 1856, the Workingmen's Party of California, and the reform charter of 1898 had

---

[31] Judd Kahn, *Imperial San Francisco: Politics and Planning in an American City, 1897–1906* (Lincoln: University of Nebraska Press, 1979); Ernest R. May, *Imperial Democracy: The Emergence of America as a Great Power* (New York: Harper and Row, 1961); Stuart Creighton Miller, *"Benevolent Assimilation": American Conquest of the Philippines, 1899–1903* (New Haven: Yale University Press, 1982), 129–218.

political, not social origins. These political origins are observable where participants engaged one another in rational debate about the governing relations of their state and society. The public sphere was structured by institutions, principally the press and political parties, and by spontaneous, uninstitutionalized crowds, speeches, and meetings. The meaning of political action in the public sphere was structured by slowly changing "discourses," or finite patterns of words and ideas, that can also be thought of as "scripts" for the behavior of actors on the political public stage.[32]

What exactly is a "public sphere"? My use of this term is derived primarily from the work of Jürgen Habermas, but also from that of Hannah Arendt. Habermas argues that the public sphere came into being in the late eighteenth century, when private persons came together to contest the governing relations of the state and society. It can be conceived of as the metaphorical space *between* the state and the world of social labor. The public sphere in the sense used here should not be confused with the state proper or with the "public sector," which is that portion of the economy controlled by the government. Neither is the public sphere the same as "public space," which is simply a geographic area like a park or a street in which persons may meet. The public sphere arose in the eighteenth century primarily through the vehicle of political journalism to constitute the independent realm in which criticism of state authorities became possible. It was the world of communication, constructed especially by the revolutionary bourgeoisie during the American and French revolutions, in unofficial institutions like coffeehouses, salons, and political parties, and in the media of speech, pamphlets, and newspapers.[33]

The substance of the public sphere is communication: "a realm of our social life in which something approaching public opinion can be formed." It also inscribes action: "A portion of the public sphere

32 The concept of political culture as a script is derived from Keith M. Baker, in Baker, ed., *The Political Culture of the Old Regime*, vol. 1 of *The French Revolution and the Creation of Modern Political Culture* (Oxford: Pergamon Press, 1987), xii. Individuals were constrained by these scripts, but not trapped. Improvisation led eventually to the rewriting of the entire script.

33 The principal work by Jürgen Habermas, on the theory of the public sphere, is *The Structural Transformation of the Public Sphere: An Inquiry into a Category of Bourgeois Society*, tr. Thomas Berger and Frederick Lawrence (Cambridge: MIT Press, 1989). For critical appraisal, see especially the essays collected in Craig Calhoun, ed., *Habermas and the Public Sphere* (Cambridge: MIT Press, 1992). My own use of the theory is stated in greater detail in Philip J. Ethington, "Hypotheses from Habermas: Notes on Reconstructing American Political and Social History, 1890–1920," *Intellectual History Newsletter* 16 (1992): 21–40.

comes into being in every conversation in which private individuals assemble to form a public body."[34] In a specific way, I have also drawn on the work of Hannah Arendt to conceptualize the public sphere as it appears in this book. Arendt's version of the public sphere is heavily grounded in classical understandings of "public" and "private." The "private" in her framework comprised the household functions of worldly production and biological reproduction; these were irrelevant to public life. The latter was the sphere of the polis, where men competed to achieve greatness and immortality in the production of the common good.[35] Arendt's rather nostalgic model is useful not because it describes the "reality" of nineteenth-century American political culture, but because it provides a bright window on the way male political leaders through the Civil War understood the division between public and private spheres. Arendt, the philosopher, presents a useful yet normative and ahistorical model of the public sphere, whereas Habermas, the sociologist, provides one that it is grounded specifically in the bourgeois era of capitalist market relations. The "private" sphere of the household was no longer ideologically irrelevant in the nineteenth century. Rather, women had acquired a visible, publicly acclaimed political task of raising virtuous citizens. That task proved the entering wedge for women's eventual transgression of the public–private boundary.[36]

Deliberative bodies like city councils or legislatures are but pale imitations of the critical discourse of the public sphere that needs to be the creation of private people free of state power.[37] The weak American state of the nineteenth century, however, frequently blurred such hard-and-fast boundaries. A citizen did not cease, once he (and later she) became an officeholder, to play a critical role in the discourse of the public sphere. Tocqueville, for instance, saw an interplay between the profusion of local offices and the pro-

[34] Jürgen Habermas, "The Public Sphere," *New German Critique* 1:3 (Fall 1974): 49.

[35] Hannah Arendt, *The Human Condition* (Chicago: University of Chicago Press, 1958), 38–78.

[36] Glenna Matthews, *The Rise of Public Woman: Woman's Power and Place in the United States, 1630–1970* (New York: Oxford University Press, 1992); Linda Kerber, *Women of the Republic: Intellect and Ideology in Revolutionary America* (Chapel Hill: University of North Carolina Press, 1980); Mary Beth Norton, *Liberty's Daughters: The Revolutionary Experience of American Women, 1750–1800* (Boston: Little, Brown, 1980); see also Nancy Cott, "Privacy," in *Companion to American Political Thought*, ed. Richard Wightman Fox and James T. Kloppenberg (Oxford: Basil Blackwell, forthcoming).

[37] Habermas, *Structural Transformation of the Public Sphere*, 83 and Chapter 13.

fusion of the print media: "The extraordinary subdivision of administrative power has much more to do with the enormous number of American newspapers than the great political freedom of the country and the absolute liberty of the press."[38] Tocqueville conflates constitutional political offices with voluntary associations in the common category of "associations."[39] Yet nonstate associations are the original home of the entity referred to in this book by the terms "public sphere" and "political public sphere."

It is also very important to distinguish the public sphere from public space. Public spaces in the nineteenth century, such as streets and the squares in front of city halls, did accommodate many activities of the public sphere, but the public sphere resides in communication, and language greatly overflowed the capacity of outdoor face-to-face assemblies to contain or mediate it. Public spaces and the print media overlapped as the core forums, or media, of the nineteenth-century public sphere. On the one hand, meetings were organized through newspapers, or were held to debate issues raised in newspapers, and on the other hand, journalists reported and commented on public meetings, in effect widening their audience and continuing the cycle of discussion. How the public sphere operated as the site of urban political culture is the story told in the following chapters. In this introduction, however, it is useful to establish concretely the outlines of the forums of the public sphere (being careful not to confuse the two phenomena): places of public assembly and the press.

The Spanish and Mexican periods of San Francisco had bequeathed to the city's American conquerors a central public square several blocks from the waterfront. Bounded by Washington, Kearny, Clay, and Dupont streets, its official name was "Portsmouth Square," after the vessel that carried Captain Montgomery to raise the American flag in 1846. San Franciscans of every language group, however, preferred the original European name for this space: "the Plaza." The Plaza actually formed a steep slope, at the foot of which, on Clay Street, stood the sandstone front of the three-story, neoclassical City Hall. Adjacent to City Hall stood the equal-sized, brick-faced El Dorado, San Francisco's largest and most prestigious

---

[38] *Democracy in America*, 411.

[39] Still, Tocqueville concludes that "if there were no newspapers there would be no common activity." *Democracy in America*, 409.

gambling house, saloon, hotel, and brothel. "What Boston Common is to Bostonians," one historian complained, "Portsmouth Square is, or should be, to San Franciscans – a place to be regarded with affection and deep interest."[40] Instead, it is today a small open space serving just one neighborhood in the heart of modern Chinatown. (See Plates 1.1 and 1.2.)

As the city grew in physical size, other squares became important places for large public meetings. During the Civil War, Union Square, at the foot of Nob Hill, become one such place, and later, in the 1870s, socialists and the Workingmen's party held large weekly meetings even farther out, on the empty spaces at the corner of McAllister and Market known as the "sand lots." But streets, as Le Corbusier once recalled, belonged to the pedestrians before the advent of the automobile. It was easy enough then to hold a large public meeting at any street corner.[41] Still, the demand for public space was so great that providing it in the warm, weatherproof indoors was quite profitable. Saloons provided easily accessible, masculine space for small groups engaged usually in the informal discussion of current events. In San Francisco, as in all other cities, there were hundreds of these from the earliest times. Some became headquarters for neighborhood-level political organizers.[42] Meeting halls, some with a very large capacity, played an important role in the structure of the urban public sphere. "Dashaway Hall," erected by the Dashaway Temperance Society in the 1860s, specialized in bookings for meetings, but theaters and music halls, like the Olympic and Platt's, also made a steady business of renting their space to voluntary, labor, and political organizations. City Hall, in fact, was originally the Jenny Lind Theater, built by the impresario Tom Maguire and sold to the city in 1853 when poor ticket sales made the imposing sandstone edifice unprofitable.[43]

40   "If all the historical spots in its neighborhood were properly marked, the Square could be fenced by tablets, and a part of its surface paved as well." Helen Throop Purdy, "Portsmouth Square," *California Historical Society Quarterly* 3:1 (April 1924): 30–44.

41   Le Corbusier quoted in Kenneth T. Jackson, *Crabgrass Frontier: The Suburbanization of the United States* (New York: Oxford University Press, 1986), 164–5. For the uses of the street, see Susan G. Davis, *Parades and Power: Street Theatre in Nineteenth-Century Philadelphia* (Philadelphia: Temple University Press, 1986).

42   Jon M. Kingsdale, "The 'Poor Man's Club': Social Functions of the Urban Working-Class Saloon," *American Quarterly* 25 (October 1973): 472–89.

43   Henry G. Langley, *San Francisco Directory* (San Francisco: Commercial Steam Press, 1861), 473; Lois Foster Rodecape, "Tom Maguire, Napoleon of the Stage," *California Historical Society Quarterly* 20 (December 1941): 296–301.

Even larger indoor space was provided by the "Mechanic's Pavilion," of which there were five between 1857 and 1906. Because of the rising value of real estate near the central business district, the owners of the Mechanic's Pavilion kept moving it farther from downtown, enlarging it as they did. By 1882, the fifth structure could hold more than ten thousand persons.[44] Churches were used not infrequently for public-sphere functions. In the 1870s the Baptists, under the leadership of Isaac Kalloch, built one of the biggest churches in the United States in the large, class-mixed, South-of-Market neighborhood. Called the Metropolitan Temple, it was modeled on Kalloch's earlier pulpit, the giant Tremont Temple in Boston. Tremont Temple was a theater converted into a church; the Metropolitan Temple was a church built like a theater, with a three-thousand-seat auditorium on the first floor (with standing room for two thousand more) and a one-thousand-seat auditorium on the second floor. From the pulpit in this "People's Church" the Reverend Isaac Kalloch gained the popular strength to win the mayor's office on the Workingmen's ticket in 1879.[45]

The greatest organ of the public sphere was the press. It is impossible to overestimate the importance of the press as the central institution of the public sphere. As scholars have repeatedly demonstrated, the active, participatory public sphere of the American and French revolutions through the revolutions and upheavals of the nineteenth century was literary as much as it was oral.[46] A profusion of pamphlets, lettersheets, broadsides, newspapers (morning, evening, semiweekly, and weekly), magazines, and books circulated the discourse of the nineteenth-century public sphere. The values and institutions of the early Republic had produced, by 1850, a nation of readers. American literacy rates, probably the highest in the world, had almost reached 90 percent by 1850 and would top it by 1860.[47] The urban commercial mass-circulation

---

[44] U.S., Work Projects Administration, *San Francisco Theatre Research*, Lawrence Estavan, ed., vol. 15, Monograph 27, *Theatre Buildings* [mimeograph] (San Francisco: 1940), 247–56.

[45] See Chapter 6.

[46] Eric Foner, *Tom Paine and Revolutionary America* (New York: Oxford University Press, 1976); Robert Darnton, *The Great Cat Massacre and Other Episodes in French Cultural History* (New York: Basic Books, 1984); Robert Darnton and Daniel Roche, eds., *Revolution in Print: The Press in France, 1775–1800* (Berkeley: University of California Press in collaboration with the New York Public Library, New York, 1989).

[47] Scholarship on American trends in literacy rates is summarized in Carl N. Degler, *At Odds: Women and the Family in America from the Revolution to the Present* (New York: Oxford University Press 1980), 308.

press had been evolving for almost twenty years by the time of San Francisco's founding. Benjamin Day and James Gordon Bennett in New York City had demonstrated in the 1830s that a market existed for low-priced daily circulations reaching the tens of thousands.[48]

Journalist-entrepreneurs seized upon the market for news as rapidly as readers from every nation stepped off the ships. During the 1850s an average of seven English-language newspapers were started *every year*, and no fewer than thirty-six foreign-language papers – published in Chinese, French, German, Spanish, Hebrew, and Italian – enjoyed at least a brief life. Competition was fierce because demand for news was high, a pattern that would continue for decades.[49] When the U.S. Census published its extensive survey of the periodical press in 1880, San Francisco, the nation's ninth largest city, had the third highest per capita circulation rate and, with its twenty-one dailies, ranked behind only New York City (which had twenty-nine) and Philadelphia (twenty-four) in the total number of papers in circulation. By 1900 the city's per capita circulation rate had increased still further. And despite the dramatic increase in the scale of the industry, there were now twenty-three dailies, two more than Philadelphia, a city almost three times as large. San Francisco produced, as later chapters will detail, one of the founders of mod-

[48]   The definitive narrative overview of the American press is Frank Luther Mott, *American Journalism: A History of Newspapers in the United States Through 260 Years: 1690 to 1950*, rev. ed. (New York: Macmillan Co., 1950). An important study, but one that does not explore the political dimension of the American press sufficiently, is Michael Schudson, *Discovering the News: A Social History of American Newspapers* (New York: Basic Books, 1978). Much more attentive to the political dimension is Dan Schiller, *Objectivity and the News: The Public and the Rise of Commercial Journalism* (Pittsburgh: University of Pennsylvania Press, 1981), 12–17.

[49]   The origins and evolution of the California press is incomparably chronicled in Edward C. Kemble, *A History of California Newspapers, 1846–1858*, reprinted from the Supplement to the Sacramento *Union* of 25 December 1958, edited and with a Foreword by Helen Harding Bretnor (Los Gatos, Calif.: Talisman Press, 1962). Included in this volume is a valuable index by Bretnor to the newspapers and editors chronicled by Kemble. The richest modern treatment of the political dimension of the California press is Robert Joseph Chandler, "The Press and Civil Liberties in California during the Civil War, 1861–1865" (Ph.D. diss., University of California, Riverside, 1978). The later evolution of the San Francisco press is covered in a remarkable series undertaken by the Work Projects Administration. Specific citations here are U. S., Work Projects Administration, *History of San Francisco Journalism* Emerson L. Daggett, Supervisor, vol. 4, *Frontier Journalism in San Francisco* [mimeograph] (San Francisco: Work Projects Administration, 1939), 14–20; idem, vol. 1, *History of Foreign Journalism in San Francisco* (San Francisco: Work Projects Administration, 1939), [mimeograph] i.

ern illustrated mass commercial journalism, William Randolph Hearst.[50]

"It ought never to be forgotten," E. L. Godkin wrote in 1865, "that a republic without a press is an impossibility, almost a contradiction in terms." Paeans to the press – especially among journalists – were frequent enough to become commonplace,[51] but Godkin's captured the structural political role of periodicals politics as communicative action: "The modern newspaper is the equivalent to the Greek agora, the only means possessed by the citizens of interchanging thought and concerting action."[52] By equating the newspaper with the physical space used both for market and for assembly in the ancient world, Godkin's observation indicates that political communication in the American republic under liberal conditions had overflowed the capacity of central squares like San Francisco's Plaza. Like the popular assembly, the nineteenth-century press was a discursive, deliberating medium. Each physical newspaper was read by more than one person, often aloud, in taverns, on the streets, or in homes. Editors constantly engaged one another in fierce debates, a practice indicating that a great many readers habitually read more than one paper each day.[53]

Newspaper owners and editors (they were usually the same person in San Francisco) were simultaneously political and business men and women. It is hard to find a political leader who had not at one time owned or edited a newspaper. Running a newspaper and running for office, in fact, were similar and deeply intertwined activities.

[50] S. N. D. North, "The Newspaper and Periodical Press," in U.S. Department of the Interior, *Tenth Census of the United States*, vol. 8 (Washington: Government Printing Office, 1884), 77; U.S. Department of the Interior, *Census Bulletin*, no. 216 (28 June 1902), 15; U.S., Work Projects Administration, *History of San Francisco Journalism*, vol 4. Emerson L. Daggett, Supervisor, *Trends in Size, Circulation, News and Advertising in San Francisco Journalism, 1870–1938* (San Francisco, 1940) [mimeograph]; W. A. Swanberg, *Citizen Hearst: A Biography of William Randolph Hearst* (New York: Charles Scribner's Sons, 1961).

[51] A poem entitled "The Press" by one Ebenezer Elliot, printed without comment on the front page of the San Francisco *Alta*, 11 July 1860, concluded with the following stanza: "The second Ark we bring: / 'The Press' all nations sing; / What can they less? / O! pallid want; O! labor stark; / Behold, we bring the second Ark – / The Press! The Press! The Press!"

[52] E. L. Godkin, "The Newspaper and the Reader," *Nation*, 10 August 1865, 165–6, cited in Schiller, *Objectivity and the News*, 74.

[53] "It may be assumed," writes S. N. D. North, "that every paper published and circulated is read by an average of at least two persons, the majority of those issued penetrating into families numbering from three to four persons." *Newspaper and Periodical Press*, 78.

Since the rise of the commercial press, newspapers had relied heavily on street sales for business. This gave editors a daily interest in finding a larger audience and in identifying popular issues.[54] Because newspapers were, as Godkin pointed out, the media of republican communication, a candidate or anyone else interested in reaching the public absolutely depended upon access to the press. Running a newspaper, then, was simply part of the political modus vivendi, but it was not merely a means of expressing the positions of the major political parties.

Even well into the Progressive Era and the rise of professional, "objective" journalism, editors had no fear of partisanship, in any sense of that term.[55] The partisanship of the press, in fact, bears comment. In the scholarship on newspapers, it has been common to distinguish between the "party" press of the mid-nineteenth century and the "independent" press of the Progressive Era.[56] Any close scrutiny of the press from the Jacksonian era to the First World War, however, causes such neat categories to disintegrate. Bennett founded his *Herald* on the principle of independence from party, but he took intense partisan stands on political issues of banking and labor, among many others. When Frederic Hudson published his history of journalism in the United States in 1873, he labeled the entire period from 1835 to 1872 as that of the "Independent Press."[57] Certainly, many principal papers served as loyal party organs. The San Francisco *Chronicle* was always Republican, and the *Examiner* was nearly always Democratic.[58] But newspapers were also business enterprises with valuable advertising space to sell. The profitability of a party association had to be weighed against the profitability of an independence that enabled an editor to switch stands rapidly rather than share the fate of a party out of power. The city's leading newspaper from 1849 through the 1870s, the *Alta California*, adopted this latter strategy and remained remarkably independent during its entire forty-two-year lifespan.[59]

---

54 Schiller, *Objectivity and the News*, 2–75.
55 Cf. Michael Schudson, *Discovering the News*.
56 Mott, *American Journalism*, 411–15.
57 *Journalism in the United States, from 1690 to 1872* (New York: Harper and Bros. 1873), 428–769.
58 See discussions in following chapters.
59 Kemble appropriately called his *Alta California* "the Mother of Newspapers" in California. A long string of editors and owners maintained its trenchant independence from the first

In no single decade can one point to a decisive shift in the kind of journalism practiced; sensationalism, partisanship, and commericalism typified the entire period, although in different measures. Very important, albeit incremental and disjointed, developments did take place, however, in the structure and content of printed communication. Change in the sheer scale of the newspaper enterprise is the most impressive. San Francisco's first newspapers were printed on hand-operated single-platen presses that had advanced very little technologically since the days of Gutenberg. A substantial daily newspaper could be established for as little as a few hundred dollars and with as small a staff as six. Such low start-up costs undoubtedly contributed to the large number of papers in the early years. The introduction of industrial technology, however, steepened the barriers to entering the newspaper business and, simultaneously, the barriers to reaching a public. Already by 1849 the New York *Sun* had sold for $250,000. The most advanced press of the Civil War era, the Hoe "lightning" press, cost more than $20,000. When the *Evening Bulletin* installed one of Hoe & Company's "web perfecting" steam-driven presses in 1877, capable of printing both sides of a continuous roll of paper, its maximum output had reached 18,000 folded copies per hour. Little more than a decade later, William Randolph Hearst invested an enormous sum in two giant Hoe presses – which he named "Monarch" and "Jumbo" – capable of producing 576,000 papers per hour.[60]

As newspaper companies expanded their circulations, they also built the tallest buildings in the cities that they served. In a construction competition repeated in New York City, Philadelphia, Boston, and San Francisco, publishers believed that they had to symbolize

issue on 4 January 1849 through the last, of 2 June 1891. The founding proprietor-editors were Edward Gilbert, Edward C. Kemble, and G. C. Hubbard, "all practical printers, and natives of one district in Northern New York," in Kemble's words. The "salutary," or statement of purpose, in the first issue reads: "This press will be independent of all parties, cliques, and persons. The cause which it will assert is the cause of California – the interests which it will endeavor to advance are the interests of California." Kemble, *History of California Newspapers*, 88–9. As this book should make clear, that pledge was roughly adhered to for decades. The valedictory editorial of the *Alta* expresses the regret that the kind of principled political independence it had maintained was now eclipsed by the commercial consumer independence of William Randolph Hearst. "Finis," *Alta* 2 June 1891.

60 U.S., Work Projects Administration, *History of San Francisco Journalism*, vol. 6, Charles Holmes and Isom Shepard, *History of the Physical Growth and Technological Advance of the San Francisco Press* (San Francisco, 1940) [mimeograph], 109.

their paper's dominance with the edifice that housed their enterprise. San Francisco's first tall newspaper buildings of the 1870s
were surpassed when Michael de Young built the city's first steel-
framed skyscraper for the *Chronicle* in 1890. Not to be outdone,
Claus Spreckels built the twenty-five-story *Call* building across Market Street. (see Plates 5.2 and 7.1). From the Plaza of the 1850s to
these skyscrapers of 1900, the structures of communication shaped
the conduct and the content of the public sphere.

THE PUBLIC CITY AND URBAN POLITICAL HISTORY

The ultimate victory of the pluralist-liberal language and practice of
social groups over the republican-liberal language and practice of
politics took place in the public sphere; it was the human product
of public political contestation and not the natural outcome of socioeconomic change. This, a central thesis of the present study, needs
to be further developed by distinguishing the approach of this book
from that of the studies of urban politics on which it builds.

In his study of Philadelphia, *The Private City* (1968), Sam Bass Warner, Jr., coined the term "privatism" as a label for what he claimed
to be the "American tradition," under which "the first purpose of
the citizen is the private search for wealth; the goal of the city is to
be a community of private money makers." Warner argued that the
"twentieth-century failure of urban America to create a humane environment" was "the story of an enduring tradition of privatism in a
changing world."[61] Warner's formulation has a solid kernel of truth.
Liberal private property relations have indeed stood at the center of
American urban development. Surrounding those private property
relations, however, has been a thick and changing political culture,
in which the meaning of private interests has been continually
reconstructed. The "privatism" thesis needs to be modified by
Tocqueville's admonition to discover "how each man will understand his personal interest."[62] This book argues that the story of political change is not reducible to the story of social change; that the
institutions of the state and of the public sphere were relatively
autonomous from the "social base"; and that the public sphere

---

[61]   Sam Bass Warner, Jr., *The Private City: Philadelphia in Three Periods of Growth* (Philadelphia:
      University of Pennsylvania Press, 1968), x–xi.
[62]   Tocqueville, *Democracy in America*, 417.

is every bit as important to reconstruct historically as the private. Indeed, the meaning of the "private" is much broader in this study than just "private property."[63]

Warner's *Private City* is a representative work within a body of scholarship that stretches back to the social surveys conducted by the settlement house activists beginning in the 1890s. The social-survey approach to urban studies has the tendency to portray political institutions and political behavior as epiphenomenal, or dependent upon, changes in civil society.[64] In recent years sociologists, political scientists, and a handful of historians have created an alternative framework, dubbed the "new institutionalism," which emphasizes "the relative autonomy of political institutions, possibilities for inefficiency in history, and the importance of symbolic action to an understanding of history."[65] Historians working within the new institutionalist approach have recently written studies of urban politics that treat the institutions of the state as relatively autonomous from the social base. As Richard L. McCormick puts it, we need to "ask political questions" about political life, "recognizing that nineteenth-century parties led semi-autonomous lives – independent, in

63   For a sampling of the diverse social meanings of privacy, see Samuel D. Warren and Louis D. Brandeis, "The Right to Privacy," *Harvard Law Review* 4:5 (December 15, 1890): 193-220; Cott, "Privacy"; and Jean Bethke Elshtain, *Public Man, Private Woman: Women and Social and Political Thought* (Princeton, N.J.: Princeton University Press, 1981); the question of public and private property in the law of municipal corporations is treated with great subtlety in Hendrik Hartog, *Public Property and Private Power: The Corporation of the City of New York in American Law, 1730–1870* (Ithaca, N.Y.: Cornell University Press, 1983).

64   Geoff Eley and Keith Nield, "Why Does Social History Ignore Politics?" *Social History* 5:2 (May 1980): 249-71.

65   James G. March and Johan P. Olsen, "The New Institutionalism: Organizational Factors in Political Life," *American Political Science Review* 78 (1984): 734. For all the attention given to "politics," leading up to the rebellion of the "new social history" in the 1960s, it is ironic, as Stephen Krasner observed in 1984, that "from the late 1950s until the mid-1970s, the term state virtually disappeared from the professional academic lexicon." Krasner, "Approaches to the State: Alternative Conceptions and Historical Dynamics," *Comparative Politics* (January 1984): 223. "States matter," Theda Skocpol writes, "because their organizational configurations, along with their overall patterns of activity, affect political culture, encourage some kinds of group formation and collective political actions (but not others), and make possible the raising of certain political issues (but not others). "Bringing the State Back In: Strategies of Analysis in Current Research," in Peter B. Evans, Dietrich Rueschemeyer, and Theda Skocpol, eds., *Bringing the State Back In* (Cambridge: Cambridge University Press, 1985), 21. This approach does not entail replacing an older social determinism with a newer political determinism. Rogers M. Smith suggests that we "stress how background structures *shape* values and interests, not to speak as if they have interests of their own." Rogers M. Smith, "Political Jurisprudence, the New Institutionalism, and the Future of Public Law," *American Political Science Review* 82:1 (March 1988): 100.

significant ways, of the social conditions out of which they came."[66] Michael Hanagan writes that "class consciousness cannot be separated from the political structures which give it form and meaning."[67]

Possibly the largest obstacle to overcome when studying the operation of political life in the nineteenth century is the image of corrupt party "machines" run by nonideological "bosses" who dispensed city jobs, turkeys, and coal to needy constituents in return for votes.[68] This image, promoted first by reformers in the 1870 overthrow of "Boss" William Marcy Tweed in New York City, was given intellectual authority in James Bryce's *American Commonwealth* (1888) when he pronounced his much-quoted verdict that American cities are the one "conspicuous failure" of American political institutions. The boss/machine model of nineteenth-century urban politics gained greatest popularity during the Cold War, when "bosses" like Boston's James Michael Curley were celebrated in works of history and in novels as pragmatic forerunners of the welfare state.[69]

By asking political questions about political history, several scholars, including Jon Teaford, Terrence McDonald, and Robin Ein-

---

[66] Richard L. McCormick, "The Social Analysis of American Political History – After Twenty Years," in McCormick, *The Party Period and Public Policy*, 137–8.

[67] Michael Hanagan, "Response to Sean Wilentz, 'Against Exceptionalism: Class Consciousness and the American Labor Movement, 1790–1920,'" *International Labor and Working Class History* 26 (Fall 1984): 36; Amy Bridges carries this line of research to its logical but startling conclusion, asserting that "in a complex society, community does not come naturally, but is a product of politics." Amy Bridges, *A City in the Republic: Antebellum New York and the Origins of Machine Politics* (Cambridge, U.K.: Cambridge University Press, 1984), 3; and Bridges, "Becoming American: The Working Classes in the United States before the Civil War," in *Working-Class Formation: Nineteenth-Century Patterns in Western Europe and the United States*, ed. Ira Katznelson and Aristide Zolberg (Princeton, N.J.: Princeton University Press, 1986), 157–96. Richard Oestreicher makes a similar case in "Urban Working-Class Political Behavior and Theories of American Electoral Politics, 1870–1940," *Journal of American History* 74:4 (March 1988): 1257–86.

[68] "The machine has existed because of the very large numbers of dependent or semidependent people who have been found in the modern American city, and because it has been better able to respond quickly and directly to their needs." John M. Allswang, *Bosses, Machines, and Urban Voters: An American Symbiosis* (Port Washington, N.Y., 1977), 150. See also Charles N. Glaab and A. Theodore Brown, eds., *A History of Urban America*, 3d ed. (New York: Macmillan Publishing Co., 1983), 206–28.

[69] The classic historical work presenting this point of view is Oscar Handlin, *The Uprooted* (Boston: Little Brown, 1951); in sociology, the model is Robert K. Merton, "The Latent Functions of the Machine," in Merton, *Social Theory and Social Structure: Toward the Codification of Theory and Research* (Glencoe, Ill.: Free Press, 1949); in fiction, Edwin O'Connor, *The Last Hurrah* (Boston: Little, Brown, 1956).

horn, have successfully challenged the centrality of machines to the study of urban politics, especially for the period before the 1920s. Teaford directly challenges Bryce's verdict of "conspicuous failure" by demonstrating that municipal fire, park, sanitation, and education departments in most major American cities were run by career professionals who were relatively autonomous from party organizations. Systematic analysis throws into question the very idea that urban political "machines" were widespread at all. Brown and Halaby's survey of more than forty cities shows that centralized party organizations that actually maintained a grip on urban political office may have appeared in most cities, but only sporadically. The heyday of such machines did not arrive until after 1920. In San Francisco during the period covered by this book, 1850 to 1900, a machine-style party organization controlled access to city government for only one period, from 1882 to 1891. The work of McDonald and Einhorn specifically refutes the most basic claim of the machine model: that urban politicians stayed in power through a nonideological distribution of government patronage to needy voters. McDonald's study of fiscal policy in San Francisco shows that nineteenth-century urban rulers were not nonideological; they operated within powerful ideological boundaries of fiscal conservatism. The so-called "bosses" in San Francisco were loathe to spend money or to raise taxes. Einhorn's study of Chicago shows clearly that municipal government revolved around property owners and not immigrant masses looking for expensive social services. Even so traditional a bastion of party patronage as the city police department was, in San Francisco, free from party manipulation long before the reformers arrived in the seat of power in the 1890s.[70]

Some of the best scholarship in recent political science has relied on the unwarranted assumption that city governments stayed in

[70] David P. Thelen, "Urban Politics: Beyond Bosses and Reformers," *Reviews in American History* 7 (1979): 406–12; Jon Teaford, *"Finis* for Tweed and Steffens: Rewriting the History of Urban Rule," *Reviews in American History* 10 (1982) 133–49; M. Craig Brown and Charles N. Halaby, "Machine Politics in America, 1870–1945," *Journal of Interdisciplinary History* 17:3 (Winter 1987): 587–612; Terrence J. McDonald, *The Parameters of Urban Fiscal Policy: Socioeconomic Change and Political Culture in San Francisco, 1860–1906* (Berkeley: University of California Press, 1986); Terrence J. McDonald and Sally K. Ward, eds., *The Politics of Urban Fiscal Policy* (Beverly Hills, 1984); Robin Einhorn, *Property Rules: Political Economy in Chicago, 1833–1872* (Chicago: University of Chicago Press, 1991); Jon Teaford, *The Unheralded Triumph: City Government in America. 1870–1900* (Baltimore, 1984); Philip J. Ethington, "Vigilantes and the Police: The Creation of a Professional Police Bureaucracy in San Francisco, 1847–1900," *Journal of Social History* 21:2 (Winter 1987): 197–228.

power by dispensing patronage, to develop institutional models of political development and social change.[71] This book was originally planned to reconstruct the sources of political participation without relying on the dubious machine model.[72] The following chapters, then, are informed by the new institutionalist scholarship stressing the relative independence of political development from social development and by a rejection of the belief that machines are the central story in a city's political history.

This book draws heavily on the scholarship from the social-historical tradition. The empirical wealth of that literature has enabled me to explore questions not previously addressed about the mobilization of constituencies in the public sphere.[73] This is not an economic history of San Francisco, although the operation and performance of the market is a key element of my analytical narrative. Indeed, this study would have been quite impossible without the large corpus of histories, such as the massive "works" of Hubert Howe Bancroft written about San Francisco, and California, almost since the founding of the city itself.[74] Recent histories of San Francisco,

---

[71] "Machine politics was of course not peculiar to New York City. The machine was the characteristic form of government in the cities of the United States; the boss and the reformer were the most prominent urban antagonists for nearly a century." Bridges, *City in the Republic*, 154; Ira Katznelson, *City Trenches: Urban Politics and the Patterning of Class in the United States* (Chicago: University of Chicago Press, 1981); Martin Shefter, "Trade Unions and Political Machines: The Organization and Disorganization of the American Working Class in the Late Nineteenth Century," in Katznelson and Zolberg, eds., *Working-Class Formation*, 197–276.

[72] McDonald's study of fiscal policy in San Francisco strongly suggested that urban political participation would need to be explained without recourse to the patronage theory, and with a central role for ideological persuasion.

[73] The social-historical approach to American city history may have underestimated the independence of political institutions, but it did produce a wealth of findings about the formation and vitality of class, ethnic, and racial consciousness, about the gendered nature of social life, about standards of living and the relative rates of occupational and geographic mobility, and so on.

[74] The first important history of San Francisco, co-written by three insightful journalist-politicians, provides important contemporary observations and data to any modern student of the city. Frank Soulé, John H. Gihon, and James Nisbet, *The Annals of San Francisco: Containing a Summary of the History of the First Discovery, Settlement, Progress, and Present Condition of California, and a Complete History of all the Important Events Connected with Its Great City: to which are added, Biographical Memoirs of Some Prominent Citizens* (New York: D. Appleton & Co., 1855); John S. Hittell, *A History of the City of San Francisco and Incidentally of the State of California* (San Francisco: A. L. Bancroft and Co., 1878). Nonacademic history reached its highest achievement in the thirty-nine volumes comprising the massive *Works* of Hubert Howe Bancroft and his uncredited employee-historians, including Henry L. Oak, William Nemos, and Frances Fuller Victor. These volumes are, as one historian later observed, both "an immense drifting miscellany" and perhaps "American historiography's greatest single achievement." To undertake the research and writing of these works Bancroft

especially on social mobility, ethnic communities, working-class formation, race relations, political development, unions, and other subjects, provided indispensable groundwork upon which this study builds.[75] Far from attempting to supplant all previous studies, this book begins with different questions and reconstructs the story of San Francisco from a very different angle – that of the public sphere.

THE POLITICAL COMMUNITY

To complete this introductory overview, we need a preliminary outline of the people who occupied the public sphere by participating in it. We can call the sum total of participants in the political life of San Francisco at any given time its "political community." Because any activity performed in the public sphere having the governing relations of the state as the object of discussion was a *political* activity, we must recognize as members of the total political community in its broadest sense not only those enfranchised few who cast ballots, but anyone who engaged in a spontaneous crowd action or street-corner meeting. Such events were as diverse as a women's rights meeting, as Chinese merchants protesting discriminatory laws, as African Americans holding a "Negro Citizens" meeting, or as a saloon argument over a newspaper article. The political community can be conceived as a pyramid with an extremely unstable base. At the top were the career politicians who organized the durable major parties. At the bottom were the disenfranchised who nonetheless participated from time to time in some political activity or, like blacks and women, who organized for the purpose of becoming enfranchised. Above these were the enfranchised who

assembled a huge library of rare books, pamphlets, and manuscript materials. Bancroft even began what is probably the earliest systematic collection of oral histories in the United States. These materials, which later became the core collection of the magnificent Bancroft Library of the University of California, were the indispensable foundation for this study of San Francisco. Walton Bean and James J. Rawls, *California: An Interpretive History*, 5th ed. (New York: McGraw Hill, 1988), 205–6; John Walton Caughey, *Hubert Howe Bancroft: Historian of the West* (Berkeley: University of California Press, 1946).

75 The founding work in the "new urban history" on San Francisco is Roger Lotchin's *San Francisco, 1846–1856: From Hamlet to City* (New York: Oxford University Press, 1974). Authors to which this study is especially indebted include Lotchin, Robert A. Burchell, Robert Chandler, Robert Cherny, Peter R. Decker, Steven Erie, William Issel, Michael Kazin, Kevin Mullen, Alexander Saxton, and Jules Tygiel. See bibliography and references throughout the text for the works by these authors.

participated in just one or two elections before moving out of the city, as thousands did each decade. Between the enfranchised occasional voter and the leadership was the core political community: enfranchised citizens who voted in more than a few elections, lived in the city for more than a few years, and comprised the stable "electorate." Because the enfranchised voters had an immense normative weight in defining the meaning of "political" during the nineteenth century, I shall discuss mainly that group who could and did vote as the "political community" in the pages and chapters that follow.

The political community thus defined requires careful explication as the center of political activity, something the following chapters will address. Crowd and other forms of political activity enter this study throughout, but the voters will dominate the discussion just as they dominated the agenda and participated in defining what was legitimate and illegitimate political activity and in defining who was to receive the privilege of the franchise and who would not. Historians have widely and for the most part uncritically acclaimed the high levels of voter participation in nineteenth-century America. It is essential for the arguments made in this study, however, to understand that voter turnout in San Francisco was always low during the nineteenth century, and that it was especially low in municipal-only elections, well before the Progressive Era and the much-studied dropoff in voter participation during that period. Terrence McDonald's analyses demonstrate these trends: "On average, 42 percent of men aged twenty-one and over voted for president, 37 percent for governor, 34 percent for mayor, and 31 percent for the board of supervisors."[76]

Urban voting was *not* a mass phenomenon, despite the effusive language among recent historians about the "virtually full mobilization of the electorate" during the late-nineteenth century.[77] Such language gives the false impression that nearly every man who could vote did so and that members of all socioeconomic classes asserted an equal voice at the polling booth. Exclusivity and white male supremacy were the unspoken goals behind the formation of

[76] Terrence J. McDonald, *The Parameters of Urban Fiscal Policy: Socioeconomic Change and Political Culture in San Francisco, 1860–1906* (Berkeley: University of California Press, 1986), 120.

[77] Quotation is from Paul Kleppner, *Who Voted?: The Dynamics of Electoral Turnout, 1870–1900* (New York: Praeger, 1982), 43; Michael E. McGerr, *The Decline of Popular Politics: The American North, 1865–1928* (New York: Oxford University Press, 1986). For more skeptical views of high levels of voter turnout, see McDonald, *Parameters of Urban Fiscal Policy*, 118–22; and Frances Fox Piven and Richard A. Cloward, *Why Americans Don't Vote* (New York: Pantheon, 1989), 26–63.

San Francisco's political community in the 1850s. In a freshly organized state already yielding uncounted riches from its soil and in its real estate, economic opportunity was very much a creature of political power. The state legislature had the power to govern access to the mines, and the city government had control of millions of dollars in rapidly appreciating "public" property to be sold at auction or otherwise transferred to "private" use.[78] White males, therefore, lost no time in restricting access to political power.

The California Constitution of 1850 limited the franchise to white male citizens who had resided in the state for six months and in the county for thirty days.[79] The lure of gold and the disruptions of the Taiping Rebellion brought roughly twenty-five thousand Chinese immigrants (almost all were men) to California by 1852, making the Chinese the largest single minority group in the state. The California legislature fortified the political and economic power of the white, Anglo male citizenry by enacting prohibitive "foreign miner's taxes" in 1850 and 1852, which effectively barred the state's skilled Mexicans and determined Chinese from the mines.[80] Blacks and Native Americans were barred from testifying in court in 1850.

[78] Christian G. Fritz, "Politics and the Courts: The Struggle over Land in San Francisco, 1846–1866," *Santa Clara Law Review* 26:1 (Winter 1986): 127–64; Bruno Fritzsche, "San Francisco 1846–1848: The Coming of the Land Speculator," *California Historical Quarterly* 51:1 (Spring 1972): 17–34. For the normative tendency to transfer public property to private hands, see Hendrick Hartog, *Public Property and Private Power: The Corporation of the City of New York in American Law, 1730–1870* (Ithaca, N.Y.: Cornell University Press, 1983), 101–42.

[79] The exact wording is "Every white male citizen of the United States, and every white male citizen of Mexico who shall have elected to become a citizen of the United States under the treaty of peace exchanged and ratified at Queretaro, on the thirteenth of May, eighteen hundred and forty-eight, of the age of twenty-one years, who shall have been a resident of the state six months next preceding the election, and the county or district in which he claims his vote thirty days, shall be entitled to vote at all elections." Theodore H. Hittell, *The Codes and Statutes of the State of California*, 2 vols. (San Francisco: A. L. Bancroft and Co., 1876), 1:43. Although by both treaty and the state constitution Mexicans were allowed access to citizenship and suffrage de jure, the numbers who actually became citizens and participated in politics was not large in the northern, most populous part of the state. The *Alta California* estimated in 1863 that the number of Spanish-speaking voters statewide was only 5,000, or about 5% of the total electorate. *Alta*, cited in Chandler, "Press and Civil Liberties in California," 47–8. Several upper-class Californios, such as the Vallejos and De La Guerras did take a prominent part in California politics, mainly on the basis of their "Spanish" identity. Mexicans who immigrated after the Treaty of Guadalupe-Hidalgo were de facto treated as part of the underclass. Albert Camarillo, *Chicanos in California*, (San Francisco: Boyd and Fraser, 1984), 13–30. Until 1870 the U.S. Constitution was silent on the qualifications for suffrage, leaving this to the discretion of the states. See Chapter 5 for a full discussion of election law.

[80] Robert F. Heizer and Alan J. Almquist, *The Other Californians: Prejudice and Discrimination under Spain, Mexico, and the United States to 1920* (Berkeley: University of California Press, 1971), 138–77; Walton Bean and James J. Rawls, *California*, 125, 127.

In order to ensure that Chinese were included in the official under-class, the California Supreme Court ruled in 1854 that the words of the 1850 act, "No Black, or Mulatto person, or Indian shall be al-lowed to give evidence in favor of, or against a White man," were intended to encompass the Chinese as nonwhite.[81]

The relationship in San Francisco – as elsewhere in the United States – between the membership of the political community and participation in the public sphere was a close one, although not automatic. Those excluded from the privileged status of "electors" (voters) contested their exclusion at the margins of the dominant public sphere. But by excluding women, blacks, and Chinese from the franchise, white male citizens intended to exclude them from the public sphere altogether. Denying them the ballot implied that they were to have no public voice and were to remain solely *private* beings. The Gold Rush, however, coincided with the first women's rights convention at Seneca Falls, New York, in 1848, and the grant-ing of statehood to California in 1850 marked the beginning of a sectional crisis that would evolve into the first civil rights movement after the Civil War. Thus, although white males were able until the end of the Civil War to avoid significant discussion of group exclu-sion in the political debates of the public sphere, they were forced to discuss those exclusions increasingly in the decades after the Civil War. And when they did discuss them, participants in the public sphere gradually constructed social-group identities as the most salient features of the political community. Stated another way, exclusion had enabled the white male citizens to construct ide-ologies stressing indivisible public interests; challenges to exclusion forced the participants to articulate interests as properties of groups.

Each chapter develops the story of changes in the political com-

---

[81] Leonard Pitt, *The Decline of the Californios: A Social History of the Spanish-Speaking Californians, 1846–1890* (Berkeley: University of California Press, 1966); Heizer and Almquist, *The Other Californians*, 92–194; Thomas W. Chinn, ed., *A History of the Chinese in California: A Syllabus* (San Francisco: Chinese Historical Society of America, 1969), 23–8; Linda C. A. Przybyszewski, "Judge Lorenzo Sawyer and the Chinese: Civil Rights Decisions in the Ninth Circuit," *Western Legal History* 1:1 (Winter/Spring 1988): 23–56; Alexander Saxton, *Indispensable Enemy*, 3–66; Bean and Rawls, *California*, 126–8. The 1854 California Supreme Court opinion overturned the conviction of a white man for murder on the testimony of a Chinese witness. Written by the twenty-nine year old Chief Justice Hugh C. Murray, it intended to close the possibility that Asians might be considered "white": "The same rule which would admit them [Chinese] to testify, would admit them to all the equal rights of citizenship, and we might soon see them at the polls, in the jury box, upon the bench, and in our legislative halls." Therefore "The use of these terms [Black, Mulat-to, and Indian] must, by every sound rule of construction, exclude every one who is not of white blood." *The People v. George W. Hall* 4 California 399. Quoted at pp. 403–4.

munity through time. Several dimensions of political participation are examined in each section of the book. These are the institutions (party, press, law) that structured individual choices; the demographic mobility that pulled and pushed enormous numbers of people through the city; the mobilization of voters to participate; the choices voters made when they voted; the formation of group (class and ethnic) voting blocs and group identities; the content of ideological appeals made by political leaders; the modes of communication between participants; and the challenges made by outsiders (blacks and women) to participate.

Two long-term patterns in political participation can be clarified at the outset. The first has to do with social groups and the second with the relationship between geographic mobility and membership in the political community. The presence of social groups in civil society is treated as an open question throughout this book. Using census manuscript samples, voter registration records, city directories, and social-scientific techniques, I have grouped thousands of San Franciscans by occupational stratum, native origins, ethnic stock, household status, and other sociological categories, for the purpose of testing hypotheses about the behavior of individuals and groups. The most basic question I have used these data to answer is, Does social class or ethnicity explain patterns in urban political participation? The most basic answer is that these group categories do not help us explain political participation in the early years, but are increasingly able to do so by the later years of this study. The most important finding, however, is that social groups as historical agents and political institutions are not separable. The process of political mobilization, beginning especially with the Civil War, made social-group identities increasingly salient in the communication of the public sphere. The antebellum decade was remarkable for the rudimentary formation of social groups as the defining criterion of individual identities. Those group identities that did profoundly shape individual self-understanding – race and gender – provided the criteria for exclusion from the public sphere rather than providing the lines of contestation within it. But within the circle of white male political citizenship, group identities of class and ethnicity mattered as yet very little. By the end of the nineteenth century, leaders in the political community claimed to represent whites, blacks, the working class, Catholics, employers, and women, and few doubted that these were principal divisions within society. The crucial issues are whether the discourse of the public sphere indicated that groups matter and whether individuals behaved as though they belonged to groups. By the end of this book, covering the period when the political culture of social groups and their needs had finally matured, it will be shown that social groups had become the fundamental building blocks of political activity, but that the groups themselves were still highly plastic. Skillful leaders in the public sphere could either mobilize groups or avoid that mobilization.

The other long-term pattern requiring some introduction is the relationship between geographic mobility and membership in the political community. High rates of population turnover characterized all American cities in the nineteenth century; researchers have found that as many as half of a city's residents would not remain more than ten years. A wealth of social-historical data has made it easy to categorize the urban transients. Stephan Thernstrom and others have shown that less successful members of the urban social economy were far more likely to disappear from the city from one decade to the next and that, conversely, those who persisted were better off and more likely to experience upward economic mobility.[82]

We can easily deduce from these sociological findings that individuals belonging to the lower occupational groups would vote in fewer elections than those of upper occupational status.[83] Kenneth J. Winkle has demonstrated this in his careful analysis of voting patterns in Ohio and Illinois during the 1850s. Using poll books, which recorded the names of individuals who actually cast ballots, Winkle shows that geographic persisters were wealthier, worked in higher skilled occupations, and were much more politically active. By casting ballots in many more elections per decade, these individuals had a disproportionately salient presence in the electorate. In terms of ballots, their presence was magnified far beyond their actual numbers.[84]

---

[82] Stanley Engerman, "Up or Out: Social and Geographic Mobility in the United States," *Journal of Interdisciplinary History* 3 (Winter 1975): 469–89; Stephan Thernstrom, *The Other Bostonians*; idem, *Poverty and Progress: Social Mobility in a Nineteenth Century City* (New York: Atheneum, 1964).

[83] See Charles Stephenson, "A Gathering of Strangers? Mobility, Social Structure, and Political Participation in the Formation of Nineteenth-Century American Workingclass Culture," in Milton Cantor, ed., *American Workingclass Culture: Explorations in American Labor and Social History* (Westport, Conn.: Greenwood Press, 1979): 31–60.

[84] Kenneth J. Winkle, "A Social Analysis of Voter Turnout in Ohio, 1850–1860," *Journal of Interdisciplinary History* 13:3 (Winter 1983): 411–35; idem, *The Politics of Community: Migration and Politics in Antebellum Ohio* (Cambridge, U.K.: Cambridge University Press, 1988). John Mack Faragher, in his study of a small Illinois town, shows how the same rift between a

Levels of voter turnout in municipal-only elections were about fifteen percent lower than in national-level elections in San Francisco from 1850 through 1900. The clear divergence between municipal and national levels of participation indicates the operation of what I shall call a "dual urban political universe." Political leaders attempted to mobilize voters on a wide range of issues, from the local property tax rates to the abolition, of slavery in the southern states. It stands to reason that propertyless individuals who circulated through San Francisco without developing strong local interests would be easier to mobilize on the basis of issues and loyalties that would be effective outside of San Francisco. The following chapters support this hypothesis. Local elections, if held separately, had only local issues, such as the tax rate and levels of expenditure, to attract voters who would logically be the most stable residents (mainly the property holders) of the city. State and national elections, however, gave free rein to the great national parties to mobilize the electorate on a host of extraurban issues, from nativism, slavery, Chinese exclusion, and Free Silver, to the foreign policy of Pacific imperialism, and of course through loyalties to the Republican and Democratic parties themselves. The persisters and the transients among the voters were sifted by occupation, property, and other resources. The manipulation of the dual political universe by political leaders is a recurrent theme in this book, although the results varied dramatically from decade to decade.

SUBJECT MATTER AND METHODS

The theoretical framework of this book, taking the public sphere of communicative action as the site of intersection between civil society and political institutions, has already been presented. A word on the subject matter and the methods is in order here. The history of San Francisco is filled with extraordinary people and extraordinary events. From David C. Broderick and James King of William in the 1850s, through Denis Kearney and Laura de Force Gordon in

minority of persisters and a majority of transients structured politics in that small town during the 1830s through the 1850s: "In the congressional races of 1836 and 1838, for example, electors from original settler families gave the Whig candidate approximately six in ten of their votes, while men from families relatively new to the creek voted in almost the same proportion for the Democrat. Because the persistent were usually owners, the transient largely squatters, this political division followed lines of economic cleavage." *Sugar Creek: Life on the Illinois Prairie* (New Haven and London: Yale University Press, 1986), 149. Faragher, like Winkle, uses poll books for his analysis.

the 1870s, to Charlotte Perkins Gilman, William Randolph Hearst, Adolph Sutro, and James Duval Phelan in the 1890s, the historian has the lives of an abundance of fascinating public figures to recount, to explain, and to fit into an overall narrative of San Francisco history. I attempt to do justice to the lives of these people by putting their actions into the context of their own understanding of alternatives (not ours), by giving them credit for actually believing in the ideologies they espoused (without taking their words at face value), and by conceptualizing them as creative beings rather than as representatives of some group or institutional interest (without divorcing them from their group or institutional context). The individuals that appear throughout this study, then, are presented not as colorful biographic digressions, but as actors who mediated creatively between structures they could not have chosen and goals that they could.

There are also several thousand individuals appearing in this study without names, in the form of "statistics." A major goal of this study is to recover the sense of creativity and of participation that ordinary people had in the building of a great city and its public life. By aggregating these people by social-scientific attributes, such as occupations, ethnicity, and marital status, I hope to have captured the ways that these different identities came to the fore in different contexts, under the influence of leaders or events that persuaded individuals to act sometimes in patterned ways and sometimes in unpredictable ones.

Concerning social groups, the role of San Francisco's Chinese presented a painful problem in the design and execution of this book. Given that so large a proportion of the city's population during the nineteenth century had been born in China and spoke Cantonese, it would have been ideal to construct this analytical narrative not only around the dominant (and dominating) English-language political culture, but also from within the Chinese-language political subculture. Unfortunately, the vast majority of primary and secondary sources necessary for such a task are available only in Chinese, a language I do not read.[85] English-language stu-

---

[85] For a survey of the historiography of Chinese Americans, see Him Mark Lai and Wei-Chi Poon, "Notes on Chinese American Historical Research in the United States," *Amerasia* 12:2 (1985–6): 101–11; Him Mark Lai, *A History Reclaimed: An Annotated Bibliography of Chinese Lanaguage Materials on the Chinese in America* (Los Angeles: Asian American Studies Center, 1986).

dies of the San Francisco Chinese community in the nineteenth century, furthermore, have only begun to appear in the years since I embarked on this book. Even where I have been able to draw on this recent work, the radical exclusion of Chinese from the ruling political culture of the city left the experience of that community beyond the scope of my narrative. There was almost no communication between these segregated populations on political terms. The Chinese of San Francisco play a role in this book primarily as the "other" against whom European and African Americans defined their own identities and privileges. Those looking for a multicultural history of the city with the Chinese portrayed as they should someday be, will not find such a narrative in this book. The public city of the San Francisco Chinese awaits its historian.[86]

I have chosen to narrate and analyze events by several criteria. The first kind are obvious ruptures in the political development of the city. The Vigilance Committee of 1856, the Workingmen's party of 1877–81, and the charter reform campaigns of 1894–8 are perhaps the three most significant such ruptures. Explanations of these episodes, fascinating narratives in their own right, are a basic requirement of any history of the city stretching from 1850 to 1900. Any model of urban social and political change must be capable of accounting for these episodes. From the work of the philosopher Josiah Royce on the 1856 Vigilance Committee through the numerous works by twentieth-century historians concerning these episodes, interpretations have served to advance one or another sociopolitical theory. The model presented in these chapters differs markedly from most accounts: It emphasizes public, political causes as the most important source of the ruptures and of the course these upheavals took.

A major objective of this book, however, is to reconstruct the "normal" operation of urban political culture in San Francisco, in order to find the general patterns not only for that city but for other major American cities as well. This has required close attention to

---

86 A modern and critical social history of the Chinese is now beginning to appear in such works as Sucheng Chan, *Asian Americans: An Interpretive History* (Boston: Twayne Publishers, 1991); Ronald Takaki, *Strangers from a Different Shore* (Boston: Little, Brown, 1989); Roger Daniels, *Asian America: Chinese and Japanese in the United States Since 1850* (Seattle: University of Washington Press, 1991); Judy Yung, *Unbound Feet: A Social History of Chinese Women in San Francisco.* Berkeley: University of California Press, 1995.

the periods prior to and following the periods of dramatic rupture. I discuss yearly and even seasonal patterns of political participation, along with a great many minor episodes of legislation, charter revision, and municipal elections throughout this book. Emphasis on locating the typical patterns in urban political life also has led me to abandon traditional periodization. This book begins with the last years of the Jacksonian era and ends with the first years of the so-called Progressive Era, endpoints justified by the criteria of the city's own history, beginning with the American period of the city's history and ending after the adoption of the reform charter of 1898. Taking up and leaving off the story in disregard of the traditional periodizations allows me to reassess the impact of the usually designated turning points, such as the Vigilance Committees, the Civil War, the "Great Upheaval" in industrial relations of 1877–89, and the Panic and Depression of 1893–4.

Finally, this study is about the linkages between state and society in the urban setting. It therefore privileges the opportunities for participation in political life over the occasions for legislative or administrative policy-making. Policy-making at the urban level, and at the state and national levels having a bearing on urban politics, plays an important role in this study. Any study of politics is largely justified by the understanding we gain from it about the performance of our political institutions. There are two main measures of "performance": inputs and outputs, or participation and policy-making. This book stresses the inputs, or the participatory dimension of political life, conceiving of the linkages between state and society as the way leaders in the public sphere mobilized citizens to participate in institutions of self-government.[87]

OUTLINE OF THE ANALYTICAL NARRATIVE

The chapters of this book simultaneously narrate and analyze the historical activities that took place in San Francisco's political public sphere from 1850 to 1900. The cumulative effect of that history resulted in the emergence of pluralist liberalism and the social-group understanding of political mobilization that characterized

---

[87]   I am able to focus my energies on the participatory dimension of urban political life in large part because of Terrence McDonald's superb study of fiscal policy in San Francisco; see McDonald, *Parameters of Urban Fiscal Policy.*

American political culture during the Progressive Era. Although no particular date can be identified as the point at which republican liberalism died and pluralist liberalism was born, a clear rupture in the historical process did occur during the Civil War and Reconstruction. This book, therefore, is organized around the 1860s as the midpoint. The first four chapters reconstruct the operation of the republican-liberal political culture; the last four examine the rise and triumph of the pluralist-liberal one.

Chapter 1 establishes the broad structural features of the city's political culture for the period covered by the first half of the book. Chapter 1 is an anatomy of the intersections between state and society in the antebellum public sphere. Analysis of the extremely fluid composition of the population reveals that modern sociological categories can be applied only heuristically. Capturing the contemporary understanding of social categories requires a framework that is ethical and characterological, one that is knowable only in relation to the construction of identities in the public sphere. The theatrical operation of that public sphere is explained as a "small republic," structured through a severely gendered division between public and private spheres. The final two sections of Chapter 1 explain the agony of organization, participation, and authority on a neoclassical, masculine, and deadly public stage. Participation was limited to a handful of privileged citizens who threw their loyalties to men who could demonstrate their honor in the pursuit of the common good. Because the common good was presumed to be indivisible, it tended to be nonnegotiable, and because men's selfhood was a function of public will, advocacy of principle frequently led to death.

Chapters 2 through 4 are analytical narratives, explaining historical events in time, with pauses to interpret the overall patterns and meanings at work. Each chapter has a dual purpose: to narrate compellingly and analyze convincingly the specific chain of events in San Francisco, and to illustrate the overall transformation at work in American political culture. Chapter 2 reexamines the vexed question of the origins of the infamous Vigilance Committees of 1851 and 1856. Since Josiah Royce's account in the 1880s, these events have been interpreted as the surface manifestation of deep social processes. My account grounds these events in the logic of republican-liberal political culture and in the visible actions of men in the contested public sphere. I argue, in short, that these famous political organizations had *political* origins, not *social* ones. Chapter 3 examines the "movement culture" created by the Committee of 1856. For ninety-nine days the Vigilante Executive Committee drew most of the city's voters into an armed paramilitary government that executed political prisoners and adopted the ancient republican practice of ostracism. This organization created a local party organization that ruled the city until the end of the Civil War.

Chapter 4 examines the transposition of the rules of political mobilization during the Civil War. By following the careers of representative party leaders and their methods of mass mobilization, I trace the ways in which the rights revolution of the Civil War unleashed the genie of social groups from within the republican logic of tyranny, dependence, and corruption. The crucial event was the conversion of race from an identity of exclusion from citizenship into a fault line of mobilization within citizenship.

Chapter 5, opening the second half of the book surveys the arrival of new structural features for the urban political public sphere in the immediate post–Civil War years. The signal transformation was the entry of women into that sphere. Women orators, lawyers, and politicians reenacted the eighteenth-century bourgeoisie's creation of a public sphere in the nineteenth century, carving a space for the assault on privilege that was the lynchpin of republicanism. This chapter next examines the attempt to shape the electorate through complex registration and election laws, introduced for the first time now that the exclusive political community had been invaded by the rights revolution of the Civil War and Reconstruction. A statistical portrait of the urban electorate over the course of the postwar decades reveals a "dual urban political community," in which larger turnouts in national elections brought a wider array of voters into the circle of mobilization. Political leaders understood and attempted to manipulate this effect, by separating or joining local and national elections. New forums of mass communication appeared in the aftermath of the Civil War to further restructure the possibilities of mobilization. Commerical newspapers managed on the logic of group marketing and the rise of working-class evangelism presaged the politics of class that exploded in the 1870s.

Chapters 6 through 8, like 2 through 4, are analytical narratives. Chapter 6 reinterprets the rise and fall of the Workingmen's Party of California (WPC), a party dramatic enough to catch the hopeful attention of Karl Marx. As the first act in the "Great Upheaval" (ca. 1877–89), which saw the rise of insurgent labor parties across the

United States, the WPC, like the Knights of Labor, has been interpreted as the eruption of class conflict into "mainstream" party politics. A close narrative analysis of political campaigns during the turbulent 1870s reveals clearly, however, that a politics of class was the creation of "mainstream" party politicians and journalists who introduced a language of class in the effort to mobilize voters. Ironically, the leadership of the WPC continued to use the now-dysfunctional republican language of politics. Statistical analysis shows that the electorate began voting by class long before the creation of the WPC in 1877. Political mobilization in the public city most dramatically led the formation of class identities in civil society.

Chapters 7 and 8 together examine the origins of "progressivism" in San Francisco, detailing the triumph of the pluralist-liberal political culture by the end of the century. Generations of scholars, writing within the social-group paradigm, have sought to describe the Progressive Era (ca. 1890–1920) as a set of distinctive regulatory, centralizing, and ameliorative policies linked to specific social groups thought to be responsible for those policies. I argue instead that progressivism was an institutionalized structure of political action and understanding, marking the arrival of a politics of social groups and their needs. Chapter 7 details the specific institutional arrangements – interest-group lobbies, sensational jouralism, the reorganization of group identities, the politization of women, and the party-weakening secret ballot – that made such a politics possible, locating the sources of that politics in the contraditions of party government.

Chapter 8 explains how a diverse cast of characters and organizations successfully created, within a newly operative pluralist liberalism, a "politics of needs," in which policy-making for specific groups became legitimate and even necessary. Intellectuals, women's rights activists, labor leaders, ethnic group leaders, suburban homeowners, business leaders, political entrepreneurs, and mass media titans mobilized voters to vote on the issues of woman suffrage in 1896 and the reform municipal charter of 1898. These two events are analyzed as emblematic of the central features at work in the emergence of a social-group conception of politics that we call progressivism.

The end of this book refers back to its beginning. The new political culture of the Progressive Era revolved around the political claims of social groups and their needs and provided the practical example of political life from which the social-group paradigm of modern social science was drawn. That paradigm, through its later incarnations as the liberal pluralism of the 1950s and the "new urban history" of the 1960s and 1970s, raised the questions this book tries to resolve.

CHAPTER I

The agony of authority:
People, public, party, and power, 1849–1859

"O the terrible anxiety of my mind," Phineus Underwood Blunt confided to his diary one sad day in November 1850; "here I am in San Francisco without a dollar of money and a family dependent on me." Phineus Blunt had come to California from Boston the previous spring with golden dreams, only to have them dashed. "I feel to put my whole trust in God," Blunt, a Baptist, had written to himself the previous April, "hoping He will direct me in my efforts to obtain some gold to take home with me." But Blunt, a lamb among wolves, was too timid to take big risks. Instead, he hedged his bets by working for wages on other men's ventures. Swindled on a claim, then robbed outright, he fled the hostile mountains for the regional metropolis in search of steady work. "I had hoped to have gone home to my family with a large sum of money, but some heartless villain stole it from me and all my hopes of going home to my family at present."[1] To relieve the anxiety of his mind, Blunt procured a job on the city police force, entered politics as a minor Whig party activist, and eventually persuaded his wife and family to join him in San Francisco.

David C. Broderick had arrived in San Francisco a year earlier than Blunt, although under very different circumstances. Son of an Irish immigrant stone carver, he watched, in the early 1820s, his father sculpt the capitals that adorn the columns and pilasters of the U.S. Capitol building. Later, growing up in New York City, David lost his entire family to illness and accidental death, tragedies incident to working-class life in the industrializing metropolis. Saddled with supporting a fatherless, and then a motherless, family, Broderick plied his father's trade. He gained ownership in

---

[1] Diary of Phineus Underwood Blunt (1809–97), 25 November, 9 April, 25 November, 1850, Bancroft Library, Berkeley, California.

1840 of a tavern in Greenwich Village called "The Subterranean," an artisan-oriented gathering place for the Loco Foco wing of New York City's Democratic party. News of California gold reached Gotham while the Loco Focos were out of power, so Broderick, aged only twenty-nine but soon to become U.S. senator from California, invested in a joint-stock venture calling itself "The Republic Co." and headed for California, setting sail for a three-month voyage around the tip of South America in the spring of 1849.[2]

Tom Maguire, future "Napoleon of the Stage," also arrived in San Francisco in the first wave of Argonauts, along with his wife Emma Maguire. A tall, handsome young man on the make, Maguire had clawed his way from the occupation of hack driver to become, in 1846, joint operator of the bars on the second and third tiers of New York's Park Theater. Tom and Emma Maguire responded to the news of California gold by setting sail with enough capital to invest in the leading saloons and gambling houses at the center of San Francisco, the Plaza. Having experimented with theater management in New York, Maguire opened San Francisco's first full-sized theater "dedicated to the drama," the "Jenny Lind," in October 1850. Over the decades, until his death in 1896, Maguire would remain the city's leading impresario, drawing the great Shakespearean actors from the eastern seaboard. His theater operations produced a string of national stars and his protégés included David Belasco, who would return East to lead the New York theater world.[3]

David S. Terry was among the small minority of early San Franciscans who arrived via land, and among the substantial minority who came from the slave South. Terry was born in Kentucky in 1823. His mother moved his family to Texas while that region was still part of Mexico in 1833. Belonging to the elite planter class, young Terry's personality and ideology took shape during two wars against Mexico. In the first (1836) he participated while only thirteen (by his own account); in the second (1846) he served as a private. News of gold found Terry dissatisfied with a courtship,

[2] David A. Williams, *David C. Broderick: A Political Portrait* (San Marino, Calif.: Huntington Library, 1969), 3–30.

[3] Lois Foster Rodecape, "Tom Maguire, Napoleon of the Stage," *California Historical Society Quarterly* 20 (December 1941):289–96; ibid., 21 (September 1942): 239–75; William Winter, *The Life of David Belasco*, 2 vols. (New York: Moffat, Yard, and Co., 1918), 1:70, 87, 105, 113, 242–4.

and, having been defeated for the office of Galveston district attorney, he joined an expedition of prospectors that included slaves, arriving in California in September 1849. Like most professionals, Terry quickly discovered that the best opportunity was not to be found in the mines but in the cities. Establishing a legal practice in Stockton, Terry threw himself into the affairs of the Democratic party, becoming a leader of the "Chivalry," or proslavery faction of the state party. "His character was moulded in a tempest," an early biographer wrote of this man, whose extraordinary career can be marked by his achievement of high elective office and also by his frequent, highly formalized acts of violence. He used his Bowie knife in the courtroom, against editors who denounced him, and, while a justice of the California Supreme Court, against the officers of the 1856 Committee of Vigilance. While chief justice of that court in 1859, he fought a momentous duel with Senator Broderick. After serving as an officer in the Confederate army, Terry returned to California and championed the Workingmen's party in 1879, then fittingly closed his career by meeting death in an assault on U.S. Supreme Court Justice Stephen Dudley Field in 1889.[4]

When Blunt, Broderick, Maguire, and Terry arrived in San Francisco, they were met by an elite of Boston and New York merchants who had established a presence in the Pacific port during the Mexican period, years before the Gold Rush, connecting San Francisco to world markets chiefly by trading in hides. In 1845, William D. M. Howard, acting for his family's merchant banking firm, purchased the Hudson Bay Company's Yerba Buena store and became the city's leading merchant by 1848, able to place the first profitable orders in the speculative frenzy following upon the news of gold.[5] It was to Howard that Phineus Blunt appealed when he arrived "without a dollar of money" in San Francisco. Blunt successfully presented a recommendation from Howard to the city marshal, Malachi Fallon (previously a keeper at the Tombs Prison in New

---

[4] A. Russell Buchanan, *David S. Terry: Dueling Judge* (San Marino, Calif.: Huntington Library, 1956), 3–19; A. E. Wagstaff, *Life of David S. Terry: Presenting an Authentic, Impartial and Vivid History of His Eventful Life and Tragic Death* (San Francisco: Continental Publishing Co., 1892), 17.

[5] The pre–Gold Rush hide trade is most famously described by another New Englander, Richard Henry Dana in his *Two Years Before the Mast* (New York: Modern Library, 1936); Peter R. Decker, *Fortunes and Failures: White Collar Mobility in Nineteenth-Century San Francisco* (Cambridge, Mass.: Harvard University Press, 1978), 9–11.

York)[6] securing him a policeman's position: "So at last the awful suspense I was in is ended and I am once more in employ."[7]

Merchants such as Howard had been the American advance guard, enabling the easy conquest of California, and now they represented the networks of trade and communication that determined the sources of population influx. Centuries of trade with the Americas by Xianggang (Hong Kong) merchants fixed the channels of Chinese immigration primarily from Guangdong Province through the city of Guangzhou (Canton). New England and New York merchants (accustomed to trading with their Hong Kong counterparts) established lines of transportation that brought 80 percent of the U.S. immigrants from New England or the Middle Atlantic states (fewer than half of all Americans lived in those regions) through Boston or New York City.[8]

As this handful of biographical sketches should begin to indicate, even in the most turbulent period of its history the elements of San Francisco's political and social structures are identifiable, and even rationally ordered. The individuals who built the city's political life came from predictable backgrounds (New England and New York primarily, but also the slave South); they followed predictable pathways to the new city; they belonged to political and economic networks before they arrived and they joined already established ones upon arrival. Further, they made sense of the new city and each other's behavior according to structures of discourse imported at a very significant time in the political history of the United States. It is the task of this chapter to introduce the several distinct ingredients that went into the making of San Francisco's antebellum political culture. These elements can be considered "structural" in the sense that each provided the context within which individuals pursued economic and political goals. We begin with the most basic structure, the peculiar composition of the city's population, and then we address another kind of structure: social class. The chapter next begins to sketch the institutional structures within which San Francisco's political history was enacted, starting with the public

[6] Bernard Moses, "The Establishment of Municipal Government in San Francisco," in *Johns Hopkins Studies in Historical and Political Science*, ed. Herbert Baxter Adams, 7 Ser., vols. 1–2 (Baltimore, 1889), 62.

[7] Blunt Diary, 26 November 1850.

[8] Sucheng Chan, *Asian Americans: An Interpretive History* (G. K. Hall and Co. and Twayne, 1991), 5; Decker, *Fortunes and Failures*, 23.

sphere. But structures are not static entities; they are created by patterns of individual behavior. The last sections of this chapter discuss the origins of political participation in the city, first with the troubled construction of political parties, next with the participation of voters in parties and elections, and finally with an examination of political leadership and the cultural structuring of authority, the bond between leaders and the led.

THE PEOPLE OF SAN FRANCISCO IN THE 1850s

The distinguishing characteristic of San Francisco's population in its earliest years was a massive sex-ratio imbalance.[9] One estimate puts the female proportion in 1849 at 2 percent (one in fifty). According to the 1852 California census, only 15 percent of the population was female (about one in seven persons). By 1860 39 percent of the population was female, and by 1900, there still was a male-to-female imbalance of 55 to 45 percent. These later decades experienced a slow equilibration, but a rapid initial adjustment in gender distribution occurred in the middle of the 1850s. Most of the overall urban growth in population in that decade is attributable, in fact, to an influx of women and minors. Between 1852 and 1860, the number of adult males actually *decreased* slightly, from twenty-four thousand to twenty-three thousand, while the number of women and minors increased from about twelve thousand to about thirty-four thousand (almost tripling), during the same eight years.[10]

The near absence of women and girls in the earliest years of San Francisco and their later rapid influx profoundly influenced the overall structure of political life in the city, from the membership of the political community to the operation of the public sphere. The first American women in the city were mostly sex entrepreneurs and mainly single. By 1860 the vast majority of women and girls were members of family units. The population by that year represented a secondary migration of families who intended to make San Francisco their home. Of a sample of the adult male population in 1852, only 5 percent could be located in the U.S. Census of 1860. This eight-year turnover rate of 95 percent far outstrips the

---

9   For the population of San Francisco, see Appendix.
10   Manuscript schedule of the California Census of 1852, "Recapitulation," 812; U.S. Bureau of the Census, *Eighth Census*, (Washington, D.C., 1864), 1: 31, 34–5.

ten-year rate of 50–60 percent that Stephan Thernstrom and
others have found to be typical of American cities of the nineteenth
century. San Francisco's rate of population turnover remained relatively high in subsequent decades, but settled down to about 70 percent per decade by the 1870s.[11] Whereas the general population
experienced extraordinary rates of transience in the 1850s, the political leaders were many times more persistent. Political activists
were the most stable members of antebellum urban society. Out of
a sample of 335 political convention delegates, party officials, candidates for office, and elected officials during the years 1850–1852, 35
percent could easily be found in the city in 1860. Their rate of persistence was seven times higher than that of all adult male citizens
and three times higher than for white-collar residents.[12] Political
activists provided the political community with a "core leadership,"
who were in a position to direct the course of San Francisco's political culture while ordinary citizens circulated through it.[13]

Antebellum San Francisco was remarkable also for the youthful-
ness of its residents. Phineus Blunt, the hapless Baptist pioneer, was,
at forty-one years of age, an old man. The mean age of adult males
(twenty-one or older) in 1852 was only thirty-one and the maximum
age was sixty. By 1900 these figures were forty and ninety, respectively. San Francisco lacked a Nestorian stratum of wizened men
with authority built from years of leadership and institutional mas-

[11] Stephan Thernstrom, *The Other Bostonians: Poverty and Progress in the American Metropolis,*
1880–1970 (Cambridge, Mass.: Harvard University Press, 1973), 9–28; Peter R. Knights,
The Plain People of Boston, 1830–1860: A Study in City Growth (New York: Oxford University
Press, 1973); Stanley Engerman, "Up or Out: Social and Geographic Mobility in the Uni-
ted States," *Journal of Interdisciplinary History* 3 (Winter 1975): 469–89; Decker, *Fortunes and*
Failures, 171.

[12] Names of "political activists," defined as any member of a party convention, party official,
candidate for office, or holder of an elected office, were culled from newspaper reports
and official records for the period 1850–2. These names were then "traced" into the index to the 1860 manuscript schedules of the U.S. Census for California. By drawing my
sample of activists from the years 1850–2, I have subjected these political elites to a much
tougher test of persistence than the random sample of adult male citizens from the 1852
California census. The political activists lasted up to ten years in this test, whereas the
adult white males had only to last eight years, from the 1852 census to the 1860 census.
San Francisco *Alta,* 26, 28 February, 1, 13 March, 13 August 1850; 13 August, 10, 12, 14
October 1852; San Francisco Board of Supervisors, *Municipal Reports* (San Francisco,
1860–), vol. 1 (1856–60), contains lists of all city officeholders retrospectively since 1850.
All of these names from 1850–2 were included in my sample; Bryan Lee Dilts, ed. *1860*
California Census Index (Salt Lake City: Index Publishers, 1984).

[13] For the concept of "core leadership," see Richard S. Alcorn, "Leadership and Stability in
Mid-Nineteenth Century America: A Case Study of an Illinois Town," *Journal of American*
History 61 (December 1974): 685–702.

tery. Instead, public authority was left in the hands of men who were still building their careers, businesses, and families. The Chief Justice of the California Supreme Court, Hugh C. Murray, was only twenty-nine-years old when he wrote the opinion that Chinese were to be considered "Indians" and therefore were disqualified from the privileges and immunities of citizenship in state laws.[14] William Tell Coleman, a "leading merchant," was only twenty-seven years old when he first took command of the Vigilantes in 1851, and David C. Broderick was only in his early thirties as he vied for mastery of the California Democrats. The volatility, instability, ideological stridency, and violence of the 1850s may well have been encouraged by this situation in which young men led young men in the Romantic era, during the rise of the Young America movement.[15]

Ethnically, San Francisco has always ranked with New York and other seaport cities in having among the highest proportion of foreign-born and foreign-stock residents. In 1852 San Franciscans born outside of the United States outnumbered the native born; by 1900 three-quarters of the city's 343,000 residents had at least one foreign-born parent.[16] Nevertheless, it was a predominantly native-born group who founded the city's political institutions and culture. Of the eligible voters in 1852, only 18 percent were foreign born. The sources of the city's eligible voters born in the United States reflected the major nodes of emigration. The largest cohort, 36 percent, hailed from the Middle Atlantic states, and those were primarily from New York City. The next largest groups came from New England (primarily from Boston) and the South (funneled through the seaport of New Orleans), at about 20 percent each. Midwestern states, far from the seaports and their clipper ships – the most common route to San Francisco – provided only 5 percent, and western states, the closest to California but as yet only sparsely settled, sent only 2 percent.[17]

Although the foreign-born voters were only a minor part of the

[14] For Murray's age, Walton Bean and James J. Rawls, *California: An Interpretive History* (New York: McGraw-Hill, 1988), 127; the case was *People v. George W. Hall* 4 California 399.

[15] On the Young America movement and political culture, see David M. Potter, *The Impending Crisis, 1848–1861*, completed and edited by Don E. Fehrenbacher (New York: Harper and Row, 1976); Sean Wilentz, *Chants Democratic*, 328.

[16] U.S. Census Bureau, *Twelfth Census*, 1:868. See Appendix.

[17] Analysis of study data. See Appendix.

Gold Rush contingent (roughly 1849–54), they rapidly established themselves as major participants in the political community by mid-decade. By 1860 about two-thirds of the eligible voters were natives of foreign countries. As in the cities from which they migrated, the Irish were the principal foreign-born group, followed by the Germans and then by those from the British Isles. Scandinavians, French and southern Europeans, and Chinese (ineligible for citizenship or voting) were the next largest foreign groups. These proportions held during most of the nineteenth century.[18]

This capital city of the "Wild West," then, was really a "New New York," with a heavy dose of New Englanders and Southerners giving it an ideologically contentious antebellum political culture. Activists from New York, Boston, and the South predominated in the cast of its early political leadership.[19]

SOCIAL CLASS: SOME PRELIMINARY OBSERVATIONS

Few questions about a polity are more important than those concerning the social class of the participants. Did social class characterize the divisions in civil society? If so, when did a working-class consciousness develop; how did it develop; and what was its relationship to political behavior? Rather than re-open the vast, contentious debate on social class in American history, we can make some preliminary observations about the state of class formation in San Francisco in the antebellum decade by drawing some conclusions from the social history of American class formation in the nineteenth century.

At the moment of San Francisco's founding, the United States had experienced at least a half century of economic, social, and political development. In the largest cities and the smallest towns, capitalist, wage-labor relations of production had long since taken firm root, displacing, if not fully replacing, the corporatist economy of artisanal production and merchant patronage. Susan Davis, Alan Dawley, Thomas Dublin, Herbert Gutman, Leon Fink, David Montgomery, Steven J. Ross, Christine Stansell, Sean Wilentz, and many others have demonstrated that working-class formation took place in the United States throughout the nineteenth century, not

---

[18] See Appendix.
[19] Moses, "The Establishment of Municipal Government in San Francisco"; Roger W. Lotchin, *San Francisco, 1846–1856: From Hamlet to City* (New York: Oxford University Press, 1974), 136–63, 213–44, and passim; Decker, *Fortunes and Failures*, 3–31.

uniformly, but episodically, unevenly, and in a segmented fashion. Class formation took place in confrontations over the introduction of industrial wage-labor relations in key contexts: the artisanal worlds of Philadelphia and New York City; the mill towns of New England; the industrial cities of Pennsylvania or Ohio.

Sean Wilentz, in his rich study of class formation in New York City, demonstrates that journeymen and master artisans evolved differing interpretations of the revolutionary ideology of republicanism to support their diverging positions in the new capitalist economy. Masters who became entrepreneurs of the emerging industries touted the independence and autonomy of the small producer. Artisans who now faced a lifetime of wage labor rather than the previously expected rise to master craftsman stressed, in their strikes and political movements, the mutual obligations of virtuous citizens promoting the commonweal. By the 1830, according to Wilentz, "celebrations and symbols" of the artisan republican heritage still appeared, "but to define the rifts of class between masters and journeymen, not to celebrate the harmony of craft."[20] It is clear from the work of Wilentz and other leading labor historians that urban class formation, having clearly reared its head in episodes like the Working Men's party of 1829–31, was quite incomplete at the beginning of the antebellum decade. Some trades, like the making of clothing, shoes, and furniture, had undergone the deepest transformation, with employers relying on unskilled, "sweated" labor, whereas others, such as shipbuilding, remained organized by the skilled artisanal crafts.[21]

Several historians have also identified the distinct emergence of an urban "middle class" by the middle of the nineteenth century. Mary Ryan, Paul Johnson, and Stuart M. Blumin show that many of the entrepreneurs and individuals in white-collar occupations had self-consciously adopted distinct lifestyles in the home and in public to differentiate themselves from the working-class or artisanal world.[22] The same changes in relations of production that the

---

20 Wilentz, *Chants Democratic*, 96.
21 Wilentz, *Chants Democratic*, 107–42; for a study with the same perspective, see Bruce Laurie, *Working People of Philadelphia, 1800–1850* (Philadelphia: Temple University Press, 1980).
22 Mary P. Ryan, *Cradle of the Middle Class: The Family in Oneida County, New York, 1790–1865* (New York: Cambridge University Press, 1981); Paul Johnson, *A Shopkeeper's Millennium: Society and Revivals in Rochester, New York, 1815–1837* (New York: Hill and Wang, 1978); Stuart M. Blumin, *The Emergence of the Middle Class: Social Experience in the American City, 1760–1900* (New York: Cambridge University Press, 1989).

labor historians have reconstructed led to a profusion of consumer goods enabling the growth of retail businesses and the cultivation of new patterns of consumption available to the upwardly mobile, but not wealthy, bourgeois household. Mirroring the expansion of unskilled wage work was a steady expansion of "new, nonmanual roles that were being generated by early industrial development." Summarizing data from Boston, Philadelphia, San Francisco, and Poughkeepsie, Blumin estimates that "the proportion of nonmanual businessmen and employees ... reached or exceeded 40% of the total workforce" by mid-century. The very architecture of the eastern cities had begun to reflect the emergence of a middle-class lifestyle by the 1850s, with glass-fronted retail showrooms for manufactured consumer goods – from bonnets to jewelry to books to carpets – clearly separated from the workshops that produced those goods. Like the studies of the emergence of a working class, however, studies of middle-class formation conclude that the emergence of such a "class" was far from complete by the 1850s. Blumin concludes firmly that "a middle class was *not* fully formed before the Civil War," placing the completion of that process toward the end of the nineteenth century.[23]

Working and middle classes were still ill-formed in antebellum San Francisco, but an upper class was entirely missing. San Francisco lacked the kind of established families of great wealth dating from the merchant princes of the eighteenth century seen in the older cities of Boston, New York City, and Philadelphia. Robert Dahl, Sam Bass Warner, Jr., Frederic Cople Jaher, and David C. Hammack have detailed the political and social decline of these families in east coast cities during the second half of the nineteenth century. In those cities, the rise of a new industrial elite displaced the older mercantile one, transforming the ethos of the city at the same time. In San Francisco, as in other western cities created in the nineteenth century, the dynamic was quite different.[24] Here the "nouveaux

23   Blumin, *The Emergence of the Middle Class*, 13, 71, 74, 93–107. See also John S. Gilkeson, Jr., *Middle-Class Providence, 1820–1940* (Princeton, N.J.: Princeton University Press, 1986).
24   Frederic Cople Jaher, *The Urban Establishment: Upper Strata in Boston, New York, Charleston, Chicago, and Los Angeles* (Urbana: University of Illinois Press, 1982); Robert A. Dahl, *Who Governs?: Democracy and Power in an American City* (New Haven: Yale University Press, 1961); Sam Bass Warner, Jr., *The Private City: Philadelphia in Three Periods of Growth* (Philadelphia: University of Pennsylvania Press, 1968); David C. Hammack, *Power and Society: Greater New York at the Turn of the Century* (New York: Russell Sage Foundation, 1982), 65–78; On the western variation, see Jaher, op cit., 453–709; Robin Einhorn, *Property Rules: Political Economy in Chicago, 1833–1872* (Chicago: University of Chicago Press, 1991), 28–60.

riches" displaced no established class but grew, rather, out of the plebeian-entrepreneurial mass of the antebellum years. By the 1870s the San Francisco elite, "Robber Barons" of the railroad and mining industries most conspicuously, would flaunt their wealth in "Nob Hill" mansions. Those same Robber Barons in the 1850s, however, were indistinguishable in socioeconomic terms from the likes of William D. M. Howard, William T. Sherman, David C. Broderick, and thousands of other opportunists. Until they arranged to benefit from the Pacific Railway Acts during the Civil War, the "big four" "railroad kings," Leland Stanford, Collis P. Huntington, Charles Crocker, and Mark Hopkins, were small businessmen. Huntington and Hopkins ran the hardware store in Sacramento where these four first met to form the Central Pacific Railway Company.[25]

San Francisco took shape in the 1850s at a point midway along the long process of class formation in the United States, after classes had begun to form but long before they constituted major divisions in society. Further, San Francisco during the 1850s was a place and time in which class formation was least likely to occur largely as a product of the relations of production or consumption. There were no established, artisanal networks of journeymen and masters whose world would be disrupted by industrial-capitalist production relations, as in Philadelphia or New York City; there were no industrial textile mills drawing on a rural or an immigrant precapitalist population, as in New England; and there was not yet heavy industry to proletarianize a formerly semiindependent skilled labor force, as in Cincinnati and Pittsburgh in the late nineteenth century.[26]

The Gold Rush and its aftermath in San Francisco during the 1850s threw the processes of class formation into utter confusion, at

[25] Bean and Rawls, *California*, 154–63.

[26] The literature on working-class formation is vast, but see especially the essays in Michael H. Frisch and Daniel J. Walkowitz, eds, *Working-Class America: Essays on Labor, Community, and American Society* (Urbana: University of Illinois Press, 1983); Amy Bridges, "Becoming American: The Working Classes in the United States before the Civil War," in *Working-Class Formation: Nineteenth-Century Patterns in Western Europe and the United States*, ed. Ira Katznelson and Aristide Zolberg (Princeton, N.J.: Princeton University Press, 1986), 157–96; Alan Dawley, *Class and Community: The Industrial Revolution in Lynn* (Cambridge, Mass.: Harvard University Press, 1976); Francis G. Couvares, *The Remaking of Pittsburgh: Class and Culture in an Industrializing City, 1877–1919* (Albany: State University of New York Press, 1984); Steven J. Ross, *Workers on the Edge: Work, Leisure, and Politics in Industrializing Cincinnati: 1788–1890* (New York: Columbia University. Press, 1985).

a time when class formation was only in its nascent stages in the nation as a whole. The barriers to arriving in San Francisco served as a social filter for the new city. The cost of the sea voyage, by which route the great majority emigrated, precluded the penniless and greatly favored those of white-collar occupation. The upper stratum of blue-collar workers were able to come in large numbers also – mainly through joint-stock companies – at prices as low as $150. These constraints had the effect of narrowing the occupational and wealth spectrum of the antebellum city: "for the rich and powerful would not come to toil, and the very poor could not well gain the distant land."[27]

By their very act of emigration across such great distances in the pursuit of wealth the initial generation of San Franciscans had intentionally put their occupational identities in abeyance; they expected opportunity and hoped for upward mobility. Such expectations of change indicate a rejection of former identities. The economic magic of gold conjured opportunity out of every corner of San Francisco. Each factor of production – land, labor, and capital – soared in value every day.[28] Unskilled and semiskilled labor in the city commanded astronomical prices of eight to twenty dollars per day due to the labor shortage created by the lure of the mining districts. The first prostitutes in the city, independent entrepreneurs, could earn two hundred dollars a night. Downward occupational change by the criteria of classic sociological categories, therefore, could present an opportunity for upward mobility.[29] The labor historian Ira Cross writes of "the building of a brick warehouse in San Francisco in 1849, on which thirty 'carpenters' were employed, of whom three were preachers, two were lawyers, three were physicians, six were bookkeepers, two were blacksmiths, and one was a shoemaker."[30] "Thus were the grades re-

27 Decker, *Fortunes and Failures*, 13–15; Hubert H. Bancroft [William Nemos and Frances Fuller Victor], *History of California*, 7 vols. (San Francisco: History Co., Publishers, 1884–90), 7:227.

28 Bruno Fritzsche, "San Francisco 1846–1848: The Coming of the Land Speculator," *California Historical Quarterly* 51:1 (Spring 1972): 17–34; Roger Lotchin, *San Francisco*, 45–99.

29 By 1860 wages had fallen to normal levels. The U.S. Bureau of the Census reported average daily wages for carpenters in the year 1860 to be $4.43. *Eighth Census*, 4:512; Ira B. Cross, *A History of the Labor Movement in California* (Berkeley: University of California Press, 1935), 19–28.

30 Cross, *History of the Labor Movement in California*, 13. Bancroft reports the same phenomenon: "The laboring man might gain the footing of employer; the clerk the position of principal; while former doctors, lawyers, and army officers could be seen toiling for wages, even as waiters and shoe-blacks." H. H. Bancroft, *History of California*, 6:227.

versed," Bancroft writes, "fitness to grasp opportunity giving the ascendancy."[31]

Our best "objective" measure of occupation and class is the five standard sociological occupational categories: high white-collar, low white-collar, skilled manual, semiskilled manual, and unskilled manual workers. This five-level scale is used throughout this book. By drawing a line beneath the two white-collar categories, we obtain the basic Marxian class categories of bourgeoisie and proletariat. A sample of men drawn from the 1852 census manuscripts reveals a relatively even distribution of these occupations. Subsequent censuses reflect a predictable refinement of the occupational structure as the city's economy matured and evolved (see Appendix). But occupational categories do not tell us how the persons themselves understood their positions in the socioeconomic structure of the city. More important than objective measures of occupational status are indications of a consciousness of class membership, or at least a sentiment of such membership.

Social class, best conceived as a relationship constructed by cultural interpretations of one's self and others, is highly dependent upon the discourse or language within which individuals understand their position in society. Significantly, recent labor historians agree that the American "language of class" was a political one, being that ideological formation known as "republicanism." It is a central argument of this book that republicanism was a discourse that did not exist in isolation, but as part of an amalgam I term *republican liberalism*. Republican liberalism was a language of the public sphere (its home institution) that legitimated both political and market ethics. At this point, it will be useful to discuss the republican side of this amalgam somewhat in isolation, because that side played so powerful a role in the public world of San Francisco.

Drawn from the *Politics* of Aristotle, from Machiavelli, from James Harrington and Algernon Sydney, and from the Baron de Montesquieu, and further elaborated in the ideological workshops of the American Revolution, republicanism was a political worldview, paradigm, or model of public life about the conditions necessary for the survival of a republican form of government. Its central tenet was that rulers and citizens of a republic must practice "civic virtue" by promoting the public interest while possessing public power. If these individuals promoted instead their private inter-

[31] Bancroft, *History of California*, 6:227.

ests then society would disintegrate under the weight of virtue's nemesis: corruption. Virtue, in turn, rested on the autonomy, or independence, of a republic's citizens. Citizens could recognize the public interest only if they were free to exercise their own reason, and they could do that only by remaining independent of one another. Dependent persons (slaves, women, children, those receiving the patronage of others) were incapable of seeing beyond their own immediate needs. Corruption, in Drew McCoy's succinct definition, was "the encroachment of power on liberty." It led to a loss of independence and to the rule, eventually, of despots, who would use their own wealth and the power of the state to make some citizens pliable and to destroy the liberties of the rest.[32]

Republicanism was a protean discourse. The generic content just described found countless variations among those who drew upon it in the first decades of American national life. Bourgeois women articulated a "republican motherhood," winning the political responsibility in their private lives to educate virtuous citizens for a self-governing society. Workers articulated artisanal variations on republicanism to contest the emerging wage-labor relations of capitalist society. Slaveowners recast republicanism to justify slavery in a liberal state. And, throughout the antebellum years, Daniel Walker Howe observes, one finds the "pervasive vocabulary of Whig–Democratic debate – virtue, balance, luxury, degeneration, restoration."[33] Republicanism was the companion of liberalism. It was no mere anachronism, but an adapted discourse that enabled the liberal ethic of individual pursuit of private gain to attain legitimacy. Neoclassical republicanism in the early republic, McCoy observes, could envision "commerce as the vital stimulus to industry that would establish Americans as a virtuous people."[34]

Typical of republican discourse is the tendency to frame what the twentieth-century mind understands as socioeconomic categories in

[32] My interpretation of republicanism is a selective synthesis of the the work of two scholars in particular: J. G. A. Pocock, *The Machiavellian Moment: Florentine Political Thought and the Atlantic Republican Tradition* (Princeton, N.J.: Princeton University Press, 1975); and Gordon S. Wood, *The Creation of the American Republic, 1776–1787* (Chapel Hill: University of North Carolina Press, 1969). For the early national period, I draw heavily on Drew R. McCoy, *The Elusive Republic: Political Economy in Jeffersonian America* (Chapel Hill: University of North Carolina Press, 1980). Quotation is from McCoy, *Elusive Republic*, 67.

[33] Daniel Walker Howe, *The Political Culture of the American Whigs* (Chicago: University of Chicago Press, 1979), 78.

[34] McCoy, *Elusive Republic*, 237.

ethical, characterological terms. A journalist in 1852, for instance, wrote of "all classes of society – the enlightened and the educated – the honest and the dishonest – the business men and the men of leisure – the philanthropist and the pickpocket...."[35] A merchant, two decades later, used the same phrase, "all classes," and similarly broke them down into "the idle and the industrious, the vicious and the virtuous, the ignorant and the educated."[36] In these expressions, the notion of social class hinges on the ideas of virtue and industriousness. What separated a philanthropist and a pickpocket was not wealth, but that one gave and the other stole money. Only after considering the embeddedness of class consciousness within the republican discourse is it possible to decipher David C. Broderick's perplexing statements on his own position in society. On the one hand, he was clearly conscious of class. In the U.S. Senate he said that he could not afford to "forget my connection with ... the class of people to whose toil I was born" or "deny that I sprang from them." Yet in emigrating to San Francisco, he was one of those who had distanced himself from the class ("them") into whose toil he had been born. Now he voiced criticism: "They submit too tamely to oppression, and are too prone to neglect their rights and duties as citizens."[37] Broderick's New York training in the idiom of artisanal republicanism led logically to characterological and political diagnoses of the social condition. In short, he identified class attributes in political terms.

Although it had many uses among many groups in American society, republicanism was essentially a *political* language. It traced the welfare of civil society to the ethical conduct of those who governed, that is, to citizens and officeholders. It was, therefore, a property of *public life*. American social historians, following the dominant trends in the social sciences since the beginning of the twentieth century, usually attribute social-group formation to processes located in civil society. Broderick, however, exemplifies the dimension of class formation excluded by that bias among social historians. Broderick's milieu was the artisanal-republican one recovered by Sean Wilentz. Broderick had named his tavern after the radical newspaper the *Subterranean*, published by his friend, the Working Men's party

35 San Francisco *Alta California*, 25 August 1852.
36 Clancey J. Dempster, "Statement" [n.d., 1870s] for H. H. Bancroft, MS in Bancroft Library, Berkeley, California.
37 U.S. Senate, *Appendix to the Congressional Globe*, 35th Cong., 1st Sess., 193.

organizer, Mike Walsh.[38] Yet Broderick was neither employee nor employer; his class identity would not be formed in either of these production relations. The structuring of his social consciousness, like that of the men he worked with and led, was largely a product of his public political life: In that context, he and others would make sense of the relations found in civil society.

The demonstrated importance of republicanism in the formation of group identities provides a very strong clue that a major source of social-group formation has been excluded from American social history: the political discourse of the public sphere. An adequate picture of the formation of social classes and other group identities (race, gender, ethnicity) can be achieved only through a reconstruction of the contexts in which individuals spoke with one another, sharing, comparing, and contesting one another's identities, and within which leaders exhorted the many to identify themselves according to patterns provided by the discourses available at a given place and time. We turn, therefore, to the urban public stage.

THE ANTEBELLUM PUBLIC SPHERE

Antebellum San Francisco was a small republic. Isolated from the national polity by thousands of miles, it might as well have been an autonomous city-state. At its center stood a forum, the physical place where citizens most easily constituted the "public sphere," defined in the last chapter as the realm of communication arising when private persons come together to debate the governing relations of state and society. This public sphere was much more than a mere public place: It arose in the medium of scores of newspapers, but also, quite easily, out of doors, in public space.

The central physical space of San Francisco's public sphere was the Plaza (officially known as Portsmouth Square), bounded by Washington, Kearny, Clay and Dupont streets. The Plaza, shaped by a steep slope, formed a natural amphitheater, at the foot of which, on Clay Street, stood the sandstone front of the three-story neoclassical City Hall. Adjacent to City Hall stood the equal-sized

---

[38] Williams, *David C. Broderick*, 6; Wilentz, *Chants Democratic*, 326–35; Alexander Saxton, "George Wilkes: The Transformation of a Radical Ideology," *American Quarterly* 33:4 (Fall 1981): 437–58.

brick-faced El Dorado, San Francisco's largest and most prestigious gambling house, saloon, hotel, and brothel.[39] (See Plate 1.1.)

During the antebellum decade so much of the activity of the public sphere of San Francisco took place in this central forum of urban life that public space and publicity were fairly inseparable; the public sphere was essentially a public stage. The connections between political and theatrical institutions were quite literal. David Broderick, as he built the first party organization in the state, lived in a theatrical milieu, residing at the home of his friends from New York, Tom and Emma Maguire. Tom Maguire, from 1849 through 1851, built and rebuilt ever-larger saloons and theaters on the Plaza. After the great fire of May 1851, Maguire ordered a supply of pink sandstone from Australia and built the Jenny Lind III in neoclassical, austere republican style. The ambitious Maguire attracted to this stage the aging Junius Brutus Booth and his young son, Edwin, in July 1852. But Maguire had overbuilt and failed to turn a profit. That summer, his friend Broderick helped him to engineer the sale of the Jenny Lind III to the city of San Francisco to serve as its proud new City Hall.[40]

The theatricality of public life in the 1850s points to the deeper structural feature of the early urban public sphere. The public sphere arose in tandem with the private sphere. Habermas stresses the origins of the public sphere in the bourgeois celebration of privacy, where members of the bourgeoisie came to understand themselves as autonomous and rational, capable of constructing a polity in which truth, not authority, makes the law. The public sphere was formally institutionalized, then, when Americans safeguarded that privacy through the rights guaranteed by their liberal constitution. The ideology of female domesticity, so well researched by historians of American women, was the ethical source enabling the practice of

---

[39] Representative accounts of public gatherings on "the Plaza" appear in San Francisco *Alta* 11, 26 March 1850; Frank Soulé, John H. Gihon, and James Nisbet, *The Annals of San Francisco; Containing a Summary of the History of the First Discovery, Settlement, Progress, and Present Condition of California, and a Complete History of all the Important Events Connected with its Great City: to which are added, Biographical Memoirs of Some Prominent Citizens* (New York: D. Appleton & Co., 1855) (hereafter, Soulé et al, *Annals*), 269–72; *Alta*, 4 June 1850; 23 February 1851; 2 September 1852; San Francisco *Daily Herald* (hereafter *Herald*), 15 May, 3 June 1856; *Daily California Chronicle* 3 June 1856; *Alta*, 26 October 1856; San Francisco *Examiner*, 31 July 1867.
[40] Rodecape, "Tom Maguire," 20: 296–301; Lotchin, *San Francisco*, 223.

CITY HALL, SAN-FRANCISCO CAL.

Plate 1.1. "The Plaza," or Portsmouth Square, in the early 1850s. Through the end of the Civil War this was the central space of urban public life. The Plaza, shaped by a steep slope, formed a natural amphitheater, at the foot of which stood the three-story neoclassical City Hall, built in austere republican style from Australian sandstone. The adjacent El Dorado was the city's leading gambling saloon. Meetings, protests, Fourth of July celebrations, and the 1859 funeral of Senator David Broderick were held on the Plaza. City Hall was originally the Jenny Lind III, built by the impresario Tom Maguire after the "great fire" of 1851 destroyed the second of his theaters. Maguire, a longtime confidant of Broderick, attracted to this stage the aging Junius Brutus Booth and his young son, Edwin, in July 1852. The intersection of government and theater in this space neatly illustrates the theatricality of politics and the political-ethical resonance of Shakespearian drama. Courtesy of Bancroft Library.

public life by (male) citizens. It was also the Janus-faced gate barring women from participation in the public sphere and at the same time justifying their entry into it (thanks to the private sphere's avowed political role) at a later date. The male leaders of commerce and politics performed their public roles on San Francisco's public stage, just as they had in New York or Boston.

But this particular public sphere was highly unusual. San Francisco, for several years, *lacked a private sphere.* The near absence of women and girls in the city for at least three years indicated, of course, a near absence of families. According to the precepts of public life in the American Republic, however, a public man drew his autonomy and his virtue from his home, wife, and family. To solve this problem, the city's early male elite joined forces with the only female elite there was. The first several hundred women in the new American city were sexual entrepreneurs, "parlor" prostitutes who commanded extremely high prices until brothel and dance-hall competition arrived in volume by 1852. By all available accounts they constituted the "ladies" of society and were shown full respect by men of every class. "Hats were removed and bows executed as they passed on the street."[41] These lady-prostitutes provided men with the cover they needed to conduct legitimate public business.

That prostitutes performed this role naturally outraged the actual married matrons who arrived in the earliest years to establish leadership of the female private and public spheres. The growth of a private sphere in San Francisco began when bourgeois matrons first began to displace madams as the legitimate visible companions of public men. Married women and daughters, as Mary Ryan has shown, were given the ceremonial role of vestal virgins in the party politics of the nineteenth century. They appeared at party meetings or parades to lend moral and ethical legitimacy to the proceedings of the men.[42] Sarah Royce, mother of the future Harvard philosopher and California historian Josiah Royce, scored the first victory for the bourgeois private sphere in 1850 when she expelled Irene McCready, a leading sex entrepreneur and the lover of the El Dorado's proprietor James McCabe, from a benevolent benefit held in Royce's home.[43] By 1852, when women in families outnumbered prostitutes by only slightly better than two to one, the "Ladies of San Francisco" presented a silk banner to the "Young Men's Whig Club" in an elaborate ceremony.[44] Decorously witnessing the proceedings from the sidelines as male politicians performed the actual banner presentation "on behalf of the ladies," these

[41] Jacqueline Baker Barnhart, *The Fair But Frail: Prostitution in San Francisco, 1849–1900* (Reno: University of Nevada Press, 1986), 14–33, quotation on 20; Soulé et al., *Annals,* 259.

[42] Mary Ryan, *Women in Public: Between Banners and Ballots, 1825–1880* (Baltimore: Johns Hopkins University Press, 1990).

[43] Sarah Royce, *Frontier Lady: Recollections of the Gold Rush and Early California* (New Haven: Yale University Press, 1932), 114.

[44] *Alta* 2 September 1852.

women were acting out a boundary ritual. A product of the home was passed, as it were, over an invisible line into the public sphere, where this political emblem would thereafter be handled only by men. It took until 1855 before the final showdown between madams and matrons occurred. In that year Arabella Ryan, known as "Belle Cora," took up a seat in the American Theater next to her lover, the gambler Charles Cora, and directly behind the U.S. Marshal W. H. Richardson and his wife. Mrs. Richardson demanded of her husband that he have the Coras removed. When the management refused to comply, the Richardsons walked out. Two days later, Cora killed Marshal Richardson in a quarrel over the incident.[45]

Such public confrontations re-drew the lines between public and private to replace the extraordinary jumble of the earliest years with a public-private boundary system that conformed to the standards of the classical and modern republics. Thereafter, family men were the privileged participants in public life, and sexuality was hidden in the private worlds of the family and discreet commercial establishments and away from the central thoroughfares.[46]

Participation in the public sphere was essentially a rhetorical experience. The formation of a public sphere, as we have seen, took place when private individuals joined one another in debates about the governing relations of their state and their society. Since the eighteenth century, as Kenneth Cmiel demonstrates, those individuals had evolved highly self-conscious public personae. They sought to present themselves in specific rhetorical forms drawn from Cicero's *De oratore* and modified by theorists of the Scottish Enlightenment. Cicero taught orators to use ornate language "to establish relationships of authority between speaker and listener" before publics that "included many unrefined listeners." Strategies for political leadership during the Enlightenment, however, turned on high levels of education among the "public" and sought the goal of persuasion through reason. Late-eighteenth-century rhetoricians

[45] Hubert Howe Bancroft, *Popular Tribunals*, 2 vols. (San Francisco: History Company, 1887), 2:29–34; Lotchin, *San Francisco*, 197–9; Ryan, *Women in Public*, 104–6; Barnhart, *Fair But Frail*, 34–7.

[46] Hannah Arendt, *The Human Condition* (Chicago: University of Chicago Press, 1958), 22–78; John D'Emilio and Estelle B. Freedman, *Intimate Matters: A History of Sexuality in America* (New York: Harper and Row, 1988); Carroll Smith-Rosenberg, "The Female World of Love and Ritual: Relations between Women in Nineteenth-Century America," in Smith-Rosenberg, *Disorderly Conduct: Visions of Gender in Victorian America* (New York: Oxford University Press, 1985), 53–76.

"argued that rhetoric should teach how to forcefully communicate one's reasoned arguments."[47] Contemporaries in the early national period took oratory so seriously that the book that established the Enlightenment theory of rhetoric, Hugh Blair's *Lectures on Rhetoric* (1783), was second only to Adam Smith's *Wealth of Nations* (1776) as the most widely owned book in American libraries by 1813.[48]

By the middle of the nineteenth century the learning of rhetoric was no less valued than it had been by the revolutionary generation, but the styles available now ranged from the refined speech of Daniel Webster in the Senate to the popular rhetoric of Mike Walsh in the *Subterranean*. As Cmiel makes clear, however, these rhetorical divergences did not result from or produce class stratification. Rather, a new, powerful, "democratic idiom" emerged, best exemplified in the rhetoric of Abraham Lincoln. Lincoln, and in a very different way Henry Ward Beecher, developed a "middling rhetoric" that "married the high and the low," joining Latinate, biblical, or Shakespearean vocabulary with the folksy expressions of the rural and urban masses.[49] Broderick's self-education, like Lincoln's, was intended to equip him with the vocabulary and syntax necessary to lead men in a republic. Befriended by Townsend Harris – whose dedication, to the education of those without means, led him to help found the Free Academy (which later became the City University of New York) – Broderick studied history, literature, and political economy while making the transition from stone carver to tavern keeper and political activist. His education continued as he surrounded himself with friends like George Wilkes, founder of the *Police Gazette* and author of a plebeian critique of Shakespeare.[50]

The close association of Broderick with the stages of New York and San Francisco, through his friendship with Tom Maguire, indicates a vital dimension of the supremacy of middling public culture in antebellum San Francisco. For Maguire, an Irish Bowery B'hoy on the make who some have claimed was illiterate, to have assumed command of the city's cultural establishment by staging Shakespeare in his own sandstone theater, could have been possible only in a social context that had not yet stratified into "high" and "low"

---

47 Kenneth Cmiel, *Democratic Eloquence: The Fight Over Popular Speech in Nineteenth-Century America* (New York: William Morrow and Co., 1990), 35–6.
48 Ibid, 40, n. 57.
49 Ibid, 55–93.
50 Williams, *David C. Broderick*, 4–5, 8–9; Saxton, "George Wilkes."

expressions of culture, conforming to upper and lower, or bourgeois and working, classes. Lawrence Levine, in his study of Shakespeare in nineteenth-century America, explains why the Shakespearean stage occupied an important place in the political culture of the antebellum republic. "The same Americans who found diversion and pleasure in lengthy political debates, who sought joy and god in the sermons of church and camp meeting, who had, in short, a seemingly inexhaustible appetite for the spoken word, thrilled to Shakespeare's eloquence, memorized his soliloquies, delighted in his dialogues."[51] Levine's valuable point is that the American stage, at midcentury, along with museums and opera, were hybrids of what we today call high and low cultural forms. Audiences of all classes filled the same auditoriums for evenings of *Hamlet, Lear, Richard III*, and *Macbeth* (the most popular) – with high-wire shows, jugglers, and farces stuffed between the acts. Maguire opened his first Jenny Lind in October 1850 with "a performance somewhat in the nature of a variety show: a Madame Von Gulpen Korinsky sang, as did one James Nesbitt, balladist, while Herr Rossiter performed feats of magic and slack-wire marvels." Three days later he staged John Banim's *Damon and Pythias*, followed by William Bayle Bernard's farce *Dumb Belle*.[52] Maguire's competition, "Doc" Robinson, meanwhile, attracted audiences at the latter's Dramatic Museum, across the Plaza from the Jenny Lind, with a mix of concerts and circus performances. Remarkably, one local paper observed a "comparatively small attendance" for the burlesque material, and counseled Maguire "that a series of representations from Shakespeare will be the most acceptable performances that can be brought before this community."[53] By 1852, with the Adelphi and American theaters boasting seating capacities – about two thousand each – to match that of the Jenny Lind III, Maguire acquired Junius Brutus Booth, to draw-off his competition's crowds.[54]

Broderick lived in the Maguires' San Francisco home, building an audience for the Democratic party while Maguire built an audience

---

[51]   Lawrence W. Levine, *Highbrow / Lowbrow: The Emergence of Cultural Hierarchy in America* (Cambridge, Mass.: Harvard University Press, 1988), 36.

[52]   Rodecape, "Tom Maguire," 20:294; Banim (Irish) Published "Damon and Pythias" in 1821, and Bernard (American) published "Dumb Belle" in 1831. *British Authors of the Nineteenth Century*, ed. Stanley, J. Kunitz (New York: H.W. Wilson, 1936), 31–3; *American Authors*, 1600–1900 (New York: H.W. Wilson, 1936), 73–4.

[53]   Rodecape, "Tom Maguire," 295.   [54]   Ibid, 296.

for drama. Maguire's theatrical stage and Broderick's party platforms had much in common. Levine recounts an 1856 performance
of *Richard III* in Sacramento interrupted by disapproving showers of
vegetables and an 1854 performance in San Francisco of *Romeo and
Juliet*, which "fascinated and entranced" a "walnut cracking audience." Both drama and politics contained "numerous folkish elements, including a knowledgeable, participatory audience exerting
important degrees of control."[55] "Shakespeare was popular," Levine concludes, "first and foremost, because he was integrated into
the culture and presented within its context." Levine correctly
observes that American society actually resembled in important
ways the social and political landscape of the Bard's creations. One
contemporary explained that Shakespeare's characters resembled
"actual persons, so that we know them as well and remember them
as distinctly as we do out most intimate friends."[56] Shakespeare's
histories and tragedies wove morals about good and evil, tyranny
and freedom, that substantially formed the outlook of political
figures from Broderick to Abraham Lincoln.[57]

When we observe political figures in the following chapters evoking scenes from the stage or from the Roman forum (or from both at
once, as in *Julius Caesar*), we are not observing mere bombast or
flowery rhetoric draped on policy issues to dress them up. We
observe deadly serious public actors evoking the strongest moral,
ethical, and political lessons they knew – ones they shared with a
well-tutored audience, thanks to the popularity of Maguire's stage.

THE AGONY OF ORGANIZATION AND PARTICIPATION

Theatrical though it was, political leadership in the public sphere
had a concrete purpose: establishing party organizations necessary
to achieve office. In October 1849 the editor of the *Daily Alta California* set an inauspicious tone for party activists of the 1850s:

There is evidently a disposition on the part of scheming factionists in this
place and elsewhere, to attempt the basis of party structure; to mark the

---

[55] Levine, *Highbrow / Lowbrow*, 28–30.
[56] Henry Norman Hudson, *Lectures on Shakespeare*, quoted in Levine, *Highbrow / Lowbrow*, 36.
[57] For Lincoln on Shakespeare and his favorite play, *Macbeth*, see "Letters to James H.
       Hackett, August 17, November 2 1863," in Don E. Fehrenbacher, ed., *Abraham Lincoln: A
       Documentary Portrait through His Speeches and Writings* (Stanford: Stanford University Press,
       1977), 236–8.

lines of distinctions, raise the necessary hue and cry, and thus early sow the seeds of division and political discord.[58]

San Francisco party leaders had the misfortune of founding political institutions at the very moment when faith in the Jacksonian Democratic and Whig parties had begun to collapse.[59] The construction of San Francisco's urban polity took place within the larger story of the sectional crisis over slavery, which eventually destroyed the Whig and Democratic parties during the antebellum decade.[60]

The *Alta*'s report of the first efforts at party organization not only reflects the disillusionment with parties on the eve of the sectional crisis; it illustrates as well the vitality of republican political norms. To describe Whig and Democratic leaders as "factionists" and to equate party organization in general as sowing seeds of "division and political discord" was to declare allegiance to faith in a single public good that required no party label or organization to represent it. Long after the appearance of the Whigs and Democrats in the 1830s many continued to believe that parties advanced only the interests of the clutch of men who ran them.[61] Even the first Whig president, William Henry Harrison, after the most famous of partisan contests, the "Log Cabin and Hard Cider" campaign of 1840, declared in his inaugural that "if parties in a republic are necessary to secure a degree of vigilance sufficient to keep the public functionaries within the bounds of law and duty, at that point their usefulness ends. Beyond that they become destructive of public virtue."[62]

Voters registered this suspicion of parties by withholding their loyalties and demonstrating independence at the polls. "By the way, while on the subject of politics," Robert S. LaMotte, a minor Whig party activist, wrote to his mother in 1851, "the San Franciscans on that score as well as most others, are a very independent people and will not be bound to party if they don't like the candidates."[63] Twenty-five years later, Andrew Jackson Bryant, a lead-

58   *Alta*, 18 October 1849.
59   See Michael F. Holt, *Political Crisis of the 1850's* (New York: John Wiley & Sons, 1978); and J. Mills Thornton, *Politics and Power in a Slave Society: Alabama, 1800–1860* (Baton Rouge: Louisiana State University Press, 1978).
60   Potter, *The Impending Crisis*, 90–120.
61   Richard Hofstadter, *The Idea of a Party System: The Rise of Legitimate Opposition in the United States, 1780–1840* (Berkeley: University of California Press, 1969).
62   Daniel Walker Howe, ed., *The American Whigs: An Anthology* (New York, John Wiley & Sons, 1973), 77.
63   Robert S. LaMotte to Mother, 31 August 1851, LaMotte Family Letters, Bancroft Library, Berkeley, California.

ing Democrat, made a similar remark, recorded by an interviewer: "Mr. Bryant's experience in politics has led him to believe that men vote more independently in California than any other State of the Union."[64] The record of party voting in San Francisco and California amply supports these contemporary observations.[65] In San Francisco the loyalty of voters was so uncertain that no national party held municipal office for more than four years consecutively during the entire period from 1849 to 1881. "As California is a very fast state," observed the *Alta* in 1852, "it is natural that parties should run their course quickly as well as other things."[66] The only party that held municipal office for longer than four years was the "independent," overtly antiparty People's party, which held office for eleven years straight, from 1856 to 1867. From 1850 to 1856 the party in power in San Francisco changed every year. Party decomposition and recombination accompanied the disloyalty of the voters. By 1854 seven different parties hawked their tickets to the voters: "Whig," "Customs House Whig," "Citizen's Reform" (Know-Nothing), "Independent Citizen's," "Democratic," "Floating," and "Ciudado."[67] From 1850 to 1900, eight different parties held office in San Francisco: Democrat, Whig, Know-Nothing, People's, Union, Independent-Taxpayer's, Workingmen's, and Republican.[68]

David C. Broderick and William Gwin were among those who came to San Francisco "to attempt the basis of party structure," in the *Alta*'s pejorative words. A careful examination of the development of party structure in the 1850s shows that party activists built a house without a foundation. In return, the political community

---

[64] Bryant was chair of the California Union party during the Civil War, chair of the Democratic California State Central Committee after the war, and mayor of San Francisco from 1875 to 1879. Andrew Jackson Bryant, Dictation for H. H. Bancroft, Bancroft Library, Berkeley.

[65] Paul Kleppner, "Voters and Parties in the Western States, 1876–1900," *Western Historical Quarterly* 14 (January 1983): 49–68; idem, "Politics without Parties: The Western States, 1900–1984," in *The Twentieth-Century West: Historical Interpretations*, ed. Gerald Nash and Richard Etulian (Albuquerque: University of New Mexico Press, 1989), 295–338.

[66] *Alta*, 13 August 1852.

[67] *Alta*, 6 September 1854; Although the "Ciudado" ticket was evidently an organization of Californios, nothing further is known about it, and no further separatism among Spanish-speakers could be identified.

[68] May 1850–May 1851, Democratic; May 1851–January 1852, Whig; January 1852–November 1852, Democratic; November 1852–October 1853, Whig; October 1853–October 1854, Democratic; October 1854–July 1855, Know-Nothing; July 1855–November 1856, Democratic; November 1856–67, People's; 1867–9, Democratic; 1869–75, Independent-Taxpayer's; 1875–9, Democratic; 1879–81, Workingmen's.

showed a supreme independence from party loyalty, harbored a deep distrust of leaders' motives, and primed themselves for open rebellion when the depravity of the "professional politicians" seemed incontrovertible.

The Democratic leadership held the first "mass meeting" for the party on 25 October 1849, and although most of the Democratic ticket was elected two weeks later in the first general elections, another meeting had to be called in January 1850 "for the purpose of effecting an organization of the Democratic party."[69] Already at this second meeting the Democrats split into their famous anti- and pro-slavery factions. The Whigs began to organize in February, and in response, the Democrats attempted to close ranks, holding a "harmony" meeting on the first of March, followed by another "mass meeting" on the ninth. The object of all this activity was to prepare for the upcoming county elections, with the sheriff's office at the top of the ticket. During the rest of that month the two great parties held more meetings, then primaries, then nominating conventions, followed by mass ratification meetings and street entertainments on the eve of the election.[70]

Despite this assiduous courting of public support by the party leaders, the much-anticipated county election went to an independent candidate named Colonel John C. "Jack" Hays, a veteran and "hero" of the Mexican War. Why, in the much-touted era of Jacksonian "mass" parties, did the first important election in San Francisco go to an independent candidate? To answer this, we need to assess the extent to which urban parties were in fact mass-based organizations.

All three of the leading candidates for sheriff in 1850 were supposedly "colonels": Colonel Townes, the Whig candidate, Colonel J. J. Bryant, the Democratic, and "Jack" Hays, the independent. Early on, the contest was drawn between the Democrat Bryant and Hays, the "Texas Ranger." Throughout the campaign, Bryant, owner of a fine hotel on the Plaza, hired a band to play music from his hotel balcony, "while the finest liquors were gratuitously dispensed at the well-stocked bar to all who chose to drink."[71] True to Jacksonian forms, the candidates held their respective "mass"

[69] *Alta*, 1 November 1849; 15 November 1849, p. 2; 22 January 1850, p 3.
[70] *Alta*, 9, 11, 22 January 1850; *Alta*, 26, 28 February 1850; 1 March 1850, p. 2; Soulé et al., *Annals*, 267–8.; *Alta*, 11 March 1850, p. 2.
[71] Soulé et al., *Annals*, 269–72.

rallies in the Plaza on the Saturday before the election. Sharing this central space for public life, the Hays rally took place during the day, and the Bryant rally at night. Bryant's fête was clearly lavish:

The whole plaza was covered with men, horses, and wagons, and was illuminated with flaming torches and other lights, which blazed from the speakers' stand and hundreds of vehicles admirably arranged for the effect.... whilst, at regular intervals cannons were fired to give effect and increase the excitement.[72]

Both meetings ended in a procession.

Voting also took place on the Plaza, which was again transformed into a gala spectacle, thronged with voters and spectators: "We never struggled harder to exercise our right of suffrage," the *Alta* reported.[73] Both candidates made appearances, "greeted with cheers long and loud whenever they were discovered."[74] Bryant staged a final display of entertainment: "a procession of mounted men, and carriages filled with musicians, with banners and flags waving above them," coursed through the square at noon. But in the midst of the excitement thus produced by the Bryant procession, *The Annals of San Francisco* (1855) reports,

Col. Hays, mounted on a fiery black charger, suddenly appeared, exhibiting some of the finest horsemanship ever witnessed. The sight of the hero, as he sat bare-headed and unattended upon his noble animal, took the people by surprise, and called forth the admiration and patriotism of the vast multitude of spectators.

If liquor and entertainment won votes in Jacksonian America, as many historians would have us believe, Bryant would have been the clear winner. But Hays had added an intangible element to the campaign: charisma. "Men crowded around him on every hand, some seizing the bridle, others clinging to his clothing and stirrups, and each anxious to obtain a grasp of his hand. The cause of Col.

---

[72] Soulé et al., *Annals*, 269–72.

[73] Quotations like these are potentially misleading, and probably account for the mistaken belief in full voter mobilization in nineteenth-century American cities. A public space could be very crowded with thousands of individuals, and yet the turnout still only accounted for less than half of the adult white male population. Contemporaries did not say that "everyone" had come out to vote, only that it was crowded.

[74] *Alta*, 2 April 1850, p. 2.

Bryant was abandoned, and a vast majority of votes were given in favor of the "Texas Ranger."[75]

Out of an adult male population of perhaps 25,000 in 1850, about half of whom were citizens eligible to vote, a "vast majority" translates into 3,058 votes for Hays, 1,131 for Bryant, and only 262 for the Whig nominee.[76] This obscure election, coming as early as it did in the long history of San Francisco politics, nevertheless represents several persistent features of the city's political culture. First, regardless of the widespread hyperbole about "nearly universal" white male suffrage, the actual numbers of men participating was quite small relative to the eligible population, perhaps 30 percent in this case (uncertainty about the population before 1852 makes a more accurate estimate impossible). Second, party forms and practices did not necessarily lead to victory.[77] Third, the intangible element of face-to-face personal charisma, in this case a war hero on a fiery charger, provided a fundamental source of authority. In sum, parties would prove important, but not all-important, to winning power in antebellum San Francisco. To understand why, we need further to refine our definition of this institution.

Although the Jacksonian parties are typically praised as mass-based, egalitarian institutions, they were surprisingly limited and closed in nature when compared with more recent European socialist parties. Comparing organizational structures and activities, Maurice Duverger defines organizations like the modern French Partie Socialiste as "branch" parties, characterized by a network of local organizations whose roles are recruitment, propaganda, education, and community involvement. Branch parties maintain a constant level of activity between elections, meeting locally every two to four weeks. As Duverger correctly observes, the typical American party organization is characterized by a nearly opposite organizational behavior: "It consists of a small number of members, and seeks no expansion. It does not indulge in any propaganda with a view to extending its recruitment." It is a closed, not an open organization: "You do not get into it simply because you desire to do so: membership is achieved only by a kind of tacit co-option or by for-

[75] Soulé et al., *Annals*, 269–72.   [76] *Alta*, 4 April 1850, p. 2.

[77] Jean H. Baker, "The Ceremonies of Politics: Nineteenth-Century Rituals of National Affirmation," in *A Master's Due: Essays in Honor of David Herbert Donald*, ed. William J. Cooper, Michael F. Holt, and John McCordell (Baton Rouge: Louisiana State University Press, 1985), 169–71.

mal nomination." Nor does this "caucus" style of party meet regularly. "Outside of the election period," Duverger observes, the American caucus-style party "lives through a period of hibernation in which its meetings are neither frequent nor regular."[78]

Duverger's distinction between European "branch" and American "caucus" parties provides a sobering counterpoint to awe-inspired assessments of American party organizations. Close observation of party activity after the interelection hibernation period closed yields a finite inventory of organizational steps:

1. Meet to organize (or reorganize)
   (a) Choose "general" or "central" committee
2. Call a primary or convention
3. Hold primary, choose delegates to convention
4. Hold convention
   (a) Draft platform
   (b) Choose candidates ("slate")
5. Hold ratification meeting
6. Stage parades and stump speeches
7. Organize election-day mobilizations

Of these steps, only (3) and (7) call for popular participation. The rest of the organizational cycle, even if all the steps were followed faithfully (which they were not) was a formula for self-replicating petty oligarchs.

But primaries, the only point in the process that opened the possibility for democratic participation before elections, were notoriously manipulable. Primary elections required slates of candidates and prepared tickets, and these were crafted behind the scenes by the central caucus or by factions of the central caucus. Setting the date of the primary, or of the meetings to organize the primaries, was a decision controlled by the central caucuses. The *Alta* complained that "the Democratic – so called – primary election" of 16 May 1853 was "the result of an order pretendedly emanating from a pretended county committee":

The pretended meeting of the pretended committee, it is pretended, was held on the second instant, but the public was not notified ... a very nice

---

[78] Maurice Duverger, *Political Parties: Their Organization and Activity in the Modern State*, trans. Barbara North and Robert North (New York: Science Editions, 1963), 24.

start for those in the secret, in which to concoct, scheme, log-roll, pipe-lay and mystify.[79]

Whigs disliked primaries. The political philosophy of Whiggery distrusted popular input; the best men should, many Whigs believed, educate the people, not vice versa.[80] Whigs in San Francisco first appeared from behind the scenes in an "Address of the Whig General Committee to the Whigs of the District of San Francisco," on 26 February 1850, setting forth the principles of the "party." John J. R. DuPuy, chair of the Whig party, abruptly announced a meeting to be held that evening at the St. Francis Hotel "To choose a committee to nominate a Whig candidate for Assembly for this district." Twenty-one men constituted themselves into a nominating committee that night and chose candidates.[81] (The following month, however, this handful of Whig leaders belatedly submitted their choices to the voting Whigs in a "primary."[82])

As we have already seen, the Whig sheriff candidate attracted all of 262 votes to reward the chair DuPuy for his disdain. Voters were capable of turning out in large numbers in primaries, but they were equally capable of ignoring them.[83] "The proceeding was very quiet and extremely farcical," reported the *Alta* about a Whig primary: "There was no degree of interest manifested by anybody except those desirous of going to the convention."[84] Either way, the voters had little real input in the process; primaries merely ratified a slate chosen by the central committee for yet another central caucus meeting, the convention, a farce of participation that did not go unnoticed. "The whole system of primary elections and caucuses is a cunning device by which a few shrewd men can control and sway the masses to their will and make them subservient to their personal ends," complained one editorial.[85] But again, as the Texas Ranger's performance indicates, there was a nonorganizational way for men

[79] *Alta*, 16 May 1853, p. 2.
[80] Howe, *Political Culture of the American Whigs*.
[81] *Alta*, 26 February 1850, p. 2; 28 February 1850, p. 2.
[82] This primary drew so little interest that the papers failed to report its results.
[83] A Democratic primary held on 25 March 1850 drew 2,471 voters, which was, curiously, a thousand more votes than J. J. Bryant, the Democratic candidate at the top of the ticket, received in the actual election that followed. This corroborates the evidence that the magnetic personality of the independent Jack Hays pulled away voters from the Democratic ranks. Other high-participation primaries: *Alta* 5, 12 October 1852; 17, 28 May 1853; 23 June 1853; 14 July 1853; 10, 11 August 1854; 18 May 1855; 25 February 1856.
[84] *Alta*, 23 June 1853.   [85] *Alta*, 11 August 1854.

to "control and sway the masses to their will." Colonel Hays seems to have run his own campaign, leading a "cadre formation" of men grouped around a single charismatic personality.[86]

Such was the political process at the top of the participatory structure. What did the bottom of that pyramid, the voting members of the political community, experience as their own segment of the city's political life? As in the sheriff's election of 1850, voters had more than a mere voting presence in the process. Sheriff Hays enjoyed the direct acclaim of the political community as it assembled en masse in the Plaza. The leadership of the regular parties attempted to court this kind of mass approval as well, in the context of "mass ratification meetings," part of the traditional election ceremonies. Ratification meetings were held after conventions in order to receive popular approval of the platform and the slate of candidates chosen by the party elite. As Jean H. Baker observes, the ratification meeting was necessary to resolve the contradiction between the reality of elite direction of the party process and the ideal that candidates and platforms be the "people's choice."[87] In fact, these ratification meetings were carefully planned by the party elite, like the rest of the process to that point. "The Whigs are making preparations," LaMotte wrote during the Whig convention of September 1852, "for a demonstration on the receipt of the names of our candidates, which we expect to get by next week, then we will *do* something."[88]

In San Francisco the largest ratification meeting of the 1850s was attended by fewer than two thousand people.[89] Although these meetings were given grandiose names by the press, such as "Great Democratic Rally," they represented only a small minority of the actual votes cast, much smaller than the real crowd pleasers of that

---

[86] On "cadre formations," see Ronald P. Formisano, "Federalists and Republicans: Parties, Yes – system, No," in Paul Kleppner et al., *The Evolution of American Electoral Systems* (Westport, Conn., 1981).

[87] Baker, "Ceremonies of Politics," 170; idem, *Affairs of Party: The Political Culture of Northern Democrats in the Mid-Nineteenth Century* (Ithaca, N.Y.:Cornell University Press, 1983), 291–92.

[88] Robert S. LaMotte to Dan [brother], 15 September 1852, LaMotte Family Papers, Bancroft Library, Berkeley. Emphasis in original.

[89] For example, *Alta* 1, 13 August 1852; San Francisco *Herald*, 16, 20; *Alta*, 26 October 1856; *Alta*, 30 September 1860. The largest ratification meeting in the U.S. during the antebellum years was attended by 12,000 people in May 1840 to ratify the choice by the Whig convention of William H. Harrison for president. Jean Baker, "Ceremonies of Politics," 169.

decade: Vigilance Committee meetings and public executions. Whereas the 4 November 1856 Democratic vote for James Buchanan in San Francisco totaled 5,306, the 25 October Democratic ratification rally drew, by one account, "probably over one thousand" participants.[90] By contrast, a support rally for the Vigilance Committee of 1856 drew more than ten thousand people, as did the second legal execution in the city in 1854.[91]

Not long after these so-called mass ratification meetings came the election itself. Elections of the nineteenth century have often been described as festive public occasions, but there was a distinctly physical dimension to voting as well. The polls on election day were surrounded for a block or two with throngs of party workers, band wagons, or processions. A typical account in San Francisco ran: "The way to the polls, for a considerable distance, on either side, was completely blocked up by roughly dressed men, who thrust their favorite tickets into the hands of every newcomer, with loud exclamations for the parties for whom they were working."[92] The fact that ballots were printed and distributed by parties necessitated this crowding of the poll approaches with ticket hawkers. One account described the ticket hawker as a man "whose duty it was to yell at the pitch of his lungs the ticket he espoused and the utter folly of the opponent's 'paper.'"[93] Simply to reach the ballot box, a voter had to wade through a scene of tumult and noise, with "every other man holding in his hands big bundles of tickets."[94]

Just as they had managed the primary, convention, nomination, and ratification steps, the party leaders tried to manage this last step in the election process by controlling the distribution of ballots. Much was at stake here. Ticket vendors frequently clashed, contesting each other's right to stand near a poll. A common trick was to print ballots that looked like the opponent's ballot, but which had different names printed thereon.[95] Voters, being jostled

90 *Alta*, 26 October 1856; *Alta*, 14 November 1856.
91 *Alta*, 29 July 1854, p. 2; San Francisco *Daily Herald*, 15 June 1856; *Alta*, 15 June 1856.
92 Soulé et al., *Annals*, 265.
93 *Alta*, 30 May 1855.
94 *Alta*, 7 November 1860.
95 "Peddling spurious tickets," as one account phrased it. *Alta*, 30 May 1860. This practice eventually led the state legislature to pass the "Vignette Ticket Act," to regulate the appearance of ballots, in 1878. Each party thereafter had to file a party logo, or "vignette," with the office of the Registrar before the election, and stiff penalties for forgery were enacted. See Chapter 5.

about and shouted at, naturally had occasion to lose their tempers. And of course, liquor was much in evidence during election day.

That such a scene would generate violence is not surprising. What is surprising is the level of violence considered acceptable by contemporaries. It is almost impossible to find an election report that does not include multiple cases of violence at various polls. Even those contests pronounced, as the 1860 presidential election was, "one of the quietest ever known in San Francisco," included "a few – only a few – disturbances" in which "pistols were drawn."[96] By comparison with previous elections, the May 1855 city election was conducted "more peacefully than has been usual." "It seemed to be the feeling," the *Alta* reflected, "that whoever got into a fight would do injury to his party, *and so both sides kept up an armed neutrality through the day*."[97] Such "armed neutrality" included "a brisk fisticuff affair ... between a Democrat and a K. N. [Know-Nothing] ... the former accused the latter of peddling spurious tickets. Revolvers were drawn and the matter looked decidedly threatening, the Democrat hitting the K. N. over the head with the weapon."[98] By the September elections of 1858, the *Alta* was greatly impressed that "never in the history of this city has there been a more orderly and quiet election." Of course, there were "trivial exceptions," including: "First District ... Jas. P. Kelly was arrested for illegal voting, and afterwards assaulting an officer with a deadly weapon. Fifth District ... Two Germans arrested for interfering with voters, and two for disorderly conduct."[99]

Once at the ballot box, the struggle to vote was not yet finished. The only guard against illegal voting came from the watchfulness of party observers. At the May 1855 election, "so rigid was the scrutiny of some of the wards that voters were challenged three and sometimes four times to ascertain the place of residence, length of time in the country, and other legal matters."[100] To guard against tampering with the vote count, party workers often kept "outside tally lists," counting the number of voters entering and exiting the poll.[101] Poll watching often revealed how badly a party's candidate was doing and called for redoubled efforts at that poll to distribute more ballots. Sometimes the solution was more desperate. In

---

[96] *Alta*, 7 November 1860.   [97] *Alta*, 29 May 1855. Emphasis added.

[98] *Alta*, 30 May 1855.   [99] *Alta*, 2 September 1858.

[100] *Alta*, 30 May 1855.   [101] *Alta*, 6 September 1855.

several dramatic cases, hired men charged in and stole the whole ballot box, smashing it to bits in the street and scattering the ballots. As a result, the Democrats had to deploy in one primary election an indestructible steel boiler for a ballot box.[102]

After the closing of the polls, counting the tickets was a complicated and time-consuming affair. Although preliminary reports usually made general results known, a complete count was usually not finished until a week after the election and up to a month later for statewide results. At the very least, officials were awake all night counting ballots. What made the task so difficult was the practice of "scratching" names from the party ballots, otherwise known as "ticket splitting." The independence of San Francisco voters during the party-disintegrating 1850s found expression in this widespread practice of adjusting party nominations to suit a voter's preference. A report of the counting progress at the Seventh Ward reads:

They had assorted the tickets at 15 minutes after 12. Know-Nothing tickets, 417; Whig and mongrel tickets, 215; straight Democratic tickets, 400; Democratic split tickets, 150; Know-Nothing split tickets, 300; general split tickets 180. The counting will proceed all night.[103]

The counting process was the final chance for party activists to influence the outcome of an election. Election officials, usually partisans themselves, were often alone, having cordoned off the poll for the night. To influence the outcome at that point, of course, they had to commit fraud. Evidence of vote-counting fraud in San Francisco indicates that some offices were fraudulently won, but it does not indicate that whole party victories were achieved in this manner.[104]

Two general conclusions emerge from this discussion of the voting process. First, it required considerable effort merely to participate. A level of physical contact, and even violence, was inherent in the normal conduct of voting. "To deposit one's vote," one writer encouraged, "is a bit of a public duty which no citizen should shirk, albeit a bruised corn or an elbow in the ribs is the penalty paid for the task."[105] Second, the procedures adopted – distributing official and bogus tickets (almost forcefully) and challenging and counting voters and ballots – generated a hostile tension

102   *Alta*, 5, 12 October 1852.   103   *Alta*, 6 September 1855.
104   Robert M. Senkewicz, S. J., *Vigilantes in Gold Rush San Francisco* (Stanford, Calif.: Stanford University Press, 1985), 104, 116–19.
105   *Alta*, 30 May 1855.

throughout. Casting a ballot meant far more than depositing a slip of paper; it entailed a physical presence and required a personal resilience to being jostled, shouted at, and challenged. No wonder, then, that one often-repeated euphemism for ballots was "paper bullets." The warlike terminology of electioneering – "campaigns," "the battle" – had more than metaphorical significance, although the meaning is lost in the genteel procedures of modern American elections.

THE AGONY OF AUTHORITY

In her account of politics in the ancient polis, Hannah Arendt captures the dialectical relation between equality and freedom that can also be identified in the public sphere of republican San Francisco:

> To belong to the few 'equals' (*homoioi*) meant to be permitted to live among one's peers; but the public realm itself, the *polis*, was permeated by a fiercely agonal spirit, where everybody had constantly to distinguish himself from all others, to show through unique deeds or achievements that he was the best of all (*aien aristeuein*).[106]

In its ideological construction and even in certain objective characteristics, political life in San Francisco imitated that of the ancient polis. The Romantic republican idiom of political discourse turned San Franciscans toward Athens and Rome as serious models for political leadership. The Romantic understanding of history was not historicist. Ancient examples, drawn from Plutarch's *Lives*, Cicero's works, and the popular plays of Shakespeare, were taken as immediate ones, worthy of close scrutiny and imitation. The republican ideological construction of the political community was not, as we have begun to see in the preliminary discussions of participation, democratic. Only a select few of the residents participated in the city's self-government. All of them of were of course white male citizens, but not all white male citizens participated. White male citizens possessed a privileged status denied to most of the adults in the city: immigrants, Chinese, blacks, and women (who, while citizens, had sharply curtailed rights). The ever-present institutional fact of constitutionally protected chattel slavery encouraged

---

[106] Arendt, *The Human Condition*, 41.

contemporaries to feel themselves part of a republican tradition that made ancient examples fully relevant to the present day.[107]

The city's steep social gradation ran not from owners to workers merely, but from white male citizens to disfranchised women, to officially inferior disfranchised Chinese and African-Americans, and to chattel slaves. This social gradation was constructed along a *political* axis, not an economic one; high status and privilege was conferred through citizenship and self-mastery; medium status was enforced through denial of citizenship; and lowest status enforced through the nonpersonhood and absolute denial of freedom in slavery, a legal (not originally economic) condition. San Francisco's Plaza, then, was hardly the rude space where men equalized by the state of nature (as in Frederick Jackson Turner's frontier myth) built a democratic political nation from the ground up. It was the city's agora – marketplace and site of deliberation – where citizens who qualified through legal privilege to participate in self-government met and struggled to build a following sufficient to carry their version of the public good to success in policy outcomes.

On the other hand, of course, San Francisco was no polis, but a public corporation chartered by the state of California in the midst of a liberal, bourgeois revolution in human relations. The liberal revolution in market and human relations entailed no simple, linear development, but instead a jumble of seemingly anachronistic and "modern" cultural forms. Merchant capital, the early modern vanguard of liberalism, had itself revived slavery from an ancient past and made it a living, worldwide institution in the nineteenth century. It was, as Elizabeth Fox-Genovese and Eugene Genovese aptly observe, Janus-faced: "The confrontation, the violence, the ambiguous social and political ramifications of commerce and finance all challenge the imagination of those who would bring a measure of theoretical order to a disorderly historical experience."[108] San Francisco, preeminently a city of merchant – not industrial – capital, summoned reasonable analogues from the ancient polis and the Renaissance city-state. An entrepôt for the plunder of

---

[107] Though slavery was prohibited by the California constitution, slaveowners frequently brought their slaves in bondage through the state, and California Democrats were deeply divided between the Free-Soil and proslavery wings, led by David C. Broderick and William M. Gwin, respectively.

[108] Elizabeth Fox-Genovese and Eugene D. Genovese, *Fruits of Merchant Capital: Slavery and Bourgeois Property in the Rise and Expansion of Capitalism* (New York: Oxford University Press, 1983), 3. and passim.

gold from the land of a native people, it was the site of organization for ghastly exploitation marking the endpoint of a process that had begun with Hernán Cortés in Mexico.[109] Indeed, the original municipal government of San Francisco in the American period consisted of U.S. citizens occupying offices implanted in New Spain by Cortés and his successors: the *alcalde* – a Moorish colonial administrative officer with judicial and executive powers – and the *ayuntamiento* – or town councilors. So many historical forms present at the height of the liberal bourgeois revolution in market and human relations may have served only to intensify the reliance by public men on the republican idiom.

Romanticism was also present in this ambiguous sociopolitical environment; it was the cultural expression of the contemporaries themselves. Romanticism was not borrowed but *enabled* the borrowing. Romanticism simultaneously exalted the individual person and situated that person in nostalgic historical contexts, referencing his or her performance to models of heroic or moral individuals understood as having embodied certain pure types, available for emulation by later generations. Historians have identified several variations on the theme of republicanism in American history, including the Enlightenment republicanism of Jefferson and Adams; the domestic republicanism of Abigail Adams or Catherine Beecher, the plebeian style of Tom Paine and Fanny Wright, and the artisanal republicanism of the New York Working Men's party. But a distinct style of republicanism flourished at midcentury that deserves attention, one we could call "Romantic republicanism." Romantic republicanism was perhaps the last gasp of that political culture that organized political discourse around the central keywords of "virtue" and "corruption" and existed only as long as the myth of a single public good could be maintained.

Romantic republicanism was a volatile mix of liberalism and republicanism. It drew very heavily on the Romantic cult of character and mixed that priority with the republican cult of virtue, to exalt the honor of men who would lead in the quest to achieve the public

---

109 As to the ghastly exploitation of California's native people, see Edward D. Castillo, "The Impact of Euro-American Exploration and Settlement," in *Handbook of North American Indians*, vol. 8, general ed. William C. Sturtevant, 99–127 (Washington, D.C.: Smithsonian Institution, 1984). 99–107; Robert F. Heizer and Alan J. Almquist, *The Other Californians: Prejudice and Discrimination under Spain, Mexico, and the United States to 1920* (Berkeley: University of California Press, 1971).

good of all. The liberal variation on classical republican statesmanship, in sum, was a cult of charismatic, heroic leadership. Two great
philosophical treatments of heroic authority arrived almost simultaneously with the American conquest of San Francisco. The optimistic version was Ralph Waldo Emerson's *Representative Men* (1850),
which was modeled in turn on Thomas Carlyle's *On Heroes, Hero
Worship, and the Heroic in History* (1847).[110] Emerson explains that
divine essence (morality, or virtue), present in humanity at large, becomes manifest in exemplary individuals, who happen to possess
more of this transcendent goodness than others. "He is great,"
writes Emerson, "who is what he is from nature, and who never re-
minds us of others."[111] Melville's negative rendition of the charismatic leader Ahab in *Moby-Dick* (1851) captures the destructive
energy of both modern bourgeois and premodern slaveowning
authority.[112] In either optimistic or pessimistic form, the leader
commands authority by embodying those character traits shared by
the masses.

The point is not that most San Franciscans read Emerson and
Melville, but that Emerson and Melville read American political
culture at midcentury and redacted its practice into literary texts.
The practice of Romantic republicanism is all too apparent in antebellum San Francisco, where men wielded authority through an intense public rapport. William Walker, the "Grey-Eyed Man of
Destiny," raised his filibuster armies in San Francisco to conquer
first the Mexican state of Sonora, then Nicaragua. When he returned from his failed expedition to rule Sonora in 1854, he was
lionized in the city. A feeble attempt to convict him for violating neutrality laws brought out many prominent citizens in his
defense.[113]

The most revealing product of Romantic republicanism in antebellum San Francisco was formalized political violence. Violence
among the city's political leaders was rooted in the struggle to build
authority in a social milieu that privileged the intangible trait of

110   Thomas Carlyle, *On Heroes, Hero Worship, and the Heroic in History* (London: Chapman and
       Hall, 1872). On Carlyle and political consequences of his theories, see Ernst Cassirer, *The
       Myth of the State* (New York: Doubleday, 1955), 235–79.
111   R. W. Emerson, *Representative Men: Seven Lectures* (Boston: Phillips, Sampson, and Co.,
       1850), 12.
112   Michael Paul Rogin, *Subversive Genealogy: The Art and Politics of Herman Melville* (Berkeley:
       University of California Press, 1985).
113   William O. Scroggs, *Filibusters and Financiers: The Story of William Walker and His Associates*
       (New York, 1916); Lotchin, *San Francisco*, 220.

virtue – something that cannot be bought or displayed and yet has to be demonstrated through outward signs. The process of middle-class formation entailed a deep suspicion of outward forms, forms available to "confidence men and painted women" thanks to the success of urban capitalist consumer production.[114] Again, the problem of demonstrating that one truly possessed the masculine or the feminine virtues was rendered more difficult by the unstable social features of early San Francisco. For women, as we have seen, the struggle took place in bourgeois drawing rooms and in the seating arrangements of the theater. For men, however, the struggle to demonstrate one's virtue took a most violent form.

The supreme expression of political violence in antebellum San Francisco was the formal duel, performed according to the rigorous and antique *code duello* by dignified, leading citizens who were considered paragons of the order-loving citizenry. The duel was an integral – though frequently reviled – part of American political life during the first two-thirds of the nineteenth century. Aaron Burr, Alexander Hamilton, James Barron, Stephen Decatur, Andrew Jackson, Charles Dickenson, Thomas Hart Benton, Charles Lucas, John Randolph, Henry Clay, and many others fought widely publicized duels, and many died. One of the last of the infamous political duels in the United States took place on 13 September 1859 between U.S. Senator David C. Broderick and California Supreme Court Chief Justice David S. Terry.

Major political figures fought duels at least once a year in San Francisco from 1852 through 1861. David Broderick survived a duel with Judge Caleb B. Smith in 1852 when Smith's bullet struck Broderick's watch fob. Broderick encouraged a duel between city alderman John Cotter and John Nugent, editor of the Democratic San Francisco *Herald*, in the same year. In 1854 Benjamin F. Washington, Democratic chieftain, and Charles A. Washburn, editor of the San Francisco *Alta California*, dueled. Another prominent editor, James King of William, whose slaying sparked the 1856 Committee of Vigilance, was repeatedly challenged to duels as he attacked politicians in the columns of his paper, the San Francisco *Evening Bulletin*.[115]

Claiming to oppose the *code duello* on religious and ideological

---

[114] Karen Halttunen, *Confidence Men and Painted Women: A Study of Middle-Class Culture in America, 1830–1870* (New Haven: Yale University Press, 1982).

[115] On King's opposition to dueling and rejection of challenges, see T. H. Hittell, *History of California*, 3:465–6.

grounds, King nevertheless succumbed to the cultural logic that gave rise to the duel. One year before he was shot down in the street by one of his editorial targets (County Supervisor James P. Casey), James King delivered the following challenge to another opponent, referring to himself in the first person plural:

Mr. Selover, it is said, carries a knife. We carry a pistol. We hope that neither will be required, but if this recontre cannot be avoided, why will Mr. Selover persist in periling the lives of others? We pass every afternoon about half past four to five o'clock, along Market street, from Fourth to Fifth street. The road is wide and not so much frequented as those streets further in town. If we are to be shot or cut to pieces, for heaven's sake let it be down there.[116]

Indeed, newspaper editors occupied so sensitive a position in the political culture that they continued to draw fire long after the formal duel had fallen from fashion. San Francisco saw two assaults on editors in 1870 alone. The *Chronicle's* de Young brothers were shot at repeatedly during the 1860s and 1870s. While sitting behind his desk at the *Chronicle*, Charles de Young finally received a fatal shot in 1879 from the mayor-elect's son.[117]

Slurs on the characters of San Franciscans engaged in the fateful struggle over slavery during the tumultuous years before the Civil War resulted in three fatal duels, each involving a Northern and a Southern partisan and each ending in the death of the antislavery politician. On 21 August 1858 two close friends and fellow Democrats, William I. Fergusen and George Pen Johnston – who differed on the slavery issue – fought each other over remarks made by Fergusen at a political convention. After three probably intentionally timid shots, the principals finally hit one another. Fergusen eventually died on September 14 after lingering for three weeks at the Union Hotel, the headquarters of his and Broderick's faction, the Douglas, or Anti-Lecompton, Democrats.

Exactly one year later, Broderick himself lay in the same hotel, dying from a mortal chest wound. The Broderick–Terry duel resulted from remarks made by Terry during a Democratic convention and by Broderick during a political dinner. A later chapter

---

[116]   Quoted in Edward McGowan, *Narrative of Edward McGowan*, 19.
[117]   Henry G. Langley, comp., *San Francisco Directory for 1870*, 33–6; Hittell, *History of California*, Vol. 4:656.

analyzes that duel. And finally, on 25 May 1861, two state assembly-men faced one another with rifles at forty yards. Charles W. Piercy, Unionist Democrat, took Daniel Showalter's bullet in the mouth and died instantly. This, the last political duel in California, re-sulted from Piercy's having changed his mind on a caucus vote for U.S. senator.[118]

This gruesome record of political violence during the 1850s pro-jects a clear political-cultural pattern. The practice of dueling has been strongly associated with the putatively premodern Southern slaveowning culture.[119] But at least half of the duelers in San Fran-cisco were Northern men. The sheer effort to establish authority in a political discourse dominated by the idea of virtue could produce a practice of dueling in the liberal marketplace of San Francisco as well as anywhere else, however. "Courage," Julian Pitt-Rivers writes, "is the *sine qua non* of honor, and cowardice is always its con-verse. Willingness to stand up to opposition is essential to the acqui-sition, as the defense, of honor, regardless of the mode of action that is adopted."[120]

PRELIMINARY CONCLUSIONS

The several structural and practical features of antebellum political culture in San Francisco have now been presented in a preliminary way, to introduce the volatile elements that participants brought to-gether to create the political organizations and events of the 1850s. Discussions of exemplary individuals, population demographics, class and gender group identities, the public sphere, political par-ties, political participation, and the Romantic republican struggle for authority culminating in the duel have all been presented here in a somewhat artificial way, abstracted from the narrative flow of events that makes them real elements of the historical process. Social-scientific methods require this sort of parsing in order to analyze and, if possible, to build models capable of making sense of the relations between the state and society.

---

[118] Hittell, *History of California*, 4:279.
[119] Bertram Wyatt-Brown, *Southern Honor: Ethics and Behavior in the Old South* (New York: Oxford University Press, 1982); Kenneth S. Greenberg, "The Nose, the Lie, and the Duel in the Antebellum South," *American Historical Review* 95:1 (February 1990): 57–74.
[120] Julian Pitt-Rivers, "Honor," in *International Encyclopedia of the Social Sciences*, 18 vols., ed. David L. Sills (New York: Macmillan Co., 1968) 6:505.

Here some preliminary conclusions about the relationship between urban state and society in the formative years of San Francisco are in order. First and foremost, there can be no easy identification between social groups and political behavior because social groups were at best nebulous, ill-formed entities. To complete their formation, as we shall see in later chapters, leaders had to mobilize individuals in the public sphere, persuading them to think and act like members of the classic sociological groups: as a class and as racial, gendered, and ethnic beings. For the time being, the public sphere was dominated by participants who mobilized followers according to variations on the Romantic republican script, which in Whig, Democratic, Know-Nothing, and People's party variants recognized only a single public good. The possibility of mobilizing groups that, in name at least, did not easily represent the entire political community (white male citizens, of course) was foreclosed by the structure of discourse itself, which lacked a context of plural interest and multiple publics that eventually arose in the late-nineteenth century.

The urban public sphere of the 1850s was a closed, unitary arena for the pursuit of organization, power, authority, and policy. In that sphere of practice the elements discussed in this chapter were inextricably intertwined. The white male dominated political community of privileged citizens guarded access to a public sphere against invasion from women and people of color. That public sphere, in turn, was the arena in which party activists had to pursue their goal of organizing Whig and Democratic electoral victories. The apparent secrecy and manipulation of caucus-style party organizations, however, clashed fundamentally with the normative republican expectations of political power publicly gotten from debates among assembled or reading citizens. Assembling or mobilizing citizens required authority, which meant honor, built from the reputation of being virtuous. To prove their possession of such character traits, men frequently dueled, and frequently died. The duel and the paraviolent nature of political participation also reinforced the boundaries of the public sphere. As long as political participation entailed behavior of this kind, men would find it inconceivable that women should gain the franchise.

The very operation of the urban public sphere, moreover, as an arena of antagonistic equality, where men met to set policy in the interests of the assembled "public," contained the elements of a fundamental legitimation crisis. Where, in a fatal discourse about absolute qualities like "virtue," was there room for disagreement? In the next two chapters, the extraordinary rise of the committees of vigilance and the long-lived "People's party" are examined in detail. These political events were the product of political mobilization in the political public sphere. To understand them properly is a goal far more important than simply to understand the curious aspects of San Francisco's particular historical development (although it is that also). Understanding the vigilante movement is to understand the centrality of the public in mid-nineteenth-century American cities. It is, as we shall see, impossible to reduce political history to social history, that is, to explain political outcomes by reference to some underlying social "facts" about group interests or group behavior.

CHAPTER 2

Republican terror: The origins of the Vigilante movements of 1851 and 1856

In the name of heaven, Catalina, how long do you propose to exploit our patience? Do you really suppose your lunatic activities are going to escape our retaliation for evermore? Are there no limits to this audacious, uncontrollable swaggering? Look at the garrison of our Roman nation which guards the Palatine by night, look at the patrols ranging the city . . . the entire body of loyal citizens massing at one single spot!

          – Marcus Tullius Cicero, 63 B.C.E.[1]

The People – long suffering under an organized despotism which has invaded their liberties – squandered their property – usurped their offices of trust and emolument – endangered their lives – prevented the expression of their will at the ballot-box, and corrupted the channels of justice, have now risen in virtue of their inherent right and power. All political, religious, and sectional differences and issues have given way to the paramount necessity of a thorough and fundamental reform of the social and political body.

          – San Francisco Committee of Vigilance, 1856 C.E.[2]

In the spring of 1856 the constitutional polity of San Francisco collapsed completely. What arose in its stead was the most extensive and interesting of American vigilante movements, the Vigilance Committee of 1856. A broadly based political and social movement, the committee drew its fearsome power from a republican under-

---

[1] "Against Lucius Sergius Catalina," 7 November 63 B.C.E. in *Selected Political Speeches of Cicero*, trans. Michael Grant (New York: Penguin Books, 1969), 76.

[2] Broadside [n.d.], San Francisco Committee of Vigilance, 1856, Papers, Huntington Library, San Marino, California. This broadside is signed "Secretary" [Isaac Bluxome, Jr.], and carries the seal of the Vigilance Committee. Although not dated, it seems to have been issued in the first week of June 1856, after Governor Johnson declared the city of San Francisco to be in a state of insurrection.

standing of public ethics. Thanks to the myths constructed by Frederick Jackson Turner and as seen in a thousand Hollywood movies, vigilance committees are routinely treated as cases of "frontier justice," interpreted in terms indigenous to the national history of the United States. In their own view, however, the Vigilantes were reenacting a political script written in Rome nineteen centuries earlier by the champion of republican liberties, Cicero. Historians since Turner have insisted on interpreting political development in terms of socioeconomic causation. To Turner, who used the San Francisco case as evidence in his famous essay "The Significance of the Frontier in American History," the process of settling the open frontier environment led to a distinct political outcome: Democracy was reaffirmed by the elemental process of establishing government where none had existed before. Social historians over the last three decades have traced political events like the vigilante movements to class and other underlying group conflicts. But the Vigilance Committee of 1856 was a political movement arising from political causes.[3]

The Vigilantes claimed, in the name of "The People," that "an organized despotism" had "invaded their liberties – squandered their property – usurped their offices of trust and emolument – endangered their lives – prevented the expression of their will at the ballot-box, and corrupted the channels of justice."[4] These were political complaints. This chapter shall endeavor to show that this political language must be taken seriously. The "Committee of '56" arose from a complex amalgam of local and national political conditions during the 1850s. Men who understood their role in history not as pioneers re-creating democracy, nor as members of a socioeconomic or ethnic group, but as republican statesmen faced with an ancient challenge to liberty, led a movement that needs to be understood in political, not social terms.

---

[3] Frederick Jackson Turner, "The Significance of the Frontier in American History," in Turner, *The Frontier in American History* (1920; University of Arizona Press, 1986). References to Hubert Howe Bancroft's *Popular Tribunals* and Charles Howard Shinn's *Mining Camps* appear at p. 33 of this edition. Turner and Shinn were both graduates of the Johns Hopkins Seminary of History and Politics; William Cronon, "Revisiting the Vanishing Frontier: The Legacy of Frederick Jackson Turner," *Western Historical Quarterly* 28:2 (April 1987): 157–76.
[4] Broadside [May 1856], San Francisco Committee of Vigilance Papers, Huntington Library, San Marino, California.

A BRIEF OUTLINE OF THE SAN FRANCISCO
VIGILANCE COMMITTEES

The two San Francisco committees of vigilance were part of a long American tradition of organized extralegal law enforcement, beginning with the South Carolina Regulator movement of 1767–9. Richard Maxwell Brown identifies 326 such movements nationwide since the Regulators, and David A. Johnson has counted 380 in California alone between 1849 and 1902.[5] In California, the tradition first appeared at "Hangtown" (now Placerville), where miners hanged three men in January 1849.[6] In San Francisco that July, Samuel Brannan, Hall McAllister, Isaac Bluxome, Jr., and other future Vigilantes organized several hundred volunteers into an extralegal police force to capture, try, and banish a gang known as the "Hounds."[7]

The first San Francisco Committee of Vigilance began in June 1851 with the capture and hanging of an alleged burglar named John Jenkins. It officially enrolled more than seven hundred members; it maintained a headquarters where it incarcerated and interrogated its suspects – trying them without benefit of counsel; and it met in plenary session. Besides executing four men, its activities included defying writs of habeas corpus, policing the city, investigating disreputable boardinghouses, boarding and inspecting vessels, deporting immigrants, and training and parading its militia. The Committee of 1851 operated in defiance of the local authorities, but it did not attempt to assume such regular governmental functions as fiscal and legislative responsibilities. The most visible of its activities ended with the fall elections in September 1851, but its Executive Committee continued to hold meetings until sometime in 1853.

The second Committee of Vigilance was very much a continuation of the first one, with many of the same leaders. Its official seal reads: "Reorganized 15th May, 1856." The "constitution" from the

---

[5] Richard Maxwell Brown, *Strain of Violence: Historical Studies of American Violence and Vigilantism* (New York: Oxford University Press, 1975), 103; David A. Johnson, "Vigilance and the Law: The Moral Authority of Popular Justice in the Far West," *American Quarterly* 33:5 (Winter 1981): 558–86.

[6] Hubert Howe Bancroft, *Popular Tribunals,* 2 vols. (San Francisco: History Co., Publishers, 1887), 1:144–5.

[7] Roger Lotchin, *San Francisco, 1846–1856: From Hamlet to City* (New York: Oxford University Press, 1974), 190–1; Bancroft, *Popular Tribunals,* 1:97–102.

first committee was adopted on that date, with few amendments. Despite the continuity, this second committee broke radically with the American vigilante tradition. Whereas previous vigilante movements, including the Committee of 1851, were concerned exclusively with civil crime, the Committee of 1856 was concerned, from the outset, with politics and political crimes. The shooting of James King of William[8] by James P. Casey, the event that brought the committee into being, was a political duel. The committee's first victim was a county supervisor, and its final act was to establish a political party. The Committee of 1856 was also enormous in size. By the time of the "Grand Parade," held to celebrate its disbandment on 11 August 1856, about six thousand men, a majority of the political community, not only had enrolled, but were participating daily in the fifty or so military companies that marched through San Francisco from June through September.

The Committee of 1856 maintained a group of large buildings – fortified with gunny sacks and cannon – as its headquarters, which contained large assembly halls, meeting rooms, a military kitchen, an infirmary, an armory, and several prison cells. Like the first committee, it executed four men. But the body count of the second committee really stands at five, considering the suicide of James "Yankee" Sullivan, who killed himself out of terror while in the Vigilantes' custody. Like the first committee also, the second one patrolled the streets, conducted investigations, held trials without benefit of counsel for the accused, deported citizens, and defied writs of habeas corpus. The Committee of 1856 far surpassed the open rebelliousness of its precursor, however. The hallmark of a popular rebellion has always been the defection of the constitutional government's militia to the ranks of the rebels. Led by the largest militia company, the California Guards, every militia company in San Francisco save two (and these were gentlemen's sporting companies) defected to the Vigilantes.[9] The Committee of 1856 captured a shipment of federal arms destined for the enfeebled state militia and arrested, imprisoned, and tried the chief justice of the California Supreme Court.

---

8 James King adopted the patronymic "of William," reportedly, to distinguish himself from other James Kings in his hometown.
9 Bancroft, *Popular Tribunals*, 2:93.

INTERPRETATIONS

Such extraordinary events have naturally attracted much scholarly attention: so much, in fact, that it is necessary to present a critique of that literature before proceeding to the argument presented in this chapter. The best histories of the committees are still two of the earliest ones: Hubert Howe Bancroft's two-volume, 1,521-page *Popular Tribunals* (1887), and Mary F. Williams's 543-page *History of the San Francisco Committee of Vigilance of 1851* (1921).[10] The many treatments written in more recent times leave Bancroft and Williams unsurpassed in their comprehensive factual and narrative coverage. Indeed, all subsequent histories have sought only to offer new interpretations of the Vigilante movements, challenging the judgments of Bancroft and Williams, and adding only selectively to the store of empirical knowledge about those episodes.[11]

It is the political nature of the second Committee of Vigilance that has kept the historical mills grinding for so many years, and the political nature of that movement has confounded every historian except Bancroft. Only Bancroft, who lived through the second movement and based his study on the oral histories of the leaders of the committees, understood that the rebellion of 1856 was politically motivated. Other historians, beginning with the Hegelian philosopher Josiah Royce (1886) and continuing through the most recent histories of Roger Lotchin (1974), Richard Maxwell Brown (1975), Peter R. Decker (1978), and Robert Senkewicz (1985), have argued that the Committee of 1856 was the result of allegedly deeper, more fundamental divisions in San Francisco society, for which the political trappings and stated goals were mere disguise.

The most recent interpretation is Robert Senkewicz's *Vigilantes in*

---

[10] Williams was the first twentieth-century historian to reexamine Bancroft's enormous archive material, as one of the editors of the University of California's project to publish the documents from the first committee. Mary F. Williams, *History of the San Francisco Committee of Vigilance of 1851: A Study of Social Control on the California Frontier in the Days of the Gold Rush* (Berkeley: University of California Press, 1921).

[11] The most recent in a very long line of historical studies of vigilante movements is Robert M. Senkewicz, S.J., *Vigilantes in Gold Rush San Francisco* (Stanford, Calif.: Stanford University Press: 1985). Senkewicz provides an excellent historiographical essay as an appendix to his book. Other important recent histories that are discussed are Roger W. Lotchin, *San Francisco, 1846–1856: From Hamlet to City* (New York: Oxford University Press, 1974), esp. 245–75; Richard Maxwell Brown, *Strain of Violence*, Peter R. Decker, *Fortunes and Failures: White Collar Mobility in Nineteenth Century San Francisco* (Cambridge, Mass.: Harvard University Press, 1978); David A. Johnson, "Vigilance and the Law," 558–85.

Gold Rush San Francisco. Senkewicz begins with the same erroneous assumption that has beguiled most twentieth-century interpreters of the Vigilantes: that the nature and causes of the committees can be deduced from the fact that the Vigilante leadership was composed of the city's leading merchants. Senkewicz asserts that the true cause of both Vigilante episodes was the psychological frustration of the merchant elite during slow business months and their "need for scapegoats" to exorcise internal discontent.[12] The enemies of the Vigilantes, in Senkewicz's opinion, were not real but imagined enemies, serving as proxies for the true demons of the Vigilantes' collective soul. Of the first committee, Senkewicz writes:

It was not so much an increase in crime as the merchants' fear of crime, on which they could blame their uncomfortable feelings of not doing very well in the gold rush city.... More probable, perhaps, than that makeshift explanation [crime], is another, that the merchants were groping toward a scapegoat.[13]

Senkewicz has a similar explanation of the Committee of 1856. It was not political corruption or election fraud that motivated the Vigilantes, but a deep jealousy felt for the politicians by the merchants of the city during a business slump.[14]

Senkewicz's account of the Vigilantes shares a theoretical parentage with other recent accounts. All of these attempt to deduce the meaning of the committees from their mercantile leaderships, and all proffer something other than the stated goals of the Vigilantes as the real source of their actions. Richard Maxwell Brown asserts that "the mercantile complexion of the Vigilance Committee [of 1856] is the key to its behavior."[15] To him, the Committee of 1856 was a movement of the Yankee merchant elite against the immigrant poor; a successful effort to end the rule of an extravagant Irish working-class political machine in order to restore the city's credit in the East.[16] Brown conducted the first systematic analysis of the approximately 2,300 surviving membership applications. In his thumbnail sketch of the membership, Brown emphasized white-collar occupations. The majority of those accepted applications,

---

12 Senkewicz, *Vigilantes in Gold Rush San Francisco*, 62–77.
13 Senkewicz, *Vigilantes in Gold Rush San Francisco*, 76–7; 82. Senkewicz goes so far as to attribute the origins of the first committee to "boredom" on the part of the merchants.
14 Senkewicz, *Vigilantes in Gold Rush San Francisco*, 156–202.
15 Brown, *Strain of Violence*, 137.   16 Brown, *Strain of Violence*, 142–3.

however, were made by blue-collar workers, as the data displayed in Table 2.1 show.[17]

Peter R. Decker makes a case similar to those of both Brown and Senkewicz, again inferring the nature and course of vigilantism from its merchant-elite leadership:

When the members of the city's elite in the years 1852 to 1856 experienced sudden and dramatic shifts in their careers, they selected vigilantism as the solution to their plight, unaccustomed as they were to working with the democratic procedures available. . . . The formation of the Vigilance Committee of 1856 was in itself an admission by the elite of their failure to maintain their occupational and financial status in the community.[18]

What recent historians share in their conceptualizations of vigilantism is an implicit model that assigns political behavior to a secondary role in relation to society. The Committee of 1856 arose primarily from a political crisis, however, which had its source in the republican script for political action.

COMPOSITION OF THE TWO COMMITTEES

Who were the Vigilantes? A picture of the membership may be the most logical place to start an investigation of the vigilante movements. What kinds of men joined may provide some clues as to why they joined. Most recent historians have focused only on the elite leadership when describing its members. Focusing on the merchants who led the committees is not new. Friends of both committees pointed to the large number of wealthy members in order to establish their legitimacy and to differentiate these organizations from lynch mobs. Enemies, on the other hand, pointed to the wealthy as a method of casting aspersions on committees' motives, appealing to the populist sentiments about the common man. Responding to this repetitive chorus in 1922, Mary F. Williams assured her readers that the majority of the first committee "were clerks or small tradesmen, and are unknown to posterity except as sons or grandsons carry on their names."[19] Evidence on the membership of the first committee is very scant. Based on a careful trace of the surviving names in the city directories, however, it is possible to say

---

[17] Brown, *Strain of Violence*, 137.   [18] Decker, *Fortunes and Failures*, 139–40.
[19] Williams, *History of the San Francisco Committee of Vigilance of 1851*, 188–9.

with certainty that the majority were not, as Williams concluded, merchants.[20]

When the Committee of 1856 disbanded, its members held a "Grand Parade" through the city, six thousand strong in full battle dress. This parade provided a chance for the friendly *Alta* to defend the committee against "all which has been said against them. They were not, as has been invidiously insinuated by the 'law and order' journals, made up entirely of 'merchants,' or 'speculators,' though these, as well as others, were joined with them. The masses were the 'bone and sinew,' whom political orators love to flatter, the 'hard-handed' mechanics, and laboring men of San Francisco."[21] Bancroft not only agreed but offered a rather comprehensive list:

This body was composed of all classes and conditions of men. Every nationality, every political and religious sentiment, every trade, profession, and occupation was represented, the only qualifications necessary for admittance being honesty and respectability. There were Catholics and Protestants, Jews and Gentiles; believers and unbelievers; know-nothings, democrats, republicans; merchants, mechanics, clerks, porters, bankers, barkeepers, draymen, stevedores, lawyers, doctors, butchers, bootblacks, hotel-keepers, and ship-captains. There were Americans and Irishmen; Frenchmen, Germans, Italians, and Spaniards; Englishmen, Welshmen, Scotchmen, and all the rest of the white-skinned races, represented in this anomalous assemblage.[22]

Friends and enemies of the committees had, depending on the circumstances, a motive for emphasizing either the wealthy or the common, native or foreign, membership of these organizations. Thanks to the survival of about 2,300 accepted membership applications to the Committee of 1856, it is possible to make a more concrete accounting of the Vigilantes than historical testimony has provided. These membership applications, held in the Huntington Library in San Marino, California, preserve the name, occupation, age, place of birth, date of application, and membership serial number of each applicant and the names of the applicant's sponsors for membership. Using a sample of adult white males drawn from the 1860 U.S. Census manuscript as a baseline for comparison, it is

---

[20] For an in-depth consideration of the 1851 Vigilance Committee membership, see Philip J. Ethington, "*The Structures of Urban Political Life: Political Culture in San Francisco, 1850–1880*" (Ph.D diss. Stanford University, 1989), 102–12.

[21] *Alta*, 19 August 1856.

[22] Bancroft, *Popular Tribunals*, vol. 2, 84–5.

Table 2.1. *Occupational distribution and relative risk estimate of joining the Vigilance Committee of 1856*

Occupational group	1860 Census sample, S.F. ($N = 328$)		1856 Vigilantes ($N = 2,204$)		Relative risk
	(%)	(N)	(%)	(N)	
Merchants	8.8	(29)	17.4	(384)	2.0
Petty Proprietors	14.6	(48)	19.8	(436)	1.4
Clerks and Salesmen	5.2	(17)	8.1	(179)	Even[a]
Skilled Workers	31.7	(104)	36.2	(799)	Even[a]
Semiskilled Workers	25.9	(85)	14.4	(318)	0.5
Unskilled Workers	11.9	(39)	1.4	(32)	0.2

Notes: The difference in proportions between these two samples is statistically significant: Chi-square test for a row by column contingency table = 155.4, $P < .0001$
[a] Although the proportions may *look* different for these two groups, they are not statistically so.
Sources: Membership Applications to the 1856 Committee of Vigilance, San Francisco Committee of Vigilance Papers, Huntington Library, San Marino, California; Manuscript schedule of the U.S. Census of San Francisco of 1860.

possible to conduct reliable statistical tests and to summarize the composition of that committee with some accuracy.[23] First, merchants were more likely than any other occupational group to join. Table 2.1 displays the distribution of occupational groups within the census, or control group, and within the 1856 Vigilance Committee. It also displays estimates of the "relative risk" that a given individual from each occupational group would have joined the committee. (See Appendix for further explanation).

[23] San Francisco Vigilance Committee of 1856, Membership Applications, Huntington Library, San Marino, California. The surviving applications represent 76% of all the applications taken by the Vigilance Committee. There were about 6,000 members of the second committee, 3,000 of whom had already joined by 25 May, when the earliest application is dated. The Vigilantes did not begin using applications until that date, so most of the difference between the membership of 6,000 and the 2,300 applications can be accounted for by this simple fact. The surviving applications were acquired by the Huntington Library in the 1920s from two separate sources. Because these applications would have been extremely damaging evidence had the Vigilantes come to trial, and were kept privately in a clandestine manner for three-quarters of a century, we can assume that the remaining 700 applications were simply lost or destroyed in a statistically random manner. Using the 1860 U.S. Census manuscript for comparison is justifiable because of the supporting evidence that the population had stabilized by 1856, so that the populations of 1856 and 1860 should not have been substantially different.

On the surface, it seems from Table 2.1 that a clear class bias was present in the membership of the Committee of 1856. Although working-class men (considering all blue-collar occupations together for the moment) comprised the majority (52%) of the committee, they were underrepresented relative to the figure of 69.5 percent for skilled, semiskilled, and unskilled workers of the city's adult white males. The top and bottom of Table 2.1 deliver a clear message. The relative risk estimates show that merchants were two times more likely than members of other occupational groups to join, and that petty proprietors (shopkeepers, etc.) were 1.4 times more likely than members of other occupations. At the bottom of the scale, semiskilled workers (sailors, longshoremen) were only half as likely to join, and unskilled workers were one-fifth as likely as members of other groups to join.

There is no particular reason, however, to draw a line in the middle of Table 2.1 between "white-" and "blue-" collar workers and to focus on the top and bottom of the occupational scale alone. Indeed, the table divides more significantly into *three* groups: the middle two occupational ranks, clerks and salesmen, and skilled workers, present the most interesting case. These two groups were just as likely to join as not to join; they were, in other words, proportionately represented in the committee. Skilled workers, moreover, comprised the largest single occupational bloc of Vigilantes: More than one-third of the total membership were the "bone and sinew" of San Francisco's adult white male population.

Another interpretation of Table 2.1, then, would be that the committee was composed of the same groups of men who composed the political community at large: the occupationally skilled and residentially stable. Semi- and unskilled workers (as Chapter 1 suggested and as we will see with greater certainty in Chapter 5), were typically left out of the urban political community, so their underrepresentation in the Committee of 1856 should not surprise us. This leaves only one remarkable feature of the occupational composition of the committee: the overrepresentation of merchants. There can be no doubt that merchants played a key role in the committee. They dominated the leadership and were twice as likely to join than were members of other occupational groups.

There was, however, something very peculiar about the merchants who joined the Committee of 1856: They were extraordinarily young. Only 14 percent of merchants in the city at large were

younger than thirty, whereas 43 percent of the merchants in the
Vigilance Committee were. Indeed, the entire committee was composed of men younger, on average, than the mean age for the city's
adult white males (a mean of 31.3 compared to 32.5).[24] In terms of
the relative risk estimate, men in their twenties were 1.4 times more
likely to join the Vigilantes than men aged twenty-nine or older. But
the age difference for the merchants was much more dramatic. The
mean age of the city's male merchants was 36.8 years, whereas the
mean age of the Vigilante merchants was only 33.7.[25] Again in terms
of the relative risk estimate, a merchant in his twenties was *four times*
more likely to join the Committee of 1856 than a merchant aged
thirty or older.[26]

For a mass movement claiming to represent the city's indivisible
general interests, it is hardly surprising that the merchants would
provide the leadership. Analyses that have focused on the *class* of
the merchants have failed to notice their *age*, however. Within the
climate of Romantic republicanism, the attractions of a movement
of this sort to young men of the highest occupational group would
have been very great. It was an idealistic chance to assert the republican ideals of unity and virtue; it promised military distinction and
an opportunity to prove one's courage, will, determination, and
character. It was a reenactment of the heroic deeds of the Founding
Fathers, a striking down of corruption and tyranny with the valor of
the Minutemen.

The ethnic breakdown of the Vigilante membership is also very
revealing. Native-born men were 2.3 times more likely to join the
committee than members of other national groups. Frenchmen,
who joined the committee in large blocs of French militia companies, were 2.8 times more likely to join. Germans and men born
in the British Isles and Canada were equally likely to join as not to
join. At the other end of the scale, Irish-born men, who comprised
19 percent of the city's population, made up less than 2 percent of
the Vigilance Committee. They were only one-fifth as likely to join

---

[24] $N = 2104$ for the Vigilantes, 333 for the city. The difference between these two population
means is significant according to a t-test, $P = .01$. The ages of the control census group
were adjusted downward for the increase (of 1.4 years) in the mean age of the city's adult
male population between 1856 and 1860.

[25] N for Vigilantes = 326; N for city = 29, $P = .05$.

[26] N for the Vigilante merchants = 326; N for the city's merchants = 29. Chi-square = 8.7,
$P = .003$; 95% Confidence Interval for the Relative Risk estimate = 1.5, 11.6.

the committee as members of other ethnic groups.[27] Many of the Irish who did join the committee, moreover, were careful to qualify their applications with such disavowals as "Protestant," "Londonderry," "Belfast," or "North of Ireland."[28]

This kind of ethnic bias in the committee's membership raises the real possibility that ethnoreligious conflict between Protestants and Irish Catholics was a major source of the Vigilante movement, as some historians have claimed. Indeed, the first two victims of Vigilante terror in May of 1856, James P. Casey and Charles Cora, were Catholics. The motto of the 1856 committee, however, was "No Party, No Creed, No Sectional Issues." The Vigilantes strenuously claimed that they were interested only in purifying the city's political institutions. Should we believe them? One negative corroboration of their claim is that in none of the committee's thousands of pages of surviving documents, nor in any newspaper source, could I find a single statement of anti–Irish Catholic motivation by a Vigilante. Given the extreme nature of overt anti-Catholic nativism then present in cities like Boston and New York, the lack of nativist language in the Committee of 1856 causes us to wonder about the meaning of the ethnic composition of the committee. This riddle can only be unraveled through an examination of the sources of the Vigilante movement, to which this analysis now turns. In the following pages, it will be possible to explain the significance of both the heavy participation by stable, skilled occupational groups and the avoidance of the committee by the Irish Catholics.

"DOWN IN FRONT!": CRIME AND THE POPULARITY OF EXECUTIONS

Because the leaders of the 1856 Vigilance Committee established a political party that was to rule the city from 1856 through the end of the Civil War, because the 1851 and 1856 committees were both dominated by merchants, and because of the ethnic bias in the Committee of 1856, some historians have doubted that there was any substantial connection between crime and the formation of the

---

27 Chi-squared tests showed the relative risk, or likelihood, of Irish joining the 1856 Vigilance Committee to be .18, with a confidence interval of .15 to .22 (Chi-square = 217.6), and a p-value of less than .001.

28 Membership Applications, San Francisco Committee of Vigilance Papers, Huntington Library, San Marino, California.

committees. The complaint about crime, they maintain, was really just a cover for other motives. Indeed, to support their claims about ulterior motives – ethnocultural, economic, and psychological – Richard Maxwell Brown, Peter R. Decker, and Robert M. Senkewicz, respectively, have concluded from newspaper analysis that crime rates were not unusually high before the formation of the two committees.

Kevin Mullen has confirmed, in a comprehensive study of all reported crimes in San Francisco from 1849 through 1853, that neither the crime rate nor the murder rate was unusual. Mullen, however, argues that the *perception* of crime and the failure to punish those arrested were the real sources of support for the Vigilantes of 1851.[29] A close reading of the evidence for the period leading up to the Committee of 1851 shows that the issue was not crime itself, but was, as Mullen suggests, punishment. "The most daring criminals," Robert S. LaMotte complained to his mother, "after being arrested have either been let off by the inefficiency of the authorities, or have escaped with but trivial punishment, so that they have boldly declared that they are not afraid of being arrested or convicted."[30]

By making this distinction between actual crime and perception of crime at the outset, we return the question of crime, punishment, and vigilantism to the public sphere, where it belongs. Lynchings are a particular, collective kind of murder. By extinguishing a human life in public – leaving the body for view and sometimes abusing it – crowds and their leaders intend to transform the individual into a collective symbol. Such terrorism is an act of communication as well as an act of murder. Its motives are inherently public, so we need not seek private, covert sources for vigilante behavior. The association of vigilantism with the frontier derives from the frontier's *newness* rather than from its alleged rawness or inherent lawlessness. The difficulty of erecting effective means of arresting, detaining, and trying suspects exacerbated a popular frustration with slowness and acquittals imposed on American jurisprudence by republican standards. Even in the older states, the delays of the courts and the success of defendants in securing acquittals had generated vigilante demands for extralegal punishment.

---

[29] Kevin J. Mullen, *Let Justice Be Done: Crime and Politics in Early San Francisco* (Reno: University of Nevada Press, 1989).

[30] Robert S. LaMotte to Mother, 3 and 10 June 1851. LaMotte Family Letters, Bancroft Library, Berkeley.

"Vigilantes and lynch mobs, in other words," writes legal historian Lawrence M. Friedman, "were pathologies of a system with too many checks and balances for public opinion."[31]

The fascinating story of penal reform in Europe and America illustrates central features of the historical process at work in San Francisco during the 1850s. Through the end of the eighteenth century, punishment was oriented toward the audience, not the criminal. Public execution day was deeply valued by magistrates and ministers, historian Louis Masur writes, as a time when "the entire community assembled for an effective lesson in morality and piety."[32] Until Enlightenment and Romantic concerns with reform and the individual soul took hold, moreover, executions were notable for meting out various degrees of physical torture or dismemberment, depending on the severity or type of crime. Branding, drawing and quartering, live burials, and the stockade were all legitimate elements of the "theater" of public punishment prior to the reforms of the late eighteenth century. The elimination of corporal punishment, the appearance of the first American penitentiaries in the 1790s, and the gradual elimination of capital punishment for all but first-degree murder were steps in the rationalization and romanticization of penal law, as prominent reformers such as Benjamin Rush sought to turn the object of a sentence from punishment of the convict to reform of the criminal, and from the body to the soul. By the mid-nineteenth century, Foucault writes, "the body as the major target of penal repression had disappeared," to be replaced by the target of the soul. Reformers like Rush, who had hoped to eliminate capital punishment altogether, were disappointed by the public pressure to retain it, but the spectacle of public torture had given way to the rapid public executions of the trap-door gallows and, in France, the guillotine.[33]

A most crucial moment in this history of penal reform in the United States was the legislative movement to eliminate public executions and to conduct them inside prison walls. This constituted a significant alteration in the shape of the public sphere, for it

31 Lawrence M. Friedman, *A History of American Law* (N.Y.: Simon and Schuster, 1973), 253.
32 Louis P. Masur, *Rites of Execution: Capital Punishment and the Transformation of American Culture, 1776–1865* (New York: Oxford University Press, 1989), 96.
33 Friedman, *History of American Law*, 248–53; David J. Rothman, *The Discovery of the Asylum: Social Order and Disorder in the New Republic* (Boston: Little, Brown, 1971); Michel Foucault, *Discipline and Punish: The Birth of the Prison*, trans. Alan Sheridan (New York: Vintage Books, 1979), 8.

removed from the sphere of collective political communication an act central to the operation of the state and thereby diminished the possibilities for citizen participation in self-government. Pennsylvania, in 1834, first removed executions from public view. New York, New Jersey, and Massachusetts followed in 1835. By 1845 all of the New England and Middle Atlantic states had eliminated public executions. Why? Critics charged that public executions constituted "a spectacle at once revolting and injurious to society." Louis Masur makes a compelling argument that the banishment of public hangings can be attributed to "the formation of middle-class sensibilities, characterized by a suspicion of the public arena, disgust with seemingly senseless cruelty, and a desire to withdraw into an exclusive social setting." The popularity of the execution, Masur finds, was deeply unsettling to the emerging bourgeoisie in the Whig-Jacksonian era. Members of the middle and upper classes began to desert the scene of executions at about this time, while "legislators, editors, ministers, and merchants decried public hangings as festivals of disorder."[34]

Masur's account, however, is too tidy; there is no room in it for the widespread practice of extralegal executions, or lynchings, in which respectable members of the middle and upper classes widely participated, a practice that long outlasted the withdrawal of official killing indoors.[35] California's first legislators, in fact, did not bother with the new fad of indoor executions at all. The lessons of mining camp justice fresh in their minds, they considered public executions a valuable state practice and retained it until 1858.

The primitive state of California's early criminal-justice system, however, and its "sievelike" wooden jails, delayed the successful conviction of anyone for a capital crime until 1852.[36] This long delay in the official delivery of an execution generated widespread impatience, visible in the words of several members of and sympathizers with the 1851 Vigilance Committee.[37] Robert S. LaMotte, the minor Whig official we met in the previous chapter, was an

---

[34] Masur, *Rites of Execution*, 5, 95.

[35] Nowhere in Masur's otherwise excellent study does he mention vigilantism or jurisprudence west of the Mississippi.

[36] The first legal execution in California was that of José Forni, on 10 December 1852. San Francisco *Alta* 11 December 1852; San Francisco *Call*, 31 March 1882, p. 3, col. 7; *Call*, 9 April 1882, p. 1, col. 8; San Francisco *Examiner*, 2 October 1887, p. 15, col. 3.

[37] On the impatience with the rate of punishment, see M. F. Williams, *History of the San Francisco Committee of Vigilance of 1851*, 163–85.

official member of the first committee, who sat among the ninety men who "tried" and condemned John Jenkins to death for the offence of burglary. "It is well known," LaMotte wrote to his mother, "that there have been within the last twelve months fifty-four murders committed in San Francisco alone not one of which has ever been punished." LaMotte contrasted San Francisco with his idea of his mother's Philadelphia, "where crime is punished and peace and quiet reigns."[38] Neither LaMotte's claims about the number of unpunished murders nor his idea of a pacific Philadelphia can be believed. Both, obviously, are exaggerations. The point here is that LaMotte *perceived* the principal problem in San Francisco circa 1851 to be the failure to administer punishments.

Another witness to these events was a lawyer of upper-class pretensions from New York City. John McCracken sympathized with but did not join the first committee, for reasons of his professional oath to uphold the laws. The lack of punishment is again the operative concept in McCracken's account: "It is most certain, our laws are sadly deficient in the punishment of crime, and the worst villains have escaped punishment, others taking encouragement have ... continued their depredations."[39] Phineus Blunt, the unhappy religious policeman, also sympathized with the Committee of 1851, but like McCracken did not actually join. Blunt noted the formation of the committee, for the purpose, as he saw it, "to look after and see that the laws are executed in regard to criminals." Blunt believed that the failure to execute the laws "had been caused by the long delay of the courts and the frequent escapes of prisoners from the city prison."[40]

Observers frequently used the word "terror," or forms of it, in their defense of the executions. McCracken approvingly wrote: "When the people saw these things they felt themselves outraged, and decided that none but the most severe punishment would terrify these felons." McCracken, with others, recognized that Jenkins's

---

38 LaMotte to Mother, 3 and 11 June 1851, LaMotte Family Letters, Bancroft Library, Berkeley California. LaMotte clearly fantasized about the level of crime and violence in Philadelphia. Philadelphia had, in fact, crime rates on par with other eastern cities during these years. See, for example, Roger Lane, *Violent Death in the City: Suicide. Accident, and Murder in Nineteenth-Century Philadelphia* (Cambridge, Mass.: Harvard University Press, 1979).

39 John McCracken to Mary [his sister], 12 June 1851, Letter #145, McCracken Family Letters, Bancroft Library, Berkeley, California.

40 Phineus U. Blunt Journal, p. 153, 10 June 1851, Bancroft Library, Berkeley.

alleged crime of burglary was a noncapital offense, "yet I cannot but think it required a terrible example to convince these scoundrels of their [the people's] determination."[41] LaMotte, an actual Vigilante, wrote of "punishing every offender in such a manner as would strike terror to the evil doers."[42]

The Vigilantes of 1851 filled this public vacuum with four executions, and the much-lamented deprivation of a legal execution was finally rectified in December 1852, with the hanging of a "Spaniard" named José Forni. The opportunity for another public killing did not come again until July 1854 with the execution of William B. Sheppard. Both of these events were immensely popular. The sheriff chose for the site of Forni's gallows the top of Russian Hill, which, the *Alta* observed, "overlooks the entire surrounding country and can be seen from every point in the city."[43] Uneasy about the location, the officials decided to "move the gallows from the top of the hill about one hundred yards west, which hid it from the view of the city." Nevertheless, "a continuous line of human beings were pressing up the hill all morning, until a crowd numbering three thousand at least had gathered together.... At least one-fourth of the number composed of youths, women, and children."[44] (See Plate 2.1.)

Even more spectacular was the execution of Sheppard in July 1854. The gallows were constructed in an open valley near the Presidio, which served as a natural amphitheater. "The surrounding slopes were covered with a sea of heads ... numbering about ten thousand." The festivity of the event horrified the editor of the *Alta*: "There was a most unfeeling manifestation of heartlessness among many in the crowd; the doomed man's ears being saluted with loud shouts of 'hats off,' and 'down in front,' accompanied with rude jests and ribald laughter which was perfectly disgusting."[45] The public enjoyment of the 1852 execution of Forni had drawn similar condemnation: "But what was most shocking was to see respectable looking parents taking their little sons and daughters into such a heterogeneous crowd, to witness such a terrible spectacle."[46]

---

[41] John McCracken to Mary [his sister], 12 June 1851, Bancroft Library, Berkeley.
[42] Robert S. LaMotte to Mother, 3 and 10 June 1851, LaMotte Family Letters, Bancroft Library, Berkeley.
[43] *Alta*, 10 December 1852, p. 2.   [44] *Alta*, 11 December 1852, p. 2.
[45] *Alta*, 29 July 1854, p. 2.   [46] *Alta*, 11 December 1852, p. 2.

EXECUTION OF JOSE FORNER, DEC. 10, 1852.
on Russian Hill San-Francisco,
FOR THE MURDER OF JOSE RODRIGUES

Plate 2.1. The Execution of José Forni, 1852. By 1845 all New England and Middle Atlantic states had eliminated public executions, yet this first official execution in San Francisco was an immensely popular event. The sheriff chose the top of Russian Hill, visible for miles around as the site of the execution. "A continuous line of human beings were pressing up the hill all morning," reads a contemporary account, "until a crowd numbering three thousand at least had gathered together.... At least one fourth of the number composed of youths, women, and children." Indeed, women and children in respectable attire are plainly depicted in this illustration. Executions were such a powerful form of public communication in San Francisco that legislators finally recoiled from the implications of direct, democratic participation in ceremonial killing and banished the practice to the insides of prisons in 1858, in keeping with the laws of the eastern states. This lettersheet, the equivalent of a modern postcard, celebrates the event for broadcast through the mails. (Forni's name is misspelled on the lettersheet.) Courtesy of Bancroft Library.

The popularity of executions soon became intolerable to the members of the California legislature. "Familiarity with such scenes," warned the *Alta*, "tends to rob them of their terror."[47]

[47]   *Alta*, 29 July 1854.

The bill to abolish public executions was passed in 1858, limiting witnesses to the number of five and banning the presence of "any person under age."[48] But the officials who sought to maintain the horrific impact of capital punishment by depriving the public of its enjoyment at least partially misunderstood the uses of terror. Whatever the effect of terror in the way of deterrence, a public death retained an extraordinary popular appeal that the bourgeois sensibilities of the *Alta* could not accommodate: the appeal of vengeance.

Phineus Blunt is a good source for insight into this phenomenon because he was not overly philosophical, he did not belong to the Committee of 1851 and therefore had no personal stake in justifying it, and he was writing only to himself: "Thus again the people have taken the law into their own hands for the purpose of avenging crime."[49] Blunt did not emphasize deterrence, as some did, but instead used the verb "to avenge." In this simple and private phrase the subtlety of the crowd-pleasing effect of terror becomes clearer. The public death of an alleged or convicted criminal rectified the injustice felt by the law-abiding citizens for having been wronged. For, as Michel Foucault observes, "capital punishment remains fundamentally, even today, a spectacle that must actually be forbidden."[50]

The illegal executions by the Vigilantes and the legal executions of Forni and Sheppard suggest that the bourgeoise's separation from the working-class crowd and their preference for privacy posited by Masur had not yet taken hold in San Francisco. If Masur is right, then the publicity-loving merchants of San Francisco were not fully bourgeois. It makes more sense, however, to stop prioritizing class when considering this pivotal moment in the transformation of urban political culture. The executions by the Vigilantes were an exercise in political communication within a political culture that was still intensely public. Reformers who sought to put executions indoors were indeed attempting to privatize one of the central functions of the state (the monopoly over the right to kill). Opponents of indoor executions, however, pointed out that privacy was inconsistent with republicanism. "If this idea of hanging men . . . is

---

48   Theodore S. Hittell, *The Codes and Statutes of California* (San Francisco: A. L. Bancroft and Co., 1876), Chapter 14, section 229., p. 1351.; San Francisco *Bulletin*, 8 February 1858, p. 2.; Sacramento *Union*, 20 March 1858, p. 2.

49   Phineus U. Blunt Journal, 11 July 1851, Bancroft Library, Berkeley.

50   Foucault, *Discipline and Punish*, 15.

correct," Wendell Phillips challenged, "then why do you not make your executions as public as possible?"[51]

Here was the point at which Romantic liberalism clashed with Romantic republicanism. The thrust of the former was to reduce punishment to a private experience of the criminal, his soul, and his god. The thrust of the latter was to retain the collective experience of punishment as theater enacted in the public sphere, as communication between the members of the political community in affirmation of their rule over the city. The living and dead bodies of the condemned men were made to signify the presence of the law where the apparatus was lacking (as in the mining regions and the first San Francisco Committee of Vigilance) and to signify the advent of a new political order, as in the Committee of 1856. This communication was only possible, however, because of a deep rapport between the merchant elite who ran the committees and the plebeian mass who joined them.

THE POPULAR ORIGINS OF THE COMMITTEE OF 1851

And as if, indeed, the stones had turned avengers, men rose as from the ground; whole blocks emptied in an instant their contents upon the thoroughfares.[52]

Hubert Howe Bancroft, 1887

The Vigilante leadership wielded the authority to lead the popular mass. "When we say of somebody that he is "in power,"" Hannah Arendt writes, "we actually refer to his being empowered by a certain number of people to act in their name."[53] The merchant

---

51 Phillips quoted in Masur, *Rites of Execution*, 113.
52 Bancroft, *Popular Tribunals*, 2:57.
53 "Power corresponds to the human ability not just to act but to act in concert. Power is never the property of an individual; it belongs to a group and remains in existence only so long as the group keeps together." Hannah Arendt, *On Violence* (New York: Harcourt, Brace and World, 1970), 44. Arendt's conception of power differs fundamentally from that of Weber, who defines power as force, or the capacity of one individual or group of individuals to subsume another's will to their own. Arendt, and more recently Jürgen Habermas, shows that such a capacity is a property of a cultural hegemony, which itself must be the actual locus of "power." See Arendt, *On Revolution* (New York: Viking Press, 1965), 179; Jürgen Habermas, "Hannah Arendt's Communications Concept of Power," *Social Research* 44 (Spring, 1977): 3–24. The equation of wealth and power is usually true but rarely examined critically in its cultural dimension. See, for example, Gabriel Kolko, *Wealth and Power in America: An Analysis of Social Class and Income Distribution* (New York: Frederick A. Praeger, 1962).

leaders of both committees, men like Samuel Brannan or William Tell Coleman, had to earn their authority and then use that authority to discipline what began as lynch mobs. "Coleman saw this danger from the beginning," Bancroft writes, ". . . and throughout the whole reform movement the difficulty was not in going forward but in holding back."[54] Historians are fond of quoting Royce's observation that the Committee of 1856 was a "Business Man's Revolution." Yet the first half of the sentence in which Royce's felicitous phrase appears is never quoted: "They avoided mob law, pure and simple, only by organizing the most remarkable of all the popular tribunals, whereby was effected that unique historical occurrence, a Business Man's Revolution."[55]

William Tell Coleman, Samuel Brannan, and other major merchants of San Francisco earned their authority to lead, and their role as Vigilantes, in a struggle with the "horror hungry populace" in February 1851.[56] On the night of 19 February 1851 a gang of eight professional thieves led by James Stuart went to the dry goods store of C. J. Jansen, following a tip that this merchant had ten to fifteen thousand dollars on the premises. Wearing cloaks for disguise, the men asked Jansen about blankets and then "hit him on the head with a slung shot" and made off with $1,586 in gold coin, leaving Jansen for dead.[57] Three days later city police made the tragic mistake of arresting a man who looked very like the suspected Stuart. This man, Thomas Berdue, came near losing his life several times until finally, in June of that year, the real James Stuart was discovered, and Berdue, sentenced to die for one of Stuart's many crimes, was exonerated and released, penniless but alive.

Immediately following the arrest of Berdue and of a supposed accomplice named Windred, "several thousands had gathered around the court-house and the Recorder's room was filled." Mere arraignment did not satisfy the crowd, however:

At the moment the Court was adjourned the cry of "Now's the time" was raised, and a general rush was made for the prisoners. Benches, desks and

54 Bancroft, *Popular Tribunals*, 70.
55 Josiah Royce, *California, from the Conquest of California in 1846 to the Second Vigilance Committee in San Francisco: A Study in American Character* (New York: Houghton Mifflin Co., 1886; Santa Barbara: Peregrine Publishers, 1970), 346.
56 "Horror hungry populace" is Bancroft's phrase. *Popular Tribunals*, 279.
57 This description is based on the confession of James Stuart in Mary F. Williams, ed., *Papers of the San Francisco Committee of Vigilance*, vol. 3 (Berkeley: University of California Press, 1919), 233.

railings were broken to pieces, and the prisoners would certainly have been taken from the room had not the Washington Guards, who had been parading during the day, rushed in with fixed bayonets and, mounting the desk and benches drove the people away."[58]

Without prior organization a serious crisis had developed, and by evening the city authorities were forced to deal with "a much larger crowd [that had] gathered around City Hall."[59] At this point the crowd elected William D. M. Howard (the merchant who had helped Phineus Blunt get a job) as president of the "meeting." Mayor John White Geary (future governor of Pennsylvania) and a brace of judges then attempted to appease the masses, finally succeeding by the appointment of twelve citizens to decide on the future course of action. These twelve included many, such as Samuel Brannan, William D. M. Howard, Henry F. Teschemacher, and A. J. Ellis, who were to create the Committee of Vigilance four months later. First, however, they had themselves to survive the wrath of the crowd. The committee of twelve called another mass meeting for the following day at 10:00 A.M. on the Plaza.

By 11:00 A.M. that Sunday six thousand people had assembled. Hoping that a swift trial would satisfy the crowd, Mayor Geary proposed "that a committee of twelve citizens be appointed to sit with the examining justice to-morrow as a jury, and that their verdict would be final."[60] But tomorrow was not soon enough. "On the contrary," Coleman later recalled, "all moved forward in a solid, sullen mass, surrounding the building and pressed against every entrance."[61] Five days short of his twenty-seventh year, William Tell Coleman made his public debut. He mounted a balcony and addressed the anarchic crowd, proposing that a committee be selected to try and punish the prisoners immediately. The motion was carried, the city courtroom was commandeered, and Coleman was appointed prosecuting attorney. No magistrate would serve as judge, so the crowd selected one. Reluctantly, Judge D. O. Shattuck served as poor Berdue's defense attorney and succeeded in sowing in the minds of the appointed jury some doubt about the true identity of the accused.

The jury failed to find a verdict, and Coleman was compelled

---

[58] *Alta*, 23 February 1851, p. 2, cols. 3–4.   [59] *Alta*, 23 February 1851.

[60] *Alta*, 24 February 1851, p. 2.

[61] William T. Coleman, "San Francisco Vigilance Committees: By the Chairman of the Committees of 1851, 1856, and 1877," *Century Magazine* 43 (November 1891): 134.

to admit this failure to the masses. "I was literally forced to walk over the heads and shoulders of the thickly packed mass of people," Coleman recalled. Coleman's announcement provoked an "indignation meeting" against him and threats to hang him and his fellow proto-Vigilantes.[62] The following day a man was found allegedly stealing something near the wharves,

and when collared drew a pistol to shoot his captor but was disarmed, had his face pounded flat, was tied to a dray while as many draymen as could stand round kept throwing in the string [whipping him] until he fainted or pretended to faint. He was then taken to the dock with a rope round his neck, pitched into the filthy mud, dragged along till the water got deep and at last when about half drowned was delivered into the hands of the Police.[63]

The fury of the crowd that year was fearsome indeed. During the great fire of 4 May 1851, two people accused of arson were simply beaten to death in the street.[64]

By early June, then, when Sam Brannan, his clerk, and two fellow merchants decided to organize a permanent vigilance committee, they could well predict that the people would be ripe for mobilization at the next opportunity to administer extralegal justice.[65] Indeed, during the fourth meeting of the fledgling committee, on 10 June, a number of citizens caught one John Jenkins in the act of robbery and decided to take him to the Vigilantes instead of to the police. Brannan argued for immediate execution. Coleman tried to intervene, arguing that it was cowardly to hang a man at night. "But the town was rousing to a high pitch of excitement, and the majority [of the committee] feared delay."[66] The news of the committee's activities, in turn, generated even more excitement, adding enrolled members to the committee and creating pressure on the Vigilantes to do something decisive with Jenkins. Hanging Jenkins

---

[62] Coleman, "San Francisco Vigilance Committees," 135. Williams, *History of the San Francisco Committee of Vigilance of 1851*, 175.

[63] Robert S. LaMotte to Mother, 20 February 1851, LaMotte Family Letters, Bancroft Library, Berkeley.

[64] The beatings to death and other episodes of these months are described in Mary F. Williams, *History of the San Francisco Vigilance Committee of 1851*, 163–85.

[65] Williams, *History of the San Francisco Committee of Vigilance of 1851*, 203–7. Brannan's merchant accomplices in the initial organization were James Neall, Jr., and George Oakes. They drew up a constitution before the night when Jenkins was hanged.

[66] Williams, *History of the San Francisco Committee of Vigilance of 1851*, 210–11.

at this point was hard to avoid. Brannan and the committee had made bold claims about swift justice, and now the clamorous crowd demanded exactly that. Jenkins was hanged, not by the merchants, but by the crowd.

Dragnet patrols of the first committee on 1 July 1851 caught a man in the act of robbery who turned out to be the real James Stuart, whom authorities still believed they had in custody in the person of Thomas Berdue, then in Marysville awaiting execution for Stuart's crimes. Stuart, undoubtedly under some kind of pressure, broke down in the Vigilante rooms and allegedly delivered a stunning confession, detailing scores of unsolved crimes and exposing his fellow career criminals – men with street names like "Jimmy-from-Town," "Billy Sweet Cheese," "Long Charley," "Long Bill," and "Activity."[67] Stuart's confession led to yet another confession, by his former partner, Samuel Whittaker.[68] These two men also exposed a Mrs. Hogan (who seems to have been both men's lover). Hogan's "house was a crib for stolen property," according to Stuart. She seems to have been a madam as well. The Vigilantes arrested her, but lacking evidence besides the confessions, released her.[69] The confessions of Stuart and Whittaker seemed to prove that there had been, lurking beneath the surface of everyday life, a terrible conspiracy of professional crime and wanton immorality, operated by men who did not marry their mates in the boarding-houses used for prostitution. "You would be astonished," LaMotte wrote to his family in Philadelphia, "at the enormous amount of evidence that has been collected, and at the stupendous combination and system of villainy that has been unravelled."[70]

As if the exposure of a vast, organized criminal underworld were not enough to justify the actions of the first committee and seal the fates of Stuart and Whittaker, their confessions revealed that these two common criminals were comparable to the greatest of conspiracies a republic had to face. Stuart's gang had watched in anger when the police falsely arrested Berdue for their own crime in Jan-

---

67 Williams, *Papers of the San Francisco Committee of Vigilance*, 3:481–3; Bancroft, *Popular Tribunals*, 1:348.
68 The confessions of Stuart and Whittaker are among the surviving papers of the first committee in the Bancroft Library. They have also been published in Williams, ed., *Papers of the San Francisco Committee of Vigilance*, 3:223–7; 472–87.
69 Bancroft, *Popular Tribunals*, 1:347.
70 Robert S. LaMotte to Father, July 9–11, 1851, LaMotte Family Letters, Bancroft Library, Berkeley, California.

sen's store. "We did not intend to do anything more,' ' Stuart allegedly confessed, "until the arrested parties got clear of the scrape, as we did not wish to see them hung, as they had nothing to do with it – we all agreed on Sunday night that if they hung them to burn the town down."[71] Another account of this confession reads: "We would have shot fifty men rather than have them hung. We all agreed that if those men were hung ... we would fire the town on Saturday night in several places."[72] A senseless but systematic plan of wanton slaughter and arson such as this had only one precedent: the Cataline Conspiracy that Cicero exposed in 63 B.C.E. Can it be coincidental that Cicero, in his first speech against Cataline – widely known to the educated men leading the first committee – found precisely the same situation plaguing the good citizens of Rome?

> What is unbearable is that these spiritless, stupid, drunken, somnolent brutes should be plotting to cut down citizens who are pre-eminent for their courage and wisdom and sobriety and energy. For as these individuals ... embrace their harlots, dazed by wine and stuffed with food ... the vomit which issues from their mouths consists of talk about massacring every loyal citizen and burning the city to the ground.[73]

It hardly seems likely that Stuart and Whittaker would on their own think to include among their particular crimes the notorious Cataline plan to "burn the city to the ground." This element at least seems to betray the help they had in composing their "confessions" and the importance to the Vigilantes of legitimating their emergency measures through reference to the very strongest republican precedents. Roman forms were followed throughout the evolution of vigilantism as a public principle. During the trial of the "Hounds" in 1849 William M. Gwin remembered the Roman practice of banishment and introduced it in order to avoid illegal executions. The Hounds were "sent out of the country" on a U.S. ship of

---

71 Williams, *Papers of the San Francisco Committee of Vigilance*, 3:234.
72 Whittaker similarly claimed that "Stuart, and indeed all engaged in the Jansen robbery, and many others, declared their intention to burn the city in case Windred and Berdue were executed; it was to be fired at night in four or five places." Bancroft, *Popular Tribunals*, 1:291, 345.
73 "Against Lucius Sergius Catalina," 9 November 63 B.C.E., in *Selected Political Speeches of Cicero*, trans. Michael Grant (New York: Penguin Books, 1969), 98.

war and the solemn practice – so full of symbolism for the purification of a community – was repeated by the 1851 and 1856 Committees alike for crimes less heinous than murder.[74]

Whittaker and another gang member, named McKenzie, were
also condemned to die, but the Texas Ranger, Sheriff Jack Hays,
managed to liberate Stuart and Whittaker from the Vigilante headquarters. The committee responded angrily, abducting them from
the city jail and hanging them within an hour.[75] Stuart was "tried"
and, in a formal ceremony, executed from a derrick on Long Wharf,
cannon and flags marking his death. Stuart further secured the
legitimacy of the first committee by blessing their deeds from the
gallows. Phineus Blunt watched Stuart's execution. "He didn't
complain but said his sentence was just," Blunt recorded in his
laconic style.[76] The nearly universal consensus of approbation for
the work of the first committee in following years is so clear that
even the opponents of the second committee prefaced their critical
words with a claim to membership in the Committee of 1851.[77]
The practical effect of this legitimacy was to keep vigilantism alive
as a viable option in times of severe crisis. It had, after all, proven
effective against organized bands of professional criminals. The
next stop on the road to 1856 was the discovery of professional criminals in the municipal government. In order to understand this, however, we need to examine the rise and fall of the Know-Nothing
order.

---

74 It is significant that Gwin tells the story not as a direct reference to Roman custom, but
    as a memory he had, in 1849, of General Andrew Jackson in Florida decades earlier.
    Jackson had been faced with the decision to execute a Spanish officer. Jackson himself
    was called "the 'Old Roman' for his firmness and decision at all periods of his life,"
    Gwin recalls, and goes on to explain how Jackson was persuaded by analogy to exile
    rather than execute the officer. "Memoirs of Hon. William M. Gwin," *California Historical
    Society Quarterly* 19:2 (June 1940): 167–8. Gwin and the Vigilantes thought of Roman
    parallels because the stories were a part of the contemporary lore about being a repub-
    lican leader in antebellum United States.
75 Williams, *History of the San Francisco Committee of Vigilance of 1851*, 261–93; Bancroft, *Popular
    Tribunals*, 1:296–7; 350–64.
76 Phineus Blunt Journal, Friday, 11 June 1851, Bancroft Library, Berkeley; Williams, *His-
    tory of the San Francisco Committee of Vigilance of 1851*, 270–1.
77 See, for example, the opening words of John Nugent's *Herald* article, opposing the forma-
    tion of the second committee and earning him the leadership of the opposition: "The
    Editor of this paper sustained the Vigilance Committee in times past to the peril of
    his life and fortunes; but ... we have arrived at the conclusion that it can never be
    revived." *Herald*, 14 May 1856.

THE CASE OF THE NONNATIVIST KNOW-NOTHINGS

Begun in 1850 as a secret society in New York under the leadership of James W. Barker, the Order of the Star Spangled Banner was a nativist organization that preached as a panacea for the nation's political ills the exclusion of foreign-born citizens from public office and a stiffening of naturalization requirements. The Know-Nothings (their members were required to say that they "knew nothing" in response to queries about the organization) spread their lodges like wildfire from New York City and that base of American ideological movements, the upstate, or "burned-over district," of New York, achieving a national membership by 1853 and holding a national council in June of 1854.[78]

The order entered politics in those years by secretly backing either its members or approved candidates and by winning elections in the most mysterious way. Often they did not publicly announce their slates, or they did so only on the day before the election. Born from a profound distrust of the machinations of professional (and foreign-born) politicians, the Know-Nothings' secrecy was a counterorganizational tactic of an ironic nature. They combated conspiracy with conspiracy, manipulation with manipulation. And yet their brand of secrecy was extremely popular. What the Know-Nothings wished to accomplish with their secret organization varied significantly from state to state, and locality to locality. Its original issue, nativism, provided the core program on the national and on most local levels. The Know-Nothings laid the blame for political corruption and professionalism at the door of Irish Catholics and other foreign-born groups, who had recently begun to do very well as political activists, and seriously entertained the possibility that the pope would assume control over Roman Catholics in the United States. Temperance was another important Know-Nothing issue, inherited from the Whigs. But the Know-Nothing phenomenon was symptomatic of a deep crisis in American political culture. It "capitalized on the forces that destroyed the Jacksonian party system," writes William E. Gienapp; "It's appeal

---

[78] This discussion of national Know-Nothingism is based on Michael F. Holt, "The Antimasonic and Know Nothing Parties," in Arthur M. Schlesinger, Jr., ed., *History of United States Political Parties*, 2 vols. (New York: Chelsea House Publishers, 1973), 1:575–620; and Holt, "The Politics of Impatience: The Origins of Know-Nothingism," *Journal of American History* 60 1973): 309–31.

integrated a virulent nativism with pro-temperance overtones and an abiding hostility to the existing parties as corrupt and unresponsive." The San Francisco pattern of Know-Nothingism supports in a particular way the findings of Michael Holt that the dramatic course of party disintegration and formation in the 1850s reflected first of all a political crisis with political causes.[79]

By 1855 all of the New England states except Vermont were under Know-Nothing control, and the Know-Nothings had become the primary anti-Democratic party in the Middle Atlantic states, most of the slave states, and California. San Francisco, whose largest American contingent hailed from New York and New England, naturally joined this movement, founding a Know-Nothing lodge in May 1854.[80] The appearance of Know-Nothingism in San Francisco was anomalous within the national pattern. There the nativist and temperance components of the national program were very weak. The first item on the San Francisco Know-Nothings' agenda was a critique of the "professionals" who ran politics for their own aggrandizement. Despite the fact that Irish-born politicians were numerous in the highest councils of the city's political structure, nativism was almost absent from the local order's platform. On the appeal of antiparty, antipolitician reformism alone, the secret order gained almost instant success in the city, winning the mayoralty and all but two aldermanic seats in the September elections of 1854.

The Know-Nothings operated much like other nineteenth-century secret fraternities, such as the Odd Fellows or the Freemasons. Membership entailed rising through three hierarchical "degrees," each initiated by the performance of symbolic secret rituals. In all of these rituals, the nationally approved oaths were revised in San Francisco to delete anti-Catholic phrases.[81] The relative unimportance of ethnoreligious feeling in the San Francisco order is most succinctly illustrated by the fact that they nominated a Roman Catholic, Lucien Hermann, for mayor in their first convention.

---

[79] William E. Gienapp, *Origins of the Republican Party, 1852–1856* (New York: Oxford University Press, 1987), 92–102, quotation is on p. 99. Michael F. Holt, *Political Crisis of the 1850's* (New York: John Wiley and Sons, 1978).

[80] Peyton Hurt, "The Rise and Fall of the Know Nothing Order in California," *California Historical Society Quarterly* [two parts] 9:1 (March 1930): 16–48; and 9:2 (June 1930): 99–128.

[81] Peyton Hurt describes the complete rituals and oaths, along with the deleted phrases, in "Rise and Fall of the Know Nothing Order," 21–3; 119–25.

Anti-Catholic Know-Nothings responded angrily to Hermann's nomination, however, and forced his removal from the ticket on the day before the election. This was not, however, a substantial victory for the nativist Know-Nothings. In the words of Peyton Hurt, the most thorough student of the party in California, the last-minute switch "occurred more as an afterthought than as the result of careful observance of the fundamental doctrine of Know Nothingism."[82]

In this cosmopolitan port city, any party tied to a nativist doctrine was handicapped from the start. Democrats, Whigs, and independents alike denounced its "proscriptive" doctrine, despite the efforts made by the Know-Nothings themselves to downplay this aspect of their movement in San Francisco. The Democrats, with the largest foreign-born constituency, were loudest in abuse. Their platform of May 1855 declared that the Know-Nothing party was: "antagonistic to every principle of Democracy; and if permitted to engraft its pernicious and proscriptive doctrines on the Legislation of the country, will produce the most dangerous results, if not altogether subvert the Government itself".[83] Whigs also joined in denunciation, devoting an entire "mass meeting" to repudiations of Know-Nothing nativism.[84]

During the months, however, when the Know-Nothings took root in the city and gained enough popularity to capture the city government in its first race, opponents were afraid to oppose the order. The Democratic convention of August 1854 defeated a resolution against the new order that declared it to be a "secret politico-religious organization ... inconsistent with our republican institutions." The leadership of the convention objected to the resolution, saying it was "injudicious to hazard the success of the ticket by bringing the party in contact with a secret society."[85] The major parties were at first unable to combat the great popularity of the Know-Nothings, which derived, no doubt, more from its reformism than from its nativism. The antiparty *Alta* summed up the situation nicely:

It is said that beside their peculiar principles of proscription to all citizens of foreign birth, they intend to select men for office who are not mere poli-

[82]   Hurt, "Rise and Fall of the Know Nothing Order," 28–9.
[83]   *Alta*, 14 May 1855, p. 2.   [84]   *Alta*, 30 August 1855, p. 2, col. 3.
[85]   *Alta*, 13 August 1854.

ticians, but men who will administer the government with economy and a desire for the welfare of the people. If they should succeed in this they will deserve the thanks of the community, even though their proscriptive principles should meet with no favor from the large majority of the people.[86]

In the anti-party climate of those years, the term "mere politicians" had become a synonym for "men ... who live upon politics and who intend to make enough out of one election to last them till the next ensuing one."[87]

The rapid decline of the Know-Nothings is as interesting as their rapid success. Throughout California, the order was on the rise only in the early months of 1855, achieving its first successes in the municipal elections in the spring of that year, and winning the governorship that September.[88] The success of the Know-Nothings in the municipal elections of September 1854 brought the warring factions of the Democratic party back together temporarily after a "harmony" convention in May 1855, sarcastically called a "grand love feast" by the *Alta*.[89] Cynical or not, the anti-Know-Nothings had found it easy to kill the order in San Francisco on the nativist issue, and keep it dead. The Know-Nothings failed in the June city elections and fared even worse in San Francisco in the September elections. Although California voters put the Know-Nothing candidate, J. Neely Johnson, in the governor's chair, Johnson and the Know-Nothings were soundly defeated in San Francisco. The demise of Know-Nothingism in San Francisco in 1855 enabled the *Alta*, after Johnson's triumph, to prophesy that "Know Nothingism will never raise its head again."[90]

The *Alta*'s prophecy was far more portentous, however, than just this observation about the Know-Nothings. "It is fair to presume," the editor wrote in September 1855, "that within the next year there will be a complete breaking-up of all parties in San Francisco, as they are now organized."[91] Indeed, the Democrats, Know-Nothings, and Whigs had all fallen to pieces by September 1856, and a new organization, the People's party, had taken the city by storm.

The source of this party disintegration was an exaggerated local

---

86 *Alta*, 2 September 1854.   87 *Alta*, 11 August 1854.
88 Winfield J. Davis, *History of Political Conventions in California, 1849–1892* (Sacramento: California State Library, 1893), 38–9.
89 *Alta*, 14 May 1855.   90 *Alta*, 7 September 1855.   91 *Alta*, 7 September 1855.

focus on the reformist, antiparty ideology that had provided the initial strength of the Know-Nothings. In the previous chapter it was shown that the complaint against the major-party activists during the 1850s was directed at their secrecy and confinement within caucuses and conventions, far above the heads of the electorate. "The great object of the rank and file of the Know Nothings," the *Alta* approved in early May 1855, "is more to preserve the purity of the ballot box and prevent caucus corruption than to get office."[92]

By the end of the Know-Nothing convention of May 1855, however, the new party had already replicated the methods of old parties. "We had been told that the Know-Nothings had improved on old party tactics ... but so far as we can see, it is the same thing in a more objectionable shape."[93] Indeed, the double irony of the Know-Nothings' secrecy finally caught up with them when they changed from an insurgent, antiparty organization to an office-holding party bent on winning more elections. The *Alta* suddenly disapproved: "The secrecy attending their councils only keeps their deeds from coming openly before the public, while plots and counter-plots are carried on as successfully as in the open convention."[94]

Opportunism had indeed come to the Know-Nothings. The newfound unity of the "harmonized" Democrats proved disastrous to that once-dominant party. The escalating furor over the sectional question, recently revived by the Kansas–Nebraska bill, made it impossible for pro-Southern Democrats and Free-Soil Democrats to share the same party leadership. The Free-Soil leader, David C. Broderick, who presided over the harmony reunion, was intolerable to such proslavery politicians as David S. Terry, who joined the Know-Nothings that year and received their nomination for his future office as chief justice of the California Supreme Court.

By the opening months of 1856, a presidential election year that many believed would determine the fate of the Union, the continued dominance of the Broderick wing of the Democrats drove a huge portion of the Democrats out of the party. Their departure in February 1856 was dramatically framed in the language of antipartyism, which had proven increasingly successful in recent years. More than one thousand Democrats signed a manifesto published on 26 February of 1856, denouncing the leadership of the Democratic party. "The men in whom high trust is reposed, we believe

---

[92] *Alta*, 14 May 1855.   [93] *Alta*, 23 May 1855.   [94] *Alta*, 23 May 1855.

to be under the dominion of persons composing a political oligarchy at war with the views of our party, and more burdensome and
obnoxious to freemen than the worst of despotism."[95]

All parties, by 1856, had to suffer the stigma of professionalism
and disregard of true "principles." The charge of opportunism
meant that politicians, in their race for compromise and office, no
longer answered to the burning issues of the day. In a series called
"The Living Issues," the *Alta* pronounced dead the famous Jacksonian issues of banks, tariffs, and internal improvements, and devoted
a long article to each of three new issues: sectionalism, temperance,
and Know-Nothingism. In fact, party politicians were trying to
avoid the sectional and other divisive issues in order to embrace
as many voters as possible, but the project backfired in two ways:
First, antebellum voters wanted their most deeply held worries to
find a voice in their government. Second, dodge issues, like Know-
Nothingism (itself largely an attempt to avoid sectionalism), were
themselves divisive, leading the Know-Nothings to fudge on their
original nativism. Yet fudging on divisive issues led to further
charges of opportunism. The apostasy of politicians had in fact become the most volatile issue during the year 1855. It could be called
a popular dissatisfaction loop: The more dissatisfied that the voters
became, the stronger the issues they demanded, and the harder it
became for politicians not to look professional and self-serving. In
order for the loss in legitimacy of the party organizations to be complete, however, the politicians had to appear not merely opportunis-
tic and professional, but boldly contemptuous of the popular will.

VIOLATING THE BALLOT BOX; OR, "A CRIME OF THE DARKEST DYE"

Casting a ballot in the United States in 1850 was an act invested
with world-historic significance. For the privileged men who did so
(as we have seen, they were a small subset of the total population),
this act very likely reminded them that they were virtually alone in
the world in their privilege of self-government. "The ballot box is
the palladium of republicanism," the *Alta* intoned. In a certain real
sense, voters went to the polls as to a civic shrine. One of a series of
toasts at a typical Democratic party dinner was offered to "The

---

[95] *Alta*, 26 February 1856.

Republican Spirit of the Age – May the Genius of Liberty animate the hearts of the people of all climes, and Heaven aid them in the efforts of the brave to release the oppressed of every nation from the thralldom which bears them to earth." This toast was followed by the Marseillaise anthem.[96]

Louis Napoleon's 1851 coup d'état against the Second Republic of France was roundly condemned in San Francisco and the revolutions of 1848 were warmly remembered: "The history of the last European revolution is yet fresh in the memory of all," proclaimed the *Alta*. Even though a failed revolution, it was "a blessing. It struck an additional blow at hereditary monarchy and its legitimacy."[97] At their annual May Day parade, the Germans carried a "republican tricolor" abreast with the American flag; all understood that America was still the vanguard of the world republican movement.[98]

In the language used to discuss the ballot box, the words "sanctity" and "purity" appear most frequently. Indeed, the shape and operation of a ballot box fitted not only to religious but also to sexual metaphors: "It is well that people are jealous of the purity of the ballot box.... They should be as sensitive of its purity as is the husband of the honor of his wife."[99] "Sovereignty," "the people," and "republicanism" were so closely identified with the ballot box that only verbs like "outrage" and "violate" could express the response to election fraud: "There is one outrage, however, to which the people will not submit. They will not permit their sovereignty to be trifled with, and when they see the ballot-box violated, they feel that the basis of republicanism is gone, and that society is reduced to its original elements."[100]

The deepest trouble for the party politicians in San Francisco began, therefore, when a series of election frauds came to light, especially in connection with the elections of 1854 and 1855. The Democrats, always more professionally adept than their opponents, drew most of the charges of fraud. Already by 1853 the *Alta* had taken a step familiar enough in regimes of dubious legitimacy; it recommended a boycott of the polls at the Democratic primary: "Better avoid the polls than approach them only to give them the respectability of recognition."[101]

Charges of election fraud began in earnest after the election of

[96] *Alta*, 24 May 1855.   [97] *Alta*, 26 February 1854.   [98] *Alta*, 7 May 1854, p. 2.
[99] *Alta*, 24 May 1855.   [100] *Alta*, 24 May 1855.   [101] *Alta*, 16 May 1853.

September 1854. An inspector of elections alleged that the reputed Democratic chieftain Edward "Ned" McGowan had offered him two thousand dollars to alter the returns in San Francisco's Second Ward.[102] The Vigilantes later collected reams of testimonies to document the systematic fraud, or more accurately, attempts at fraud, during the elections of 1854 and 1855.[103] The evidence of this and other incidents is convincing to anyone perusing the Vigilante files. Reports of fraud surfaced again after the spring elections of 1855.[104] The *Alta*'s language can be taken as a foretaste of the popular rage to be felt the following year:

We look upon an act of this kind as a crime of the darkest dye, and whoever has been guilty of it – whether Whig, Democrat, or Know Nothing – we hope may never know the blessings of liberty again. May he be shut up in a prison till he is taken out to be hanged, and may every friend of free institutions, every advocate of popular rights, never mention his name but to hiss out maledictions against it.[105]

In the fall of 1855 James King of William, a former Democratic activist and a recently ruined banker, began his meteoric rise to civic martyrdom by founding the *Daily Evening Bulletin* and filling its columns with high-quality business and international news mixed with lurid and abusive exposés of corruption and crime in high places. Within a year King had outstripped the circulation of all other papers in the state, including the *Alta*, reaching ten thousand copies a day for San Franciscans, a weekly edition for the state, and a semimonthly edition with subscriptions reaching not only to the eastern seaboard but to Europe as well.[106]

King, in his reckless articles, naturally focused on the reports of election fraud. King, whose reformism was complicated by a personal banking vendetta against a pro-Broderick banking house, insisted that the system of fraud and corruption was run as a single iniquitous machine by David Broderick:

---

[102] Charges reported in *Alta*, 27 September 1854, p. 2.
[103] "Papers Relating to Ballot-Box Stuffing and Fraudulent Elections," San Francisco Committee of Vigilance Papers, Huntington Library, San Marino, California.
[104] James P. Casey was formally arraigned on charges of riot and fraud on 26 August 1855. *Alta*, 27 August 1855.
[105] *Alta*, 30 May 1855.
[106] Sketch of the *Bulletin* in Samuel Coville, *San Francisco City Directory for the Year Commencing October 1856* (San Francisco, 1856), 26.

Of all the names that grace the roll of the political wire-workers in this city, the most conspicuous of all ... as high over his compeers as was Satan over the fallen angels, and as unblushing as determined as the dark fiend, stands the name of David C. Broderick[107]

James King also liked to refer to Broderick as "David Cataline Broderick," in reference to the conspirator of the Roman Republic.[108]

The overnight success of King's new newspaper was the product of successful marketing. Newspapers were important business enterprises in San Francisco, and King's had impressive investors. He did not invent popular outrage at election fraud, but rather fed on it, and fed it in turn through his bulging circulation. His art was to locate issues important to potential consumers and create stirring articles to match and enflame those concerns. San Francisco in fact became an important source of this technique. It led, eventually, to the very large and sensational, or "yellow," journals of the late nineteenth century, one of which was William Randolph Hearst's San Francisco *Examiner*.

The genealogy of antiparty, conspiratorial language long predates King, as we have seen. The *Alta* vented it against the Whigs, Democrats, and even the Know-Nothings. It appeared again in the first resolution in the manifesto signed by more than the one thousand Democrats who repudiated their party's leadership in February 1856:

FIRST. The ballot-box has been placed almost exclusively under the control of men in whose character and fidelity to the Democracy, we do not confide.[109]

One of these who had become notorious was James P. Casey, inspector of elections for the Sixth Ward and recently elected county supervisor from that ward. His notoriety resulted from an arrest for election-day violence in the spring elections and from the remarkable feat of gaining his election to the Board of Supervisors in the September elections without having been a candidate. (Reports charged that not liking the results in his ward he stuffed enough of his own ticket into the ballot box at the eleventh hour to win.)

King's exposé of Casey's past as a convict in New York's Sing Sing prison provoked Casey to confront King with a revolver and

---

[107] *Evening Bulletin*, 12 October 1855.   [108] *Evening Bulletin*, 17 October 1855.
[109] *Alta*, 26 February 1856.

kill him, on 14 May 1856. The popular outrage against the death of King was the collective venom concentrated from years of hostility toward the political process and months of mounting evidence that the professional politicians were contemptuous of the most basic beliefs and institutions of the republican polity, conspiratorial in their methods, and criminal in their character.

Casey's shooting of King was the moment that brought together the strands of republicanism and vigilantism in the third week of May 1856. A crowd quickly appeared at the scene of the shooting and took the initiative; just as quickly calls were made for a Vigilance Committee, both to control the crowd and to carry out its will. From the start the movement focused on the ballot box and politicians as its animating objects: to protect the one and punish the other.

It is remarkable how widespread was the belief that grave political crimes had been committed. A measure of this consensus is the extent to which opponents of the committee agreed with the Vigilantes on their charges. John Nugent, the stubborn editor of the Democratic *Herald*, who denounced the committee beginning with the issue of 15 May, had this to say about James P. Casey in his first antivigilance editorial:

The fact that Casey has been an inmate of Sing-Sing prison in New York, is no offence against the laws of his state. Nor is the fact of his having stuffed himself through the ballot-box as elected to the Board of Supervisors from a district where it is said he was not even a candidate, any justification ... to shoot Casey, however richly the latter may deserve to have his neck stretched for such fraud upon the people.[110]

The *Herald*'s ground for opposition to the committee was procedural and legal. Morally, Nugent agreed with the thousands who joined and the thousands more who sympathized with the committee.

Another context in which to witness the strength of the collective sense of political injustice is the attempt to hold a "mass meeting" in opposition to the committee on 2 June 1856. The Executive Committee of the Vigilantes tried in vain to keep its members and sympathizers away from the antivigilance demonstration by posting broadsides throughout the day and even displaying banners during the demonstration, reading "FRIENDS OF THE COMMITTEE: COME OUT

[110] *Herald*, 15 May 1856, p. 2.

OF THE SQUARE." Fearing a riot, the Vigilantes kept two thousand men under arms nearby.[111] The majority of the crowd was *hostile* to the proceedings and kept the speakers tied to a single subject: the ballot box. Frequent interruptions on this issue forced the speakers to address it. The first speaker, Judge Alexander Campbell, "said he had no doubt there had been in times past ballot box stuffing."[112] Colonel Edward D. Baker, Abraham Lincoln's friend, also attempted to speak against the committee, but he was forced to answer the crowd about the ballot box instead: "Our best, our noblest, our wisest men would come out and vindicate the majesty of the law. They have no sympathy with the ballot-box stuffers."[113] The crowd, however, was not interested in the majesty of the law. At this point in Baker's speech, a model of a ballot box, "a tin box on a long pole," was elevated by someone in the jeering crowd, mocking the anti-Vigilante activists.[114]

The ballot box was the supreme icon of the Vigilante movement. At the head of the elaborate engraving that embellished the membership certificates of the Committee of 1856, is a ballot box, depicted with the goddess Justice fallen before it, her scales scattered useless on the ground, while the goddess Liberty soars above the box, bringing vengeance to the enemies of republicanism. The most prized possession of the committee was a false-bottom ballot box, allegedly used for years by the Democrats. Displayed at public occasions and kept prominently in the center of their main committee room, the famous false-bottom box had a secret compartment to hold extra ballots, which would be released into the main compartment with the slip of a hidden panel. The Vigilantes also collected testimony about the etiology of this trick ballot box: "Nicholas Parazon, carpenter, thinks he built the ballot box.... Gallager and Parazan are couzins ... [he] ... thinks Gallager ordered the box made in '52."[115]

William T. Sherman's letter of 17 May records his first meeting of

---

[111]   *Daily California Chronicle*, 3 June 1856.   [112]   *Herald*, 3 June 1856.

[113]   *Daily California Chronicle*, 3 June 1856.

[114]   *Daily California Chronicle*, 3 June 1856; *Herald*, 3 June 1856. The antivigilance activists called themselves the "Law and Order" party.

[115]   Membership certificate, Committee of Vigilance Papers, Huntington Library, an illustration of the false-bottom ballot box can be found in H. H. Bancroft, *Popular Tribunals*, vol. 2 (San Francisco: History Company, 1887), 7; undated note, "Papers Relating to Ballot-Box Stuffing and Fraudulent Elections," San Francisco Committee of Vigilance Papers, Huntington Library, San Marino, California.

negotiation with the president of the committee, William Tell Coleman, "in which Coleman said the purpose of the association was not to subvert the law but to assist it in purging the community of the clique of shoulder-strikers, ballot-box stuffers, and political tricksters generally." Coleman went on to claim "that the courts and juries had become of no use, and that they must be purged or spurred on."[116] The inability to secure a conviction for election fraud, after years of reports, supported the belief that the courts and juries were willing members of the network of conspiracy against the people. Himself a believer in this network, the historian Bancroft gave a succinct illustration:

Let us now set the thing going and see how it works: Sullivan wants Casey elected, and Casey desires to place on the bench a judge after his own heart, so that when he or any other gentleman wishes to kill some unreasonable citizen, or any worker silly enough to complain of reasonable bleeding at the hands of the non-workers, no one shall be hurt for it. It is all in the family; the fraternity are to elect their ticket.[117]

Note also that Bancroft, writing in the 1880s, divided society into two classes: workers and nonworkers, the latter being, of course, professional politicians. This echoes the division established by the antiparty activism of the Know-Nothings in San Francisco during the 1850s and helps explain the popularity of the committees amongst the skilled workers who belonged to them.

One of the alleged "shoulder-strikers" and "ballot-box stuffers" was James "Yankee" Sullivan, a former inspector of elections. Sullivan was a legendary prizefighter whose name was still a household word in New York, whence he had migrated.[118] Days after the death of King and the execution of Casey, and before he himself committed suicide (believing he was to be hanged, Sullivan slashed his brachial artery), Sullivan provided the Vigilantes with a confession that played the same role in the second committee as the con-

116   William T. Sherman to Major Turner (St. Louis), Sunday, 18 May 1856, "Sherman and the San Francisco Vigilantes: Unpublished Letters of General W. T. Sherman," *Century Magazine* 43 (December 1891):299.
117   Bancroft, *Popular Tribunals*, 2:7.
118   In his infamous 1905 discourses on machine politics, Tammany chieftain George Washington Plunkitt told the reporter William L. Riordan that "by the water's edge in my district where boatmen drink their grog ... the only ornaments are a three-cornered mirror nailed to the wall, and a chromo of the fight between Tom Hyer and Yankee Sullivan." William L. Riordan, *Plunkett of Tammany Hall* (New York: E. P. Dutton, 1963), 86.

fessions of Stuart and Whittaker had in the Committee of 1851. Published by the Vigilante press, Sullivan's confession shockingly revealed the ways that the people had been deceived, and it justified the committee in all its subsequent work. The committee, which was supported by the biggest papers and thus had channels of propaganda at its disposal, published the confession with the names deleted, in order not to impair its investigation, but heightening thereby the impression of conspiracy:

The first money I received on the day of the election was from Mr. _____, about half past six o'clock in the morning. He gave me ten dollars, and promised, after the election was over, to give me ninety dollars more if I would 'see Mr. _____ through.' _____, the candidate for _____, came out in the course of the morning and gave me twenty dollars. . . .

The second day after this election _____ and _____ came to me in the street from Gallagher's drinking saloon, and _____ said, let us put _____ on the returns instead of _____. I said, I don't care, anybody but _____ You make out the returns and I'll sign them.[119]

The galvanizing effect of this confession was tremendous. A burst of enrollment followed its publication, adding literally thousands of men to the ranks of the committee.[120] The "Revolution of the People," as one broadside phrased the movement, had begun.[121]

CONCLUSION

The 1856 San Francisco Vigilance Committee is an archetypic political movement with obvious social reverberations. The interest-group paradigm has taught us to look at movements of this kind as outcomes of social conflicts. The method implied by that paradigm has been to discount the stated goals of the political movement and try to find the unstated goals of the supposed social movement lying behind it. The republican paradigm within which the antebellum generation conducted their public lives, however, did not share this ' essentially social understanding of political life. Indeed, theirs was a political understanding of social life, at least insofar as the social was

[119] *Daily California Chronicle*, 3 June 1856, p. 2, col. 4.
[120] See the analysis of the dates of application to the second committee in the following chapter.
[121] [Broadside] "Revolution of the People," San Francisco Committee of Vigilance Papers, Huntington Library, San Marino, California.

public. The origins of the spectacular Committee of 1856, as we have seen, were not social but political.

One riddle still left unresolved by this analysis, however, is the question of why there were so few Irish in the committee. Studies written within the interest-group model have deduced from this kind of evidence the existence of a more basic source of the committee: ethnocultural conflict. There would seem to be good reason to argue that the committee was a nativist organization. First, the Vigilance Committee of 1856 followed several years of smoldering conflict between leaders of the Irish minority in San Francisco and nativist Protestant spokesmen.[122] One of these latter was James King of William, patron saint of the Committee of 1856, who had been intensely anti-Catholic in his scathing *Bulletin* columns. The Irish in San Francisco understandably assumed that the committee shared King's anti-Catholicism.

Second, most of the Vigilantes' victims were Irish Catholics. The feeling that they were under seige by the Vigilantes must have been clear. The Irish Catholics of that time left us little but chiseled inscriptions to mark their outrage. Within the graveyard walls of the eighteenth-century Mission Dolores there are three conspicuous monuments. These mark the graves of three of the five victims of the Committee of 1856: Charles Cora, James P. Casey, and James "Yankee" Sullivan. To the tourists who daily stroll the peaceful churchyard these graves must mean very little, even though the message is clear to historians, amateur and otherwise. Sullivan's headstone reads: "Who died by the hands of the V.C.," and displays a bitter "anthem":

> Thou shall bring my soul out of
> Tribulation, and in thy mercy thou
> Shall destroy mine enemies

The Mission Dolores, founded by Father Francisco Palóu in 1776, was the most hallowed Catholic ground in the city. The friends

122   Robert M. Senkewicz, "Religion and Non-Partisan Politics in Gold Rush San Francisco," *Southern California Quarterly* 61:4 (Winter 1979): 351–78. Senkewicz recounts several episodes of Irish–Protestant conflict in San Francisco during the first half of the 1850s, focusing on public school questions. The remarkable thing about those conflicts, however, is how tame they were compared with similar conflicts in Massachussets and elsewhere in the East. Senkewicz even shows that the Know-Nothing city government of 1855 willingly supported Catholic schools financially! The Know-Nothing movement itself was distinctly nonnativist in San Francisco.

who paid for these messages had them placed in one of the few strongholds of an outnumbered minority.

The present interpretation diverges from recent accounts of the role of ethnicity in the Vigilante movement in the argument that nativism had a lopsided effect. Irish Catholics had every good reason to suspect the Vigilantes of nativism, but nativism cannot even begin to explain the Vigilante movement. The motto of the Committee of 1856 was "No Party, No Creed, No Sectional Issues." The "No Creed" phrase was meant to distance the committee from the nativist, Know-Nothing party in which James King of William, the man whose death sparked the committee, had been active. In hundreds of official committee documents and the newspaper accounts of all their activites, I could find no indication that an ethnic animus informed the committee's thinking or behavior. On the contrary, the opponents of the committee were apt to raise the ethnic issue. Pointing, in the pages of the *Herald*, to the large French-speaking contingent in the committee, John Nugent declared: "But the worst feature in this organized defiance of the ministers of the law, is the admixture of an alien element in the ranks of the rebellious band."[123] Given the overt language typical of American nativism in those years, it should not have been hard to find evidence of anti-Irish sentiment somewhere in the voluminous surviving documents of the committee, had such animus typified the proceedings of the body's leadership. Robert A. Burchell, the leading historian of San Francisco's Irish community, corroborates these findings in his account of the Vigilantes.[124]

A subtle but very important distinction seems to be in order to separate the probable anti-Irish sentiments of much of the committee's rank and file from the practical absence of such among the committee's leadership. The Vigilante leadership's role had been to harness the spontaneous mass demonstrations demanding vengeance for the murder of James King of William. From that moment, the committee could be equated with nativism only by the Irish, and may have been so connected by those who accepted William Tell Coleman's leadership of the movement. Burchell makes this crucial distinction as well:

---

[123]   *Herald*, 4 June 1856.
[124]   Robert A. Burchell, *The San Francisco Irish, 1848–1880* (Berkeley: University of California Press, 1980), 125–33.

Even if the committee had never decided explicitly to proscribe the foreign-born in general, and the Irish most particularly, the results had been in that direction, so that for some years many Irish Democrats appeared to turn their backs on city politics and to wait for more favourable opportunities.[125]

It was the nature of the Vigilante leadership to direct the purposes of the movement according to the republican ethical script, and that script was not derived from nativism, as the analysis in this and the following chapter should make clear. For the time being, we can observe that Coleman, just three years after the committee disbanded, headed the list of subscribers for the erection of a towering granite monument in memory of the leading Irish Catholic San Francisco politician of the 1850s, David C. Broderick.[126]

[125] Burchell, *San Francisco Irish*, 132. Burchell goes on to point out, however, that many Irishmen were nominated by the Vigilante-founded People's party and held high municipal offices during the height of Vigilante power from 1858 to 1863.
[126] The story of the monument to David Broderick, erected during the Civil War in the Laurel Hill Cemetary, then razed in 1937 during the removal of that cemetary, is told in San Francisco *Chronicle*, 1 December 1969. A bust of Broderick done in the Roman republican style is all that remains of this monument. It is now held by the California Historical Society in San Francisco. For the list of subscribers, *Alta* 24 September 1859.

CHAPTER 3

Though the heavens fall: The Vigilante movement culture of 1856

After 1856, San Francisco became a one-party town whose politics hinged on the municipal dimension of the political community. Returned to power at each election by comfortable majorities or pluralities, the "People's" party, founded by the Vigilantes, ruled the city for ten years. The Vigilante-People's regime grounded its success in blood, propaganda, and respectability. The Vigilantes took the feeble reformist programs of municipal nonpartisanship and fiscal conservatism from New York and Boston and made them succeed in San Francisco through a revolutionary experience: the fraternal solidarity forged during three months of ideologically charged activites and the guilt shared by six thousand men for illegal executions, searches, and deportations. The Vigilante leadership seized an opportunity to impose direction on the shape of group identities during a period in which the capitalist mode of production made many alternative identities possible. They did so by espousing an ideology of mutualistic relations between the potentially hostile strata of society. The Vigilante rank and file internalized that ideology by participating in what Lawrence Goodwyn, in another context, has called a "movement culture."[1]

The merchants and professionals of the thirty-member Executive Committee of the Committee of Vigilance, men like the Democrat William Tell Coleman, the Republican and future People's party mayor Henry F. Teschemacher, and the physician and future People's party police chief Martin J. Burke, achieved through the Vigilante movement an ideological hegemony in the city by reifying the mutualist vision of social classes integral to republicanism. I shall use the term "mutualism" in this chapter to put a name on that aspect

---

[1] Lawrence Goodwyn, *The Populist Moment: A Short History of the Agrarian Revolt in America* (New York: Oxford University Press, 1978).

of the republican idiom that I outlined in the Introduction: the belief that the public good was indivisible and that although "interests" existed, they were not legitimate actors in the formation of public policy.

The Vigilantes forged the latent elements of republican political understanding – antipartyism, mutualism, the indivisible public good – into a working and ruling ideological formation that legitimated the rule of a self-avowed apolitical party run by a secret executive committee on business principles. During the reign of the Vigilante-People's regime, the merchant elite of the city defined the public good, and the majority of urban voters supported their definition. That "majority," however, was among a political community that became even more restricted under the Vigilante-People's regime than it had been prior to 1856. Conspicuously absent from the winning Vigilante-People's constituency were the Irish Catholics and the low-blue (semi- and unskilled) workers. With very good reason, these men believed that the People's party was merely an outgrowth of the Know-Nothing movement that had died in 1855. Inadvertently, then, the People's party's mutualism looked like mutual exclusion to the Irish Catholics and fostered a smoldering group consciousness, which, by the end of the Civil War, would burst forth in the form of an openly Irish Catholic city regime and the beginning of the politics of class in San Francisco.

There was nothing intrinsic about the class or social structure of San Francisco that would have produced the Vigilante movement of 1856. It arose from the peculiar intersection in San Francisco of weak party organizations, intense political participation by a limited political community, a crumbling national party structure, a loss of legitimacy by the party elite in the city, the beginning of a vigilante tradition in 1851, and some spectacular political violence in 1855 and 1856. Having arisen politically, the Vigilante movement imposed on civil society a reigning conception of social identities. For about ten years, during the Vigilante-People's hegemony, winning political mobilization was achieved by appealing to mutual, not to class, interests. Vigilante mutualism taught that prosperity depended upon low municipal expenditures, low taxation, and the prevention of professional politicians (i.e., national political parties) from gaining a foothold in municipal affairs.

As an urban political realignment arising from a legitimation crisis, the Vigilante-People's movement operated in a distinctly

dialectical fashion. Half of its energy was directed at the delegitimation of the established authorities, and the other half was directed
toward constructing an alternative authority structure. The process
was dialectical because the creation of a new authority structure
took its strength and legitimacy from the disgrace of the old, and
the disgrace of the old order grew worse with the success of the new.
The following discussion first examines this process and then presents a series of perspectives on the creation of new cultural norms.

PATTERNS OF THE COMMITTEE:
NINETY-NINE DAYS

From the "reorganization" of the Committee of Vigilance on 15
May 1856 until the disbandment of their army of six thousand on
18 August, the Committee of 1856 lasted exactly ninety-nine days.
The patterns of enrollment that occurred during the activities of
the committee are most revealing of the way this movement operated to draw the political community into a consensual ethics of
public purpose. Ironically, historians purporting to write a "social
history" of the Vigilance Committee merely have stressed the social
class origins of its elite leadership. Only by turning attention to the
thousands of men who composed the rank and file, most of whom
were working-class, is it possible to understand the meaning of vigilantism in San Francisco.[2]

To celebrate their demobilization and their enormous popularity,
the full force of the Vigilantes staged a "GRAND PARADE AND REVIEW
OF THE VIGILANCE COMMITTEE" on 18 August 1856. Veterans of the
Mexican–American War remarked that the six thousand men on review presented a larger force of men and arms than General Winfield Scott led when the U.S. Army captured Mexico City in 1847.[3]
Accounts report crowded sidewalks and windows at every point of
the parade. Businesses closed their doors for the day, and the city
was decorated as though it were the Fourth of July. In the midst of
their entourage, the Vigilantes pulled a large replica of "Fort Gunnybags," the committee's headquarters, made of painted canvas and
embellished with five protruding cannon. High above the streets,

---

[2]   The historiography of the two San Francisco Vigilance Committees is discussed at length
in Chapter 2.
[3]   *Alta*, 19 August 1856.

sympathizers had suspended so many banners that the newspapers could list only a few.[4] Between two of the tallest buildings "was suspended a frame in the shape of a quarter circle, with the word 'Vigilance' on either side – a large eye, emblematic of the seal of the Committee, just above it."[5] This "Grand Parade" marked the end of an extraordinary episode in American political and social history. For more than three months a majority of the city's voting citizens and a majority of its most respected public leaders had openly defied the laws of the state. The Confederate States of America, just five years later, would also enjoy this much legitimacy in rebellion, but no other rebellion on this scale has gone unpunished to such an extent. Vigilante participants were considered heroes in San Francisco through the end of the century. How did they win such long-lived legitimacy?

The six thousand members of the Committee of 1856 did not all join at once. At least three phases of the committee's lifespan, each characterized by a pattern of enrollment, must be distinguished. The previous chapter explained the origins of the Committee of 1856 in the response to a political assasination, the killing of the editor James King of William by the County Supervisor James P. Casey on 14 May 1856. This shooting provoked the first wave of enrollment, a rapid enlistment of twenty-eight hundred men prior to the Vigilante executions of James P. Casey and Charles Cora on 22 May. The demand for admission to the reorganized committee was so great, in fact, that the Executive Committee halted enrollments by 17 May in order to concentrate on abducting Casey and Cora from the city authorities, in whose custody they were being held.[6] On 24 May the committee began requiring formal, written applications for admission. Most of these these written applications survive, enabling a systematic analysis of patterns of enrollment from that day forward.

Surrounded by almost three thousand armed Vigilantes and faced with a cannon at the door, the police "surrendered" Casey and Cora on 18 May. James King of William actually died from his

---

[4] *Bulletin*, 19 August 1856; *Alta*, 19 August 1856. [5] *Alta*, 19 August 1856.

[6] Clancey J. Dempster reports as follows: "Upon Saturday afternoon [17 May] the admission of applicants desiring to enroll ... was suspended and President Coleman and Marshall [Charles] Doane planned a movement of the Committee by which the jail was to be surrounded." Clancey J. Dempster, Dictation for H. H. Bancroft, p. 49, Bancroft Library, Berkeley.

mortal wound two days after that, on 20 May. After a grand procession and furneral for King, the Vigilantes returned to their headquarters, "Fort Gunnybags," and hanged Casey and Cora from
the windows of a warehouse. The death of King and the killing of
Casey and Cora had an extraordinary effect on the city. "He is
dead!" lamented the *Alta*: "On his tombstone let there be written
the simple word RESURGAM! He will arise! His memory will be
embalmed forever as a martyr.[7] Bancroft called this period "the
loosing of latent law," and recalled (in characteristic prose) that
"half the town by friction of electrical words were stirring the atmosphere in the invocation of cleansing storm."[8] Clancey J. Dempster,
a member of the the Executive Committee, recalled the "long rows
of men standing day after day in single file in Sacramento street
awaiting their turn for examination and admission."[9] His melodramatic account suggests the gravity of the application process:

The eager men who stood so patiently in front of the Vigilance Quarters
with flashing eyes and compressed lips were almost universally silent with
that solemn sense of demeanor which betokens a sense of deep responsibility.... The occasional remarks exchanged by acquaintances were generally uttered in the low tones which men use when in the vicinity of sorrow or
death.[10]

Businesses were closed for many days, either from the participation
or by the uncertainty of their owners. Most ominously, the bi-weekly
steamer of 20 May carried the second largest shipment of gold to
date from San Francisco, raising fears of an exodus of capital.[11]
Dempster's description of the burst of enrollment following the executions of Casey and Cora is well supported in Figure 3.1, which
plots the frequency of applications from 25 May through the middle
of July, when virtually the full membership of six thousand had been
reached.

After the deaths of Casey and Cora, the supporters of the com-

[7]   *Alta*, Wednesday, 21 May 1856.
[8]   H. H. Bancroft, *Popular Tribunals*, 2 vols. (San Francisco: History Co., Publishers, 1887),
2:60.
[9]   Clancey J. Dempster, Dictation for H. H. Bancroft, p. 46, MS in Bancroft Library,
Berkeley.
[10]   Clancey J. Dempster, Dictation, p. 18.
[11]   *Mercantile Gazette and Shipping Register*, 19 June 1856, p. 3. The *Mercantile Gazette* insisted that
it was not capital in flight from the Vigilante excitement, but rather was the coincidental
removal of funds by a large French investment house.

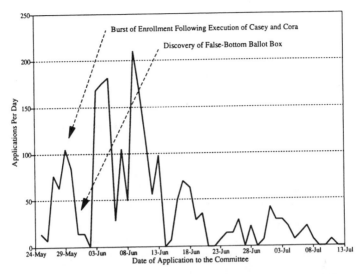

Figure 3.1. Frequency of membership applications per day to the 1856 Committee of Vigilance

mittee justified its continued operation and helped define its future goals. "It is a fact which cannot be denied," explained the *Alta*, "that the present crisis of affairs in San Francisco and the State of California has been brought about mainly by the baneful influence of election frauds. An unholy alliance had been formed between political office seekers and ballot-box stuffers."[12] To combat this "unholy alliance" the *Alta* warned that the three thousand armed men of the committee were "backed by the entire moral force of the city and State, who will stand by them until the work of regeneration is completed."[13] A Vigilante broadside phrased this moral urgency in the republican language of the body, of a single organism: "the paramount necessity of a thorough and fundamental reform of the social and political body."[14]

Nothing, however, guaranteed that the movement might not fade away at this point. The killing done, little else may have occurred to maintain interest in enrollment or participation. Specifically, the committee might have faded away had the promise to root out professional political criminals not been fulfilled. Indeed, we can

[12] *Alta*, Wednesday, 28 May 1856. [13] *Alta*, 24 May 1856.
[14] Broadside, [n.d.], San Francisco Committee of Vigilance Papers, Huntington Library.

observe a sudden drop in enrollments by 30 May in Figure 3.1. As it happened, spectacular discoveries of political fraud in the third week of the committee enflamed the city once again.

Following the two executions, the committee's military units searched the city in predawn raids and domiciliary searches for political criminals and evidence of their crimes. A "Communication," possibly by the Executive Committee, appeared in the *Alta*, which proclaimed: "Some terrible work must be done to regain our lost civil liberty and legal rights. The people must rise and search every man's tent, and put away the evil from among them."[15] On Thursday, May 29, the committee's men found the infamous "false-bottom ballot box" in the house of a Democratic activist named "Woolley" Kearney. The use of the false-bottom ballot box to defraud democracy, along with other incidents of election rigging, were confirmed suddenly in the publication of the confession of James "Yankee" Sullivan, then in the custody of the Vigilantes under suspicion of ballot box stuffing.[16]

The Vigilantes displayed the false-bottom ballot box in the center of their Executive Committee meeting room and trotted it out periodically for public display.[17] The committee certainly appreciated its value: "This cunningly contrived specimen of rascality gave them at least a thousand good fighting men."[18] Analysis of the dated membership applications confirms Bancroft's offhand guess. During the week following the ballot box discovery and confession of Sullivan, a furious burst of enrollment began, again clearly visible in Figure 3.1. "The public pulse ran up to a fever heat again yesterday, and the stirring scenes of last week were renewed."[19] More than nine hundred new members joined the committee by Sunday, 8 June, and eight hundred fifty more had enrolled by the mass meeting of Saturday, 14 June. At least ten thousand people turned out in support for the committee that Saturday to listen to lengthy speeches and to view the amazing false-bottom ballot box.[20]

---

[15] *Alta*, Friday 30 May 1856.   [16] See previous chapter for these events.

[17] Bancroft claimed that someone offered the committee $5,000 for this box. In fact, the committee's treasurer eventually sold the "patent double-action ballot-box" after the committee disbanded for $500 as part of a fund-raising drive to settle the Vigilantes' sizeable debts. Treasurer's report reproduced in Bancroft, *Popular Tribunals*, 2:542–3.

[18] Bancroft, *Popular Tribunals*, 2:99.

[19] *Alta*, Sunday, 1 June 1856.

[20] *Alta*, Sunday morning, 15 June 1856, p 2. For further consideration of the size of this meeting, see note 39.

The final, and perhaps the most important, phase of the committee's career began during the month of June, when the organized opposition, calling itself the "Law and Order" party made a concerted, though feeble, attempt to defeat the Vigilantes. David S. Terry, a justice of the California Supreme Court, had positioned himself as Governor J. Neely Johnson's chief adviser during the Vigilante movement. After the suicide of Yankee Sullivan, Terry began issuing writs of habeas corpus, demanding that the Vigilantes produce prisoners Billy Mulligan and Martin Gallagher, whom the Vigilantes had captured as known "shoulder strikers" and "election bullies." The Vigilantes ignored the writs. On Tuesday, 3 June, Governor Johnson declared the city of San Francisco to be "in a state of insurrection" and commanded William T. Sherman to call out and enlist new men into the militia. Sherman faced an impossible task. On 21 May, when the Vigilantes numbered three thousand, Sherman wrote "At no time ... could I count on more than one hundred inexperienced men."[21] Following the governor's proclamation, Sherman redoubled his efforts. By 15 June the governor had raised, at the most, four hundred seventy-five men loyal to him.[22] By that time the armed Vigilantes numbered fifty-two hundred men.

By 15 June the official opposition to the Vigilantes had begun to collapse. Sherman had resigned his post as major-general of the California militia in exasperation on 7 June, after a strenuous week of negotiations with William T. Coleman and the Vigilantes. He was succeeded by Volney Howard, a member of Terry's political circle. Major-General Howard had none of Sherman's prestige, leaving the Vigilantes much more confident, although they still feared some imminent attack, for the committee was in open rebellion against both California and the United States.[23]

The climax of the committee's career arrived when Governor Johnson managed to procure, on the ship *Julia*, a load of federal arms and tried secretly to send them into San Francisco to his miniature militia units. The Executive Committee, which had spies in most important places and learned easily of the plot against them,

21   William T. Sherman to Hon. Thomas Ewing, 21 May 1856, in "Sherman and the San Francisco Vigilantes," *Century Magazine*, 43 (December 1891), 301.
22   "The highest estimate we have heard of those who were mustered into the service of Gov. Johnson ... is 475." *Alta*, 15 June 1856, p. 2.
23   T. H. Hittell, *History of California*, 4 vols. (San Francisco, 1885–97), 3:566–7.

ordered a seizure of the federal arms on 21 June. In the ensuing fray, Justice Terry drew his notorious Bowie knife and stabbed a Vigilante policeman named Sterling A. Hopkins in the neck. Terry was then arrested and the committee proceeded to capture and disarm Major-General Howard's militia units. By nightfall, the state's forces had been dismantled without a shot fired. One hundred of the governor's men were briefly imprisoned and two thousand stand of government arms had been captured.[24]

By 22 June the Vigilance Committee had absolute control of San Francisco. In response to a petition for aid from the governor of California, President Franklin Pierce and Secretary of State William L. Marcy expressed alarm, but refused to help, believing the rebellion would not last until their reply could reach California.[25] In the meantime the Executive Committee was stuck with a dilemma. They could not try Terry for murder unless Hopkins died, which the latter stubbornly refused to do. On the other hand, the committee was reluctant to release Terry, for he would be their judge should the Vigilantes come to trial themselves. Their solution was to demand Terry's resignation from the bench in return for his release. Once again a battle among political elites was decided by the issue of a man's character. William T. Sherman recorded Terry's response: "He would rather die than be dishonored."[26]

The membership enrollment patterns during this third phase of the committee's life, as Figure 3.1 indicates, became irregular. The bursts of enrollment do not seem to correlate with any one of the events occurring during that phase. But enrollment did continue to grow steadily, adding another seven.hundred members from 15 June onward.

Terry kept his captors in a quandary throughout July. Finally the Executive Committee found him guilty of resisting arrest by a Vigilante officer and of assault. His sentence was to have this verdict read to him and to advise him strongly to resign his position on the bench. Released quietly at 2:00 A.M. on 7 August, Terry swiftly boarded a riverboat to Sacramento, and the Executive Committee,

[24]   Hittell, *History of California*, 3:567.; *Alta*, 24 June 1856, p. 1.

[25]   The dispatches from the governor to the president and the replies are all reprinted in Bancroft, *Popular Tribunals*, 2:358–62.

[26]   William T. Sherman to Turner, 2 July 1856, in "Sherman and the San Francisco Vigilantes," 306.

having long ago accomplished its goals, immediately made plans to disband the Vigilantes.[27]

DISGRACE OF THE ELECTED OFFICIALS

Primarily because the committee earned so much popular support, the political-cultural authority of its leaders grew steadily throughout the movement's ninety-nine-day duration. Opponents of the committee were left holding empty badges of authority as the rebellion delegitimated the constituted government. How thorough this process was can be appreciated only by examining it in some detail.

The opponents of the committee called themselves the "Law and Order" party, but the variety of their previous political affiliations confounds any attempt to fit the configuration of either support or opposition with previous political alignments. Its leading members were John Nugent, David S. Terry, David C. Broderick, and Edward D. Baker. Nugent, the editor of the *Daily Herald*, turned his columns against the committee from the very first night of its organization and consequently lost, within a single day, most of his advertising business for this stance. The *Herald of* 14 May 1856 was a full-sized newspaper, three-feet long and two wide. From 15 May onward, however, it was a midget among the San Francisco press, falling to half of its original size after the powerful auctioneers withdrew their patronage.[28] "This is not all," Nugent complained: "A number of valorous commercial gentlemen on Front street gathered together a number of the *Heralds* of yesterday morning, and making a pile of them in the street, burned them amid great rejoicing."[29]

Nugent provided the instrument of communication for the Law and Order party, but he shared little else politically with the rest of the opposition. David Terry, the California Supreme Court justice who helped to lead the Chivalry, or pro-Southern faction, of the Democratic party, had temporarily joined the Know-Nothing party and now supported his fellow party member, Governor J. Neely Johnson. David C. Broderick, leader of the Free-Soil wing of the

---

[27]   *Alta*, 8, 9 August 1856.   [28]   *Herald*, 14, 15 May 1856.
[29]   San Francisco *Daily Herald*, 16 May 1856, p. 2, col. 1. Nugent also reports that 212 persons withdrew their subscriptions on 15 May.

Democratic party, stood shoulder-to-shoulder with Terry, who three years later would kill him in a duel over control of the California Democrats. These mismatched men were joined by yet another odd ally: Edward D. Baker, a leading western Whig-cum-Republican, Abraham Lincoln's bosom friend from Illinois, and widely renowned as a brilliant and moving orator.[30]

Given their irreconcilable party or factional affiliations, one possible explanation for these men's purpose in leading the Law and Order party is principle, expressed plainly in the name they chose. They not only denounced the flaunting of the Constitution and civil liberties but also feared the destruction of California's commerce. Another motivation, however, was honor. Merely by their remaining neutral, Terry and Broderick, as longtime leaders of their respective wings of the Democratic party, would have given tacit admission of the truth of their own corruption. According to the rules of honor, only active opposition could recover their already threatened reputations. "The touchstone of character is action," Bancroft wrote about Coleman, a phrase that was just as appropriate for his contemporaries.[31] The Law and Order party was led by men of sterling reputations. Although each man's honor was too strong for the committee to defeat him personally, collectively they simply failed to build their own following. This outcome was in part produced by their own unwillingness to support the elected officials of San Francisco. Nugent himself supported the goals, if not the methods, of the committee in the columns of his paper.[32]

During the first few days of the committee the loss of official legitimacy was so great that most of the governor's own militia units dissolved and joined the Vigilantes en masse, marking their transition by adding the cognomen "Independent" to their previous names: the "Independent Washington Guards," the "Independent City

---

[30] Baker delivered the oration at the funeral of David C. Broderick in 1859; see Chapter 4.

[31] Baker's reputation was threatened because he had, reluctantly in fact, been Charles Cora's defense attorney in August 1855, during Cora's legal trial for the murder of U.S. Marshal Richardson. Baker, an extremely able lawyer, succeeded in having Cora acquitted. The Vigilantes considered this an unjust verdict, and charges of purchased jury votes appeared in the earliest columns of James King of William's newspaper, the *Bulletin*. The charges were undoubtedly unfair, and Baker had not been associated with corruption before or after these events. His opposition to the committee must have been charged with his indignation at the Vigilante trial and execution of Cora.

[32] Their "only object is to purge the body politic," even the *Herald* echoed the Vigilantes' claims. *Herald*, 12 June 1856, p. 2.

Guards," or the "Independent Wallace Guards."[33] Even in the midst of his sincere efforts to put down the Committee, Major-General Sherman wrote disparagingly of the men he was forced by duty to defend: "The public offices heretofore [have] been controlled absolutely by politicians who did not scruple to use such men as Casey, Billy Mulligan, Charley Duane, *et hoc genus omne*, all graduates of New York prisons or political clubs."[34]

By the first day of June even Nugent – the central spokesman for the opposition – showered the mayor and sheriff with contempt for their impotence: "The complete abandonment of their sworn duties by the municipal and judicial officers in this city ... has rendered them the pliant tools of that body [the Vigilance Committee], and they are no longer the officers intended by the Constitution and laws."[35] The discovery of the false-bottom ballot box on 29 May and the publication of Sullivan's confession on 2 June cast serious doubts on the legitimacy of the standing authorities. On 5 June the notorious "election bully" Billy Mulligan supposedly ratified his own deportation from the decks of the steamer taking him away. In a statement that was probably elicited in trade for his life and the opportunity to be deported, Mulligan delivered a further indictment of the city's elected officials:

I know that my punishment is just.... I find no fault with the Committee. They are all respectable gentlemen and are acting rightly.... There is not an officer in the city or county of San Francisco who is legally elected. They are all thieves from the Mayor down, and should be driven from office. I hope to hear that they have all been made to resign.[36]

Whether it had been fraudulently won or not, the authorities' popular mandate to rule had evaporated.[37] The spell of doubt "smirched if it did not thoroughly blacken every incumbent."[38]

---

[33] These companies are listed in the account of the Fourth of July festivities, *Alta*, 5 July 1856.

[34] "In haste," W. T. Sherman to Hon. Thomas Ewing, 21 May 1856, letter reprinted in "Sherman and the San Francisco Vigilantes," 301.

[35] San Francisco *Daily Herald*, 1 June 1856.

[36] Bancroft, *Popular Tribunals*, 2:280.

[37] Neither the investigations of the Vigilance Committee nor the work of subsequent scholars have supported the charge that most of the city government had been elected fraudulently; Robert M. Senkewicz, *Vigilantes in Gold Rush San Francisco* (Stanford, Calif.: Stanford University Press, 1985), 116–19.

[38] Hittell, *History of California*, 3:634.

Mayor James Van Ness and the rest of the city government lost so much legitimacy that even City Attorney Bailie Peyton, in an astonishing move, chaired the huge public demonstration of 14 June in support of the Vigilance Committee. Estimates of the size of this demonstration range from the hostile *Herald*'s improbable number of three thousand to the *Bulletin*'s figure of fifteen thousand; but the *Alta*'s estimate of ten thousand seems most credible.[39]

With the false-bottom ballot box at his side, Peyton addressed the crowd from the balcony of the Oriental Hotel:

I ask you, fellow-citizens, has there been in San Francisco for the past several years any Government which emanated from a free expression of the popular will? [cries of no! no!]. The men who have made the laws and executed them, so far as the voice of the people goes, have acted as your agents without authority. They have acted under a fraudulent power of attorney not derived from you but from those who have worked together to overthrow the popular will. . . . What kind of Government could be built on stuffed ballot boxes?[40]

Following Peyton's long address, a series of pro-Vigilante resolutions were read and passed. The vote (by raised hands) was nearly unanimous. The unsympathetic *Herald* counted only two dissenting votes (which would have included the reporter's own). One of these resolutions declared: "That we have the fullest confidence in the people, and in the people's organization known as the Committee of Vigilance of San Francisco, and in their ability and determination to maintain the common safety. . . ."[41] About ten thousand people – the approximate size of the electorate – voted together to delegitimize the standing government. More people – and the accounts do not exclude women from the crowd – voted for the Vigilantes that day than had voted for any party or person since the founding of the city.

After this vote of support, the meeting began to slip from the control of Bailie Peyton and into the hands of more radical leaders.

---

[39]   The actual size of the meeting can be read between the lines of the opposition *Herald*'s account. The terse phrase in that account – "The meeting was a large one." – betrays the mendacity of the *Herald* in the face of an overwhelming show of popular support for the committee. Meetings of only 3,000 people rarely received such a description. The rest of the account is also revealing. The *Herald* observed only two votes in the crowd against the resolutions at the meeting, and it recorded only positive shouts of approval from the crowd. San Francisco *Daily Herald*, Sunday morning, 15 June 1856; *Alta*, 15 June 1856; *Bulletin*, 15 June 1856.

[40]   San Francisco *Daily Herald*, 15 June 1856.   [41]   Ibid.

First, someone forwarded a resolution to organize auxiliary support for the committee, "and when ... the emergency of the case demands it, to perfect such a plan, by calling together our fellow-citizens, [and] enrolling their names ..."[42] By their unanimous support for this resolution, the crowd in effect greatly enlarged the size of the committee over its official strength on that day of fifty-two hundred.

William Sharon, one of the founders of the Bank of California, then took the speaker's place on the balcony and proposed a resolution to demand "the resignation immediately of the City and County officers, the Judges (with the exception of Shattuck and Norton), and the members of the Senate who hold over to the next term."[43] "The crowd seemed to relish the proposition mightily," reported the *Herald*. Before a vote could be taken, however, Peyton hustled Sharon aside and adjourned the meeting. Unsatisfied, Sharon "mounted a truck on the opposite side of the street and succeeded in getting a majority in favor of their adoption from a portion of the meeting."[44]

Sharon's resolution began a persistent call for the resignation of the city's elected officials. William Sharon and Ira P. Rankin organized another mass meeting on 12 July, this one having been called for the express purpose of petitioning the standing officials to resign. The petition quickly sported some six thousand signatures.[45] In fact, some of the city and county officials had already been required to resign on the first of July, 1856, in accordance with the new "Consolidation Act" charter of the city and county of San Francisco. The Consolidation Act, passed in 1855, superseded the old city charter on 1 July, but a new city and county government was not to be elected until the general elections in November.[46] The act of 1855 left the mayor and a number of other officers in place, alongside a transitional Board of Supervisors appointed by three justices of the peace.

This statutory coincidence confused and further weakened the authority of the elected officials and soon the petition for resignations

---

[42] Ibid.
[43] San Francisco *Daily Herald*, 15 June 1856; Hittell, *History of California*, vol. 3:634–5.
[44] *Herald*, 15 June 1856.
[45] *Alta*, 11, 24 July 1856; Hittell, *History of California*, 3:635.
[46] There was no connection between the legislation of 1855 and the Vigilance Committee except, in the eyes of the committee, happy coincidence.

demanded that the transitional government step down as well![47] The rules of honor made these voluntary resignations impossible, however. To resign would be tantamount to an admission of one's holding office fraudulently. As the *Alta* observed, the mayor and others kept their offices to "preserve their reputation and vindicate their character."[48]

Ironically, the republican reputations of the Vigilance Committee's elite prevented them from forcing or even openly advocating the resignation of the standing officials.[49] Such a move would, they knew, show that the Executive Committee was motivated by a selfish desire for power.[50] Clancey Dempster referenced the fear "lest some shadow of pretense might be afforded for reproach of office seeking." The validation of this charge, which the Law and Order party frequently made, would have seriously discounted "that purity of motive and ... self-denial which had actuated the organization and of which it justly was proud."[51] The only way these conservative men could justify their flagrant violations of the law was to cast their actions in the purest, most disinterested light possible.

Further, by avoiding comprehensive governance of the city, the Vigilantes exempted themselves from responsibility for, and criticism of, budgetary and other inevitably controversial decisions. With six thousand Vigilantes patrolling the streets unchallenged even by the president of the United States, with local officials disgraced, and with the status of some local officials in doubt, the committee provided the only real political authority in town, and probably on the entire west coast as well. "We are, as it were,"

---

[47]   *Daily California Chronicle*, 3 July 1856; *Alta*, 11, 24 July 1856.
[48]   *Alta*, 24 July 1856.
[49]   On the day following Bailie Peyton's mass meeting and the Sharon resolutions for resignations, William Tell Coleman convened an Executive Committee to appoint a committee to investigate the question of resignations and to report on which of the current officers might be asked to resign. This was a very delicate approach, however, and the appointed committee never got around to making its report. Hittell, *History of California*, 3:635.
[50]   "... when we have insured to our citizens an honest and vigorous protection of their rights, then the Committee of Vigilance will find great pleasure in resigning their power into the hands of the people, from whom it was received." Broadside, "To the People of California," [n.d.], San Francisco Committee of Vigilance Papers, Huntington Library, San Marino.
[51]   Clancey J. Dempster, Dictation, p. 16.

lamented the *Daily California Chronicle*, "a body politic without a head."[52]

The Vigilance Committee visibly supplanted the elected officials in one important area, that of policing the city. The Executive Committee employed full-time a police force of special officers – the only paid Vigilantes – who arrested particularly wanted criminals.[53] On one occasion, the Executive Committee purchased a schooner and sent the Vigilante police all the way to Santa Barbara on it in search of the much-wanted Democratic chieftain Edward "Ned" McGowan. On a day-to-day basis the many companies of the committee covered all points of the city in constant vigilance, making arrests that the regular police would have been expected to make.[54] Concerned primarily with professional and political crimes, Vigilantes turned ordinary criminal suspects over to the regular courts.[55]

DISCIPLINARY AUTHORITY

If anything, the Vigilance Committee was too popular. The evidence just presented indicates that the Executive Committee frequently sought to *restrict* enrollment into its official ranks. Enrollment was suspended days after the shooting of King by Casey, then resumed again only after the printing of formal applications. At the mass meeting led by Bailie Peyton and William Sharon on 14 June the crowd had voted itself an auxilliary force, but the Executive Committee consipicuously declined to enroll these new volunteers. The leading Vigilantes were imposing discipline on a relatively spontaneous movement, the likes of which are usually only found during genuine revolutions.

At every step, the Vigilante leadership built its authority in the most careful way. The first ritual enacted by the committee was the

---

[52] *Daily California Chronicle*, 3 July 1856.
[53] John L. Durkee, "Statement," MS in Bancroft Library, Berkeley. Durkee was the only member of the legitimate police to defect to the Vigilantes. He was eventually given command of the Vigilante police and later stood trial for piracy in the capture of the ship *Julia*. H. H. Bancroft, *Popular Tribunals*, vol. 2:375–6; 501–6.
[54] For example, *Alta*, 24 June 1856.
[55] Philip J. Ethington, "Vigilantes and the Police: The Creation of a Professional Police Bureaucracy in San Francisco, 1847–1900," *Journal of Social History* 21:2 (Winter 1987):197–228.

choosing of its president. According to an unwritten republican formula for political virtue, individuals were expected to "decline the
honor" several times before accepting high positions, which demonstrated that they had to make a personal sacrifice for the sake of the
community. Following this custom, several leading merchants en-
treated William Tell Coleman to lead the reorganization of the
committee within hours of the Casey–King shooting.[56] Coleman's
Romantic character was no doubt flattered by the potential of leading a republican revolution. He had, two years earlier, publicly supported William Walker when that infamous filibuster had faced
charges of violating U.S. neutrality laws.[57] But Coleman, a leading
merchant with much to lose, must also have thought about his own
skin. And his very first concern, drawing on his experience leading
the first committee in 1851, must have been to discipline whatever
movement emerged. "On two conditions will I accept the responsibility," Coleman replied, "absolute obedience, absolute secrecy."[58]
"No dictator could have it more absolutely than I," Coleman later
boasted; "it was always so in such matters."[59] He eventually became
primus inter pares, sharing his authority with a group of about
thirty oligarchs who composed the Executive Committee.

All the members were issued membership numbers in consecutive
order as they enrolled. Coleman commanded that numbers 1
through 100 stand together to form a company and elect a captain,
that numbers 101 through 200 do likewise, and so on, "and to begin
drilling at once." "This last order," Coleman explained, "was given
for three reasons":

First, the absolute necessity that no time should be lost in getting into
shape for subsequent action; second, that the men might from the start
appreciate the fact that they were not independent units in a mob, but
simply members in an association that was subject to a centralizing
power; and third, that incendiary discussion might be checked, and the
riotous inclinations of the men sobered into earnest, organized effort.[60]

---

56 "Coleman acquiesced in their sentiments, thanked them for their offer of leadership, but
     declined, saying he would assume his share of the risk and responsibility, but would serve
     in the ranks only." Bancroft, *Popular Tribunals*, 2:65.
57 See Chapter 1.   58 Bancroft, *Popular Tribunals*, 2:74.
59 "Statement of William T. Coleman on the Vigilance Committee," [n.d.] Dictation for
     Theodore H. Hittell, for his *History of California*, in Theodore H. Hittell Collection, Ban-
     croft Library, Berkeley, California.
60 "The Vigilantes of '56: William T. Coleman's Record of the Early Days, The Secret
     Archives of a Moral Earthquake ... ," San Francisco *Morning Call*, 20 April 1884, p 1.

Once disciplined, the Vigilantes issued "several thousand good flint-lock muskets" to the rank and file, procured from a speculator who had bought the outdated weapons from the U.S. government in hopes of outfitting the filibusters or the Indian expeditions of those years.[61] The flintlocks, equipped with long bayonets, were literally leftovers from the very first years of the Republic. They must have had the effect of reinforcing the Vigilantes' sense of themselves as "citizen soldiers," in the tradition of the revolutionary war.[62] Surviving broadsides and lettersheets, such as the one depicting the execution of Casey and Cora in Plate 3.1, show these thousands of bristling bayonets brandished at every appearance of Vigilante power.

SYMBOLS AND SWORD RITUALS

The Committee of 1856 was a genuinely popular movement. As the analysis in the previous chapter demonstrates, more than half of the membership had blue-collar occupations and the total number of official members amounted to a clear majority of San Francisco's enfranchised citizens. Like any popular movement, the Vigilance Committee cemented itself together with symbols and rituals drawn selectively from current discourse to legitimate the cause. The committee's elaborate iconography helped attract new members, define the movement's ideology, and unify its authority. A look at these symbols and rituals clarifies the meaning the movement held for its mass participants.

The committee's favorite symbol, the all-seeing – or vigilant – eye, was displayed most prominently wherever the committee's authority reached. Plate 3.2 shows one of the silver medals struck by the committee for members who could afford them. Beneath the eye on the obverse is the personal identification number "2688," indicating that its owner joined the committee on 17 or 18 May.[63] The eye was also the main part of the seal used on all

---

61 Bancroft, *Popular Tribunals*, 2:89.
62 Broadside, "The Revolution of the People," San Francisco Committee of Vigilance, Huntington Library, San Marino, California.
63 Surviving official documents usually refer only to a member's number, not his name, so we do not know to whom this medal belonged. The "List of Certificates to be Issued," San Francisco Committee of Vigilance Papers, Huntington Library, San Marino, California, gives each member's number alongside the date he joined. Member 2688 falls between members who joined on the 17th and the 18th of May.

Execution of *CASEY* & *CORA*,
by the San Francisco Vigilance Committee
May 22ª 1856.

Plate 3.1. The "execution" (lynching) of James P. Casey and Charles Cora by the Vigilance Committee of 1856. This public killing was committed from the windows of a warehouse in the commercial district that served as the Vigilante headquarters. On occasions like this, the committee displayed its fearsome strength. The rigid military discipline signified the orderly, lawlike way these men were put to death. Barely visible are the thousands of revolutionary war vintage, bayonet-tipped muskets. These antiquated weapons, although deadly enough, served primarily to represent symbolically the revolutionary struggle for liberty. Courtesy of the Bancroft Library.

official committee documents, such as deportation decrees or press releases.[64]

There can be little doubt as to the origin of the all-seeing eye. It was the eye used by the Freemasons, for whom it served as an Enlightenment symbol of universal knowledge, culture, and civilization. In contrast to the rationalistic and atheistic French lodges, Freemasonry in America was openly Christian. To American Masons, therefore, the eye directly symbolized God, the all-seeing, all-

[64]   Facsimile of the official seal can be found in Bancroft, *Popular Tribunals*, 2:10.

Plate 3.2. Silver medallion sold to some members of the Vigilance Committee of 1856. The eye, borrowed from Freemasonry, was the master symbol of the movement, expressing the committee's exposure of criminals through vigilance. The reverse displays a figure of Justice who is conspicuously unblindfolded. Above her head are the two Vigilante slogans (see text for explication).

knowing One.[65] The Vigilantes amended this symbolism still further. Their employment of the eye in connection with the term "vigilance" – as in the banner suspended over the city at the Grand Parade of 18 August – endowed the eye with the meaning of social discipline. The viewers of this eye might have read in it Masonic notions of theistic ubiquity, but they certainly saw in it as well the meaning of human authority. And although it is doubtful that the Vigilantes' eye stirred in its viewers the Masonic meanings of scientific and aesthetic knowledge, they quite likely saw in that eye knowledge of another type: surveillance.

To the public the committee gave a promise to accompany the eye, seen in the two slogans, one in Latin and one in English, appearing on the reverse of the medal in Plate 3.2: "FIAT JUSTICIA RUAT COELUM: BE JUST AND FEAR NOT." Both of these phrases were a common part of contemporary school lessons and served to exemplify the highest ideals of the American republic.[66] The Latin motto,

---

[65] The same eye, of course, adorns the Great Seal of the United States, symbolizing God's completion of the pyramid of thirteen states.

[66] I am indebted to J. Mills Thornton III for the identification of these phrases.

meaning "Let justice be done though the heavens fall," dates from the Roman Republic. Its message is plain; catastrophic means are justified in the pursuit of justice as an end. Like the references to Cicero and Cataline, this Roman epigram fixed the Vigilantes' purpose firmly in the antique, recurrent struggle to maintain liberty.

The English phrase, "Be Just and Fear Not," is from Cardinal Wolsey's advice to his servant Cromwell in Shakespeare's *King Henry VIII*. Wolsey's entire phrase was widely quoted, used in the mastheads of newspapers as well as in school primers: "Be just, and fear not; / Let all the ends thou aim'st at be thy country's, / Thy God's and truth's."[67] The popularity of this phrase stemmed from and reinforced the republican conception of politics, which importuned the political community to rise above their individual self-interest and practice thereby "civic virtue." If the Vigilantes hoped to capture the legitimacy lost by the disgraced municipal officials, it was necessary for them to fend off charges of selfish motives by wearing Wolsey's advice as a shield.

Whatever meaning these slogans held for those outside the committee, the iconography of the Vigilantes served the clear internal purpose of unifying the cause of a "thorough and fundamental reform and purification of the social and political body."[68] A description of the main drilling room on the first floor of committee headquarters gives a sense of this usage: "As if to impress the beholder with the eternity of watchfulness which the vigilance principle demanded, an immense emblematic eye glared from the southeast corner of the room, and attracted the attention of each member as he entered."[69] Another wall-mounted eye hung in the large meeting room on the second floor as well, bearing the inscription "NUNQUAM DORMIO," or "I NEVER SLEEP." Only Vigilantes and their prisoners could enter these rooms. Ironically, the rooms were used at night for dormitories.[70]

The sword is the symbol of state power. The significantly unblindfolded figure of Justice on the reverse of the medal in Plate 3.2 (she is vigilant, or "wide awake," as a popular phrase would have put it) stands with the sword at her side. Officers, in the modern age of rapid-fire sidearms, wield swords primarily to symbolize their authority. Sometime in June the members of the various Vigilante

---

[67]   *King Henry VIII*, act 3, scene 2.   [68]   Broadside, "To the People of California."
[69]   Bancroft, *Popular Tribunals*, 2:99.   [70]   Bancroft, *Popular Tribunals*, 2:99.

units began presenting their commanders with costly dress swords in formal sword-presentation ceremonies, to express their obedience to the authority of the committee and its purposes. Each week the various companies presented "a sword of honor," "a beautiful sword," or "an elegant sword," until the *Alta* began its reports with the weary title "Another sword presentation."[71] The men who served under Colonel J. B. Badger gave him "the usual full dress sword, with silver mountings, and heavy gilt scabbard, [which] cost $150.00."[72] In what must have been the typical routine, the men of the Pioneer Guards chose from themselves a representative to make a short speech:

We are proud of you as our commander, we are proud of you as a military commander, and we respect and admire you as a true-hearted gentleman.

Take this sword, and lead us into the good work that has commenced. Take it, and never sheath it until the whole race of murderers and assassins, rowdies and ballot-box stuffers have been exterminated.

In response, Colonel Badger feigned utter surprise and protested that he was only doing his duty, having no ambition for glory. This said, he delivered an evidently rehearsed response:

I assure you, gentlemen, that this token of your esteem shall never be drawn in disgrace, nor, when drawn, sheathed in dishonor. Gentlemen, I thank you. As your speaker has said, I will lead you on in this good cause, until the name of murderer is a disgrace, that of ballot-box stuffer unknown, and official corruption unheard of.[73]

Ceremonies of this sort, akin to the mass meeting of 14 June, erected the authority of the Vigilante elite on the firm cultural ground of popular power.

SCENES OF POLITICAL-CULTURAL CHANGE

During the reign of the Vigilance Committee, six thousand men, a majority of the city's political participants, took part in the city's affairs for a duration and with an intensity that completely overshadowed any prior political campaign, or even any voluntary associations, such as fraternal lodges or fire and militia companies. It

---

[71] *Alta*, 21, 25, 26 June, 5 July 1856.
[72] *Alta*, 26 June 1856.   [73] Ibid.

was a movement with revivalistic fervor, militaristic commitment, and a mutually conditioned consensus. The "vigilance principle" worked within and without the committee to establish the basis of a political culture that would shape the city's political development for decades to come.

The Vigilante movement greatly furthered the project of establishing the male exclusivity of the political public sphere discussed in Chapter 1. In addition to their civil employment, the rank and file of the committee spent time in the committee rooms most days of the week, and spent at least one whole night per week at the headquarters or on patrol.[74] Devoting so much time to the committee meant, of course, time away from families and the private world of women. By establishing their headquarters as the new source of public authority, the Vigilantes also reinforced the gender-defined public–private boundary. The committee resembled other institutional enclaves of male sociability, such as militia companies or saloons, that were intentionally hostile to women. The committee documents record a simple incident to illustrate this boundary. A woman applied to the committee headquarters one night "for permission to spend the night with her husband. The request was not granted."[75] This kind of exposure must have reinforced the sacrificial, fraternal lessons of the committee's program as well as the myth that the "people," in the political sense, were male.

A set of Vigilance Committee documents "relative to denounced members and other suspicious characters," in the form of sworn testimonies and letters to the Executive Committee from the rank and file, reveals the uses of the committee's authority to enforce political-cultural norms.[76] About half of these pertain to political crimes: ballot box stuffing, fraudulent voting, election violence, graft,

---

[74]   Robert S. LaMotte's description of life in the first committee should serve as an accurate portrayal of the routine of the second committee as well: "I ... dine at half past 4, return to the office till dark, then go to the rooms of the Vigilance Committee to hear the news and take part in the proceedings, and if I am not on duty (which duty happens once a week and generally keeps me up until morning) return home at 9 or ten, turn in and sleep." Robert S. LaMotte to Father, 22 July 1850, LaMotte Family Letters, Bancroft Library, Berkeley.

[75]   *Alta*, 18 June 1856.

[76]   "Correspondence, depositions, & cetera from the files of the Investigating Committee, relative to denounced members and other suspicious characters." Hereafter, "Files of the Investigating Committee." San Francisco Committee of Vigilance Papers, Huntington Library, San Marino. These records also include correspondence from sympathetic nonmembers.

and corruption. Addressing himself to the executives, Alfred Clarke (number 723) began his denunciation with a preamble: "Gentlemen, as much of the evils we are organized to prevent & cure, have been thrust upon us through the Ballot Box, I understand that to purify the Ballot Box is one of the duties we have undertaken to perform." Clarke then stated his charge: "I feel it is my duty to inform you that about four Months ago John McCann boasted in my presence of having voted *seven times* at the last Election."[77]

Although multiple voting was only a misdemeanor under the laws of California, it potentially merited enforced deportation under the rule of the Vigilantes. Other "crimes" were not so specific, however. Numerous testimonies against James S. Colby earned him the ire of the committee. "Among the charges," reads the Investigating Committee's notes, was that Colby was "an associate and friend of a class known as 'Shoulder Strikers.'"[78] Colby's worst offense, it seems, was the low esteem in which his character was held. L. M. Quimby stated that "he would not trust him in *any secret society*." Another Vigilante, L. P. Hassbruch, added the following concrete allegation: "[Colby] belonged to the Knownothing [*sic*] Lodge, in this he proved false to his obligations, and is in every respect a trader [traitor] to the party."[79]

Even when the Vigilantes denounced members and nonmembers for nonpolitical crimes, most charges had a political connection. J.G. Chappel (number 2738) reported that one Peter Burns had assaulted him with a gun while the latter was a city policeman in September 1855. Chappel claimed that Burns nearly killed him, the bullet passing through his "hare." The point of the story, however, was that "the Would Be murder[er] is now in the Custom House Employ."[80] Chappel's statement supported the committee's raison d'être: the alleged entrenchment in official capacities of criminals and men of low character.

The relationship between the regulation of public and private behavior is illustrated by a document in which W. R. Reynolds "complained of" Henry Borchees: "Said Borchees was on duty on the

---

77 Emphasis in original. In "Files of the Investigating Committee."
78 The term "shoulder striker" enjoyed widespread use in San Francisco. It denoted a violent man who picked fights, and more specifically, it referred to hired "election bullies," who were, allegedly, employed to intimidate voters. The term seems to have derived from professional pugilism, meaning one who "strikes from the shoulder."
79 Records clipped together under "Colby," "Files of the Investigating Committee."
80 Ibid.

morning of the 24th and on coming home he beat his wife, and broke every thing in the house, threatening to Kill his wife." After this, Mrs. Borchees took refuge in Reynolds's house, and Henry Borchees reportedly "came to the house of Mr. Reynolds last night between 9 and 10 o'clock seeking for his wife, threatening her life, and d —— g the Vigilance Committee." This document bears the simple judgment of the Investigating Committee: "Suspend Him."[81]

Through the Vigilantes' concern with the proprieties of domestic household life a larger function of the committee comes to light. One man was denounced to the committee by a member who admitted: "He can not of his own Knowledge give any testimony for or against him other than his general reputation which is bad."[82] Similarly, Executive Committee member Clancey J. Dempster could write of society that it was composed of "all classes, the idle and the industrious, the vicious and the virtuous, the ignorant and the educated."[83] The intangibility of these references needs to be contextualized by exploring the Vigilantes' method of identifying men with good reputations.

During the committee's reign, numerous ministers supported its actions from the pulpit. In his "Sermon on the Death of Jas. King of William," the Reverend Walter Frear drew freely from Emerson's 1850 text *Representative Men* to make King and Casey stand for the two opposed elements in society:

James King of William and James P. Casey – the sufferer, and the head actor in this tragic scene – do not appear before us to-day, merely as individuals. They are *representative men*: One stands as the representative of the working, honest people; the other, of idle tricksters and the breeders of corruption. One stands for the order-loving, well-meaning men, who are the bone and sinew of the land; the other for that roving, dissolute class who live by the art of cunning; creeping about our cities and towns, and here and there gathering themselves in knots ... like the hissing stacks of serpents that are sometimes met with on the banks of the Amazon.[84]

Still, these distinctions between virtuous citizens and evil serpents would have lacked enforceability without more concrete markers.

81   "Files of the Investigating Committee."
82   "John A. McCrea, San Francisco, June 18th 1856," "Files of the Investigating Committee."
83   Clancey J. Dempster, "statement" for H. H. Bancroft, MS in Bancroft Library, Berkeley, reverse of p. 24.
84   Emphasis in original. Rev'd Walter Frear, *A Sermon on the Death of Jas. King of William, Preached at Iowa Hill, on Sunday, May 25, 1856* (Iowa Hill [Calif.]: Miller and Olmstead, 1856), 6. Copy in Huntington Library.

In "A Discourse for the Times," the Reverend Dr. William A. Scott explained to the parishioners of the Calvary Presbyterian Church how the city's ills could be overcome through the triumph of family life in San Francisco:

There is one great principle in human nature on this subject ... and although it may not be as strong in men as in women, still the best preventive of crime is to have them [men and women] in such as situation as will call out their natural feelings of husband and wife, father and mother, in the purest manner. But this cannot be done if men live as hermits or monks, separated by many long months, and even years, from the society of their wives and children.[85]

Significantly, in the Vigilantes' "thorough and fundamental reform and purification of the social and political body," none of the four executed nor thirty-two deported men was married.[86]

A distinctive demographic shift took place in San Francisco at mid-decade, after which the number of women and families in San Francisco increased dramatically. In 1855 the *Alta* published an editorial discussing ways to deal with "the reign of violence" in the city. "We want population," the *Alta* declared, "we want law-loving people to come here to abide with their families."[87] Now that the Vigilantes were able to define the public sphere by reference to the clear boundary between it and the private sphere, an important concrete test of character was a man's household status. When Alfred Clarke denounced John McCann for boasting of voting seven times in one election, he closed his complaint with the statement: "He is (I believe) a single man. The City would lose nothing by his absence."[88]

Good government, according to both republican and bourgeois formulas, was unthinkable without virtuous women ensconced in domestic households. From the outset of the committee there was an assumption that married family heads were the movement's natural constituency. Liberty, the republican formula taught, was

---

[85] Rev. Dr. Wm. A. Scott, *A Discourse for the Times: Delivered in Calvary Church, Sunday, July 27, 1856* (San Francisco, 1856). Copy in Huntington Library.

[86] Broadside, [n.d.] San Francisco Committee of Vigilance Papers, Huntington Library. Charles Cora in fact married Belle – on the day of his execution. His prior relationship with her, a known prostitute, was a crucial mark against him in his trials and in King's *Bulletin.*

[87] *Alta*, 31 August 1855, p. 2, col. 2. This is, ironically, an antivigilante editorial, written in opposition to vigilance committees in the interior of the state. The events of May 1856, however, transformed the *Alta* into one of the strongest supporters of the vigilantes.

[88] "Files of the Investigating Committee."

dependent first of all on a supply of selfless, virtuous, public-minded men to fill the places of power. During the early national period the ideology of "republican motherhood" evolved to place responsibility for the training of virtuous, self-governing men in the hands of women. Equally important in the republican formula for good government was the "cult of domesticity," for a mother was also a wife, the moral flywheel to the publically striving husband. The world of commerce and power was corrosive to morals; the morally pure home was essential to the regulation of men's ethical conduct.[89]

Although it is shown here that the Vigilantes enforced the ideal of bourgeois domesticity, it has already been demonstrated that the committee's origins were political, not social ones. The demand for family-based citizens was drawn from political ideology and enforced institutionally. Josiah Royce, helping to construct the social conception of politics in the 1880s, fudged these clear lines of causality to argue that the Vigilance Committee was a manifestation of moral family life. Likewise, later historians would trace the committee to deeper social processes. Observing the committee carefully, however, we see how social formations were the object of the Vigilantes' actions; we observe them in the act of social construction.

In point of fact, the Vigilante elite were not paragons of Victorian morality; they left purity to the care of their wives and daughters. A great many of the leaders and the rank and file were engaged in the liquor trade and stories of hard drinking pepper the accounts of meetings.[90] Gerritt Ryckman, a leader of the first committee, refused to join the second one because, in his words, "I went down to one of their meetings, and they were about half of them tight."[91] Hubert Howe Bancroft felt it necessary to explain the drinking of the heroic Vigilante elite to his sensitive readers: "It was the custom, a most deplorable one, among all classes in those days to drink ... when not absolutely thirsty."[92] Indeed, Bancroft's

---

89   Mary Beth Norton, *Liberty's Daughters: The Revolutionary Experience of American Women, 1750–1800* (Boston: Little, Brown and Co., 1980); Linda Kerber, *Women of the Republic: Intellect and Ideology in Revolutionary America* (Chapel Hill: University of North Carolina Press, 1980); Nancy Cott, *The Bonds of Womanhood: 'Woman's Sphere' in New England, 1780–1835* (New Haven: Yale University Press, 1977); Barbara Welter, "The Cult of True Womanhood," *American Quarterly* 18 (Summer 1966): 151–74.

90   "Membership Applications," San Francisco Committee of Vigilance Papers, Huntington Library, San Marino.

91   G. W. Ryckman, Dictation for H. H. Bancroft, p. 18, MS in Bancroft Library.

92   H. H. Bancroft, *Popular Tribunals* 2:64.

research materials reveal him in the act of creating a myth of the Righteous Vigilantes. Clancey J. Dempster, after reading the manuscript of *Popular Tribunals*, corrected Bancroft on an "allusion which would indicate that I had always been a steady attendant at Church, whereas ... I am quite indifferent to what many would consider the *duty* of regularly listening to preaching."[93] Engaged in a project of constructing the ideology of the sacred home, the Vigilantes brought the separate-spheres ideology to life by solidifying the boundaries of public and private, a distinction essential to restoring the ethical sphere for the operation of liberal-capitalist relations of production.

MUTUALISM FOR SAN FRANCISCO

The language of the Vigilantes asserted that the meaningful divisions in society arose not from the type of work men did (criminal behavior was not considered work), but from the way they did it (honestly or dishonestly). From the two starting points of character and republicanism, the Vigilantes imposed a mutualistic vision of the socioeconomic world on San Francisco's political universe. The mutualist vision is amply represented in a lithograph by Charles Nahl, executed to adorn the membership certificates issued to the members of the committee during the committee's reign at two dollars apiece.[94] The original, too large and detailed to reproduce here, measures 18 by 15 inches. Into that space Nahl crowded allegorical figures, symbols, and objects that not only tell the story of the Vigilante movement, but also embed that movement in the mutualist vision of society. Nahl was a leading California artist during the nineteenth century but is now best known for his large oil paintings portraying the romantic life of the gold miners and of the Mexican Californians. His mendacity in those paintings accords with the idealization of society found in the lithograph under examination here.[95]

At the top of the certificate is the vigilant eye overlooking society

---

[93] C. J. Dempster to H. H. Bancroft, 20 October 1878, Bancroft Library, Berkeley.

[94] "List of Certificates to be Issued" recorded the distribution of these. The sale of the certificates to the members was one method of fund raising for the Vigilantes. Huntington Library, San Marino, California.

[95] See Walton Bean and James J. Rawls, *California: An Interpretive History* (New York: McGraw-Hill, 1988), 87, 208.

and glaring at the viewer. Beneath the eye is the drama of the committee's creation: Justice fallen senseless to the ground before the violated ballot box, battle-clad Liberty flying overhead to smite the enemies of republicanism ("NUNQUAM DORMIO" on her shield), and beside these figures the legions of the Vigilantes assembling to reclaim their city, with "Fort Gunnybags" in the foreground. At the base of the lithograph Nahl depicted, with a profusion of objects, the entire preindustrial economy. Two allegorical figures sit amongst the tools and products of commerce and agriculture: on the left a goddess of agriculture reposes on a cornucopia of agrarian output; on the right a goddess of commerce holds a clipper ship in her lap and rests an oar on her shoulder, with fishes in her hair to match her sister's wheat-stalk laurel crown.

The crucial configuration of the certificate, however, is the balance of the figures on the right and the left. Here Nahl presented mutualism in its purest form. Holding a slogan-filled banner across the center of the certificate are Hercules (or Samson) on the left and an angel of culture and learning on the right. Hercules, symbolizing the "bone and sinew" of society, stands among the tools of the mechanical arts: the carpenter's saw, chisel, and mallet; the miner's pickax; the blacksmith's anvil and tongs, and so on. The angel of learning stands amidst the artifacts of high culture: a globe, telescope, chemistry equipment, a painter's palette, and so forth. This angel holds a quill pen to balance Hercules' club and points with her right finger to Heaven, eyes upturned. She symbolizes the art and attainments of civilization, practiced and perpetuated by the society's learned, professional, and moneyed elite.

On closer view, the two figures are also engaged in a mutual task to combat the ills plaguing San Francisco and threatening civilization. While Hercules crushes underfoot a multiheaded, claw-footed monster, overcoming the force of evil, the angel, with "MORAL POWER" on her side, deftly extinguishes the spirit of evil itself, in the form of the stealthy serpent. While the blue-collar and shopkeeping members of the rank and file broke down doors and surrounded the governor's armories, the merchant elite directed the movement from the rooms of the committee, condemning men to death and banishing scores of others on their authority as the honored guardians of the moral power of natural law. Dempster, a merchant and member of the Executive Committee, expressed the spirit of Nahl's lithograph when he begged "to enlarge on the cheerful sacrifice of their time by laboring men and the risks they took which did not, to such an extent at least, affect the more prominent members of the Committee."[96]

Mutualism was far more than a theory or something to be idealized in pictures, however. It was the concrete personal experience of the Vigilantes, seen in the process whereby men joined the committee. Applicants were required to have two current members of the committee sponsor them for admission. The sponsors' names appeared at the top of the form. Men mainly chose sponsors of higher occupational status than themselves to sign their applications. Most applications by blue-collar applicants, moreover, were sponsored by white-collar members.[97] The explicit language of the application states that the sponsors "do hereby consider ourselves RESPONSIBLE for his GOOD CONDUCT." These sponsorships represent personal bonds of loyalty and responsibility between the merchant and the mechanic classes; the camaraderie of the committee's reign could not have failed to have reinforced those bonds.

THE USES OF CULTURAL AUTHORITY

The movement of 1856 placed the Vigilante leadership in an unusually powerful position to make their vision of society the one that counted. We have seen how public men needed to keep their characters spotless, their reputations respected, and their honor recognized. Shame was naturally a very potent weapon. In recognizing the power of the Vigilante elite to shame them, targets of the committee certified the committee's cultural authority.

After David S. Terry's capture he wrote a note to the Executive Committee asking them politely: "To give me an opportunity of vindicating my fair name which is dearer far than life I request the charges against me be submitted to a legal tribunal in this City."[98] The refusal of the Executive Committee to release Terry made it imperative for him never to show the slightest contrition. William

---

[96] Bancroft, *Popular Tribunals*, 2:398.

[97] This analysis was conducted by tracing the sponsors' names on 110 applications, using LeCount and Strong's *San Francisco Directory (San Francisco*, 1856) for October 1856. Of the 100 applications, 53 could be traced, and of these 37 had sponsors with higher status occupations than the applicant. Most of these, moreover, were white-collar sponsors of blue-collar applicants.

[98] David S. Terry to Vigilance Committee, 23 June 1856, San Francisco Committee of Vigilance, 1856, Papers, Bancroft Library, Berkeley, California.

T. Sherman's observation of Terry's attitude was no doubt accurate: "He would rather die than be dishonored."[99]

David C. Broderick, although ruthlessly assailed by James King of William as the "dark fiend" and mastermind of all evil in San Francisco, enjoyed an unimpeachable character in the city and the state.[100] Although the Vigilantes easily denounced many of Broderick's fellow Democrats, men like Ned McGowan or Billy Mulligan, they stood clear of the honored Broderick. As James O'Meara, a contemporary of these events, observed, "Any harm to him, by that body, would have been the occasion of very serious trouble."[101] The Executive Committee were unsure of what to do about this respected man, because the fallen martyr King had assured everyone that Broderick was greatly to blame. Failure to arrest Broderick would also be construed as cowardice, perhaps the worst form of dishonor. Although McGowan, Charles P. Duane, Mulligan, and others had been banished by the first week of June, and twenty-four of the thirty-two total deportees had been given the enforced exile decree by 21 June, it took the Executive Committee until 19 July to issue a Vigilante warrant for Broderick's arrest.[102] Broderick's reputation, however, was strong enough to defeat even the Vigilance Committee. He called on his friend, old Gerritt W. Ryckman, known as the "Nestor" of the Committee of 1851, but not a member of the present one, to intercede on his behalf. Broderick complained to Ryckman that, "to be overhauled by the Committee would destroy his popularity as an aspirant for senatorial honors." Ryckman somehow managed to have the Executive Committee rescind the order for Broderick's arrest.[103]

99   William T. Sherman to [Henry S.] Turner, St. Louis, 2 July 1856, in "Sherman and the San Francisco Vigilantes," 308.
100   King's phrase appears in his *Daily Evening Bulletin*, 12 October 1855. The leading modern biographer of Broderick, David A. Williams, explains that Broderick purposely kept his personal life above reproach: "Pride and aspiration kept him from indulgence in the soft pleasures of the flesh, which were so prominent in his milieu. In the midst of a battle for his political life he declared that no man could truthfully say that he had ever seen Broderick in a gambling hall or a brothel." Williams, *David C. Broderick: A Political Portrait* (San Marino, Calif.: The Huntington Library, 1969), 10.
101   [James O'Meara], *The Vigilance Committee of 1856: By a Pioneer Journalist* (San Francisco: James H. Barry, Publisher, 1890), 56.
102   *Alta*, 21 June 1856, lists "The Catalogue" of "notorious persons" who had been banished from the city by that date.
103   Mary F. Williams, *History of the Vigilance Committee of 1851*, (Berkeley: University of California Press, 1921), 194–5; Gerritt W. Ryckman, Dictation for H. H. Bancroft, p. 19, Bancroft Library, Berkeley, California; David A. Williams, *David C. Broderick*, 133.

Broderick's friend Thomas Maguire, "Napoleon of the Stage" proprietor of Maguire's Opera House, the most popular theater in San Francisco, suffered a more serious threat. Maguire received the dreaded banishment decree of the Vigilantes declaring him a "notoriously bad character" and sentencing him "to leave the State by the 5th of July next, never to return."[104] The decree was a crushing blow to Maguire. His theater, alternating a highbrow program with baudy comedies, was, as we saw earlier, a natural rendezvous not only for many politicians but also for the type of citizen the Vigilantes deplored: gamblers and prostitutes.[105] Maguire wrote a pathetic letter to the committee begging them to postpone his deadline and give him a chance to answer the charges against him. He sought to separate his character from that of his patrons: "I have never been a brawler or disturber of the peace. I have never used or carried weapons of any kind. I have been a hard working, industrious man, endeavoring in all things to deal justly with my fellow men." Maguire then presented his credentials as a virtuous citizen. He was a genuine family man:

I have a Mother and two Sisters who are supported by me alone. My wife has gone to New York for the purpose of bringing to California my Mother and Sisters, and they are now or soon will be on their way. If your sentence against me is carried out, with what shame will they who now hope to form an honorable and happy household here, find on their arrival that I am driven into exile with the brand of infamy upon me!

"My misfortunes," Maguire concluded, on a note of filial piety, "will bring the gray hairs of my Mother in sorrow to the grave."[106] The Vigilantes eventually allowed Maguire to remain in the state upon "his written parole to thenceforward act the part of a good citizen."[107] They had disciplined this impresario of the public sphere with the most damaging weapon a public person could face: calumny.

The most prominent of those whom the committee succeeded in dishonoring through banishment fought tenaciously to restore their

---

[104] Hittell, *History of San Francisco*, 3:559.
[105] Michael H. de Young, Dictation for H. H. Bancroft [1875], MS in Bancroft Library, Berkeley.
[106] Thomas Maguire to the Executive Committee, 28 June 1856, "Files of the Investigating Committee."
[107] Hittell, *History of California*, 3:617.

reputations. Two of these were Edward ("Ned") McGowan and Charles P. ("Dutch Charley") Duane. McGowan, a chieftain of the Democratic party in San Francisco, had long been connected with charges of election fraud and was thought to be an accomplice of James P. Casey in the killing of James King of William.[108] He had very good reason to fear for his life and managed to escape the Vigilante dragnets. His repeated evasions of a powerful private army chasing him for months across the state earned him the moniker "Ubiquitous." Early in 1857 he surfaced in Sacramento in order to clear his name and publish his defense, entitled the *Narrative of Edward McGowan: Including a Full Account of the Author's Adventures and Perils, While Being Persecuted by the San Francisco Vigilance Committee of 1856.*[109] McGowan stood trial in San Francisco for aiding and abetting in the murder of James King and was acquitted in June 1857. But the *Alta* reported that "McGowan is expected to return quickly to Sacramento, as he is very unpopular in San Francisco."[110]

Charles P. Duane was positively reckless in his attempt to return to San Francisco. Exiled under the death ban on the southbound steamer the *Golden Age*, Duane disembarked at Acapulco and tried to board the *John L. Stephens* back to San Francisco eleven days later. The captain insisted that Duane would be hanged the instant he returned and refused to allow him on board. "Let them do with me what they please," Duane is reported to have said, "I cannot go elsewhere and hold up my head." Rebuffed, Duane stowed away and appeared on deck once the steamer was at sea. Captain Pearson, convinced Duane was in mortal peril, forced him at sea to board the southbound steamer *Sonora*. Duane gave up and went on to New York, where he plagued the committee with expensive lawsuits for a number of years. Duane finally returned to San Francisco in 1860. He again took up a number of lawsuits, but his political career had been ruined.[111]

---

108   McGowan's prominence in San Francisco's Democratic organization prior to the Committee of 1856 is seen in the following reports: *Alta*, 17 May 1853; 13 August 1854.

109   "Ned McGowan in Sacramento," *Alta* 2 March 1857, p. 2; Edward McGowan, *Narrative* (San Francisco: Published by the Author, 1857).

110   "Trial of Edward McGowan," *Alta*, 5 June 1857, p. 1.

111   H. H. Bancroft, *Popular Tribunals*, 2:597–600; "The Answer of Robert H. Pearson, of San Francisco California, to the Libel of Charles P. Duane ..." U.S. District Court, San Francisco, MS dated 25 April. 1861, signed "Hall McAllister, Proctor for the Defendant," private collection of Winifred H. Medin, Santa Rosa, California.

"A PEOPLE'S PARTY FOR LOCAL PURPOSES"

The Vigilantes had never intended to remain in power for so long. Members of the Executive Committee had neglected their businesses for months, the organization cost thousands of dollars per week to sustain, and the Vigilantes were marking time against the day when the federal government would be forced to recognize that the state of California was powerless before a self-governing city. During the last week of July, rumors spread that U.S. warships were preparing an assault on the rebellious city.[112] The release of their last captive, Justice Terry, on 7 August finally enabled the committee to disband; the Executive Committee made plans that very day for the Grand Parade of 18 August, to be preceded by an "open house" public display of the committee rooms.[113]

The Vigilante elite also moved quickly to transform their movement into a legitimate political organization capable of carrying its popular principles into municipal policy. "The leaders of public opinion now realized," Dempster continued, "that peace secured by bayonets alone might be wisely and securely entrusted to ballots for enduring maintenance."[114] The very day after Terry's release, an elaborate notice "TO THE CITIZENS OF THE CITY AND COUNTY OF SAN FRANCISCO" appeared in the pro-Vigilante newspapers announcing the formation of a "People's party." The text of this announcement included the platform of the proposed party, each element of which began with the sonorous phrase, "We need – and the public voice demands...." The announcement called for a public meeting to be held the following Monday for the purpose of ratifying the party and its platform.[115]

The People's party platform was a formal redaction of the far-reaching republicanist ideology of the Vigilante movement. The

---

112 The weekly disbursements of the committee from 15 May to 11 August 1856, averaged $3,225. See Bancroft, *Popular Tribunals*, 2:542–3; on rumors of a federal attack, *Alta* 24 July 1856.

113 *Alta*, 9 August 1856; Bancroft, *Popular Tribunals*, vol. 2:526–31.

114 "The exertions of the Vigilance Committee had been required to clear the field, to relieve the community of the terror inspired by the association of the 'rough' element with corrupt rings of the plunderers of the city, and to protect the timid from ... gangs of "patent ballot box' owners." Clancey J. Dempster, "Statement," [n.d.], for H. H. Bancroft, pp. 16, 18–19, MS in Bancroft Library, Berkeley.

115 *Alta*, 9 August 1856; *Bulletin*, 9 August 1856.

first principle of the new party was "that it was necessary to separate the local municipal government from the general party politics of the State and Nation."[116] To this end, the People's party pledged "not to interfere" with the "several political parties to which we all have more or less affinity" in the November presidential and general elections. The language of the speakers at the first mass meeting was even stronger: "Already parties are organizing for the fall elections; in the ranks of these are found the old campaigners [whose goal is] to hoodwink and control the voters, to secure office for themselves."[117] The People's party would focus only on the local elections, including municipal offices and the state legislative seats from San Francisco only. The *Alta* neatly summarized the rationale behind a separate city party organization:

What matters it to the people of San Francisco, whether the President of the Board of Supervisors [mayor], or the Police Judge, be a 'Democrat,' a 'Republican,' or an 'American' [Know-Nothing]? Can his belief or disbelief in the propriety of the Kansas Nebraska Bill, or distribution of public lands, or the right of the General Government to enter upon a system of internal improvements, affect or interfere with the performance of his duties as a presiding officer, or dispenser of justice to evil doers?[118]

The People's party leaders argued that the divisive national political issues aided the professional party managers to "hoodwink and control the voters" so that "corrupt rings of the plunderers of the city" stayed in municipal power.[119]

True to the diagnosis of political ills that had led to the committee's formation, the People's party platform denounced the "fraudulent manoeuvers of nominating conventions" and the farce of party primaries.[120] The organizers worried most of all that "perennial office-seekers, who have as many faces as Janus, and would join any party to obtain office" might obtain control of the new party, making it "as corrupt as other parties" and turning it "into a mere party machine."[121] The People's organizers accordingly won from the crowd assembled on Monday, 11 August, a mandate to inaugurate a new system of choosing candidates for city office: a "nominating committee" of twenty-one men, empowered to choose a

---

[116]   Dempster, "Statement," p. 18, Bancroft Library, Berkeley.
[117]   *Alta*, 12 August 1856.   [118]   *Alta*, 9 August 1856.
[119]   These quotations are cited earlier.
[120]   *Alta*, 9 August 1856.   [121]   Ibid.

slate of People's party candidates from outside the ranks of the professional politicians.

This was the last time the public had anything to say about the leadership of the People's party. The nominating committee, known thereafter as the "Committee of 21," reproduced itself each year by selecting its own successors. The Committee of 21 always met in secret to defend against the infiltrating "worms of party," and simply published the People's slate for public review.[122] Hardly a party at all, the People's party was really a self-selected nominating organization, modeled in part on the Know-Nothings. The new party, like the Vigilantes, was enormously popular. A city that had seen no party stability before 1856 became a one-party town for the next decade.

The organizers of the People's party capitalized on the mutualist message conveyed by the Vigilante movement. Speaking to the mass meeting of 11 August, E. H. Washburn claimed that "the idea [for a People's party] was suggested by business men and mechanics. They had long groaned under the evils of packed conventions."[123] The professional politicians, so broadly compromised by the work of the Vigilantes, were portrayed as a class unto themselves, preying on the "industrious laboring classes of all conditions of life" (i.e., mechanic *and* merchant). "How often, we would ask," another speaker asked the crowd, "have the merchants ever been represented in the Legislative body? . . . How often, we demand, has the mechanic or the laboring man been represented by one of his own type?"[124] The Vigilantes' version of the mutualist message held that merchants and mechanics, joined by a bond of interest in the prosperity of their city, should vote together for "sound men, and well approved citizens, who will faithfully discharge their duties without [any] other object than the public good, the public peace, and common prosperity."[125] The belief in an "identifiable common good," as Amy Bridges has shown in the case of New York City during the same decade, was an increasingly antiquated one, not consonant

---

[122] The story of the People's party has never been told in detail. Various short discussions appear in a number of works. The best early treatment is Bancroft, *Popular Tribunals*, 2:640-8. The best recent treatment is Terrence J. McDonald, *The Parameters of Urban Fiscal Policy: Socioeconomic Change and Political Culture in San Francisco, 1860-1906* (Berkeley: University of California Press, 1986), 92, 124-8, 136-40. The quotation "worms of party" is from *Alta*, 9 August, 1856.

[123] *Alta*, 12 August 1856.   [124] Ibid.

[125] *Alta*, 9 August 1856.

with the class, ethnic, racial, and gender conflicts emerging from the industrial system of production. The Vigilante movement had made mutualism not only believable but workable in San Francisco.

The mutualist phrasing of the People's platform – "the public good, the public peace, and common prosperity" – is vague; the People's leadership had a concrete program of great simplicity to match it: fiscal conservatism. The city in 1856 was heavily indebted, and taxes were much higher than they were to be after the People's party came to power.[126] The fiscal plank in the People's platform was simple and direct: "We need, and the public voice demands – a faithful guardianship and an economical administration of the public funds."[127] In the plain words of Clancey Dempster, this meant putting the city's finances "on a 'pay as you go' basis."[128] "The People's party," declared another Vigilante executive, "was formed irrespective of national politics and solely to carry on the city government on an economical basis and manage it as businessmen would manage their own affairs."[129]

The preamble to the People's platform begins with a demographic background to the city's political problems: "It is well known, that hitherto, ... almost our whole population has been transient, no one seeming to cultivate an attachment to the soil, but each one steeled his heart beforehand against the conclusion that California should be his home."[130] The Vigilante movement was victory for "men of sterling worth," in the words of the Reverend Benjamin Brierly of the Washington Street Baptist Church, " – men with families, men whose interests are with us, and upon whom the public might rely."[131] The executed and banished men all seemed to be the opposite of this ideal. They were single, violent, and of dubious occupational status.

Even in the defensive account of James O'Meara, an opponent of the Vigilantes, the banished men seemed the antitheses of good citizens. Charles P. Duane "had a reputation as a 'handy man in a fight.'" He had "killed a Frenchman in a difficulty, was tried for

126   McDonald, *Parameters of Urban Fiscal Policy*, 125–6.
127   *Alta*, 9 August 1856.
128   Clancey J. Dempster, "Statement," p. 19, Bancroft Library, Berkeley.
129   Martin J. Burke, Dictation for H. H. Bancroft, p.6, MS in Bancroft Library, Berkeley.
130   *Alta*, 9 August 1856.
131   Rev. Benjamin Brierly, *Thoughts for the Crisis: A Discourse Delivered in the Washington St. Baptist Church. San Francisco, Cal., On the Sabbath Following the Assassination of James King of William By James P. Casey* (San Francisco: Eureka Book and Job Office, 1856).

the deed, and acquitted." Billy Mulligan "was the incarnation of fearlessness, fight, and frolic – dangerous frolic." Bill Lewis "was a great, powerful, terrorizing fellow, desperate and unscrupulous." Woolley Kearney was "the homeliest, ugliest looking mortal I ever saw."[132] Such were hardly "men of sterling worth ... upon whom the public might rely." The banishment of such men, the idealization of the good citizen as a family head with long-term interests in the city, and the emphasis on fiscal conservatism in the People's program focused the emerging political culture on the socioeconomic top and center of the electorate. The clear intent was to appeal to taxpaying, property-owning residents. Clancey J. Dempster reported that some of the People's organizers even advocated limiting the electorate to taxpayers, hoping "thus [to] escape the many evils attendant upon 'taxation without representation.'"[133] Indeed, the People's party changed its name briefly after the Civil War to the "Taxpayer's" party.[134]

Like the ideology of mutualism, fiscal conservatism was certainly not unique to San Francisco. The urban historian Jon Teaford observes that "taxpayer revolts were common as early as the 1850s, with angry citizens in New York City, Philadelphia, and Milwaukee complaining of public extravagance and corruption and already urging a more frugal, businesslike administration of municipal government."[135] The significant achievement of the People's party was to realign the urban polity in such a way as to make reformist, antiparty, fiscally conservative government the ruling political passion, resting on stable majorities for many years.

The evidence does not support the argument that the fiscal conservatism of the People's party was a self-interested policy of the Vigilante merchant elite, employed to shore up their own fortunes.[136] The party was popular across class and party lines. Whereas a number of the city's wards were typically Democratic in

---

132 [James O'Meara], The *Vigilance Committee of 1856: By a Pioneer California Journalist* [pamphlet] (San Francisco: James H. Barry, Publisher, 1890), 46–51.
133 Clancey J. Dempster, "Statement," p. 18, Bancroft Library.
134 McDonald, *Parameters of Urban Fiscal Policy*, 92.
135 Jon Teaford, *The Unheralded Triumph: City Government in America, 1870–1900* (Baltimore, 1984), 5.
136 Robert M. Senkewicz, S.J., *Vigilantes in Gold Rush San Francisco* (Stanford, Calif.: Stanford University Press: 1985), 156–202; Peter R. Decker, *Fortunes and Failures: White Collar Mobility in Nineteenth Century San Francisco* (Cambridge, Mas.: Harvard University Press, 1978), 137–143; Richard Maxwell Brown, *Strain of Violence: Historical Studies of American Violence and Vigilantism* (New York: Oxford University Press, 1975), 141–3.

state and national races, and others were typically Republican in those races, *all* wards except the First delivered People's party majorities or pluralities in almost every election from 1856 through the end of the Civil War. The First Ward, comprising the waterfront, had more semi- and unskilled residents than any other ward. Its residents lived primarily in boardinghouses; the males were typically single, working as sailors, boatmen, draymen, and laborers. It was the most transient ward in the city and therefore the antipode of the People's targeted constituency. Middle-class wards, by contrast, delivered the largest majorities for the People's party. The Fifth and Eighth Wards voted up to 69 percent for the People's slate.[137]

Although the target of the Vigilantes had been the local leadership of the Democratic party, the People's party was clearly supported by men who voted loyally for both Republicans and Democrats in the national races. The president of the committee himself, William Tell Coleman, was a steadfast Democratic party leader. Dr. Henry P. Coon, People's party mayor of San Francisco during and after the Civil War, stated flatly that "the majority of the supporters of the People's ticket had come from the most respectable portion of the Democratic party."[138]

Not only the galvanizing experience of the Vigilante movement sustained the popularity of the People's party, but also the nagging fear of retribution for the committee's crimes. Loyalty to the People's party went fist in glove with support for the ever-popular Vigilance Committee. In the midst of an attempt by opponents of the committee in the State Capitol to embarrass the Vigilantes, through special appropriations for the Law and Order party and other measures, a state senate seat became vacant.[139] In a special election in February 1857, Vigilante executive F. A. Woodworth ran for office on the People's ticket. "Why is this choosing of a Senator ... regarded with such a deep concern?" the *Alta* asked rhetorically. "It is a simple question of Vigilance and Anti-Vigilance.

---

[137] This summary is based on an analysis of the voting results in the San Francisco *Alta*, 14 November 1856; 9 September 1857; 5 September 1858; 14 September 1859; 10 November 1860; 23 May 1861; 21 May 1863; 17 May 1865; San Francisco *Examiner*, 14 September 1867; and on analysis of samples from the manuscript schedules of the California census of 1852 ($N = 536$) and the U.S. Census of 1860 ($N = 334$).

[138] Henry Perin Coon, "Annals of San Francisco," Dictation for H. H. Bancroft, p. 26, MS in Bancroft Library.

[139] The Law and Order party never ran a slate of candidates. It was merely an organization formed to oppose the Vigilantes.

This is the only inquiry involved.... It is a bald fact – a unity – a proposition denuded to the very skin – an individualized measure, having no party antipathies or affinities."[140] Woodworth won his seat by a large majority.[141]

As long as the People's party maintained its appeal to the cross-section of stable urban burghers from both parties, it confounded the patterns of national party politics and confounded as well the formation of public identities based on class. It did not, however, confound the formation of *ethnic* public identities; indeed, it fostered them. The Irish voters never forgot the seeming connection between the Vigilantes and the Know-Nothings (an illusion, as we have seen, but a justified one, given James King's role as the committee's official martyr). The majority of the Vigilantes' most prominent targets were Irish-born as well. Although the absence of a nativist ideology in the Vigilante movement precludes the possibility that the Vigilantes targeted Irish men *because* they were Irish, the foreignness of the Irish obviously contributed to their already threatening public profiles as single men who frequently engaged in violence and had links to election fraud.

As suggested in the last chapter, then, there was a lopsided ethno-cultural conflict at work in antebellum San Francisco. Irish Catholics stayed away from the Vigilante-People's regime and remained in the Democratic party, both locally and nationally, where they felt at home. This sequestering of the Irish wholly within the Democratic party left many Irish activists in a position to become leaders in the emerging politics of pluralism when the end of the Civil War brought the Democrats back to local power.

CONCLUSION

The People's party ruled the city directly through the end of the Civil War.[142] Regardless of the duration of their direct rule, however, the People's party and its Vigilante ethos had a lasting impact on the political life of the city for many decades, even until

---

[140]   *Alta*, 24 February 1857.
[141]   The returns for this election gave Woodworth 57 percent of the 7,956 votes cast, while his nearest competitor in the three-way race received 36%. *Alta*, 25 February 1857.
[142]   A People's municipal administration was in power as late as 1873. McDonald chose that date as the end of the party's reign, but I am inclined toward the shorter estimate of the party's duration.

the end of the century. Antiparty political discourse became firmly engrained in the local political culture. Years after the last People's government, when national parties had resumed control of the city's politics, editorials entitled "No Party Politics in Municipal Affairs" were quite common.[143] The ideology of fiscal conservatism was even more successful. Terrence McDonald, the most thorough student of the city's fiscal history, summarizes the People's party's impact:

Almost regardless of party or persuasion, political actors in San Francisco between 1860 and 1882 shared a consensus on fiscal policy containing these three principles: first, a low tax rate; second, low expenditure; and third, no indebtedness, and therefore, construction of capital improvements on a 'pay as you go' basis.[144]

As we shall see in Chapter 7, the city's only genuine "boss," Christopher A. Buckley, was careful to select Washington Bartlett, a former Vigilante, to head the Democratic city ticket in 1882.[145]

The Vigilante-People's era significantly diverted San Francisco's urban political development from the paths followed by other major North American cities. The early success of antipartyism as a popular political cause in the city and the dramatic delegitimation of urban party politics made the wishes of many urban reformers actually come true. The city's police department offers a striking example. Police departments in New York, Boston, and Philadelphia remained unprofessional political adjuncts to the party-patronage networks throughout most of the nineteenth century. Long before the Progressive Era and the war on municipal corruption, however, and even before the civil service reform movement of the 1870s and 1880s, the San Francisco police developed a professional bureaucracy that was relatively free from partisan control, run by career officers, and staffed by highly paid dedicated patrolmen who made more arrests per week than police in any other department in the country. The San Francisco police department was a direct creation of the Vigilante movement, put in power by the People's

[143]   San Francisco *Chronicle*, 1 May 1875. The *Chronicle*, moreover, was the strongest Republican paper in the city.
[144]   McDonald, *Parameters of Urban Fiscal Policy*, 117.
[145]   William A. Bullough, *The Blind Boss and His City: Christopher Augustine Buckley and Nineteenth Century San Francisco* (Berkeley: University of California Press, 1979), 117; McDonald, *Parameters of Urban Fiscal Policy*, 155–6.

party, and institutionally embedded by the long reign of that party.[146]

Through the People's party, the Vigilante elite was able to maintain the independence of San Francisco's municipal politics from the political fortunes of the state and the nation through the end of the Civil War. During the ten years from 1856 through 1866, San Francisco's politics were driven by the local dimension of the political community, that small core of political participants whose occupational skills, property ownership, and geographic stability enabled them to set the agenda for the municipal polity while the great national parties were held at bay. The Civil War, however, brought to bear on the local polity pressures too great for the People's coalition to resist and ultimately brought its downfall. But the Civil War unleashed a new, and longer-lasting set of political conflicts, which is the story of the next chapter.

[146] Ethington, "Vigilantes and the Police."

CHAPTER 4

Race and reaction: Civil War political mobilization

The experience of the Civil War was the turning point in the gradual transition from a republican-liberal to a pluralist-liberal political culture. The most important sources of urban political development sometimes lie outside municipal boundaries.[1] The only major city in the entire region beyond the Rockies, San Francisco's strategic, symbolic, and demographic importance to the Union made it the center of administration for the far western theater of the war. The Vigilante-People's party, called upon to perform their patriotic duty of assuring public support for the war, became embroiled in policy conflicts that Democratic and Republican party leaders used to mobilize their respective constituencies. But the demise of the People's party was merely a byproduct of a much more profound transformation in political culture that this chapter seeks to explain. By the end of the political mobilization for and then against the war, public leaders had invented the elements of a social conception of political action by forcing partisan differences to hinge on social identities rather than on invisible and indivisible markers, such as character, virtue, and honor.

Neither the complex story of Civil War origins nor even San Francisco's role in the Civil War can be treated comprehensively here.[2] This chapter undertakes only to trace the main elements of

---

[1] For comparable studies see Robin L. Einhorn, "The Civil War and Municipal Government in Chicago," in Maris A. Vinovskis, ed., *Toward a Social History of the American Civil War: Exploratory Essays* (New York: Cambridge University Press, 1990), 117–138; J. Matthew Gallman, *Mastering Wartime: A Social History of Philadelphia during the Civil War* (New York: Cambridge University Press, 1990).

[2] For the origins of the Civil War, see David M. Potter, *The Impending Crisis, 1848–1861* (New York: Harper and Row, 1976), 51–121; Kenneth Stamp, *The Imperiled Union: Essays on the Background of the Civil War* (New York, 1980). For the history of California and San Francisco in the Civil War, see Benjamin Franklin Gilbert, "The Confederate Minority in California," *California Historical Society Quarterly* 20:2 (June 1941): 154–70; Robert

the changing strategies used by leaders to mobilize followers during the social revolution unleashed by the sectional crisis and the Civil War.[3]

OUTLINE OF PARTY CONFLICTS

The instability of political regimes in California, amply exemplified by the Vigilance Committee of 1856, can be read as a series of rehearsals for the Civil War. The four years between the insurrection of the Vigilantes and the insurrection of the Confederacy marked a protracted legitimation crisis in the American polity generally and in San Francisco in particular. The Vigilance Committee experience prepared a majority of the voting citizens of San Francisco to identify and act upon tyrannical threats to their liberty, as diagnosed by the master script of republicanism. The logic of republican mobilization continued to operate during the sectional crisis and the Civil War, but it produced erratic partisan results. The republican discourse that typified the Civil War period in San Francisco contained a crucial new ingredient, race, which forced a profound transformation in the way leaders mobilized voters by the end of the war. To follow the ultimately ironic course of republicanism during the Civil War years, we begin with the role of its last martyr, the stonecutter's son David C. Broderick.

A brief overview of the main lines of partisan development is necessary. Beginning with the passage of the Kansas-Nebraska Act in 1854, which effectively repealed the Missouri Compromise and thereby potentially opened the Western Territories to the formation of states with slave constitutions, there were really two Democratic parties in California. The dominant faction of the Democratic party was its "Chivalry," or proslavery, wing. Led by William M. Gwin, Milton S. Latham, and David S. Terry, this wing of the party favored the Buchanan administration, the Dred Scott decision, the proslavery Lecompton constitution for Kansas, full enforcement of the Fugitive Slave Law in nonslave states, and the

Chandler, "The Press and Civil Liberties in California, 1861–1865" (Ph.D. diss., University of California, Riverside, 1978); and the references throughout this chapter.

3 For the thesis that the American Civil War unleashed a social revolution, See David Montgomery, *Beyond Equality: Labor and the Radical Republicans, 1862–1872* (New York: Alfred A. Knopf, 1967); idem, *The American Civil War and the Meanings of Freedom* (Oxford: Clarendon Press, 1987); Eric Foner, *Reconstruction: America's Unfinished Revolution, 1862–1877* (New York: Harper and Row, 1988).

freedom of slaveowners to settle in the Territories. Opposed to all of these policies were the leaders of the Free-Soil Democrats, led by David C. Broderick and John Bigler. The division of these two factions of Democrats after the Kansas-Nebraska Act had opened the way for the Know-Nothing gubernatorial victory of 1855. In their last act of cooperation, Broderick's and Gwin's supporters engineered an exchange of support that handed both men the two open seats in the U.S. Senate, in the legislative session of 1857.[4]

In March 1856 Edward D. Baker, Cornelius Cole, Collis B. Huntington, Leland Stanford, Charles Crocker, and several other men met to form the Republican Party of California. What brought these men together was a "firm and uncompromising opposition to the extension of slavery" and a deep dissatisfaction with the timid positions of the Whig, Know-Nothing and Democratic parties vis-à-vis the 1854 repeal of the Missouri Compromise. These organizers of the Republican party were staking out the ideological left wing of the opposition to slavery. In contrast to Broderick, who insisted upon adherence to the Lewis Cass doctrine of popular sovereignty, the Republicans were committed to prohibiting "the admission of any more slave states."[5] The Republicans got off to a late start in California. Ironically, their first presidential candidate, John C. Frémont, onetime hero of the California Republic, was unpopular on the west coast because of his disputed claim to the dubious Las Mariposas Mexican land grant.[6] Unpopular in the mining districts, the Republicans were strongest in San Francisco, where a majority of the city's votes went to the losing Republican gubernatorial candidate, Edward Stanly, in 1857. During the Buchanan administration, there were essentially three parties in California (the Know-Nothings rapidly disappeared after 1856).[7]

---

[4]   A detailed contemporary summary of these party fortunes is contained in "Political Movements – Past and Present," Sacramento *Union*, 2 February 1859, p. 2.

[5]   Catherine Coffin Phillips, *Cornelius Cole: California Pioneer and United States Senator* (San Francisco: John Henry Nash, 1929), 77–9; Gerald Stanley, "Slavery and the Origins of the Republican Party in California," *Southern California Quarterly* 60:1 (Spring 1978): 1– 13. For the origins of the Republican party nationally, see William E. Gienapp, *The Origins of the Republican Party, 1852–1856* (New York: Oxford University Press, 1987). Quotation is from the party's first manifesto, cited in Stanley, "Slavery and the Origins of the Republican Party in California." 1.

[6]   Walton Bean and James J. Rawls, *California: An Interpretive History* (New York: McGraw Hill, 1988), 121–3.

[7]   Gerald Stanley, "Racism and the Early Republican Party: The 1856 Presidential Election in California," *Pacific Historical Review* 43:2 (May 1974): 171–87; idem, "Civil War Politics in California," *Southern California Quarterly* 64 (Summer 1982): 115–32.

From the moment they arrived in Washington, D.C., in December 1857 Broderick and Gwin became bitter opponents.[8] Both men were attempting simultaneously to build party organizations in California and to uphold strong ideological policy positions. Gwin almost immediately won the federal patronage appointments for his faction, and Broderick was left with only ideology to fight with. His central policy concern was to oppose the admission of Kansas under the notorious Lecompton, or proslavery, state constitution.[9] Since 1854, settlers from the slave and the free states had been migrating to Kansas. The minority proslavery settlers succeeded, after a series of boycotted and fraudulent elections, in sending their proslavery constitution to Washington. President Buchanan's approval of this Lecompton constitution ranks as a major cause of the Civil War. It divided the Democrats as never before and turned Stephen A. Douglas into the leading opponent of slavery extension among Northern Democrats. In this battle Broderick cast his lot with Douglas and the handful of Democratic senators and congressmen willing to vote against Buchanan and risk destroying the Democratic party.[10] "His class of men" in the Senate, Lincoln said of the Democrats willing to oppose Lecompton, "numbered *three* and no more."[11]

DAVID C. BRODERICK IN DEFENSE OF WHITE FREEDOM

After the first session of the 35th Congress, Broderick's Free-Soil wing of the Democratic party decided to break completely with the Chivalry-dominated Democratic party organization by founding an "Anti-Lecompton Democratic party" from scratch. While Lincoln and Douglas waged their historic debates in Illinois, Broderick stumped California, desperately trying to organize this new Democratic party on the policy of opposing the Lecompton constitution.

8　David A. Williams, "California Democrats of 1860: Division, Disruption, Defeat," *Historical Society of Southern California Quarterly* 55:3 (Fall 1973): 239–52.

9　Potter, *The Impending Crisis*, 297–321

10　David A. Williams, *David C. Broderick: A Political Portrait* (San Marino, California: Huntington Library, 1969), 148–55, 171–5. On the ideological nature of Broderick's career, see Alexander Saxton, "George Wilkes: The Transformation of a Radical Ideology," *American Quarterly* 33:4 (Fall 1981): 437–58.

11　In addition to Douglas and Broderick, these three included Senator Charles E. Stuart of Michigan. Williams, *David C. Broderick*, 171–94; Lincoln, "Speech at Springfield, Illinois," 17 July 1858, *Abraham Lincoln: Speeches and Writings, 1832–1858*, ed. Don E. Fehrenbacher (New York: Library of America, 1989), 466. The point of Lincoln's statement was not to praise Douglas, Broderick, and Stuart, but to show how many more Republicans opposed Lecompton.

Broderick's philippics against the Buchanan administration merit careful attention. In them, Broderick crafted a critique of aggressive despotism and a defense of political freedom that reenacted the script of the 1856 Vigilantes in all respects except one: Broderick's diagnosis of despotism centered on the westward expansion of slavery by a cabal in the South and in Washington.[12]

Broderick's assault on the "Slave Power" began with his most famous Senate speech, made during the winter 1857–8 session. He was responding to South Carolina Senator John P. Hammond's political-economic defense of slavery, in which Hammond denounced Northern laborers as the "white slaves," the "mud sills" of society. "In all social systems, there must be a class to perform the drudgery of life," Hammond began. "Our slaves are black, of another and inferior race.... Yours are white, of your own race; you are brothers of one blood." Hammond's analysis linked labor systems to political institutions: "Our slaves do not vote. We give them no political power. Yours do vote, and being the majority, they are the depositaries of all your political power." Hammond predicted that, were these exploited laborers to learn the "tremendous secret" of their political power, "your society would be reconstructed, your Government overthrown ... "[13]

Broderick's Romantic and republican response to Hammond likewise linked political with economic institutions. At forty, the youngest member of the Senate, Broderick responded in the language of "Young America": "Slavery is old, decrepit, and consumptive; freedom is young, strong, and vigorous. The one is naturally stationary and loves ease; the other is migratory and enterprising."[14] It was the independence of free labor that made it expansive and vigorous: "Wherever there is land for settlement, [free white laborers] will rush in and occupy it, and the compulsory labor of slaves will have to give way before the intelligent labor of free men."[15] Broderick's response was strongly grounded in his pride in being one of those free laborers whom Hammond disparaged. In a moving dramatic

---

[12]   My analysis in this section is heavily indebted to Eric Foner, *Free Labor, Free Soil, Free Men: The Ideology of the Republican Party Before the Civil War* (New York: Oxford University Press, 1970); and J. Mills Thornton III, *Politics and Power in a Slave Society: Alabama, 1800–1860* (Baton Rouge: Louisiana State University Press, 1978).

[13]   Congressional Globe, 35th Congress, 1st Session, Appendix, p. 193.

[14]   For a discussion of the relation between the Young America movement and the sectional crisis, see, Potter, *The Impending Crisis*, 14, 142, 178.

[15]   Quoted in Williams, *David C. Broderick*, 192.

gesture, Broderick recalled the scene of his own youth in Washington, D.C.: "Pointing to the intricate sculpturing on the columns of the Senate chamber, he said they were the work of his father."[16] In 1853 he was responsible for a party platform that declared, "The Democratic party cherishes as among the best features of the constitution of this state, those which protect the laborer from degradation and oppression."[17]

It would be a mistake, however, to trace Broderick's ideological position to his class position in a capitalist society; it proceeded more clearly from his position in a republican polity. Indeed, Broderick declared in this same speech that "I have not the admiration for the men of the class from whence I sprang that might be expected; they submit too tamely to oppression, and are too prone to neglect their rights and duties as citizens."[18] To Broderick and his contemporaries, social relations were the product of political institutions and policies. In the second half of his response to Hammond, Broderick denounced the Lecompton constitution in terms nearly identical to those of the Vigilantes who had delegitimated the Democratic government of San Francisco through exposure of election fraud. The Lecompton constitution "was a fraud from its very inception," Broderick declared, continuing, "Every election in that Territory, looking to this constitution as a result, was founded in fraud." Adding his voice to those of scores of Republicans, he recited case after case of ballot box stuffing and poll list mendacity in Kansas. In one precinct, "twelve hundred and sixty-six votes are reported as having been polled. The census shows forty-seven white inhabitants." Broderick did not shrink from tracing these frauds to the president himself. Castigating "the fading intellect, the petulant passion, and the trembling dotage of an old man on the verge of the grave," Broderick asked: "Will not the world believe [that the president himself] instigated the commission of these frauds, as he gives strength to those who committed them?"[19]

Incensed by Broderick's speech, the Chivalry Democratic majority in the California legislature passed resolutions of censure against

---

16 Williams, *David C. Broderick*, 180. Actually, all we know is that Broderick's father was one of the master stonecarvers who did the most intricate work on the Capitol's architectural elements. It is likely, but not certain, that he carved the marble on the interior of the Senate chamber.

17 Quoted in Williams, *David C. Broderick*, 78.

18 Ibid., 193.

19 *Congressional Globe*, 35th Congress, Appendix, p. 193.

him in January 1859 for his "disrespectful" language. Broderick, knowing that his fledgling Anti-Lecompton Democratic party needed all his help in the gubernatorial election of 1859, returned to California in April to campaign against his opponents.[20] This would be his last campaign. Its outcome – his death, interpreted as an assassination – would supply to the antislavery parties the same galvanizing effect as had the assassination of James King of William to the formation of the Vigilance Committee in 1856.

Broderick in California hammered away at the nefarious designs of the Chivalry Democrats. They were "men who, elevated by your votes, have usurped power and used it to public injury, who have tainted the channels of justice and attempted to enslave the people, and who now seek to prostrate their rule by corrupt, reckless and indecent expenditure of the public money. [Prolonged cheering]"[21] In response, William M. Gwin, Broderick's colleague in the Senate, blasted the junior senator for having "joined the Black Republicans, the enemies of Democracy."[22] Broderick, painting the Buchanan and Chivalry Democrats as complicit in a monstrous scheme of despotism, portrayed his failure to win the federal patronage as a badge of virtue: "I was not a lackey, under the nod of an unscrupulous appointing power. I was the representative of a great and independent state – I was a free man. [Cheers]"[23] He made what could be interpreted as a factional fight for patronage into a defense of free and independent people everywhere: "I knew that the people of California would never give their consent to the enslavement of a free people, and I exercised every power I could command to prevent the perpetration of this foul wrong upon the people of Kansas."[24]

Broderick, as the Vigilantes had earlier done, invoked the legitimacy of rebellion to executive tyranny in defense of liberty:

The people of California, in the formation of our State Constitution, decided that we should not have slavery nor paper money banks.... Suppose that the General Government said that we should have both or remain out of the Union! There is not a free white man within the sound of

[20] T. H. Hittell, *History of California*, 4 vols. (San Francisco, 1885–97), 4:249; Williams, *David C. Broderick*, 207.
[21] Sacramento *Union*, 11 July 1859, p. 1.
[22] Donald E. Hargis, "The Issues of the Broderick – Gwin Debates of 1859," *California Historical Society Quarterly* 32:4 (December 1953): 313–25. Quotation at 321.
[23] Ibid.   [24] Sacramento *Union*, 11 July 1859, p. 1.

my voice who would not have been willing to shoulder his rifle and again court the battle for free thought, free speech, and Independence. [Cheers. A VOICE – "You're talking sense, now."][25]

This outline of political corruption and exhortations to defend independent manhood convinced William Tell Coleman, the president of the Committee of 1856, to sign on in support when Broderick launched the San Francisco *News* as the organ of the Anti-Lecompton Democrats in May of 1859.[26]

A FUNERAL ORATION AND PARTISAN REALIGNMENT

It is somewhat fitting that Broderick's attempt to mobilize voters with the republican language of the Vigilantes would ensnare him in a fatal duel with an erstwhile ally from that conflict of 1856. In an important convention speech to the Chivalry Democrats, David S. Terry, now the chief justice of the California Supreme Court, called the members of the Anti-Lecompton party "personal chattels of a single individual, whom they are ashamed of. They belong, heart and soul, body and breeches, to David C. Broderick." Broderick, furious at this insult, reminded a group of men gathered in a San Francisco hotel that he had stood by Terry when the judge was imprisoned by the Vigilantes. "I once considered him," Broderick continued, "the only honest man on the Supreme bench but I take it all back."[27] Immediately after the election Terry challenged Broderick to a duel for making these remarks, and Broderick accepted. In their meeting on 13 September near Lake Merced, just over the San Mateo county line (to evade the San Francisco police), Broderick's weapon discharged prematurely after the signal to fire, the bullet striking the ground. Terry's shot tore through Broderick's right lung, wounding him too seriously to recover. Broderick's friends watched over him for three days until he finally died on the morning of 16 September.[28]

This was not the first time either Broderick or Terry had fought a

---

[25] Ibid. This speech was delivered on 9 July at Placerville.

[26] San Francisco *Alta*, 19 May 1859; San Francisco *News*, 22 May, 6 June 1859, cited in Williams, *David C. Broderick*, 208.

[27] Quoted in Williams, *David C. Broderick*, 232.

[28] San Francisco *Alta*, 14, 16, 17, 18 September 1859. The most thorough accounts of this duel are Williams, *David C. Broderick*, 230–44; and A. Russell Buchanan, *David S. Terry of California: Duelling Judge* (San Marino: Huntington Library, 1956), 83–110.

formal duel. Duels, as we saw in Chapter 1, were actually a routine
fact of life for leading politicians in San Francisco. But this particular duel, which was widely anticipated during the campaign and
alleged to have been plotted by Terry, symbolized nothing less than
the aggressive despotism of the Slave Power. "They have killed
me," Broderick claimed as he lay dying, "because I was opposed
to the extension of slavery and a corrupt administration."[29] "The
larger part of the community almost apotheosized him," the historian Theodore Hittell wrote in the 1890s, "and for years his name
was used as a battle-cry of freedom."[30]

The U.S. Senate and House of Representatives went into official
mourning for Broderick for thirty days.[31] In San Francisco all public
buildings were draped with black crepe. On the morning of 18 September a crowd of ten thousand began to assemble in the Plaza to
cast their final vote for this extraordinary political champion. Workers had assembled a twenty-foot-square catafalque at the base of the
Plaza's flagpole, "covered with black muslin with white laid over
in stripes equidistant." At mid-afternoon the pallbearers brought
Broderick's body from his longtime headquarters, the Union Hotel
(adjacent to City Hall), and laid the casket at the base of the flagpole, covered with flowers. Formal funeral orations in antebellum
America were self-consciously neoclassical. Pericles's oration of
431 B.C.E, in particular, over the bodies of the Athenian soldiers who
had died in battle with Sparta, "became the most famous oration
of its kind, a model endlessly copied, praised, and cited – especially
... during America's Greek Revival." Edward Everett refined the
genre in his dedications of monuments to the revolutionary war heroes
at Bunker Hill (1833, 1850, 1857) and Lexington (1835) and, of
course, in his two-and-a-half-hour speech that preceded Lincoln's
address at Gettysburg (1863).[32]

Colonel Edward D. Baker, longtime friend of Lincoln's and

---

29 These words were ascribed to Broderick by his close friend and ally, E. D. Baker. Baker
spent many of Broderick's last hours with the dying senator. San Francisco *Alta*, 19 September 1859.
30 Hittell, *History of California*, 4: 229.
31 "Remarks, Delivered in the Senate and the House of Representatives of the United
States, on the Announcement of the Death of Hon. David C. Broderick, of California,
Late a Member of the Senate of the United States in the Thirty-Fifth Congress. In the
Senate of the United States, February 13, 1860," [pamphlet], Bancroft Library, Berkeley.
32 Garry Wills, *Lincoln at Gettysbury: The Words that Remade America* (New York: Simon and
Schuster, 1992), 41–62, 271 n. 23.

reputed to be the greatest orator on the Pacific Coast, was the obvious choice to deliver the funeral oration over the body of Broderick. Baker's oratorical gifts won him adulation throughout his wide-ranging career. As a young Whig colleague of Lincoln's in Springfield, Illinois, he was chosen "Orator of the Day" for the prestigious Fourth of July celebrations of 1836 and 1837. This honor was repeated in 1838 (he was then only twenty-seven), when he stood on the cornerstone of the new Illinois State Capitol building in Springfield to deliver the dedication address. He also joined that year with Lincoln in the debates of the Young Men's Lyceum.[33] Baker was recognized as having a unique power to persuade his audiences. He demonstrated this most dramatically when he closed for the defense of Charles Cora, the reviled gambler, in that man's trial for the murder of U.S. Marshal William Richardson in 1855. Dazed, the jury deadlocked and left Cora awaiting a new trial (which the Committee of 1856 later supplied, along with a guilty verdict, without recourse to Baker or any defense counsel).[34]

Baker's funeral oration for Broderick was a step in his own path to the U.S. Senate and to even greater oratorical renown. He had just been defeated by the Chivalry in the September elections and afterward moved to Oregon, where the Republicans and Douglas Democrats elected him to the Senate a few months later. Baker's funeral oration of September 1859, then, was an intrinsically political event, printed in pamphlet form as a campaign document.[35] Like Everett's and Lincoln's orations, Baker's speech followed the Periclean format, with a review of the hero's virtues, praise of the political system that the hero had died defending, and an exhortation to the audience not to waste Broderick's sacrifice. But Baker

---

[33] Baker gave an address on 13 January that went unrecorded, eleven days before Lincoln's now-famous speech on political violence. Harry C. Blair and Rebecca Tarshis, *The Life of Colonel Edward D. Baker: Lincoln's Constant Ally* (Portland: Oregon Historical Society, 1960), 1–13; Lincoln, *Speeches and Writings, 1832–1858,* 28–36; William H. Herndon and Jesse W. Weik, *Herndon's Life of Lincoln* (New York: Albert and Charles Boni, 1936), 152–4.

[34] The defense of Cora is reproduced in Oscar T. Schuck, *Masterpieces of E. D. Baker* (San Francisco: Oscar T. Schuck, 1899), 287–318. See also Chapter 2.

[35] *Speech of Hon. Edw. D. Baker, U.S. Senator from Oregon, Delivered at A Republican Mass Meeting. Held at the American Theater, in the City of San Francisco, Friday Evening. October 26th. 1860* (San Francisco, 1860), facsimile of cover page in Blair and Tarshis, *Life of Colonel Edward D. Baker,* 174; *Oration of Col. E. D. Baker, Over the Dead Body of Broderick,* [pamphlet, n.d.], Bancroft Library. This oration was in print as late as 1889: *Oration of Colonel Edward D. Baker Over the Dead Body of David C. Broderick, A Senator of the United States, 18th September, 1859* (New York: De Vinne Press, 1889), [pamphlet], Harvard College Library.

clearly also followed another, more analogous model: that of Marcus Antonius over the body of the assassinated Julius Caesar in 44 B.C.E. Shakespeare's sympathetic rendering in Anthony's "Friends, Romans, countrymen, lend me your ears" oration was certainly familiar to the audience. They may have read Plutarch's version of it in school or at home as well.[36] Like Plutarch's and Shakespeare's Anthony, Baker called attention to the bloody shroud wrapping the fallen leader's body. Like Shakespeare's Anthony, Baker called the death a brutal political assassination. "His death was a political necessity, poorly veiled beneath the guise of private quarrel." Like Anthony, he admitted that the fallen leader had been "ambitious" (a republican vice), but, like Anthony, he turned this fault into a virtue, reminding the audience "of the many good purposes" this ambition "was intended to effect."[37]

Despite their separate party affiliations, Baker and Broderick had been close political allies and friends.[38] Baker and Broderick had stood together in opposition to the Committee of 1856, and Baker had long attempted to bring the Republicans into a merger with Broderick's Anti-Lecompton organization. Now he tied his friend's death to Slave Power's intrigue: "It has been a system tending to one end, and that end is here." The embeddedness of this oration in the republican ethos and its Romantic veneration of classical heroes constructed its political impact: "You read in his history," Baker proclaimed, "a glorious imitation of the great popular leaders who have opposed the despotic influences of power in other lands and in our own."[39]

To appreciate the public power of Baker's funeral oration it is necessary to view it within the context of his brief role as a Republican party mobilizer in the West and the East. After his election by the Oregon legislature to the U.S. Senate, Baker stopped on his way to Washington on the eve of the 1860 national election to deliver a speech at San Francisco's American Theater, with John C. and Jessie Benton Frémont in the audience, against slavery's extension, for the Union, and for Lincoln. This "American Theater Speech" so

---

[36] *Julius Caesar*, act 3 sc. 2; Plutarch, *The Lives of the Noble Grecians and Romans*, trans. John Dryden and rev. Arthur Hugh Clough (New York: Modern Library, n.d.), 1112–13.

[37] *Oration of Col. E. D. Baker, Over the Dead Body of Broderick;* the full text of Baker's oration can also be found in the San Francisco *Alta*, 19 September 1859.

[38] Broderick had spent the night before the duel drinking coffee with Baker. Williams, *David C. Broderick*, 237.

[39] *Oration of Col. E. D. Baker, Over the Dead Body of Broderick.*

electrified the audience that Californians celebrated phrases from it for decades, especially the passage on freedom: "In the presence of God – I say it reverently – freedom is the rule, and slavery the exception.... As for me, I dare not, I will not be false to freedom! (Applause.) Where in youth my feet were planted, there my manhood and my age shall march."[40] In the climax of the two-and-a-quarter-hour oration, Baker chided his compatriots for allowing slavery to march unchecked in the land of the free, while republicans in Germany and elsewhere looked to America for global liberation. At this point a dignitary on the stand lost control of himself: "It is true! It is true!" the man exclaimed, running to the footlights with his arms extended, "We are slaves, compared to the rest of the world."[41] Republicans in the Senate maneuvered to put Baker on the floor in key exchanges during the Secession Winter, and he capped his oratorical career as a speaker at the massive Union Square rally of one hundred thousand people in New York City on 19 April 1861, following the firing on Fort Sumter. His stirring message to New Yorkers was martial: "My mission here to-day is to kindle the heart of New York for war – short, sudden, bold, determined, forward war." Baker practiced what he preached, and he died in command of three Pennsylvania regiments and the First California Regiment at the Battle of Ball's Bluff, 21 October 1861.[42] In the Senate it was Baker's turn to be eulogized; Charles Sumner did him this honor. Had he lived, Baker would undoubtedly have joined the Radicals in the prosecution of the war and Reconstruction.[43]

As in the aftermath of Anthony's oration for Caesar, Baker's Oration for Broderick was followed by a massive political realign-

---

[40] The passage continues: "Where in youth my feet were planted, there my manhood and my age shall march. I will walk beneath her banner. I will glory in her strength. I have seen her, in history, struck down on a hundred chosen fields of battle. I have seen her friends fly from her; I have seen her foes gather around her; I have seen them bind her to the stake; I have seen them give her ashes to the winds, regathering them that they might scatter them yet more widely. But when they turned to exult, I have seen her again meet them face to face, clad in complete steel, and brandishing in her strong right hand a flaming sword red with insufferable light! (Vehement cheering.)." Blair and Tarshis, *Life of Colonel Edward D. Baker,* 209.

[41] "The American Theater Speech," in Schuck, *Masterpieces of E. D. Baker,* 115–16; also reprinted in Blair and Tarshis, *Life of Colonel Edward D. Baker,* 200–10.

[42] Schuck, *Masterpieces of E. D. Baker,* 234; Baker's military command at Ball's Bluff is detailed in Blair and Tarshis, *Life of Colonel Edward D. Baker.* 147–55.

[43] *Brigham and Baker: Two Speeches of Sumner,* 10 and 11 December 1861 (Washington, D.C.: no publisher), 7-page pamphlet in Harvard College Library.

ment. The realignment of 1859–60 drained the Chivalry Democratic organization of voters and filled both the Anti-Lecompton Democratic and Republican parties with new adherents. In the three-way gubernatorial race of 1859 the Chivalry candidate, Milton Latham, had won 44.3 percent of the city's votes, against 27.4 percent for the Anti-Lecompton and 22.3 percent for the Republican candidates. In November 1860, days after Baker's American Theater Speech, the Chivalry-nominated Breckinridge presidential electors took only 17.7 percent of the city's vote, against 27.9 percent for Douglas and 47.9 percent for Lincoln. Combining the Anti-Lecompton and Republican party votes for San Francisco yields a clear antislavery vote of 75.8 percent; that figure totaled just 49.7 percent in 1859. By the gubernatorial election of 1861 this antislavery vote had swelled to 91.8 percent, against the remnant Chivalry party's mere 8.2 percent.[44] For the state of California as a whole, Gerald Stanley has demonstrated that the rise of the Republican party resulted from an "genuine realignment" rather than continuity between the Whigs, Know-Nothings, and Republicans constituting merely a change in name. Stanley found that Whigs were more likely to join the Democratic party than the Republican, and that Republicans were more likely to have become politically active for the first time when they joined their new party. Further, counties voting for the Broderick wing of the Democratic party correlated with those voting in 1856 for the first Republican candidates, whereas Know-Nothing counties did not.[45]

Deciphering what happened among voters in San Francisco through statistical analysis of ward-level voting returns correlated with 1860 census data from those wards, we find further confirmation of a realignment taking place, especially among unskilled and semiskilled workers. These low-blue-collar voters correlated with the Chivalry Democrats ($r = .54$) in the election of 1859 but swung around and correlated with the Douglas (Broderick) Democrats (.50) in 1860. This low-blue-collar bloc correlated negatively with the Re-

[44] Walter Dean Burnham, *Presidential Ballots 1836–1892* (New York: Arno Press, 1976), 292–3, 300–1; Winfield J. Davis, *History of Political Conventions in California, 1849–1892* (Sacramento: California State Library, 1893), 74, 84, 108, 127, 128, 201, 267; San Francisco *Alta*, 12 September 1859, 10 November 1860, 7 September 1861.

[45] "Out of 643 Whigs only thirty-eight became Republicans while fifty-one became Democrats." Stanley's study is apparently exhaustive, based on a sample of 1,285 Republicans and 2,193 Democrats, culled from party conventions and state legislative sessions. "Slavery and the Origins of the Republican Party in California," 4–7 and passim.

publicans in each of these elections ($-.53$ and $-.58$), which suggests that they fled the Chivalry for the Anti-Lecompton Democrats after Broderick's death, but did not support the Republicans. That Democratic alignment would prove crucial when, after the Emancipation Proclamation of 1863, Democrats began mobilizing voters on the basis of strong class and race appeals.

Skilled, white-collar, and Irish voters also seem to have changed their behavior after the apparent assassination of Broderick. Skilled workers, unlike their low-blue-collar neighbors, correlated negatively with the Chivalry in the 1859 election, and the white-collar workers correlated positively with the Republicans in the same election, but both groups showed no significant correlation in 1860. Apparently, the pull of ideological persuasion in that four-way race between Bell, Breckinridge, Douglas, and Lincoln scattered these votes too widely to appear in statistical measures. Irish voters, who showed positive correlation with Broderick's party in both 1859 and 1860, showed no correlation with the Chivalry in 1859. After the death of the Irish Catholic hero Broderick, however, this group registered a strongly negative ($-.73$) correlation with the Chivalry Democrats in 1860.[46]

During the Secession Winter of 1860–1, a majority of the city's voters joined the Union movement with the same enthusiasm they had poured into the Vigilante movement four years earlier. As in the Vigilante movement, the cause of the Union transcended party lines. "This is patriotism not partyism," the *Alta* declared.[47] The California legislature convening in January had gained a sudden majority of Douglas Democrats and proceeded to pass new resolutions expunging the censures of Broderick and hailing him as a visionary. By February patriots had organized a grand Union parade estimated at fourteen thousand people and founded ward-based Union military clubs.[48] The cause of patriotism overshadowed distinctions between parties in the city. The *Herald*, previously a hostile Breckinridge paper, suddenly discovered Unionism after

---

[46] The discussion in the last two paragraphs is based on analysis of 1860 census study data and election returns from San Francisco *Alta*, 12 September 1859, 10 November 1860, 7 September 1861, 5 September 1863. See Appendix for description of 1860 census sample.

[47] San Francisco *Alta*, 27 April 1861.

[48] *Alta*, 23 February 1861; Bancroft, *History of California* 7: 275–87; on the Union clubs and their relation to the Vigilantes, see Robert J. Chandler, "Vigilante Rebirth: The Civil War Union League," *The Argonaut: Journal of the San Francisco Historical Society* 3:1 (Winter 1992): 10–18.

the firing on Fort Sumter. Editor John Nugent no doubt remembered his loss of readership when he opposed the Vigilantes in 1856.[49]

RACE AND FREEDOM: THE REPUBLICANS AND CIVIL RIGHTS

What drew the Free-Soil Democrats under Broderick together with the Republicans under Baker was a united front against slavery and the despotic designs of the Slave Power, visible in the republican discourse of mobilization that these two men deployed. That discourse now injected into the San Francisco political culture a vocabulary of race, which became the city's wedge issue par excellence. But republicanism, as a political discourse, is at bottom neither democratic nor liberal. It rests on a hierarchical division of human beings into independent and dependent persons, the latter identified as Chinese, blacks, Indians, women, and children. The institution of slavery was the ideal type of despotism; it undoubtedly enabled the archaic language of republicanism to thrive much longer than it should have in a liberal-capitalist constitutional order. But the origins of a civil rights movement attacked republicanism with the natural rights tradition of constitutional liberalism.

The republican ethos of Broderick or Baker left them constantly contrasting themselves and their audiences negatively with slaves while at the same time denouncing slavery and flirting with abolitionism. The critique of slavery as an institution, in turn, opened Douglas Democrats and Republicans to the charge of being friendly to blacks in a polity founded on legalized white supremacy. Republican party founders were forced to disown abolition, claiming they opposed only the extension of slavery, and this "solely on behalf of free white labor of the North"[50] Despite their own denunciations of "nigger-worshippers," these Republican activists were throughout the 1856 campaign attacked by mobs who accused them of abolitionist sentiments.[51] Marked exceptions among the Republicans were Charles Crocker and Edward D. Baker. "Abolition chokes in your throat!" Baker chided his Douglas Demo-

---

[49] San Francisco *Herald*, 1 August, 4 October 1860; *Alta*, 27 March 1861, gloated over this about-face.
[50] Frank M. Pixley, a Republican activist and later the editor of the San Francisco *Wasp*, quoted in Stanley, "Racism and the Early Republican Party," 178.
[51] Stanley, "Racism and the Early Republican Party," 177.

cratic rivals in the American Theater Speech: "For us it always thunders on the right."[52]

The language of race entangled itself at the intersections between political virtue and economic independence so vital to republican political ethics. A distinction can be made between the endemic *racism* of American whites prior to the Civil War and the growing political category of *race* during the Civil War. These bear the same relation as the endemic class *sentiments* and the politically articulated class *consciousness* discussed in Chapters 1, 6, and 7. What would emerge gradually after the war was a political culture organized around group categories; the crucial development was the conversion of inchoate attitudes into central means of political mobilization. The hybrid discourse I have identified as republican liberalism fell in the balance with the emergent pluralist liberalism during the Civil War, through the contradictions at the heart of political mobilization in republican terms. The most destructive source of contradictions was between the racial hierarchy of dependence central to republicanism and the commitment to equal rights central to liberalism. Both Republican and Democratic party leaders were *racist*, but only the Republicans were willing to commit themselves and their political fortunes to equal civil rights among racial groups.

At one speech in Santa Cruz, Broderick castigated a heckler by saying: "Are you a white man? If you are, you should conduct yourself properly at this meeting." He then went on to assert: "This is the real issue. You, fellow citizens, who are laborers and have white faces, must have black competitors, and it is for you who have white faces, and labor with your hands, to say whether this corrupt Administration shall be overthrown or not."[53] Likewise, the new Republican organ, the San Francisco *Daily Times*, argued that Republicans should attempt "to crush out all third parties [meaning Broderick's] and have a direct and distinct issue of free labor and white men on one side, and slave labor and niggers on the other."[54]

Though obviously racist, the antislavery coalition mobilized by Broderick and Baker temporarily empowered enough white allies to enable the small but active black community to break into the public sphere for the first time during the Civil War. Blacks were

---

[52] Schuck, *Masterpieces of E. D. Baker*, 113.
[53] Sacramento *Union*, 31 August 1859.
[54] San Francisco *Daily Times*, 1 July and 1 August, cited in Williams, *David C. Broderick*, 206–7.

not only disfranchised in California by the state constitution of 1850, but statutes of 1850 and 1851 also barred them from testifying against whites in courts of law. Numbering less than one percent of the California population, blacks in San Francisco launched their public voice with the weekly *Mirror of the Times* in 1856, and later added the *Pacific Appeal* and the longer-lived *Elevator.*[55] These papers coordinated a systematic assault on discrimination on street cars and in schools, as well as a petition campaign to repeal the bans on black testimony. The petitions signed by four thousand blacks submitted in 1857 and 1858 were stiffly rejected by the Chivalry Democratic majority, but the black and white antislavery forces came together in the same political mobilization that produced the defeat of the Chivalry Democrats.[56]

In January 1858, as Broderick began his assault on Buchanan and Lecompton, a young slaveowner named C. V. Stovall attempted to return to Mississippi with his slave named Archy Lee. In what became California's Dred Scott case, Archy Lee liberated himself with the help of the black community in Sacramento, was arrested, was freed by one judge, and then was re-arrested "and, followed by a great crowd of sympathetic whites and negroes, led back to his cell." Archy Lee's case was then brought before the Supreme Court of California, Chief Justice David S. Terry presiding. Terry ruled that Stovall had resided in California too long to maintain his slave property, but that "under the circumstances we are not disposed to rigidly enforce the [constitutional] rule for the first time" because the slave's master was young, did not understand the law, and "being in poor health, had need of the services of his slave."[57] The white press, no less than the black, met the Terry decision with howls of derision: "The Constitution never operates against a young man traveling for his health." The conflict now shifted to San Francisco, where blacks and whites prepared to prevent Stovall from removing Lee from the state by placing guards at all docks and

[55] Robert J. Chandler, "Friends in Time of Need: Republicans and Black Civil Rights in California during the Civil War," *Arizona and the West* 24 (Winter 1982): 320–7.

[56] Rudolph M. Lapp, *Blacks in Gold Rush California* (New Haven: Yale University Press, 1977); idem, *Afro-Americans in California* (San Francisco: Boyd and Fraser, 1979), 4–17.; James A. Fischer, "The Political Development of the Black Community in California, 1850–1950," *California Historical Quarterly* 1 (1971): 256–66; Rudolph M. Lapp, "Jeremiah B. Sanderson: Early California Negro Leader," *Journal of Negro History* 53 (1968): 321–33.

[57] Lucile Eaves, *History of California Labor Legislation* (Berkeley: University of California Press, 1910), 100–1.

police officers on every outgoing ship in the harbor. With a warrant of kidnapping sworn out against him, Stovall was arrested, and Edward D. Baker pleaded Lee's case, winning his emancipation by a decision of a U.S. commissioner.[58]

The struggle for civil rights in California focused on the issue of black testimony as soon as the war commenced. On 29 October 1861 a white man named Rodney B. Schell, knowing that his victims could not testify against him, robbed a black-owned millinery shop. After George W. Gordon, a black civil rights activist, complained to the police, Schell shot and killed him. As Schell was being prosecuted for these crimes in the spring of 1862 the California legislature was forced by floods in Sacramento to convene in San Francisco. This legislature, the first with a majority of Douglas Democrats and Republicans (soon to unite as the Union party), took up the repeal of the testimony ban. The trial itself presented a shocking spectacle of injustice. One witness, who claimed himself to be a "dark skinned Portuguese," was examined by two doctors, who found that his hair, when studied under a microscope, exhibited a "kink" that proved him to be at least one-eighth African, and, therefore, not allowed to testify against a white man. Still, the bills enabling civil and criminal testimony of blacks failed in the state senate, where Democrats were able to block them.[59]

Republican sponsorship of the civil and criminal testimony bills proceeded from the liberal assault on the illiberal foundations of republicanism. No doubt many Republicans agreed with the Democrat who called advocacy of black testimony "political suicide." But the wartime emergency steadily empowered the republican Radicals, not only in the U.S. Congress, but in the Union states as well. Following the Union party victory in September 1862, the testimony bills were rapidly passed and signed into law by the new Republican governor Leland Stanford in March 1863. Remarkably, however, blacks won this hard-fought battle at the expense of California's most unprivileged political caste, the Chinese. To win approval for their own citizenship rights, some black leaders felt it necessary to contrast themselves with people even more unfree.

---

[58] San Francisco *Bulletin*, 5, 6, 7 March 1858; San Francisco *Alta* 6, 7 March 1858, cited in Eaves, *California Labor Legislation*, 102; Rudolph M. Lapp, *Archy Lee: A California Fugitive Slave Case* (San Francisco: Book Club of California, 1969).

[59] James A. Fisher, "The Struggle for Negro Testimony in California, 1851–1863," *Southern California Quarterly* 51 (1969): 313–24; Chandler, "Friends in Time of Need," 325–7.

The editor of the *Elevator* in 1865 compared blacks' "American ideas, Christian religion, and family connections" with the Chinese, "with their filthy habits, idolatrous worship, and cortezan companions." The civil and criminal testimony bills still excluded the testimony of "Indians, Mongolians, and Chinese."[60] These racist concessions made by Republicans at the height of their wartime empowerment prefigured the powerful political reaction mobilized against them by the Democrats beginning with the Emancipation Proclamation of January 1863.

RACE AND REACTION: THE CONVERSION OF HENRY HAIGHT

"What were his politics?" queried a researcher working for Hubert Howe Bancroft's "History Company" in 1878. "He was a strict democrat in every sense of the word," the former aide replied about his former boss, the late Governor Henry Huntley Haight: "a very strict Jacksonian Democrat and always in favor of democratic principles."[61] Haight's aide, who had not met him until 1867, either forgot or considered it irrelevant to his answer, that Henry Haight had been the chairman of the Republican State Central Committee in 1859. Haight was the party stalwart who blocked his party from uniting with Broderick's Anti-Lecompton Democrats in that year.[62] In 1891 Theodore H. Hittell wrote that Haight "was then [in 1859] known as one of the straightest of the so-called Straight Republicans – men who were not only Republicans but such uncompromising Republicans that they were in favor of running a straight Republican ticket at the hazard of defeat."[63] Haight campaigned vigorously for Lincoln in 1860, but after the war began he suddenly became a Democrat. By 1864 he was active in the presidential campaign of Democratic candidate George B. McClellan, and by 1867 this erstwhile "straightest" of Republicans was the standard-bearer for the triumphant return to power of the Democratic party.[64]

---

[60] *Elevator*, 15 December 1865, cited in Chandler, "Friends in Time of Need," 329, 338.

[61] "Interview with un-named person re Haight," [n.d.], MS in Bancroft Library, Berkeley. From the statements of the person it is clear that he was a close aide of Haight's during his governorship and a family friend as well. This aide only came to know Haight during the campaign of 1867, however.

[62] David A. Williams writes that Haight's address "to Republicans of California," Sacramento *Union*, 30 August, 1859, "closed the door to fusion." *David C. Broderick*, 225 n. 49.

[63] Hittell, *History of California*, 4: 407–8.   [64] *Alta*, 30 October 1864, for example.

What happened? Hittell, baffled by Haight's conversion, guessed that Haight might have "changed his opinion on the subject of slavery or had in fact never been in favor of abolition." Or perhaps, Hittell suggested, Haight had "considered himself slighted by the Republican party."[65] In reality, Haight did not convert; he merely took part in the surrounding realignment patterns in order to stay true to his beliefs. In doing so, he contributed to the subtle but decisive reformulation of antebellum republicanism. Retracing Haight's steps in this process illuminates the pathway from the republican language of politics to the liberal language of interest groups.

Henry Haight came to his political maturity just as slavery became an issue that could not be buried. Born in 1825 in Rochester, New York, an important site of antislavery agitation during the 1830s, he graduated from Yale in 1844 and joined his father in the practice of law in St. Louis, Missouri. On the border of both the slave South and the disputed territories, St. Louis was a most important political frontier in the struggle over slavery. While in St. Louis the young Haight published a Free-Soil newspaper and most probably worked with Francis P. Blair, founder of the Free-Soil party and son of the elder Francis P. Blair, Andrew Jackson's influential advisor.[66] Haight left for California in 1849, before the Blairs formed and led the Missouri Republican party, but his Free-Soil political initiation in the city of the Blairs and of Thomas Hart "Bullion" Benton marked him as a Jacksonian, hard-money, anti-monopoly, pro-labor, antislavery ideologue.

Haight was a perfect specimen of those politicians Eric Foner has termed the "Democratic-Republicans": former Democrats who became Republicans.[67] The source of loyalty to the new Republican party for these men was their strong ideological debt to the core concept of "free labor," a basic building block of republican (small *r*) political economy. The elder Blair was the patriarch of this faction; their "producerism," so popular among northern artisans and small farmers, clashed fundamentally with the idea and reality of slavery extension. Not coincidentally, Haight's career paralleled

[65] Hittell, *History of California*, 4: 408.
[66] These details are found in Hittell, *History of California*, 4:407; Bancroft, *History of California*, 7: 325 n. 10, 750 n. 13.; Davis, *History of Political Conventions in California*. 599–600; Arthur M. Schlesinger, Jr., *The Age of Jackson* (Boston: Little, Brown, and Co., 1945), 70–2.
[67] Foner, *Free Soil, Free Labor, Free Men*, 149–85.

that of the younger Blair, who by 1868 had deserted the Republican party to run for vice-president on the Democratic ticket with Horatio Seymour.[68]

But the Republican party was a hybrid affair, embracing significant policies of the Whigs, including centralization of government and promotion of a banking network and paper currency. These policy positions were bound to come into conflict with the Jacksonian version of producerist republicanism. By assessing Haight as a "strict democrat," (small *d*), his aide meant that he was an austere man in the humble style of classic republicanism. "He never much went into society proper," recalled the aide, and "never wore a claw hammer suit [coattails] in his life, always wore the same clothes: dark olive cloth, the whole suit of the same."[69] Haight preferred to sit at home reciting to his children from memory his favorite poets, Sir Walter Scott and William Cullen Bryant.[70]

Henry Haight's earliest political activities after his arrival in 1850 in San Francisco are unclear. By 1856 he was among the handful of intrepid founding Republicans in the state, campaigning for John C. Frémont. Haight had also in the meantime married a Missourian, Anna Bissell, and the two were devoted parishioners at the Calvary Presbyterian Church. Therein hangs the first tale of Henry Haight's turn away from the Republican cause. In May 1861, months prior to the first Battle of Bull Run, the Haights' pastor, the Reverend Dr. William A. Scott, took the political step of praying for "all presidents and vice presidents," meaning Abraham Lincoln, Hannibal Hamlin, Jefferson Davis, and John C. Breckinridge. Scott's prayer, and a later endorsement of the rebellion during the Presbytery of California held in his own church, contrasted unfavorably with the patriotic sermons delivered by the city's fiery young Unitarian minister, Thomas Starr King. Scott's sectional sermons prompted patriots to hang him in effigy opposite his church, with a sign reading "Dr. Scott, the reverend traitor." Scott prudently disappointed the Unionist crowd that gathered that day to hear him utter treasonous prayers. By 1 October he and his family had fled the city for Europe.

68   Eric Foner, *Reconstruction: America's Unfinished Revolution: 1863–1877* (New York: Harper and Row, 1988), 339–45.

69   "Interview with un-named person re Haight." The term "claw-hammer," used here to designate a formal dinner jacket, is a clear case of plebeian metaphor.

70   Dictation of Anna Bissell Haight, 1890, MS in Bancroft Library, Berkeley.

The flight of Scott profoundly affected the Haights, who hated to see him hounded out of the city by a patriotic mob.[71]

Scott's exile was a major element in Haight's wartime rejection of the Republican party, a conversion that followed neatly the prescriptions of republican political ethics.[72] "Our unhappy country is still bleeding at every pore," Haight wrote to Scott. "I confess my faith in the practicability of [r]epublican government is extremely feeble – If human nature were perfect the case would be different," he lamented.[73] Haight took up another cause that pitted him squarely against the administration and enabled him to articulate everything he found threatening in the war policies of the Republican party. By the Legal Tender Act of 25 February 1862, Congress put into circulation $450 million in "greenbacks," for which no specific gold reserve was set aside nor any date set for redemption into hard coin.[74] Greenbacks were "fiat" money and therefore anathema to Californians, whose economy was synonymous with gold. Furthermore, the California constitution expressly forbade the issue of currency by private banks; all business in the state was transacted in gold, sometimes great piles of it. When New York banks suspended specie payment and the U.S. Treasury issued "fiat" money, San Francisco merchants resolved together to trade only in gold

[71] Scott had been hanged in effigy once before, during the 1856 Vigilance Committee crisis. The most detailed accounts are Chandler, "Press and Civil Liberties in California," 151–4, 157–9; Clifford Merrill Drury, *William Anderson Scott: 'No Ordinary Man'* (Glendale, Calif.: Arthur H. Clark Co., 1967), 250–67; a short account appears in Hittell, *History of California*, 4:288; Charles W. Wente, *Thomas Starr King: Patriot and Preacher* (Boston: Beacon Press, 1921), 69–119.

[72] His disillusionment coincided with the exile of the Reverend Scott, but followed a very wide set of political convictions. Haight detailed these in a long letter to his brother-in-law on 3 May 1861, in which he denounces – in high republican style – *both* parties: "Party spirit has always been the bane of Republics – this is an ancient maxim of truth of which the present crisis furnishes a deplorable evidence.... I will frame my indictment first against the Democratic party, & then against the Republicans." Reprinted in A. Russell Buchanan, "H. H. Haight on National Politics, May 1861," *California Historical Society Quarterly* 31:2 (June 1952): 195.

[73] Haight sent a string of sad letters to Scott during the latter's exile, expounding on "the deep grief felt by myself and family at parting from a pastor and friend we love so much." Haight to William A. Scott (London) [1862], William A. Scott Papers, Bancroft Library, Berkeley.

[74] Bray Hammond, "The North's Empty Purse, 1861–1862," *American Historical Review*, 68 (October 1961): 1–18.; Robert P. Sharkey, *Money, Class, and Party: An Economic Study of the Civil War and Reconstruction* (Baltimore, 1959); Clifton K. Yearley, *The Money Machines: The Breakdown and Reform of Governmental and Party Finance in the North, 1860–1920* (Albany: State University of New York Press, 1972).

or in greenbacks only at their gold value. In 1863 the state legislature added teeth to this defiance of national currency policy by enacting the "Specific Contract Law," which allowed parties to a contract to specify the currency in which payment was to be made (meaning gold). As a result of these actions, greenbacks hardly circulated in California, and the state did not experience the severe inflationary trends of the rest of the nation during the period 1863–78.[75]

The local ban on greenbacks was not just a gold-region cause. It was also a Jacksonian one. Andrew Jackson had destroyed the Second Bank of the United States and Thomas Hart Benton had proclaimed the virtues of specie money because, in the political economy of producer republicanism, only hard money had real value. It was, therefore, with great relish that Henry Haight took up the defense of James Lick when the latter refused to accept payment in greenbacks for rent from his tenant, one William Faulkner. Haight intended to challenge the constitutionality of the Legal Tender acts. "The sole question," Haight argued, "is the validity of the provision making these notes a tender in the payment of debts."[76] But Haight, in his brief before the California Supreme Court, went much further and attacked the expansion of governmental authority during the war in general.

As in Broderick's crusade against the Lecompton constitution, Haight's critique of the Legal Tender acts followed the republican script that unified ideas about labor, economy, citizenship, popular sovereignty, power, and tyranny. The authority of the Legal Tender acts, he argued, derived only from the dangerous war-power theory. "If a state of war, *ipso facto*, abolishes constitutional provisions and limits," Haight warned, "the result must follow in case of a war with any power. A war with New Grenada would be as potent to accomplish the result as a war with all Europe."[77] Denouncing "this shallow nonsense which attempts to connect loyalty to the

[75] Joseph Ellison, "The Currency Question on the Pacific Coast during the Civil War," *Mississippi Valley Historical Review* 16:1 (June 1929): 50–66; Gordon M. Bakken, "Law and Legal Tender in California and the West," *Southern California Quarterly* 62:3 (Fall 1980): 239–57; Ira B. Cross, *Financing an Empire: History of Banking in California*, 2 vols. (Chicago: S. J. Clarke Publishing Co., 1927), 1:289–361.; Hittell, *History of California*, 4:346–7; Terrence J. McDonald, "Appendix A: The 'Greenback Era' in San Francisco and Its Effect on Prices," in *Parameters of Urban Fiscal Policy*, 285–8.

[76] H. H. Haight, "The Currency Question," Argument for Appellant, "In the Supreme Court of the State of California, James Lick, Appellant, vs., William Faulkner, et al., Respondents" (San Francisco: B. F. Sterett, Printer, 533 Clay St. [1864]).

[77] Haight, "The Currency Question," 17.

Government with this wretched legal tender scheme of finance," Haight asserted that the government, "having then become possessed of this absolute power" can subvert "not only the courts [but] our whole system of elections and every other safeguard of liberty, without any exception whatever."[78]

Haight was not drawing a fantastic picture. During the war provost marshals were posted in every city to oversee the conduct of the civilian population, committing several notorious violations of civil liberties.[79] Opposition politicians were arrested, habeas corpus was frequently suspended, and newspapers were shut down for criticizing the war.[80] In San Francisco, People's party chief of police Martin J. Burke made regular arrests of citizens for "uttering treasonous language."[81] Haight argued his case while campaigning for Democratic presidential candidate George B. McClellan.[82] At the height of that campaign, General Irvin McDowell, commander of the Army of the Pacific, arrested Charles L. Weller, chairman of the Democratic state committee, after the latter had criticized the administration's war aims. Weller was kept imprisoned in Fort Alcatraz for a month.[83] With the chairman of his own party in prison, Haight lamented: "The Roman apothegm, '*Inter arma silent leges*,' is gravely stated as a fit and proper rule to be literally applied to our system of government."[84]

It was terrible enough that civilians engaged in political opposition should be harassed and imprisoned, but in the Legal Tender

---

[78] Haight, "The Currency Question," 2, 16.

[79] The most notorious of these cases were the arrest and deportation to the South of Ohio Democrat Clement Vallandingham and the suspension of habeas corpus in the military arrest and imprisonment of Pennsylvanian Democrat John Merryman. Coming to Merryman's aid, the aged Chief Justice Roger Taney said he believed he "had been kept alive for just such an occasion." Jean Baker, *Affairs of Party*, 158; In general, see Mark E. Neely, Jr., *The Fate of Liberty: Abraham Lincoln and Civil Liberties* (New York: Oxford University Press, 1991); for San Francisco and California, the definitive account is Chandler, "Press and Civil Liberties in California."

[80] San Francisco *Morning Call*, 11 October 1862.

[81] San Francisco *Municipal Reports*, vol. 1862–63, p. 130; vol. 1863–64, p. 122; *Alta*, 7, 11 October 1864. More arrests were made by the Provost Marshal, Davis, *History of Political Conventions in California*, 192, 203.

[82] *Alta*, 30 October 1864.

[83] Davis, *History of Political Conventions in California*, 203; Robert J. Chandler, "The Press and Civil Liberties in California During The Civil War, 1861–1865" (Ph. D. dissertation, University of California, Riverside, 1978), 290–344; Hittell, *History of California*, 4:389–99. Weller was arrested on 25 July 1864 and released 18 August.

[84] Haight, "The Currency Question," 17. The Latin translates roughly as "during war law is silent"; Chandler, "Press and Civil Liberties in California" 309–20.

acts, Congress had subverted the very basis of republican society. Gold specie was, in Haight's understanding, much like the Constitution; it guaranteed the liberty and well-being of the people.[85] This kind of governmental usurpation struck at the very labor of citizens:

The pillars upon which all national greatness (especially in a Republic), rest, are the prosperity and resources of the industrial classes, whose interests and prosperity all depend upon a sound and stable currency, the destruction of which is the destruction, by inevitable sequence, of all business, of all guaranty for a reward of industry, enterprise, or capital.[86]

Threatening the value of citizens' labor was a presumption of power too tyrannical to bear. "Scandalous frauds" would be "forced upon the people by the thumbscrew pressure of tender laws."[87]

Although Henry Haight saw himself during the war as a defender of republican virtue against the depredations of a corrupt and tyrannical government threatening the freedom of its citizens, he was in fact helping to turn the republican paradigm into an interest-group paradigm. His critique of the Republican party and its beneficiaries was becoming a critique of the industrial capitalists whose fortunes had been wedded to the policies of the Republican party during the war. Chief among these were California's new railroad moguls and Republican party leaders, Leland Stanford, Charles Crocker, and Collis P. Huntington.

EMANCIPATION AND THE REVERSAL OF PARTY FORTUNES

Thanks to the Emancipation Proclamation, the gubernatorial election of 1863 was the first election since 1856 in which the state Democratic party stood unified. Party leaders such as Haight wrote

---

[85] Constitutional conservatism in this period was not just the ideology of the Democrats, it was so pervasive that even the Radicals were limited by it. See Michael Les Benedict, "Preserving the Constitution: The Conservative Basis of Radical Reconstruction," *Journal of American History* 61 (1974): 65–90.

[86] Haight, "The Currency Question," 30.

[87] Ibid., 30. The transforming impact of the "greenback imbroglio" on party reorganization is told for the eastern states in Montgomery, *Beyond Equality*, 340–56. The configuration of allies in California on this issue was much different than that for the East, however. Whereas divisions over this issue split both the Republican and Democratic national conventions of 1867, they amounted to very little in California. On the Pacific coast, Haight could speak for everyone, from manufacturers and San Francisco bankers to retailing shopkeepers and wage-earning laborers, because the state had completely avoided the greenback inflation, and everyone stood to loose by the introduction of paper money.

the terms of their opposition into the forceful platform at the July state convention:

> *Resolved,* That we denounce and unqualifiedly condemn the emancipation proclamation of the President of the United States as tending to protract indefinitely civil war, incite servile insurrection, and inevitably close the door forever to a restoration of these states.[88]

Democrats listed under the heading 'administrative usurpation of extraordinary and dangerous powers, not granted by the constitution," the following depredations:

> The subversion of civil by military law in states not in insurrections or rebellion – the arbitrary military arrest, imprisonment, trial, and sentence of American citizens ... the suppression of freedom of speech and the press – the open and avowed disregard of states rights.[89]

These, the central planks of the California Democratic platforms from 1863 through 1867, flowed especially from "the fanatical attempt to place the negro on a social and political equality with the white race."[90] The 1864 platform of the California Democrats had refined the anti-emancipation formula:

> That the war as at present conducted by the abolition party, is not prosecuted in a manner to restore the Union.... On the contrary, the object of those in power is simply to abolish slavery and, in the event they succeed in this, to revolutionize the government, and establish a centralized power.[91]

William Tell Coleman, who joined in one battle after another against encroaching governmental tyranny, marched as the president of the McClellan (Democratic) Union Central Club in the torchlight procession of 5 November 1864. Beside Coleman rolled a float that depicted, simply, "The Temple of Liberty," signifying the defense of republican institutions against the Lincoln regime.[92]

Early in the 1864 campaign the state Democratic convention met in San Francisco, formerly the undisputed stronghold of the Union party. "Two years ago I attempted to address the Democrats of this

---

[88] Davis, *Political Conventions in California*, 199.
[89] Ibid., 198.   [90] Ibid.   [91] Ibid., 208.
[92] San Francisco *Alta*, 3 November 1864. The date of this citation precedes the actual event because the Democrats printed the order of march days prior to the event, a method of publicity popular at the time.

city," Judge William T. Barbour reminded the audience, "but was prevented by hireling Republicans, who crowded into the Hall." Now he and the Democrats were free "to use the dearest birthright of the American people – the freedom of speech."[93] Calling themselves "Broom Rangers," the Democrats of 1864 marched with thousands of kitchen brooms, to symbolize their peace platform and their determination to sweep the Republican despots from power.[94] Although they only polled 42 percent of the city's presidential vote against the 58 percent majority for Lincoln, the Democrats were recovering steadily. After observing the Ninth Ward Democratic Club meeting in April 1864, a journalist for the Union party *Daily Morning Call* reported ominously: "Unless one visits these meetings of the Democracy and sees the number of persons who have heretofore worked hand and heart with the Union party of California, he cannot realize the strength of the McClellan party."[95] In the spring municipal elections of 1865, the Democratic candidate Isaac Rowell came within just a hundred votes of recapturing the mayoralty for the Democrats for the first time since 1855.[96] By September the Democratic senatorial candidates polled 57 percent majorities.[97] In the 1867 gubernatorial race, Henry Haight's campaign had pushed this Democratic majority to 61 percent.[98]

The unpopularity of the Emancipation Proclamation and of the wartime policies of the Lincoln administration not only launched the Democratic party to recovery, it broke up the Union party coalition and shattered the isolation of the municipal People's party as well. The symptomatic organizational event of 1865 was the breakup of the Union party into the "Short Hair" and "Long Hair" factions. The Short Hairs' moniker derived from their members adopting the hairstyle fashion of prizefighters; their opponents' title was simply applied by contrast.[99] The Short Hairs were led by John Conness, formerly an ally of Broderick's in the Anti-Lecompton Democratic party. These party activists had ties to the working-class world of prizefighters like Yankee Sullivan, but their outrageous, violent behavior within the Union coalition eventually cost them

93   "Democratic State Convention," San Francisco *Daily Morning Call*, 11 May 1864.
94   The *Alta*, 12 October 1864, actually counted 1,050 brooms in a procession of 2,830 marchers on 11 October 1864.
95   San Francisco *Daily Morning Call*, 7 April 1864.
96   *Alta*, 18 May 1865.   97   *Alta*, 8 September 1865.
98   San Francisco *Examiner*, 14 September 1867.
99   Hittell, *History of California*, 4:393–4.

their old support and equated them merely with patronage deals and underhanded, violent party conventions.[100] The Long Hairs, who formed the majority of the Union party, were, roughly speaking, former Republicans. Conness managed to wrench control of the convention and primary process away from the Long Hairs in 1863, ousting Leland Stanford as the party's gubernatorial candidate and replacing him with Frederick Low. But at the Union convention of 25 July 1865 the Short Hairs, unable to nominate their choice for U.S. senator, resorted to violence. The convention broke up in a frightful brawl, in which "spitoons flew from side to side like bomb-shells on a battle field. . . . Pistols were drawn and used as substitutes for clubs. . . . Several [combatants] jumped out of the windows, others who were badly hurt were assisted out of the building." The scene was so notorious that Governor F. F. Low, the Short Hairs' choice, was forced to repudiate the use of his name. Again in 1867 a Union party meeting in San Francisco devolved into mayhem.[101]

The mounting unpopularity of the war eventually caught up with the formerly independent People's party. After the outbreak of the war, Vigilante-People's police chief Martin Burke transformed the police into the elite units of a five-hundred-member voluntary Union Brigade, which drilled menacingly in the streets to dissuade disloyalty. Burke trained his police in civilian riot-control techniques. Charles Weller, even after spending a month in Alcatraz for disloyalty, criticized Burke's intimidations. During one McClellan parade in 1864 a crowd hissed Burke and his police battalion as they approached. Burke dismounted and pushed through the crowd, challenging the hecklers to identify themselves.[102] This behavior identified the People's party with the violations of civil liberties criticized by Haight, and eroded the image of disinterested civic virtue cultivated by the People's party from 1856 to 1861. The pressure of national politics, which had been banished by the People's organizers, now rushed in to tie that party to national party fortunes. Supporters of the party attempted to shield it from national alliances as soon as the war broke out, by shifting the time of elections

[100]   These developments are detailed in Ethington, "The Structures of Urban Political Life: Political Culture in San Francisco, 1850–1880" (Ph.D. diss. Stanford University, 1989), 235–41.
[101]   Davis, *Political Conventions in California*, 217, 246; Bancroft, *History of California*, 7:317.
[102]   *Alta*, 7 October 1864; Philip J. Ethington, "The Vigilantes and the Police: The Creation of a Professional Police Bureaucracy in San Francisco, 1847–1900," *Journal of Social History* 21:2 (Winter 1987), 205–6.

from the fall to the spring in 1861. National party leaders, hoping to displace the local party from its valuable patronage posts in San Francisco, however, switched the date of the city elections back to coincide with general elections in the session of 1865–6. This move attached the People's party to the declining fortunes of the Union party; both parties were defeated in the triumph of the Democrats under the antiwar Haight in 1867.[103]

Political violence in San Francisco climaxed on 15 April 1865, when the telegraphic news of Lincoln's assassination provoked Unionist crowds to attack the offices of Democratic newspapers. Chief Burke, with his well-trained riot force, somehow failed to check this crowd until it had destroyed the *Democratic Press*, the *Occidental*, the *Monitor*, the *Franco-Americaine*, and the *News-Letter*. As captured in the remarkable photograph in Plate 4.1, Burke's force went into action when the crowd tried to dismantle the offices of the *Echo du Pacifique*, which rented space in the Unionist *Alta California*. Again, the press, as the central institution of the public sphere, had proven a flashpoint at the intersection between state and civil society.[104]

Telling incidents of symbolic class conflict begin to appear in the 1864 campaign. During torchlight parades, supporters signaled their approval by lighting their homes along the line of march. One Union man closed down his house during a McClellan torchlight parade and went to a bar downtown. Meanwhile, his Democratic servants invited their friends over and lighted up the man's house, cheering the Broom Rangers as they passed.[105] Likewise, during a Lincoln parade, the proprietor of a hotel sent his cook to the roof to hoist a brand-new Union flag, but the cook hoisted it upside down, leaving the proprietor to explain himself to the Union press.[106] The city's trade unions, mounting their Eight-Hour movement in 1865, endorsed the Democratic party through the

[103]   *Statutes of California*, Fourteenth Session: "An act to change the time for holding municipal elections in the City and County of San Francisco, and to define the terms of certain officers," 22 April 1861; "The object of the change in the time of the election was to separate our local elections altogether from state or national politics," *Alta*, 15 May 1861; *Statutes of California*, Sixteenth Session: "An act to change the time for holding municipal elections in the City and County of San Francisco and to define the official terms of certain officers thereof," 2 April 1866.

[104]   *Alta*, 16–20 April 1865; Bancroft, *History of California*, 7:311–12; Chandler, "Press and Civil Liberties in California," esp. 290–344.

[105]   *Alta*, 8 November 1864.   [106]   *Alta*, 9 November 1864.

Plate 4.1. San Francisco police defending newspaper offices from rioters attempting to destroy the press of the Democratic newspaper *Echo du Pacifique* on 15 April 1865, after the assassination of President Lincoln. Crowds had succeeded in wrecking five other "disloyal" presses before arriving at this scene. The *Echo* rented its space from the Unionist *Alta California*, whose building (the middle white building with black crepe on the second-floor balcony) the police were careful to protect. Like modern radio and television stations, newspaper offices were the targets of military action and collective violence in an unstable polity. The de Young brothers acquired their original press equipment for the *Chronicle* by salvaging the wreckage from this crowd. This rare photograph shows the police deploying their newly learned riot-control training under the command of the Vigilante-People's party police chief, Dr. Martin J. Burke. The irregular colors of the uniforms indicates that Burke had also mobilized the volunteer Police Battalion. Courtesy of The Lincoln Museum, Fort Wayne, Indiana.

newly formed "Industrial League."[107] Democratic party leaders and their pro-labor press in the years 1863 to 1867 wove the strands of republican political economy together with the republican understanding of power, corruption, and white supremacy to produce a language of race and class for political mobilization by 1867. That the low-blue-collar vote, as we saw earlier, began to shift to the Democrats in 1863 indicates the growing unpopularity of the war among the working class and the Irish. The full articulation of a language of class would not be crafted until the party competitions of the 1870s, as will be explained in Chapter 6.

THE POLITICAL ORIGINS OF RACIAL MOBILIZATION

The engine of the Democratic party's complete recovery by 1867 was, as the foregoing suggests, the ability of Democratic leaders to portray the wartime policies of the Lincoln administration and the California Union-Republican regime as tyrannical in design. These leaders mobilized a reaction against civil rights for all nonwhites, against emergent corporate-industrial leadership, and toward a new, class- and interest-based formulation of political ideology. The class and race conflict in San Francisco stimulated by the war followed the pattern experienced in its most severe form in the 1863 New York City Draft Riots, in which working-class rioters attacked blacks and capitalists as representatives of the injustices they felt the war had imposed.[108]

How did social groups become elements of political mobilization? Analysis of San Francisco during the Civil War offers an opportunity to trace a precise answer to this question in the case of racial identities. Here we need to pause and consider the complex relationship between race, class, and politics. From the perspective of political theory, there are two general tendencies in the historical literature concerning the relation of race to political action. One is to treat racial ideology as more fundamental than class, material, and political interests, a position argued most forcefully by George M.

---

[107] *Examiner*, 23 December 1865; Sacramento *Union*, 2 February 1866; *Examiner*, 5 March 1866; Sacramento *Union*, 2, 3 May 1867. The eight-hour movement and its connections to the Democratic party is described in Ira B. Cross, *History of the Labor Movement in California* (Berkeley: University of California Press, 1935), 47.

[108] Iver Bernstein, *The New York City Draft Riots: Their Significance in American Society in the Age of the Civil War* (New York: Oxford University Press, 1990); Foner, *Reconstruction*, 32–3.

Fredrickson.[109] The other is to treat class relations as the fundamental source of racial, material, and political ideologies, a view expounded by Eugene D. Genovese.[110] Both of these widely employed theses about the priority of racial ideology, however, relegate political ideology and action to a secondary role vis-à-vis either race or class. Barbara J. Fields argues a middle ground, maintaining a fluid definition of race "in connection with surrounding ideologies."[111] The foregoing analysis supports Fields's position by suggesting that racial ideology in California only makes sense as an integral part of political discourse about political and economic institutions.

California, with its large population of Chinese, presents a special case of American race relations. The state's five thousand black inhabitants amounted to less than 1 percent of the population, but the 1870 census showed fifty thousand Chinese residents, almost 9 percent of the population. This proportion actually represents a decline; as early as 1852 10 percent of the state's population had been Chinese. Most of these were men who had immigrated to work in

---

[109] In this view, whites of all classes were united in a common social and political illusion of rough equality, based on a fundamentally shared "creed" of white supremacy. The political outcome was, Fredrickson and others have argued, a truce between the owning and working classes of whites in both the North and the South. Fredrickson's use of the term "Herrenvolk Democracy" is borrowed from Peter L. van den Berghe, who typifies Herrenvolk Democracies as those, like the United States and South Africa, that "are democratic for the master race but tyrannical for the subordinate groups." *Race and Racism; A Comparative Perspective* (New York, 1967), 17–18, cited in George M. Fredrickson, *The Black Image in the White Mind: The Debate on Afro-American Character and Destiny, 1817–1914* (New York: Harper Torchbooks, 1971), 61; see also 61–8, 320–5.

[110] Of southern slave society, Genovese writes: "Its history was essentially determined by particular relationships of class power in racial form." Genovese avoids reductionism while maintaining the "centrality of class relations" in the formation of all ideologies. *Roll, Jordan, Roll: The World the Slaves Made* (New York: Vintage, 1972), 4.

Alexander Saxton's *The Indispensable Enemy: Labor and the Anti-Chinese Movement in California* (Berkeley: University of California Press, 1971), portrays race and racism as a byproduct of class and political conflict. Saxton reduces the problem of white supremacist ideology to material and practical interests. Race became a building block of political action, his argument implies, because it was in the interests of three key groups to be racist: semi- and unskilled white workers facing direct competition from the Chinese; skilled workers not in competition with the Chinese but needing allies in their political fight to maintain their newly formed trades unions; and Democratic politicians in need of "issues" with which they could defeat the Union party after the war. *Indispensable Enemy*, 67–91.

[111] These issues are discussed at length in Barbara J. Fields, "Ideology and Race in American History," in J. Morgan Kousser and James M. McPherson, eds., *Region, Race, and Reconstruction: Essays in Honor of C. Vann Woodward* (New York: Oxford University Press, 1982), 143–77; quotation is from 152.

mining, but a substantial urban working and middle class began to develop in the 1860s, as Chinese were forced out of the mining economy by discriminatory legislation such as the foreign miner's tax. Opportunities for Chinese in San Francisco – especially in manufacturing – expanded rapidly in the 1860s, increasing the Chinese population of the city during the Civil War decade. In 1860 only 8 percent of the state's Chinese lived in San Francisco, whereas more than 25 percent did in 1870. In that year the San Francisco Chinese numbered twelve thousand, more than ten times the number of blacks and one in twelve San Franciscans. Families were growing slowly among this preponderantly male population; two thousand Chinese were adult women, but only three hundred Chinese had been born in the state by 1870.[112]

With so many Chinese in the state since 1852, it is extraordinary that anti-Chinese politics did not arrive until the end of the Civil War. In 1861 the Democratic San Francisco *Herald* almost pleaded that "the Cooley question *should* be made a public issue in the State," indicating that it was not already.[113] In his influential 1971 study of labor and the anti-Chinese movement in California, Alexander Saxton traces postwar anti-Chinese politics to three crucial developments that occurred after the Civil War: after Chinese workers began to find employment in factories and construction during the Civil War, labor-market competition motivated unskilled white workers (especially among the Irish) to form "Anti-Coolie Clubs" to protest Chinese employment; the rapid formation of skilled trades unions at the end of the war; and the need of the Democratic party for an issue. "Party leaders were scanning the horizon" in 1867, Saxton argues, and found in the anti-Chinese issue a lever to return themselves to power.[114] Saxton's fine work may never be surpassed as a study of the role of racism in the California labor movement, but as an explanation of political development it is limited by the priority it gives to social process over political process. To portray race and class conflict as arising in civil society and then being captured by cynical

[112]   Population figures from U.S. Census, 1870, vol 1., *Population*, p. 91; *Langley's San Francisco Directory* (San Francisco, 1871), 11; For a detailed discussion of the changing Chinese population, see Saxton, Indispensable Enemy; 3–5.

[113]   Quoted in Robert J. Chandler, "'Anti-Coolie Rabies': The Chinese Issue in California Politics in the 1860s," *Pacific Historian* (Spring 1984): 34. Emphasis added. As Chandler observes, the *Herald*'s suggestion indicated that anti-Chinese racism was *not yet* a political issue.

[114]   Saxton, *Indispensable Enemy*, 67–91.

politicians in need of issues misses the political construction of those conflicts.

Political leaders, from Broderick to Haight, had found race to be an indispensable element of political mobilization since 1856, but the issue until the end of the war had been blacks, not Chinese. Chinese Californians, already barred from obtaining citizenship by U.S. naturalization laws, with almost no civil or political rights in the state, became the object of racist political mobilization because of the threat that they would become citizens under the policies of the Radical Republicans, not because of their competitive position in the labor market. In the late 1860s and the 1870s, the labor-market competition would become the political issue at hand, but it is essential to identify the original source of racist political mobilization. The crucial development making anti-Chinese political racism possible arrived when Republican party leaders Crocker, Hopkins, Huntington, and Stanford won the federal contract to build the western half of the transcontinental railroad in 1862. When work began in earnest at the end of the war, the Central Pacific management learned to exploit the Chinese for the hard labor of cutting a railroad grade through the Sierra Mountains. From 1866 through the completion of the railroad link to the East in 1869, the Central Pacific employed ten thousand Chinese, an almost inconceivable payroll for the American economy at that time.

Henry Haight, in his conversion to the Democratic party, saw in the Republican leadership the rise of a political-economic despotism. As standard-bearer for the Democrats in 1867, he fully exploited the linkages between wartime federal policies, the Republican party leaders, and the Chinese workforce. Haight's opponent in the gubernatorial race was George C. Gorham, who was forced to answer for the sins of the wartime Union party. "Corruption has gotten possession of the reins of government," the *Examiner* wrote, "and run riot over the land, committing frauds, thefts, peculations in all the public offices, and oppression of the people with high taxes."[115] Gorham's vulnerability stemmed from his reportedly underhanded nomination in the Union primaries and conventions, his lobbying on behalf of the railroad corporations and payment by them, and the responsibility of the Union party for the Radical

[115] *Examiner*, 10 September 1867.

Reconstruction acts in Congress.[116] Most revealing about the political intersections between race and class was the scene at the "Democratic Mass Ratification Meeting," in San Francisco's Union Hall, in July 1867. The hall was packed with a "vast assemblage of persons, principally mechanics and other workingmen." The chair of the meeting, Colonel Joseph P. Hoge, asked rhetorically, "What means equality before the law, as [Gorham] puts it forward? It is that black men and Chinese are to have seats in the Legislature, sit on juries, testify in the Courts – in a word, to be levelled up to equality with the Anglo-Saxon race."[117] Hoge did not mention Chinese laborers; he focused instead on civic participation.

It was the design of the Union party, Hoge explained, "to organize a black party and then train the negro to vote the Radical ticket."[118] Blacks and Chinese, the white supremacists of California held, were unworthy of citizenship and suffrage because they had no independence or intelligence and could therefore be manipulated, or "trained to vote," by scheming politicians. "The science of handling and manipulating organizations so as to secure every advantage has been used without stint by Gorham," the *Alta* warned early in the campaign.[119] Such a notoriously corrupt and unscrupulous organization was of course capable of depriving whites of their vote, which was, as Colonel Hoge put it, "manhoods's voice."[120]

Gorham's party *had* disfranchised white voters in the former Confederate states, through the Military Reconstruction acts of March and July 1867. Haight focused on these events with vigor during the campaign, detailing the despotism of Radical Reconstruction: "The policy of reconstruction at present is simply this: Congress by military force overrides the right of the States to regulate suffrage, for the purpose of transferring political power from whites to blacks. I can never sanction the means nor the object."[121] Haight could not sanction the "means" because they were despotic, nor

---

[116] The primary process that resulted in the nomination of Gorham began with the violent meeting in San Francisco of 25 to 31 May 1867. The Short Hairs at that meeting decided not to hold the primary according to the newly enacted Porter Primary Law, but instead hold it by methods it could better control. Davis, *Political Conventions in California*, 246–7; *Alta*, 16 July 1867.

[117] *Alta*, 10 July 1867.   [118] Ibid.

[119] *Alta*, 11 June 1867.   [120] *Alta*, 10 July 1867.

[121] "Speech of H. H. Haight, Democratic Candidate for Governor, Delivered at the Great Democratic Mass Meeting at Union Hall, Tuesday Evening, July 9th, 1867," [pamphlet, n.p., n.d], pp. 2–3, Bancroft Library, Berkeley. Another and similar speech by Haight is quoted in Hittell, *History of California*, 4:410–11.

the "object" because it would flood the electorate with pliable tools for despots:

'Manhood Suffrage' is insisted upon by Republican leaders. . . . We believe that this doctrine if carried into effect would be our destruction. There are 40,000 or 50,000 Chinese in this State it is supposed, nearly all of whom are males over twenty-one years of age. The Chinese can all be naturalized upon this theory and then all can vote. About twenty-five cents a head – say twelve thousand dollars, would throw the Chinese vote one way or the other, and the price would rise according to the competition.

The despots on the horizon, Haight need hardly have pointed out, were the employers of the majority of the Chinese in the state: "The Central Pacific Railroad with ten thousand Chinese laborers, could out-vote the entire voting population of the mining counties, through which the road passes. Gangs of Chinese would be imported for their voting as well as their working qualities."[122]

Just as controversial in California as the Military Reconstruction acts was the Freedman's Bureau bill of 1866, the ongoing program to educate and aid freed slaves. The *Examiner* denounced it as one of "the most bare-faced . . . swindles on the rights of white humanity." It represented millions of dollars "to be squandered on the worthless blacks, while they would not bestow a dollar upon an indigent white man to keep him from starving."[123] Another article, entitled "WHITES TAXED FOR NEGROES," deprecates indebting the country for the sake of freed blacks and to the benefit of rich men, at the expense of the "toiling millions of white people."[124]

The Democratic leadership found its way to class language through the concrete connections of political reasoning about race. Emancipation and civil rights for blacks and Chinese made non-whites a threat to whites because these supposedly pliant tools were to be used by the Union party and the capitalists to oppress the free, white, taxpaying male citizenry of California. The full implications of this shift to the advocacy of social groups in the polity had not yet fully polarized into a language of working versus owning class; that development had to wait until the 1870s.

---

[122]   Ibid., "Speech of H. H. Haight . . ."
[123]   *Examiner*, 17 February 1866.
[124]   *Examiner*, 16 March 1866.

CONCLUSION

The Civil War was the last act of the Romantic, republican-liberal political culture of the nineteenth century. Hallmark attributes of that political culture, such as formal duels among political leaders, suddenly disappeared. The dramaturgical public of the antebellum period, which drew so seriously on classical models and from Shakespeare's many lessons about liberty, corruption, ambition, and tyranny, was fundamentally transformed by the experience of the war. The years of appalling violence must have undermined the Romantic self-presentation of politicians as heroic defenders of liberty. But something more subtle had been at work in all the conflicts of the sectional crisis and the Civil War. The political conception of society, which was the core feature of republicanism, was decisively displaced by the social conception of politics, which was the core feature of liberalism. Because these two conceptions had been intertwined in that Romantic amalgam I have termed republican liberalism, it would not become apparent for many more years that the political conception of society had been laid to rest. With the unleashing of social-group identities as handles for political mobilization, however, the function of political action was increasingly seen as a tool for social-group conflict.

At San Francisco's largest theater, Maguire's Opera House, the great antebellum tragedian Edwin Forrest brought his last San Francisco tour to a close on 29 June 1866 with a performance of Shakespeare's *Macbeth*.[125] "The aisles were thronged, the lobby crowded to excess; the stairs to the parquette were taken possession of, and even the ladies were forced to stand during the performance. It was an ovation, the like of which has never been extended to an actor in our city."[126] *Macbeth* was the ideal tragedy for a Civil War audience of 1866. The story of a nation torn to shreds, of political leaders corrupted by ambition, crime, and fear, must have struck home to the generation of Americans who had lived through the most destructive war of the century. "I think nothing equals

---

[125]   *Langley's San Francisco Directory* (San Francisco, 1867), 20, indicates that the last performance was on 29 June 1866.

[126]   *Alta*, 2 June 1866, quoted in Work Projects Administration, *San Francisco Theater Research*, vol. 11 Lawrence Estavan, editor, *Monographs 22. Edwin Forrest, and 23. Catherine Sinclair* (San Francisco: WPA 1940), 11.

Macbeth," Lincoln wrote in August of 1863.[127] Lincoln, of course, was killed in a theater by a Shakespearean who shouted "Sic semper tyrannis!"[128] John Wilkes Booth's father, Junius Brutus, was himself named for the mythical hero of republican Rome. With Broderick, Baker, Lincoln, and so many other opponents of "tyranny" dead, and with the Confederacy subdued at the ruthless hands of that one-time San Francisco banker William T. Sherman, the audience must have been particularly affected by Malcolm's lament in the fourth act:

> But for all this,
> When I shall tread upon the tyrant's head,
> Or wear it on my sword, yet my poor country
> Shall have more vices than it had before,
> More suffer and more sundry ways than ever,
> By him that shall succeed.[129]

The prolonged political battles, first against slavery and then against the Lincoln administration's war policies and Radical Reconstruction, had armed San Francisco with a new and more socially divisive political culture. Major party politicians were now increasingly trying to mobilize voters on the basis of direct appeals to class and race.

---

127   Lincoln to James H. Hackett, 17 August 1863, in Don E. Fehrenbacher, ed., *Abraham Lincoln: A Documentary Portrait through His Speeches and Writings* (Stanford, Calif.: Stanford University Press, 1964), 237.

128   "Thus ever to tyrants!"

129   *Macbeth*, act 4, sc. 2. That Forrest used this scene is strongly indicated by its inclusion in his 1868 promptbook. George H. Clarke, prompt annotations for Edwin Forrest's *Macbeth*, [1868], Shakespeare Promptbooks, number 188, Harvard Theater Collection, Houghton Library.

CHAPTER 5

The postwar reconstruction of the urban public sphere

The Civil War released the genie of interest-group politics from the municipal bottle. It took another decade of political conflict, however, before an emerging politics of class would expose the contradictions within republican liberalism and force interest-group liberalism to the surface as America's dominant political culture. In the immediate postwar years a new configuration of the urban public sphere laid the groundwork for the practice of a politics of group conflict. We have seen, in Chapter 4, how the political agenda of the Civil War forced group identities of race and – hazily at first – of class, into the public discourse of San Francisco. In addition, the identity of gender boldly arrived in the public sphere in the form of the women's rights and woman suffrage movements.[1] The woman suffrage movement, like the first civil rights movement during the Civil War, posed an ultimately fatal challenge to the republican-liberal discourse because it exposed privilege as the basic conceptual and practical unit of political rationality in a liberal, contractual political economy.

This chapter examines a cluster of interrelated changes in the urban public sphere of the postwar years: the women's rights challenge to "patriarchal" male political privilege; the white male legislative reaction to challenges of class, race, and gender; the social composition of the electorate during the late nineteenth century; and the origins of mass communications media as a vital organizing element of the restructured public sphere. The national

---

[1] For the emergence of gender politics in the struggles of the Civil War and Reconstruction, see Ellen Carol DuBois, *Feminism and Suffrage: The Emergence of an Independent Women's Movement in America, 1848–1869* (Ithaca, N.Y.: Cornell University Press, 1978); idem, "Outgrowing the Compact of the Fathers: Equal Rights, Woman Suffrage, and the United States Constitution, 1820–1878," *Journal of American History* 74:3 (December 1987): 836–62.

process of Reconstruction sparked in California a partisan struggle to maximize electoral fortunes in an emerging politics of group identities. Legislators during this period erected a fascinating body of election law, epitomized by the Registry Act of 1866, which established the most extensive and effective system of voter registration in the United States. The new voter registration system of 1866, in turn, permits an accurate measurement of the composition of the urban electorate from the late 1860s through the end of the century. Analysis of the electorate indicates a complicated relationship between classes and voting in San Francisco, which I describe as a "dual urban political universe," in which the local patterns and rules of the political game differed from those governing the national and state levels of political action within the same city. The chapter closes with consideration of the new commercial press in the San Francisco *Chronicle* and *Examiner* and of the arrival of an extraordinary Baptist evangelical named Isaac Kalloch. These agents reshaped the public sphere in its most essential aspect: as a structure for communicative action. As institutions in their own right, these new media promoted the new interest-group language of political life.

WOMEN AS ORATORS, LAWYERS, AND POLITICIANS: NATURAL RIGHTS VERSUS THE MASCULINE PUBLIC SPHERE

"I am glad that I live in the nineteenth Century," a young Spiritualist named Frank Tallmadge wrote to a fourteen-year-old adolescent named Laura de Force in 1856: "whose so many mighty truths, are being unfolded." Laura de Force (later Gordon) was born in Pennsylvania and spent her years of early adulthood as a "trance medium," communicating publicly with departed spirits in the most radical phase of religious liberalism in the nineteenth century. The women's rights and woman suffrage activists since the Seneca Falls Convention of 1848 drew heavily on Spritualism for its supply of women public speakers. As an extension of Romanticism and transcendentalism, Spiritualism's theorists (including the communitarian socialist Robert Dale Owen) found in women's moral natures the rhapsodic gift of communication with the spirit world. Trance mediums provided a conduit for American audiences to see and hear eternal truths and to learn the way toward "Progress."

Their hallmark was the ability to speak spontaneously but authorita-
tively on subjects selected by the audience.[2]

Laura de Force Gordon gained her apprenticeship in public speaking in the Spiritualist movement, traveling widely through New
York and New England before her arrival in California, where she
would launch the woman suffrage movement in that state. In 1860
the eighteen-year-old de Force appeared in Boston, the setting for
Henry James's critical portrayal of just such a trance medium –
women's rights radical in the character Verena Tarrant of *The
Bostonians* (1886).[3] Spiritualism provided de Force with vital ideological tools for breaking and entering the masculine public sphere.
Young Frank Tallmadge was "glad to be in the present age," he
wrote to "Miss Force," because

> Woman will take her place, before the world which Duty designed and
> created for her, in far times, ages preceding this, the Masculine Element
> ruled, and they were ages of force, they ruled, over the Feminine Element
> greatly to their Detriment, all Power was monopolized, [including] the
> right to public teaching.[4]

The protofeminist program of the Spiritualists followed logically
from their belief in radical individualism, and in woman's special
gift to know justice. Spiritualists understood that "public" and
"authority" were coterminous. Tallmadge had written "the right
to rule" before crossing it out and rewriting "right to public teaching" in the letter just quoted.[5]

---

2   Frank W. Tallmadge to Laura de Force, 17 February 1856, Laura de Force Gordon
    Papers, Bancroft Library; Berkley; Ann Braude, *Radical Spirits: Spritualism and Women's
    Rights in Nineteenth-Century America* (Boston: Beacon Press, 1989); Robert Dale Owen's tract
    on Spiritualism was *Footfalls on the Boundary of Another World* (1860). See Sydney E. Ahlstrom,
    A Religious History of the American People (New Haven: Yale University Press, 1972), 488–
    90. I am indebted to Deborah Coon for my appreciation of the political importance of
    Spiritualism.
3   Tallmadge to de Force, 24 April 1860, Laura de Force Gordon Papers.
4   The passage continues, in Tallmadge's mispunctuated but fascinating prose, thus:
    "Denied, we are taught, from the higher life, that the new era now dawning upon the
    world, unlike the former, will place the Feminine Element in preponderance, for a time,
    for the purpose of regaining the lost Equilibrium, if that be true (and I believe it) we can
    easily understand how the future will be an Age of Refinement governed by the principle
    of Love, because the female mind poseses [sic] more of that inmost principle of the Divine
    which is Love." Tallmadge to de Force, 17 February 1856, Laura de Force Gordon Papers.
5   Tallmadge to Laura de Force, 17 February 1856. Tallmadge eventually confessed to de
    Force that he felt more toward her than "an ordinary friend," and that his Spirit "guar-
    dians" had "foreshadowed" his meeting such a "Lady, with whom they have indicated my
    future life was to be connected." But "Lola," as her friends called her, was to marry

One of the peculiar features of San Francisco's political history is the absence of a women's rights movement prior to the immediate postwar years.[6] San Francisco's intensely masculine, agonal public life must have been particularly hostile to women. To participate in the city's public political world until 1868 required the masculine Romantic virtues of character, courage, and honor. The only appropriate match for heroic masculine Romantic orators like Edward D. Baker, then, was a feminine Romantic orator to be found in the Spiritualist movement. Laura de Force Gordon boldly entered Platt's Hall on the night of 19 February 1868 to deliver the first lecture in the city on the subject of woman suffrage and women's rights.[7] The event was sparsely attended, however, and when in August of the following year, 1869, the "Woman's State Suffrage Association" was organized, "there were just sufficient members to fill the offices."[8]

Presence in the public sphere required possession of print media. By their own accounts, the organizers of the California suffrage movement had been inspired by Susan B. Anthony's newspaper, *The Revolution*.[9] Gordon had sold subscriptions to *The Revolution* on her way to California, and in January 1869 another reader of that journal was inspired to break the male monopoly of the central medium of nineteenth-century political communication. A schoolteacher named Emily A. Pitts bought a minor paper called the *California Weekly Mercury* and converted it into the first woman suffrage paper in the West. Ignoring the advice of supporters to change the name of the journal to the *Liberator*, the *Emancipator*, or the *Reformer*, she named it *The Pioneer* instead. On the masthead ran the subtitle: "Devoted to the Promotion of Human Rights."[10]

---

another in 1862. That she kept these letters all her life can indicate many private things, of course, which we can never know. One, however, may have been Tallmadge's rich Spiritualist discussions of women's rights. Tallmadge to de Force, 29 May 1858, 24 April 1860, 16 March 1861, 6 April 1861, Laura de Force Gordon Papers.

6 Elizabeth Cady Stanton, Susan B. Anthony, and Matilda Joslyn Gage, eds., *History of Woman Suffrage*, vol. 3 (New York: Susan B. Anthony, 1886), pp. 749–68. Most of the California chapter in Stanton et al. was authored by Elizabeth T. Schenk, one of the first five organizers of woman suffrage in California.

7 De Force had married a Scottish physician named Charles H. Gordon in 1862 and accompanied him to California.

8 Stanton et al., *History of Woman Suffrage*, 3:751–2.

9 The influence of Anthony's *Revolution* is recounted in Almira H. Eddy to Laura de Force Gordon, 20 January 1881, Laura de Force Gordon Papers.

10 Sherilyn Cox Bennion, "The Pioneer: The First Voice for Women's Suffrage in the West," *Pacific Historian* 25:4 (Winter 1981): 15–21.

Affiliating their new organization with Elizabeth Cady Stanton and Susan B. Anthony's New York–based National Woman Suffrage Association, Emily Pitts, Elizabeth T. Schenk, Laura de Force Gordon, and Sarah Knox Goodrich provided a core of leaders who stamped the San Francisco movement with an extraordinary natural-rights agenda.[11] The majority of California's original organizers were Spiritualists, a striking fact that helps explain the strident natural-rights content of their program.[12] Another source of that radicalism was the reverence these women orators had for the Radical Republican Edward D. Baker. Oregon suffragist Abigail Scott Duniway, on a visit to San Francisco, "was inspired by Pitts' example to launch the major suffrage publication of the Pacific Coast, the *New Northwest*." Duniway, also a Spiritualist, wrote an epic poem about Baker and kept a photograph of herself with the image of the fallen hero superimposed above her head, as her guiding "spirit friend."[13] Clara Shortridge Foltz, who in 1878–9 would team up with Gordon to win the right of California women to enter the state's law school and to practice before the State Supreme Court, found her way to the San Francisco circle of radical women through Duniway in Oregon. Foltz's biographer, Barbara Allen Babcock, reports that Foltz carried a lecture on Edward D. Baker in her portfolio.[14]

Gordon and her cofounders of the western woman suffrage movement may have acquired public voices, but they needed to pry open the lips of their sisters who lacked the skills necessary for public personae. At the first meeting of the California State Woman Suffrage Society, held at Dashaway Hall on 26 January 1870, nine regional suffrage associations had sent delegates, 120 of whom were admitted to the convention. Gordon, however, found that these delegates did not yet behave as political beings, which is to say, they had not yet found *their* public voice:

---

[11]   San Francisco *Alta California*, 12, 13, 15 July 1871; Stanton et al., *History of Woman Suffrage*, 3:749–66; Bennion, "The Pioneer," 15–21

[12]   "Of the nine women listed in the *History of Woman Suffrage* as holding suffrage meetings during the 1870 campaign, six also appear in the [Spiritualist] *Banner of Light's* List of Lecturers." Of the remaining three, only one cannot be positively identified as a Spiritualist. The single man on the list, John A. Collins, served as president of the Society of Progressive Spiritualists in San Francisco." Braude, *Radical Spirits*, 193.

[13]   The arresting photograph of Duniway/Baker is reproduced in Ruth Barnes Moynihan, *Rebel for Rights: Abigail Scott Duniway* (New Haven: Yale University Press, 1983). For Duniway's association with Baker, which began in Illinois, see 24, 70–1, 98, 133, 171, 174.

[14]   Barbara Allen Babcock, "Clara Shortridge Foltz: First Woman," *Arizona Law Review* 30:4 (1988): 678–81.

Mrs. Gordon said she had noticed that when questions were put to the meeting not more than a dozen timid voices could be heard saying "aye," or "no." The ladies must not sit like mummies, but open their mouths and vote audibly. This disinclination to do business in a business-like way, is discreditable. (Cheers). Mrs. Gordon's hint was taken, and unequivocal demonstration of voices was made thereafter upon the taking of each vote.[15]

In this one scene we can see the process by which private individuals came together to constitute (in this case, to reconstitute) the urban public sphere.

"We shall insist upon woman's independence – her elevation, socially and politically, to the platform now solely occupied by man," declared the twenty-four-year-old editor Emily Pitts in the first issue of *The Pioneer*. "We shall claim for her each privilege now given to every male citizen of the United States. In short, we shall claim for her the right of suffrage."[16] Pitts promised independence, the touchstone of republican citizenship, for women. But in doing so she was reversing the formula employed so effectively to keep the electorate restricted. In their philippics against black and Chinese suffrage, Democratic party leaders such as Henry Haight insisted that the franchise rested on economic independence. Delegitimating the claims to suffrage of ex-slaves and Chinese laborers by this route reinforced the emergent social conception of politics.[17]

Pitts and her comrades exposed the lie in the republican formula by demonstrating that the state bestowed social power through political privilege. Drawing on the lessons of the struggle for enfranchisement by the freed slaves, they identified the franchise as a source, not a result, of independence.[18] In 1871 the California State Woman Suffrage Association proudly hosted a long speaking tour by

---

[15]   Stanton et al., *History of Woman Suffrage*, 3:753.

[16]   Bennion, "The Pioneer," 17.

[17]   Jürgen Habermas provides a cogent diagnosis of the relationship between the restrictive franchise of the liberal state and the universal pretensions of the bourgeois public sphere. On the one hand, "the public sphere of civil society stood or fell with the principle of universal access," but the restricted franchise of the early liberal state "did not necessarily have to be viewed as a restriction of the public sphere itself as long as it could be interpreted as the mere legal ratification of a status attained economically in the private sphere." Since Adam Smith the bourgeoisie could argue that the attainment of economic status in the private sphere *was* consistent with the principle of universal access, and so the fiction of universal access was transferred to the political franchise. Habermas, *The Structural Transformation of the Public Sphere: An Inquiry into a Category of Bourgeois Society*, trans. Thomas Burger (Cambridge, Mass.: MIT Press, 1989), 85–6.

[18]   For the close relationship between abolitionism, the woman suffrage movement, and Reconstruction, see DuBois, *Feminism and Suffrage*.

their champions, Stanton and Anthony. On 12 July Anthony spoke before a large crowd at Platt's Hall on "The Power of the Ballot," developing this theme that the ballot was not an expression of social power, but a source of it. She frightened the *Alta* with talk of forming leagues of working women, empowered by the ballot, who could then "inaugurate strikes, as men do, and obtain from their employers better wages and easier times." She made a concrete connection between the franchise and social power in other realms of life. Women strikers, she explained, "were not maintained by newspapers because they were not voters; if they had been, the press would not dare to disrespect their power." Anthony then illustrated how the apparatus of the state, rather than being constituted by society, itself constituted the configurations of social life: "She referred to the changed condition and standing of negroes, produced by the ballot, and insisted that it was not because colored people were more respected now than then, as a class, but because they had the power of the ballot, and it could not be disrespected."[19]

The previous night, Elizabeth Cady Stanton had offered friendship to whatever party might promote their cause, but threw out a defiant challenge to the male electorate nonetheless: "She said it was not the intention to petition or beg or pray for their rights. They propose to get their names registered as voters, possessing the right to vote, and if refused, they will sue the officers."[20] The state's 1866 voter registration system, intended as a vehicle of suffrage *restriction*, was hardly in place when the woman suffrage movement attempted to use it for suffrage *expansion*.[21] Several women marched into City Hall during the month of August to have their names, as U.S. citizens, registered as voters in California.[22] Their claims were eventually defeated when the California Supreme Court ruled that female citizens could not gain access to the franchise through the Fourteenth Amendment.[23]

[19]   San Francisco *Alta*, 13 July 1871.
[20]   *Alta*, 12 July 1871. On Stanton's political philosophy in general, see Lois W. Banner, *Elizabeth Cady Stanton: A Radical for Woman's Rights* (Boston: Little, Brown, 1980).
[21]   The California State Woman Suffrage Convention met annually in San Francisco from 1870 onward. San Francisco *Alta*, 1 January 1870; 3 January 1871; 12, 13, 15 July 1871; 14 August 1871.
[22]   Henry G. Langley, *City Directory of San Francisco* (San Francisco, 1871), "Chronological History of Principal Events," 35–6.
[23]   Van Valkenberg v. Brown (43 Cal. 43); The U.S. Supreme Court finally ruled the same way on this question in 1875 in Minor v. Happersett (21 Wall., 162).

The *Alta* favorably reported Stanton's lectures, which avoided the ideas of labor radicalism, applauding her ideas about "the purifying effect the right to vote by women would have upon society" and praising her denunciations of free love.[24] The movement in San Francisco was somewhat hobbled in 1873 when Emily Pitts's enemies succeeded in painting her (now Pitts-Stevens) as a free love advocate and forced her from control of *The Pioneer*. Her successor, Mrs. C. C. Calhoun, promised that the paper would no longer be "tainted" with the "pestilential atmosphere of FREE LOVE, so called."[25] Calhoun let the paper die within a few months, and the lecture visit the following year by Victoria Woodhull to San Francisco, advocating not only free love but also sundry revolutionary doctrines, added to the sources of dissension.[26] Pitts-Stevens herself was horrified by the association with free love, and she turned her attention to the temperance crusade, joining the growing reform movement in the San Francisco Woman's Christian Temperance Union.[27]

The withering away of *The Pioneer* hardly diminished the energy of the movement's leaders, however. By 1871 Gordon, Schenk, Pitts, and Knox had been joined by Ellen Clark Sargent, whose husband, the Republican Aaron A. Sargent, was to introduce the "Susan B. Anthony" woman suffrage amendment in the U.S. Senate in 1878.[28] By 1871 these women were operating as strategists for the woman suffrage amendment. Ellen Sargent cautioned Gordon, who was organizing the statewide California convention, not to associate Aaron Sargent with suffrage openly, because as a congressman he was just then campaigning for the U.S. Senate in the California legislature. She warned of the danger of "enemies who would be only too glad to get some new excuse for opposing his claims" to the Senate seat. If the women laid low, Sargent explained, "Mr. S. is willing to help us to his ability . . . and if he should get elected as Senator, it will greatly increase his influence."[29]

24 *Alta*, 12 July 1871; 15 July 1871.
25 Cited in Bennion, "The Pioneer," 21.
26 Woodhull's speeches are reported in the *Alta*, 2, 3 June 1874.
27 Bennion, "The Pioneer," 21; see also Joan M. Jensen and Gloria Ricci Lothrop, *California Women: A History* (San Francisco: Boyd and Fraser, 1987), 61–7.
28 Mari Jo Buhle and Paul Buhle, *The Concise History of Woman Suffrage* (Urbana: University of Illinois Press, 1978), 307.
29 Ellen Clark Sargent to Laura de Force Gordon, 21 October 1871, Laura de Force Gordon Papers.

Gordon developed a network of political alliances with men. In 1871 she was nominated by the San Joaquin Independent party for State Senate and actually won two hundred (male, of course) votes.[30] Unlike Sargent, Gordon was a Democrat. By 1873 she owned a newspaper in Stockton, and from 1876 through 1878 she was the editor of an important Democratic paper across the Bay from San Francisco, the Oakland *Daily Democrat*.[31] It was from this position of institutional strength that Gordon joined forces with Clara Shortridge Foltz to gain admission to the state-run Hastings College of Law in San Francisco. These first women admitted to the California Bar also engineered the passage of the "women's lawyer's bill" in the state legislature. As Barbara Babcock has demonstrated, Foltz and Gordon managed a lobbying campaign like political experts during the California Constitutional Convention, winning the inclusion of two historic clauses: one guaranteeing equal access for women to "any lawful occupation," and another guaranteeing women's access to California's higher educational institutions.[32] The stature achieved by Gordon within male political circles is evidenced by a list of candidates for delegates to the Constitutional Convention of 1878, which displays Gordon's name appeared alongside that of David S. Terry and the names of the major party chieftains of the state, men such as the Democrats Henry Haight, John S. Hager, and Joseph P. Hoge and the Republicans Eugene Casserly and Morris M. Estee.[33]

Despite her male alliances Gordon's message was always as contentious as that of her friend and comrade, Susan Anthony.[34] Gordon's and Foltz's respective law practices and need for self-support kept them from graduating from Hastings. The first beneficiary of their effort was a younger woman, Mary McHenry, who became the first female graduate of Hastings College of Law and in turn became an influential leader during both of the constitutional amendment campaigns of 1896 and 1911.

[30] Corinne L. Gilb, "Gordon Laura de Force," in *Notable American Women, 1607–1950: A Biographical Dictionary*, ed. Edward D. James, 3 vols. (Cambridge, Mass.: Belknap Press, 1971), 2:68–9.
[31] Gordon to "Ma and Pa" [from Stockton, n.d, 1874–5]; Gordon to Parents, 19 January 1877, Laura de Force Gordon Papers.
[32] The history of Gordon and Foltz in these years is masterfully told in Babcock, "Clara Shortridge Foltz: First Woman," 673–717.
[33] [List of candidates for Delegate to the California Constitutional Convention of 1878–9], Laura de Force Gordon Papers.
[34] Susan B. Anthony to Laura de Force Gordon, 8 November 1869, 9 February 1871, 15 May 1876, 18 March 1877. Laura de Force Gordon Papers.

It was a commonplace defense of the male franchise to argue that suffrage was a *privilege* and not a *right*. "In the United States suffrage is a privilege, franchise or trust conferred by the people upon such persons as it deems fittest to represent it in the choice of magistrates," reads George W. McCrary's authoritative 1875 *Treatise on the American Law of Elections*.[35] McCrary, writing in the midst of myriad challenges to widen the franchise, was very careful to explain why suffrage restriction was compatible with self-government:

The right to vote is not a natural right, such as the right to personal security, personal liberty, and the right to acquire and enjoy property. It is not such a right as belongs to a man in the state of nature.... In the United States the people are the source of all political power, and it is within their power to give, refuse, or restrict the elective franchise.[36]

This distinction between the perfect freedom of contract theory and the restrictive privilege of the franchise was a central contradiction in the bourgeois public sphere.[37] In the 1890s Mary McHenry Keith would seize upon this contradiction in her lecture "Is the Franchise a Privilege or a Right?" She forced the defense of privilege back to its "democratic" origins in the city-state: "Ancient Democracy, after all, was only class government, a broader Aristocracy. Its franchise was truly an exclusive privilege possessed by a minority." Speaking from the position of historical strength, she lambasted the defense of "privilege after privilege has been destroyed and rights substituted in their place."[38]

The home ground of the woman suffrage argument was natural rights theory, and the language of natural rights was the home ground of liberalism.[39] The woman suffrage movement, therefore, had established itself as a fountainhead of the new liberal discourse and steadily helped to submerge the republican discourse. This

[35] George W. McCrary, *A Treatise on the American Law of Elections*, 4th ed., ed. Henry L. McCune (Chicago: Callaghan & Co., 1897), 2.

[36] McCrary, *Treatise on the American Law of Elections*, 2, 5.

[37] Habermas, *The Structural Transformation of the Public Sphere*, 57–8.

[38] Mary McHenry Keith, "Is the Franchise a Privilege or a Right?" MS. in Keith-Pond Papers. The dividing line between the rights and privileges arguments, however, was not always clear. Virginia Minor was to argue before the Supreme Court in 1872 that suffrage was *both* a right and a privilege. See Barbara Babcock et al., *Sex Discrimination and the Law: Causes and Remedies* (Boston: Little, Brown, 1975), 11–19.

[39] Josephine Donovan, *Feminist Theory: The Intellectual Traditions of American Feminism* (New York: Frederick Ungar Publishing Co., 1985); Stephen M. Buechler, *The Transformation of the Woman Suffrage Movement: The Case of Illinois, 1850–1920* (New Brunswick, N.J.: Rutgers University Press, 1986). On the grounding of liberalism, see Introduction.

liberal language, in turn, was a direct predecessor of the pluralist liberalism shortly to achieve predominance in the Progressive Era. McHenry Keith's role in the creation of the interest-group paradigm at the end of the century will be explored in Chapters 7 and 8.

ELECTION LAW: THE PARTISAN STRUGGLE TO RESHAPE THE POLITICAL COMMUNITY

Until 1870 the U.S. Constitution was silent on the qualifications for suffrage. Each state was free to confer the franchise on whomever it chose.[40] The qualifications imposed by the states, in contrast, have been minutely detailed and extensive. During the nineteenth century, states limited the franchise by the criteria of citizenship, sex, race, age, property, education, payment of taxes, moral behavior, and length of residence. Although historians frequently applaud the disappearance of property qualifications by the late antebellum period and remark on the great import of "universal suffrage," it must be remembered how grossly oversimplified these terms of analysis really are.[41]

The California Constitution of 1850 extended the elective franchise to every white male citizen of the United States who had resided in the state at least six months, and in the county at least one month, before an election. Within the context of the high rates of geographic mobility displayed by nineteenth-century Americans, a residency requirement could disqualify a great number of people. In addition, laws bearing on the conduct of elections, such as the timing of an election, can have a significant impact on the number of people who can or will exercise their elective franchise. The shape of the electorate was highly mutable, therefore, and never anything so simple as a fixed figure of adult males.

The struggle over the Fifteenth Amendment coincided with the be-

---

[40]   The Fifteenth (1870), Nineteenth (1920), Twenty-fourth (1961), and Twenty-sixth (1971) amendments to the U.S. Constitution limit the power of the states to create the electorate through their constitutions and statutes. But these amendments impose only the broadest guidelines about race, sex, the use of poll taxes, and age, respectively.

[41]   Most states barred black citizens from the franchise until after the Civil War. Citizenship, moreover, is the first prerequisite for suffrage, and until 1870 the U.S. Congress limited naturalization to "any alien being a free white person," in which year naturalization was opened to "aliens of African nativity and to persons of African descent." An act of May 1882 decreed that "hereafter no State court or court of the United States shall admit Chinese to citizenship." McCrary, *Treatise on the American Law of Elections*, 59.

ginning of the postwar woman suffrage movement in San Francisco and meshed with the movement toward suffrage restriction through election laws. When Democrat George Rogers of San Francisco took his seat as speaker of the California Assembly in December 1869, he declared that "the people had sent him there ... to place the seal of condemnation on the Fifteenth Amendment."[42] When Governor Henry H. Haight transmitted that amendment to the California legislature, he sternly recommended its defeat, and the legislature defeated it by an almost unanimous vote. In the California Senate, John S. Hager sounded the alarm felt by these beleaguered white men:

Every intelligent, reflecting man must feel our institutions are now, and for some time have been, undergoing an ordeal of more terrible severity than they have ever encountered before – an ordeal that may decide the cause of self government and republican institutions for ourselves, and perhaps for the world, now and forever.[43]

During the 1860s and 1870s, legislators passed a spate of election laws changing the times of elections, regulating the process of elections, establishing a system of registration, and altering the constitutional qualifications for the elective franchise.

A remarkable aspect of the decade of the 1850s, by contrast, had been the absence of significant legislation on elections. As we saw in the first three chapters, election fraud was a constant theme in San Francisco, and the alleged existence of a ruling clatch of political criminals was the primary cause of the Vigilante uprising of 1856. The route chosen for purifying the electoral process, however, was not the passage of regulatory statutes, but visual vigilance among the participants. For years the Vigilante-People's party organized an army of poll watchers to maintain vigilance – the central theme of their movement – at the polls.[44]

The Board of Supervisors also experimented with mechanical aids to election purity. After the discovery of the false-bottom ballot box in 1856, several designs for tamper-proof ballot boxes emerged. Hoping to market a new product, the Dennis Wire Works presented

---

[42] Quoted in T. H. Hittell, *History of California*, 4 vols. (San Francisco, 1885–97), 4:425.

[43] "Speech of Hon. John S. Hager, of San Francisco, In the Senate of California, January 28, 1870, on Senator Hager's Joint Resolution to Reject the Fifteenth Amendment to the Constitution of the United States." [pamplet] Bancroft Library.

[44] *Alta*, 23 August 1857, 4 September 1858, 8 September 1859.

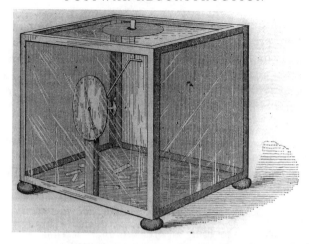

Plate 5.1. "The Glass Ballot Box." Prior to 1864, San Franciscans relied upon visual surveillance rather than penal law to prevent election fraud. This glass ballot box, designed by an optician, is equipped with a mechanical counter and a bell to announce the addition of each ballot. It represents an Enlightenment construction of political participation, with a stress on open, public knowledge about the machinery of the state. *Source*: Hubert Howe Bancroft, *Popular Tribunals* 2 vols. (San Francisco: History Co., Publishers, 1887), 2:12.

a prototype wire ballot box to the *Evening Bulletin* prior to the November elections of 1856: "The invention is bullet, brick-bat, and burglar proof, is tight and gracefully constructed of brass wire.... The wires are so woven so that great strength is given, and by no possible means can a ballot be dropped in and hidden from view."[45] A local optician named Roach produced a more elegant and ingenious design, however, in the form of a supposedly bullet-proof glass ballot box (see Plate 5.1).[46]

On 24 October 1856 the Board of Supervisors met to consider the purchase of the ingenious glass ballot boxes, but balked at the price of one hundred dollars each.[47] The reliance during the 1850s on personal surveillance and on equipment that resembled magician's

[45] *Alta*, 27 September 1856.
[46] "Through a small hole in the circular brass plate fitted into the top the ticket was thrust, and as it passed in it touched a spring which struck a small bell and turned the hands of a dial. The bell and dial were both within the box, so that they could not be tampered with. The dial could be arranged so as to count five thousand." H. H. Bancroft, *Popular Tribunals*, 2 vols. (San Francisco: History Co., Publishers, 1887), 2:12.
[47] *Alta* 24 October 1856; Roach's invention eventually sold for $500 to go on exhibit in the interior of the state. Bancroft, *Popular Tribunals*, 2:12.

props contrasts sharply with the reliance on election laws that characterized the decades of the 1860s and 1870s. The concrete source of the election legislation of the Civil War and Reconstruction periods was the partisan struggle between the Union party and its rivals.

As we saw in Chapter 4, the Douglas Democrats (friendly to the Vigilante-People's movement) in the state legislature of 1861 moved the municipal elections from the general date in the fall to the off-season time of May. They did so in fear that the mounting pro-war Unionist movement would threaten the blissful isolation of municipal politics that had protected the People's party from national party influences.[48] That particular statute demonstrates the extent to which party leaders understood the effect of changes in the scheduling of elections as well as the operation of what I describe as a "dual urban political universe," whereby the residentially stable and occupationally skilled dominated the local political universe, while the transient and propertyless provided the dynamic margin of votes needed to win in national- and state-level elections. "The object of the change in the time of the election," the *Alta* stated, "was to separate our local elections from state or national politics."[49]

Thus insulated from the national party turnouts, the People's party survived until the Union party finally managed in 1866 to change the city's municipal elections back to the fall.[50] The goal of the Union party legislators, who knew that their strength lay in national, not local, allegiances, was to make municipal politics dance to the national tune. They understood the dual political universe no less well than did the legislators who had changed the elections to the off-season date of May. Ironically, the change made by the Union party benefited the Democrats. In 1867 the statewide resurgence of the Democratic party gave San Francisco a Democratic mayor for the first time since 1855.[51]

---

48 *Statutes of California*, 14th Session (1861–2), "An Act to change the time for holding municipal elections in the City and County of San Francisco, and to define the terms of certain officers," approved 22 April 1861.

49 *Alta*, 15 May 1861.

50 *Statutes of California*, 16th Session (1865–6), Supplement 45, "An Act to change the time for holding Municipal Elections in the City and County of San Francisco, and to define the Official Terms of certain Officers therein mentioned," approved 2 April 1866.

51 See previous chapter for the rise of the Democratic party in California after 1863. San Francisco *Examiner*, 23 December 1865; Sacramento *Union*, 2 February 1866; *Examiner*, 5 March 1866; Sacramento *Union*, 2, 3 May 1867. The labor movement's association with the Democratic party is described in Ira B. Cross, *History of the Labor Movement in California* (Berkeley: University of California Press, 1935), 37–59.

In 1864, the Union party, at the peak of its legislative strength but facing serious challenges for the first time since the war began, passed three new election laws. Since the Emancipation Proclamation in 1863, the Democrats had been gaining strength slowly but steadily. The rising Democratic opposition to the war in 1864 put the Union party into a rather desperate phase of defensiveness. In addition to an act providing for California soldiers in the field to vote as Californians, the Union legislators passed the first law since 1851 to regulate elections, creating an elaborate procedure for challenges to a voter's suffrage qualifications and adding misdemeanor fines and jail terms for violations.[52]

The other election law passed by the Union party in the year 1864 was an act to redistrict San Francisco. The Union party's opponents charged that U.S. Senator John Conness planned the redistricting scheme "to throw the control of the metropolis into the hands of the rough element, sometimes known as 'the boys.'"[53] The Conness wing of the Union party did thrive on the extraurban allegiances of patriotism and loyalty to the party of Lincoln, as we saw in the previous chapter. Because the redistricting increased the number of wards south of Market Street (where the greatest number of working-class voters lived), and enlarged the transient First Ward, it is possible that Conness had such a plan in mind.[54] In any case, the redistricting did not keep pace with the movement of population westward, and within a few years the suburban wards greatly outnumbered, in population, the waterfront wards. None of the 1864 laws, enacted during the sway of the Conness wing of the Union party, had a lasting effect on the city's political universe, but they do indicate how well the political elite understood the operation of the dual political universe.

The elections of 1865 brought the Union party back to power in the California state legislature, but not the Conness, or "Short

[52] The judges and inspectors were to conduct a preliminary interrogation about the voter's citizenship and length of residence, then to accept an oath of qualification if the preliminary investigation proved inconclusive. Significantly, however, this act left challenges to take place on election day, at the scene of the polling place itself. *Statutes of California* 15th Session (1863–4), Chapter 272, "An Act to provide for the support of the privilege of Free Suffrage during the continuance of the War," approved 1 April 1864; Chapter 413, "An Act amendatory and supplementary to an Act, passed March the twenty-third, A.D. eighteen hundred and fifty, to regulate Elections," approved 4 April 1864.

[53] Hittell, *History of California*, 4:393–4.

[54] *Statutes of California*, 15th Session (1863–4), Chapter 200, "An Act to re-district the City and County of San Francisco," Approved 21 March 1864.

Hair," faction of that party. The violent and clearly devious organizational tactics of the Conness wing discredited that faction and brought the "Long Hairs" to power for one last term before the revival of the Democratic party in 1867. The Long Hairs, mostly former Republicans, enacted two very important election laws with the hope of limiting the strength of the Short Hairs and the Democrats. One of these was the Primary Election Law, also known as the Porter Primary Law. Enacted in 1866, this was the first law in the United States attempting to regulate the conduct of primary elections among voluntary political organizations (i.e., parties).[55] A reaction to the notorious Conness-run primaries, which had deprived the Long Hairs of majorities in the Union conventions, the Porter law extended the laws regulating regular elections to primaries *if* the party volunteered to hold their primaries under its provision. Within a short time, party leaders opted to hold their primaries without the aid of the new law. It would eventually require a constitutional amendment to create a mandatory primary law.[56]

By far the most important election law enacted during the 1860s was the Registry Act, approved on 16 March 1866.[57] This law required for the first time in California that qualified electors be recorded on official documents prior to the election in which they wished to vote. Prior to the Registry Act, the burden lay with those who sought a restrictive enforcement of the suffrage requirements, to challenge suspected illegal voters. Now the burden suddenly came to rest on the shoulders of all potential voters. Those wishing a restrictive enforcement still had to maintain vigilance over the registration process, but the law alone did most of the work by requiring an additional act of participation by the potential electors.

As a rule, suffrage restriction or expansion is a partisan strategy. Registration of voters was already an old idea by 1866. The first such law was enacted in Massachusetts in 1800, but the pressures to open the franchise and reduce suffrage requirements shortly thereafter suppressed the idea for several decades. The rise of great

---

[55] C. Edward Merriam, *Primary Elections: A Study of the History and Tendencies of Primary Election Legislation* (Chicago: The University of Chicago Press, 1908), 9.

[56] Winfield J. Davis, *History of Political Conventions in California, 1849–1892* (Sacramento: California State Library, 1893), 242, 244, 249, 260, 281; see Chapter 7 for further discussion of the attempt to regulate primaries.

[57] *Statutes of California*, 16th Session, Chapter 265, pp. 288–301.

immigrant populations and transient urban centers during the later antebellum years revived the concept of registering voters. As often happened, a New York law provided the example for Californians. In 1859 the New York legislature passed a statewide, but weak, registration law.[58] The California Registry Act was a partisan move authored by Long Hair Unionists who sought to clip the wings of rivals. Horace Hawes, the bill's author, deserves a prominent place in the story. Similar registration systems in Philadelphia, New York, and Chicago proved much weaker than the California law due to loopholes carefully planted in the legislation. But Hawes, an intense autodidact of artisanal origins like Broderick, was a master legislative artist whose chefs d'oeuvre stood the test of time.[59] As prefect of San Francisco under Mexican law between the conquest and California's admission to the United States, Hawes prosecuted the "Hounds" gang. As a Democratic property owner, he was the author of the economy-minded Consolidation Act of 1856, which remained the charter of San Francisco for almost a half-century, until it was finally replaced by popular vote in 1898. The Consolidation Act placed severe constraints on the power of the Board of Supervisors to spend or to incur debt and saved revenue by consolidating the city and county governments. The timing of the Consolidation Act was fortuitous, going into effect in time for the People's party to take credit for the radical cuts in taxation and expenditure.[60]

Now Hawes was a member of the Long Hair faction of the Union (Republican) party faction seeking to prevent the frauds they feared both Short Hair Unionists and Democrats used to achieve power. Hawes took the enfeebled New York registry law of 1859 and forti-

---

[58] In 1865, as a partisan move aimed at the Democratic organization in New York City, the Republican state government at Albany amended the law to make it applicable only to cities. Joseph P. Harris, *Registration of Voters in the United States* (Washington, D.C.: The Brookings Institution, 1929), 65–90.

[59] Born in 1813 in Danby, New York, Hawes was apprenticed by his impoverished parents at an early age to learn carpentry and cabinetmaking. He was apparently something of a prodigy, for he managed while learning his trade not only to educate himself but also to pass a teacher's examination by the age of sixteen. Hawes then proceeded to learn and practice law, settling in Utica, New York, then Erie, Pennsylvania – both frontier commercial centers. Hawes was active in Democratic party politics during the Jacksonian years, and by 1847 he was rewarded with an appointment by President Polk as consul to the Society Islands. From that post he made his way to San Francisco during the Gold Rush and joined the handful of men who built and led the political apparatus of the city during its formative years. Hittell, *History of California*, 3:385, 4:189, 514.

[60] Hittell, *History of California*, 4:689.

fied it, giving his Union party a bulwark against the return of the Democratic party. Suspicion of opponents served greatly to ensure passage of the bill before it could be weakened. The Long Hair faction feared the Conness, or Short Hair, faction's penchant for election fraud, and both Long and Short Hair Unionists feared the legend of Democratic electoral shenanigans. The act empowered the county clerk to maintain lists, to be called the "Great Registers," enrolling the names of qualified electors. It established procedures for proving citizenship, but most importantly it required that registration was to take place *three months before an election*. Much of the act also stipulated how the Great Registers were to be organized and kept, when they were to be updated, the criteria for removing and appending names, and how poll lists were to be produced for use on election day. Finally, Hawes's long and complex bill created a "State Board of Registry" and prescribed misdemeanor penalties for the violation of the act.[61]

Passage of the Registry Act was planned during a special Union caucus held one evening in January 1866. When it reached the Senate floor, John S. Hager, leading the Democrats, stamped the law as partisan, charging that the Union caucus planned "to vote down any amendments proposed by anyone outside that caucus."[62] The bill was passed quickly in the Senate by a Union majority of twenty-four to seven, but the large minority of Democrats in the Assembly waged a noisy fight against the bill, attempting parliamentary delays and even to shout down the proponents when the debate grew hot. The sections that drew the greatest objection were those specifying the criteria to be used in determining the citizenship of applicants for the franchise. In their opposition, however, the Democrats were at a disadvantage, for, especially since the Vigilante movement, no one dared suggest advocacy of anything but the purest election standards. One of the most vigorous opponents, for instance, proposed that "if the law would stop election frauds and perfect the election law, in God's name pass it." Another opponent admitted he "was in favor of a Registry Law that should conduce to the purity of the Ballot-Box, and protect the rights of all citizens, native and foreign; but he was opposed to an act like this."[63]

The Democrats' chief complaint was that the bill, "by requiring

---

[61] *Statutes of California*, 16th Session, Chapter 165.
[62] Sacramento *Union*, 25, 31 January 1866.   [63] Sacramento *Union*, 24 February 1866.

extraordinary proofs of citizenship," was intended to "exclude from voting a majority of the naturalized citizens." In other words, they feared the bill was aimed at the Irish voting bloc concentrated in the Democratic party, a bloc now promising to support a winning party again. In clearest terms, then, Assemblyman Jesse D. Goodwin charged that:

This bill was drawn ... as an act of hostility to the Democratic party, in order to disfranchise a portion of the voters of California, supposed to be inimical to the party now in power. It was that which had united the Union party in favor of the bill.

Another Democrat, who denounced the bill as "a fraud and a swindle, compared to which all the ballot-box stuffing which ever occurred in California was not a 'circumstance,'" tied the timing of the legislation to the rise of the Democratic party:

The gentleman who had hatched out this bill, seeing by the recent news that there was a fair prospect that his party would go down and another come up, had slipped in various provisions to prevent men who had been naturalized from voting for freedom.[64]

Significantly, both Union and Democratic party leaders clashed on this bill from a position of suffrage restriction. The very first response of the Democrats to the bill was to attempt to have the word "white" inserted in it. They clearly feared the erosion of white male privilege as the postwar years began. "The bill would rob white citizens of their constitutional right of suffrage," one Democrat cried, "and thus pluck the brightest jewel from the diadem of the Goddess of Liberty."[65]

The provisions in the Registry Bill for enrolling naturalized citizens who had lost their naturalization papers caused the greatest alarm. The bill required two alternative tests in this case. One was the "testimony of at least two registered citizens, being householders and legal voters of this state," that the applicant was indeed a naturalized citizen.[66] Failing any other proofs, the applicant was required to have resided in the state for one full year. This was consistent with the requirement then in force in the courts for ob-

---

[64] All of the quotations in this paragraph are from the Sacramento *Union*, 24 February 1866.
[65] Sacramento *Union*, 24 February 1866.
[66] *Statutes of California*, 16th Session, Chapter 165, p. 290.

taining a second set of naturalization papers, but it seemed to *double* the requirement of six month's residency in the state for suffrage already in the California Constitution. Both requirements, in fact, tied the qualification for suffrage to stable residency. The required testimony of two householders was a product of the stable burgher mentality of the Vigilante-People's party movement, and came very close to a property requirement for the franchise.

These provisions, and the Democratic opposition to them, again show a clear understanding of the dual electorate. The Democrats were well aware of the source of their strength in the more transient, blue-collar strata of the citizenry. John S. Hager in the Senate had moved to amend the bill so that applicants could "prove their citizenship by their own affidavits." He said, with the high rates of geographic turnover in mind, that "very few men in California would be able to prove it by other testimony." Horace Hawes, the bill's author and representative of the Vigilante way of thinking, was equally certain that qualified voters would be known and stable citizens. He replied by claiming "that the amendment was unnecessary, because all well known citizens would be recorded as such by common repute."[67]

The Union party wanted this bill badly enough to fend off serious amendment in the Assembly and, after a long evening session that lasted until midnight, the bill was passed on 27 February 1866.[68] The test of the Democratic complaints against the Registry Act would be the impact of the new registration system on the turnout and outcome of the September election of 1867, the first election in which the act was in effect. Throughout the campaign of that year the Democratic press, led by the new *Examiner*, sent up a howl of alarm against the bill. Calling the act the "Hawes Bilk," the *Examiner* warned voters to "be undeceived, and register at once."[69] Opponents even organized an "indignation meeting" in protest of the law to be held on election day, 4 September 1867.[70]

The election of 1867, however, resulted in a triumphant landslide victory for the Democrats. Democratic fears of disfranchisement vanished with reports of an increased turnout over the previous year, and the puzzling fact that fewer people voted than had registered.

[67] Sacramento *Union*, 20 January, 1866.
[68] Sacramento *Union*, 28 February 1866.
[69] San Francisco *Examiner*, 25, 31 July; 1, 2, 8, 27 August 1867.
[70] *Examiner*, 31 July 1867. There was no report of the demonstration ever taking place.

The neutral impact of the registration law may, in fact, be accounted for by the heavy effort invested by the Democrats in mobilizing their electorate to register. "ENROLL! ENROLL! ENROLL!" one headline shrieked.[71] The great Democratic triumph of 1867 taught the Democrats suddenly to favor the new law and fear for their own sake the chicanery of the Republicans in the following elections. The Democratic legislature of 1868–9 actually strengthened the Registry Act by changing the classifications of violations from misdemeanors to felonies.[72]

Several election laws passed during the 1870s vividly illustrate the quandary in which party leaders found themselves in that decade. Two of these laws attempted to regulate the shape and appearance of the party tickets used in the elections. Until the Australian, or secret, ballot was adopted in California in 1891, parties printed and distributed their own ballots. This practice is often cited as a lever of control exercised by the parties over the voters, because the distinctive ballots could easily be monitored at the polls by party watchers.[73] But historians have not paid enough attention to the loss of control engendered by the party ballot. Because a voter's choice was mediated by a pathway of party loyalty, imitation of a party's ballot appearance was an easy route to victory for independent candidates or breakaway factions.[74] In the tumultuous period of party competition that prevailed during the 1870s, near pandemonium reigned at the polls as hawkers purveyed bona fide and bogus tickets side by side.[75]

An example of the difficulty parties had in maintaining control of the electorate is provided by an oral history given by Michael H. de Young, cofounder and editor of the San Francisco *Chronicle*, in 1875. De Young recounts the election of 1871 in which the People's party and the *Chronicle* opposed the candidacy of Delos Lake for district judge. Lake received the nomination of the Democrats and had the backing of William C. Ralston, president of the Bank of California.

71   San Francisco *Examiner*, 30 July 1867.
72   *Statutes of California*, 17th Session, Chapter 482, pp. 647–55.
73   For example, William Issel and Robert W. Cherny, *San Francisco, 1865–1932: Politics, Power, and Urban Development* (Berkeley: University of California Press, 1986), 117–18.
74   Joseph P. Harris, *Election Administration in the United States* (Washington, D.C.: The Brookings Institution, 1934), 151–52.
75   *Examiner*, 14 September 1867, 16 September 1869, 22 September 1871, 19 September 1873, 11 September 1875, 10 September 1877, 8 September 1879. Observers commented on an extreme level of "scratching," or altering tickets, by 1875. *Alta*, 2 September 1875.

The People's party, favored to win in that election, had nominated a man named M. C. Blake for the same judicial office. Ralston had thousands of counterfeit People's tickets printed with the name Lake substituted for that of Blake. The de Young brothers had already printed the People's tickets when they discovered on the morning of the election the Ralston-Lake counterfeits:

The result was [the People's party] were compelled to get out another ticket – a new ticket – and abandon the old one. We had hardly got it out before they had an imitation of it.... We devoted the whole day running around to the polling places, tearing up these bogus tickets, fighting and trying to secure a fair election.[76]

Elections such as these led legislators to enact two laws for the regulation of ballots. The first, passed in 1874, sought to remove the source of counterfeiting by requiring that "every ticket be of paper, uniform in size, color, weight, texture, and appearance."[77] The printing layout of the ticket remained unregulated, however, so counterfeiting went unchecked. In 1878 the legislature passed the "Vignette Ticket Act," officially entitled "An Act to prevent the Circulation of Bogus Tickets and to Prevent Frauds upon Voters." The "vignette" referred to the symbolic design or logo used by the various parties at the head of their ticket. With the paper quality and appearance regulated, the design came to be the only thing left to counterfeit, and to prevent this the Vignette Ticket Act required that each party deposit a sample of its vignette before each election and each party use only that vignette on its tickets.[78]

A third law indicates how little knowledge or control the party leaders had over the electorate. This was the so-called Piece Club Act of 1878. The origin of the term "piece club" is entirely obscure, but some authors have, in confusion, altered it to read "price club," a term much more appropriate in meaning but nonetheless incorrect. The full name of this act was "An Act to Prohibit

---

[76] M. H. de Young, *Dictation for H. H. Bancroft* [1875]. Typescript in Bancroft Library, Berkeley.

[77] A ballot was technically defined as a folded ticket, the latter being the piece of paper with the candidates' names printed upon it. Alfred Clarke, *A Compilation of Laws Relating to Elections, Now in Force in the State of California* (San Francisco: A. L. Bancroft and Co., Printers and Lithographers, 1875), sections 1187, 1191, 1197, 1198.

[78] Louis Kaplan, *Extracts from the United States Statutes, the Constitution of the State of California, and the Political and Penal Codes. Relating to the Elective Franchise, Registration of Citizens, and Elections* (San Francisco: Board of Election Commissioners, 1878), 40–1.

'Piece Clubs,' and to Prevent Extortion from Candidates for Office."[79] Operators of piece clubs approached candidates and pretended that they headed political clubs of voters. The scam was to demand a campaign contribution from the candidate, ostensibly for the costs of printing handbills and holding rallies. These confidence men would adopt some vague name for their invisible club, the most ingenious being the "Independent Democratic Liberal Republican Anti-Coolie Labor party." The candidate, rather than risk losing the promised hundreds of votes, usually paid the extortion money.[80]

This phenomenon of piece clubs, and the act to prohibit them, strongly indicates that the politicians knew so little about their electoral base that they could be fooled by such a simple scam. These acts to regulate the electorate, passed during the ideological and electoral instability of 1866–78, occurred during the period that included Reconstruction, the depression of the 1870s, and the rise of the Workingmen's Party of California. They represent the fear party leaders held not only of their opponents, but of the electorate. It is certainly not accidental that party leaders suddenly devised ways to restrict and control the electorate at the moment when blacks gained the franchise and Chinese and women threatened to do so. In Chapter 6 the insufficiency of these laws for staving off voter independence will be examined. We next turn to a detailed examination of the social composition of the electorate, made possible by Hawes's efficient Registry Act.

THE SHAPE OF THE URBAN ELECTORATE DURING THE THIRD PARTY SYSTEM

Historians widely assume that the shape of the urban electorate was broad and mass-based prior to the electoral reforms of the Progressive Era. Measuring turnout at state and national levels, political historians have argued that the "third-party system" (1860–94) was characterized by "full voter mobilization" and by participation of all socioeconomic classes eligible to vote. Urban historians, most

---

[79] Kaplan, *Extracts*, 62.
[80] Quoted in Issel and Cherny, *San Francisco*, 119.

without conducting their own tests, have assumed that patterns within the cities reflected and even exaggerated this pattern, with working-class residents participating even more assiduously than white-collar urbanites.[81]

Using the individual-level data on occupation and nativity contained in the California Great Registers, it is possible to test the "full voter mobilization" model of urban political participation directly. Table 5.1 compares the distribution of occupations among eligible male voters in the 1870 census manuscript as a "control group" with that in the Great Register of 1867. Using a Chi-square test of significance, we can estimate the likelihood that members of specific occupational groups would register to vote. This is expressed as a "relative risk," which estimates how much more or less likely a group was to register than all the other groups.

The most striking finding displayed in Table 5.1 is the obvious difference between occupational strata. The three white-collar groups (merchants, petty proprietors, and clerks and sales workers) were just as likely to register as not to register; the test group was not significantly different than the control group. Skilled workers, however, were 1.3 times more likely than members of other groups to register. Semi- and unskilled workers were significantly less likely to register to vote as were members of other groups. If registering to vote is a good indication of the propensity of a person to participate

---

[81] The very high rates of nineteenth-century voter turnout in the nation and by regions (but significantly not by *cities*) have been demonstrated especially by Walter Dean Burnham, "The Changing Shape of the American Political Universe," *American Political Science Review* 54 (March 1965): 7–28; idem *Critical Elections and the Mainsprings of American Politics* (New York: W. W. Norton, 1970); and Paul Kleppner, *Who Voted?: The Dynamics of Electoral Turnout, 1870–1980* (New York: Praeger, 1982). The urban historian's version of Walter Dean Burnham's well-known "System of 1896" thesis is the so-called Hays thesis. Samuel P. Hays, "The Politics of Reform in Municipal Government in the Progressive Era," *Pacific Northwest Quarterly* 55 (1964): 157–69. Progressive reform is supposed to have put to an end a golden age of mass, immigrant, working-class, neighborhood-based urban politics. A typical application of this thesis is Charles N. Glaab and A. Theodore Brown, eds., *A History of Urban America* 3d ed. (New York: Macmillan Publishing Co., 1983), 206–28. Most recently, Martin Shefter uncritically applies Burnham's nationwide data to his study of the urban machine, assuming that the "extraordinarily high level of popular involvement in party politics" amounted to "the mobilization of the working class" into urban politics. Martin Shefter, "Trade Unions and Political Machines: The Organization and Disorganization of the American Working Class in the Late Nineteenth Century," in *Working-Class Formation: Nineteenth-Century Patterns in Western Europe and the United States*, ed. Ira Katznelson and Aristide R. Zolberg (Princeton, N.J.: Princeton University Press, 1986), 210.

Table 5.1. *Occupational composition of the San Francisco registered electorate,*
1867, compared to census of 1870

Occupational group	Relative risk	95% Confidence interval	Chi square	P-value
Merchants	1.0	.8, 1.4	.2	.69
Petty Proprietors	.8	.7, 1.1	2.2	.13
Clerks and Salesmen	1.2	.9, 1.7	1.9	.16
Skilled Workers[a]	1.3	1.1, 1.6	7.7	.005
Semi-Skilled Workers[a]	.8	.6, .9	4.8	.03
Unskilled Workers[a]	.75	.6, .9	3.9	.05

[a] Occupational groups showing significant differences between samples. *P*-values of
.05 or less are significant.
Sources: Random samples of eligible male voters drawn from the manuscript schedule of the 1870 U.S. Census for San Francisco, $N = 314$; and the California Great
Register for San Francisco (Sacramento, 1867), $N = 325$.

by voting, then voter participation in the late 1860s was *not* evenly
distributed across occupations, but clearly skewed. But the composition of the electorate was not simply skewed upward on the occupational scale. Skilled workers were the most likely to register. As I
have indicated in earlier chapters, the prominence of skilled workers in the electorate held vital importance. This large and residentially stable group clearly attracted the attention of party leaders
and municipal policy makers. Their class identity, however, was ambiguous. They could be convinced to join with merchants in the
Vigilance committees, as previous chapters demonstrated; and they
could be convinced to join the "Workingmen," as the next chapter
will demonstrate.

Ethnically, the composition of the electorate was not very complicated. The Great Registers allow us only to measure *nativity*, not
ethnicity, because the nativities of the voter's parents are not given.
Table 5.2, then, must underestimate the likelihood of the two principal white ethnic groups, Irish and Germans, to register.

Democratic party lawmakers had feared that the Registry Act
would disenfranchise naturalized Irish voters, but Table 5.2 plainly
shows that Irish-born citizens were just as likely to register as not.
Democrats, pleased with the results of the election of 1867, in which

Table 5.2. *Native composition of the San Francisco registered electorate, 1867,*
compared to census of 1870

Country born	Relative risk	95% Confidence interval	Chi square	P-value
United States[a]	1.41	1.2, 1.7	16.6	.001
Ireland	.9	.75, 1.1	.9	.34
Germany[ab]	.8	.6, .9	5.0	.025

[a] Native groups showing significant differences between samples have *P*-values of .05 or less.
[b] Includes all eligible male voters born in German-speaking countries.
Sources: Random samples drawn from the manuscript schedule of the 1870 U.S. Census for San Francisco, $N = 314$; and the California Great Register for San Francisco (Sacramento, 1867), $N = 325$.

an Irish American, Frank McCoppin, was elected mayor, not only stopped complaining about the Registry Act thereafter but, as we saw, actually strengthened it. Neither do the data summarized in Table 5.2 indicate a Hibernian invasion of the political community. Irish-born adult males composed 25.5 percent of the city's population and 23 percent of the registered electorate in 1867. The lower likelihood of adult males born in German-speaking countries to register may be explained by the greater number of more recent immigrants among that group.[82]

As California's labor historians have shown, the racial line of social-group cleavage was by far the dominant one in San Francisco from the Civil War through the First World War. Ethnic-group identity formation among European people in the political public sphere was not a leading source of division in this city, where the Chinese were the "indispensable enemy." The Civil War, through the Fourteenth and Fifteenth Amendments, had converted race from an uncontested exclusive boundary into a contested boundary requiring constant vigilance among the privileged. This dynamic, suppressing intra-European ethnic conflict, is what made California and San Francisco, in Carey McWilliams's phrase, "the great

[82]   Again, the use of nativity rather than ethnicity here artificially decreases the likelihood that foreign-stock groups would register to vote.

exception" to the relative weakness of class politics in American history.[83] In the emerging politics of group interests, class interests among white males would become the predominant political cleavage within the official electoral politics of the public sphere.[84]

Did the 1866 Registry Act and subsequent election laws have a restrictive effect on the urban political community? The evidence just presented does not indicate that voter registration excluded white ethnic groups, but it may have restricted the participation of the lower economic strata, whose transience may have prevented them from meeting the three-month advance registration requirement. However, evidence from the late 1860s and early 1870s seriously qualifies such a prediction. The return of the national parties to the municipal political contests of San Francisco – made possible by the paired timing of municipal and general elections from 1867 onward – coincided with a massive influx of blue-collar workers into the city. The completion of the transcontinental railroad in 1869, and the continued prosperity of California for two years after the depression of 1873 began in the East, helped to nearly double the city's population during the 1870s. Analysis of the Great Registers for the years 1869 through 1871 reveals a clear rise in the proportion of low-blue-collar workers who registered to vote. Unskilled workers, for instance, jumped from an estimated relative risk of .75 in 1867 to an estimate of 1.35 in 1869. In other words, in the 1869 Great Register Sample $(N = 325)$, these low-blue-collar workers were suddenly 1.3 times more likely to be registered to vote than members of other occupational groups.[85] In the 1871 Great Register Sample $(N = 299)$, unskilled workers were just as likely to register as not to register (relative risk of 1).[86]

---

[83] Alexander Saxton, *Indispensable Enemy: Labor and the Anti-Chinese Movement in California* (Berkeley: University of California Press, 1971); idem, "San Francisco Labor and the Populist and Progressive Insurgencies," *Pacific Historical Review* 34 (November 1965): 421–38; Michael Kazin, *Barons of Labor: The San Francisco Building Trades and Union Power in the Progressive Era* (Urbana: University of Illinois Press, 1987); idem, "The Great Exception Revisited: Organized Labor and Politics in San Francisco and Los Angeles, 1870–1940," *Pacific Historical Review* 55:3 (August 1986): 371–402; Carey McWilliams, *California: The Great Exception* (New York, 1949).

[84] Albert Camarillo, *Chicanos in California* (San Francisco: Boyd and Fraser, 1984); Robert F. Heizer and Alan J. Almquist, *The Other Californians: Prejudice and Discrimination under Spain, Mexico, and the United States to 1920* (Berkeley: University of California Press, 1971).

[85] 95% Confidence bounds = 1, 1.8; Chi-square = 5.4, $P = .02$.

[86] 95% Confidence bounds = .8, 1.3; Chi-square = .03, $P = .85$.

Table 5.3. *Occupational composition of the San Francisco registered electorate, 1880, compared to census of 1880*

Occupational group	Relative risk	95% Confidence interval	Chi square	P-value
Merchants[ab]	1.3	.96, 1.8	3.5	.06
Petty Proprietors	1.1	.9, 1.4	1.9	.17
Clerks and Salesmen	.8	.7, .99	3.6	.056
Skilled Workers[a]	1.3	1.1, 1.5	11.5	.001
Semiskilled Workers[a]	.7	.6, .8	17.4	.001
Unskilled Workers	.9	.7, 1.1	.5	.47

[a] Occupational groups showing significant differences between samples. P-values of .05 or less are significant within the 95–100% confidence bounds.
[b] The result in this category was significant within 90–95% confidence bounds.
Sources: Random samples of eligible male voters drawn from the manuscript schedule of the 1880 U.S. Census for San Francisco, $N = 422$; and the California Great Register for San Francisco (Sacramento, 1880), $N = 493$.

By 1880, as Table 5.3 indicates, the likelihood that low-blue-collar workers would register to vote fell again to the levels found in 1867. The Registry Act itself and the batch of election regulation laws enacted from 1866 to 1878 do not seem to have prevented the mobilization of low-blue-collar working-class voters. The biggest infusion of working-class voters, which lasted through 1871, had occurred despite the addition of felony penalties to the Registry Act. The high rates of mobility among those potential voters, however, probably extracted most of these new entrants from the electorate again later in the 1870s. Ominously, merchants were suddenly more likely to register to vote than not, in a ratio similar to that of the highly mobilized skilled workers (whose ratio remained unchanged from 1867 to 1880). The increased mobilization at the top of the occupational scale spelled serious trouble for class relations in the city, a development explored in detail in the Chapter 6. The relative risk for the principal nativity groups remained about the same in 1880 as it had been in 1867, which further suggests that the action of the 1870s would take place among class, not ethnic-group cleavages.

Combined with the evidence of low municipal-level voter participation presented in Chapter 1, these analyses of the social composition of the Gilded Age urban electorate do not support the idea of a fully mobilized electorate. "There was hardly a millionaire on Algonquin Avenue who knew where the ward meetings of his party were held," John Hay wrote in his conservative novel *The Breadwinners* (1884), lamenting the failure of the owning classes to participate in city affairs; but "there was not an Irish laborer in the city but knew his way to his ward club as well as to mass."[87] Hay, like recent urban social and political historians, thought the urban polity was especially open at the bottom end of the social scale, permitting democratic participation that was both broad and deep. Yet in San Francisco the actual patterns tell a very different story. The urban electorate was skewed, unevenly, toward upper occupational groups, but the bulwark of participation was the middling burgher stratum: the skilled workers. It was possible, however, for low-blue-collar voters to flood into the active political community. Their transience left them without the possibility either of developing durable community ties or of developing into a durable constituency.

This is the dual urban political universe. Low-blue-collar voters were available for mobilization from time to time, especially on the basis of symbolic issues of race, class, or national party loyalties, which did not require a local vested interest and could be carried from city to city. Meanwhile, another set of urbanites formed the stable core community of the local political community. These groups included especially the low-white-collar and skilled population, whose numbers made them the largest segment of the electorate. Whether they would ally themselves with the upper or lower occupational groups of the dual political universe depended largely upon the logic of political mobilization and party programs, which is the subject of the remaining chapters.

THE ORIGINS OF MASS COMMUNICATION AT THE DAWN OF AN INTEREST-GROUP DISCOURSE

The central institution of the political public sphere had always been, since the seventeenth century, political journalism. Two new newspapers appeared in San Francisco to provide a platform for the changed discourse of political actors. These began to prioritize the language of class: the *Examiner* and the *Chronicle*. As a mea-

---

87   *The Bread-Winners: A Social Study* (New York: Harper and Bros., 1884), 229.

sure of their historical precocity, from among a field of scores of dailies only these have survived as the principal newspapers of San Francisco. Rapidly eclipsing the *Alta California*, these papers represented a new kind of journalism: commercial and sensational.

These new papers were instrumental in bringing about the new interest-group discourse by the very nature of their commercialism. Their editors saw the postwar opportunity to exploit an emerging consumer market. "The old political issues upon which the people in their partizan contests, in past years, rallied at the polls, have become obsolete," the Democrat William S. Moss declared in the first issue of his new, Democratic, *Examiner* on 12 June 1865. "Never before did more important duties devolve upon the press," Moss calculated: "New issues ... the status of the revolted states ... the future political and social position of the negro ... how the people are to be alleviated of the burdens of taxation" had come to the fore. He even appealed to the Irish component of the party by proposing the landing of one hundred fifty thousand Irish-American Civil War soldiers in Ireland to liberate it from Great Britain.[88]

The *Chronicle* was created by a pair of young Radical Republicans, Michael H. and Charles de Young, as the appropriately named *Dramatic Chronicle* in 1865. By Michael de Young's own account, the two brothers acquired the equipment for their new paper by picking it up in the streets, following the rioters who were sacking the offices of Democratic newspapers in anger at the news of President Lincoln's assassination. "I followed the mob from behind," Michael recalled, "taking items."[89] (See Plate 4.1.) From the destruction wrought by a furious crowd they snatched up enough type to print a small listing and review of the San Francisco stage. Ambitious and resourceful, the de Youngs distributed their paper free until they had acquired a readership; by 1867 investors were making offers on the promising paper. During the 1870s, the de Young brothers were to compete with the *Examiner* and the *Call* (another new paper, first published in 1859) for the readership of the city's working class. In so doing, they helped powerfully to shape emerging class identities.

During the 1870s another medium of mass communication appeared on the scene. In 1875 the dynamic Baptist preacher Isaac S. Kalloch arrived in town. By the time he took up life as a San

---

88 *Examiner*, 12, 13 June 1865.
89 Michael H. de Young, Dictation for H. H. Bancroft, MS in Bancroft Library, Berkeley.

Plate 5.2. The Chronicle Building at the northwest corner of Bush and Kearny streets, sometime in the 1880s. As the central institutions of the public sphere, San Francisco's largest newspapers began competing to build the most impressive structures, beginning with buildings such as this. It housed the *Chronicle* from 1879 until 1890, when Michael H. de Young, in competition with William Randolph Hearst, constructed the city's first steel-ribbed skyscraper on Market Street. Newspapers were participatory media. This photograph shows a crowd typically gathered to learn the news of some event. Charles de Young was assassinated in his office on the top floor of this building by the mayor's son in 1880. Courtesy of Bancroft Library, Berkeley California. Wyland Stanley Collection.

Franciscan, Kalloch had accumulated a stormy past. His story begins in Rockland, Maine, where, as the son of a Baptist minister, growing up during the excitement of the Second Great Awakening, he proved a prodigy. By the age of sixteen Kalloch was locally renowned as the "Boy Preacher." Kalloch not only stood out as an evangelical preacher during a time of remarkable evangelicals, he also was physically striking. In the words of his biographer:

He was a giant of a man, weighing 240 pounds, slim-hipped and big-shouldered, with a shock of flaming red hair and pink whiskers around his chops. He dressed elegantly. He had a magnetic platform manner, a voice of gold, and he always attracted crowds of unparalleled size.[90]

Kalloch's fame as a handsome and effective abolitionist rapidly spread beyond Maine. In 1853, at age twenty-three, he was recruited by the abolitionist radicals of Massachusetts, Theodore Parker and William Lloyd Garrison among them, to take the pulpit of the nation's largest Baptist congregation, Tremont Temple of Boston.[91]

Populistic by theology and style, the Baptists tended to build enormous churches. In 1857 the "Sorrel Stallion," as he came to be called, left his loyal Boston congregation of thousands to build a new one in the heart of the antislavery war: Lawrence, Kansas.[92] The last pulpit he occupied in Kansas was the massive new structure in the state's leading city, Leavenworth, seating one thousand parishioners. "The Baptist Church is so large," the *Leavenworth Times* reported, "that the society has been puzzled to know what to do with it, but Mr. Kalloch has solved this problem."[93] Kalloch was restless, however, and in the fall of 1875 he and his family suddenly disappeared, leaving a note that they were moving to California.

Kalloch made an instant splash in San Francisco; the local Baptist deacons fulfilled his wishes for a gigantic new church, the Metropolitan Temple. Surpassing in size even the Tremont Temple, the Metropolitan Temple became the largest Baptist church in the United States. Like the Tremont Temple, the interior was built as an amphitheater. It seated three thousand, and two thousand

---

90 M. M. Marberry, *The Golden Voice: A Biography of Isaac Kalloch* (New York: Farrar, Straus and Co., 1947), vii.

91 Tremont Temple had fallen into financial difficulty, and Kalloch was believed capable of saving the church. Originally a large theater, it had been acquired by abolitionists in the 1830s and converted into a "free church," intended to appeal to poor whites and blacks alike. Kalloch built a huge following there, only to become the subject of a major scandal. It was alleged he had become intimately involved with one of his parishioners. Charges of sexual misconduct were to accompany his entire career. Marberry, *The Golden Voice*, 195–222.

92 Kalloch lived in Kansas for almost two decades, improving, during those years, his methods of mass appeal, founding and editing newspapers, and even serving a term in the Kansas legislature. Like the de Youngs, he was a Republican. And like the de Youngs, he had a powerful business sense. In Kansas he also invested in the railroads and sat as director of one. Marberry, *The Golden Voice*, 195–222.

93 Marberry, *The Golden Voice*, 219.

more typically stood in the aisles to hear Kalloch's sermons. Strategically built in the city's huge, class-mixed South-of-Market Tenth Ward, the building was really a temple of mass instruction. On the second floor was another auditorium seating one thousand. Eleven other rooms were used for libraries, lecture rooms, gymnasia, day nurseries, and sewing and manual training. Religious training was offered every day of the week. In short, the Metropolitan Temple was a dynamic community center aimed at the city's marginal classes in the midst of a great depression.[94]

Like his Baptist contemporary and counterpart in Philadelphia, Russell Conwell (whose Temple University, built for Philadelphia's working people, closely resembled Kalloch's temple), Kalloch preached to the poor an invigorating message of self-help through piety, sobriety, and the work ethic. True also to the abolitionist radical mission of the Tremont Temple, Kalloch's church originally reached out to the Chinese. Kalloch for some time maintained the largest Chinese Sunday School in the city.[95]

Together, these new newspapers and Kalloch's Metropolitan Temple offered something that the structures of communication within the older republican discourse could not: a forum for the promotion of class and group identities. The *Alta* was the ideal newspaper for republican San Francisco. Nonpartisan, it always claimed to promote the interests of all San Franciscans. It reflected and reinforced the republican assumption of an indivisible public interest. This shift from newspapers providing a unitary urban *agora* to commercial newspapers consciously targeting marketable subpopulations is a development misunderstood by media sociologists beginning with the influential urbanist Robert Park. Park, in his 1915 essay "A Natural History of the Newspaper," established a modernization framework to portray the newspaper as a medium allowing communication across space and communities that had been fragmented, dispersed by the socioeconomic forces of modern industrial capitalism. David Paul Nord, in a recent restatement of this view, suggests that the new newspapers created a "public community." Ironically, this ecological model seems to be backward. The antebellum press had addressed a quintessentially "public community" already: one in which social divisions were difficult to recognize. The

---

94 Sacramento *Union*, 6 January 1878, 10 December 1887.
95 Cross, *History of the Labor Movement in California*, 120.

postwar press began fragmenting that community into the urban communities of class, race, and ethnicity. Moss, the de Youngs, and the Reverend Kalloch targeted subcommunities to market their public goods.[96]

There are many ways to reconstitute the public sphere; I have examined several of these in this chapter. The public sphere, which provides the structures of practice in self-government, also shapes the meaning of discourse taking place in its media. The reconstitution of the San Francisco public sphere by women simultaneously altered the boundaries of the "private" and weakened republicanism by strengthening the natural-rights tradition of liberalism. The introduction of election and registration laws was a partisan attempt to regulate the membership of the active citzenry within the climate of the social revolution unleashed by the Emancipation Proclamation. The dual urban political universe defined in this chapter reveals that active citizenry to have been highly malleable and uneven in its social composition. Indeed, politicians were well aware of these changes among mass participants and sought to manipulate them. Politicians and the new media entrepreneurs, as we shall see in the next chapter, worked frenetically within this altered public sphere to sharpen the identities of class and race in San Francisco.

---

[96] As an examination of William Randolph Hearst in Chapters 7 and 8 will indicate, the commercial-sensational press further reinforced and capitalized on social divisions. David Paul Nord, "The Public Community: The Urbanization of Journalism in Chicago," *Journal of Urban History* 11:4 (August 1985): 411–42; Robert Ezra Park, *Society: Collective Behavior, News and Opinion, Sociology and Modern Society* (Glencoe, Illinois: The Free Press of Glencoe, 1955).

CHAPTER 6

A language of politics in a politics of class: The Workingmen's Party of California

"California is very important to me," Karl Marx wrote to his American correspondent Friedrich Sorge in November of 1880, "because nowhere else has the upheaval most shamelessly caused by capitalist concentration taken place with such speed."[1] The "upheaval" that had gained his attention in this particular instance was the Workingmen's Party of California (WPC). The WPC was, in turn, only the opening act in a remarkable outpouring of political insurgency that historians would come to call the "Great Upheaval." During the 1880s parties with names like "Workingmen," "Labor," or "United Labor," headed by labor leaders and lower middle-class militants, and usually affiliated with the Knights of Labor, gained political power in more than a hundred cities and towns across the United States. With significant regularity, however, the lifespan of these parties was very short, averaging less than two years. By 1889, little political trace was left of the urban labor parties.[2]

The Great Upheaval originated in the nationwide rail strike of 1877, was punctuated by the Haymarket Square bombing and the strike wave of 1886, and continued through the Homestead and Pullman strikes of 1892 and 1894. It overlapped with the rise and fall (1888–96) of the Farmers' Alliance and People's party movements. Whether measured by numbers of people either participating in strikes or voting for labor or farmer radical parties, the Great Upheaval presents an impressive example of widespread protest politics on the part of hundreds of thousands – if not millions –

[1] Karl Marx to Friedrich A. Sorge, [London], 5 November 1880, in *Karl Marx and Frederick Engels, Letters to Americans, 1848–1895: A Selection*, ed. Alexander Tractenberg, trans. Leonard E. Mins (New York: International Publishers, 1953), 126.

[2] For a recent overview, see Bruce Laurie, *Artisans into Workers: Labor in Nineteenth-Century America* (New York: Hill and Wang, 1989), 141–75. The finest detailed account to date is Leon Fink, *Workingmen's Democracy: The Knights of Labor and American Politics* (Urbana: University of Illinois Press, 1983).

of ordinary American people, white and black, men and women, immigrant and native born.[3]

Scholars have asked for a full century now whether the political parties with working-class names and themes, formed during the Great Upheaval, amounted to a serious challenge to the political economy of laissez-faire industrial capitalism, to the wage system of labor, or to the continued dominance of the two major American political parties. The most recent wave of scholarship, called the "labor-republican synthesis," argues that the insurgent parties of the Great Upheaval resulted from the gradual introduction of an industrial wage-labor system in the United States. That new, industrial-capitalist political economy clashed fundamentally with expectations of autonomy, independence, and citizenship among American working people, these scholars argue. The injustice felt at the workplace and in communities, especially during times of depression or overt repression from the 1830s through the 1890s, created a genuine working-class consciousness that took a form identified as "republican."[4]

Labor republicanism, according to these scholars, was that ideology, worldview, or discourse that focused on the vital importance of civic virtue for the survival of republican government, identified small producers (skilled workers, farmers, or middle-class businessmen) as the source of all wealth, and proclaimed the independent citizen-producer to be the surest repository of virtue. Wage labor, in this conception, reduced men and women to the status of dependency and was therefore corrosive to the republic because destruc-

---

[3] The basic facts of the upheaval are provided in Jeremy Brecher, *Strike!* (Boston: South End Press, 1972); Philip S. Foner, *The Great Labor Uprising of 1877* (New York: Monad Press, 1977). For nuanced analyses of the cultural and political dimensions of nineteenth-century class conflict, see especially Herbert G. Gutman, *Work, Culture and Society in Industrializing America: Essays in American Working-Class and Social History* (Oxford: Basil Blackwell, 1977); and Steven J. Ross, *Workers on the Edge: Work, Leisure, and Politics In Industrializing Cincinnati: 1788–1890* (New York: Columbia University, Press, 1985).

[4] The literature on republicanism and its importance relative to liberalism is very large, but see especially J. G. A. Pocock, *The Machiavellian Moment: Florentine Political Thought and the Atlantic Republican Tradition* (Princeton, N.J.: Princeton University Press, 1975); Joyce Appleby, "Republicanism in Old and New Contexts," *William and Mary Quarterly* 43 (January 1986): 20–34.; John Patrick Diggins, *The Lost Soul of American Politics: Virtue, Self-Interest, and the Foundations of Liberalism* (New York: Basic Books, 1984); idem, "Comrades and Citizens: New Mythologies in American Historiography," *American Historical Review* 90 (June 1985): 614–38; idem, "The Misuses of Gramsci," *Journal of American History* 75:1 (June 1988): 141–45; and a very welcome synthesis: James T. Kloppenberg, "The Virtues of Liberalism: Christianity, Republicanism, and Ethics in Early American Political Discourse," *Journal of American History* 74:1 (June 1987): 9–33.

tive of citizenship and virtue. As the much-quoted preamble to the constitution of the Knights of Labor put it, "We declare an inevitable and irresistible conflict between the wage-system of labor and the republican system of government."[5]

Organized in the aftermath of the nationwide railroad strike and the San Francisco anti-Chinese riots of July 1877, the Workingmen's Party of California achieved several state and municipal electoral victories beginning in February 1878. By the fall of that year, the WPC took a significant minority bloc of delegates to, and set the agenda for, the California constitutional convention. In 1879 the city of San Francisco had a WPC mayor, and several state supreme court judges had been elected under the WPC banner, but by that time the party had already gone into decline. Known as "Kearneyism" to contemporaries, the Workingmen's Party of California has long been a painful embarrassment to new labor historians. Marked by the violent demagoguery of its leader, Denis Kearney,[6] and by rabid anti-Chinese racism, the WPC has been neglected by the most recent revisionists in favor of the many noble political experiments of the Knights of Labor.[7]

5   See Herbert G. Gutman, *Power and Culture: Essays on the American Working Class*, ed. Ira Berlin (New York: Pantheon Books, 1987), 329–56; Sean Wilentz, "Against Exceptionalism: Class Consciousness and the American Labor Movement, 1790–1920," *International Labor and Working Class History* 26 (Fall 1984): 1–24. Fink's most complete study is his *Workingmen's Democracy*, but see also his "The Uses of Political Power: Toward a Theory of the Labor Movement in the Era of the Knights of Labor," in Michael H. Frisch and Daniel J. Walkowitz, eds., *Working-Class America: Essays on Labor, Community, and American Society* (Urbana: University of Illinois Press, 1983): 104–22.; idem, "The New Labor History and the Powers of Historical Pessimism: Consensus, Hegemony, and the Case of the Knights of Labor," *Journal of American History* 75:1 (June 1988): 115–36; Peter S. Rachleff, *Black Labor in the South: Richmond, Virginia, 1865–1890* (Philadelphia, 1984); Susan Levine, *Labor's True Woman: Carpet Weavers, Industrialization, and Labor Reform in the Gilded Age* (Philadelphia, 1984). Knights of Labor constitution quoted in Wilentz, "Against Exceptionalism," 14.

6   There has always been confusion over the spelling of Kearney's given name. Many contemporary newspaper reporters and the historians H. H. Bancroft, T. H. Hittell, and Ira B. Cross all spelled it "Dennis," while other reporters and the historians James Bryce and Alexander Saxton spelled it with one "n." The latter is correct. Mary Frances McKinney interviewed Kearney's son and daughter, William R. Kearney and Mildred Kearney, in July 1939. They were positive that their father spelled his name "Denis." Mary Frances McKinney, "Denis Kearney, Organizer of the Workingmen's Party of California" (Master's thesis, University of California, Berkeley, 1939), 8.

7   The most important accounts of the Workingmen's Party of California are Henry George, "The Kearney Agitation in California," *Popular Science Monthly* 17 (August 1880): 433–53; James Bryce, "Kearneyism in California," in his *The American Commonwealth*, 2 vols., (London: Macmillan and Co., 1889), 2:372–95; Helen H. Ingels, "The History of the Workingmen's Party of California" (Master's thesis, University of California, Berkeley, 1919); Ira B. Cross, *A History of the Labor Movement in California* (Berkeley: University of California Press,

Through a narrative analysis of the origins of the Workingmen's Party of California – the first successful "labor" party of the Great Upheaval – this chapter presents a very different account than those of the labor-republican synthesis. As with so many other historical attempts to explain political outcomes in social terms, the labor-republican explanation of the insurgent parties of the Great Upheaval mistakenly begins with the conflicts in civil society. Ironically, adopting the ethical plotline promoted by the insurgents themselves, recent social and labor historians have overlooked the sympathetic role of "mainstream" politicians of the two major political parties in fomenting what I shall call a "politics of class." Almost invariably, the major party leaders are depicted as cynical defenders of the status quo; their own ideology, appeal, and language are either ignored or simplified with the label "bourgeois." The language and culture of the insurgents, on the other hand, are lavished with extensive attention. In a representative passage, Richard Oestreicher writes of "the bourgeois resistance one would expect to any challenge to capitalist power in a capitalist system."[8]

The mainstream politicians and the major newspapers, as we have seen in previous chapters, were essentially in control of the institutional apparatus of the public sphere. A transformation in the

1935), 88–129; McKinney, "Denis Kearney"; Ralph Kauer, "The Workingmen's Party of California," *Pacific Historical Quarterly* 13 (1944): 278–91; Alexander Saxton, *The Indispensable Enemy: Labor and the Anti-Chinese Movement in California* (Berkeley: University of California Press, 1971), 113–56; Steven Philip Erie, "The Development of Class and Ethnic Politics in San Francisco 1870–1910: A Critique of the Pluralist Interpretation" (Ph.D. diss., University of California, Los Angeles, 1975); Neil L. Shumsky, "San Francisco's Workingmen Respond to the Modern City," *California Historical Quarterly* 55:1 (Spring 1976): 46–57; Michael Kazin, "Prelude to Kearneyism: The July Days in San Francisco, 1877," *New Labor Review* 3 (June 1980): 5–47; idem, "The Great Exception Revisited: Organized Labor and Politics in San Francisco and Los Angeles, 1870–1940," *Pacific Historical Review* 55:3 (August 1986): 371–402; William Issel and Robert W. Cherny, *San Francisco, 1865–1932: Politics, Power, and Urban Development* (Berkeley: University of California Press, 1986), 125–30. For a detailed treatment of the WPC within the context of San Francisco political history, see Philip J. Ethington, "The Structures of Urban Political Life: Political Culture in San Francisco, 1850–1880" (Ph.D. diss., Stanford University, 1989), 301–60.

8   Sean Wilentz, *Chants Democratic: New York City and the Rise of the American Working Class, 1788–1850* (New York: Oxford University Press, 1984); Fink, *Workingmen's Democracy*; Lawrence Goodwyn, *The Populist Moment: A Short History of the Agrarian Revolt in America* (New York: Oxford University Press, 1978); David Scobey "Boycotting the Politics Factory: Labor Radicalism and the New York City Mayoral Election of 1884," *Radical History Review* 28–30 (1984): 300; Steven J. Ross, "The Politicization of the Working Class: Production, Ideology, Culture, and Politics in Late Nineteenth-Century Cincinnati," *Social History* 11:2 (May 1986): 171–95.; quotation is Oestreicher, "Urban Working-Class Political Behavior and Theories of American Electoral Politics, 1870–1940," *Journal of American History* 74:4 (March 1988): 1272.

language of political contestation would most logically have begun among politicians and journalists whose daily task it was to find marketable appeals. The Civil War and its political resolution in Reconstruction, as we saw in Chapters 4, and 5, unleashed through the Emancipation Proclamation and the Fourteenth and Fifteenth Amendments, the origins of social-group identities of race, class, and gender. During the 1870s, leaders of argumentation in the public sphere managed to legitimate the use of group identities for the definition of ethical political policy. The efforts of parties and newspapers to win constituencies during the competitive 1870s led to a mobilization of the political community along class lines. In 1877–8, the leaders of the Workingmen's Party of California briefly captured this already-mobilized class constituency, but they failed to maintain it. Why they failed is the greatest irony of all. The language of mobilization used by the WPC was not a language of class, but a language of politics. In the last major use of republican liberalism as a script for the production of a political drama, the WPC sought to explain social ills in terms of political corruption.

Before examining the origins of the Workingmen's Party of California from within a polity charged by class language and an electorate mobilized along class lines, the role of class in the languages of republicanism and liberalism requires some clarification. The WPC illustrates a crucial moment in the transition from republican liberalism to pluralist liberalism, a transition traced throughout this book. Political contestation in late-nineteenth-century America was conducted within a hybrid discourse, containing elements drawn from classical and neoclassical political theory, Christian doctrine, commonsense philosophy, revolutionary traditions, racial sentiments and ideologies, gender ideologies, imported ethnic oppositional cultures (like those of the German 48'ers and the Irish), artisanal worldviews, liberal ideology, and even folk traditions.[9] A comprehensive analysis of political discourse would account for the

---

[9]   For a mere sampling of these varied discourses, see Kloppenberg, "Virtues of Liberalism"; Steven Hahn, *The Roots of Southern Populism: Yeoman Farmers and the Transformation of the Georgia Upcountry, 1850–1890* (New York: Oxford University Press, 1983); David Thelen, *Paths of Resistance: Tradition and Dignity in Industrializing Missouri* (New York: Oxford University Press, 1986); Nick Salvatore, *Eugene V. Debs: Citizen and Socialist* (Urbana: University of Illinois Press, 1982); Carroll Smith-Rosenberg, *Disorderly Conduct: Visions of Gender in Victorian America* (New York: Oxford University Press, 1985); Ava Baron, ed., *Work Engendered: Toward a New History of American Labor* (Ithaca, N.Y.: Cornell University Press, 1991); Kerby A. Miller, *Emigrants and Exiles: Ireland and the Irish Exodus to North America* (New York: Oxford University Press, 1985).

influence of these and other strains, but for the purposes of this chapter, I would like to isolate the operation of two mixed and yet ultimately contradictory paradigms, or models, of human society. The earlier paradigm was essentially political whereas the later one was essentially economic. Republicanism belonged to the older, political paradigm whereas liberalism and the language of class belonged to the newer, economic paradigm.[10] What distinguished these two paradigms was the attribution of cause and effect in their explanations of social phenomena. The language of republicanism, with its vocabulary of virtue, corruption, and tyranny, attributed social distress and happiness to the behavior of political leaders and to the constitution of political power. Liberalism and its offspring, the language of class, attributed the prosperity or distress of society to the operations of the economy and to the behavior of agents within the economy. This is, in Joyce Appleby's words, what "was truly revolutionary in the liberal world view: the replacement of the economy for the polity as the fundamental social system."[11]

Describing the emerging political discourse of the 1870s as being characterized by a "language of class" is not to suggest that anyone who spoke in terms of "capital" and "labor" had a socialistic class analysis of society as opposed to an individualistic-liberal one. Indeed, these terms seem much more typically to have been used in the sense of classes as competing interest groups. It is to insist, however, that labor republicanism does not at all qualify as a "language of class" because it grounded the source of social distress not in the economy, but in the polity. Republicanism, including labor republicanism, was as much a discourse about *leaders* as it was a discourse about *citizens*. Authors of the labor-republican synthesis correctly characterize that half of republican language that stresses the necessary conditions for independent, virtuous citizenship, but they neglect the much more fateful emphasis in all forms of republicanism on the character of the rulers as the ultimate source of corruption, dependence, and loss of liberty in the citizenry as a whole.[12]

---

[10] This distinction is derived from J. G. A. Pocock, "Virtue, Rights, and Manners: A Model for Historians of Political Thought," in Pocock, *Virtue, Commerce, and History: Essays on Political Thought and History, Chiefly in the Eighteenth Century* (Cambridge, U.K.: Cambridge University Press, 1985), 37–50.

[11] Joyce Appleby "Republicanism and Ideology," *American Quarterly* 37:4 (Fall 1985): 470.

[12] See for example Wilentz, "Against Exceptionalism"; Fink, "The New Labor History," 115–36. For the basic orientation of republicanism toward rulers, see J. G. A. Pocock, *Politics, Language and Time: Essays on Political Thought and History* (Chicago: University of Chicago Press, 1989), 80–103.

PARTY COMPETITION AND THE ORIGINS OF
A POLITICS OF CLASS

We need to begin any investigation of the Great Upheaval long before the unrest of the period following the nationwide strikes of 1877. A much more appropriate place to start is the immediate postwar years, when the Republican and Democratic parties were struggling to build or rebuild constituencies and, with them, political power. Forced to combine under unstable "Union" parties during the Civil War, riven by the divisive issues of currency and emancipation, and forced to take controversial positions vis-à-vis a congressional radical vanguard and a reactionary executive, Republicans and Democrats at the state level sought to restore their previous organizational integrity in the decade following Appomatox. Because, as David Montgomery and Eric Foner have shown, the Civil War and Reconstruction opened a veritable Pandora's box of social conflict, party leaders had no shortage of opportunities to define clear platforms and appeal for voter support. Emancipation, war subsidies and funding, and especially the Fourteenth and Fifteenth Amendments brought race, class, and women's rights to the center of mainstream political conflict. Although it was clear enough that the enfranchisement of free blacks or funding of the Freedmen's Bureau Bill would provoke deep feelings, it was not yet clear how the "social question" would play at the polls.[13]

We need first of all to recapture the sense of struggle faced by party leaders in the postwar years. Too often, recent historians have depicted party loyalties during the "third party system" (ca. 1860–94) as being so durable that Democrats or Republicans only had to get out the loyal vote through spectacular parades.[14] It is true enough that only two parties managed to maintain durable national organizational structures for most of the nineteenth century

---

[13]   David Montgomery, *Beyond Equality: Labor and the Radical Republicans, 1862–1872* (New York: Knopf, 1967), 230–386; idem, *The American Civil War and the Meanings of Freedom* (Oxford: Clarendon Press, 1987); Eric Foner, *Reconstruction: America's Unfinished Revolution, 1863–1877* (New York: Harper and Row, 1988), 1–175.

[14]   Paul Kleppner, *The Third Electoral System, 1853–1892: Parties, Voters, and Political Cultures* (Chapel Hill: University of North Carolina Press, 1979). I am not interested in disputing the precise endpoints of the third party system. For a very reasonable synthesis, see Jerome M. Clubb, William H. Flanigan, and Nancy H. Zingale, *Partisan Realignment: Voters, Parties, and Government in American History* (Beverly Hills: Sage Publications, 1980), Chapter 1.

and that these two parties maintained core voters in national elections for Congress and presidents. There is no justification to assert, however, as Amy Bridges does, that "to be an independent voter in the nineteenth century was unthinkable, considered as absurd as the idea of a third sex."[15] If Bridges were right, it would be impossible to account for the myriad independent parties that gained voter support throughout the nineteenth century. In local elections, parties with neutral-sounding names like "Taxpayers'" or "Citizens" or "People's" or "Law and Order" were common and persistent in every major city from Boston and New York to Chicago and San Francisco. Even on the national level, where Democrats and Republicans had the greatest advantages, the millions of votes cast for the Greenback, Prohibition, and People's parties came from something more routine than a "third sex." Antipartyism, as Richard L. McCormick demonstrates, was a persistent theme accompanying the supposed golden age of party politics.[16] Independent parties held the mayoralty for half of the years between 1850 and 1900 in San Francisco. In New York City, despite the vaunted powers of Tammany, "reform" candidates won seven of the nine mayoral elections held from 1870 through 1886. As David Hammack observes, "When Tammany did not join in a fusion campaign [with reform parties] during those years, its candidates were usually defeated."[17] Bessie Louise Pierce observes that in Chicago "the formation of successful independent parties, particularly in the 'seventies, began first and went farthest in the realm of municipal politics."[18]

As we saw in the last chapter, during and immediately after the Civil War political leaders in California changed party membership at a bewildering pace. Former antislavery Democrats like Henry Huntley Haight and Andrew Jackson Bryant became Republicans or Unionists during the war, then switched back to the Democrats,

---

[15] Amy Bridges, "Becoming American: The Working Classes in the United States before the Civil War," in *Working-Class Formation: Nineteenth-Century Patterns in Western Europe and the United States*, ed. Ira Katznelson and Aristide Zolberg (Princeton, N.J.: Princeton University Press, 1986), 193.

[16] Richard L. McCormick, *The Party Period and Public Policy: American Politics from the Age of Jackson to the Progressive Era* (New York: Oxford University Press, 1986), 228–59.

[17] "Even when Tammany candidates did begin to win with some regularity after 1886," Hammack writes, "they generally attracted less than 45 percent of the vote." David Hammack, *Power and Society: Greater New York at the Turn of the Century* (New York: Columbia University Press, 1982), 119–20.

[18] Bessie Louise Pierce, *History of Chicago*, vol. 3 (New York: Knopf, 1957), 344.

citing disagreement with Radicalism or the course of Reconstruction.[19] As organizers built and rebuilt parties, they dragged along the memory of David C. Broderick, former standard-bearer for the antislavery or Free-Soil Democrats in California.[20] Bryant, Democratic mayor of San Francisco from 1875 to 1879, founded the Broderick Republican Club in 1871. As Republicans like Haight and Bryant became Democrats again, however, and as the Democrats sought to rebuild their reputation as the defenders of the citizen-producers of the Republic, they increasingly emphasized Broderick's working-class identity. At the head of a parade for the eight-hour day on 3 June 1867, stonecutters carried a bust of Broderick and a sign that read, "Broderick was one of us."[21]

If party leaders frequently switched their organizational membership and redefined their symbols, we can expect the voters to have been as willing to switch their allegiances as well. San Francisco delivered mainly Democratic majorities before the war, Republican and Union majorities during the war, and then alternated between Democratic and Republican majorities after the war. Reflecting national patterns, competition between the Democrats and Republicans in San Francisco during the 1870s was fierce and closely balanced.[22] To the chagrin of major party leaders, however, voters assiduously split their tickets, and minor parties annually entered the field. In the mayoral election of 1873 seven organizations advanced a slate of credible candidates for city office: "Citizen's Independent," "Democratic," "Liberal Reform," "Citizen's Union," "People's Union," "Republican," "Taxpayer's and People's."[23] Neither Democratic party leaders nor their Republican counterparts could take their constituencies for granted. Instead, they had constantly to compete for the favor of an independent, skeptical, and critical community of voters.

The intensity of political competition was augmented by the rapid

19   Theodore H. Hittell, *History of California*, 4 vols. (San Francisco, 1885–97), 4:408; "Interview with un-named person re Haight," [n.d.], MS in Bancroft Library, Berkeley, California; Andrew Jackson Bryant, "Dictation for H. H. Bancroft," MS in Bancroft Library, Berkeley.

20   *Congressional Globe*, 35th Congress, 1st Session, Appendix, 191–3.

21   Saxton, *Indispensable Enemy*, 69.

22   Clubb et al., *Partisan Realignment* 47–118; Kleppner, *Third Party System*.

23   Winfield J. Davis, *History of Political Conventions in California, 1849–1893* (Sacramento: California State Library, 1893), 324.

increase in the size of the urban electorate, which kept the party leaders scrambling to build or maintain majorities. During the single term of Governor Henry Haight, from 1867 to 1871, the size of San Francisco's voting electorate increased by almost 50 percent, from 17,314 to 24,995 voters.[24] Two population surges, one following the completion of the transcontinental railroad in 1869 and the other following the economic downturn of 1873 in the East, caused the city's population to grow at a rapid rate through the end of the decade, increasing by 63 percent from 1870 to 1880. This meant a jump of 84,000 people and an increase of 10,000 new registered voters.[25]

As party leaders scrambled for the favor of this dynamic urban electorate, they sought, of course, to develop politically profitable appeals. Before turning to a look at those appeals, it is essential to describe kinds of voters the political leaders sought to mobilize. In particular, one must recognize the crucial position held by skilled workers in the late-nineteenth-century city. Comprising 35 percent of the registered electorate in 1867, skilled workers were also, as we saw in the previous chapter, 1.3 times more likely to register to vote than any other occupational group. Occupationally skilled and residentially stable, skilled workers held a respected and feared position in the electorate through the Progressive Era, when the Building Trades Council led the successful drive for a closed-shop city. Although it is easy enough to identify the proportions of the five principal occupational groups (high- and low-white-collar, skilled, semiskilled, and unskilled) in the city's electorate, it is much more difficult to determine the size or the membership of the "working class." If, in 1867, we count the skilled workers (35%) with the semiskilled (15%) and unskilled workers (6%) in the registered electorate as "working class," then the working-class voters totaled 56 percent of the San Francisco electorate. If, on the other hand, they identified with the clerks, salespeople, and petty proprietors (30%) and/or the

---

[24] San Francisco *Examiner*, 14 September 1867, 22 September 1871.

[25] Already by 1873 the San Francisco *Chronicle* reported a shortage of dwellings relative to the demand and a sharp increase in rents. *Chronicle*, 2 May 1873. Population figures are from: United States Bureau of the Census, *Ninth Census*, 3 vols. (Washington, D.C., 1872), 1:91; idem, *Tenth Census*, 22 vols. (Washington, D.C., 1883–8), vol 1:671. For number of registered voters, *California Great Registers* (Sacramento, 1871–80); Henry G. Langley, *San Francisco City Directory for the Year 1880* (San Francisco, 1880), 11. The number of registered voters in San Francisco in 1880 was 43,775.

high-white-collar voters (14%), the "working-class" proportion of the electorate would be only 26 percent.[26]

Indeed, much of the public discourse of the 1870s involved an effort to define, or construct, the class identities of the city's citizens. As recent work by Mary Ryan, Karen Haltunnen, Martin J. Burke, and Stuart M. Blumin has shown, the "middle class," no less than the working class, was in the process of formation throughout the nineteenth century, a process not yet complete at the onset of the Great Upheaval.[27] Before asking how the "working class" was politicized, then, we need to ask how any group of citizens gained the identity of working class in the public sphere. The new labor historical literature agrees on the emergence of a class-conscious, working-class identity in the urban United States by the last decades of the nineteenth century, composed primarily of wage-earning blue-collar workers. Following this rough consensus, I shall hypothetically define the skilled workers in the registered electorate as part of the "working class," along with the semiskilled factory operatives and longshoremen, and the unskilled day laborers. Whether the skilled workers, an occupational group on the border of the blue- and white-collar classes, identified with the working class or not will be indicated through statistical observation of this hypothetical grouping. Using statistical analyses of voting behavior, then, it is possible to estimate the point in time at which the working class, defined by the Marxian criterion of one's relation to the means of production, began to vote as a bloc.

A narrative jaunt through the campaigns of San Francisco during the 1870s reveals nothing more clearly than that "mainstream" party politicians and journalists – dismissed a priori as "middle

---

[26]   Sources: Random samples drawn from the manuscript schedule of the 1870 U.S. Census for San Francisco, N = 314; and the 1867 California Great Register for San Francisco (Sacramento, 1867), N = 325; The method of analysis was to use a Chi-square test of the difference in proportions of occupational groups between the registered voter sample and the 1870 census manuscript sample. From this statistic the likelihood ratio is calculated. For occupational categories, see Stephan Thernstrom, *The Other Bostonians: Poverty and Progress in the American Metropolis, 1880–1970* (Cambridge: Harvard University Press, 1973), "Appendix B: On the Socioeconomic Ranking of Occupations," 289–302.

[27]   Mary P. Ryan, *Cradle of the Middle Class: The Family in Oneida County, New York, 1790–1865* (New York: Cambridge University Press, 1981); Karen Haltunnen, *Confidence Men and Painted Women: A Study of Middle-Class Culture in America, 1830–1870* (New Haven: Yale University Press, 1982); Martin J. Burke, "The Conundrum of Class: Public Discourse on the Social Order in America" (Ph.D. diss., University of Michigan, 1987); Stuart M. Blumin, *The Emergence of the Middle Class: Social Experience in the American City, 1760–1900* (New York: Cambridge University Press, 1989).

class" or "bourgeois" by much recent scholarship – unabashedly turned to an escalating language of class in their desperate efforts for office and for circulations. As they mobilized the voters and increased their readerships with a language of class, the mainstream party politicos and journalists also managed, as we shall see, to create a working-class voting bloc prior to the Great Upheaval.

The Democratic party of San Francisco, starved for office by years in the political wilderness, staged a comeback during the "Great Reaction" of 1867, by joining Democrats throughout the North in the formulation of a racial and class-based critique of the wartime and Reconstruction policies of the Republican party.[28] By doing so, the Democrats set a new agenda for the distressing 1870s. This critique was cast within the still-valuable republican discourse, so that in the Democratic explanation of events, the Republican party and the railroad corporations were headed down the well-worn path to tyranny with the imposition of the Fourteenth Amendment, the corrupt acquisition of railroad subsidies, and the employment of Chinese labor. The Fourteenth Amendment was allegedly part of a plan by the California Republican party chieftains and the Central Pacific Railroad executives Leland Stanford and Charles Crocker to enfranchise their dependent Chinese employees (cast as slaves) to further the oppression of the white workingman. Within this republican shell, however, a mounting drumbeat of interest groups and classes could be heard. "Capital, in a mere encounter of endurance," the Democratic San Francisco *Examiner* warned, "has ever proved too powerful for labor."[29] The need for legislative defense of the "labor" interest was urgent, lest the "capital" interest do irreparable harm to republican institutions.

This message was enormously popular among the wage-earning working class. At the "Democratic Mass Ratification Meeting" in July 1867, the daily *Alta California* reported that the Union Hall was "packed with a vast assemblage of persons, principally mechanics and workingmen." The Chair of this meeting asked the crowd rhetorically: "What means equality before the law ... ? It is that black men and Chinese are to have seats in the Legislature, sit on juries, testify in the Courts – in a word, to be levelled up to equality with the Anglo-Saxon race."[30] Henry Haight, the Democratic candidate

28   Foner, *Reconstruction*, 307–16.
29   *Examiner*, 6 August 1867.
30   San Francisco *Alta California*, 10 July 1867.

for governor, then stepped to the lectern and explained what the Republican tyrants had in mind: "The Central Pacific Railroad with ten thousand Chinese laborers, could out-vote the entire voting population of the mining counties, through which the railroad passes. Gangs of Chinese would be imported for their voting as well as their working qualities."[31] Their opposition to the Fourteenth Amendment, Chinese labor, and continued railroad subsidies and support of the eight-hour law gave the Democrats the governorship of the state and the mayoralty of San Francisco in 1867.[32]

It was in this environment that Henry George began his remarkable career as an American labor and reform leader. Climaxing in his nearly successful bid for mayor of New York City in 1886, George's career helps to illustrate the sources of the Great Upheaval in the activities of the mainstream parties and mainstream press. Migrating to California on the eve of the Civil War, George cast his first ballot there for Abraham Lincoln. An apprentice typesetter, George ascended through the journalistic ranks in a way that was not uncommon as late as the 1860s and 1870s. He achieved the transition from compositor to editorial writer and then editor by writing timely essays for San Francisco's leading dailies in the aftermath of the Civil War. George's rapid success as a political journalist illustrates how the phenomena of popular appeal, party organization, and ideological development were intertwined. After publishing in 1869 an article in Horace Greeley's *Tribune* on the danger of Chinese immigration to the interests of white workers, George gained the attention of the Democratic governor Henry Haight, which in turn led George to the editorship first of a Democratic paper in Oakland and then of the statewide party organ, the *Reporter*, in 1870. During the 1870s George was a loyal Democrat, who, as editor of the San Francisco *Post*, helped shape the party's prolabor attack on Republican party policies. He ran for a state assembly seat from San Francisco in 1871, but lost in a Republican sweep of that year.[33]

Henry George, in fact, wrote his reformist masterpiece, *Progress and Poverty* (1879), while enjoying a Democratic patronage sinecure

---

31   "Speech of H. H. Haight, Democratic Candidate for Governor, Delivered at the Great Mass Meeting at Union Hall, Tuesday Evening, July 9th, 1867," [pamphlet], Bancroft Library, Berkeley.
32   *Examiner*, 14 September 1867; Saxton, *Indispensable Enemy*, 67–91.
33   San Francisco *Call*, 30 August 1871; *Examiner* 21 September 1871.

as a gas inspector in San Francisco.[34] Granted by Governor William S. Irwin in gratitude for the editorial support George had supplied, the gas inspectorship was frankly acknowledged as a sort of writing fellowship, "more than anything else a tribute to intellect," according to the governor's private secretary.[35]

Once the Democrats developed a marketable ideology, however, they had no power to corner the market on that formula. The Republicans, after their defeat of 1867, rushed to recover their support among the crucial skilled, semiskilled, and unskilled workers of the city and the state. The Republicans' bid for recovery was aided by the failure of the Democratic governor Haight to maintain in office the image of race and class crusader that he had projected during his victorious campaign of 1867. Haight and his party won valuable racial capital with a ringing rejection of the Fifteenth Amendment, but lost it again when Haight extended to visiting Chinese diplomats the common courtesy of an official banquet.[36] The Republican banners in the campaign of 1871 attest to Haight's tarnished racial image: "Brother Haight will preach at the Chinese Mission in Canton in 1872"; "God Speed Haight and Brother Chinamen"; "Ah Sin – elder Brother of H. H. Haight"; "I say Governor, how did you like that Chow-Chow at the Occidental?"[37]

The dissatisfaction of voters on the Chinese issue went beyond that about the symbolic act of a governor dining with Chinese diplomats, however. From 1870 to 1876 the San Francisco Board of Supervisors passed a series of harassment ordinances directed against the Chinese. The first of these was the "Cubic Air" law of 1870, which required a minimum of 500 cubic feet of air space for every resident of a building (directed against the crowded Chinese tenements), and another ordinance in that year forbade walking on sidewalks while carrying poles (the traditional Chinese method of carrying loads). The Board of Supervisors passed the nation's first zoning ordinance in 1873, with a ban on laundries in certain sec-

---

34　George's early career as a political journalist is compellingly explained in Saxton, pp. 92–101; John P. Young, *History of Journalism in California* (San Francisco, 1915), 78–9, 102.

35　Charles Albro Barker, *Henry George* (New York: Oxford University Press, 1955); Henry George, Jr., *The Life of Henry George* [1900] (New York: Robert Schalkenbach Foundation, 1960), 232, 269–300.

36　"Speech of Hon. John S. Hager, of San Francisco, In the Senate of California, January 28,1870, on Senator Hager's Joint Resolution to Reject the Fifteenth Amendment to the Constitution of the United States." [pamphlet], Bancroft Library, Berkeley.

37　*Alta*, 5 September 1871.

tions of the city. This was struck down in the courts but passed again in 1876, when it was again struck down.[38] All parties who attempted to resolve the Chinese issue knew (or rapidly discovered) that stopping the flow of Chinese immigration and curtailing Chinese employment were goals that could be accomplished only at the state and national levels of legislation. Even knowing that failure was inherent in anti-Chinese measures within a local jurisdiction, the mainstream parties returned to the issue like an addictive drug, steadily exacerbating their image as bungling, deceptive, or corrupt politicians and hastening their own defeat at the polls.

Snatching the oppositional initiative from the Democrats, the Republican platform of 1871 denounced the employment of Chinese as "offensive to the exalted American idea of the dignity of labor, detrimental to the prosperity and happiness of our laboring classes, and an evil that ought to be abated."[39] Making promises on the Chinese issue was of course aimed at harvesting low-blue-collar voters. Accordingly, the Republicans, who had once feared the low-blue-collar immigrant voters enough to pass the sweeping voter registration law of 1866, now extended a "cordial welcome" to the white immigrant worker-voters just then pouring into the city.[40] The San Francisco Republicans openly courted the naturalized voters with slogans like "Garibaldi is a Republican."[41]

The Democrats also stumbled in their appeal to the skilled workers at the outset of the turbulent 1870s. Haight's gains from advocacy of the eight-hour law were politically nullified when it came to light that the contractors in charge of constructing the new State Capitol had – right under Haight's nose – been skimming profits from the wages of the building tradesmen hired to do the work. "If he does not protect the workingman now," one constituent asked, "will he in the future?"[42] At the mass Republican procession

[38]   Sucheng Chan, *Asian Americans: An Interpretive History* (Boston: Twayne Publishers, 1991), 45–102; Linda C. A. Przybyszewski, "Judge Lorenzo Sawyer and the Chinese: Civil Rights Decisions in the Ninth Circuit," *Western Legal History* 1:1 (Winter/Spring 1988): 23–56; Saxton, *Indispensable Enemy*, 67–112.

[39]   Davis, *History of Political Conventions in California*, 308.

[40]   The debates on the Registry Act are reported in the Sacramento *Union*, 24 February 1866; Davis, *Political Conventions in California*, 308.

[41]   *Alta*. 5 September 1871.

[42]   *Alta*, 4 September 1871.

through San Francisco two days before the election, the Iron Workers Union marched in line with the Republican faithful, carrying a transparency[43] showing Haight as a convict for his alleged collusion in defrauding the State Capitol workers. Other Republicans carried a banner that read: "Labor must be protected against combined capital."[44] Democratic party activists with trade union ties now broke with Haight, calling this austere Jacksonian Democrat a representative of the "kid-glove Democracy."[45]

Soon after, the Republicans returned to power at the state and city levels in 1871 (thus depriving Henry George in his bid for a state assembly seat). However, it was their turn to suffer at the hands of the class-and-race critique. The unfolding of several scandals during the period 1874–77 conveniently reinforced the Democratic thesis that Republican politicians were corrupt oppressors of the white workingman. In 1874 the Republican license collector, coroner, public administrator, and assessor were found to have committed frauds.[46] Newton Booth, the governor whom the cynical Republicans had nominated on an antirailroad platform, was curiously silent once in office on the issue of railroad regulation. Charges of his collusion with the Central Pacific Railroad were later confirmed in the notorious "Colton Letters."[47]

On 26 August 1875 the Bank of California, unable to meet its obligations, closed its doors. The failure of the leading financial institution west of the Mississippi was entangled with the disgrace of its flamboyant president, William C. Ralston, who had spent the bank's millions on extravagant projects as if the depositors' money were his own and then tried to save the bank by attempting to sell the Spring Valley Water Company, the city's supplier of water, to

---

[43] A transparency was a back-lit banner, widely used in the nighttime parades of the nineteenth century.

[44] *Alta*, 5 September 1871.

[45] *Chronicle*, 19 July 1871; Davis, *Political Conventions in California*, 295–7.

[46] John S. Hittell, *A History of the City of San Francisco and Incidentally of the State of California* (San Francisco: A. L. Bancroft and Co., 1878), 399.

[47] When the Central Pacific Railroad's political lobbyist David D. Colton died in 1878 and the Big Four tried to cheat his widow of a fair share of his fortune, Ellen M. Colton retaliated by making her husband's letters public. These, the "Colton Letters," showed, among other things, that the antirailroad crusader Newton Booth had actually been on the railroad's payroll, and one of its warmest friends. See Walton Bean and James J. Rawls, *California: An Interpretive History* (New York: McGraw-Hill Book Co., 1988), 216 18, 224.

B 1802 Birdseye View of San Francisco, towards Palace Hotel and Nob Hill. *Tabor* Photo. San Francisco.

San Francisco for a five-million-dollar profit.[48] The plan so outraged even the city's wealthy conservatives that the *Bulletin*, usually
friendly to the big investors, denounced Ralston's scheme and the
politicians who had participated in it.[49] The bank's Board of Directors, suddenly aware of Ralston's profligacy, removed him from his
position as president. Hours later he was found dead in the San
Francisco Bay, an apparent suicide.[50] The local economy finally
joined the eastern economic collapse two years late as the failure of
the Bank of California precipitated the city into a terrible economic
decline.

Ralston's sudden demise symbolized the precarious state of class
relations in San Francisco. Like the capitalists in the 1920s, Ralston
and the Central Pacific Railroad magnates who built their mansions
on Nob Hill during the 1870s at least enjoyed the relatively secure
reputation of having led the economy to great prosperity. Ralston
had financed the construction of the lavish, eight-story Palace Hotel
at the corner of Market and New Montgomery, towering literally
and figuratively between the upper-class mansions of Nob Hill and
the working- and middle-class homes of the sprawling South-of-
Market neighborhood. (See Plate 6.1.) After the collapse of the

[48]   Issel and Cherny, *San Francisco*, 124–5.
[49]   John S. Hittell, *History of San Francisco*, 405; Issel and Cherny, *San Francisco*, 124–5.
[50]   The coroner's jury ruled the death an accidental drowning. Ralston regularly swam in the
         bay, and may have been swept out by a rip tide. Many believed at the time, however, that
         Ralston took his own life. T. H. Hittell, *History of California*, 4:555.

Plate 6.1. San Francisco seen from the South-of-Market neighborhood, looking
north toward Nob Hill. The huge white structure in the upper left is the Palace
Hotel, financed by Bank of California president William C. Ralston, who fancied
himself the Lorenzo de Medici of San Francisco. In the upper right, the gothic
mansion of railroad magnate Mark Hopkins is plainly visible. The sunny South of
Market was the home of thousands of working-class families whose identities and
allegiances were not predictable. Many lived in homes they owned, or they rented
comfortable flats. Until the mid-1870s, many may have gazed upward to the mansion of the millionaire Mark Hopkins with admiration. After the collapse of the
Bank of California and Ralston's disgrace, however, the language of class created
in the campaigns from 1867–75 could more easily persuade members of the middling social strata that they were members of a working class. Many more would
now see Hopkins's residence as the dark castle of an oppressive Railroad Baron.
Carrying torches like furious villagers, many would follow Denis Kearney to the
top of Nob Hill, cheering his denunciations of "miserable felonious bank-
smashers." Courtesy of Bancroft Library.

Bank of California and Ralston's disgrace, however, the language of class created in the campaigns from 1867 to 1875 could more easily persuade the middling members of the working class, those who owned their homes or rented comfortable flats for their families in the sunny South-of-Market wards. Many may have gazed upward to the gothic mansion of the millionaire Mark Hopkins with admiration; many more would now see it as the dark castle of an oppressive Railroad Baron. Many would soon follow Denis Kearney to the top of Nob Hill, carrying torches like furious villagers, to cheer his denunciations of the "miserable felonious bank-smashers."

The Democrats, enjoying their traditional status since the days of the Loco Focos as the party of the workingman, were able to profit much better from the mobilization of the working class than the Republicans. Thanks in part to the efforts of prolabor, antimonopoly journalists like Henry George, the municipal elections of 1875 and 1877 brought victories for the Democrats, who twice elected Andrew Jackson Bryant to the troubled mayoralty of San Francisco.[51]

ESTIMATING CLASS MOBILIZATION

Fortunately, we can do much more than merely speculate on the impact of the changed discursive activity of the early 1870s on mass political behavior. Using reliable samples of individuals drawn from the lists of registered voters, categorizing them by class and ethnicity, and aggregating them by ward-level election districts, it is possible to estimate the sources of political mobilization from 1867 through the career of the Workingmen's Party of California. Indeed, the interpretive models presented by authors of the labor-republican and the party-structural syntheses yield hypotheses susceptible to rigorous quantitative testing. Combining the most persuasive elements of these works yields the following general model of the Great Upheaval: The major political parties normally achieved voter loyalty on the basis of ethnocultural appeals and other, durable community ties. Class consciousness was, according to the recent trends in scholarship, acquired outside of the mainstream political system. Movement cultures arising from the labor

[51]   San Francisco *Examiner*, 7 September 1875; 10 September 1877.

and agrarian conflicts of the 1870s, 1880s, and 1890s produced tidal waves of "politicization," which then broke up on the Democrats' or the Republicans' obdurate, co-optive organizational structures.[52]

According to the labor-republican and the party-structural syntheses, we would expect to find ethnicity to be superior to class as a predictor of party preference until the appearance of a "labor" party, which would temporarily tap what Oestreicher calls an underlying "reservoir" of class sentiment. After the career of this labor party, voter preference should again be explained best by variables describing the ethnicity of the voters.

Multivariate linear regression analysis of presidential, gubernatorial, and mayoral elections in San Francisco does not support the idea that major parties were the bane of class politics. Indeed, we find the opposite. Table 6.1 displays the results of tests in which the percentage of "working class" registered voters in each ward plus the percentage of Irish-born (the city's dominant ethnic group) registered voters in each ward were the two independent, or "explanatory," variables, and the percentage voting for Democratic and Workingmen's party candidates or measures was the dependent, or "outcome," variable.

The results displayed in Table 6.1 tell a very interesting story. In the elections of the late 1860s, when the Democratic party leaders were reassembling their party followers, the regression tests support the familiar picture of ethnocultural voting. The percent Irish-born in each ward was strongly and positively associated with the percent voting for Democratic candidates in each ward. The percent working class, on the other hand, did not have a significant explanatory value toward the voting in each ward. Moreover, these models are quite good. The fourth column, "Adjusted R^2," tells us how much of the variance in the Democratic vote is accounted for by the two independent, or explanatory, variables: class and Irishness. In the elections of 1867 through 1869, the models explain most of the variance in the Democratic vote.

During the years from 1871 through 1873, however, we can observe a transition underway as the party leaders and editors stepped up their competition for working-class votes by using an increasingly strident language of class. The percent Irish in each ward loses its

---

[52] See preceding discussion of literature.

Table 6.1. *Linear regression estimates of class and ethnic voting for Democratic and Workingmen's Party candidates and issues: 1867–1882*

Percent vote for	% Working class β	% Irish β	Adjusted R^2
Dem. Governor Candidate 1867	.15	.58**	.63
Dem. Mayor Candidate 1867	.25	.51*	.60
Dem. President Candidate 1868	.24	.53**	.63
Dem. Mayor Candidate 1869	.21	.68**	.61
Dem. Governor Candidate 1871	.26 (*)	.40	.59
Dem. Mayor Candidate 1871	.18	.42	.43
Dem. President Candidate 1872	.20	.45	.49
Dem. Mayor Candidate 1873	.09	.49*	.44
Dem. Mayor Candidate 1875	.61***	−.10	.76
Dem. President Candidate 1876	.54***	−.19	.84
Dem. Mayor Candidate 1877	.37***	.02	.87
Workingmen's Party Delegates to Constitutional Convention 1878	1.16***	−.42	.77
Workingmen's Party Mayor Candidate (Isaac Kalloch) 1879	.96***	−.22	.75
Dem. President Candidate 1880	.67***	−.14	.72
Dem. Mayor Candidate 1881	.48**	.37	.67
Dem. Mayor Candidate 1882	.60**	−.28	.65

Notes: All data aggregated by wards ($N = 12$). The asterisks denote the levels of significance for the beta coefficients (β) in the second and third columns. Figures without an asterisk were not significant; Those with an asterisk were significant, at the following levels: " * " = p-value of .05 or lower, " ** " = p-value of .01 or lower; " *** " = p-value .001 or lower, "(*)" denotes almost significant, with a p-value of between .05 and .1.

Sources: The values of the independent variables for Percent Working Class and Percent Irish were calculated from the registered voter samples nearest to the election date in time. Samples used were: 1867, $N = 325$; 1873, $N = 341$; and 1880, $N = 496$. Election returns collected from newspapers: San Francisco *Examiner,* 14 Sept. 1867; 13 Nov. 1868; 17 Sept. 1869; 21 Sept. 1871; 13 Nov. 1872; 19 Sept. 1873; 7 Sept. 1875; 17 Nov. 1876; 10 Sept. 1877; San Francisco *Chronicle,* 22 June 1878; 13 May 1879; San Francisco *Alta California* 6 Oct. 1879; *Examiner,* 4 Nov. 1880; *Chronicle* 9 Sept. 1881; 11 Nov. 1882.

significance as an explanatory variable during these transitional elections, and class was almost significant in the 1871 gubernatorial election. Moreover, the models become weaker as well, with less than half of the variance in the Democratic vote explained by a combination of class and ethnic variables.

Next, in the elections from 1875 through 1882, we can observe the impact of the emergent class language on the behavior of voters. In 1875, the vote for the Democratic mayoral candidate Andrew Jackson Bryant was strongly and positively associated with the percent of working-class voters in each ward, whereas the percent Irish in each ward was insignificant. This election also marks a jump in the amount of the Democratic vote explained, or accounted for, by the two explanatory variables. Indeed, the most striking results of this table are conveyed in figures for the 1875, 1876, and 1877 elections. Class remained a strong predictor of the Democratic vote in each of these elections, and the percentage of the vote accounted for by the model increased to an extraordinary 87 percent in the mayoral election of 1877, which was held in September, one month *prior* to the organization of the Workingmen's Party of California.

Once the Workingmen's party appeared on the scene, its leaders continued the pattern begun by the Democrats, mobilizing the working class to vote even more tightly for a single party, with a one-to-one correspondence between the percent working class in each ward and the percent voting for the Workingmen's party delegates to the constitutional convention in the spring of 1878. The Workingmen's party mayoral candidate, Isaac Kalloch, achieved a similarly tight mobilization of the working class in 1879. But note also that the class and ethnic variables explain a decreasing amount of the vote for the Workingmen's candidates and the new constitution, compared to the amount of the Democratic vote of 1877 explained by those variables. In other words, there were two "peaks" of working-class mobilization in the 1870s, depending upon which yardstick we use. The first was achieved by the Democratic party and its journalistic supporters, in the election of 1877. Class and ethnicity alone, without considering intangible variables not included in these models, explained nearly nine-tenths of the Democratic vote, and only class was significant. Class as a variable increased in explanatory power in the elections of 1878 and 1879, but the amount of unexplained variance increased as well.

The last phase of electoral evolution is displayed in the results for the elections of 1880, 1881, and 1882. After the collapse of the Workingmen's party in 1880, the Democrats hung on to the mobilized working-class voting bloc, but both the strength of association between the working-class variable and the overall variance explained decreased steadily from the peaks reached between 1875 and 1879.[53]

To summarize these results most succinctly, the Democratic party managed to mobilize the San Francisco working-class voters as a bloc years before the appearance of the Workingmen's Party of Califorrnia. Indeed, we can even confirm from this table an observation made by James Bryce and other contemporaries: the Workingmen's party was actually a pirated version of the Democratic party. The Workingmen's Party, under the leadership of Denis Kearney and Isaac Kalloch, merely picked up a constituency that the Democrats had already mobilized along class lines. These findings seriously call into question the assumption made by recent studies of the Great Upheaval labor parties, that the political insurgents mobilized class constituencies against mainstream parties that had neglected, avoided, or patched over class issues. It appears that the ballot box was not at all, as Alan Dawley claims, the "coffin of class consciousness."[54] It may in fact have been the cradle.

The Democratic party had reached a troubling pinnacle of success in the fall of 1877. Having mobilized the working class with strident appeals to class and race hostility, it could no longer control that hostility. A prescient writer for the San Francisco *Chronicle* summarized Andrew Jackson Bryant's predicament as follows:

Mayor Bryant ... spends his evenings in indicting virulent harangues projected against the water monopoly and the Chinese hoards, and during the nights is troubled with an oppressive nightmare, in which he represents himself as struggling desperately with a gigantic Spring Valley bug and a Mongolian behemoth.[55]

The electorate had been mobilized and the working class politicized, but the mayor's office could do no more about the Chinese

---

[53] For explanations of multiple linear regression, see K. H. Jarausch and K. A. Hardy, *Quantitative Methods for Historians: A Guide to Research, Data, and Statistics* (Chapel Hill: University of North Carolina Press, 1991); M. S. Lewis-Beck, *Applied Regression: An Introduction* (Beverly Hills, Calif.: Sage Publications, 1980).

[54] Alan Dawley, *Class and Community: The Industrial Revolution in Lynn* (Cambridge: Harvard University Press, 1976), 70.

[55] *Chronicle*, 2 September 1877.

issue than the Board of Supervisors had accomplished years earlier. Collective violence against the Chinese had already broken out in the "July Days" riots that left at least one Chinese dead and tens of thousands of dollars lost in property damage.[56]

When Denis Kearney appeared as a soapbox orator in the aftermath of the riots, the San Francisco *Chronicle*, owned and edited by the combative Radical Republicans Charles and Michael de Young, became Kearney's most important mainstream sponsor. The de Young brothers, as we saw in Chapter 5, were expert market analysts who had gladly entered the competition for working-class favor during the 1870s by appealing to class sentiments. Without this mainstream sponsorship, neither Kearney nor the WPC might ever have found a following. Whether or not the de Youngs or other "bourgeois" managers of public sphere communications were cynical opportunists is immaterial from a phenomenological standpoint. Kearney's project and their own, profitable editorial war against "capitalists" like William C. Ralston overlapped. In an editorial of February 1878 entitled "The Cause of the Crisis," the de Youngs voiced what, to judge by the voting patterns, had become the majority view among the members of the political community: "That capital is the aggressor in the impending conflict there is no shadow of a doubt."[57]

A LANGUAGE OF POLITICS

There was nothing unusual about the tiny organization calling itself the "Workingmen's Trade and Labor Union," formed in the last few weeks before the September 1877 elections by an obscure Irish-born drayman named Denis Kearney and a trade unionist named John Day.[58] Contemporaries assumed it was just one of the many fraudulent "piece clubs" set up to extort campaign contributions from the leading candidates by claiming to control large blocs of voters, with phony catch-all names like the "Independent Democratic Liberal Republican Anti-Coolie Labor party."[59] Kearney

---

[56] Kazin, "Prelude to Kearneyism," 20–26; Kauer, "The Workingmen's Party of California," 279.
[57] *Chronicle*, 10 February 1878.
[58] Cross, *Labor Movement*, 94–5.
[59] The origin of the term "piece club" is entirely obscure, but some authors have, in confusion, altered it to read "price club," a term much more appropriate in meaning but none-

and his fellow organizers, then, faced the same competitive environment as any other aspirants for political power. Their challenge was
to set themselves off from the politicians already controlling the
field. They arrived on the scene to find a constituency already mobilized by a politics turning on the keywords "capital" and "labor" –
which is to say, by a language of class.

The success of Kearney's club rested on the temporary popularity
of its latest formulation of labor republicanism. Because the incumbent leaders of the two major parties had promised the working people more than they could deliver, the leaders of the Workingmen's
Party of California easily dusted off the arsenal of republican oppositional discourse: blaming the distress of the long depression not on
economic factors, but on the fallen virtue of political leaders, ostensibly corrupted by, or dependent upon, the aristocratic corporate
capitalists. This formula tapped many resonant chords, among
them the revolutionary heritage and Christianity. But, although the
WPC enjoyed temporary, spectacular success, its leaders could ride
the working-class tiger only until the dysfunctionality of republicanism as a language of class undermined their drive for power.

The WPC's republican formulation is best observed in a four-
sided canvas tableau constructed by the Kearney group, mounted
atop a wagon that they parked on the street to advertise their meetings:

On each side of the canvas was painted a conspicuous sketch, consisting of
three life-size figures. In the center of the group stands a workingman. The
words "Our turn to rule," precedes him from his mouth. On his left is a
sinister-looking Democrat, and on his right an urbane Republican. Both
of these politicians grasp him lovingly by the elbows. "The man I have
duped" extends in large letters from the Democrat's mouth. The Republican exclaims, "The man I have crushed!"[60]

This tableau should look familiar to the reader of recent social and
labor histories. Kearney and his associates built their movement by
constructing the very melodrama that later historians were to adopt

theless incorrect. The example is quoted in Issel and Cherny, *San Francisco*, 119. The
practice had grown so burdensome that the legislature of 1878 passed "An Act to
Prohibit 'Piece Clubs,' and to Prevent Extortion from Candidates for Office." Louis
Kaplan, *Extracts from the United States Statutes, the Constitution of the State of California, and the
Political and Penal Codes, Relating to the Elective Franchise, Registration of Citizens, and Elections*
(San Francisco: Board of Election Commissioners, 1878), 62. (See Chapter 5.)

60   *Chronicle*, 2 September 1877.

as the explanatory model for the origins, course, and destruction of those movements.

One of the many ironies buried in the contribution of the WPC to national political culture is that it began its career by suppressing San Francisco's socialistic Workingmen's Party of the United States (WPUS). Following the September 1877 elections, Kearney began his weekly orations in vacant "sandlots" where the new City Hall was under construction, competing for the favor of an audience that had been assembled by the socialists. Thomas H. Bates of the WPUS had long held meetings on the sandlots to educate the masses about class conflict and capitalist exploitation. Kearney's explanation of the economic crisis was not at all economic, however, but racial and political. Kearney cast Bates as a race traitor and directed his twelve hundred listeners one Sunday to silence the socialists: "You will have to mob these white Sioux and white pigtail men first. You will have to shoot them down in the streets, before you begin on the Chinese." The crowd obeyed, in part at least, by destroying the wooden WPUS platform and chasing the socialists off the sandlots.[61] Later, the WPC included in its platform a declaration that "We utterly repudiate all spirit of communism or aggrarianism [*sic*]."[62]

Having smashed the only organization with a Marxian class analysis of society, Kearney and his associates then appropriated its name, replacing "of the United States" so that it became the "Workingmen's Party of California." This new organization made its first official appearance at Dashaway Hall in San Francisco on 5 October 1877. Denis Kearney and his lieutenants, John G. Day, Henry L. Knight, and William Wellock, had prepared a menacing manifesto that was adopted by the one-hundred-fifty-member meeting as the party's first platform. "The Republic must and shall be preserved," declared the platform, "and only workingmen will do it." Proposing to "unite all poor and working men and their friends into one political party," the platform planned "to wrest government from the hands of the rich" and to "place it in those of the people, where it properly belongs." Because "the rich have ruled us until they have ruined us," the new party must "destroy the great money power of the rich by a system of taxation that will

---

61 Quoted in Davis, *Political Conventions in California*, 367.
62 WPC platform adopted 3 June 1879. Davis, *Political Conventions in California*, 396.

make great wealth impossible in the future." The WPC platform promised also "to rid the country of cheap Chinese labor as soon as possible ... because it tends still more to degrade labor and aggrandize capital."[63] These were the two central themes of the party: first, to end political manipulation "by thieves, peculators, land grabbers, bloated bondholders, railroad magnates, and shoddy aristocrats – a golden lobby dictating [legislative] proceedings," and second, to use the purified political process "to vote the moon-eyed nuisance [Chinese] out of the country."[64]

"This is Communism," the Sacramento *Record-Union* concluded after this first appearance of the WPC.[65] In fact, of course, it was republicanism. Or rather, to be more accurate, it was a lopsided blend of the three vocabularies of republicanism, class, and race used by the mainstream politicians during the 1870s. It stood out from the mainstream discourse in several ways. First, it was obsessively focused on defining the figure of the "workingman" as the citizen-savior of the Republic. Second, it followed the republican script of tyrannical corruption versus virtuous, innocent citizenship down the same political dead-end road on which the Knights of Labor were later to travel. Both the WPC and the Knights adhered to a political vision claiming that the source of social and economic distress was the corrupt misrule by an evil cabal of capitalists and politicians.[66]

After its first meeting in October 1877, the movement grew rapidly, gained regular press coverage, and provoked repressive actions by the city police. Kearney's legitimacy, however, reached a dizzying height when he was released from jail in time to play grand marshal in the citywide Thanksgiving Day parade. Sitting enthroned on his own drayman's cart, Kearney led some ten thousand San Franciscans up Market Street in an impressive show of support for the WPC message.[67] (See Plate 6.2.)

In January 1878 Kearney's reputation prompted the Democrats and Republicans in the state legislature in Sacramento to send a "Joint Committee on Labor Investigation" down the river to San

---

[63] *Chronicle*, 6 October 1877. This platform is reprinted in Davis, *Political Conventions in California*, 366–7.
[64] *Chronicle*, 16 October 1877.
[65] Sacramento *Record-Union*, 8 October 1877.
[66] Fink, "The Uses of Political Power."
[67] Saxton, *Indispensable Enemy*, 119.

Plate 6.2. Thanksgiving Day Parade, 1877, led by Denis Kearney and the officers of the Workingmen's Party of California (WPC). After its first meeting in October 1877, the WPC grew rapidly, gained regular press coverage, and provoked repressive actions by the city police. In spite of his incendiary, violent language, Kearney's credibility as a republican tribune of the people was for a time greater than that of the frightened Democratic or Republican party leadership. His public authority reached a dizzying height when he was released from jail in time to play Grand Marshal in the citywide Thanksgiving Day parade. Sitting enthroned on his own drayman's cart, Kearney led some ten thousand San Franciscans up Market Street in an impressive show of support for the WPC message. This lithograph was published in E. Benjamin Andrews, *The History of the Last Quarter-Century in the United States, 1870–1895*, vol 2. (New York: Scribner's Sons, 1896), 374. Andrews's caption reads: "Denis Kearney being drawn through the streets of San Francisco after his release from the house of correction. The procession passing the Lotta Fountain in Market Street. Painted by Howard Pyle from photographs by Taber and a description by Kearney himself." Courtesy Harvard College Library.

Francisco in order to assess the danger posed to public order by the Kearney movement. The Joint Committee, it turns out, was ultimately just another opportunity for the Democratic majority to demonstrate that they were the workingmen's friends. The questions were friendly and the legislators even arranged to hold a special sandlot meeting – with the Joint Committee calmly flanking Kearney on the platform as he gave one of his notorious, incendiary speeches! The majority (Democratic) report was sympathetic to the WPC, criticized attempts to link it to the July 1877 riots, and was critical of the harassment of the WPC by the San Francisco police. The Joint Committee's hearings, like those of the U.S. Senate's "Committee Upon the Relations Between Labor and Capital" held in 1883, provide a rare opportunity to observe direct, public dialogue between participants engaged in the construction of social conflict and social identities. This stage in the WPC movement also generated a flurry of texts, from hearing testimonies to transcribed public speeches to pamphlets, all of which we can examine to see how the WPC attempted to mobilize the electorate with their version of labor republicanism and with the "workingman" identity that fit into their essentially political diagnostic schema.[68] Throughout the WPC movement, it is also striking how conscious the participants were about language. Witnesses were often asked to define terms like "workingman" and even, as we shall see, to explore the relationship between language and action.

"Virtue" was the central and superior term used in the construction of the WPC's workingman. A workingman was an honest man. He was not simply a man who worked with his hands (but forms of manual labor were most easily recognized as honest). Thus one Mr. Clark "said the term workingmen means all who earn their bread by the sweat of their brows, and that all such are eligible for membership."[69] The biblical passage, of course, suggests the ethical component of the WPC program. Another strong component was the revolutionary language of aristocracy, citizenry, and slavery (always the Chinese). The unnamed authors of a pamphlet entitled *The Labor Agitators; Or the Battle for Bread: The Party of the Future: The Work-*

---

[68]   The Joint Committee held public hearings on 2, 3, 4, and 16 February 1878. These were reported in detail by the San Francisco *Chronicle*, 3, 4, 5, and 17 February 1878. The committee published majority and minority reports in the *Appendix to the Journals of the Senate and Assembly*, 22d Session, 1877–8 (Sacramento, 1878), vol. 4.

[69]   *Chronicle*, 4 January 1878.

ingmen's Party of California explained that "the workingmen of California are not stupid peasants. They are scholars, skilled artisans, soldiers, and know how to live and how to die.... They see their situation between the Aristocrat and the Chinaman, and they will scatter both like chaff before the wind." This pamphlet portrayed the workingmen as "an honest middle class who love their country and each other better than all the shoddy aristocrats on earth; and safer for the great Republic."[70] Universal membership, reflecting the republican tendency to strive toward the Rousseauean "General Will," was another theme. William Wellock, one of Kearney's chief lieutenants, explained to the Second Ward Club of the WPC that "the party was intended to embrace all classes of people without any distinction of class or political party."[71]

Denis Kearney thought that only 20 percent of society did not qualify as workingmen: "What the workingmen – and eight-tenths of the community are workingmen – want for their guide is common honesty and common sense."[72] He assured this same audience that "the reporters of the newspapers are workingmen, like ourselves – working for bread and butter. But for the villainous serpents, the shiny imps of hell that own these newspapers I have the utmost contempt." Why were the newspaper proprietors "shiny imps of hell"? Not, it seems, because they owned rather than worked, but because they could be bought by the "first thief that comes along with his purse of gold stolen from the masses." "I have known," Kearney explained, "some of the dirtiest drunkenest men that God Almighty ever put breath into write articles for the newspapers condemning this honest uprising of the people."[73] Everywhere the distinction made by WPC leaders follows this line of reasoning. Virtue made a workingman, and all the vices made his enemy. Increasingly, anyone who opposed Kearney by definition possessed all the vices and earned his utmost contempt.

Although the WPC retained part of the class vocabulary by con-

---

70 *The Labor Agitators; Or the Battle for Bread: The Party of the Future: The Workingmen's Party of California, Its Birth and Organization – Its Leaders and Its Purposes: Corruption in Our Local and State Governments: Venality of the Press* (San Francisco: George W. Greene, Publisher, [1878]). Copy in Bancroft Library, Berkeley. In my judgment, this pamphlet was not printed later than early February 1878.

71 *Chronicle*, 4 January 1878.

72 *Speeches of Dennis Kearney, Labor Champion* (New York: Jesse Haney & Co., 1878), [pamphlet], 6–7, Stanford Library, Stanford California.

73 *Speeches of Dennis Kearney*, 6.

trasting "workingman" with "capitalist," the party's spokesmen preferred the term "shoddy aristocrats," a term much truer to the republican tradition of the eighteenth century. The shoddy aristocrat was just as much a construction as the workingman. Activists of the WPC used this term so much that they eventually conjured up a whole party of such beings, referred to simply as the "shoddys," or the "shoddyites."[74] The preference for morally pejorative terms – "monopoly robber," "blood sucker," "bloated bondholders," "shoddyite," "miserable felonious bank smashers" – to the economic term "capitalist" demonstrates the republican location of social distress in the *character* rather than the *interests* of rulers and elites.

Thus the WPC found fault with wealth only insofar as it was illgotten or corrupting. "It is well to make money," testified Henry L. Knight before the Joint Committee on Labor Investigation, "and to make all that can be made. But there is an excess of wealth that becomes dangerous to the public." Knight, the author of the WPC's first platform, showed how little the leadership cared about problems with the relations of production, such as the wage-labor system or even the traditional labor issue of the hours of labor.[75] Knight's definition of the problem was moral: "As to money monopoly, I think that it enables the great capitalist to commit the grossest outrages, to seduce his neighbor's wife or daughter, as he is a man above the law."[76] Knight went on to explain how the wealth of those who had accumulated more than $100,000 or six square miles of land might be decreased, through massive taxation and through limits to the size of landholdings. State Senator Fowler then asked Knight: "How much money is a man allowed to have?" Knight thought that "an income of $5,000 to $10,000 a year will enable a man to live in just as high style as a modest gentleman and a citizen of the Republic ought to desire to live and is proper."[77]

The republicanism of the WPC was a reiteration of the rural republicanism of Richard Henry Lee or the urban version of Sam Adams during the War of Independence.[78] The Workingmen's

[74] *Chronicle*, 3 May 1879.
[75] Stedman and Leonard, *The Workingmen's Party*, describes Knight as the author of the first WPC platform, but Kearney and Day must have had a hand in drafting it as well.
[76] *Chronicle*, 4 February 1878.
[77] Ibid.
[78] Pauline Maier, *The Old Revolutionaries: Political Lives in the Age of Samuel Adams* (New York: Knopf, 1980).

Party of California, declared one pamphlet, "will help to found the true republic, in which none will have feathers and gewgaws till working people are comfortably fed, clothed, and sheltered. It will ... confine the rich to a rational and virtuous life in strict obedience to a righteous law."[79] Pamphleteers wrote as though individuals consciously belonged to the ranks of either the honest or the dishonest: "Let the rich who have made their money honestly and use it like gentlemen come out from among the greedy rascals who have stolen what they have and use it for still further corruption and fraud!" declared one pamphlet.[80] Once all such "workingmen" had joined hands in one great party for the salvation of the Republic, legislation might be possible to secure virtue once again. But how to identify the elect now that the Judgement Day had supposedly arrived? When Denis Kearney promised "to build a monument on the rotten carcasses of the Democratic and Republican parties" (indirectly making clever use of the central republican term "corruption"), the movement seemed clear enough. The practical task of gathering together only the virtuous within one party, however, was of course impossible.

The structures of political practice in San Francisco, thanks to the labors of the mainstream politicians, forced the WPC to adopt different guises while mobilizing the different classes of the political community and at the same time trying to maintain the republican assertion that virtuous character mattered more than material interests. The leadership of the WPC – like the leadership of most Great Upheaval political insurgent groups – came from a mixed-class background of workers and petty proprietors.[81] To dwell on this fact, however, would be to miss the much more significant fact that

---

[79] *The Labor Agitators* [no pagination].

[80] Ibid.

[81] Of the top WPC leadership, President Kearney was a drayman with one or two carts; Vice-President William Wellock was a boot and shoemaker and soldier turned evangelist of Christ, and Secretary Henry M. Moore was a tailor and self-educated lawyer who had lost several small ventures, including a hotel, on his trail from Orange County, New York, to San Francisco, where he operated with a partner as a real estate agent. Treasurer Thomas Donnelly owned several pieces of property in the city and provided the bail for Kearney during his many arrests. Frank Roney, a member of the party's Executive Committee and leading personality, was a master ironworker. Biographies are included in Stedman and Leonard, *History of the Workingmen's Party*, 95–109; information verified in Henry G. Langley, *San Francisco Directory for the Year Commencing February, 1878* (San Francisco, 1878); Cross, *History of the Labor Movement in California*, 322; and Saxton, *Indispensable Enemy*, 116–27.

these parties attempted to construct a political identity for themselves that was disembodied from class interests and invested instead in a moral image of the citizen "workingman." Why such a project failed is observable in the way that the WPC leadership was forced to use republicanism – a language of politics – within an emergent interest-group discourse and practice, what I call a "politics of class."

Denis Kearney, the workingman's ideal, had to play the role of class chameleon in his organizational task of building a party. An episode in which Kearney seized control of a meeting of property holders illustrates the dilemma of building a party on the language of politics within a polity activated by the language of class. In 1878 the Spring Valley Water Company tried once again to sell its stock at an eight-million-dollar profit to the city of San Francisco, whose water it supplied. As it had in 1875, this scheme brought a storm of protest from the city's taxpayers. On 16 March hundreds of prominent citizens, leading landowners in the city, gave their names to an announcement calling a mass meeting to protest the Spring Valley bill. Although the meeting was hastily called, Union Hall the following night was densely packed for what the San Francisco *Call* termed "the most exciting [meeting] ever held in this city."[82] What made the meeting so exciting was the presence of Denis Kearney, then at the height of his local power to draw crowds. The meeting was heavily attended by the city's leading property holders, and it had also drawn what seems to be at least an equal number of Kearney's followers. One of the original organizers, Samuel Hancock, tried to call the meeting to order but was prevented by shouts of "Kearney! Kearney! Kearney!" Obligingly, Kearney mounted the rostrum and admitted, "Fellow citizens, I do not know who called this meeting." At that, the organizers tried to expel him from the meeting. Eventually, he did leave the hall, but the meeting was unable to elect a chair, thanks to Kearney's followers inside. Kearney then reappeared and declared himself chairman.

Remarkably, the leading landholders did not walk out of their captured meeting. On the contrary, they gradually came around to Kearney's coarse style of leadership and in the end voted for his resolutions. To accomplish this feat, Kearney presented himself as a representative of the stable, property-owning classes of the city:

[82]   San Francisco *Call*, 16 March 1878.

[Applause] Fellow citizens, this meeting was called, not in the interest of politicians, not in the interest of bloated bondholders, not in the interest of miserable felonious bank smashers, but in the interest of the honest property-holders and honest tax-payers of San Francisco [Applause]. And as an able representative of that class I appear to you on this occasion [Applause].[83]

In return, conservatives like Frank Pixley, coeditor with Ambrose Bierce of the *Argonaut,* and Loring Pickering, owner of the *Call,* recognized (in the parliamentary sense) Kearney and stood on the stage with him. Pickering, whose paper had gladly advocated labor issues for the previous ten years, addressed the crowd after Kearney had passed the principal resolutions: "As to Mr. Kearney, I never saw him before I came here this afternoon. I have no prejudice against him. If he can do anything for the benefit of this city I shall be satisfied.... I do not think I would want to change the action of this meeting."[84] Together, then, the landowners of San Francisco joined hands in a solemn republican invocation, led by the evangelist Denis Kearney:

Resolved, that we, the electors and taxpayers of the city of San Francisco, sever every relation with the apostate senators who voted for the Spring Valley robbery bill, and denounce each and every one of them as traitors to their trust, and that every unrepentant Senator, upon his return to the home he has dishonored, be branded with the brand of infamy and turned over to the perpetual scorn of every honest man.

[Loud Applause] The resolution was carried.[85]

When speaking to the "Horny-handed sons of toil," Kearney did not, of course, project himself as the "able representative" of the "property-holders" of San Francisco.[86] "My fellow countrymen," Kearney proclaimed to one working-class crowd: "As the humble representative of the humble classes, the poor working classes, I appear before you tonight with no flowery phrases with which to garnish my speech."[87]

---

[83] *Call,* 17 March 1878.   [84] Ibid.   [85] Ibid.

[86] *The Oxford Dictionary of Quotations,* 3d ed. (Oxford: Oxford University Press, 1980), credits Kearney with the invention of this phrase, and suggests that Kearney's source was James Russell Lowell's *A Glance behind the Curtain:* "And blessed are the horny hands of toil." (pp. 288, 319).

[87] *Speeches of Dennis Kearney,* 6.

Kearney's class chameleonism illustrates to some extent what postmodern literary theory has termed "the autonomy of the text." Were we to judge Kearney by his socioeconomic status, his relations to the means of production, his wealth, his ethnoreligious or community membership, or other "objective" criteria about his place in American society, we would conclude that he was a petty bourgeois Irish Catholic. To himself and his followers, though, he was nothing less than the incorruptible Workingman, a citizen. On the other hand, political discourse in San Francisco had, long before his rise, taken on a structure in which one could speak most effectively in the idiom of classes or interest groups. In communication with the property owners he was a property owner; in communication with the poor he was a member of "the poor working classes." His public self, in other words, had to conform to the currently efficacious script for political mobilization.

By 1878 the WPC gained another important adherent, the Reverend Issac Kalloch, pastor of the city's largest church, the Baptist Metropolitan Temple; one of the largest churches in the United States.[88] The adherence of Kalloch, whose following by 1877 was numbered in the thousands, further illustrates how much the moral keyword "virtue" owed to Christian sources as well.[89] "I do not know Mr. Kearney personally," Kalloch said when he declared his conversion to the cause of the party, "but I recognize in him an instrument of Providence whose purpose is reform, and as such I know him."[90]

THE SELF-DESTRUCTION OF THE REPUBLICAN PARADIGM

The construction project of building a republican workingman took place on the discursive terrain of the public sphere, a phenomenon illustrated by the extraordinary attention paid by the WPC to language itself. Beginning its career as an election-season club that was easily confused with the con-game of "piece clubs," the WPC would have been overshadowed by the mainstream appeals to class and race unless it inflated the language of republicanism further

---

[88]   M. M. Marberry, *The Golden Voice: A Biography of Isaac Kalloch* (New York: Farrar, Straus, and Co., 1947), 195–222. See also Chapter 5.

[89]   Kloppenberg, "Virtues of Liberalism."

[90]   *Chronicle*, 10 July 1878.

than it had been stretched before. As William Wellock, the party's vice-president explained: "In the beginning of this agitation harsh language was necessary. It needed the fearless words of Kearney to arouse the fighting qualities of the people, borne down by monopolies and so long accustomed to the heavy hand of oppression to doubt the power of speech."[91] As Wellock's explanation indicates, the rhetorical mobilization of voters by the mainstream parties had exhausted the credulity of the electorate.

Finding a formulation of republicanism forceful enough to gain the attention of word-weary San Franciscans was a difficult task during a century remarkable for the use of extreme language by public figures. Kearney solved this problem, however, thanks to the ready availability of the gothic genre. It is probably not accidental that the only major American writer of gothic literature since Edgar Allan Poe was the leader of San Francisco's literary establishment, Ambrose Bierce. Bierce's stories, some extolling suicide, most starring monsters or ghosts, sold well in the city's magazines throughout the last three decades of the century.[92] "American gothic," writes Michael Paul Rogin, "depicts a titanic struggle between the forces of good and evil, in which the world is under the devil's sway." It is "an art of dualism, of haunted characters, violence, and horror. Although it claims to stand for good, it is fascinated by evil."[93] Kearney's fascination with evil was a trademark of his oratory. Opposition newspaper editors were "villainous serpents ... shiny imps of hell." "The whole vocabulary and epithets have been heaped upon us," Kearney told one crowd, "and the holy cause in which we have risen[,] by the thieving vampires that threaten the life-blood of the workingmen. [Applause.]"[94]

Kearney cast himself in a Romantic struggle with the "classical" language of his detractors. Boasting that he used "no classical language with which to fool my hearers," Kearney denounced "classi-

---

[91] *Call*, 3 January 1878.

[92] During the 1870s, Bierce wrote essays and stories for the San Francisco *News Letter* and the San Francisco *Argonaut*. Some of his most macabre work seems to have been written during this period. *The Ambrose Bierce Satanic Reader: Selections from the Invective Journalism of the Great Satirist*, comp. and ed. Ernest Jerome Hopkins (Garden City, N.Y.: Doubleday & Co., 1968). Richard O'Connor, *Ambrose Bierce: A Biography* (Boston: Little, Brown and Co., 1967). For Bierce's career during the 1870s, see Carey McWilliams, *Ambrose Bierce: A Biography* (New York: Albert and Charles Boni, 1929), 119–40.

[93] Michael Paul Rogin, *Ronald Reagan, The Movie: and Other Episodes in Political Demonology* (Berkeley: University of California Press, 1987), 19.

[94] *Speeches of Dennis Kearney*, 11.

cal thieves and legal pirates."[95] He also denounced the Associated Press as a "villainous, thieving, infamous band of scalawags that are aiming to control public opinion." Kearney on one occasion assessed his own vocabulary: "The English language, I believe, contains in the neighborhood of sixty thousand words. I am in possession of a few hundred of those words, and I use them.... I use my humble, plain, unvarnished words to extol virtue and condemn robbery."[96] True to the Romantic republican tradition, Kearney spoke as though he were the voice of natural virtue, risen "plain" and "unvarnished" from the common stock of workingmen. Speculators, shoddy aristocrats, capitalists, politicians, indeed the whole edifice of contemporary civil authority, was under the sway of evil, and this pervasive, beguiling, corrupting, oppressing network of villainy needed to be purged and uprooted.

The attention shown by contemporaries to language and its relation to action was in fact widespread. Some of Kearney's supporters insisted that his violent language was not meant literally. "What little things they [the WPC] did say," testified one follower, "were only used as metaphors."[97] The judge who set Kearney's bail at twenty-one thousand dollars on charges of incitement to riot, however, disagreed. "I think language is an overt act. I know of no acts done save [by] language."[98] Police captain Isaiah W. Lees thought the crowd's support of Kearney's tongue proved that the threats were real. Captain Lees made a practice of monitoring the WPC meetings and observed that

whenever Kearney would use the most violent language he would call for a show of hands, and it would be a perfect sea of hands.... When people stand there for three hours in a pouring rain to listen to these speeches it is an insult to their intelligence to say that they are not in dead earnest.[99]

The end of the WPC was as gothic as Kearney's language. The contradictions of using republicanism – a language of politics –

---

[95] The reference to "classical" language supports the analysis of Kenneth Cmiel, who demonstrates that a battle was underway during these years between advocates of a refined, latinate form of expression, and advocates of a simple, supposedly more popular style. See Cmiel, *Democratic Eloquence: The Fight over Popular Speech in Nineteenth-Century America* (New York: William Morrow and Co., 1990), 176–205.

[96] *Speeches of Denis Kearney*, 6.

[97] *Chronicle*, 17 February 1878.

[98] *Chronicle*, 3 February 1878.

[99] Ibid.

within the politics of class brought about, simultaneously, both the WPC's greatest triumph and its disintegration during the campaign of June 1878 for delegates to the California constitutional convention of 1878-9. Sweeping all thirty of San Francisco's delegates and winning enough delegates statewide to set the agenda of the convention, the WPC momentarily achieved the starkest stratification of the electorate by class lines yet reached, as we saw in Table 6.1.

But Kearney and the WPC had achieved a mobilization of the working class in spite of themselves. His republican, political conception of social distress never wavered: The evil character of rulers alone was the root cause of unemployment and low wages. Politicians were too corrupt, too beholden to the Shoddy Aristocrats (the railroad and other corporations who employed the Chinese), to pass the necessary legislation to expel the Chinese from the state. The WPC constructed the Chinese as slaves: the supposedly degraded labor of the latter, whom Kearney and his compatriots simply called "lepers," enabled the capitalist-aristocrat to hold the workingman in bondage as well.

Because this program was morally defined, because the republican definition of the public good (centered on "virtue") was indivisible, Kearney tended, like Robespierre, toward a totalistic dictatorship of the General Will. A visible cult of the leader grew up around Kearney as he was repeatedly arrested for inciting to riot, incendiarism, and so on. "But I tell you," Kearney warned, "and I want Stanford and the press to understand, that if I give an order to hang Crocker, it will be done.... The dignity of labor must be maintained, even if we have to kill every wretch that opposes it."[100] "I am the voice of the people," Kearney is supposed to have said on another occasion, "I am the dictator until the people put someone else in my place."[101] After a memorable torchlit address in front of the Stanford and Crocker mansions on Nob Hill and another arrest, Kearney's supporters spoke of "this martyrdom of our leaders [that] will in the end redound to their glory, and the liberation of the workingmen of California from the thralldom of capital and the incubus of the Chinese."[102] But the party activists who

[100] *Bulletin*, 1 November 1877.
[101] Quoted in Cross, *History of the Labor Movement in California*, 106.
[102] Davis, *Political Conventions in California*, 373.

wanted to translate the WPC momentum into some concrete gains for organized labor quickly grew tired of Kearney's republican millenialism.

John Day, cofounder of the party, was the first to go. He did so, the trade unionist said, because "he was tired of hearing [Kearney's] nonsensical speeches about what he is going to do if things don't go the way he wants them."[103] In May 1878 Frank Roney, another trade unionist and later to play a major role in building organized labor's political power in the city, and several others held a rival state convention and tried to expel Kearney from the party. "We have been compelled to this course by the following considerations," the breakaway faction declared in a published address. Their complaints, significantly, were complaints against the core meaning system of republicanism. No matter how much it had been bent into service as a "language of class," it ultimately located social distress in the corruption of rulers. "Denis Kearney has," the Roney faction charged, "from the first, assumed the role of a dictator who would brook no opposition to his will, suspecting everybody of treason who dared to differ with him in opinion, ... he has charged all officers of the party with being wire-pullers, political tricksters, traitors, and thieves."[104]

Kearney maintained control of the party, however, and steered it over the precipice. Kearney drove not only bona fide labor leaders but also the vital San Franciso *Chronicle* to desert and oppose him as well. By the spring of 1879 the constitutional convention had concluded its labors, having written one of the longest constitutions in the world, an instrument that, much amended, still frames the government of California. The WPC, having sent a large but minority bloc of delegates, set the tone of the convention, but did not control it. In spirit, the new constitution embodied republican distrust of politicians and their corrupters, the corporations. Article IV enumerates literally hundreds of laws that the legislature *cannot* pass. But in particulars, the leading members of the two major parties were responsible for the document's final form. The constitution attempts several objects: to shift the tax burden from ordinary citizens by limiting the power of authorities to incur debts and by making previously exempt or undertaxed categories of property subject

---

[103] Quoted in Kauer, "The Workingmen's Party of California," 281.
[104] *Bulletin*, 7 May 1878.

to taxation; to increase the liability of corporations and banks for obligations and embezzlement; to regulate the monopolistic railroad by establishing a Board of Railroad Commissioners; and, in answer to the overwhelming popularity of the anti-Chinese movement, to prevent by all possible means the employment of Chinese.[105]

In the campaign for the ratification of the new constitution, and the municipal elections that followed, the de Young brothers, having broken with Kearney, created a "New Constitution party" and denounced not only the WPC (which also campaigned for the new constitution) but also the "railroadized [R]epublican party."[106] Now the de Youngs were the political opponents of both Kearney and Kalloch, two easy targets for a sensational, commercial newspaper. "The hoodlums and the ... followers of the dirty demagogue Kearney, will naturally gravitate toward the ticket headed by the lecherous and unprincipled parson Kalloch," declared the *Chronicle* during the 1879 municipal elections. The de Youngs had rediscovered Kalloch's scandalous past and let loose a barrage of abuse:

KALLOCH'S CAREER: A Course of Lust, Fraud, and Hypocrisy. Juvenile Amours and Adolescent Debauchery. Testimony of Witnesses at Adultery Trial. Notorious in Boston for His Hatred of the Irish: He Publically Denounces them as the Scum of the Earth, Fit only to Associate with Brutes: His Swindling Attempts in Massachusetts and Kansas.[107]

The Reverend Kalloch responded in kind, preaching the next day on the moral depravity of the de Youngs' mother. This was too

---

[105] The unabridged text of the California constitution is widely available, thanks to the fascination of Lord Bryce, who reprinted the entire document in fifty pages of his *American Commonwealth*. Bryce's multivolume work was revised, abridged, and reprinted many times after the first edition appeared in 1888, but the California constitution can be found in the appendix to the first volume of nearly every edition. The story of this important convention is woefully neglected by historians. The best recent treatments are Bean and Rawls, *California*, 181–5; Andrew Rolle, *California: A History*, 4th ed. (Arlington Heights, Ill.: Harlan Davidson, 1987), 314–19; Morton Keller, *Affairs of State: Public Life in Late Nineteenth Century America* (Cambridge, Mass: Belknap Press, 1977), 113–14; Barbara Allen Babcock, "Clara Shortridge Foltz: Constitution-Maker," *Indiana Law Journal* 66:4 (Fall 1991): 848–940; and Carl B. Swisher, *Motivation and Political Technique in the California Constitutional Convention, 1878–1879* (Claremont, Calif.: Pomona College, 1930). See the thousands of pages of transcript in the *Debates and Proceedings of the Constitutional Convention of the State of California. Convened at the City of Sacramento, Saturday, September 28, 1878*, 3 vols. (Sacramento: State Office, J. D. Young, Sup't., 1880–1).

[106] *Chronicle*, 21 August 1879.

[107] *Chronicle*, 22 August 1879.

much for the choleric Charles. He sat in a carriage outside of the Metropolitan Temple and shot Kalloch, wounding but not killing him, days before the election. A year later Kalloch's son marched up to the editorial rooms of the *Chronicle* and killed Charles de Young at his desk.[108] The bathos of this spectacle has a solid core of rationality to it. A movement built on the morally grounded discourse of republicanism, which emphasized above all else the character of leaders, logically culminated in the self-destruction of the insurgent elite.

CONCLUSION: ON THE SURVIVAL OF THE "MAINSTREAM PARTIES"

E. L. Godkin noted with alarm in 1867 the emergence of a "politics of class feeling" that clashed with his liberal belief in abstract, universal equality.[109] There are many routes to class consciousness and class formation. Work cultures evolving at the workplace and in the communities, as David Montgomery, Herbert Gutman, and many others have clearly demonstrated, promoted persistent, if segmented, class sentiments throughout the nineteenth century and well into the twentieth. Class consciousness in Gilded Age America may have come also from many nonpolitical sources, but the sustained agitation and legislation carried out by mere Democrats and Republicans from at least 1866 forward is the sine qua non of explanatory variables for the burst of labor politics in the 1880s.

The friendly labor legislation enacted in the midst of the nationwide party disarray of 1866–8 marked perhaps the very origin of a politics of class in the United States. From George W. Julian's sponsorship of the federal eight-hour bill in 1867, making eight hours the limit for the workday of federal employees, and its passage by both houses of Congress in 1868, the mainstream party leaders stamped the most popular demand of the American labor movement with the legitimacy of the national state. Ordinary party politicians in most of the nation's industrialized states acted likewise, so that by 1868 Connecticut, New York, Pennsylvania, Illinois, Missouri, Wisconsin, and California had all enacted eight-hour laws. These laws

---

[108] These complex events are best described in Saxton, *Indispensable Enemy*, 127–56; and Kauer, "The Workingmen's Party of California," 286–91.

[109] *Nation*, 27 June 1867, cited in Foner, *Reconstruction*, 484.

have been widely dismissed by historians because of their ineffectuality. "Liberty of contract" clauses gave employers an easy route to evasion, and most employers ignored the new laws.[110] But the greatest import of these laws may not have been contained by their enforceability. After the passage of an eight-hour bill in Ohio in 1886, as Steven Ross observes, "an individual who ... demanded an eight-hour day now spoke not as a selfish worker, as manufacturers had previously claimed, but as a citizen seeking his or her lawful right."[111]

Democratic and Republican organizers had little trouble in 1880 reassembling their constituencies after the gothic spectacle of the de Youngs, the Reverend Mayor Kalloch, and Denis Kearney. But it cannot be said that the major party politicians "co-opted" the movement; they were simply picking up where they had left off when Kearney pirated their voters in the winter of 1877–8.[112] The language of mobilization favored by the mainstream politicians had centered on race and class: Mobilizing identifiable groups was a lot easier than attempting, as the WPC had attempted, to play St. Peter and separate the elect from the corrupt. The intersection of the mainstream discourse with that of the WPC turned out to be race: Republicanism thrives on the master – slave metaphor, and the Anglo Californians had long equated the African Americans with the Chinese. Dutifully enacting a law requiring corporations chartered by the state to fire their Chinese employees, the Democratic state legislature sought to put the new, antimonopoly constitution into action. The following year the demands of western workingmen and workingwomen, translated in Washington as California's prospective electoral votes, won them passage of the Chinese Exclusion Act, the first door to slam closed on the long-open immigration policy of the United States.[113]

The disastrous career of the Workingmen's Party of California had repercussions that went far beyond the history of class formation in San Francisco. Kearney's gothic republicanism enabled

---

110 Foner, *Reconstruction*, 481–2.
111 Ross, "The Politicization of the Working Class," 184.
112 That the WPC merely stole the Democratic party's institutional structure is demonstrated in Issel and Cherny, *San Francisco*, 125–30.
113 On the women in the WPC, see Mary P. Ryan, *Women in Public: From Banners to Ballots* (Baltimore: Johns Hopkins University Press, 1990), 160–1; Roger Daniels, *Asian America: Chinese and Japanese in the United States since 1850* (Seattle: University of Washington Press, 1988), 29–66.

opinion makers like *Harper's Monthly* cartoonist Thomas Nast to construct the counterimage of the workingman: the anarchistic death figure featured in his "Social Science Solved" cartoon of 10 April 1880. Nast's images constitute a part of the long process of both working-class and middle-class formation that the Great Upheaval no doubt brought close to completion. Because republicanism proper – an attempt to reform the character, or virtue, of the rulers – had no clear mode of implementation other than continued opposition (it always had provided the ideal oppositional vocabulary), it had begun to appear senseless within a political environment that had been structured around the pursuit of realizable goals for working people and consumers, such as working-hours legislation and railroad-rate regulation. Additionally, the extreme form of republicanism wielded by Kearney and the WPC contributed to the criminalization of radicalism that would continue through the Haymarket trials and the First World War.[114]

After finishing *Progress and Poverty*, which he composed and published during the lifespan of the WPC, Henry George responded directly to Nast's cartoon and sought to explain "The Kearney Agitation in California" to the nation's educated readership in a *Popular Science Monthly* article. "There has not been in San Francisco any outbreak of 'foreign communism,'" George wrote, "nor ... anything socialistic or agrarian. This movement has in reality been inspired by ordinary political aims."[115] George, as we have seen, was in a position to know of what "ordinary political aims" consisted. Perhaps the Democrats and even the Republicans had created a monster that they could not control; perhaps they had fanned a class conflict that they did not really desire; and perhaps the party leaders and mainstream press editors were utterly cynical during the ten long years prior to the nationwide strike of 1877, when they courted the votes of working-class men and promoted a language of class in the public sphere. The overwhelming lesson of this story, however, has been that the major parties and the mainstream press were indeed responsible for "politicizing" the working class in San Francisco.[116]

---

[114]   Rogin, *Ronald Reagan, The Movie*, 44–81.

[115]   Henry George, "The Kearney Agitation in California," 433–53. George describes the Nast cartoon and responds to it at the beginning of his article, p. 434. James Bryce relied heavily on George's interpretion in his *American Commonwealth*, 2 vols. (London: Macmillan, 1889), 2:372–95.

[116]   Cf. Steven J. Ross, "The Politicization of the Working Class."

The rise and fall of the WPC illustrates in a dramatic way that republicanism, essentially a language of politics, had begun to outlive its usefulness by the onset of the 1880s. The widespread, if brief, success of the local insurgent parties sponsored by the Knights of Labor in the late 1880s no doubt attests to the continued popularity of the republican idiom in Gilded Age political culture. The violent racism of the WPC may have been a unique experience among labor insurgencies, structured by the unusual conditions of California. But all local cases of labor politics in the Great Upheaval were unique, and all, like that of the WPC, came to fruition only after prolabor politicians and journalists had politically legitimated the social conflict between "labor" and "capital." Leon Fink's rich analysis of the Knights of Labor–backed parties in five cities in the 1880s demonstrates that the leadership of insurgent labor parties drew strength from their strong ties to the major parties. In Richmond, Virginia, a national stronghold of the Knights, in fact, it was the Republican party that the Knights chose as their labor-reform vehicle.[117]

The competitive party period that lasted from the Civil War through the 1890s did not allow mainstream politicians to rest contented with a stable core constituency from election to election, because it was the *marginal*, independent voters that they sought to win and retain. At the local level, moreover, party politics bore little resemblance to the closed, two-party oligopoly so often described at the national level. The crisscrossing of party leaders from one party to another, the profusion of independent parties, and the rampant ticket splitting among voters shown here for San Francisco was not at all unique. In Chicago, for example, Bessie Louise Pierce documents "the marked degree of party irregularity, the crossing of political lines, and the making of new combinations in the elections of 1871, '72, and '73." Like California's Henry Huntley Haight and Andrew Jackson Bryant, Illinois's Lyman Trumbull and Governor Palmer shifted from the Republicans to the Democrats.[118]

The uncertainties that major party politicians faced in the immediate postwar years forced them to take positions that would then reverberate throughout civil society in the form of identities and ideologies. Any careful history of the parties or the press in the 1870s will show the almost cavalier adoption of a language of class

117 Fink, *Workingmen's Democracy*, 38–218.
118 Pierce, *History of Chicago*, vol. 3 (New York: Knopf, 1957), 344.

among the mainstream party leaders. Editors of the daily press, also locked in a fierce competitive struggle for the favor of urban workers, gladly opened their columns to prolabor writers. Beginning in 1873, Chicago's otherwise conservative Republican Joseph Medill ran a regular column on labor issues by an English-born ex-Chartist named Mrs. W. D. Wynkoop.[119] In Boston, the labor writers for the "mainstream" *Globe* and the *Herald* in the 1880s included Cyrus Willard and Francis Pickett, both leading organizers of the city's Central Labor Union and Knights of Labor.[120]

The language of politics used by Kearney and the WPC owed more to the Vigilantes than it did to the origins of class politics in the United States during the 1870s. The term "workingman" was synonymous with "virtuous citizen" to the leaders of the WPC. Its definition did not admit of multiple "interests" in society or politics. Rather, the workingman label served to identify the virtuous, and these were the only legitimate members of the political community. That there was a single, identifiable common interest was never doubted by Kearney. Politicians had failed society by subverting that common interest to their own selfish greed for power and money. Labor leaders like Frank Roney, who peeled themselves from this unwieldy electoral apparatus, had a very different idea about interests, as the next chapter demonstrates.

---

[119]   Karen Lynn Sawislak, "Smoldering City: Class, Ethnicity, and Politics in Chicago at the Time of the Great Fire, 1867–1873" (Ph.D. diss., Yale University, 1990), 299.

[120]   Jama Lazerow, "'The Workingmen's Hour': The 1886 Labor Uprising in Boston," *Labor History* 21:2 (Spring 1980): 207–8.

CHAPTER 7

The institutional preconditions of progressivism

During the two decades following the California constitutional convention of 1879, the structures and practice of political life in San Francisco underwent a decisive transformation. By the beginning of the twentieth century, the frame of municipal government, the leadership of the political parties, the structures of communication in the public sphere, the political mobilization of the citizenry, and, most important, the policy issues on the public agenda, all had evolved so far from their institutional origins in the antebellum city that their operation has to be considered part of a separate political culture.

This chapter and the next trace the maturation of changes on several levels of government and society that were to produce what has come to be called the "Progressive Era" (ca. 1890–1920). Justifiably recognized as the birthplace of the American welfare state, of modern feminism, of an urban, immigrant, and consumer society, of a triumphant white-collar social class, of interest-group politics, of weak political parties, of centralized expert authority structures in business and government, of mass commercial journalism, of low levels of political participation, and of the social-scientific professions themselves, the Progressive Era has been richly described by generations of scholars, but its origins remain obscure. Why did so many changes in the American polity take place during this intense period of political and social upheaval?

Historians have for decades identified "progressivism" as a set of policies intended to solve the myriad facets of the crisis of industrial urban modernity: to curb the abuses of the industrial Robber Barons, regulate or control immigrant life, maintain racial hierarchies, bridge the yawning chasm between classes and ethnic groups, introduce social welfare programs to protect working children, women, and men abused by the industrial mode of production, destroy the corrupt power of political party organizations, eliminate vice and crime, and achieve an almost endless list of smaller goals derived from these. Although there have been many interpretations of progressivism, most have been variations on the social-group paradigm, assigning political change in the period to the work of one or another social group in their respective drives to achieve political power in the closing decades of the nineteenth century.[1] Working within the social-group paradigm, historians have now produced an enormous literature that ascribes a pivotal role in the creation of this reform agenda to every social class in society and to both genders. Tracing political changes to social relations has established many links but few explanations.

In this chapter and the next I analyze the sequential steps by which the political culture we have come to call progessivism came about. The term "progressivism" in this study signifies a discursive environment, much in the same sense that the term "Enlightenment" signifies a period in the intellectual, cultural, economic, and political history of the transatlantic world a century or so earlier. Just as there was no single "Enlightenment," so there was no single "progressivism." Progressivism was neither a discrete set of new policy goals, nor the expression of the interests of a particular social group. Instead, progressivism was a reorganization of the public sphere that enabled the pursuit of interests by groups and their leaders. To understand how such a reorganization was accomplished, this chapter explains the origins of new structures that began to channel political participation by the 1890s.

A SPECIES OF FORCE: THE CONTRADICTIONS OF
ORGANIZATIONAL PARTY POLITICS IN THE 1880S

Every note in the chorus of the State's complaint grows out of the hostility to the Southern Pacific Railway monopoly . . .

— Julian Ralph (1895)[2]

---

[1] "Apart from their differences," Stephen Skowronek writes, "the major interpretations of Progressive reform have tended to focus on the environmental disruptions and social interests that propelled American institutional development forward and to treat the state as an adaptive response mechanism providing the appropriate institutional instruments under the guiding light of timely reform principles." Stephen Skowronek, *Building a New American State: The Expansion of National Administrative Capacities, 1877–1920* (Cambridge, U.K.: Cambridge University Press, 1982), 17.

[2] "California's Great Grievance," *Harper's Weekly* 39 (2 March 1895): 204.

Patronage would not go around or even approximately go around.
— "Boss" Christopher Buckley[3]

The operation of political power in the decade of the 1880s is in many ways the most important of all the background sources of progressivism. It was the apogee of the organizational party system that had begun with Andrew Jackson and ended with the rise of progressivism in the early 1890s. It was also the period of severe contradictions for the American party system. The years from 1881 to 1891 are the only ones during the five decades of this study in which the "boss" and the party "machine" made a genuine appearance. Christopher Augustine Buckley, the "Blind Boss" of the Democratic party, is typically credited with dominance in this period, although his power has been vastly overestimated by historians.[4] Buckley's power lay in his control of the party apparatus, a position he had in common with his Republican rivals, William T. ("Bill") Higgins, Martin Kelly, and Phil Crimmins.[5] These party leaders would have been astonished to learn that their rule was founded on satisfying the needs of voters distressed by the strains of immigration and industrial life, as Oscar Handlin, Richard Hofstadter, and Robert K. Merton claimed in classic accounts, or that their rule grew from the neighborhood basis of socioeconomic life, as commentators as widely spaced as Jane Addams, Robert Woods, Samuel Hays, and John Allswang believed.[6] Their rule derived from four essential features of the "third" American party system: (1) complete control of the primary elections and party conventions, (2) linkage with the state and national election process, (3) a severely conservative

3   Christopher Buckley, "The Reminiscences of Christopher Buckley," ed. James H. Wilkins, San Francisco *Bulletin*, 28 January 1919. This memoir ran every day from 31 August to 9 October 1918, and from 23 December 1918 to 5 February 1919. It will be cited hereafter as Buckley, "Reminiscences," followed by the date.
4   Callow calls Buckley "the undisputed overlord of San Francisco." Alexander Callow, Jr., "San Francisco's Blind Boss," *Pacific Historical Review* 25 (August 1956): 261–79; William R. Bullough, *The Blind Boss and His City: Christopher Augustine Buckley and Nineteenth-Century San Francisco* (Berkeley: University of California Press, 1979).
5   Another "boss," Abraham Ruef of the United Labor Party, appeared in 1901, later to be successfully prosecuted by Hiram Johnson in the graft prosecutions of 1907. His complex story lies beyond the scope of this investigation, however. See Walton Bean, *Boss Ruef's San Francisco* (Berkeley: University of California Press, 1972); James P. Walsh, "Abe Ruef Was No Boss: Machine Politics, Reform, and San Francisco," *California Historical Quarterly* 51:1 (Spring 1972): 3–16.
6   Robert K. Merton, "The Latent Functions of the Machine," in *Social Theory and Social Structure*, rev. and enl. (New York: Free Press, 1957), 71–82; Richard Hofstadter, *Age of Reform* (New York: Vintage, 1955); Oscar Handlin, *Boston's Immigrants*, rev. and enl. (Cambridge, Mass.: Belknap Press of Harvard University Press, 1979).

fiscal ideology, and (4) rivers of revenue from a variety of nontax-payer sources. In short, organizational politicians had institutional, not social, resources. Institutional change not social change ended their reign and began the Progressive Era.

"The old boss business was bad," recalled Christopher Buckley. "It rested on a species of force – an utterly lawless primary."[7] By "lawless" Buckley did not mean *violent* (although organizational parties did countenance some violence); he meant *unregulated*. Every "boss" recognized that the primary was the sole source of his power and that control of primaries was possible because the parties were, juridically, merely clubs of "private" citizens, protected in their right of assembly to nominate whom they pleased for elected offices. "The law took no cognizance at all of primary elections," Martin Kelly inaccurately recalled. The ineffectual, voluntarily invoked Porter Primary Law of 1866 had at least recognized the power of primaries. But Kelly was right to conclude that before 1908 primaries "were absolutely party affairs and arranged by the all-powerful county committees." In 1867 the editor of the *Alta* made a similar observation: "The source of all power in political parties is the primary election."[8]

Until the last decade of the nineteenth century, as we have seen in previous chapters, political parties controlled almost the entire election process. Access to the American state, from the federal to the local levels, was controlled by legally "private" clubs that controlled not only the candidate-selection process but also nearly the entire election process, including printing and distributing ballots. All the "state" proper did was supply the ballot box, designate an election date, and count the ballots (but even the ballot counters were appointed by the ruling-party leaders). Such control made parties quasi-state institutions. But this control did not necessarily inhibit critical debate nor restrict voter choice. As we have seen, the 1870s were years of wild competition among numerous parties, none of which could count on durable party loyalties. In such periods, political leaders had to rely on *ideological* appeals, and when they did so, they created a working-class voting bloc and unleashed

---

[7]   Buckley, "Reminiscences." 4 February 1919.

[8]   Martin Kelly, "Martin Kelly's Story," San Francisco *Bulletin*, ran from 1 September to 26 November 1917. Quotation is from 4 September 1917. *Alta* 17 May 1867, quoted in Eric Falk Petersen, "Prelude to Progressivism: California Election Reform, 1870–1909" (Ph.D. diss., University of California, Los Angeles, 1969), 46.

the monster of the Workingmen's Party of California. Stung by the Workingmen's party, the Democratic and Republican party leaders swatted the electorate with a series of disciplinary laws from 1878 to 1881, which resulted in a much more manageable political community.

The first steps in election-law reform were the "Piece Club," and "Vignette Ticket" acts. Analyzed in Chapter 5, these acts barred solicitation of alleged campaign funds from candidates by organizations claiming to control blocs of votes – an admission that the candidates did not know who really did control the votes. Printing a ballot on a brightly colored, distinctive strip of paper with a logo at the top ensured that the act of voting was visible and very unsecret. There was a weakness in this system, however. Because the state did not regulate the printing process, entrepreneurs could disrupt it. Because of the capacity of minor parties and independent candidates to disorganize a major party's victory by printing lookalike ballots with certain names replaced, the major parties had a major headache at each election trying to suppress the "bogus" tickets of independents and rival factions. The Vignette Ticket Act provided for the registration with the election commissioner of each party's ballot design (the logo was called its "vignette"), to prevent counterfeit on election day. Again, the Democrats and Republicans are revealed here as needing the help of the state to maintain their integrity before an unruly electorate.

The final step in restoring order and discipline to the election process was the decision to switch the local date of election to November of even years. Long experience, as we have seen, had taught the politicians that this move greatly enhanced the power of the regular parties in local elections. The off-year elections had originated in 1861, to insulate the Vigilante-People's party from the influence of the national contests. The law of 1881 scheduled the next local election in November 1882. For the first time in several decades, municipal nomination on one of the major party tickets would be tantamount to election. The only uncertainty left would be which of two parties would win, a vast improvement over the agony of persuasion typical of the 1870s.[9]

These structural protections ended abruptly with the introduction

9 Terrence J. McDonald, *The Parameters of Urban Fiscal Policy: Socioeconomic Change and Political Culture in San Francisco, 1860–1906* (Berkeley: University of California Press, 1986), 160.

of the Australian ballot in 1891, which finally wrenched control of the ballot from "private" political parties and lodged it with the state. The decade of the 1880s, then, should have been a period of consistent party regularity between the top and bottom levels of the ticket. Indeed, Terrence McDonald has demonstrated that this was precisely the case:

This type of regularity reached its peak from 1882 through 1890, when four out of five mayoral elections and all supervisorial elections went the same way as the top of the ticket. This regularity dropped dramatically after 1892, when the winning supervisors were [of] the same [party] as the top of the ticket only half of the time, and the winning mayor was never of the same party as the top of the ticket.[10]

These patterns strongly suggest that the timing of local with national elections was the primary reason for the hegemony of the organizational politicians in the 1880s.

Once these laws were in place, access to government at the national, state, and municipal levels could come to rest in the primary election, as the bosses quoted earlier noted. Contrary to much writing on urban party machines depicting them as vast mobilizing organizations that tied the citizen to party loyalties, organizational politicians considered voters a necessary annoyance. Especially in urban centers, where voters were most independent and unpredictable, party leaders struggled to discipline the voter with institutional checks at every point where he had choices to make.[11] They began with the primary. Abraham Ruef, who began his political career under Kelly in the 1880s, recalled the importance of primaries and the unimportance of voters: "It made no difference to them whether the voters came to the meeting or not, so long as they could carry out their program. It was easier to carry out the program when no one was present."[12]

Primary elections selected delegates to party conventions, which drafted platforms and composed party slates. The source of power in the primary resided in the ability of the preexisting county committee to set the date and hours of the primary, to establish the credentials of party membership, and to notify or not notify the public

[10] McDonald, *Parameters of Urban Fiscal Policy*, 164–5.
[11] Comparisons with Chicago and New York City appear in Chapter 6.
[12] Abraham Ruef, "The Road I Traveled," San Francisco *Bulletin*, 6 April–15 September 1912. Quotation is from 23 May 1912.

about the primary. Gross abuse of this control – not notifying the public at all or opening the primary polls for absurdly short hours – tended to provoke press censure and bad publicity, as the rise of the 1856 Vigilance Committee made clear. Nevertheless, control of all these steps leading up to a convention was easy to maintain with the appearance of fairness. The Porter Primary Law of 1866, enacted in frustration by lawmakers after factionalism reigned supreme in the parties at the end of the Civil War, could have put control of the primaries in the hands of the official election commissioners. But the Porter law, the first of its kind in the nation, was voluntary. Parties had to choose to invoke its provisions. Not surprisingly, the influence of the Porter law was "practically nonexistent" by 1868.[13]

The Democratic and Republican parties held a series of meetings in late 1881 and early 1882 to devise the best plan of organization to ensure control over the nomination process. The Democratic plan, generally credited to the work of the rising "Blind Boss," Christopher Augustine Buckley, but actually hammered out by the oligarchy of leaders over a period of months, was known as the "precinct club plan." Again, we see the inverse relation between local organization and centralized control. According to the precinct plan, the Democratic City-County Committee would forgo the Porter Primary Law option of holding a citywide primary and instead select delegates to the municipal, state, and national conventions from the "clubs" in each precinct.[14] The system ensured discipline. In order to win nomination for an office by one of the parties, an individual needed the support of the handful of notables who could coordinate the procedures of the meetings in forty-seven precincts. The system worked precisely as it was intended. Beginning in 1882, only those candidates approved by Buckley in the Democratic party or Martin Kelly and Phil Crimmins in the Republican party (or all three, as we shall see), could get on the ticket in November, where they could ride the successful national slate to victory.[15]

The reaction of Buckley's circle to a challenge from within the Democratic party in 1884 illustrates the importance of segmented

13   Petersen, "Prelude to Progressivism," 46–54, 55.
14   San Francisco *Alta California* 23 December 1881; San Francisco *Call*, 10, 17 January, 29 March, 4 April, 6 May 1882.
15   "Address to the Voters of San Francisco," *Examiner*, 7 April 1882; San Francisco *Call*, 8 October 1882; Petersen, "Prelude to Progressivism," 77–8.

structure to centralized control. Several business leaders, dissatisfied with being shut out of the process, organized an "Anti-Boss Club," or "ABC," in 1884 and petitioned the State Central Committee for a return to citywide primaries for delegate selection. The State Committee, fearing a breakdown in the party's newly acquired discipline, denied the request, and the ABC failed to defeat Buckley's men that year.[16] The same group tried a different approach in 1886. In an effort to beat the bosses at their own game, the ABC began to set up rival precinct clubs. Again fearing a collapse of order, the State Committee this time forced Buckley to negotiate. Buckley's ruse was telling. He disingenuously proposed to make the process *more* democratic by multiplying the number of clubs to 164. Of course, only an army of thousands of volunteers could surmount the barriers of such an arrangement, but the ABC fell for Buckley's plan and lost miserably.[17]

Once the Democrats or Republicans had composed a slate, they had to overcome their old nemesis, voter choice. The concurrence of local with state and national elections, however, made this task much easier than it had been when city elections were held off year and off season. Whereas city-only elections, with their low voter turnouts, could be won, as we have seen, by either guerrilla tactics or skillful formulation of ideological appeals, winning national elections required large bureaucracies. The enlarged stakes and organizational requirements were demonstrated in July 1880, when the veteran Union Army general William Rosecrans organized the "Blue and Gray Hancock Legion" in an attempt to unite veterans behind the Democratic candidate for president. By August Rosecrans had 3,196 men organized in military fashion by precinct, throughout the city. These precinct-level fighting units were armed with the names and addresses from the Great Registers. They would call on each voter and discover his preference, trying, of course, to persuade as well. On election day, Rosecrans's soldiers sought to get all of their friendly constituents to the polls.[18]

The lesson of the Blue and Gray Hancock Legion is that a political structure that genuinely reached into every neighborhood of the city was in no wise an organic reflection of the decentralized order

---

[16] *Call*, 16 September 1883, 26 May 1884, 1 October 1884.
[17] *Call*, 5 October 1886; Petersen, "Prelude to Progressivism," 83–5.
[18] San Francisco *Alta California*, 28 July 1881; Petersen, "Prelude to Progressivism," 39–41.

of semiindustrial civil society. Samuel P. Hays, in his widely cited thesis, continues the tradition of the Chicago School positing a fit between the organization of civil society and the organization of political life. Fragmented constitutional structures are decentralized only to the unwary observer, however. To win elections within a framework, such as that provided by the labyrinthine American federal system or precentralized city charters, required a highly disciplined organization – the modern party – which could overcome the constitutional hurdles and be in hundreds or thousands of places at once while pursuing the same object.[19]

The size and complexity of these organizations underscore the need for money in the organizational party regimes of the 1880s. Printing ballots was only one of several costs the parties bore in the long process that preceded a November election. The others included conducting registration drives, subsidizing speaking tours, paying piece clubs when and where they still operated, and maintaining those far-flung "clubs." Because these segments of the public sphere were, as we saw earlier, part of the private sector, they had to be rented. Maintaining a political club in the down times of the election calendar so that it could emerge in time to control the nomination process in the spring required money. When the general campaigns were in full swing, costs mounted. Subsidizing speaking tours required money for travel and lodging. Parties rented and even built facilities for assembling huge crowds of the party faithful to hear prominent candidates and government officials speak on the issues of the campaign. In 1890 the San Francisco Republican party paid for the construction in two weeks of a temporary structure large enough to hold six thousand people, and proceeded to fill it nightly with events until the election was held.[20]

"God only knows how much money was spent" outfitting the clubs, Buckley recalled of the 1888 general election: "It is within my knowledge that within this city at least $150,000 was spent by the Democrats, and the Republicans spent more."[21] Buckley, in 1919, had reasons to exaggerate. But contemporary data are not

---

19 Samuel P. Hays. "The Politics of Reform in Municipal Government in the Progressive Era," *Pacific Northwest Quarterly* 55 (1964): 157–69; Richard Oestreicher, "Urban Working-Class Political Behavior and Theories of American Electoral Politics, 1870–1940," *Journal of American History* 74:4 (March 1988): 1257–86.
20 Petersen, "Prelude to Progressivism," 42–3.
21 Buckley, "Reminiscences," 20 January 1919.

lacking. An election law of 1893 forced disclosure of campaign expenses for the first time, the only available evidence of the amount of money required to win an election under the organizational regimes. In 1894 the Republicans reported $36,000 in campaign contributions for the whole state; Democrats reported only $9,600 for that year.[22] The parties had every reason to underreport, however, so we can take a rough guess and say that the cost of an election in San Francisco alone was somewhere between ten and one hundred thousand dollars.

"What we call machine politics," Henry George observed in 1883, "springs from the cost of elections."[23] The rising cost of elections in the 1880s, however, proved only one-half of the fatal contradiction that ensnared the organizational parties at the dawn of progressivism. Although "the expenses of organization were very heavy," as Buckley recalled, he also observed with much accuracy that "no part or parcel of it came out of the pocket of the dear people."[24] Why? Because the organizational politicians governed under the severest of fiscal ideological constraints. Buckley introduced the cornerstone of this ideology himself, a policy known as the "Dollar Limit." An ironclad pledge in both parties' platforms every year from 1882 forward, the Dollar Limit promised to levy taxes at no greater rate than one dollar per one hundred dollars of assessed value. McDonald has shown statistically how rigidly this limit was enforced, which explains why Buckley could recall that "patronage would not go around or even approximately go around."[25]

Organizational politicians were forced to walk a tightrope between the overwhelming sentiment for low taxes and low expenditures, on the one hand, and the enormous, rising cost of elections in the 1880s. This was a great dilemma. For, as Buckley himself admitted, the majority of voters were "not held overtight by party lines, ... voted pretty much as they liked and were inclined to give the boss and his lieutenants the go-by."[26] The solution, of course, was to raise money outside of the tax revenues.

[22] Petersen, "Prelude to Progressivism," 37–8.
[23] "Money in Elections," *North American Review* (March 1883), quoted in Clifton K. Yearley, *The Money Machines: The Breakdown and Reform of Governmental and Party Finance in the North, 1860–1920* (Albany: State University of New York Press, 1970), 96.
[24] Buckley, "Reminiscences," 28 January 1919.
[25] McDonald, *Parameters of Urban Fiscal Reform*, 158–202; Buckley, "Reminiscences," 28 January 1919.
[26] Buckley, "Reminiscences," 7 January 1919.

The oldest method of party fund-raising was an assessment, ranging from 2 to 6 percent on the salaries of officeholders, plus a sliding-scale contribution required of any candidate seeking office, ranging from ten dollars to several thousand dollars. Linking the local elections to the national calendar not only maximized voter turnout and partisan voting, but tied the money machinery of the federal and state organizations directly to that of the city. Still, as Clifton Yearley observes, party fund-raising was locked to holding state power: "Like the feeding of Siamese twins, the financing of political parties and of governments were inseparable acts; the starvation of one meant the starvation of the other."[27] Yearley aptly describes the parties as "parasites" who extracted money on the way into and out of the official government coffers. The ultimate sources of the big money in the campaigns in the 1880s, then, were the large corporations with franchises to obtain and regulations to stave off. By early 1884, only one corporation in the state really mattered: the Southern Pacific Railway Company, incorporated by a charter in the state of Kentucky.

The Southern Pacific (or "SP," as contemporaries knew it) began life as the Central Pacific in 1861, when its founders and principal owners, the "Big Four" – Charles Crocker, Mark Hopkins, Collis P. Huntington, and Leland Stanford – won the gigantic federal subsidy of the Pacific Railway Act. Already by the early 1870s it had what amounted to an entire department devoted to lobbying the state's party organizations and the legislature. The SP injected money into the parties in many ways, most of which were more subtle than outright bribery of legislators. One method was to retain the lawyer-legislators as counselors, an entirely legitimate practice. Another was to include men like Buckley on lucrative stock deals. And of course the SP provided thousands of dollars in campaign contributions every year.[28]

The SP also entered the politics of the crucial San Francisco party organizations in another, complicated way. At the close of the depression of the 1870s, San Francisco experienced a spectacular building boom, spreading the area of settlement past the major hills to the area then known as the "suburbs": the Western Addition, the

---

27 Yearley, *The Money Machines*, 97.
28 R. Hal Williams, *The Democratic Party and California Politics, 1880–1896* (Stanford: Stanford University Press, 1973), 9–14.

Sunset, the Richmond, and the southern extremes of the vast South-of-Market neighborhood, down through the Mission District and Noe Valley. A symbiotic relationship developed between these suburbs and the necessary infrastructural services such as gas, water, and the street railways. Proximity to a streetcar line greatly enhanced the value of real estate, both unimproved and built upon, and of course water and gas hookups were essential.[29]

The severe fiscal constraints placed by the electorate on the supervisors and the executive branch of the city government, and especially the ideological ban on redistribution, made it very difficult for the city to provide infrastructural services out of revenues.[30] The solution to this developmental problem was the same as the solution to the fund-raising problem the parties faced: lean on the corporations. Supervisors avoided the taboo of redistributing revenues by granting franchises to "private" corporations – called "quasi-public corporations" by the progressives – for periods of up to fifty years, in return for a small purchase price and, later, a small percentage of the gross receipts. This game had already begun in 1879, when the Board of Supervisors made twenty-six franchise grants. Given the rapid construction of the suburbs, these franchises, which could be bought and sold, became very valuable, and the SP managed to acquire most of them in the city by 1884, under the name of the "Market Street Railway Company."[31]

Thus, the golden age of organizational politics in San Francisco, which lasted from 1881 to 1891, was a product of institutional resources distributed so that politicians could avoid the politics of redistribution in a decade of rapid urban growth. It was not a product of social needs nor of the fragmented nature of urban society prior to the alleged centralization of the economy at the turn of the century, as the social paradigm would have us believe. It was a product of party hegemony over the primary and election processes, of election laws that disciplined the electorate, of local elections timed to match national ones, of an ideology that prevented the city government from providing services at the rate required, and of the enor-

---

[29] William Issel and Robert W. Cherny, *San Francisco, 1865–1932: Politics, Power, and Urban Development* (Berkeley: University of California Press, 1986), 117–38.

[30] Robin Einhorn, *Property Rules: Political Economy in Chicago, 1833–1872* (Chicago: University of Chicago Press, 1991), 1–28, 144–87; McDonald, *Parameters of Urban Fiscal Policy*, 116–202.

[31] Issel and Cherny, *San Francisco*, 132.

mous financial requirements of elections under these structural conditions. The collapse of this system would be a consequence of both distributive and regulatory politics. The distributive politics of infrastructural and party finance, resting as it did on major corporations, burdened the parties with an enormous ideological liability: undeniable association with the "Octopus." Regulative politics, to be taken up in the next section, brought lobbies to the halls of government and would ultimately shatter the coherence of the party oligopoly.

ORIGINS OF INTEREST-GROUP LOBBIES

The reconfiguration of the political community in San Francisco proceeded within and through these contradictory structures of the state and quasi-state insitutions in the 1880s. During the 1870s ideological electoral mobilization aggregated political participants into group identities. Next, policy demands were made by leaders who partially institutionalized these group identities formed in the public sphere. By making credible policy demands in the 1880s and 1890s, these institutionalizing group leaders reinforced group identities by forcing political contestation further to revolve around interest-provoking legislation. This process proceeded rapidly, beginning with the competitive campaigning on issues of race and class in the early 1870s and finding its first fruits in the California Constitution of 1879. By the beginning of the 1890s the process of political mobilization had created the interest-group lobbies considered to be such a natural feature of modern American political culture.

The California Constitution of 1879, which, as Morton Keller observes, was part of a nationwide reaction to postwar public policy, embedded into the state's fundamental law several forms of constituency-aggregating policies.[32] Lobbying for interest groups, in fact, can be said to have begun in that constitutional convention. Laura de Force Gordon and Clara Shortridge Foltz lobbied successfully for the two gender-equality clauses of the constitution: the one guaranteeing equal access to the state's higher education, and the other, even more remarkable, declaring that "No person shall on account of sex be disqualified from entering upon or pursuing

---

[32] Morton Keller, *Affairs of State: Public Life in Late Nineteenth-Century America* (Cambridge: Harvard University Press, 1977), 111–14.

any lawful business, vocation, or profession."[33] The Workingmen's Party of California and Granger representatives loaded the new constitution with redistributive and regulatory legislation masquerading as fundamental law, attempting to tax and regulate corporations in scores of ways and barring all corporations chartered in California from hiring Chinese. Labor politicians enshrined the eight-hour day in the new constitution as well. Most of the redistributive and regulatory content of the new constitution was invalidated by the California and U.S. Supreme Courts; the declaration of eight hours as a legal day's work was, like most eight-hour legislation, full of loopholes and unenforceable. These policy demands, promised but unfulfilled, would not go away.[34]

The politics of policy demands served simultaneously to reinforce and to undermine the organizational party regime of the 1880s.[35] The party leaders, constrained by the consensual ideology of fiscal conservatism, turned to the corporations as a way to fund their growing organizations and provide them with utility services without having to raise taxes or redistribute resources. The corporations, to avoid regulation and redistribution, turned to the parties for security. The SP did not always have its way, as R. Hal Williams makes clear in his study of the California Democratic party, "but the process had become a circular one in which initial railroad involvement and the public's demand for regulation interacted to draw the company further into politics."[36] At the same time, mobilized interest groups sought policy goals inimical to both the parties and the corporations and met, at first, an impasse. Homeowners might be kept happy for some time with seemingly costless

---

[33] California Constitution, article 20, section 18.

[34] Foltz and Gordon's role in the 1879 California Consitutional Convention is detailed in Barbara Allen Babcock, "Clara Shortridge Foltz: Constitution-Maker," *Indiana Law Journal* 66:4 (Fall 1991): 849–940. The standard account of the convention is Carl Brent Swisher, *Motivation and Technique in the California Constitutional Convention, 1878–1879* (Claremont, Calif.: Pomona College, 1930); Linda C. A. Przybyszewski, "Judge Lorenzo Sawyer and the Chinese: Civil Rights Decisions in the Ninth Circuit." *Western Legal History* 1:1 (Winter/Spring 1988): 23–56. Lucile Eaves demonstrates that the eight-hour provision in the California constitution was no more effective than the state law of 1868. *A History of California Labor Legislation with an Introductory Sketch of the San Francisco Labor Movement* (Berkley: University of California Press, 1910), 198–225; Ira B. Cross, *A History of the Labor Movement in California* (Berkeley: University of California Press, 1935), 117–20.

[35] For the distinction between distributive, regulative, and redistributive policies, see Theodore J. Lowi, "American Business, Public Policy, Case-Studies, and Political Theory," *World Politics* 16:4 (July 1964): 677–715.

[36] R. Hal Williams, *The Democratic Party and California Politics*, 12.

infrastructural improvements and rapid gas and water hookups, but the dependent relationship of the parties on the private railroad and the quasi-public utility corporations contained contradictions for the constituencies at the top and the bottom of the socio-economic scale.

In large part because of the covert lobbying practiced by the Southern Pacific, overt, public-sphere lobbies became institution-alized by the close of the 1880s. Most interestingly, interest-group lobbies formed from within the organizational parties, where they would be in a position to achieve fundamental reforms when the contradictions of the organizational regime finally caught up with it. Like a cancer within the parties, interest-group lobbies became malignant immediately after the election of 1890 and weakened the system so badly that the municipal-reform movement could feed on the remains by the end of the century.

In 1883 Ellen Colton, widow of the SP's chief political agent in the 1870s, made public, in the course of a lawsuit, a voluminous cor-respondence between her late husband and Collis P. Huntington, in which the two men openly discussed the purchase of political power in the California legislature. "It costs money to fix things," Huntington advised Colton: "I believe with $200,000 I can pass our bill, but that it is not worth this much to us."[37] The SP's lobby-ing was not, however, part of the public sphere. For one thing, it was either very illegal or patently unethical, and certainly embarras-sing. It was, in short, corrupt. And whereas the influence of the railroad was widespread and often quite legal, as in the payment of lawyer's fees to legislators, the influence was publicly illegitimate from an early date in the railroad's life span. "I have been accused of being a railroad man, which I deny," began an angry exchange at the San Francisco Democratic County Committee in 1872. "I call him to order," responded the first's accuser: "I will expose him in a minute."[38]

A truly modern lobby had to operate legitimately in the public sphere by openly advocating the interests of a specific group and pushing regularly for specific legislation. Lobbies (public) in the modern political culture accomplish what corruption (private) did

[37] Walton Bean and James J. Rawls, *California: An Interpretive History* (New York: McGraw-Hill Book Co., 1988) 217.
[38] *Alta*, 12 August 1872.

in the preceding one. Therein lies the significance of lobbies. They signal a fundamental alteration in the rules of political legitimacy. A public lobby was first introduced by labor organizations attempting to secure and widen the gains they had made in the politics of the 1870s.

As prosperity returned to the city in 1881, so too did the strength of the city's unions. Frank Roney, a socialist who had led the unsuccessful revolt against Denis Kearney in 1878, took command of a moribund organization called the San Francisco Trades Assembly in 1881 and became its chief lobbyist.[39] Roney gradually established a permanent presence of the Trades Assembly in Sacramento. The assembly's "legislative committee" prepared a list of questions for legislators and candidates to record publicly their positions on "employer's liability, factory inspection, postal savings banks, government ownership, free textbooks, weekly pay day, and the abolition of child labor."[40] Its biggest success was the establishment of a bureau of labor statistics in 1883. Based in San Francisco and with primarily San Francisco concerns, the Bureau of Labor Statistics represents the first significant institutional foothold achieved by an interest group in the state. Lacking enforcement powers, its several directors, beginning with the erstwhile Workingmen's party member John S. Enos, nevertheless supplied labor lobbyists with the hard data on working conditions they needed for drafting legislation.[41]

Meanwhile, Roney infiltrated the organizational parties and secured for himself a durable office in the City Hall boiler room; from that base he could devote himself to full-time organizing and lobbying. The scheme by which he gained this office further illustrates how the contradictions of the organizational party regime eventually brought it down. At the height of the organizational hegemony over the election process, the Democratic and Republican leaders took as few chances as possible. As the Democrats had traditionally run strong in the mostly working-class Tenth Ward, Republican leader Bill Higgins sought candidates with working-class

---

[39] Cross, *History of the Labor Movement in California*, 130–40.
[40] Cross, *History of the Labor Movement in California*, 142.
[41] After the collapse of the Workingmen's Party, John S. Enos became a Democratic representative in the Assembly, introducing bills to establish the eight-hour day and the bureau itself. He was director of the bureau from 1883–7. Peter Varcados, "*Labor and Politics in San Francisco, 1880–1892*" (Ph.D. diss.: University of California, Berkeley, 1968), 163–4.

credentials and Democratic approval for the supervisor's seat in that ward. Roney wanted a handpicked union official to get the Republican nomination. "Accordingly I visited several influential Democratic political friends," Roney recalled, "and had them call upon Higgins to urge Gilleran's nomination. Not one of these men knew Gilleran and what they did was done to oblige me." The strength of the Republican presidential ticket – headed by James G. Blaine – in San Francisco that year led to a Republican sweep of the supervisors' seats, and Gilleran was elected. Gilleran returned the favor by acquiring for Roney a patronage spot tending the City Hall boilers. His sympathetic boss "had a writing desk brought into the fireroom, and I began to work as a labor organizer in real earnest, unencumbered with strenuous labor," Roney recalled.[42]

The position of Roney within the network of party political patronage forces us to think of the rise of labor organizations in the 1880s in a different light. We saw, in the last chapter, how Henry George rose through the ranks of the San Francisco Democratic party as a newspaper propagandist and sometime candidate for office. His reward was the gas inspectorship that provided his means of support while he wrote *Poverty and Progress*.[43] The organizational parties were addicted to the money of the corporations, ironically, because they had such a competitive struggle for the voters who, Buckley distinctly remembered, "were likely to give the boss and his lieutenants the go-by." Thus, though they had been stung by the WPC, the party leaders continued to promote and court labor leaders. In fact, the "labor vote," represented as it was by the earliest institutional structure of all the Progressive Era lobbies, would rise in power only as the crisis of the organizational parties came to a head in the 1890s. As the *Chronicle* put it as early as 1886, "It is folly to pretend that labor is not capable of powerful action."[44]

The relative durability of Roney's patronage office contributed greatly to the organizational achievement of the decade: the establishment of a central labor union in San Francisco. Roney was an active organizer in all of the central labor organizations that emerged in the wake of the WPC: the Trades Assembly (1878–84),

---

[42] Frank Roney, *Frank Roney: Irish Rebel and California Labor Leader: An Autobiography*, ed. Ira B. Cross (Berkeley: University of California Press, 1931), 419–23.

[43] See Chapter 6.

[44] Quoted in Varcados, "Labor and Politics in San Francisco," 146.

the Knights of Labor (1881–6), the International Workingmen's Association (1881–7), and finally the successful and potent Federated Trades Council (1885–92).[45] These central labor unions coalesced in the crucial year of 1885–6, when, in conformance with the national strike wave, scores of new unions were formed and federated at the sector level. Having gotten as far as aggregating by the iron, building, and maritime trades, these unions needed permanent organizers to finish the work of federation. Roney supplied this, as did the idiosyncratic radical Burnette Haskell. When the Knights of Labor called a conference to discuss further legislation against the Chinese and against convict labor, Roney and Haskell engineered a takeover of the meeting and founded the "Representative Council of Trades and Labor Federation of the Pacific Coast," or Federated Trades Council (FTC) as it would be known.[46]

The FTC under Roney introduced two new methods to the San Francisco labor movement that were also evolving in other cities: the strike assessment and the boycott. The strike assessment was a redistributive mechanism, taxing unions in one sector for the support of strikers in another. As one could predict, redistributive measures led to disaffection. After costly strikes by the ironworkers, marine firemen, and streetcarmen, the steamship stevedores' and tailors' unions dropped out of the FTC, complaining of the strike assessments.[47]

The boycott was among the most effective emerging weapons in labor organizers' arsenal. It had its San Francisco origins in the anti-Chinese movement, with a white union label movement. Outside of the ideological popularity of anti-Chinese racism, though, organizing a boycott meant overcoming multiple obstacles: those between trades and between people in their roles as producers and consumers. Again, the FTC had the institutional resources to achieve this feat. A very illuminating example was the success of the Typographical Union's strike and boycott against the *Morning*

[45]   Cross, *History of the Labor Movement in California*, 130–216; Eaves, *California Labor Legislation*, 40–6; Roney, *Frank Roney*, 317–560; Varcados, "Labor and Politics in San Francisco," 66–97; Kazin, *Barons of Labor*, 36–63.

[46]   Eaves, *California Labor Legislation*, 43–4; Cross, *History of the Labor Movement in California*, 173, 177–178.

[47]   For the origins of the boycott, see David Scobey, "Boycotting the Politics Factory: Labor Radicalism and the New York City Mayoral Election of 1884," *Radical History Review* 28–30 (1984): 280–325; Cross, *History of the Labor Movement in California*, 179–85; Eaves, *California Labor Legislation*, 45.

Call and the *Evening Bulletin*, both owned by Loring Pickering and George K. Fitch, who had maintained an antiunion hiring policy for many years. In February 1886 the union demanded of Pickering and Fitch a closed shop. When the owners refused, the Typographical Union, with the FTC's blessing, called a boycott, which immediately won the support of more than fifty unions. As we have seen, it was a condition of the newspapers as well as the political parties that they needed working-class support. In just one month the boycott forced Pickering and Fitch to accede to the union's demands.[48]

On 11 May 1886, in part to celebrate the successful strike and boycott of the *Morning Call* and the *Evening Bulletin*, the FTC demonstrated a presence for organized labor that had become permanent. Ten thousand workers, in a line that reportedly stretched ten miles, marched behind Frank Roney, serving as grand marshal, in the city's first Labor Day Parade. Mobilization on this scale did not arise spontaneously from the workshops; it was the product of the carefully wrought institutional networks that Roney and others had pieced together during the years since the Workingmen's Party's demise.[49]

Not all of the strikes in the mid-1880s were successful. The most disastrous were the streetcarmen's strikes of 1886 and 1887. With carmen required to work as long as fourteen to sixteen hours a day for a wage of $2.50, the Carmen's Union had attempted since 1874 to force a reduction in hours and rise in wages. A successful streetcar strike on one line in July 1886, reducing the carmens' shifts to twelve hours for $2.50, led to a strike on the Sutter and Geary lines for similar conditions. This violent strike lasted eighty-six days: "Cars were stoned and damaged, strike breakers were beaten, one person killed, and the ... papers recorded eight explosions of dynamite." The strike was defeated in 1887. One man was found guilty of dynamiting, and the other city unions bore an assessed cost of eleven thousand dollars.[50]

Remarkably, the defeat of this spectacular strike did not end in the disintegration of the FTC. On the contrary, the defections of various unions from the FTC by 1887, as Lucile Eaves perceptively observed, *strengthened it*: "as this left a more wieldy body of

---

48 Cross, *History of the Labor Movement in California*, 179–80.
49 Cross, Ibid., 179–81; Roney, *Frank Roney*, 488–9.
50 Cross, *History of the Labor Movement in California*, 185.

genuinely interested members, who succeeded in exerting a wider influence than had been possible in any previous body." Roney's FTC lobby in Sacramento was able to build on the spectacle of the carmen's strike and achieve a law limiting the hours of gripmen, drivers, and conductors to twelve hours a day. The FTC lobby had achieved a landmark victory in this instance, for the law, signed by the governor on 11 March 1887, was perhaps the first law to regulate working conditions for a single class of persons. An almost identical bill had been vetoed by the governor in March 1874, on the grounds that it constituted "class legislation," meaning it was not aimed at the whole people. With the law limiting the carmen's hours, a milestone in political culture had been passed. Furthermore, in 1880 Governor Perkins had vetoed an attempt to establish a bureau of labor statistics on the grounds that it, too, was special legislation. The achievement of the bureau in 1883, with a broad mandate, had broken that barrier, but the carmen's hours bill much more clearly applied to a discrete subset of the population.[51]

No sooner had the FTC's organized labor lobby begun to score victories, than the merchants and manufacturers woke up to their interests as groups. The earliest trade group was the Manufacturers' Association of California, formed in 1883, by which year labor politicians had secured national legislation in the Chinese Exclusion Act.[52] Employers' associations began to appear in San Francisco in 1886 in response to strikes. The Engineers' and Iron Founders' Association was provoked by the ironworkers' strike; the Eating House Keepers' Association was provoked by the cooks' and waiters' organizing drive; and the Ship Owners' Protective Association defeated the Coast Seamen's Union (CSU) in an 1886 strike involving thirty-five hundred sailors. But again, the CSU's defeat did not come at the cost of weakening the FTC.[53]

The stage was now set for the battle of organized interest-group lobbies in the centers of legislative policy-making, beginning with

---

[51] Eaves, *California Labor Legislation*, 46; Cross, *History of the Labor Movement in California*, 184; 185; Varcados, "Labor and Politics in San Francisco," 118.

[52] "The objects of the Manufacturers' Association are: to develop and protect the producing and manufacturing interests of California; to circulate information of new districts or distant points open to our manufacturers; to prevent oppressive legislation and unfair taxation; to provide a place of meeting for the interchange of ideas and promotion of good feeling among members." The Manufactuers' Association was incorporated 13 November 1893. *San Francisco Directory*, (1890), 87.

[53] Cross, *History of the Labor Movement in California*, 182–3.

San Francisco City Hall. In June 1885 a steam boiler exploded, killing two stationary engineers. Within two weeks the FTC had drafted and submitted to the Board of Supervisors a boiler inspection ordinance, which provided for the appointment of a skilled worker as boiler inspector and for yearly inspection of boilers. Moreover, it stipulated that only skilled workers could operate boilers, and that boilers must be operated under a certificate of inspection. Two wealthy supervisors with boilers in their businesses, John S. Gibbs and Claus Spreckels, blocked the ordinance. Gibbs made the unlikely argument that San Francisco's "boilers were the best in the world and if the ordinance passed it would shut down 90 percent of them." The FTC then secured campaign pledges from the Democratic party's County Committee for a boiler-inspection ordinance. These campaign pledges were made in public, one FTC's lobbying method that distinguished them from the railroad lobby. Made in public, specific pledges were hard to break, so when the Democrats recovered a majority on the Board of Supervisors in 1888, they won the introduction again of a boiler-inspection ordinance. By this time, however, the group targeted with regulation had formed the Manufacturers' Association of California and had brought their new organization to bear against the inspection law. This organization included Andrew S. Hallidie, the founder of the city's cable car systems, and Irving Scott, owner of the city's largest boiler factory. Faced with this opposition, the supervisors faltered and allowed the ordinance to die.[54]

At the state level the FTC had greater and increasing success. Building on the 1887 carmen's bill breakthrough, which regulated the hours of labor in a private industry for the first time (perhaps because it was a "quasi-public" corporation), the FTC lobby joined with the state commissioner of labor and the San Francisco assemblyman James Maguire to enact two bills regulating the working conditions of children and women. The Child Labor Bill of 1889 provided that no male under the age of sixteen or female under the age of eighteen be required to work more than sixty hours a week. This bill ran up against that earlier product of lobbying, the equal opportunity clause of the constitution, so it was amended to apply the age of eighteen to both sexes. Another bill required the

[54] Varcados, "Labor and Politics in San Francisco," 179, 181.

provision of bathrooms and sanitary conditions if women were employed.[55]

With the rise under Roney's leadership of the FTC, labor had provoked the formation of business lobbies during the organizational party regimes of the 1880s. These groups were built on the sudden consciousness of shared interests within sectors of the manufacturing elite provoked by the threat of specific regulations. The capitalist class, however, rarely found an opportunity to see itself as such in political terms. William Issel summarizes an all-important pattern in the political activity of San Francisco's business elite: "Never a monolithic political bloc, business developed its political role in the urban policy-making process by a complex combination of bargaining and conflict with its rivals, and by accommodating to its internal differences, rather than by imposing its preferences upon the body politic."[56] It is a serious mistake to imagine that a business or corporate elite initiated progressivism in San Francisco. The business leadership was a latecomer to the foundational changes in the city's political culture that would constitute progressivism; labor organizations deserve that palm. The many sector-level business lobbies did not even manage to form "peak" associations until 1892, a full year after the pivotal reform victory – the Australian ballot – had been achieved.

Modern interest-group lobbies, then, were formed first by labor leaders in the public sphere from an institutional base in the organizational party regime of the 1880s. To perform in public, however, both parties and lobbies needed the press and had to work within a structure of discourse increasingly transformed in style and content by the rise of the mass media.

FROM COMMUNICATIONS BUSINESS TO POLITICAL-
CULTURE INDUSTRY

A truthful sensation has always been desired, its value has always been admitted ...

– William Randolph Hearst (1888)[57]

---

[55] Eaves, *California Labor Legislation*, 315–16.
[56] William Issel, " 'Citizens Outside Government': Business and Urban Policy in San Francisco and Los Angeles, 1890–1932," *Pacific Historical Review* 58 (1988): 119.
[57] William Randolph Hearst, "Pacific Coast Journalism," *Overland Monthly*, 2 Ser., vol. 2 (April 1888): 404.

The Hearst method has all the reality of masturbation
— Ambrose Bierce[58]

The rise of mass, commercial, sensational journalism was a central element in the origins of progressivism. Yet, we know little about the *work* this new media did in changing the political culture of modern America in the Progressive Era. Worse, it is not even clear what was new about the new media of Pulitzer and Hearst in the late 1880s and the 1890s. Sensationalism in the news, usually defined as reliance on lurid stories of crime, sex, monstrosities, and the bizarre intended to "excite the emotions of the reader," was, as Frank Luther Mott observed long ago, an important part of American journalism since the eighteenth century.[59] Commercialism, as well, was central to the rise of the American public sphere since long before the Civil War, as previous chapters have demonstrated. Nor was independence from political party affiliation a new feature of journalism in the 1890s.

Yet few would doubt that Joseph Pulitzer and William Randolph Hearst fundamentally restructured the news business in the last decades of the nineteenth century (making it into a major industry), and that the new journalism fed the changes in political culture in an important way. "Muckraking" journalism about the crimes of politicians and about the injustices inflicted on workers and consumers by manufacturers, corporations, and quasi-public utilities was a staple feature of progressivism. Because Hearst has gained an almost mythic status in the history of American journalism, it is necessary to situate his arrival within the longer-term trends. It should become clear that the critical difference Hearst made to the structure of the public sphere after his arrival in 1887 was a reorientation of the position of the reader vis-à-vis the state, so that by the early 1890s, citizens were steadily recast from their earlier role as participants into a newer one as consumers.

The newspaper in the 1880s and 1890s continued to provide the central forum of San Francisco's public sphere; its role in communication was little changed since the beginnings of the city in the 1850s. It is wrong to think of newspapers as a means of bridging

---

58 Quoted in Ferdinand Lundberg, *Imperial Hearst: A Social Biography*, with a preface by Dr. Charles A. Beard (New York: Equinox Press, 1936), 23.
59 Frank Luther Mott, *American Journalism: A History of Newspapers in the United States Through 260 Years: 1690 to 1950*, rev. (New York: Macmillan Co., 1950), 442–3.

the geographic distance imposed by urban growth and the development of neighborhood subcommunities.[60] The growth in size and complexity of the city had no visible impact on the basic shape or operation of the newspaper market. Citizens would continue to meet in- and out-of-doors by the thousands or tens of thousands through the end of the century. The most rapid period of residential neighborhood expansion occurred in the 1880s, but the newspaper market was extensive long before then. When the U.S. Census published its national survey of the periodical press in 1880, San Francisco, the ninth largest city, had the third highest per capita circulation rate and, with its twenty-one dailies, ranked behind only New York City (which had twenty-nine) and Philadelphia (twenty-four) in the total number of papers in circulation.[61]

Important changes in the format of newspapers, however, were underway. From the mid-1870s through the end of the century, the trend was toward smaller newspapers with less space devoted to advertising and a changed presentation of the news content. Perhaps the most interesting and fundamental of these changes was the diminishing ratio of advertising to news. In 1870 the *Chronicle* devoted about 62 percent of its total space (measured in column inches) to advertising and the *Examiner* about 70 percent. In 1880 these figures were closer to 50 percent, and by 1900 both papers filled their pages with slightly less than 40 percent advertising to 60 percent news space.[62] Further, advertising filled much or most of the newspapers' front pages in the 1870s, whereas all the major papers had banished ads to inside pages by 1891. This change may seem paradoxical within a society that historians have agreed was becoming more consumerist as industrialization brought an avalanche of new goods to the urban market. Indeed, advertising grew in the share of the newspapers' revenues as the space devoted to it shrank. The answer to this paradox is in part that advertising grew more efficient and more modern. In 1870 none of the advertising contained "sales

60   For a sophisticated statement of the view I reject here, see David Paul Nord, "The Public Community: The Urbanization of Journalism in Chicago" *Journal of Urban History* 11:4 (August 1985): 411–42.

61   S. N. D. North, "The Newspaper and Periodical Press," in U.S. Department of the Interior, *Tenth Census of the United States*, vol. 8 (Washington; D.C.: Government Printing Office, 1884), 77.

62   U.S. Work Projects Administration, *History of San Francisco Journalism, vol 4.*, Emerson L. Daggett, Supervisor, *Trends In Size, Circulation, News and Advertising in San Francisco Journalism, 1870–1938* (San Francisco, 1940) [mimeograph], 21, Harvard College Library.

appeal"; it simply listed in uniform small type the merchandise available. By the 1880s "display advertisements" became common. These were multicolumn ads with illustrations and claims about the qualities of the product being sold.[63] Such advertising was more expensive because it required artwork and more space, but it became the hallmark of an emergent consumer society.

These changes in advertising, however, do not explain the changes in news presentation. Because the basic economics of the newspaper business had not changed since the 1840s, we can assume that exciting news coverage was intended to sell advertising space in the 1860s, '70s, '80s, and '90s alike. With the banishment of the advertisements to the inside pages, surely the news had been given first priority before the reader's eyes. What *was* changing, I would suggest, was what constituted *exciting* news coverage. The authors of a Work Projects Administration study of San Francisco journalism conducted in the late 1930s were shocked by the way the city's editors in 1880 "carried little or nothing to attract readers to their columns." They give as an example the *Bulletin's* story of a kidnapping, in which the father had paid sixty thousand dollars in ransom for his son. This story took only one-and-a-half column inches "without headlines," whereas a "letter from the public" on the issue of whether the library should close at nine o'clock or remain open, was given seven-and-a-half inches, "dressed up" with headlines.[64] Certainly Hearst in the 1890s would present a story such as a kidnapping with screaming banner headlines, would provide pictures of the kidnapped child, and would send investigative reporters to develop personal-interest stories. But the journalists who wrote the WPA study, operating within the standards established by Pulitzer and Hearst, could no longer understand what would "attract" readers in the years up to 1880. Given that the *Bulletin* sold advertising space with stories about library closing hours within San Francisco's intensely competitive market, we can only assume that such stories interested the readers.

Besides, the *Bulletin*, like the *Alta*, was a relatively conservative newspaper. The use of sensation to build readership had been pioneered, as we have seen, by the de Youngs in the 1870s, when they

63   U.S. Work Projects Administration, *History of San Francisco Journalism*, vol. 6, Charles Holmes and Isom Shepard, *History of the Physical Growth and Technological Advance of the San Francisco Press* (San Francisco, 1940) [mimeograph], 87–108, Harvard College Library.
64   Work Projects Administration, *History of San Francisco Journalism*, 6:83.

exploited the WPC story to win leadership in the city's circulation wars. Their efforts climaxed in 1879 with the erection of the *Chronicle*'s tall tower at the corner of Kearny and Bush streets. This building contained the latest technology in printing equipment and signaled the end of the period in which competitors could enter the market with small capital investments. The sensationalism exploited by the de Youngs, however, always of a political nature, had invited bullets and other violent assaults several times since they began the Republican paper in 1865 in the wreckage of rioting against the Democratic press.[65] And that sensationalism finally cost Charles de Young his life when the son of Mayor Kalloch marched up the stairs of the new *Chronicle* building and killed the editor behind his desk.[66]

Not surprisingly, it was the surviving Michael de Young who introduced the urban reform program in a sensational format. In 1885, two years before Hearst acquired the *Examiner*, the *Chronicle* ran a story headlined:

FILTHY SEWERS, A SYSTEM OF ELONGATED CESSPOOLS, MILES OF DIRTY DRAINS, TONS OF ACCUMULATING OFFENSIVENESS, MUDDY MISSION FLATS, A STANDING MENACE TO HEALTH, THE CITY FRONT ENVIRONED WITH AN ILL-ODOROUS BELT OF CONTAMINATION.

Still, the notion of "sensational" journalism was not yet publicly legitimate. De Young had to accompany this story with a disclaimer: "It is not the intention to make the present article one of a sensational or alarmist nature, but it is the intention to say plainly just what the condition of things is."[67]

It is probably fair to say that, until about the mid-1880s, the plainly presented news material was exciting enough to the readers, but that entrepreneurs like de Young, who sought wider circulation, began changing the standards for excitement. To do so, they merely drew from the toolbox assembled by James Gordon Bennett and Benjamin Day in the 1830s and Joseph Pulitzer more recently. Had Hearst never acquired a San Francisco newspaper, the city's press would doubtless have changed in the same direction under the pressure of de Young's or Pulitzer's innovations. But Hearst's

[65] *Langley's City Directory* (1872), 41–2; *Langley's City Directory* (1873), 41.
[66] See previous chapter.
[67] San Francisco *Chronicle*, 15 September 1885.

arrival caused a massive speedup of the trends already underway in both the format and the content of the central institution of the city's public sphere.

The outlines of William Randolph Hearst's biography are familiar enough, known to recent generations, principally through Orson Welles's *Citizen Kane* (1941). The only child of the mining millionaire George Hearst, young William Randolph was doted on by his mother, Phoebe Apperson Hearst, a leading San Francisco society matron and philanthropist. His parents provided him education through a private academy, but the results were not good. At Harvard, which he entered in 1882, he spent his time playing expensive pranks. For his last, he sent chamber pots to each of his professors – including William James and Josiah Royce – with their pictures affixed to the inside bottom. For this he was expelled in his third year. Although he demonstrated a contempt for learning, he was fascinated with journalism. He visited the Boston *Globe*, which had begun experimenting with sensational commercial methods, and then worked on Pulitzer's *World* briefly before returning to San Francisco in 1887.[68]

Since 1865 the *Examiner* had been the official organ of the Democratic party. During the early 1870s the paper grew addicted to party fortunes by relying for its revenue on its designation as the publisher of official announcements. When the WPC temporarily ruined the Democratic party, the paper lost profitability. Meanwhile, George Hearst, an unlettered man who had made his fortune in the Homestake and other mining speculations, wanted to cap his career with a seat in the U.S. Senate. As we have seen, one needed to bring resources to the table of organizational party power in order to achieve office. Hearst acquired the unprofitable *Examiner* because it would make him a party leader in the act of purchase. He also brought an enormous sum of money to the cash-poor Democratic party, which, compared with the Republicans, could boast few millionaire benefactors.[69]

When George Hearst finally wrung his Senate seat from the state legislature in 1887, he no longer needed the pathetic *Examiner* and turned it over to his superfluous son. William Randolph, now aged

---

68 Lundberg, *Imperial Hearst*, 20; W. A. Swanberg, *Citizen Hearst: A Biography of William Randolph Hearst* (New York: Charles Scribner's Sons, 1961), 33–4.
69 R. Hal Williams, *Democratic Party and California Politics*, 65–6; Petersen, "Prelude to Progressivism," 30–45.

twenty-four, had big ideas for the little paper. Even before taking control of the paper he had arranged to be the sole San Francisco subscriber to Joseph Pulitzer's news service. "I am anxious to begin work on the *Examiner*," the son wrote to his father: "We must be alarming and enterprising, and we must be startlingly original. We must be honest and fearless. We must have greater variety than we have ever had."[70] William Randolph, however, had to find a method that would outshine the aggressive Michael de Young, and to do so he simply outspent de Young and innovated in style as rapidly as he could.

Hearst could afford to innovate without fear of losing business because the *Examiner* did not have any business to speak of and because money was of little object to him. Surrounding himself with real talent, young Hearst brought the curmudgeonly Ambrose Bierce out of retirement and hired a bevy of reporters to write or create personal-interest stories and exposés. For managing editor he hired the "drunken, profane and corrupt" Sam S. Chamberlain, who had been secretary to the elder James Gordon Bennett, editorial director of the New York *Evening Telegram*, and, with the backing of San Francisco silver millionaire John W. Mackay, founder of the Paris *Le Matin*.[71] For management Hearst hired Arthur "Brainy" Brisbane, son of the Fourierist utopian socialist Albert Brisbane, who would serve as Hearst's close friend and chief advisor for years. The presence of Brainy Brisbane was an important source of the paper's aggressive populism. And for editorial writing Hearst hired his Harvard buddy and fellow prankster Arthur McKewen.

This staff helped Hearst break into the *Chronicle*-dominated market by changing the rules of the game. Just four days after Hearst's first edition, the *Chronicle* banished advertisements from its front page. But the key alteration that Hearst forced upon the San Francisco market was a reorientation of the news content. In part, this entailed an impoverishment of language. "There is no need ever to use a word of more than three syllables in a newspaper," Brainy Brisbane lectured his writers. He admonished them that "a newspaper is mostly read by very busy people, or by very tired people, or by very uneducated people none of whom are going to hunt up

[70] Swanberg, *Citizen Hearst*, 37.
[71] John K. Winkler, *W. R. Hearst: An American Phenomenon* (New York: Simon and Shuster, 1928), 83; Lundberg, *Imperial Hearst*, 26.

a dictionary to find out what you mean."[72] This linguistic strategy may sound democratic, but it was in fact a major step in cutting the masses off from the rich language that had characterized the public sphere of earlier decades. For, as Brisbane undoubtedly knew, there was in the 1880s a raging debate among editors and educators about the appropriate form of speech in American society. By choosing the same side as Denis Kearney, who also participated in the debate by denouncing "classical speech," Brisbane was using language consciously to build a readership the same way Kearney had used it to build a political movement.[73]

In the process of forcing a place for their paper in the newspaper market, Hearst, Brisbane, and McKewen altered the condition of the reader. Because reading newspapers was an engagement in the public sphere and its political debates, Hearst's innovations had an enormous impact on the functioning of political participation. Editorialist McKewen summarized the *Examiner's* goal: "What we're after is the gee-whiz emotion."[74] Hearst's goal and achievement was to break though the critical-rational operation of the newspaper and find a reliable market somewhere below the level of debatable knowledge. Illustrations of course operated on this level. One can respond to a Nast cartoon or others in that genre, but one cannot rebut it as an argument as one can text. Hearst's staff made the text work in this way also. In his first big "scoop," Hearst sent a team of writers and illustrators in a chartered train to cover the burning of a luxury hotel in Del Monte. The writers cast the story in unmistakably erotic language: "HUNGRY, FRANTIC FLAMES LEAPING HIGHER AND HIGHER, WITH DESPERATE DESIRE."[75]

Proceeding from his motto that "there is no substitute for circulation," Hearst gave his paper the title "Monarch of the Dailies" in the first month of operation, while still far behind the circulation of the *Chronicle*.[76] Promising readers "THE MOST ELABORATE NEWS, THE BRIGHTEST SOCIAL NEWS, THE LATEST AND MOST ORIGINIAL SENSATION," Hearst adopted the strategy of the New York *World*, to let readers know that they "could depend on being startled, amazed

72 Brisbane quoted in Roy Everett Littlefield III, *William Randolph Hearst: His Role in American Journalism* (Lanham, Md.: University Press of America, 1980), 13.

73 Kenneth Cmiel, *Democratic Eloquence: The Fight over Popular Speech in Nineteenth-Century America* (New York William Morrow and Co., 1990), 176–257.

74 Lundberg, *Imperial Hearst*, 26.

75 *Examiner*, 3 April 1887.

76 *Examiner*, 12 March 1887.

or stupefied daily simply by buying the *Examiner*." But as W. A. Swanberg correctly observes, "stupefying things do not happen every day," and Hearst "solved this by creating them."[77] The creation of news, a process Daniel Boorstin describes as "the pseudo-event," completed the string of changes that reoriented the position of the reader.[78] Hearst had his reporters make news in numerous ways. These stunts included paying a couple to get married in a balloon and capturing a grizzly bear, naming it "Monarch," and after parading it through the streets, donating it to the zoo. Significantly, however, much of the stuntwork was aimed at testing the city's public services. One reporter, H. R. Haxton, an expert swimmer, deliberately fell off the San Francisco–Oakland ferry to test the company's rescue readiness. Another, reporter, Winifred Sweet "Annie Laurie" Black, faked a fainting spell, was taken to the city hospital, and then "exposed" the horrid conditions there. Winifred Black was so successful at the new project of creating news in personal-interests stories that she is credited as the first "sob sister" of American journalism. Her exploits were so admired by the time of her death in 1935 that her body lay in state, by order of the mayor, in the City Hall rotunda.[79]

The production of news at this premeditated, industrial level certainly built circulation. The *Examiner*'s circulation shot from ten thousand in 1886 to fifty thousand four years later, catching up with the *Chronicle* and surpassing de Young's paper with nearly eighty thousand by 1896: a rate of growth many times greater than the population increase over ten years.[80] But the production of news created more than readers, it created *consumers*. Whereas the reader in the newspaper market of the period up to the 1880s was in large part a participant in the print medium's substantial segment of the public sphere, the reader after the arrival of Hearst was gradually but unmistakably cast in the role of a consumer. This effect was even greater as Hearst forced concentration in the market. De Young was able to keep pace with Hearst's mounting circulation figures and signaled his intent to do battle by building the city's first

[77]   Swanberg, *Citizen Hearst*, 45.

[78]   Daniel Boorstin, *The Image: A Guide to Pseudo-Events in America* (New York: Atheneum, 1987), 7–44.

[79]   Swanberg, *Citizen Hearst*, 45–60; Walton Bean, "Black, Winifred Sweet," in *Notable American Women, 1607–1950: A Biographical Dictionary*, ed. Edward T. James and Janet Wilson James, 3 vols. (Cambridge: Belknap Press, 1971), 1:154–6.

[80]   Work Projects Administration, *History of San Francisco Journalism*, 4:64–65.

steel-ribbed skyscraper in 1890, at the corner of Market, Geary, and Kearny streets.[81] Claus Spreckels, owner of the *Call*, met Hearst's and de Young's challenge by building the soaring twenty-five-story office tower next door to the Hearst Building. But the *Alta*, that pillar of respectable, independent journalism, proved unwilling to change. In 1885 it noted the increasing use of illustrations as "A Growing But Silly Newspaper Fashion of the Day."[82] By 1891, in its fortieth year, the *Alta California* was forced to close its doors.[83] By the turn of the century, circulation wars took place between newspaper-publishing giants whose huge buildings, the largest in the city, faced each other across Market Street, in the heart of the central business district. (See Plate 7.1.)

The arrival of mass consumer journalism did not mean that the role of the press had become superficial or unreal. This is the significance of Bierce's quip that the "Hearst method has all of the reality of masturbation." The outcome was no less real for having been self-actuated. William Randolph Hearst had a strong political agenda. After Henry George, he would be the second San Francisco journalist to mount a serious campaign for mayor of New York City. Indeed, he had presidential ambitions as early as 1904. Franklin K. Lane, who built his political career within the Hearst-dominated public sphere of San Francisco, explained that Hearst "knows public sentiment and how to develop it very well.... He has great capacity for disorganization of any movement that is not his own, and an equal capacity for organization of any movement that is his personal property." Lane, then, summarized the two halves of the "Hearst method": the power to shape public opinion and the power to disorganize rivals. "He feels with the people," Lane continued, "but he has no conscience."[84]

The maturation of the political culture of pluralist liberalism in the 1890s depended very much on the reorientation of the media worked by Hearst and his competitors. In 1888 Hearst published a magazine article explaining his "method." For a newspaper to

81   John P. Young, *History of Journalism in San Francisco* (San Francisco: Chronicle Publishing Co., 1951), 135–6.

82   *Alta California*, 12 November 1885.

83   The last issue of *Alta California* was that of 2 June 1891, in which the editors claim that they preferred to go out of business rather than become a sensational paper.

84   Franklin K. Lane to Edward B. Whitney, 13 November 1905, in *The Letters of Franklin K. Lane: Personal and Political*, ed. Anne Wintermute Lane and Louis Herrick Wall (Boston and New York: Houghton Mifflin Co., 1922), 52.

Plate 7.1. The Hearst Building and the Spreckels Building, 1905, housing the *Examiner* and the *Call*, respectively. This view shows the physical center of the public city, recognizably "modern" yet still the site of participatory, even face-to-face communication. This view across Market Street toward the southwest corner of Market and New Montgomery, shows several generations of physical development at the core of the city's central business district. In the distance, toward the foot of Market Street at the Bay, the retail and office buildings are typical of the antebellum city. The eight-story building with the bay windows is the opulent Palace Hotel. Once considered giant in size (see Plate 6.1), the Palace Hotel helped shift the center of the business district from the old Plaza (see Plate 1.1) on Kearny St. to this intersection. William Randolph Hearst's 1890s structure, matching the Palace in scale, and the Spreckels *Call* building, soaring to twenty-five stories, together announce the continued centrality of newspapers in the urban public sphere. The broad space of Market Street, with its slow-moving streetcars and horse traffic, was still the domain of pedestrians. The space pictured here was capable of accommodating huge crowds. The *Examiner*, in competition with the *Chronicle* and the *Call*, attracted such crowds to its building on election nights and on other newsworthy occasions by announcing election returns from the grand balcony, within hearing distance of the street below. Courtesy of Bancroft Library, Berkeley, California. Graves Collection.

"have a large circulation" in San Francisco, Hearst explained, it "must address almost everybody, and to do that, of course, it must have articles to suit the different classes." Hearst used the term "classes" to embrace both ethnic-national and socioeconomic groups. He did not argue that such a newspaper must address issues common to all these "classes," but instead that it must address each of them separately, a strategy that must produce a physically large newspaper. Papers like the *Morning Journal* or the *Times* in New York could afford to address specific classes, he explained, because the city was large enough to provide a substantial market within that class. Because San Francisco was so cosmopolitan,

there are just as many classes in California as there are in New York. Say there are twenty. Hence if a paper speaks to a class, it speaks to one-twentieth of the reading population. In New York this would be one-twentieth of several millions; here but one-twentieth of less than half a million.[85]

Hearst was both responding to and creating a market of "classes," or social groups. He had no sense of a universal public interest, but rather sensed a segmeted one that required specific targeting. By recasting the reader from participant to consumer, the mass commercial media reconceived the citizen as a marketing target, with interests and needs to which journalists could appeal.

The three elements of political-cultural evolution traced so far – the potential for delegitimation of the major party regime of the 1880s, the rise of interest-group lobbies, and the reconstruction of communications in the public sphere – now worked to bring to maturity the group identities that had begun to arise after the Civil War and would became the basic units of twentieth-century political life.

THE REORGANIZATION OF GROUP IDENTITIES

During the 1890s the classic sociological categories – class, race, ethnicity, and gender – became institutionalized as concrete elements of the political public sphere. These group identities simultaneously became the building blocks and the stumbling blocks of

---

[85] Hearst, "Pacific Coast Journalism," 403.

political mobilization for the progressive reformers. Interest-group leaders of the newly formed lobby organizations and officeholders who saw those leaders as wielding blocs of votes now entered into the symbiotic relationship that characterizes twentieth-century American political culture. Together with the Hearst-reoriented mass press, and sensitive to markets within a rapidly commercializing public sphere, the new directors of public communication not only reified but reinforced group identities, legitimating for the first time "class legislation," or policy that openly benefited only one group.

This process was discontinuous, contradictory, and incomplete. Each new "group" was in fact just a different combination of institutional resources, capable of shaping the behavior and consciousness of individuals from the top to the bottom of the political community, and outside of it as well. Organized in the political public sphere, these group identities were constitutive of consciousness. What was experienced as overlapping sentiments about group membership at an infinite number of points in the social structure of San Francisco – in the public media, at the workplace, in the community, and in the home – could be crystallized into something more coherent, called group consciousness, at crucial junctures by actors heading institutions created to speak in the name of groups. What we are describing, then, is not a "real" group, such as the working class, and its leaders, who either represent or misrepresent them. We are describing thousands of people who could be mobilized (or mobilized against) along several lines of demarcation. Further, the occasion and ability to so mobilize people along different lines arose from within the preexisting institutional structure of the political public sphere. For that sphere has a shape with access points roughly defined at any given moment primarily by the parties and the press, but also by voluntary groups and other institutions, such as labor organizations, churches, and universities.

We have seen how the labor leaders of the Federated Trades Council, along with maverick party activists and the mass press, undermined the hegemony of the Democratic and Republican parties by the year 1891. At the same time, however, three "groups" appeared institutionally to complicate the political public sphere of the 1890s. These were the working class, Irish Catholics, and women. Taking each of these in turn, we find that the transformation of political culture in the 1890s had to happen within the context of highly mobilized groups without clear allegiances to any of the key actors in the parties, the press, or the government.

Labor was the first group identity to mature, as we have seen, in the postwar public sphere. The early maturation of that identity enabled the institutionalization of the FTC with the organizational help of the party leaders. But the organization of a labor interest was never fully tamed by the organizational party leaders. The most persistent problem was the recurrent mobilization of working-class voters by activists on the ideological left. The extraordinary political mobilization of workers by the Workingmen's Party of California never really subsided; it merely fragmented.[86] One offshoot in this fragmentation was the organization of the "International Workingmen's Association" (IWA) by the quixotic (yet sometimes effective) Burnette G. Haskell. Haskell, born in California in 1857, was educated at, but never graduated from, the University of California, the University of Illinois, and Oberlin College. In 1879 he passed his California bar exam but followed the usual pattern into public leadership by acquiring a newspaper, called *Truth*, financed by his uncle in 1882. Haskell, who fancied himself a clandestine revolutionary, organized the IWA in that year, with an explicitly Marxist platform and an encrypted cell structure that owed as much to the secret fraternal Freemasons or Odd Fellows as it did to international communism. In the estimation of the labor historian Ira Cross, Haskell was "one of the most erratic and brilliant geniuses in the history of the labor movement on the Pacific Coast." Claiming "millions of members" worldwide, Haskell's IWA numbered at most a few hundred card-carrying members at its height in the mid-1880s.[87]

Haskell's ability to mobilize even hundreds, through *Truth*, indicates the existence of a highly class-conscious working-class network in San Francisco. Analysis of the known members of the IWA reveals that the most ideologically radical participants in the political public sphere were characterized by the same occupational and geo-

[86] Michael Kazin, "The Great Exception Revisited: Organized Labor and Politics in San Francisco and Los Angeles, 1870–1940," *Pacific Historical Review* 60:3 (August 1986): 371–402.

[87] Cross, *History of the Labor Movement in California*, 156–65, 167; Issel and Cherny, *San Francisco*, 81–2.

graphic stability that characterized the core political community of the city.[88] Although in numbers the IWA was not widespread, Haskell and these members succeeded in organizing the Coast Seamen's Union in 1885, a heroic feat in itself, in an industry marked by employer repression. The IWA leadership was also instrumental in organizing the brewery workers, the Knights of Labor, and the Federated Trades Council before it broke up in the late 1880s following a failed sailors' strike and Haskell's departure with a band of settlers to found the cooperative colony at Kaweah, California.[89]

More widely, "Dr." C. C. O'Donnell presented the Democratic and Republican party leaders with a perennial labor-vote problem. O'Donnell, one of the original organizers of the Workingmen's Party of California, survived that party's demise and began to mount independent candidacies for office in 1886. Evidence about O'Donnell's appeal is scarce because he rarely appeared in the press. It is clear that he continued to organize in the WPC tradition, leading the San Francisco Anti-Coolie League in the late 1880s and early 1890s.[90] Terrence McDonald summarizes the best available evidence to conclude that "O'Donnell's yoking together of attacks on the Chinese and the rich represented working-class political consciousness circa 1879." His votes came almost exclusively from the working-class wards of the city, the waterfront and South-of-Market neighborhoods. After garnering more votes as an independent in 1884 for coroner than the winning mayoral candidate, he began running for higher office. In 1886, with no party organiza-

---

88   Through an intensive investigation of 187 members identified in Haskell's diary, Bruce Dancis reports that IWA members lived in the city slightly longer than the working-class population at large, and that native-born and German-born membership was greater than those groups' distribution in the city, while Irish-born members participated proportionally to their distribution in the labor force. Sixty-two percent were blue-collar workers, and most of these were skilled. Bruce Dancis, "Social Mobility and Class Consciousness: San Francisco's International Workingmen's Association in the 1880s," *Journal of Social History* 11:1 (Fall 1977): 75–98.

89   Varcados, "Labor and Politics in San Francisco," 200–2; Cross, *History of the Labor Movement in California*, 158–9.

90   O'Donnell also appears in building records as having built homes exclusively with day laborers, which indicates either a solicitude toward the unskilled, nonunion workers or perhaps a desire to cut costs. "Dr. C. C. O'Donnell hired 'daywork' to build five slightly peculiar homes in 1887 for four thousand dollars. Perhaps he also designed them, for the cluster at 1328–46 York Street in the Inner Mission neighborhood looks like no other in the City!" Judith Lynch Waldhorn and Sally B. Woodbridge, *Victoria's Legacy* (San Francisco: 101 Productions, 1978), 27.

tion to back him, O'Donnell took 20 percent of the city's vote for governor as an independent. Two years later he ran for mayor of San Francisco, in a three-way campaign against Democrat E. B. Pond and Republican C. R. Story, again as in independent. This time he received 28 percent of the votes cast and forced Pond to take office with a plurality of 38 percent of the citywide vote. In 1890 O'Donnell did even better, taking 31 percent of the vote for mayor, to the Democrat's 29 percent; the victorious Republican, G. Sunderson, had to take office with only a 38 percent vote mandate. Again in 1892 O'Donnell took 28 percent of the vote for mayor. That year, however, the Reform Ballot Act so undermined the major parties that another independent candidate, Levi Ellert, won office on the "Non Partisan" ticket with 30 percent of the vote. The Democrat took a mere 22 percent of the votes in that election and the Republican only 15 percent! O'Donnell's performance at the polls began to taper off in 1894, when the enormously popular Adolph Sutro won the mayoralty with 50 percent of the vote. Still, O'Donnell took 23 percent that year, to the Democrat's 7 percent and the Republican's 19 percent.[91]

What makes these showings by O'Donnell so impressive is first, that most were achieved in defiance of the major parties' control of the balloting process, and second, that the major dailies virtually ignored O'Donnell, depriving him even of the minimum publicity available to major-party candidates. His supporters had to take a ticket from the major-party distributors, strike out the name of the party candidate, and write in O'Donnell's. Unfortunately, it is very difficult to say anything with precision about O'Donnell's source of votes. Census data are lacking for the period in which O'Donnell did so well, but Terrence McDonald estimates that in the presidential elections of 1888 and 1892 "26 percent of those who voted for the Democratic presidential ticket split for O'Donnell, while 28 percent of those voting Republican did so."[92] O'Donnell drew his votes from both major parties, mainly in the most heavily working-class neighborhoods, and ran on a persistent antiwealthy, anti-Chinese platform. His candidacies testify to an institutionally uncaptured

[91]   McDonald, *Parameters of Urban Fiscal Policy*, p. 201; San Francisco *Examiner*, 9 November 1884, 24 November 1886, 24 November 1888, 30 November 1890, 12 November 1892, 8 November 1894.
[92]   McDonald, *Parameters of Urban Fiscal Policy*, 199–200.

working-class political expression that would outlive the hegemony of the two major parties in the 1880s.[93]

Overlapping the labor-group identity in the 1890s was the institutionalization for the first time of an Irish Catholic identity in the public sphere. The public construction of that identity is attributable to the efforts of a single leader, the "Fighting Priest" Father Peter C. Yorke. Born in Galway in 1864, Yorke entered St. Patrick's College of Maynooth, Ireland, in 1882, just as young John Henry Wigmore, Franklin K. Lane, and James Duval Phelan were entering the project of political reform in San Francisco. Yorke did not emigrate to the United States until he received word in 1886 that he would join the archdiocese of San Francisco. After two years of preparation at St. Mary's Seminary in Baltimore, Yorke reported to Archbishop Riordan in San Francisco in 1888, just when the city's public sphere began its rapid period of transformation. However, Yorke was being groomed as a spokesman for the archdiocese, and in 1889 he entered the new Catholic University in Washington for graduate work in Semitic languages. Energetic and intellectual, Yorke rose through the local hierarchy rapidly after returning in 1891. Teaching in the city's parochial schools, Yorke became a theorist of Catholic education. He rose from curator of St. Mary's Cathedral on Van Ness Avenue to archdiocesan chancellor by 1893.[94]

In September 1893 the American Protective Association (APA), a nativist organization that had been founded in Iowa several years earlier, opened its first chapter in San Francisco and began to spread anti-Catholic propaganda.[95] The following January Father Yorke founded, with the future police chief William Sullivan, the League of the Cross Cadets, a men's club pledged to temperance and "the cause of religion." In April, with the apparent intent of combating the APA, Archbishop Riordan appointed the militant Yorke to edit the church's official newspaper, the *Monitor*. As the long-lived editor of the official voice of Catholicism in San

93   This paragraph relies on the analysis in McDonald, *Parameters of Urban Fiscal Reform*, 199–202.

94   David Joseph Herlihy, "Battle against Bigotry: Father Peter C. Yorke and the American Protective Association, 1893–1897," *Record of the American Catholic Historical Society of Philadelphia* 62:2 (June 1951): 95–100; Bernard Cornelius Cronin. "Father Yorke and the Labor Movement in San Francisco, 1900–1910," *The Catholic University of America Studies in Economics*, vol. 12 (Washington, D.C.: Catholic University of America Press, 1943), 22–27.

95   Herlihy, "Battle against Bigotry," 97.

Francisco, Yorke launched a campaign of unremitting defense of the political interests of Catholics throughout the 1890s, to the explicit exclusion of any other issue.[96]

Yorke was a founder of clubs. In the 1890s Yorke was instrumental in the formation of the Young Men's Institute of California – a parallel to the YMCA, the Catholic Literary and Social Society, and the Women's Liberal League. As editor of the *Monitor* Yorke learned quickly about the methods of mass journalism. Following the lead of Hearst and de Young, he published a special supplement to the *Monitor* on St. Patrick's Day, on twenty pages of green paper.[97] When Archbishop Riordan objected in 1894 to the use in the city's public schools of Philip Van Ness Myer's *Outlines of Medieval and Modern History*, which contained negative material on the Catholic church, Yorke turned the *Monitor* against the city's School Committee. In November 1895 Yorke began what became his most visible debate, a protracted series of exchanges between himself and the leaders of the APA carried in the major dailies, billed by the *Examiner* as "The Great Controversy." From the pulpit of the Presbyterian church the Reverend Donald Ross had delivered a sermon on the pope's influence in American politics. Yorke challenged Ross to substantiate his charges, and the major dailies saw profit in the controversy. From 28 November 1895 through February 1896 Yorke and his detractors kept the columns filled with this debate.[98]

As Yorke must have known, the APA was pathetically weak in San Francisco, where three of every four residents were immigrants or the sons or daughters of immigrants and where the largest single group of eligible voters were Irish Catholics.[99] The 1890 U.S. Census report on the statistics of religious bodies had revealed San Francisco to be an overwhelmingly Catholic city. Of the 92,872 communicants or members of all the religious bodies in the city, 70,670, or 76 percent, were Catholics.[100] Nevertheless, Yorke had seized on a potent-sounding foil against which to build a Catholic political interest. Within this "Great Controversy," which he and the *Examiner* had literally created, Yorke made himself into a cul-

---

[96] Cronin, "Father Yorke and the Labor Movement," 25–6.

[97] Herlihy, "Battle against Bigotry," 99–100.

[98] Cronin, "Father Yorke and the Labor Movement," 29–32; Herlihy, "Battle against Bigotry," 110–16; *Examiner*, 28, 30 November 1895; *Call*, 8, 9, 11 December 1895.

[99] Analysis of study data, sample drawn from the 1900 U.S. Census manuscript, $N = 1406$.

[100] U.S. Bureau of the Census, *Report on Statistics of Churches in the Eleventh Census* (Washington, D.C.: Government Printing Office, 1894), 98–9.

tural broker within the interest-fragmented public sphere of the 1890s. Despite the disintegration of the weak APA after it failed to achieve its goals in the election of 1896, and despite the flight of Reverend Ross under a cloud of scandal in August 1897, Yorke continued to declare until the end of the century that the APA menaced religious freedom.[101] Although he would take up the issue of labor in the next century, he never wavered from his single-minded pursuit of the Catholic interest during the crucial 1890s, a pursuit that proved critical in the charter reform campaigns of 1896 and 1898.[102]

THE POLITICIZATION OF WOMEN

The entire liberal state, founded in patriarchy mystified by liberal theory as the framework of individual freedom, came increasingly under assault in the 1880s. Women, whether bourgeois or working class, active in the suffrage movement, attempted to redefine the "base" on which the state rested, that is, to redefine authority, sovereignty, freedom, justice, and the public sphere itself. During the 1880s the two founders of the women's movement in California, Clara Shortridge Foltz and Laura de Force Gordon, continued to provide the top leadership, but there arrived in the public sphere a younger generation of women, belonging to the cohort of Progressive Era political leaders. After winning admission of women to California's higher education and to the bar, and after embedding these rights in the California Constitution in 1879, Foltz and Gordon settled into the hard work of their legal practices and the long organizing struggle of the woman suffrage movement. In 1880

---

[101] For example, Yorke opposed Judge Maguire's 1898 run for governor on the ground that the Democrats had been insufficiently vigilant against the APA. "I don't care if it were true that [Republican gubernatorial candidate] Gage were tied up to ten thousand corporations," Yorke declared in defiance of the Democratic juggernaut against the Southern Pacific that year: "I know he is a man who dared to be unpopular in the cause of religious liberty." Herlihy, "Battle against Bigotry," 116–20; Cronin, "Father Yorke and the Labor Movement," 35.

[102] For example, since 1889 the Coast Seamen's Union had opposed the yearly recharter of the Ladies Seamen's Friendly Society, which, despite its benevolent name, was actually being operated as a front by a "crimp" as a recruiting boardinghouse for the ship owners. The CSU and the FTC demanded that the Board of Supervisors stop recharting the society on these grounds. Father Yorke, however, objected to the operation because he alleged it was controlled by the A.P.A and discriminated against Catholics. Varcados, "Labor and Politics in San Francisco," 191–2; Cronin, "Father Yorke and the Labor Movement," 32–3.

we find Gordon sleeping in her San Francisco law office, her parents sending her fresh clothes as she handled largely women's cases for divorce. In 1884 Gordon replaced Foltz as the head of the California State Woman Suffrage Association (CWSA) and held that position for the next ten years, heading the efforts to lobby the state legislature annually for improved property laws for married women, for other laws pertaining to women's civil rights, and for a suffrage amendment to the state constitution.[103]

Although Foltz and Gordon were unable to complete their own studies at the Hastings School of Law after opening its doors to women, others followed in their path. In 1882 Mary McHenry (later Keith), an Irish Catholic San Francisco native, became the first woman to graduate from that institution. So distinguished was her performance that the law school's deans, just a few years after trying to keep Foltz and Gordon out, chose McHenry to deliver one of four scholarly addresses at the commencement exercises at Platt's Hall. Standing on the same rostrum where ten years earlier Susan B. Anthony had spoken on "The Power of the Ballot," McHenry delivered a paper that at first glance seems as dry as those given by her male colleagues: "The Origin and History of the Last Will and Testament."[104] In fact, it was a not-so-subtle strike at the legal foundations of the patriarchal family in the liberal state. She argued that "few other legal instruments can be as directly and certainly traced" to the "tribal and patriarchal" early Roman law as the last will and testament. She traced the gradual achievement under later Roman law of "personal and proprietary independence" for women. Ironically, these gains were lost under feudal English law and McHenry lamented the loss of "an independence whose destruction has so deeply injured civilization."[105]

As McHenry gained in age and experience, she would play a

---

[103] Laura de Force Gordon to parents, 12 February 1879, 3, 16, April 1880, 8 December 1880, 25 June 1882, 27 July 1882, 9 August 1882, 21 August 1882. Laura de Force Gordon Papers, Bancroft Library; Susan B. Anthony and Ida Husted Harper, eds., *History of Woman Suffrage*, (New York: Susan B. Anthony, 1902), 4:502–8.

[104] Anthony's earlier speech is described in San Francisco *Alta* 13 July 1871; "Second Annual Commencement of Hastings College of the Law. University of California, at Platt's Hall, Monday, May 29 1882" [program] Keith-Pond Family Papers, Bancroft Library, Berkeley.

[105] Mary McHenry, "The Origin and History of Wills," MS, Commencement Address, Hastings College of the Law, San Francisco, 29 May 1882, Keith-Pond Family Papers, Bancroft Library.

prominent part in the suffrage campaigns of 1896 and 1911. But the woman movement in San Francisco remained in the hands of the older generation through the 1880s. In 1884 Clara Shortridge Foltz, Marietta L. B. Stowe, the editor of the *Pioneer* after Emily Pitts, and two other women decided on their own initiative to nominate Belva Lockwood for the office of U.S. president. Lockwood had accomplished at the national level what Foltz and Gordon had accomplished in California: In 1879 she had become the first woman admitted to practice law before the U.S. Supreme Court. Having been denied her petition by the High Court in 1876, Lockwood had enlisted the aid of the California senator Aaron A. Sargent (husband of San Francisco suffrage leader Ellen Clark Sargent) to secure passage of a bill enabling her to gain admission. Lockwood's route to the practice of law, then, paralleled that of Foltz and Gordon, and was connected with it as well. On the receipt of a letter from Foltz, Stowe, and others, Lockwood notified the press that she had been nominated by the "National Equal Rights Party," for which she promptly drew up a platform. The new party nominated Stowe for vice-president and attracted a great deal of press coverage. The San Francisco *Call* ridiculed the Equal Rights party for having called a "primary" to "ratify the nomination," and for listing the names of Lockwood and Stowe on the ticket rather than the names of their electors, implying that the party did not understand politics. In fact, Lockwood and Stowe took 4,149 votes in six states (734 in California). But Anthony of the National Woman Suffrage Association (NWSA) disapproved of the course, and the name of Laura Gordon, a staunch NWSA regular, is conspicuously absent from the notices of the new party.[106]

The platform, however, was typical of the ideology of the San Francisco suffrage leaders, especially Gordon. The first plank reads: "We pledge ourselves, if elected to power, so far as in us lies, to do equal and exact justice to every class of our citizens, without distinction of color, sex, or nationality."[107] Under Gordon, the San Francisco suffragists, as bourgeois as the leaders certainly were,

---

[106]   Belva A. Lockwood, "How I Ran for the Presidency," *National Magazine* 17:6 (March 1903): 728–33; Louis Filler, "Lockwood, Belva Ann Bennett McNall," *Notable American Women*, 2:413–16; San Francisco *Call*, 2 November 1884. Probably owing to the disapproval of Lockwood and Stowe's candidacy by Anthony, the *History of Woman Suffrage* does not cover the episode.

[107]   Lockwood, "How I Ran for the Presidency," 731.

forged early ties with working-class women and maintained those through the passage of the California suffrage amendment in 1911.

The rapid increase of women working in light industry during the 1870s and 1880s was accompanied by a significant organization of women into trade unions. Primarily employed in the hard-to-organize laundries and shoe, glove, and cigar-making industries, women workers nevertheless had a representative on the Federated Trades Council, had established a union label in the shirt factories (to which they had to call the attention of the male unions, however), and had organized a separate assembly of the Knights of Labor. These women Knights held a "mass meeting" at Metropolitan Hall in March 1888. On the platform, Laura de Force Gordon drew universalistic plans for woman solidarity in the cause of suffrage, suggesting that "the women of this city should organize themselves on the plans of the Knights of Labor." Judge Maguire of the FTC was also on hand, exhorting working women to unionize so that they could "do by combination what they cannot do individually," namely, win favorable labor legislation.[108]

The 1888 "mass meeting" held under the auspices of the women Knights was part of a greatly widening segment of the political public sphere in which women participated. Even Mayor Pond was "present on the platform," the ritual gesture of the prudent politician. In May of that year the San Francisco *Call*, perhaps looking for ways to deal with Hearst's rapid transformation of the *Examiner*, recognized a market niche in the public, political communication of women and established a "Woman's Column." This fascinating column, described in each issue as "open to correspondents for the discussion of general interest to women," ran every Friday for more than a year. An early correspondent thanked the *Call* "for giving us a little corner where we can exchange our thoughts and ideas."[109] In a great many of the letters, the correspondents spoke out on the difficulties experienced by themselves and others at the workplace and in their families as the sphere of women in civil society expanded. Some gave advice or composed critical essays on topics such as "Girls as Wage-Workers," "Women and Wages," and "Our Business Girls." Most letters were political. "I am only a woman, without a vote, and therefore of no consequence, politically

[108] San Francisco *Alta*, 16 March 1888; *Eaves*, California Labor Legislation, 314–15.
[109] San Francisco *Call*, 25 May 1888.

speaking," wrote "H. A. H.," somewhat facetiously. "But I come from good old Revolutionary stock," she intoned, and then preceded to hammer out a cogent argument against the American party and nativism, drawing on the Bill of Rights.[110]

Indeed, reading the *Call*'s Woman's Column is to experience the critical-rational operation of the political public sphere. Letters began to address previous letters and engage other writers in long-running debates. One writer praised the ongoing discussion of women's rights and the ballot, but suggested that one subject about woman had been neglected: "her relation toward her sister women." This writer, "L. A. T.," complained that "women do not try to help each other; they do not work as a body to advance the cause of woman." Early in the column's history, two San Francisco authors began a long debate on the general equality of the sexes under the title "The Woman Question." In the critical tradition of the Enlightenment public sphere, the authors wrote under pen names: "Scientia" and "C. C." Scientia, who revealed his gender, developed a case for women's disability to adopt political public roles, claiming that fathers, brothers, and sons would deny women nothing that justice requires. "Oh Scientia, read the morning papers attentively for a year," C. C. retorted, and "note down" the cases of women seeking redress for "wrongs put upon them by fathers, husbands, brothers; yea, even by the sons they have borne into the world." C. C., who also revealed her gender, composed long lists of the specific legal disabilities of women, from child custody to property rights. Later debates between these two correspondents considered relative brain sizes (both authors citing scientific sources) and the public administrative achievements of Frances Willard and the Woman's Christian Temperance Union (WCTU). Of course, always they returned to woman suffrage.[111]

The Woman's Column, however, seems to have been an outburst of pent-up discussion. After a year the debates tapered off, and the *Call* changed the format. Lead articles were now apparently written by the staff, followed by fewer letters from the public than in the

---

[110] One correspondent wrote a sentimental piece called "Thoughts of Mother," but her defensive opening indicated that she knew a nonpolitical letter was out of place in the Woman's Column forum: "Some of you who read the Woman's Column may glance at this and pass it by," she began. San Francisco *Call*, 1 June, 13 July 1888.

[111] *Call*, 8, 15 June, 6,13 July 1888.

early columns. Although the Woman's Column seems at this point to have presaged the women's sections that would typify the mass commercial press, it still carried essays on hot political topics, such as the sympathetic "Independent Women – Who Do Not Depend Upon Men to Help Them Along in the World," and a series of articles on the operation of woman suffrage and women officeholders in Wyoming and Kansas. After 1889 the column became infrequent, brought to life sporadically to cover a subject like a report from Mrs. E. P. Keeny, superintendent of franchise to the Women's Christian Temperance Union," in 1891.[112]

The decline of the Woman's Column by late 1889 seems to indicate a general failure of the suffrage leaders, Gordon, Foltz, and Stowe, to mobilize women with a radical equal rights ideology. In 1882 the membership of the California Woman Suffrage Association was only two hundred. In 1890 the annual meeting was so poorly attended that "several speakers urged that the matter [of sending a delegation to the state legislature to lobby for a suffrage amendment] be dropped and the meeting adjourn until such time as women showed sufficient interest in the proceedings to attend." Gordon did not even bother to pay for a listing of the CWSA in the city directory that year.[113]

Many times more women gained public political experience in the city's voluntary benevolent associations. These institutions, formed mostly during the mid-1870s, provided the majority of the social welfare or "public" assistance in the city through the end of the century. Some were organized by and restricted to national language groups; others eschewed limitations "as to the nativity, religion, or social condition," but scores of such organizations were administered entirely by women. The Scandinavian Ladies' Aid Society alone had as many members in 1882 as the California Woman Suffrage Association. Thousands of San Francisco women administered, through these organizations, every kind of social service, from the Little Sisters' Infant Shelter, "organized for the purpose of taking care of the young children of working women during

---

[112] *Call*, 26 July, 15, 23, 30 August 1889, 11 September 1891.

[113] *Langley's San Francisco Directory for the Year Commencing April, 1882* (San Francisco: Francis, Valentine, and Co., 1882), 82; San Francisco *Call*, 22 November 1890; *Langley's San Francisco Directory for the Year Commencing May, 1890* (San Francisco: Geo. B. Wilbur, 1890), 86–94. Hereafter these volumes are cited as *San Francisco Directory*, followed by the year.

the day, thus allowing the mother to perform a day's work," to the Old People's Home of San Francisco, with one hundred fifty members, which provided a "home for the needy, sick and destitute of all nations."[114]

Like the political parties, these women's voluntary organizations performed state functions primarily by raising their own revenues, allowing the tax rates to remain low. So much in charge of the social welfare functions were these voluntary associations that even the little money raised by the government for the purpose of relief was channeled through them. The women-run San Francisco Female Hospital, for instance, which billed itself as a lying-in hospital obviating the need for abortions ("innocents murdered in their mothers' wombs"), received three to five thousand dollars from the state and the city each year from 1870 through 1881. By 1894, when the Stanford University Department of Economics and Social Science published a comprehensive survey of public and private relief in San Francisco (excluding the city's 75 churches), 204 charitable organizations dispensed more than 1.3 million dollars, only a few thousand of which came from government revenues. Not all of these were run by women, but many of the principal ones were, like the San Francisco Benevolent Association, which provided outdoor relief with one-half of all revenues from the city's so-called police fund, or the "fines and forfeitures imposed for offense."[115]

As the organized demand for equal citizenship rights for women drifted at the end of the 1880s, the state, ironically, in effect politicized thousands of women in two significant contexts. One was the dependence of the state on the voluntary organizations to provide public relief. Another was the dependence of the municipality on women to staff the city's public schools. Teaching, the vanguard profession for nineteenth-century women, was deeply enmeshed in the city's party political-patronage structure. As early as 1864, 249 of the city's 279 teachers were women. Nearly all of the city's public school teachers in 1890 were women, and all were appointed by the

---

[114]   San Francisco Directory (1882), 91, 89; On the political role of women's voluntary associations, see especially Paula Baker, "The Domestication of Politics: Women and American Political Society, 1780–1920" *American Historical Review* 89:3 (June 1984): 620–47.

[115]   *San Francisco Directory (1882)*, 81–97; *San Francisco Directory (1890)*, 69–82; C[harles] K[elly] Jenness, *The Charities of San Francisco: A Directory of the Benevolent and Correctional Agencies, Together With a Digest of those Laws Most Directly Affecting Their Work* (San Francisco: Book Room Print, 1894), 1–15.

members of the Board of Education. Those school board members, in turn, had been elected on tickets nominated by the parties, and tions. Teachers' contracts had to be renewed at least every two years under each new school board. The result, as one activist put it in 1888, was that "teachers are forced into politics in their own protection at every change in the board" by approaching, befriending, and even bribing their neighborhood party officials."[116]

One woman politicized in just this way, gaining and losing positions in the public schools (along with her sisters) depending upon the electoral fate of her male political connections, was Kate Kennedy (1827–90). Kennedy, raised in Ireland by middle-class parents who sent her to a Catholic girls' finishing school, turned her education in the United States toward a teaching career. Kennedy, who spoke four languages, acquired the principalship in 1867 of one of the Democrats and Republicans won most of the city offices during the 1880s because of the linkage between national and local elec- the city's multilingual "Cosmopolitan Schools," established by Democrats on the school board to satisfy the city's diverse population.[117] Appointed to the State Board of Examination in 1872, Kennedy, an ally of Henry George in the Democratic party, led a successful lobbying drive in 1874 to make women eligible for election to boards of education and, most remarkably, to require all California school boards to pay women teachers an equal amount to that paid to men for equal work. This achievement was the product, like those of the labor leaders, of boring from within the party system. By the late 1870s Kennedy was active not only with the suffrage leaders but also with the Knights of Labor. She organized support for the striking street-railway workers in 1884 and composed

[116] M. W. Shinn, "Women on School Boards," *Overland Monthly*, n.s. 12 (November 1888): 547–54, quotation on p. 554; Buckley corroborates this allegation, recalling a visit he had from a teacher who thought she had to pay him, the boss, $250 to secure her position. The mistake, Buckley explains, was that she was expected to pay the party leader in her ward. Buckley, "Reminiscences," 27 January 1919; Callow, "San Francisco's Blind Boss," 269.

[117] "Many of our best citizens [were] unwilling to permit their sons and daughters to grow up to maturity, and remain forever ignorant of their native tongue. A great number . . . , native as well as foreign, were compelled to patronize private institutions." John Pelton, *Sixteenth Annual Report of the Superintendent of Public Instruction* (San Francisco: Mayer Bros., 1867), 46, cited in Daniel Perlstein, "Kate Kennedy: Patronage, Professionalism, and Politics in a Teacher's Life," 28, unpublished paper presented at the History of Education Society, Chicago, 1989.

pamphlets for the "toilers" against the monopolies run by the "puny aristocrats."[118]

Although women in rural districts rapidly gained positions on school boards, by 1888 there still had not been a woman elected to the San Francisco Board of Education. In 1886, however, the major parties made an accidental discovery. Several independent parties had nominated women for the school board, including Kate Kennedy on the United Labor party ticket, while the Democrats and Republicans had nominated only men, probably because they were hard-pressed to find enough slots for all their male party workers. The independence of the voters showed through (as in Dr. C. C. O'Donnell's candidacy that year), when five thousand voters "scratched" the names of the regular party nominees and put the women candidates in their place. Although none of these women gained enough votes to win, some party leaders learned their lesson. When a delegation of women who had formed a "Committee of One Hundred" approached the two party conventions in 1888, the Democrats still refused to nominate women. The Republicans, however, agreed because they now "had reason to believe the thing was popular," according to M. W. Shinn, one of the women organizers.[119]

In the history of urban politics, the struggle over school reform has typically been presented as a case of the party machines, in league with the ethnic neighborhood voters and teachers, attempting to preserve their neighborhood autonomy against Yankee reformers who sought to take the politics out of the public schools as a cover for their supposedly actual motive of taking control from the ethnic, working- and lower-middle-class neighborhoods. The San Francisco case tells a very different story. Here we are forced to take the demand for reform, particularly the effort to remove school boards from electoral – and therefore from party – control, as a demand sufficient in itself. Kate Kennedy, a leader in the Irish

---

[118] "An Act to make women eligible to educational offices," and "An Act to prevent discrimination against female teachers," in *Statutes of California Twentieth Session* (Sacramento, 1874), Chapter 257, p. 356, and Chapter 667, p. 938; Kate Kennedy, *Doctor Paley's Foolish Pigeons, and Short Sermons to Working-Men* (San Francisco, Cubery & Co., 1906); quotation is from Perlstein, "Kate Kennedy," 41.

[119] "In a somewhat sharp election struggle, where the body of people were known to be already discontented with municipal politics, they were glad to avail themselves of popularity." Shinn, "Women on School Boards," 553.

Catholic and working-class communities (one-half of the city's teachers were Irish in 1884), was a longtime opponent of elective school boards. Shinn's Committee of One Hundred called for a reformed city charter in which the school board would be appointive, not elected, and explicitly deprecated the attempt to convert this demand into an ethnoreligious issue. Indeed, Shinn suggested in 1888 that the mobilization of ethnic identities against school reform was a cynical ploy by the party leaders to retain their control over this valuable source of patronage.[120] Understanding the politics of municipal reform in the Progressive Era requires a recognition of the genuine ideological commitment to structural and policy innovations like the depoliticization of school boards. Unwary observers, who have depicted such programmatic policy innovations as a function of social-group power or "organization logic," have misleadingly depicted political parties as supportive of working-class or ethnic interests. In fact, the defense of those interests was quite separable from, and congruent with, opposition to political parties.[121]

The steady increase in numbers of women active in voluntary associations, teaching, and other occupations politicized by connections with the state, however, could not alone overcome the inertia felt by the CWSA in 1890 and thus advance the radical restructuring of political sovereignty portended by the woman suffrage movement. That feat had to be carried out in the public sphere by leaders who could mobilize women, in each of the public roles they had acquired, with an ideological discourse on domesticity, family,

---

[120] "While every paper in the city speaks in the friendliest manner of the movement, some one goes in secret to every Hebrew who can be reached, telling him with shrewdness, and surprising as it may seem, some effect, that this is all a crusade against the Hebrews in the schools; some one else performs the same service for the Catholics; while a third sees to it that all intense Protestants are informed that it is a Jesuit intrigue to obtain control of the schools for the Church of Rome." Shinn, "Women on School Boards," 554.

[121] Samuel P. Hays, "The Politics of Reform in Municipal Government in the Progressive Era," *Pacific Northwest Quarterly* 55 (1964): 157–69. David Hammack, *Power and Society: Greater New York at the Turn of the Century* (New York: Columbia University Press), 259–99. The study by Ira Katznelson and Margaret Weir of Chicago and San Francisco is undermined by their exclusion of Kate Kennedy's class and ethnic political activism. *Schooling for All: Class, Race and the Decline of the Democratic Ideal* (New York: Basic Books), 75–120; For a critique of the social-group perspective, see Philip J. Ethington, "Recasting Urban Political History: Gender, the Public, the Household, and Political Participation in Boston and San Francisco during the Progressive Era," *Social Science History* 16:2 (Summer 1992): 301–33.

education, social welfare, and the state. The genius for articulating that discourse appeared in the person of Charlotte Perkins Stetson (hereafter Gilman), who arrived in Oakland on 18 September 1891, just in time to join a widening network of political and social reformers. Gilman's role in remaking the urban public sphere in San Francisco will be discussed in the following chapter.

The increasing politicization of women in the late 1880s posed new problems for the men who monopolized the institutional apparatus of the state and parties, but not in the same way as the institutionalization of the group identities of class and ethnicity. Women's political consciousness and participation was as diverse as women themselves, arising in every class and ethnic context outside of the Chinese community. This fragmentation, along with their lack of the ballot, effectively neutralized women's influence as one of the emergent interest groups. The most crucial step in the remaking of San Francisco's political culture at the end of the ninteenth century, the Reform Ballot Act of 1891, was accomplished on the basis of the several action structures analyzed so far.

POLITICAL ENTREPRENEURS AND THE REFORM
BALLOT ACT OF 1891

Trying to define and explain the leadership of Progressive Era political change, historians usually offer some variant of a generational model. Most of the leaders who came to call themselves "progressives" after the turn of the century belonged to a distinct generation: They were born during the Civil War, give or take a few years. When George Mowry wrote his classic study *The California Progressives*, he depicted this leadership as that of an industrial middle class pinched between organized labor and the big corporations. Richard Hofstadter modified Mowry's thesis to depict the same generation suffering from "status anxiety." Robert Wiebe and Samuel P. Hays cast their progressive generation within rising middle and corporate classes, respectively. Robert Crunden has argued even more forcefully for the generational thesis, making a specific case that the progressive leadership was supplied by the Protestant group of young professionals, usually sons and daughters of ministers, born between 1854 and 1874. Stressing the "psychological origin of progressive achievements," he argues that this generation's upbringing socialized them to apply their parents' Protestant missionary zeal to public life beginning in the 1880s and 1890s.[122]

Here again, however, the group model of political history has worked to obscure more than it clarifies. Each wave of historiography has been written as a search for the group experience that would lead to political innovation. The burst of Progressive Era ideological and policy innovation was so dramatic, furthermore, that most have sought to explain the appearance of progressivism as a sudden break with the past. A careful eye, however, will discern a complex overlap between the generations, classes, ethnic groups, and genders in the most important phases of progressive emergence. Social and social-psychological group models are attractive and are not necessarily wrong, but there is a much more plausible and verifiable explanation at hand. It is probably accidental that the progressive generation was born at the time of the Civil War. The crucial development was not their birth or upbringing, but the crisis of the American organizational party system, which arrived at the end of the 1880s. The first generation of Americans to reach political maturity at the time of that crisis, and to be entering politics for the first time (unintegrated into the older structures of power and interest) would of course have been born between 1859 and 1866. In their twenties during the height of the party system of the 1880s, these men and women were too young to acquire leadership positions until about 1890, but they were quite old enough to read the burst of reform literature that began to appear nationally in the period 1885–90. Indeed, the young proto-progressives owed everything not to their parents or to their class, but to an older genertion of political leaders who had worked with or against the organizational parties for decades and who initiated them into the very institutions they would try to destroy.

The role and method of the early progressives is best captured with the term "political entrepreneur," defined by John Mollenkopf

122 George E. Mowry, "The California Progressive and His Rationale: A Study in Middle Class Politics," *Mississippi Valley Historical Review* 36 (September, 1949): 239–50; idem, *The California Progressives* (Chicago: Quadrangle Books, 1963); Richard Hofstadter, *The Age of Reform: From Bryan to F.D.R.* (New York: Alfred A. Knopf, 1955); Hays, "The Politics of Reform in Municipal Government," 157–69; Robert Wiebe, *The Search for Order, 1877–1920* (New York: Hill and Wang, 1967); Robert M. Crunden, *Ministers of Reform: The Progressives' Achievement in American Civilization, 1889–1920* (Urbana University of Illinois Press, 1984).

as "one who gathers and risks political capital or support in order to reshape politics and create new sources of power by establishing new programs (or 'products')." Defining the early progressives this way clarifies their role as infiltrators of the organizational parties and as transformers of the structures of political power, rather than as representatives of group interests who rose in a relatively constant political arena. "He or she thus does not simply play by the rules of the game," Mollenkopf continues, "but attempts to win the game by changing them."[123] What social-group models of political development usually fail to recognize is the way political actors have deliberately changed the political arena, or "game," so as to favor some agendas, groups, and actors over others. Political entrepreneurship is thus an activity relatively autonomus from social-group formation.

Thanks largely to organized labor, the policy goals that would come to characterize urban reform in the Progressive Era had been around for a long time before progressivism actually arrived. As early as 1881 Frank Roney had written a "Municipal Platform" for the short-lived Mechanics' Assembly. Roney's platform included the following planks: municipal ownership of gas and water; taxation not to exceed one dollar per hundred; city ownership of street-sweeping machinery; eight-hour day on all public works; increased pay for teachers; and stricter enforcement of health and sanitation laws.[124] Platforms such as these needed to be institutionally empowered to become viable policies, which means that parties needed to adopt them. For that to happen, in turn, infiltrators had to follow Roney's lead and transform the parties from within.

Policy innovation in the organizational party regime of the 1880s was enormously difficult because of that regime's principal contradiction: that between the parties' ironclad promise to voters not to redistribute their wealth in fiscal policy, on the one hand, and the parties' dependence upon the railroad and utility corporations for support, on the other. This contradiction is best illustrated by the mayoralty of Washington Bartlett (1882–7). Bartlett had been a member of the 1856 Committee of Vigilance and had served as county clerk both under the People's (1859–63) and Democratic

---

[123] John H. Mollenkopf, *The Contested City* (Princeton, N.J.: Princeton University Press, 1982), 6.

[124] San Francisco *Call*, 5 August 1881, cited in Varcados, "Labor and Politics in San Francisco," 125.

party labels.[125] Christopher Buckley's County Committee had put him on the ticket in 1881 to represent the austere fiscal promises in the party's platform. Bartlett saw his policy role in negative terms. He pushed through a reduction in the salaries of city workers and even suspended the lighting of city streets for four months in order to balance the budget. The Board of Supervisors, meanwhile, distributed utility franchises and water-rate increases to keep pace with city growth and, presumably, to keep the party's money machine running. Bartlett often vetoed franchise grants, but in his second term these vetoes were usually overridden by a Republican Board of Supervisors. San Francisco's governing record was quite efficient and even professional, but it operated by displacement through distributive policies. And yet these policies, designed to minimize conflict, threatened at any minute to alienate the mass of citizens on whom the city fathers depended for reelection. Bartlett had a motto that summarized the ideological prison in which the organizational parties dwelt: "Whenever you attempt to do anything contrary to usual methods, you are always suspected of a desire to do something wrong."[126]

So, until the major parties could be defeated in a game that they controlled, policy innovations designed to equalize the tax burden or protect citizens and workers would have to wait. The FTC's principal goal from as early as 1886, therefore, had been to change the rules of the electoral game by gaining the adoption of a secret ballot, printed by the state authorities, and distributed at the polls. This reform, known as the Australian ballot, would cut the political parties out of their long-held role of administering the most important elements of the election (although not of the primary) process. Achieving this goal in California rested on the remarkable cooperation of self-styled "mugwumps" with radical labor organizers and dissident party leaders.

Who were the political entrepreneurs in San Francisco, and how did they operate? John Henry Wigmore was born and raised in San Francisco. The son of an Irish immigrant who had become prosperous in the lumber trade, Wigmore earned a B.A. at Harvard in 1883. He returned to San Francisco, where he led several young men in the organization of an ambitious and short-lived Municipal

---

[125] Washington Bartlett Dictation, Bancroft Library, Berkeley.
[126] Robert W. Righter, "Washington Bartlett Mayor of San Francisco, 1883–1887," *Journal of the West* 3:1 (January 1964): 111.

Reform League, which sought to organize the overthrow of the political bosses in every ward of the city. The group broke up when Wigmore returned again to Boston, but two of its members, the future mayor James Duval Phelan and the future city attorney Franklin K. Lane, later formed the Young Men's Democratic League, with the Australian ballot as its central goal. Their bridge to power was the remarkable James G. Maguire, then one of the FTC's potent lobbyists.[127]

Maguire was born in Boston to Irish Catholic immigrant parents who brought him to California as a small child before the Civil War. After attending both public and private schools, he apprenticed as a blacksmith for four years. His blacksmithing came to an end with a brief stint teaching school, and in 1875 Maguire won election to the state legislature on the class-charged Democratic ticket. By 1878 he had passed his examination before the bar of the state supreme court, and in 1882 he was elected judge of the San Francisco Superior Court. From that point onward, even after he was elected to the U.S. Congress in 1892, Maguire retained the title "Judge Maguire," which gave him an aura of disinterested civic wisdom. In 1886 he briefly joined the short-lived Labor party, but otherwise was a life-long Democrat.[128]

Maguire can be thought of as an institutionalized labor politician. He proved a valuable asset to the Democrats, who, since the 1870s, had known that they could not do without overt, explicit labor appeals. Because the United States was, as Stephen Skowronek suggests, still a "state of courts and parties," judges like Maguire were essential to the maintenance of the party as a popular institution. Nor had Maguire sold out to the corporate capitalists who provided the funding for the party to which he belonged. In 1888 he made a landmark ruling in the case of a former Iron Moulder's Union worker named Le Boeuf, who had been suspended from the union for violating union rules, and who was now prevented from finding work because union members refused to work with

---

127   Keith W. Olson, *Biography of a Progressive: Franklin K. Lane, 1864–1921* (Westport, Conn.: Greenwood Press, 1979), 16–18; Varcados, "Labor and Politics in San Francisco," 158–9; Lane and Wall, *Letters of Franklin K. Lane*, 1–17.

128   Maguire's career history has been neglected by most students of San Francisco. Details can be found in *Coast Seamen's Journal*, 26 February 1890, and American Biographical Archive [microfiche]; Varcados, "Labor and Politics in San Francisco," 158. During his campaign for governor of California on the Democratic ticket in 1898, the *Examiner* referred to him as "Judge Maguire," and "Champion of the People." 1 November 1898.

him. At issue was the open shop. Maguire dismissed Le Boeuf's case of conspiracy and his ruling was sustained upon later appeal.[129]

Alone among the San Francisco proto-progressives, Franklin K. Lane fits Robert Crunden's description: Born in 1864, Lane, the son of a Presbyterian minister who had moved his family to California in 1871, was raised in a home where each Sunday evening the children confessed their sins, prayed, and sang hymns. Graduating from Oakland High School in 1880, Lane worked as a reporter throughout the 1880s while taking classes at the University of California and studying law at Hastings law school in San Francisco. Lane had an unfocused sense of mission. He campaigned for a Prohibitionist gubernatorial candidate in 1884 but called himself a mugwump by 1888 and identified with the principled Democratic leadership of Grover Cleveland.[130] Lane passed his bar examination in 1888, but complained to Wigmore in that year: "I feel all the time as if I must be engaged in some life work which will make more directly for the good of my fellows."[131]

The FTC had tried unsuccessfully in 1886 to push an Australian ballot law in the legislature, but when it tried again in 1888–9, its lobbyists had acquired a new set of allies. The Australian ballot was first secured in Massachusetts in 1889, after the effective lobbying of the Massachusetts Ballot Act League. Also in that year Wigmore's important study, *The Australian Ballot as Embodied in the Legislation of Various Countries*, appeared, but he had sent Lane a copy of the manuscript earlier, in 1888. Maguire and Lane had used the Wigmore manuscript to revise the FTC's bill, and Lane relied upon it when he addressed the assembly in favor of the bill. Allan Thorndike Rice, editor of the *North American Review*, even met with Judge Maguire to supply him with ballot-reform pamphlets and materials.[132] But the bill was understood precisely as it was intended, as an assault on the hegemony of the two major parties, and by February 1889 it had been voted down by a bi-partisan vote.[133] One party leader complained to Lane that the bill "tends to the disintegration

129 Frank Roney, *Frank Roney*, 370–1; Eaves, *California Labor Legislation*, 397–8.
130 Olson, *Biobraphy of a Progressive*, 15–16; Lane and Wall, *Letters of Franklin K. Lane*, 9–12, 18–20.
131 Franklin K. Lane to John Henry Wigmore, 9 May 1888, in Lane and Wall, *Letters of Franklin K. Lane*, 19.
132 Petersen, "Prelude to Progressivism," 94.
133 Twenty-one Republicans and twenty-six Democrats combined to defeat the bill. Petersen, "Prelude to Progressivism," 98.

of political parties and as they are essential to our national life we must not help on their destruction."[134] The FTC-led assault on the organizational parties had run aground on a central paradox: Reform legislation would have to be enacted by the organizational politicians themselves.

The arrival of party-weakening electoral law reform had to await a party-weakening electoral defeat. And the manner in which that defeat arrived illustrates how the urban party "machine" did not rest on a base of support in the neighborhoods so much as it was suspended like a marionette from above. In 1888 the Democratic municipal slate, drawn by Christopher Buckley's County Committee, was swept to power by the strength of the Cleveland vote in the city.[135] The mayor and all but one supervisor were Democrats, but Buckley, decades later, remembered the election for the "disastrous loss of the great Federal patronage." Cleveland, of course, lost in the presidential election to Harrison that year. "The transfer of the immense Federal patronage to the Republicans," Buckley recalled, "was a crushing blow to the organization, especially with a party which was almost daily more and more divided against itself in municipal policy."[136]

Buckley, it turns out, remembered correctly. His control of the County Committee began to slip as soon at the plums began to fall from the party tree that winter, and as soon as the close relationship between the parties and the franchised utility corporations appeared as a liability rather than an asset. The distributive politics of the 1880s had finally run its course by the end of the decade, especially with the appearance of a powerful new voice of criticism within the Democratic party, the newly renovated *Examiner*. As part of his expensive drive to push the *Examiner* into the local market, Hearst hired the legendary Thomas Nast for a few months. Hearst tore into the streetcar companies for their many pedestrian accidents, having Nast portray the streetcars as vans of destruction driven by his trademark skeleton man.[137] Now the genuine policy question of whether the Democratic party had served the city's residents best by promoting the unregulated and unremunerative growth of the

---

[134]   The party leader was most probably Henry Dibble. Lane to Wigmore, 17 February 1889, in Lane and Wall, *Letters of Franklin K. Lane*, 23.

[135]   *Examiner*, 24 November 1888 p. 2.

[136]   Buckley, "Reminiscences," 18, 20 January 1919.

[137]   Winkler, *W. R. Hearst*, 74.

streetcar and other utility franchises had a focused public voice in the Democratic *Examiner*. The rising criticism against the utility franchises explains Buckley's reference to a party "divided against itself in municipal policy."

The FTC's and the Young Men's Democratic League's aggressive lobbying for ballot reform, the appearance of Hearst's campaign against the streetcars, and the loss of the party's campaign lifeblood, convinced several leading Democrats to appoint a "Committee of One Hundred" to reorganize the party and remove control from Buckley, who had not only proved a failure but a liability. At the head of this Committee, ominously enough, was the ubiquitous William Tell Coleman, now entering his final reform campaign forty years after rising to the leadership of the first Vigilance Committee in 1851. Also represented was the city's Democratic wealth, including the Irish Argonaut James Phelan. These factionalists joined with the ballot reformers under the leadership of the FTC and Judge Maguire to secure a campaign pledge for the Australian ballot at the 1890 party convention.[138]

Although the Democrats lost their majority in the state legislature, the reformers had also secured written pledges from a significant number of Republican legislators. The Republicans, meanwhile, capitalized on the dissension in the Democratic ranks and handed down a grand jury indictment against Christopher Buckley in February 1891. In that month also George Hearst died in Washington, leaving William Randolph much freer to criticize his father's party.[139] The motivation of the Republican majority to damage the Democrats and look good themselves during a session otherwise known as the "Legislature of a Thousand Scandals," and the motivation of the reorganizing Democrats to purge themselves of the boss label, under pressure from the efficient lobbying of the FTC, led to the adoption in 1891 of the Reform Ballot Act, but not without complications and a major concession to the party regulars.

The days and weeks between the death of Senator Hearst on 28 February, to the signing of the bill on 12 March 1891, were marked by extraordinary machinations, resulting primarily from the scramble

---

[138] The pledge card reads: "I pledge my word of honor that I will if elected ... at all times advocate, urge and work for the reform ballot law as submitted by the Council of Federated Trades and the Legislative Committee of the California State Grange." *Examiner*, 3 March 1891.

[139] *Examiner*, 28 February 1891; Petersen, "Prelude to Progressivism,"113.

for the vacant Senate seat. A principal contender was Michael de Young, young Hearst's chief media rival. De Young's candidacy was managed by the Republican party diehard Henry Dibble, who also led the fight against a Reform Ballot Act. Dibble left no question that his opposition to the Reform Ballot Act was a defense of the party system as it had stood since the days of the Whigs and Jacksonians. The FTC-sponsored bill not only put all candidates on a single, government-printed and -distributed ballot, but it also allowed nomination of candidates by popular petition. That provision, Dibble complained, "was calculated to destroy the two major parties."[140] Dibble had to abandon his sponsorship of de Young for the Senate seat, but he blocked the Reform Ballot Act until the pledged supporters agreed to let him amend it. These "Dibble amendments" increased the number of signatures needed to make an independent nomination and, most significantly, allowed for a single mark at the head of the ticket to indicate a straight-ticket vote. With these amendments the majority for the bill soared from 36 to 63, and the bill passed with only 3 negative votes.[141]

After 1891 the parties were no longer able to link their local victories to the national party fates. Loss of that structural link brought reformers to power and led to the radical restructuring of the city government by the end of the century. It is important to observe that this breakthrough had been achieved two full years before the 1893–4 depression, a time to which historians have often pointed as an origin for progressive reform.[142] Not changes in society or the economy, or some groundswell of public opinion rising from the "base" of the polity, but specific political innovation at the top of the political structures explains the advent of progressive reform in San Francisco. We turn now to the working out of a reform agenda within the newly configured public sphere of the 1890s.

---

[140] *Examiner*, 7 March 1891.
[141] Petersen, "Prelude to Progressivism," 113–19.
[142] David Thelen, *The New Citizenship: Origins of Progressivism in Wisconsin* (Columbia: University of Missouri Press, 1972); Richard L. McCormick, *From Realignment to Reform: Political Change in New York State, 1893–1910* (Ithaca, N.Y.: Cornell University Press, 1981).

CHAPTER 8

Progressivism as the politics of needs: The mobilization of group identities

During the 1890s a new political culture emerged in San Francisco and in the rest of the nation. This chapter completes the analytical narrative begun in the first chapters by reconstructing the process by which our modern political culture of pluralist liberalism conducted within a social understanding of politics came into being. Building upon the institutional transformation of parties, interest groups, and the media that had culminated in the Reform Ballot Act of 1891, political entrepreneurs in San Francisco generated a new political culture that called itself "progressive." Progressivism was a discourse and not an ideology, a political culture and not a program. The "progressive" slogan was a normative and ultimately consensual one, wielded to bring about a politics of needs, interest groups, and government by administration rather than by party, and the constitutional structures enabling such a politics.

From this new political milieu, a host of San Francisco activists went on to join their compeers from other states to constitute "progressivism" on a national scale in the first decade of the twentieth century. Mayor James Duval Phelan and City Attorney Franklin K. Lane built on their San Francisco experiences to become prominent figures in Woodrow Wilson's Progressive wing of the Democratic party; Charlotte Perkins Gilman organized women in San Francisco during the crucial mid-1890s, developing her ideas for *Women and Economics* (1898); Edward Alsworth Ross formulated his social-control brand of the new science, sociology, during his stormy career at Stanford University from 1892 through his dramatic dismissal by Jane Stanford in 1900; Hiram Johnson skyrocketed from his reform activities in San Francisco to revolutionize California politics and then join Theodore Roosevelt on the ticket of the national Progressive party in 1912; and the claim to originating mass, commercial, sensational journalism belongs to San Francisco under the influence of William Randolph Hearst and his San Francisco *Examiner* as much as it does to New York City under the influence of Joseph Pulitzer.

The great variety of "reform" projects represented by activists as different as Phelan, Lane, Gilman, Ross, Johnson, and Hearst indicates the challenge posed by any attempt to interpret political change in the Progressive Era. Progressivism was distinguished by the way people became mobilized and integrated into relations with the state, and not by a set of groups that can be identified as "progressive." Progressivism began in San Francisco when political entrepreneurs managed to coordinate the multifarious institutionalized group-action structures in the vacuum created by the rupture in the organizational parties' hegemony over the electoral political process, a rupture that appeared as early as 1888 and burst after the adoption of the Reform Ballot Act in 1891.

In an emergent pluralist political universe, a multitude of voices spoke out in favor of and against various projects for "reform." This chapter narrates key features of the "reform" process in San Francisco during the 1890s in order to sort out and assess the relative influence of the principal voices of the transformation we call "progressivism." To tell even a limited story about the wide-ranging changes in urban political life that took place in the 1890s requires assembling a daunting cast of characters. Intellectuals, women's rights activists, suburban homeowners, labor leaders, business leaders, political entrepreneurs, mass-media titans, and of course the ordinary voters all played a significant role in the birth of a modern urban political culture of pluralist liberalism. They did so in the highly contested public sphere of critical debate, and from positions of institutional power that greatly differentiated the multitude of actors by their levels of power and their ability to speak with authority.

What did "progressivism," this new political culture, produce? The most important achievement wrought by political leaders in the new political culture of the 1890s was the adoption of a new San Francisco city charter in 1898. That charter was in effect a codification of the new political culture, providing a framework for policy innovation and administration under new principles. The most important defeat of the new political culture was the rejection of the woman suffrage amendment to the state constitution in the pivotal election of 1896. Although there were many other "reforms" on the agenda of the reconstructed public sphere in the 1890s, this chapter explains these two outcomes in order to illustrate the underlying emergence of a politics of needs.

INTELLECTUALS AND THE CITY

Intellectuals appeared as a distinct social class in the United States in the 1890s. Thanks to the founding of new universities such as the University of Chicago and Stanford University, and to the rapid growth of American higher education in general, the numbers of graduate-trained "experts" on economic, political, and social problems multiplied rapidly before the turn of the century. These men and women made themselves available as participants in the public-sphere debates about the governing relations of a society undergoing what they understood to be an urban-industrial crisis. As Christopher Lasch observes, this class, or status group, defined itself as a group apart by its role as critics of the status quo.[1] They also defined themselves as a group not at all apart, but rather as sociopolitical doctors engaged to cure the evils attendant on urban-industrial society.

By making the city the first subject of their concern in the formation of the modern social sciences, the new intellectuals articulated most comprehensively the discourse of the emergent urban political culture. The city, they observed, had generated class, ethnic, and racial conflict, had generated poverty, political corruption, disease, immorality, the "social evil," excess individualism, selfishness, greed, waste, inefficiency, and anarchism and other kinds of dangerous political radicalism. It was both the embodiment and the location of the best achievements and the worst problems of modern society. The intellectuals formulated their new social sciences, designed institutions, and promulgated policy recommendations by observing the city as a natural phenomenon, as a large-scale social fact that had resulted from long-term institutional development and from the operation of the market. These intellectuals have been praised as harbingers of the welfare state, as visionaries who saw

[1] Christopher Lasch, *The New Radicalism in America, 1889–1963: The Intellectual as a Social Type* (New York: Alfred A. Knopf, 1965).

that poverty, malnutrition, ill health, and racial and class conflicts were produced by society and the environment rather than by the personal moral failings of the poor, of the malnourished, or of the striking worker. Whether or not their social environmentalism is worthy of praise or blame, it is clear that the intellectuals articulated a shift in the political culture that also stressed social forces. By identifying society with the environment, intellectuals justified reconstructing governmental machinery and programs to respond to *social* needs.

A symbiotic relationship arose between intellectuals and the city, in which the city provided the crises and the intellectuals provided solutions. But the intellectuals were observing a crisis created, as we have seen, by political leaders in the public sphere. They were, in effect, codifying a relationship between society and the state that institutional leaders had evolved through their own relationship with constituents in the contested realm of a competitive public sphere since the social revolution unleashed politically by the Civil War. The outline of "reform" the intellectuals began to publish in the 1890s resonated very well with the projects of the political entrepreneurs who worked their way into positions of power by the middle of that decade. Those political activists were eager readers of the new social science literature; it flattered their own methods of mobilization.

At Columbia University, Frank Goodnow took a leading role in the foundation of the modern discipline of political science with his influential studies of city government: *Municipal Home Rule* (1895) and *Municipal Problems* (1897). Goodnow's studies of government signaled what was perhaps the deepest change in the political culture of the Progressive Era. The city, he declared in *Municipal Home Rule*, "should be regarded primarily as an organization for the satisfaction of local needs."[2] To satisfy those "needs," Goodnow elaborated his famous distinction between "politics" and "administration," arguing that constitutionally, the city was administrative in character and should be structurally reformed to reflect that function. Goodnow, however, did not suggest a simple centralization of authority in the city, to detach popular participation from bureaucratic administration. Indeed, he, along with E. A. Ross at

---

[2]   Frank J. Goodnow, *Municipal Home Rule: A Study in Administration* (New York: Macmillan and Co., 1895), 26.

Stanford, thought the powers and responsibilities of the city council should be enhanced, not weakened.[3]

At the University of Chicago, meanwhile, intellectual-activists in and out of academia produced an exciting sociopolitical reform agenda that can be characterized as social-democratic. Albion Small, Charles Zueblin, and W. I. Thomas in the Sociology Department; George Herbert Mead and John Dewey in the Philosophy Department; Sophonisba Breckinridge and Grace Abbott in the Graduate School of Social Work; Jane Addams, Florence Kelly, and Julia Lathrop at the independent Hull House; and Graham Taylor at Chicago Commons formed a network encouraging intellectual and political policy innovation that produced an enduring blueprint for the American welfare state.[4]

An important satellite spreading and increasing these influences sprang up in the form of the Leland Stanford Jr. University, founded in 1891, a year earlier than the University of Chicago. Like Chicago, Stanford's leading social scientists had been trained in the Johns Hopkins Seminary of History and Politics. Like Chicago, Stanford was founded with the surplus wealth created by a great industrial corporation. And like their colleagues at Chicago and Columbia University, the Stanford intellectuals were deeply concerned with questions of political and social reform. Unlike Chicago, however, the story of the relationship of those intellectuals to political development in San Francisco has yet to be told.

The leading proponent of social and political reform at Stanford was the flamboyant Edward Alsworth Ross, brought from Cornell University to the Department of Economics and Social Science by President David Starr Jordan in 1892. For nearly ten years after the arrival of Ross, Stanford was one of the most exciting centers of social-scientific thought and training in the United States. Heading the Department of Economics and Social Science was Amos G. Warner, whose magnum opus, *American Charities* (1894), became the

[3]   Michael H. Frisch, "Urban Theorists, Urban Reform, and American Political Culture in the Progressive Period," *Political Science Quarterly* 97:1 (Spring 1982): 295–315.
[4]   Steven J. Diner, *A City and Its Universities: Public Policy in Chicago, 1892–1919* (Chapel Hill: University of North Carolina Press, 1980); Mary Jo Deegan, *Jane Addams and the Men of the Chicago School, 1892–1918* (New Brunswick, N.J.: Transaction Books, 1988); Mary J. Deegan and John S. Burger, "W. I. Thomas and Social Reform: His Work and Writings," *Journal of the Behavioral Sciences* 17 (1981): 114–25; Martin Bulmer, *The Chicago School of Sociology: Institutionalization, Diversity, and the Rise of Sociological Research* (Chicago: University of Chicago Press, 1984).

standard text across the country on the principles of public relief. The authoritative statement of scientific charity, Warner's text was widely used in social work classes as late as the 1930s.[5] Warner trained the first woman Ph.D. in sociology, Mary Roberts Smith (later Coolidge), who received the doctoral degree in 1896 and was an active member of the faculty during most of the decade.[6] Others among the new faculty included Frank Fetter, whose textbook on economics would become the standard in the second decade of the twentieth century, and E. Dana Durand, who would author an influential study of New York City's finances in 1898 and become the director of the U.S. Census in 1910. Among their students were the San Francisco progressive reformer Franklin Hichborn; the suffragist Ida Husted Harper, returning to college with her daughter in 1892; the suffragist and historian Ann Martin, who nearly won a U.S. Senate seat in Nevada after the Nineteenth Amendment; and not least, that "Forgotten Progressive," young Herbert Hoover.[7]

While at Stanford, Ross made his most important contribution to social science, and to the theoretical arsenal of progressivism, in his theory of "social control." The term "social control," thanks in large part to Ross's own deep racism, rapidly came to mean the control of immigrants, the working class, and people of color by WASP experts in state bureaucracies. But in Ross's initial formulation, the concept was directed as much at the industrial corporate corrupters of society and politics as at anyone else. Ross's ideas are inextricable from the setting of California, where individualism, he thought, had run amok, producing the villainy of the Southern Pacific and its corruption of politics, the conflict between classes, and a general unraveling of social cohesion. Ross explained his theory of social

5   Amos G. Warner, *American Charities: A Study in Philanthropy and Economics* (New York: Thomas Y. Crowell and Co., 1894); idem, *American Charities*, 3d ed. rev. Mary Roberts Coolidge, with a biographical preface by George Elliot Howard (New York: Thomas Y. Crowell Co., 1918); Amos Griswold Warner, Stuart Alfred Queen, and Ernest Bouldin Harper, *American Charities and Social Work*, 4th ed. (New York: Thomas Y. Crowell, 1930). By the fourth edition the book had gone through twenty-six printings.

6   J. Graham Morgan, "Women in American Sociology in the Nineteenth Century," *Journal of the History of Sociology* 2:2 (Spring 1980): 1–34.

7   Leland Stanford Junior University, *Register*, vols. 1891/2–1899/00; Carl N. Degler, "The Ordeal of Herbert Hoover," in Barton J. Bernstein and Allen J. Matusow, eds., *Twentieth-Century America: Recent Interpretations* 2d. ed. (New York: Harcourt Brace Jovanovich, 1972), 197–214; Richard Hofstadter, *The American Political Tradition and the Men Who Made It* (New York: Vintage, 1974), 373–4; Joan Hoff-Wilson, *Herbert Hoover, Forgotten Progressive* (Boston: Little, Brown, 1975).

control as a study of "the influences that help to lead men to do *right* by their fellow men." To construct such a theory he spun out a series of twenty articles on "Law, Public Opinion, Belief, Suggestion, Religion, Ideals, Ceremony, Personality, Instruction, etc." under the heading "Social Control" for Albion Small's *American Journal of Sociology*, beginning in 1896 and published together in book form in 1901.[8]

Ross was amplifying Lester Frank Ward's concept of "telic," or guided, evolution, casting "teachers, clergymen, editors, lawmakers, and judges" as "those who administer the moral capital of society." Ross thought that these administrators should "wield the instruments of control" under the direction of a sociologist like himself, who must "make himself an accomplice of all good men for the undoing of all bad men."[9] Thus, while industrial capitalism was eroding social order under the cover of laissez-faire social Darwinism, Ross saw the "good men" as consciously guiding "the human caravan across the waste." And Ross saw the state as the key instrument in the restoration of social order: "The more a state helps the citizen when he cannot help himself, protecting him from disease, foes, criminals, rivals abroad and monopolists at home, the more he will look to it for guidance." Here Ross articulated an essential feature of the transformation of American political culture that crystallized in the 1890s, the concept of the state as an aggregation of social forces: "The State is . . . a device by which social power is collected, transmitted, and applied *so as to do work*."[10]

Ross and his colleagues evolved a curriculum at Stanford that both reflected and expressed their shared concern with the city as a location of problems to investigate and to resolve.[11] In the academic

[8] During the winter holiday from teaching, Ross sat down in the Stanford library and outlined "the thirty-four means through which society disciplines its members." Julius Weinberg, *Edward Alsworth Ross and the Sociology of Progressivism* (Madison: State Historical Society of Wisconsin, 1972), 76–105; Ross to "Mama" [M. D. Beach, his foster mother] 28 November 1897, Edward A. Ross Papers [microfilm], Madison, State Historical Society of Wisconsin, 1986; Edward A. Ross, *Social Control: A Study in the Foundations of Order* (New York: Macmillan, 1901). For a general discussion of Ross and the theory of social control, see Dorothy Ross, *Origins of American Social Science* (Cambridge, UK: Cambridge University Press, 1991), 229–56.

[9] Ross, *Social Control*, 441.

[10] Ross, *Social Control*, 82.

[11] For a survey of the sociology curriculum in general in these years, see J. Graham Morgan, "Courses and Texts in Sociology," *Journal of the History of Sociology* 5 (Spring 1983): 42–65.

year 1894–5 Ross began teaching a course for advanced students called "Cities," which he described as "a special study in sociology, economics, and politics."[12] He used the new textbook by Albion Small and George Vincent of Chicago, which was intended as a "laboratory guide" for the construction of urban social surveys.[13] Ross, Warner, and Mary Roberts Smith continued to expand the curriculum of sociology so that, by 1900, a student could choose between Social Institutions, Sociology of the Family, Race Problems, Immigration, Statistics and Sociology, Causes of Poverty, Charities, Criminology, Penology, Cities, and Social Psychology.[14] Moreover, Warner and Frank Fetter taught courses on city administration, and Fetter even began deploying his students to conduct a social survey of the South-of-Market neighborhood in 1899.[15]

Despite the intellectual ferment in Palo Alto, the social-scientific intelligentsia failed to exert a demonstrable impact on the shape of political development. Ross entered the presidential campaign in 1896 to become the Democratic party's academic spokesman for free silver, against the conservative gold economists at Chicago and Harvard. There is no evidence, however, that he ever entered municipal politics, and only briefly did he comment on the proposal for a new charter in 1898. In that case, he opposed the plan to centralize authority in the mayor's office, as we shall see.

The leading social settlement in San Francisco best exemplifies the ironic interplay between the transformation of the public sphere and the projects of the progressive urban reform theorist-activists. Inspired by a visit of Jane Addams to San Francisco in 1895, several activists joined with University of California and Stanford faculty to found the South Park Settlement (soon renamed the "San Francisco Settlement") in the class-mixed South-of-Market

[12] Leland Stanford Junior University *Register* vol. 1894–5, p. 81, Stanford University Library.
[13] Albion W. Small and George E. Vincent, *An Introduction to the Study of Society* (New York: American Book Co., 1894), 15–17.
[14] Leland Stanford Junior University, *Register*, vol. 1897–8, pp. 89–90; vol. 1898–99, pp. 87–8; vol. 1899–1900, pp. 97–8.
[15] This survey was never published but may be discovered someday: "Immediately after college closed I went up to the City . . . meantime I put in my time learning what I could about the City, and working along with some students in the preparation of a map of a small district south of Market, showing the chief sociological features. It was a little experiment, not as successful as it can be made the next time, but may be a good lead to work more fully later. I may have it in shape to show you when you return." Frank A. Fetter to Ross [Palo Alto to Paris] 24 June 1899, Ross Papers, State Historical Society of Wisconsin.

neighborhood, funded by a bequest from Phoebe Apperson Hearst, William Randolph's mother. The organizers, led by Fred E. Haynes, a fresh Harvard Ph.D. and a Boston-area settlement activist, declared that this first settlement house west of the Mississippi should "serve as a medium among the different social elements of the city for bringing about a more intelligent and systematic understanding of their mutual obligations."[16] For this purpose by 1897 the South Park Settlement had established clubs, such as the Men's Political Economy Club, classes, and a library, "similar in their workings to those of other settlements," and had organized "many social gatherings, lectures, concerts, and entertainments, which form so important a part of the South Park Settlement life." By their own account, the San Francisco Settlement workers had chosen a neighborhood of "working people" within a few blocks of "both the wealthy and the destitute."[17]

To bridge group identities the settlement activists organized classes for children that followed "a well-developed plan and purpose to train these young thinkers in the ethics of the home, the school, the playground and the larger community life." Settlement workers reached several hundred children every Sunday for slide lectures in this vein. For the adults, the settlement workers organized clubs, which "engaged" participants "in the study and discussion of current economic and political questions, especially those of money and of the relations between labor and capital." The gymnasium was put at the service of the labor leaders of the San Francisco Labor Council and the Federated Trades Council once a month for "an interesting series of addresses from labor leaders, lawyers, business men, etc, on various phases of the labor problem. Each address is followed by discussions, when diverse opinions are freely aired." The energy of the settlement was an effort to make the public sphere more rational, more open to dispassionate, scientific ideas, and more democratic: more accessible for the working people of the neighborhood, who could participate in clubs they ran themselves. "The crying need of San Francisco is not higher wages or shorter hours, but intelligent public opinion. The Settlement

---

16 "The San Francisco Settlement Association," *Prospect Union Review* 1:15 (January 1895): 3–4.
17 Fannie W. McLean, "South Park Settlement: Characteristic Work in a San Francisco Neighborhood," *The Commons* 14 (June 1897): 1–3.

should be a source of accurate and unsensational information," one official remarked.[18]

Nevertheless, the San Francisco Settlement, with its slide shows for children, its political economy clubs, and its forums for debate between capitalists and laborers, could carve out only a small segment of the political public sphere for these purposes. That segment still floated in the sea of mass-media produced on an industrial scale by Hearst and his competitors, who maximized their appeal to specific social groups in a self-conscious strategy of targeted consumer marketing. In the marketplace of ideas some people had the ideas while others had the market. Change in the social-institutional structure of San Francisco came about through intensive activity in the city's dominant segments of the political public sphere. While the South Park Settlement, funded by the Hearst mining fortune, ministered the theory of social-group reconciliation and adaptive education to a few hundred participants in weekly club meetings, trying to foster an ethic of community democracy, William Randolph Hearst, also funded by the Hearst mining fortune, reached one hundred thousand readers a day with a discourse of group identities, fostering class, ethnic, and racial conflict.[19]

A similar summation may be reached about the intellectuals themselves. While E. A. Ross articulated his theory of social control to a handful of students who would, like Franklin Hichborn, eventually play a role in San Francisco's political dramas, political entrepreneurs like James Duval Phelan were putting together coalitions of institutional leaders to rewrite the city charter in a politically feasible way. Ross and Goodnow made careful arguments in their writings about the importance of retaining a strong city council while refashioning the city government to become more administrative and less political. Ross and Goodnow, however, brought little to the institutional table of political reform besides justifications for administrative centralization, as we shall see in the case of the drafting of the reform charters of 1894 and 1898. First, however, we need to consider the deepest challenge to the configuration of the public sphere in the 1890s: the mass entry of women into political discourse under the leadership of Charlotte Perkins Gilman.

---

[18]   Katherine Coman, "The South Park Settlement, San Francisco," *The Commons* 8 (August 1903): 7–9.
[19]   Ibid.; Lucile Eaves to E. A. Ross, 4 May, 20 November 1901; 8 August 1905.

CHARLOTTE PERKINS GILMAN AND THE POLITICAL
MOBILIZATION OF WOMEN

One of the visiting lecturers on the Stanford campus was a woman who many have described as the most original feminist thinker of the Progressive Era: Charlotte Perkins Gilman.[20] Known as Charlotte Perkins Stetson at the time of her arrival in Oakland in 1892, Gilman (as I shall designate her, to credit the name by which she is known), great-granddaughter of Lyman Beecher and heir to a long line of New England reformers, including her great aunts Catherine Beecher and Harriet Beecher Stowe, had come west to facilitate her separation and divorce from her first husband, the artist Walter Stetson. In California she became involved with a widening circle of woman suffragists, Bellamy Nationalist clubs, labor unions, women's clubs, and the Pacific Coast Women's Press Association. Settling in Oakland, across the Bay from San Francisco, Gilman became intimately involved with the reform journalist Adeline Knapp and rapidly became a local celebrity activist. Her restless mind brought her before an extraordinarily diverse constituency, from labor organizations to upper-class women's clubs, but her driving ideological commitment was toward the articulation of an original feminist ideology.[21]

Gilman's activity in the public life of San Francisco shaped her thought, and she in turn had a demonstrable influence on the burgeoning reform activity of the city during the years of her residency in the San Francisco Bay area. Gilman's biographers agree that her California period, ending in late 1895, was a key stage in her personal, intellectual, and political development. It is clear as well that those years were a key stage in the transformation of the political culture of San Francisco. By 1893 Gilman was thoroughly integrated into the cultural and political left wing of the San Francisco political community. When her relationship with Knapp ended, Gilman became involved with the populist-realist writer Edwin Markham and the leading lobbyist for the Federated Trades

---

20 For the position of Gilman in the construction of feminism, see Nancy Cott, *The Grounding of Modern Feminism* (New Haven: Yale University Press, 1987), esp. 1–50.

21 On Gilman's California years, see Marian K. Towne, "Charlotte Gilman in California," *Pacific Historian* 28:1 (1984): 4–17; Mary A. Hill, *Charlotte Perkins Gilman: The Making of a Radical Feminist, 1860–1896* (Philadelphia: Temple University Press, 1980), 187–258; Ann J. Lane, *To Herland and Beyond: The Life and Work of Charlotte Perkins Gilman* (New York: Pantheon, 1990), 158–9. Gilman's lectures at Stanford are discussed in her diary, 18–19 April 1894, Charlotte P. Gilman Papers, Schlesinger Library.

Council, Eugene Hough. Markham, Hough, and Gilman spent long nights hammering out plans to battle the Southern Pacific railroad monopoly, and they attempted to˙enlist the eccentric Joaquin Miller in the cause. In this literary-political circle, Gilman published her short book of political-personal poetry, *In This Our World* (1893).[22]

By the spring of 1894 another remarkable woman, Helen Stuart Campbell, arrived in San Francisco, fresh from studying economics under Richard T. Ely in Wisconsin and publishing a prize-winning study called *Women Wage-Earners* under Ely's editorship in 1893.[23] Campbell had helped organize the first Bellamy Nationalist Club in Boston; Gilman had been involved with the Nationalists ever since arriving in California. In May 1894 Gilman moved into Campbell's San Francisco home on Powell Street, and the two began a partnership in editing the *Impress*, the journal of the Pacific Coast Women's Press Association.

The Gilman-Campbell collaboration resulted in an outpouring of "material feminist" ideological innovation.[24] Both Campbell and

22 On Markham and Hough, see Hill, *Charlotte Perkins Gilman*, 210–11, 218, 224–5. Hough's name appeared as one of the officials of the FTC on the pledge card used by the FTC in 1891 to discipline the Democrats and Republicans in passing the Reform Ballot Act. *Examiner* 3 March 1891; Gilman, Diary, 16, 20, 31 January 1893, Gilman Papers, Schlesinger Library; Charlotte Perkins Stetson [Gilman], *In This Our World* (Oakland, Calif.: McCombs and Vaughn, 1893). Gilman describes the original publishers as "two of my Socialist friends." It was later republished several times. See Gilman, *The Living of Charlotte Perkins Gilman: An Autobiography* (1935; Madison: University of Wisconsin Press, 1990); 168–70.

23 Campbell, who had begun her writing career as a popular author of children's books (Gilman had read them as a child), evolved first into a home economist, teaching at the Raleigh, North Carolina, Cooking School, and then into a reporter for the New York *Tribune*, for which she conducted investigative stories on the lives of working women and the residential conditions of the poor. This line of work, based in the Christian missions of New York City, led her to study economics with Richard T. Ely, but at the same time she organized the National Household Economics Association. Gilman, *The Living*, 171–3, describes her relationship with Campbell ("Mrs. Campbell became like a mother to me"), 174; Ross E. Paulson, "Campbell, Helen Stuart," in *Notable American Women*, 1:280–281, gives an overall sketch of Campbell's career, but fails to mention a big and revealing work by Campbell, *Darkness and Daylight: Lights and Shadows of New York Life. A Woman's Story of Gospel, Temperance, Mission, and Rescue Work "In His Name," With Hundreds of Thrilling Anecdotes and Incidents ...* (Hartford, Conn.: A. D. Worthington & Co., Publishers, 1892). This book is a sprawling, illustrated Dickensian affair with large appended sections by Col. Thomas Knox and Inspector Thomas Byrnes, chief of the New York Detective Bureau, as well as an introduction by the Reverend Lyman Abbott. Campbell's chapters were originally written for the New York *Tribune*.

24 Gilman and Campbell's partnership in Hill, *Charlotte Perkins Gilman*, 238–49; Dolores Hayden, *The Grand Domestic Revolution: A History of Feminist Designs for American Homes, Neighborhoods, and Cities* (Cambridge, Mass.: MIT Press, 1981), 2–29, 182–277.

Plate 8.1. Charlotte Perkins Stetson [Gilman]. Shown here in San Francisco at the age of thirty-four, Gilman was just launching her career as one of the most original American feminist thinkers. As single mother, caretaker of her own dying mother, manager of a boardinghouse, editor of the reformist weekly *Impress*, lecturer, writer, and organizer, Gilman galvanized San Francisco's myriad women's organizations into a renewed movement to obtain the franchise, by organizing the Woman's Congresses of 1894 and 1895. Gilman typically presented herself in formal portraits by striking an assertive profile pose, with her chin high, indicating her public persona. This unusual image, captured by a newspaper photographer assigned to cover the controversial divorcée, theorist, and organizer, captures the thoughtful Gilman in the midst of her exhausting project to carve out of the urban public sphere a permanent place for women. On the reverse she wrote: "Un-'touched' – taken by a newspaper 1894 or 5. Pretty worn out already." Courtesy of the Schlesinger Library, Radcliffe College, Cambridge Massachusetts.

Gilman were deeply concerned with the labor economics of women and sought to merge socialism with women's rights through scientific housework intended to free working women from the second shift, and to free middle-class women from the bondage of housework.[25] In her lectures of these years, of which about sixty survive,

[25] On Campbell as a "material feminist," see Hayden, *Grand Domestic Revolution*, 185–6. Hayden points out that Campbell preferred taking housework out of the home rather than making it a cooperative enterprise, as Gilman was also later to prefer.

Gilman first formulated the message she would synthesize in *Women and Economics* (1898): the need of economic independence for women. She thus served as a bridge between two generations of women activists then overlapping in San Francisco's public sphere. In contrast to Laura de Force Gordon, who was now in her mid-fifties and focusing all of her public energies on winning the ballot, Gilman sought to widen the struggle to achieve all kinds of social reform, beginning with the relations of reproduction and production.

To represent the richness of the thought that poured from Gilman's pen and lips in these years is a task beyond the scope of this chapter. A few observations, however, are in order. Already in 1891 she argued that although motherhood was woman's special role, to fulfill it properly she needed full equality in the political and economic world. In 1892 Gilman was awarded a gold medal by the Trades and Labor Unions of Alameda County for an evolutionary, socialist essay on "The Labor Movement," crediting that movement with an avant-garde role in the history of civilization. The next year, in praise of the populist movement, she argued that "Industrial freedom makes honest reality of political freedom, and living truth of religious freedom."[26] And in a lecture of 1 February 1894 entitled "The Ethics of Woman's Work," Gilman wove these strands of socialism and feminism together:

Women need progressive organized industry as much as they need education or food or air – it is a condition of human existence and progression. That they should be deprived of such industry and relegated to the performance of those nutritive and excretory functions of the body politic, and those at the most primitive level, is wrong – grievously wrong to humanity, and to be carefully considered in the ethics of woman's work.[27]

For Gilman to speak in public about the "nutritive and excretory functions of the body politic" represents a real break, not only with the earlier women leaders of public discourse but also with the polit-

---

[26]   Charlotte Perkins Stetson [Gilman], *The Labor Movement: A Prize Essay read before the Trades and Labor Unions of Alameda County, September 5, 1892* [pamphlet] (Oakland: Alameda County Federation of Trades, 1893), Schlesinger Library, Radcliffe College; "The Labor Movement" and the other lectures cited here can be found in Larry Ceplair, ed., *Charlotte Perkins Gilman: A Nonfiction Reader* (New York: Columbia University Press, 1991), 53–79. Quotation is from "What the People's Party Means," 77.

[27]   Ceplair, *Charlotte Perkins Gilman*, 77–8.

ical discourse of men and women alike prior to the 1890s. To conceive of politics as rooted in or dependent on economics and the reproductive functions of the home was part of a larger shift marking the emergent discourse of progressivism. For Gilman, at least, it led to a certain downgrading of the long-sought goal of the ballot. "As to women, the basic need of economic independence seemed to me of far more importance than the ballot," Gilman later wrote of her San Francisco years, but, she added, the ballot "was a belated and legitimate claim, for which I always worked as opportunity offered." Gilman's growing influence in San Francisco represented a distinct shift in emphasis, then, not away from the ballot, but toward a wider ideological framework that still included the ballot and equal rights.

The most enduring achievement by Gilman in the work of transforming the public sphere of San Francisco was her role in organizing the first two widely attended Woman's Congresses in May of 1894 and 1895. The idea for the first congress originated in the Pacific Coast Women's Press Association in August 1893, probably inspired by the Woman's Congress held at the 1893 Chicago World's Columbian Exposition. As a member of the permanent Board of Managers, Gilman poured herself into the arrangements for each of the California congresses, inviting the leading men and women in every field of expertise, choosing broad themes for each congress, and organizing each congress around topical "sessions" featuring short papers followed by ten-minute discussion periods open to the audience.[28]

The 1894 congress, which took the theme "Woman and the affairs of the world as they affect and are affected by her," heard papers on dress reform, "The Relation of California Women to Politics," "Opportunities for Higher Education of Woman of This Coast," "The Business Woman's Evolution," "How To Dispense With Servants," and women's health. Much of this program had a bourgeois emphasis, but the congress also heard more critical economic papers. Gilman spoke on "What Socialism Is," which she defined as "the organic unity of the human race." Helen Campbell spoke

---

[28]   Gilman, Diary, 13–14 February, 13 March 1894. The role of Gilman in the Woman's Congresses is briefly discussed in Hill, *Charlotte Perkins Gilman*, 248–250, and Lane, *To Herland and Beyond*, 164. The best source is the newspaper coverage (see following notes) and the Charlotte P. Gilman Papers, Schlesinger Library, box 1, folders 1–15, containing the programs.

on "The General Condition of Working Women in the United States." This first Woman's Congress, reported as filling the seats to capacity each day, was but a demonstration of the range of women's public interests that could be brought together under one roof.[29]

The success of the first congress led to the spectacular success of the second, held in May 1895. Gilman and Campbell left their mark most distinctly on the program for the second congress, the theme of which was "the study and discussion of the Home, in its deepest and widest relations." The importance and publicity of this congress was greatly enhanced by the presence of Susan B. Anthony and of Dr. Anna Howard Shaw, who described it as "the most marvelous gathering I ever saw." The publicity associated with the attendance of Anthony and Shaw helped to advance the attendance and attention paid to the congress. The superintendent of schools even canceled classes one day so that Anthony could address the city's nine hundred teachers.[30] The *Examiner* devoted full-page illustrated coverage to the event and sent Hearst's star personal-interest feature writer, "Annie Laurie" (Winifred Sweet Black), to compose first-person essays about the proceedings.[31] Annie Laurie, despite her hostility to the entire congress, emphasized over and again how popular the sessions were, how women were barred at the doors to prevent dangerous overcrowding. Laurie, who preferred the "sensible" women who "said sensible things about babies or about schools," complained that "when a woman talked about the 'Slavery of Wives,' the room was not big enough for the women who wanted to argue, and they didn't talk back, they agreed."[32]

The second congress unified the equal rights suffrage radicalism of Anthony with the domestic radicalism of Gilman, and articulated a political ideology of women's authority in the private and the public household. On the one hand, a recurrent theme of the second congress was "the home is a workshop," seeking to validate women's domestic labor as socially necessary, but also to press the growing movement for community kitchens as a path to women's emancipation. "THE DOMESTIC KITCHEN DOOMED," the *Examiner* head-

29   *Examiner* 1–5, 13 May 1894.
30   Susan B. Anthony and Ida Hasted Harper, eds., *History of Woman Suffrage* (New York: Susan B. Anthony, 1902), 4:253.
31   *Examiner*, 22–26, 28–29 May 1895.
32   *Examiner*, 26 May 1895.

line declared after a day of papers on "Federated Cooking." Eliza Orr of San Francisco detailed the theory that modern economic evolution, appearing in bakeries, caterers, and telephone exchanges, portended the elimination of private housework and would result "in the modification of the whole domestic system." The *Examiner* summarized this session with the conclusion that "in the new home wherein will dwell the new women, there will be no kitchen. You will get your dinner in a box from a factory."[33]

Although numerous speakers addressed packed audiences explaining how to revolutionize the home by making its functions public, collective, or part of the world of business, just as many spoke on the transformation of the state by domesticating it. In a critique of masculine liberalism entitled "The Family is the Unit of the State," one speaker declared that "when the whole family is recognized as the unit of good Government women will be given power in the State."[34] The first of a series of resolutions ratified by the congress read: "Especially we emphasize that the home is primary ... and we would enlarge women's boundaries in order to enlarge the home and all it represents."[35] Dr. Anna Howard Shaw agreed. In her paper "The City and the Home," Shaw declared that "the street-cleaning department of the city was never intended for men to manage," for men "have not been taught to clean up." The only way to get the streets cleaned was, simply, "to put it in the hands of women who understand the work."[36]

These admonitions to usurp the administrative work of the city from men could appear very ominous. San Francisco suffragist Selina Solomons argued that human society had arisen in a "Matriarchate," subsequently lost, and that "history had begun its repetition and that a return of the same condition is expected shortly."[37] Solomons was only participating in a widespread intellectual debate of the late nineteenth century, stemming from Sir Henry Maine's *Ancient Law* (1861), in which he had claimed that the origins of Western society were to be found in the patriarchal Roman family. Taking a position on this question was fraught with political implications. We have seen that Mary McHenry chose it in her commencement address at Hastings College of Law in 1882. It was significantly raised at the first congress as well, by the Stanford

33 *Examiner*, 23 May 1895.   34 *Examiner*, 24 May 1895.   35 *Examiner*, 25 May 1895.
36 *Examiner*, 24 May 1895   37 *Examiner*, 26 May 1895.

sociologist Mary Roberts Smith, who spoke on the "Future of the Family," claiming that the "Roman idea ... based on the utter supremacy of the husband and father ... prevails pretty much in our day." But, Smith added, the "evolution of the family is far from complete."[38] The Reverend Ada C. Bowles, taking the anti-Maine view, asserted that "we had matriarchal laws before patriarchal laws."[39] Whether or not they agreed with Maine as to the original condition of human society being patriarchal or matriarchal, the women at the congress intended to evolve both the family and the state away from patriarchy, sometimes, as in Solomons's paper, threatening a return to matriarchy.[40]

In her later years Charlotte Perkins Gilman remembered her San Francisco years as ones of "failure, a repeated, cumulative failure." She remembered her reception by San Franciscans as one of hostile rejection: "the foulest misrepresentation and abuse I have ever known."[41] True, the *Impress* failed, and she left the city late in 1895 without any money. But Gilman remembered too harshly. Her contributions to the rebuilding of San Francisco's political life should not be underestimated, despite her own radicalism and her real originality.[42] She was instrumental in forging from the inchoate sentiments of domestic womanhood a politically conscious ideology of the home, as the basis of women's public institutions, and its relation to the state.[43] Through her ceaseless energy she had provided

[38] *Examiner*, 4 May 1894.   [39] *Examiner*, 2 May 1894.

[40] Indeed, this theme of a woman's ability to govern the state as she would her household was so widespread that "C. C.," the interlocutor discussed in Chapter 7, had used it in her debate with "Scientia" in the *Call*'s Woman's Column of 1888, turning Scientia's observation that "Government has followed the family in its structure" against him. "There are few families in which the woman is not the real governing power in the conduct of its affairs and the regulation of its economy," C. C. observed, and drove home the point: "If she has proved herself here ... it is but fair to presume she would be able with study to comprehend the economy of the larger family." San Francisco *Call*, 6 July 1888.

[41] Gilman, *The Living*, 76, 80.

[42] Hill observes a distinct rewriting by Gilman of her relationship with Adeline Knapp, for instance, in *The Living*. Gilman is clearly too harsh on the San Francisco public as well. See Hill, *Charlotte Perkins Gilman*, 191–210.

[43] My characterization of Gilman as a radical is based chiefly on her criticism of the marriage institution, which she had identified as immoral as early as March 1893 when she wrote a paper called "The Sex Question Answered" for the Woman's Congress of the World's Columbian Exposition in Chicago. This essay contained central ideas that would appear in her 1898 *Women and Economics*: "The essential indecency of the dependence of one sex upon the other for a living is in itself sexual immorality." (Quoted in Hill, *Charlotte Perkins Gilman*, 201). On the distinction between sentiments and politically mobilized group consciousness, see Richard Oestreicher, "Urban Working-Class Political Behavior and Theories of American Electoral Politics, 1870–1940," *Journal of American History* 74:4 (March 1988): 1257–86.

the connecting link between the women's voluntary world of political action and the moribund suffrage fight, bringing to the former a forum for articulating a domestic-public reform ideology, and to the latter new life. "Write papers, read, discuss, exhort, work," Gilman's diary for a day in June 1893 reads: "Visit local groups as desired. Make it go, St[ate] Council, Help organize. Help push. A large slow thing this. Should be a City council also."[44]

Anthony and Shaw had come to San Francisco in part to re-ignite the suffrage movement. They held on the last day of the 1895 congress a suffrage meeting "to devise a plan to secure the passage of the constitutional amendment at the next legislature." Indeed, Gilman and her colleagues who planned the Woman's Congress had primed the pump for such an effort. "In all my forty years' experience," Anthony asserted, clearly overwhelmed by the week-long experience of thousands of California women in deliberation, "I never saw such an audience assembled for work on suffrage lines." Anthony established a temporary state committee and filled it not only with the established suffrage leadership, but also with State Senators Charles McComas and Frank McGowan and Mayor Adoph Sutro. Before the end of the 1895 legislative session, the energized female and male suffragists had pushed a suffrage amendment through the state legislature, set to go before the voters in the general election of November 1896. It is a story to which we shall return.[45]

THE HOME AND THE STATE

The speakers at the second Woman's Congress were right, as it turns out, about the political character of the home in its relation to the state. They were in effect demystifying the home by historicizing classical liberalism, which had, for almost a century, conceptualized the state as resting on male individuals. Once men and women activists recovered the historical dimension of social and political structures, as they did in the debate about the patriarchal origins of modern institutions, they also recovered the sense of the polity as a household that had been central to political theory at least

---

[44] Gilman, *The Living*, 166–7.
[45] "But they didn't all stay [for the suffrage meeting with Anthony]," the hostile *Examiner* reporter added: "Fully half melted away when they found out what was going on." This observation, if true, still left Gordon's California Woman Suffrage Association with hundreds of new, mobilized volunteers. *Examiner*, 25 May 1895.

from Plato through Sir Robert Filmer. Exposing this relationship did not resolve it, however. There was not yet to be in San Francisco what Paula Baker calls a "domestication of politics," because of the persistently gendered public-private boundary. The public sphere as a site of disputation of governing relations had been predicated, as we have seen, on the severe ideology of female domesticity.[46]

Any alteration of the political public sphere had profound implications for the home, and the home structured political action along several axes. One was the economic fact of homes as real property that required municipal services. Another was the influence of the home on men's propensity to participate in politics. Most basic was the axis of gender authority, both within and outside the home, already made problematic by the discourse of the public sphere. Each of these was interlinked, but a single political tendency did not result. The home in need of services led easily to a redefinition of municipal governmental functions, but the question of who was best qualified to administer such services touched on ideologies of gender segregation and authority. Here we reconstruct the basic structuring features of urban political culture at the point of its most dramatic transformation.

The prosperity of the 1880s had brought a massive physical expansion of San Francisco outward into the "suburban" districts (all within the city limits).[47] These were the large spaces westward to the ocean, both north and south of Golden Gate Park, and southward, beyond Rincon and Potrero hills, out on the old Mission Road, now simply called Mission Street, past the eighteenth-century Mission Dolores and down to the southern city and county limits.[48] A Currier and Ives lithograph, giving a "bird's-eye view" of San Francisco shows these outer districts to be either sparsely settled or completely vacant in 1878.[49] The famous wooden "Victorian" homes surviving

---

[46] Paula Baker, "The Domestication of Politics: Women and American Political Society, 1780–1920," *American Historical Review* 89:3 (June 1984): 620–47.

[47] Assembly Districts 33, 35, 36, 37, 38, 40, and 41 are considered "suburban" in all of the following analyses, while 28, 29, 30, 31, 32, 34, 39, 42, 43, 44, and 45 are considered the older, central assembly districts.

[48] Charlotte Gilman penned a poem on the subject of city expansion during the early 1890s: "On sand – loose sand and shifting – / On sand – dry sand and drifting – / The city grows to the west; / Not till the border reaches / The ocean-beating beaches / Will it rest." Stetson, *In This Our World* (1893), 82.

[49] "The City of San Francisco: Bird's Eye View of the Bay Looking South-West," lithograph, Currier and Ives, New York, 1878, Bancroft Library, Berkeley.

today are nearly all in these suburban districts and were nearly all built during the 1880s and 1890s.[50] The development of the "suburban" neighborhoods was an important phase in the story of American middle-class formation. The stress here should lie with the word "formation," because it is not simply the case that the middle class moved to the suburbs, nor that the suburbs were overwhelmingly "middle class." Just over half (54%) of the households in the city's newly developed suburban wards were headed by men or women of white-collar occupation; the rest were blue-collar workers. Homeownership rates were more than three times higher in the suburban wards (35%) than in the older wards (11%).[51] Jules Tygiel has even shown that homeownership among a sample of family-dwelling carpenters, teamsters, and laborers (27%) exceeded the citywide rate of 24 percent. Carpenters, who would spearhead the politically potent Building Trades Council in the years after 1896, achieved a remarkable 41 percent home ownership in Tygiel's analysis.[52]

The residents of these new neighborhoods desired extensive and expensive infrastructural improvements, of course: graded and paved streets (even more expensive on San Francisco's hills than in cities like Chicago), gas and water service, sewers and drainage, lighting. To push these demands, suburban residents organized a profusion of "neighborhood improvement clubs." The improvement clubs were symptomatic of the collapse of budgetary politics of distribution, or of what Robin Einhorn calls the "segmented system" of paying for municipal services. Until the adoption of the new charter, most streets were paved and sewers laid by "special assessments" levied only on the property owners who fronted the street in question. The system had the virtue of avoiding redistribution but the fault of requiring large outlays by a small number of citizens. The high and immediate costs of infrastructural improvements pro-

---

50 A survey sponsored by the National Endowment for the Arts in 1975–6 found 13,487 homes built before 1900. Of these, 5,500 had been built in the 1890s, 3,600 in the 1880s, and 3,100 date from the 1870s. Of course, the older ones would not have survived, but the maps of these structures show that very few of the 1870s structures were built in the outer, or suburban, districts. Judith Lynch Waldhorn and Sally B. Woodbridge, *Victoria's Legacy* (San Francisco: 101 Productions, 1978), 10–31.

51 Study data, analysis of sample of 1,401 individuals from 1900 U.S. Census manuscript.

52 Tygiel, "Workingmen in San Francisco, 1880–1901" (Ph.D. diss., University of California, Los Angeles, 1975), 274, 276–7; Terence J. McDonald, *The Parameters of Urban Fiscal Policy: Socioeconomic Change and Political Culture in San Francisco, 1860–1906* (Berkeley: University of California Press, 1986), 213–14.

voked angry meetings "of indignant protestants [*sic*]" in which speakers at the "Post Street Improvement Club," for instance, denounced the Board of Supervisors' plan to extend Post Street as "the worst kind of job," which "favored the rich landowners and not the poor ones."[53] In the mayoral election of 1892, the crisis of these growth pains was apparent, but unresolved. Each of the six candidates agreed with the Democrat (of the "Reorganized" faction that had opposed Boss Christopher Buckley) Barry Baldwin, who said he was "strenuously opposed to the present system of street extensions." It imposed a burden on property holders that was "unjust and should be put to a stop at once." Most had begun to use the words "progress" and "progressive" to describe their policies for better streets and nice parks, but each was just as adamant about "economy." None of the candidates had a better idea of how to pay for improvements.[54]

In May 1895 the South Side Improvement Club joined with a host of bicycle clubs to stage a massive, lantern-lit procession of, the *Examiner* reported, ten thousand pedestrians and two thousand cyclists – "a wilderness of wheels" – to demand better roads. "Wheelmen," as they were called (although there were many women on wheels reported), wanted smooth-surfaced roads and wanted to use the roads far beyond their own neighborhoods. Organizations from the Richmond District, the Western Addition, the Mission District, and the South Side created a citywide Federation of Improvement Clubs in 1893, and by 1895 these federated groups had organized demonstration projects of street cleaning, paving, and other services in what can be seen as a remarkable example of grass roots participatory government, albeit one outside of the fiscal structure of the local government.[55] What they wanted was a redistributive, or debt-financed, method of paying for expanded services, which in turn required a reconstruction of the purposes of government (providing for needs) and of the structure of government (free of allegedly thieving party control).

The rise of the improvement clubs as a consequence of suburban development was just one way the home intersected with the state. Another way, more generally obtaining, was in patterns of political

53 San Francisco *Call*, 3 September 1892.
54 *Call*, 5 October 1892, carried interviews with all six candidates.
55 *Examiner*, 23 May 1895; McDonald, *The Parameters of Urban Fiscal Policy*, 187–8.

participation. The political community by the 1890s had been expanded by women's extensive public organizations far beyond the confines of electoral politics. But the voting, all-male section of the political community was profoundly shaped by the family and household status of potential voters. We have seen indications in previous chapters of the influence of the household status of men on their propensity to participate in voting. The data available for the turn of the century enables a much more powerful analysis of the sources of political participation. Taking a sample of 121 adult male eligible voters from the U.S. Census of 1900, and tracing them individually into the lists of registered voters from 1892 to 1904, the relative predictive value of ethnicity, occupational strata, age, homeownership, and marital status on the decision to register to vote can be estimated using multiple logistic regression analysis. Only two variables had a significant effect on the propensity to register to vote: marital status and age. Controlling for the effects of ethnicity, occupation, age, and homeownership, a man who was married was 2.6 times more likely to be registered than a single man, and every increase of ten years in age made him 1.4 times (or 0.14 per year) more likely to be registered. Analysis of voter turnout in presidential, state, and municipal elections from 1896 to 1900 yields similar results. Controlling for ethnicity, the percent of those registered to vote who actually voted is best explained by two variables: marital status and class. Of these, the percent married in each assembly district had the strongest influence.[56]

Participation in electoral politics in the last decade of the nineteenth century, then, was structurally linked to the private household through the institution of marriage and the family. The best predictor of participation was whether or not a man was married. The importance of married men within the electoral political community raised the stakes considerably when discussions of redistributing political sovereignty arose. The operation of gender identity stretched far beyond the home, however. Although the state proper was of course nearly all male (excepting a few women on the school boards), men, no less than women, participated in gender-segregated voluntary institutions outside of political parties and the

[56] Philip J. Ethington, "Recasting Urban Political History: Gender, the Public, the Household, and Political Participation in Boston and San Francisco during the Progressive Era," *Social Science History* 16:2 (Summer 1992): 301–33.

state. The most striking example of these institutions were the secret fraternal societies that exploded in membership during the last decades of the nineteenth century. An 1897 article in the *North American Review* proclaimed that the last third of the nineteenth century was the "Golden Age of Fraternity." Of 19 million adult male Americans, 5.5 million belonged to fraternal organizations. The Odd Fellows (810,000 members in 1897), Freemasons (750,000), Knights of Pythias (475,000), and Red Men (165,000) were the leading organizations, but millions more belonged to smaller secret societies and millions more than that belonged to the Knights of Labor, the Grange, trade unions, and the Grand Army of the Republic, all of which borrowed heavily from the secret societies. "The distinguishing feature and central activity" of the secret societies, writes Mark Carnes, "was the performance of elaborate sequences of initiation rituals."[57]

Secret fraternal societies proliferated rapidly in the 1880s and 1890s. As thousands of women engaged in all-female voluntary organizations and sought wider participation in the economy and polity, a process that achieved a measure of feminine solidarity and political consciousness in the Woman's Congresses of the 1890s, thousands of men rushed from the home and into all-male lodges to reinforce their masculine solidarity. In San Francisco by 1900 there were more than 260 "lodges," "tribes," or "courts" situated in every neighborhood of the city for the Free and Accepted Masons, the Independent Order of Odd Fellows, the Ancient Order of Foresters, the Foresters of America, the Improved Order of Red Men, the Knights of Honor, and the Knights of: " . . . Pythias," ". . . the Golden Eagle," ". . . Tara," ". . . the Red Branch," ". . . the Maccabees," and so on. Based on Anthony Fels's study of the San Francisco Freemasons, we could estimate a secret society membership of more than twenty thousand in 1900.[58] Although historians agree that

---

[57]   Mark C. Carnes, "Middle-Class Men and the Solace of Fraternal Ritual," in Mark C. Carnes and Clyde Griffen, eds., *Meanings for Manhood: Constructions of Masculinity in Victorian America* (Chicago: University of Chicago Press, 1990): 37–52; *North American Review*, membership figures, and quotation cited at p. 38.

[58]   The Freemasons had an average lodge membership of 258.5 in 1900. To be on the conservative side, and to assume some overlapping membership, we could choose 100 as an estimated average lodge size for the fraternal societies in general. There were 261 lodges listed in the 1900 city directory, which yields 26,000 members. Anthony Fels, "The Square and the Compass: San Francisco's Freemasons and American Religion, 1870–1900" 2 vols. (Ph.D. diss., Stanford University, 1987), 1:65; *Crocker-Langley San Francisco Directory for the Year Commencing May 1900* (San Francisco: H. S. Crocker Co., 1900), 63–73.

these organizations were heavily middle class and Protestant in membership (meaning white-collar), they were not exclusively so. Fels finds that one-third of the Masons in 1900 were working class, and we find that the Irish had their Ancient Order of Hibernians, and the working class had the Ancient Order of United Workmen.[59]

Whatever else the secret societies performed in terms of identity formation, their primary feature, beyond class and ethnicity, was that of gender solidarity. Most strikingly, whereas the speakers of the Woman's Congress exposed and criticized patriarchy, the men of the fraternal societies recognized and celebrated it. As Carnes demonstrates, the ritual of the secret societies marked a passage from the feminine-dominated world of the home and a boy's up-bringing to a world of men and of extradomestic masculinity. After following symbolic ordeals in the various initiation rites, the mem-bers approached the sanction of the masculine hierarchy. "The Patriarchal Degree of Odd-Fellowship," writes Carnes, "featured a young man's quest for the approval of surrogate fathers." In the ritual for that degree, a "high priest ... instructed the initiate to kneel. Then he intoned: 'You have toiled through the ways of doubt and error to the bosom of our Patriarchal family.'"[60]

Whether the reconstructed state of the Progressive Era would be a "matriarchate," as speakers at the Woman's Congress suggested, or a "Patriarchal family," as the rites of masculine secret-club soli-darity implied, was in fact a central and structuring question of the political discourse of the 1890s, one with profound implications for the course of American political development. The mounting insti-tutional strength of women political activists with a highly gendered ideology about reform was met by a masculine establishment with demonstrable interests in keeping the reform agenda masculine. "Women played no part in our lives," recalled one of Franklin Lane's associates during this period.[61] As we shall see presently, James Duval Phelan's vision of urban reform included an explicit dedication to keeping women in the home. To reach that stage in the narrative, however, we need to pick up the thread of political change begun in the previous chapter.

59 Fels, "Square and the Compass," 1:66–71; *Crocker-Langley San Francisco Directory ... 1900,* 65–6.

60 Carnes, "Middle-Class Men and the Solace of Fraternal Ritual," 49.

61 *The Letters of Franklin K. Lane: Personal and Political,* edited by Anne Wintermute Lane and Louis Herrick Wall (Boston and New York: Houghton Mifflin Co., 1922), 24.

PROGRESSIVES AND SILURIANS:
THE REFORM MATRIX OF 1891–1896

When the props fell away from the organizational parties after the passage of the Reform Ballot Act in 1891, the initiative in political entrepreneurship passed from the labor union leadership to the city's business leadership. Labor's business allies in the Young Men's Democratic League and the Australian Ballot fight of 1888–91 became the senior partners in the reform coalitions of the 1890s, most importantly because labor unions fell on hard times again in 1892, just when the possibilities for fundamental governmental change arrived. The most powerful underlying cause of the steep decline in the institutional fortunes of organized labor was the panic and depression of 1893–7. But the downturn began as early as 1892.[62] Most devastating, however, was the defeat of the American Railway Union (ARU) strike and boycott of the Pullman Company. Several dramatic and fatal confrontations between California railway workers and the state's militia ended in a mass arrest and the trial of two union workers for murder in San Francisco. One man was convicted and sentenced to hang. The ARU members were blacklisted and the unions were demoralized, but by all accounts, "public opinion" turned even further against the hated SP monopoly. By 1897 organized labor was the weakest it had been since the depression of 1875–9. A mere forty-one hundred workers could be counted as union members. This institutional weakness nearly eliminated the structure of mobilization on the class-identity axis necessary for labor leaders to achieve labor goals during the reform process. The bitterness left by the SP's high-handedness was free to flow into other channels of mobilization, provided especially in the populist mayoral candidacy of Adolph Sutro.[63]

Actually, the labor lobby under Frank Roney, Judge Maguire, Eugene Hough, Andrew Furuseth, and others had achieved several exemplary victories in 1892 before temporarily losing its clout. The most visible of these was the ten-year extension of the Chinese Exclusion Act. Labor leaders' success in maintaining their "indispensable enemy," the Chinese, in the status of political pariahs

[62] Lucile Eaves, *A History of California Labor Legislation* (Berkeley: University of California Press, 1910), 314.
[63] Ira B. Cross, *A History of The Labor Movement in California* (Berkeley: University of California Press, 1935), 218.

through national legislation was a lesson not lost on the political entrepreneurs of the business elite. In the spring of 1894 these business leaders combined at last into a powerful political lobby called the Merchants' Association. One of the new organizers, J. Richard Freud, "endeavored to stir the merchants up to a sense of their obligations in the community." Freud's model was organized labor: "The laborers, he said, had pushed the Chinese Restriction Act to a successful conclusion, and it was time the merchants did some legislating."[64]

But the Merchants' Association had not organized against organized labor. Their defining agenda was to reconstruct the electoral and administrative machinery of the municipal government, and these goals called for a new city charter to replace the Consolidation Act of 1856. The model developed by Samuel P. Hays to explain urban reform in the Progressive Era argues that the leaders of reform acted in the interest of the new corporate elite to overthrow the rule of ward-based machines with their ethnic and working-class constituencies. That model misreads the merchant leadership of the charter reform drives in American cities beginning in the 1890s by inferring from it an agenda to promote the interests of the corporate elite. The Merchants' Association was dominated by family-owned firms and not corporations. Their common enemy was the Southern Pacific Railroad: the corporate "octopus." Also, the Hays model makes it impossible to imagine why the electorate, already mobilized along ethnic, class, and neighborhood lines, would support a change in their government designed to close those aggregations off from participation and benefits.[65]

If the Merchants' Association had as their agenda the centralization of power in order to remove the working-class and ethnic neighborhoods from power, we would at least expect some record of this agenda to survive; yet none does survive. Instead, the reform agenda of the Merchants' Association was directed first of all at the contradictory and broken fiscal machinery of the organizational party regimes, that structure that had avoided redistribution, that had relied on "private" franchises to supply services while politicians kept taxes and expenditures to a minimum.

The political label "progressive" first arose as a dialectical nega-

---

[64] *Examiner*, 4 May 1894.
[65] Samuel P. Hays, "The Politics of Reform in Municipal Government in the Progressive Era," *Pacific Northwest Quarterly* 55 (1964): 157–69.

tion of that fiscal ideology and practice. "THEY SMOTE THE SILURIANS," ran an *Examiner* headline in May 1894; "Progressive Speakers Before the Merchants' Association," ran the subtitle. The adjective "progressive" had come into use during the previous four or five years to distinguish those who favored improvements in city services from the "Silurians," a paleontological term used locally to describe the rigid fiscal conservatism that had paralyzed growth in the neighborhoods and the modernization of city infrastructure throughout. "Silurian" was taken from geological evolutionary science, marking the period "from 405 to 435 million years ago, the fourth oldest period of the Paleozoic era."[66] McDonald, who has decoded the "Silurian" label and its significance in fiscal ideology, traces this term as well as the rise of the "progressive" label to the *Examiner* in 1888, the first year of young Hearst's control of the paper.[67]

One of the founding members of the Merchants' Association was T. T. Williams, business manager of the *Examiner*, who "said he appeared on behalf of W. R. Hearst and the EXAMINER" and "made it clear that anything he could do to aid them in their efforts to benefit the city would be done."[68] In fact, the *Examiner* had already begun to render the powerful service of recasting political discourse around the "progressive" – "Silurian" dichotomy. Who would say, in the period of Darwinian evolution's greatest cultural triumph, that she or he was "unprogressive"? Who would wish to be labeled a Silurian, fit to crawl with the earliest plants and organisms? According to the *Examiner*, "These silurians have opposed the park, have opposed decent pavements, opposed new sewers, opposed new schoolhouses, opposed everything, in short, that the city has needed and has had to be taxed to pay for."[69] Consensus slogans like "virtue" and "progressive" do not have politically viable opposites. In the 1850s there had been no alternative to seeking the labels "virtue" and "honor." These labels did not demarcate party or policy differences, but did reveal the central meaning structure of policy debate and constituency mobilization. By the 1890s, it was not acceptable to be labeled "unprogressive."

---

[66]　McDonald, *The Parameters of Urban Fiscal Policy*, 183–5, explicates the significance of the term "Silurian" and gives its etymology. Quotation is from p. 183.

[67]　*Examiner*, 6 October 1888, 30 June 1891. Cited in McDonald, *The Parameters of Urban Fiscal Policy*, 183ff.

[68]　*Examiner*, 4 May 1894.

[69]　Quoted in McDonald, *The Parameters of Urban Fiscal Policy*, 184.

The Merchants' Association, then, organized under the aegis of a consensual ideology strategically designed by the leading firm in the communications industry of the public sphere. Power in that sphere can be defined primarily by the ability to change the terms of public debate and reorient the ethical value of the privileged keywords of debate. The Merchants' Association, in fact, had organized relatively late in this process of discursive reorientation. By 1894 the major parties had lost control of the city's electoral market. The legislative session of 1891 was now known as the "Legislature of a Thousand Scandals," and the regular Democrats were suffering the ignominy of Christopher Buckley's grand jury indictment and subsequent flight to Canada. Among those who routed Buckley from within the Democratic party – the "Reorganizers" – was the august Vigilante chieftain William Tell Coleman, back now for the last of his reform battles. The regular Democratic party further lost legitimacy when it tried to deny the Reorganized Democrats a place on the new Australian ballot in the fall of 1892, even though the Reorganizers had already been recognized as the true San Francisco Democrats by both the State Central Committee and the national convention in Chicago. The result in the municipal election of 1892 was near chaos. Levi Ellert of the Citizen's Non-Partisan party won the mayoralty with a mere 30 percent of the vote; C. C. O'Donnell, with his working-class constituency, took another 28 percent of the vote; and even the reformed Democrats had to settle for third place, with 22 percent of the mayoral vote.[70]

The inchoate voter revolt became much more focused – but still more independent of the major parties – in the election of 1894, behind the candidacy of the remarkable millionaire populist Adolph Sutro (1830–98). Sutro, born in Aix-la-Chapelle of German Jewish parents, emigrated with his mother in 1850 to New York City and emerged as a young merchant in San Francisco and Stockton from 1851 to 1859. An engineer by training, Sutro spent the 1860s setting up a venture to build a drainage and ventilation tunnel through the base of the mountains to the Comstock Lode of Nevada. In doing so, the independent Sutro became an inveterate foe of the Southern Pacific, which tried to thwart his venture, and the hero of the miners, who saw his tunnel as an attempt to bring safety to the mines. In 1879 Sutro sold his stock in the tunnel

[70] *Examiner*, 8 November 1892.

venture and invested heavily in San Francisco real estate, mainly in the unsettled western districts, and became the city's largest land-owner overnight.[71]

Sutro, however, was to become a patrician populist rather than an evil landowner. He built a magnificent mansion for himself on Sutro Heights overlooking the Pacific, and around it he built the "Sutro Gardens," a sculpture park and picnic grounds open to the public. In 1894, the year of his election as mayor, Sutro completed the gigantic Sutro Baths, huge indoor swimming pools built right at the ocean's edge. Sutro's largesse, derived perhaps from some aristocratic ideal of public service learned in his native Germany, resembled in a striking, and probably consciously intended way, the bread-and-circus populism of the Roman patricians, who also built constituencies by constructing amusements and baths at their own expense.[72] Sutro's popularity skyrocketed, however, when in 1893 he challenged the Southern Pacific and defeated them at their own game. The SP-controlled streetcar company had a monopoly on the five-mile stretch of tracks used by most people to get to Sutro Heights and charged an exorbitant ten-cent fare for their service. Sutro built a parallel line to his estate and forced the SP to reduce its fare to five cents. In an era of greedy Robber Barons, Sutro looked like the great benefactor of the People. Indeed, he even pledged to give his gardens and baths to the city someday.[73]

Sutro embodied the aspirations, first of all, of the suburbanites who built homes and moved into the pleasant suburbs surrounding Golden Gate Park. He was the virtual King of Suburbia, presiding in his castle at the water's edge and protecting the little burghers from the SP dragon and providing them with pleasant leisure facil-

---

[71]   Robert E. Stewart and Mary F. Stewart, *Adolph Sutro: A Biography* (Berkeley, 1962); biographical sketch, Adolph Heinrich Sutro Papers, Bancroft Library, Berkeley; Bean and Rawls, *California*, 173–174, 219–220; Issel and Cherny, *San Francisco*, 134–5, 206.

[72]   The parallel must not be overdrawn. The Roman patricians ruled through patron-client relationships unknown in modern San Francisco. Sutro's was an imitation of Plutarch's Rome, which informed the understanding of nineteenth-century Americans. M. I. Finley, *Politics in the Ancient World* (Cambridge, U.K.: Cambridge University Press, 1983), 24–49; John E. Stambaugh, *The Ancient Roman City* (Baltimore: Johns Hopkins University Press, 1988), 36–85, 123–41.

[73]   Adeline Knapp, "San Francisco and the Civic Awakening," *Arena* 12 (March–May 1895): 245–6; Adolph Sutro to C. Henri Ware, 31 July 1895, Sutro Papers, Bancroft Library. The ultimate disposition of Sutro's estate was that the Heights (Gardens) were in fact given to the city by Sutro's heirs, but the city had to purchase the Baths. *Municipal Record* 5:36 (5 September 1912): 285.

ities. But Sutro, whose talent for broad appeal cannot be underestimated, was also a champion of the working class. He favored the workers in the Pullman strike (because he favored anyone who opposed the SP), and in the election of 1894 they looked to Sutro for relief from the SP's blacklists. Sutro even favored woman suffrage, and, as we have seen, served on the temporary committee organized by Susan B. Anthony at the end of the 1894 Woman's Congress. The People's party had little difficulty drafting Sutro to run on its ticket that year.[74]

Sutro, after defeating the SP locally, threw himself into the national campaign to keep Collis P. Huntington from achieving a fifty-year postponement of the railroad's debt to the federal government, which had finally come due on the massive subsidies that had made the Robber Barons' millions possible. This "funding scheme," one of Huntington's many public relations failures, also brought the *Examiner's* clout to bear, so that by 1894 a unified political configuration was possible joining working-, middle-, and upper-class San Franciscans in an attempt to win power back from the evil corporation at the local and the national levels. "I have lately started in to oppose the Southern Pacific Ry co.," Sutro wrote to a family member in Dresden, "the great power which rules this land, and in consequence, I have drifted somewhat into politics." His motives were both national and local: "The result has been a marvel all over the United States," he explained in a letter to Paris, "for there is hardly a paper in any state that has not commented" on his candidacy.[75]

In office, Sutro served as a coordinator of the various reform organizations. He corresponded with reformers in other cities, including his contemporary mayor, Hazen Pingree of Detroit. He received copies of William Stead's *If Christ Came to Chicago* from others, spoke at an annual sanitary convention, aided the neighborhood improvement clubs, intervened on behalf of blacklisted workers, and arranged secretly for outside experts to undermine the plans of the long-despised Spring Valley water monopoly to build a reservoir on top of a sewage swamp. He even wrote to the governor of Kentucky pleading with him to revoke the charter of the Southern Pacific,

[74] Sutro to Alex Hamilton, 27 March 1895; Millie Brogue to Sutro, 11 November 1894; Sutro to Miss Mary J. Hay and Miss Harriet Cooper, 23 March 1896, is a long statement of his prosuffrage views, Sutro Papers, Bancroft Library.

[75] Adolph Sutro to Hugo Sutro, Dresden, 17 August 1894; Sutro to Dr. George and Emma S. Merrit, Paris, 20 December 1894. Sutro Papers, Bancroft Library.

"because I look upon [it] as the curse of our country and responsible for the evil condition of the Pacific Coast." At the same time, Sutro enlisted the merchant-dominated Civic Federation to name for him the new Board of Election commissioners allowed under the Purity of Elections Act, passed in 1893.[76]

Sutro, however, was powerless to alter the deeper structural problems of the urban polity. He had even lost the one powerful tool the mayor had had over urban policy when the California Supreme Court ruled, in a complex dispute, that the mayor could no longer veto the budget. The "municipal government is now a headless thing," a former mayor explained to the Richmond District Improvement Association, "and in case of need the people have no one to turn to for guidance and protection."[77] Sutro complained that "the Mayor is merely a neglectible figure-head."[78] As a figurehead, however, Sutro could, and did, work to mobilize discontent, by fostering the delegitimation of the organizational party regime. In January 1895 a crisis occurred that seemingly laid the blame for the governing crisis of the city at the door of the Southern Pacific and the two national parties. In reward for his organizing a Republican party victory in 1890, incoming Governor Henry H. Markham appointed the Republican party "boss," Colonel Dan Burns, a staunch defender of the Southern Pacific, to fill one of the vacant spots on the San Francisco Board of Police Commissioners. This kind of appointment was usual and customary under the organizational regime. But when Burns resigned after the Democratic victory in the fall of 1894, Markham appointed "Mose" Gunst, "the keeper of a saloon and pool-room, the alleged head of a faro-bank," at the eleventh hour before the new governor took his office. Democratic Governor James Budd tried to fire Gunst, but the commissioners, thanks to the statute passed during the Workingmen's party upheaval, had lifetime tenure, and Gunst refused to resign. Sutro gladly organized a meeting at the Metropolitan Temple to protest "this outrage upon public decency." Observers saw in this

---

[76]   Sutro to Hazen Pingree, 18 February 1895; Sutro to Charles F. Hanlon, 11 March 1895; Sutro to Dr. Winslow Anderson, 15 March 1895; Sutro to Joseph Britton, 1 July 1895; Sutro to James H. Budd, 16 July 1895; Sutro to surgeon general of the United States, 5 November 1895; Sutro to Civic Federation, 27 January 1896, Sutro Papers, Bancroft Library.

[77]   Hon. Frank McCoppin, "Address on the New Charter for the City and County of San Francisco," 8 November 1896 [pamphlet], Stanford University Library.

[78]   Adolph Sutro to Civic Federation, 27 January 1896, Sutro Papers, Bancroft Library.

meeting the kind of grouping needed to overturn the organizational regime. Those in attendance were not the "martyr-missionaries of reform who in every great city sound the alarm long before the mass of good citizens are awake to danger," Adeline Knapp wrote, these were instead the "leading citizens."[79] The leading citizen who led the leading citizens, James Duval Phelan, not only articulated a program to codify the new political culture in fundamental law, but was astute enough also to lead the ordinary voters as well.

THE MIND OF AN URBAN PROGRESSIVE REFORMER: JAMES DUVAL PHELAN

The leadership of the reform coalition passed to James Duval Phelan (1861–1930) during the administration of Adolph Sutro. Phelan, whom we met in the last chapter as a Young Democrat aligned with the labor politician James Maguire, was by all accounts the central figure in the reform process of the 1890s. By the beginning of the 1890s he was a leader and/or founder of the principal reform organizations: the Citizen's Defense Association, the Merchant's Association, the Civic Federation, the Reform Charter Association, and president of the Federation of Improvement Clubs. Elected mayor in 1896, he was instrumental in orchestrating the adoption of a new charter in 1898. The reform editor Fremont Older, who would play a leading role in the Graft Prosecutions early in the next century, remembered that "it was Phelan's first administration that gave me my first social sense." Given his centrality to the remaking of San Francisco's political life, it is worthwhile to explore his ideas in detail.[80]

The son of the Irish-born Argonaut James Phelan, James Duval Phelan was born and raised in San Francisco (the first mayor born in the city). The elder Phelan had risen from grocery clerk to merchant in New York City, found further opportunity in the Gold Rush, and plowed his handsome profits on imported cash safes into real estate. By 1869 James Phelan was so wealthy that he settled into

---

[79] Julian Ralph, "California's Great Grievance," *Harper's Weekly* 39 (2 March 1895): 204–7; idem, "Reform in San Francisco," *Harper's Weekly* 39 (9 March 1895): 230–1; Adeline Knapp, "San Francisco and the Civic Awakening," 243–5.

[80] McDonald, *Parameters of Urban Fiscal Policy*, 95–7, 193–4; Issel and Cherny, *San Francisco*, 134–5, 139–40, 146–52; Petersen, "Prelude to Progressivism," 127–8; Fremont Older, *My Own Story* (San Francisco: Call Publishing Co., 1919), 27.

a gentleman's life as a rentier and leading banker, founding and presiding over what today is called the Crocker Bank, one of the largest in the state. Educated in Catholic schools, the junior Phelan graduated from St. Ignatius College (now the University of San Francisco) in 1881 and then spent one year in Hastings College of Law, briefly a classmate of Mary McHenry.[81]

The young Phelan had neither the interest nor the need to finish his law degree. Apparently desiring instead the role of political statesman, Phelan embarked on a tour of European cities, sending back articles on municipal conditions to the *Examiner*.[82] Upon returning, Phelan immersed himself in upper-class social life, became the chair of Wigmore, Lane, and Maguire's Young Men's Democratic League, and helped found the Citizen's Defense Association by 1891. A leading figure in upper-class club life, Phelan preferred literary to purely social clubs. He belonged to the exclusive (24-member) Chit-Chat Club, in which members presented and discussed papers on literary and politicoeconomic subjects.[83] In 1891 he was elected president of the Bohemian Club, founded by journalists and artists in the 1870s, originally an earnest men's forum for debate before devolving into a prankish retreat for celebrities like Henry Kissinger and Neil Armstrong in the late twentieth century. In the salonlike setting of these clubs, Phelan developed and honed his abilities as a public speaker and essayist on practical political issues. He also left enough texts from this period of his career to reconstruct his overall agenda in the leadership of urban reform culminating in his inauguration as mayor in January 1897.

Phelan was among the first to use the term "progressive" as an adjective to describe a political program. By "progressive" Phelan meant, approximately, economic growth and development within a unified, popular civic sense of common interests, by means of efficient, nonpartisan municipal administration. Arguing for a new

---

[81]   Judd Kahn, *Imperial San Francisco: Politics and Planning in an American City, 1897–1906* (Lincoln: University of Nebraska Press, 1979), 59–61.

[82]   Issel and Cherny, *San Francisco*, 34–6, 109–10, 139–40.

[83]   The Chit-Chat Club was organized in 1874 and met monthly. The program for 1891–2 included the following papers: "The Australian Commonwealth," "Large Land-Holdings in California and the Remedy," "Immigration and Naturalization," "College Athletics," "Across the Plains in 1850," "Manual Training," "Railroad Commissions: Their Uses and Abuses," "Country Roads," "Ireland, Ancient and Modern," "Utility of Bank Commissions," and "William H. Seward." Chit-Chat Club of San Francisco, "Eighteenth Annual Meeting, San Francisco, Nov. 7 1892" (San Francisco, 1892) [pamphlet], Widener Library, Harvard College.

charter in 1896, he spoke of "the great and desirable end that we may have a scientific, systematic, and responsible government which will, at the same time, be both progressive and economical." In his first mayoral address to the Board of Supervisors, Phelan gave as an example of "municipal progress" (he replaced the word "development" here with the word "progress" in revision): the city of Glasgow, Scotland, which owned its utilities and reportedly ran them so efficiently and profitably that the citizens were not even taxed! Such a city was Phelan's utopia. As McDonald has shown, Phelan's fiscal ideology attempted to straddle the fence between the penury-minded small property owners – whose leadership he had assumed as president of the Federation of Improvement Clubs – and the goal of generating growth, beauty, and public welfare though needed infrastructural expenditures. "Economy without parsimony" was Phelan's formula: "The people desire improvements," he told the supervisors at his inauguration, "but they desire the public revenues be prudently expended."[84]

Phelan the millionaire reformer was the nearly perfect embodiment of the "best men" tradition in early urban reform ideology; he could have walked out of the pages of James Bryce's *American Commonwealth*. Phelan was the wealthy man who plunged into his city's affairs to promote the general welfare and cleanse it of patronage politics. Indeed, Phelan had a lot in common with Bryce. Both were greatly influenced by Albert Shaw, a graduate of the Johns Hopkins Seminary of History and Politics. Like Phelan, Shaw (with much better training) had also taken a research tour of British and European cities.[85] The results of these investigations were published in two highly influential books, *Municipal Government in Great Britain* and *Municipal Government in Continental Europe*, both published by Macmillan in 1895.

Next to Bryce's *American Commonwealth*, Shaw's books were the most influential intellectual source for the first wave of urban reformers. In them, Shaw singled out Glasgow, with its municipally owned gas, water, and streetcar utilities that actually earned the

---

84   "Address to the Board of Supervisors," [typescript, January 1897], James Duval Phelan Papers, Bancroft Library. In the typescript of this first address to the Board of Supervisors, Phelan revised the phrase "municipal development" to read "municipal progress," indicating that these two terms were synonymous but not identical; progress meant a good deal more than mere development.

85   Lloyd J. Graybar, *Albert Shaw of the* Review of Reviews: *An Intellectual Biography* (Lexington: University Press of Kentucky, 1974), 16–45.

city a profit every year, for especial praise, and from Shaw the
example of Glasgow spread throughout reform discourse in the
1890s. New York reformer Frederic C. Howe, who attended Shaw's
lectures at Johns Hopkins in the 1890s, remembered the enthusiasm
inspired by his ideas. Shaw

> painted pictures of cities that I could visualize – cities that I wanted to take
> part in in America; cities managed as business enterprises; cities that were
> big business enterprises, that owned things and did things for people.
> There was order and beauty in the cities he described. They owned their
> own tramways and gas and electric lighting plants, and they made great
> success of them.[86]

Shaw, in his glowing optimism, was careful to show that municipal
ownership was not a question of socialism, but simply good business
sense. He cheerfully explained that "the present evils of city life are
temporary and remediable. The abolition of the slums, and the destruction of their virus, are as feasible as the drainage of a swamp
and the total dissipation of its miasma."[87] If cities "present new
problems we must meet them," Phelan declared, citing Shaw in his
campaign for mayor and the new charter in 1896: "If they require
government to put on new functions we must assume them. If they
demand new administrative undertakings we must not shirk the task.
Whatever is defective must be made whole."[88] Like Shaw, Phelan
insisted on celebrating the city. This could be read as boosterism,
of course, because Phelan's entire fortune depended on his lucrative real estate in the business districts.[89] But unlike any of his San
Francisco political predecessors, he opened the doors of municipal
services very wide: "The city has certain work to perform," he told

---

[86] Frederic C. Howe, *Confessions of a Reformer* (Chicago: Quadrangle Books, 1967), 5–6,
quoted in Graybar, *Albert Shaw*, 73–4.

[87] Albert Shaw, *Municipal Government in Great Britain* (1895; New York: Macmillan Co., 1901),
2–3.

[88] James D. Phelan, "Municipal Conditions and the New Charter," *Overland Monthly*, 2d Ser.
28 (July 1896): 105.

[89] Phelan took an explicitly pro-urban approach. "The work of a city must be done and you
must have your protection and your remedy here," he told the Young Men's Catholic
Mutual Aid Society in 1887, helping them raise funds for a library. Phelan, Address,
"Young Men's Catholic Mutual Aid Association," 27 October 1887, MS in Phelan
Papers, Bancroft Library; "Large cities are the repositories of everything that science
and art and invention have done for mankind and they are a dear possession of every
country." Phelan, "Municipal Conditions and the New Charter," 105.

the supervisors: "It must care for the health, the comfort, the education, the property and the general welfare of the people."[90]

Apart from Shaw, Phelan's other great inspiration was the emerging City Beautiful city-planning movement begun at the World's Columbian Exposition in Chicago, in 1893. Phelan served as director of the California exhibit at the Chicago Fair. There he met the creator of the White City, Daniel Burnham (he later induced Burnham to create a plan for San Francisco) and was smitten by the wide vistas and the neoclassical façades. Upon his return to San Francisco, Phelan was eager to make it into an imperial city, one that could provide a suitable western metropolis for America's burgeoning commercial and military empire in the Pacific Basin.[91] Phelan's planning of public spaces was part of a large segment of the discourse of progressivism, one that sought to overcome the social and interest-group divisions within the city and to create a new ethos of the "public interest." Unlike the social-democratic segments of the progressive discourse of urban reform, however, Phelan's vision intended to create a consciousness of the common good through the creation of inspiring statuary, imposing façades, and green, shop-lined boulevards.

Besides the fantastic White City, Phelan's actual models in this regard were Washington, D.C., and especially Baron von Haussmann's reconstructed Paris.[92] To attract business and tourists (especially now that Los Angeles had begun its boom), the city needed to be attractive. Phelan was especially attentive to the suburbs. "The suburbs of the city should have the fostering care of the municipal authorities," Phelan told the supervisors. By making them attractive, "We can recover our lost population from the bay counties

90 Phelan, "Address to the Board of Supervisors," [typescript, January 1897]; "There is nothing that is calculated to add to the health, comfort and prosperity of communities that municipalities have not undertaken." Phelan, "Municipal Conditions and the New Charter," 105.

91 For the City Beautiful movement among architects and urban planners, see J. A. Peterson, "The City Beautiful Movement: Forgotten Origins and Lost Meanings," *Journal of Urban History* 2 (August 1976): 415–34; William H. Wilson, "The Ideology, Aesthetics and Politics of the City Beautiful Movement," in Anthony Sutcliffe, ed., *The Rise of Modern Urban Planning: 1800–1914* (London: Mansell, 1980), 165–98. On the politicocultural meanings of the White City, see Alan Trachtenberg, *The Incorporation of America: Culture and Society in the Gilded Age* (New York: Hill and Wang, 1982), 208–43.

92 The most perceptive account of Phelan's planning ideology is Kahn, *Imperial San Francisco*, 57–9.

and other parts of the State, which was driven away by bad and unclean streets, neglected parks and unsanitary conditions."[93]

Phelan's adoption of the White City ideal also indicates something about his position on ethnicity and race. Like any Irish politician, he sang the praises of the freedom-loving Irish people and condemned religious intolerance. But Phelan also sought to reinforce the bonds of white ethnic immigrants to one another in contradistinction to Native Americans, Chinese, and Japanese. His plans for civic improvement and his enthusiasm for overseas empire were of a piece. He proposed to line San Francisco with heroic columns commemorating the explorers Vasco Nuñez de Balboa, Juan Rodriguez Cabrillo, the American conquerors John D. Sloat and John B. Montgomery, and so on. These pillars "should stand in our streets as an inspiration to the rising generation," Phelan explained in one of his many public speeches: "Civic capacity will follow close upon the footsteps of civic pride." Phelan personally commissioned or organized the erection of much public statuary, including the commemoration of California statehood, the statue of the Irish-American revolutionary patriot Robert Emmet, and the Goethe-Schiller monument. Perhaps most fittingly, Phelan chaired the commission that oversaw the design and construction of the monumental victory column in Union Square, commemorating Commodore Dewey's victory of Manila in the Spanish-American War.[94]

During the nationwide industrial crisis of 1893–4, Phelan's ideas crystallized in very distinct views on race, class, and gender. Looking at his speeches to the private Bohemian and Chit-Chat clubs from this period, it is possible to understand the deep anxieties and desire for white male supremacy in Phelan's particular – and successful – brand of urban reform. "The white man is actually a whited man," Phelan warned his fellow club members in a Christmas eve talk: "If the mills of Education and the gospel should close down and there would be no output of lime, man would be exactly what God made him, and that would be a catastrophe."[95] Phelan,

[93] Again, Phelan stressed progress with economy: "By attracting population to the suburbs, the assessed wealth of the city, which comes from the presence of population, will materially increase and compensate us for any unusual outlay." Phelan, "Address to the Board of Supervisors," [typescript, January 1897] Phelan Papers.

[94] Kahn, *Imperial San Francisco*, 64–5.

[95] Christmas lecture, begins "The club is bright tonight ..." 25 December 1893, Phelan Papers. To which "club" this lecture was addressed is not specified, but Phelan uses in it a freedom of expression much like the one that he used in his Bohemian and Chit-Chat Club speeches.

deeply pessimistic about human nature, asserted that the inferior races threatened civilization from below. Phelan's racism, made potent in leadership in the anti-Chinese and anti-Japanese movements of the turn of the century, was an imperial racism. It kept him at the forefront of popularity among the majority of San Francisco's European population, especially the Irish working class.[96]

A year later Phelan asserted that industrial strife threatened to let loose the floodgates of this alleged barbarism. In a speech called "Signs of the Times," Phelan spoke about the lessons of the Pullman strikes and boycotts. He was especially impressed that "the sympathy for the strikers was nearly universal." In that upheaval, "the third Estate had apparently entered upon its role. The veneer of civilization was for a moment rubbed off and revealed the average citizen in his nakedness." Claiming even that the Pullman strikes and the rise of the People's party "foreshadowed the possibility of revolution in this country when the time is ripe," Phelan proposed a solution filled with significance for understanding the brand of progressivism that succeeded in San Francisco.

Phelan's solution to the industrial crisis was not to disenfranchise the working class he apparently feared in 1894, but to lead it: "Sedulously therefore should the conditions of the laboring classes be studied with a view of removing every legitimate cause of complaint," Phelan explained:

The law should win respect by deserving it. There is a disposition on the part of the laboring classes to act together, which should be forestalled by the old parties, by wise statesmanship and necessary legislation to prevent a class alignment in political contests which is almost as much to be deprecated as a religious alignment.

Phelan here explains the significance of his life-long membership in the Democratic party. Like the most successful progressives – Robert La Follette, Theodore Roosevelt, and Woodrow Wilson – Phelan worked from within one of the "old parties." With Lane, Wigmore, and Maguire, Phelan had helped to make the Democratic party appealing to the working class. Now, in 1894, he saw in the old parties a superior solution to the industrial crisis, for

96 Alexander Saxton, *Indispensable Enemy: Labor and the Anti-Chinese Movement in California* (Berkeley: University of California Press, 1971); 229–57; Roger Daniels, *Asian America: Chinese and Japanese in the United States since 1850* (Seattle: University of Washington Press, 1991), 29–66,100–54; Sucheng Chan, *Asian Americans: An Interpretive History* (Boston: Twayne Publishers, 1991), 45–61.

"party division in the electorate on the basis of poverty and want" threatened revolution, whereas Phelan understood his own party at least as capable of bridging class lines.[97]

Phelan may have been an optimist about the capacities of the city, but he was deeply pessimistic about social reform. In a commentary on the popular Henry George and Edward Bellamy, Phelan said "there is one thing these reformers never account with, that is human nature, imperfect and selfish." Giving human nature a feminine gender, Phelan made clear his position on the emerging social-justice wing of progressivism: "If you drive her out for a time with a club – be it a single tax club or an altruistic club – she will always return."[98] Phelan's gendered hostility here was not at all accidental, for the third element of his social vision in the 1890s – a deep, misogynistic male supremacism – is an important part of the texts he produced in 1893–4, when he assumed leadership of the city's reform coalition.

Just as Charlotte Gilman and her sister activists mobilized San Francisco women to expand the boundaries of the home to include a role in running the city's public services, Phelan resisted that transformation of the boundaries of the public sphere. In February 1894, two months before the first Woman's Congress, he chose to speak on the subject "Has Woman a Vocation Outside the Home?" His answer was, emphatically, no. Women, he complained (accurately), "have taken positions in all the professions and trades." Phelan asserted that society is "governed by laws of divine origin," and that in violating such laws, "woman ... is the offender." Believing that "in a well-regulated society ... men support women," Phelan asserted that "woman's duty is ... exclusively to the family and within the family." Phelan pulled few punches in this deeply anxious speech. Not only would public activity "unsex" women, they were incapable of engaging successfully in it. "The consensus of opinion," Phelan decided, "establishes the fact that women lack in imagination, originality, creative power and invention," that they "achieve knowledge in an imitative way," and that "genius ... has been totally denied to the female sex."[99]

[97]   Phelan, "Signs of the Times," [MS], 12 November 1894, Phelan Papers.
[98]   Ibid.
[99]   Phelan, "Has Woman a Vocation Outside the Home?" also marked: "Read Before the Chit-Chat Club by James D. Phelan, February 12, 1894," MS in Phelan Papers.

Phelan was very clear about the authority relations in question. "They [women] should not appeal for the ballot to right fancied wrongs; they should appeal to men for even greater consideration."[100] Phelan's vehemence assumes importance, of course, because the timing leaves no mistake that the cause of his concern was the invasion of male privilege by his own generation of college-educated women, at least one of whom, Mary McHenry, now a contemporary political activist, had been a classmate.[101] Phelan repeated this argument in another speech of the same period entitled "The Genius of Women." These were no passing references; Phelan's progressivism was greatly defined by these attitudes on gender inequality.

Although the revived strength of women's organizations in 1894 played a significant part in provoking Phelan's intense antifeminism, it cannot be said that women's public strength had the same effect on all leaders of urban political reform in this period. Indeed, Adolph Sutro signed onto the suffrage movement in 1894 and put himself at the service of suffragists, issuing statements and funding kindergartens organized by Gilman's Woman's Press Association. Laura de Force Gordon and Ellen Sargent had cultivated a steady corps of male allies who willingly sponsored their legislation in Sacramento and Washington, D.C.

In the last analysis, a man's position on women's rights in the 1890s was a matter of personal, ideological, or psychological feelings, and Phelan, it turns out, had a very interesting love life. "In a big green box ... (key in my pocket) is Mrs. Ellon's letters and an account of our relations," Phelan wrote to his lawyer in December 1894. Phelan, in his long life, never married. The reason, apparently, was his relationship with a woman named Mrs. Florence Ellon. He had met Ellon in the late 1880s and in 1894 began suddenly to worry that she might sue him for paternity, so he wrote an account of their relationship to protect himself. "I am always afraid of women," Phelan confessed in this letter, "good in themselves perhaps but influenced by others." He explained how he had

---

100 Phelan, "Has Woman a Vocation Outside the Home?" Phelan Papers.
101 In the same speech he spends much energy deprecating women's achievements in higher education: "Perhaps it is after all only the yearning for maternity that causes the young women of our colleges to attempt creative work in art and in literature. How fondly they handle the children of their brain!" Phelan, "Has Woman a Vocation Outside the Home?" Phelan Papers.

bought Mrs. Ellon a flat and given her thousands of dollars in support. "I have no relations with her [other] than sleeping with her
occasionally," Phelan coldly declared. But the two apparently became a loving, if clandestine couple in later years. Phelan would
call her "Firenze," and Ellon would write demanding to see him
more often, in a relationship that lasted until his death in 1930.[102]

Phelan's perpetual bachelorhood, his keeping a dependent mistress, and his fear of women put his sanctimonious views of the
family and women's maternal duties in clearer light. William
Randolph Hearst also kept a mistress – in Sausalito – and his *Examiner* was staffed by bachelors who treated the women's movement
with condescending scorn. In 1892 Hearst's editorialist Arthur
McKewen singled out Gilman (then Stetson) for abuse, on the occasion of her divorce from Walter Stetson. "There are not many
women, fortunately for humanity, who agree with Mrs. Stetson that
any 'work,' literary, philanthropic, or political, is higher than that of
being a good wife and mother."[103] Even Hearst's star woman feature writer, Winifred "Annie Laurie" Black heaped abuse on the
Woman's Congress, as we have seen. And when the *Examiner*
pitched its hostility to the Southern Pacific and the railroad's corruption of the state, it did so in the name of aggrieved "manhood." At the height of the funding-scheme controversy, the
Examiner covered its entire front page with a single illustration: a
caricature of C. P. Huntington aiming a revolver at the reader's
face. The caption reads: "Hand Over Your Honor, Manhood, and
Independence, and Be Quick About It."[104]

With Phelan and the *Examiner* as the pivotal figures in the reconstruction of the urban public sphere in the crucial years in which the
frame of government was completely revamped and the structure of
public discourse reconstructed as well, we can safely conclude that
Phelan's progressivism met the political culture of women in collision and not in collusion, as some have suggested. In his project to
remake the structure and functions of municipal government so that

---

[102]   Phelan to Frank [Sullivan], 10 December 1894, Phelan Papers. In the Phelan Papers
there are 194 letters between the two lovers dating from 1905–30.
[103]   "The Wife and the Writer," *Examiner*, 19 December 1892. Lane quotes this article without reference but mistakenly attributes it to "Christmas Day." Lane's source must be
Hill, who mistakenly dates the article as 25 December 1892. Lane, *To Herland and Beyond*,
170; Hill, *Charlotte Perkins Gilman*, 321n.
[104]   *Examiner*, 1898, illustration by Homer Davenport reproduced in Walton Bean and James
R. Rawls, *California: An Interpretive History*, 5th ed. (New York: McGraw Hill, 1988), 221.

it could "care for" the health, comfort, education, property, general welfare, and sanitary conditions of "the people," Phelan had no intention of sharing authority with women who had recently claimed many of those fields as their particular areas of expertise.[105]

THE POLITICS OF MUNICIPAL CHARTER REFORM

One defining moment in urban Progressive Era reform across the nation arrived with the adoption of new city charters, a course of action strongly fostered by the intercity National Municipal League and its annual conventions, which began in 1894.[106] The provisions adopted varied from city to city, but the ideal charter sought by reformers by the turn of the century centralized administrative authority in the hands of the mayor; replaced elective departmental offices with appointive ones; replaced neighborhood-based with at-large elections of city councils; secured some measure of "home rule" insulation from state legislation; restructured the fiscal machinery, providing for increased indebtedness; adopted the initiative, referendum, and later recall; and provided for municipal ownership of utilities. Charters containing most of these features were adopted as early as the 1890s in some cities, including New York City and San Francisco. The method of drafting new charters, the choice of features, the public deliberation and popular vote

---

[105] Aileen Kraditor, *Ideas of the Woman Suffrage Movement 1890–1920* (New York, 1965); Paula Baker, "Domestication of Politics: Women and American Political Society 1780–1920s," *American Historical Review* 89 (1984): 620–47. Phelan, "Municipal Conditions and the New Charter," "Address to the Board of Supervisors," Phelan Papers.

[106] In January 1894 the Philadelphia Municipal League held the first "National Conference for Good City Government." By December of that same year, organizers had established the National Municipal League and held a "Second National Conference" in Minneapolis, and a "Third" in Cleveland the following May. Clearly, the local reform associations had overcome inertia to establish a national federation of political efforts. Philadelphia Municipal League, *Proceedings of the National Conference for Good City Government* (Philadelphia: Municipal League, 1894); National Municipal League, *Proceedings of the Second National Conference for Good City Government* (Philadelphia: National Municipal League, 1895), covers the May 1895 conference as well. The burst of communication about reform indicates that municipal reform also began in earnest in the 1890s. The number of works cited in the *Proceedings* of the first conference that were published before 1881 was only seventeen; from 1881 through 1885 there were all of twenty-three. But the publication of articles and books on the reform of municipal politics began to increase rapidly after that. Fifty-three works cited were published in the five years between 1886 and 1890; twenty-six in 1891; thirty-eight in 1892; and fifty in 1893 alone. Philadelphia Municipal League, *Proceedings of the National Conference for Good City Government*, 371–81.

on these new frames of urban government, provide an important window on the operation and preferences of the changing political culture of the 1890s. The San Francisco Charter of 1898, replacing the Consolidation Act Charter of 1856, presents a decisive point of reference for the changes analyzed in this book.

The members of the San Francisco Merchants' Association launched a drive to alter the structure of urban political power by invoking the provision of the 1879 state constitution providing for the election of a "Board of Freeholders" in 1894 to write a new charter and submit it to the voters. In the general election of 1894 the majority of the city's voters displayed their usual independence by splitting their tickets between the populist Adolph Sutro for mayor and the Merchants' Association's slate of freeholders. Only one populist freeholder was elected to the board that drafted the first reform charter. As William Issel has shown, the 1894–5 Board of Freeholders was closely allied with the business-elite leadership of the Merchants' Association and the Civic Federation. As the fifteen members began to draft the new charter, their task looked deceptively easy. The one-year-old San Francisco Labor Council, which had replaced the Federated Trades Council as the city's central labor federation, along with its organ, the *Voice of Labor*, and the important *Coast Seaman's Journal* at first joined the Civic Federation and supported its goals. Both the Republican *Chronicle* and the now independent *Examiner*, though rivals, joined in support of creating a charter on the "modern theory," meaning the latest proposals at the National Municipal League meetings held in 1894 and 1895 to centralize administration, "curtail the number of elective officers," and take the parties out of bureaucracies like the school board by implementing a civil service system and by making departmental heads appointive by the mayor.[107]

With the state superintendent of schools and the San Francisco Teachers' Club declaring early for a nonelective, five-member nonpartisan school board chosen from career teachers, consensus seemed easy on the potentially divisive issue of the school department. The long, Vigilante–People's party tradition of taking politics out of city government found expression in the representative of the

---

[107]   The best treatment of the San Francisco case is William Issel, "Class and Ethnic Conflict in San Francisco Political History: The Reform Charter of 1898" *Labor History* 18 (1977): 341–59. Quotations are from p. 344; Issel and Cherny, *San Francisco*, *141–3*.

most recent People's (Populist) party, Dr. Jerome Anderson, one of the freeholders. Anderson thought the city should be "run like any other great corporation," by "making somebody responsible."[108] In the proposed charter produced by the freeholders by the spring of 1895, the mayor's office was greatly strengthened, acquiring appointive power over several municipal department heads, including four (parks, police, fire, health) and election commissioners appointed at that time by the governor. The freeholders also enabled the city to acquire the hated private utilities and to incur bonded indebtedness for extraordinary expenses for such a purpose. The freeholders, however, required a conservative two-thirds majority for both of these innovations, leaving the minority of voters an effective veto power.[109]

The freeholders also altered the Board of Supervisors, but not in a drastic way. The Consolidation Act Charter, as amended in 1873, provided for the supervisors to be elected each from a separate ward, but by the votes of the city at large. That system was adopted to avoid the politics of redistricting the city.[110] By the mid-1890s, however, the growth of the suburban districts had made the combined at-large–by ward system patently absurd. Old wards, like the Fifth, cast as few as 464 votes in the election of 1894, while newer wards, like the Eleventh, cast as many as 18,621. That system had been a boon to the organizational politicians, who could easily control the nominations in the old small wards. Thus, when the freeholders wrote a charter in which the supervisors would represent the city at large and be voted on at large, the proposal was not controversial, although some favored an eighteen-member Board of Supervisors elected at large. The election of supervisors from each ward separately was a nonissue.[111]

The Merchants' Association, the Civic Federation, and the Citizen's Charter Association, formed in 1896 to campaign for the new instrument, however, assumed more unity among the city's active interest groups than there actually was. The first to dissent were

108 Anderson quoted in Issel, "Class and Ethnic Conflict," 343.
109 San Francisco Board of Freeholders, *Charter for the City and County of San Francisco* (San Francisco: Geo. Spaulding and Co., 1895), 22–23, 51–62, 114, 134, 153, 165, 172.
110 See Chapter 5.
111 San Francisco Board of Freeholders, *Charter* (1895), 9–10; Gustav Gutsch, *A Comparison of the Consolidation Act with the New Charter* (San Francisco: Citizen's Charter Association, 1896). [pamphlet] Stanford University Library.

the vital labor leaders. Although there was broad agreement on the general principles of the new charter, such as undermining the power of the parties and transferring appointive power over several departments from the governor to the mayor, there was considerable room for disagreement within these goals. The *Voice of Labor* and the San Francisco Labor Council condemned the new charter for not providing for popular initiatives, and for its small Board of Supervisors. Most damaging, however, was the sudden discovery in June 1896 by Father Peter C. Yorke of a nativist agenda embedded in the new charter. Yorke's opposition to the new charter only in June 1896, after more than a year of debate on the document, indicates that the priest needed the controversy more than it needed him. The freeholders had required that teachers shall have had their education in the California public schools. Yorke had been busy during the winter and spring of 1895–6 with his "Great Controversy" debate with the nativist American Protective Association leader Reverend Donald Ross, and now, apparently, he needed another target in his project to mobilize the political consciousness of the city's Catholics. He denounced the new charter as "supremely vicious" because "the trail of the A.P.A. is visible across it."[112] There is no evidence that any member of the freeholders was a member of the nearly fictitious APA, nor that the provision was intended to disqualify Catholics (it would disqualify New England Protestants as well).

Yorke knew, however, how to mobilize fear, as the majority of the city's teachers were in fact Irish Catholics. The Citizen's Charter Association, with the popular Irish Catholic reform leader and mayoral candidate James Duval Phelan at its head, tried desperately to repudiate the noxious provision, explaining that "the provision was inserted by the freeholders under a mistake concerning their powers" and that this provision, "which has provoked so much criticism and opposition in certain quarters," would be invalid because it clashed with the state's authority to set the qualifications of teachers.[113] But Yorke's *Monitor* maintained a steady opposition to the new charter. His mobilization of the Irish Catholic vote against the charter damaged its credibility so badly that Phelan

---

[112]   Yorke quoted in Issel, "Class and Ethnic Conflict," 346.
[113]   Gutsch, *Comparison of the Consolidation Act with the New Charter*, 14–15.

ceased to advocate the new charter in his mayoral campaign by October, hoping to win the mayoralty in spite of the now unpopular document.[114]

Given the already mobilized, institutionalized group identities – labor, business, Irish Catholics, suburban home dwellers, and especially consumers – achieving a new charter required leaders of the Merchants' Association to forge links with all of these groups. The task was tricky because each group (except the women's movement, which the leaders like Phelan defined out of the coalition altogether) had virtual veto power. The first attempt to replace the Consolidation Act Charter of 1856 with a new instrument in 1895–6 failed adequately to mobilize the institutionalized consciousness of the interest groups created in the post–Civil War city, and was defeated at the polls. Analysis of the patterns in voting confirms the textual evidence that Father Yorke played the pivotal role in defeating the new charter. Summarizing a large sample of households taken from the 1900 U.S. Census manuscript (1,406 individuals) by the city's eighteen assembly districts, it is possible to arrive at estimates of voting behavior while controlling for the social variables most likely to have played a role in electoral outcomes: class, ethnicity, homeownership, marital status, and neighborhood residence.

Table 8.1 indicates that ethnicity proved to be the most important variable in the charter election of 1896. The percent Irish stock in each assembly district was most clearly responsible for defeating the first reform charter of that year. For every increase of 10 percent of Irish-stock residents, there was a decrease of 6.2 percent in the vote for the charter. Class had no effect on the vote for or against the new charter, perhaps a reflection of organized labor's nadir of strength during the charter reform fights of 1894–8. The percentage of voters living in suburban wards had no effect on the patterns in the 1896 charter vote, which probably indicates a divided opinion in the suburbs over its merits on several questions, such as schools, franchises, and municipal ownership.

Analysis of the vote for Phelan for mayor in 1896 indicates that, unlike the vote on the charter, neither the Irish-stock nor any other variable had any influence on the vote. The model for that analysis

[114] McDonald, *Parameters of Urban Fiscal Policy*, Chapter 7.

Table 8.1. *Multiple linear regression analysis of voting on the 1896 city charter*

Predictor variables	Regression coefficient (β)	P-value
Working Class	.4	.88
Suburban	−.15	.79
Irish Stock	−6.2	.014[a]
U.S. Stock	−2.2	.36

[a] = Significant Relationship

Notes: $N=18$ assembly districts; model adjusted $R^2=.403$ ($p=.027$). Voting data taken from the manuscript official returns, California State Library, Sacramento. For population data, 1900 U.S. Census sample described in the Appendix.

was insignificant; none of the overall pattern in the vote is explained by it.[115] This result attests to another very important lesson from these multiple regression analyses: the unexplained variance is just as important as the patterns in voting attributable to the independent variables. That the vote for this singular progressive reform leader had no correlation with any important social-group variable casts serious doubt on the theories of progressive reform that explain political change in that period as a function of changing social-group power. The vote for or against Phelan, apparently, was *ideologically* motivated. Phelan had declared himself a partisan of very distinct new ideological positions. He claimed that the municipal government should take on new functions in the economy and the social life of the city. He stood for a redistribution of tax burdens, and he argued, even as he campaigned as a lifelong Democrat, that city administration should come under civil service rules and operate strictly on a business basis. Having made specific appeals to each of the city's potent interest groups, he left voters only with the task of deciding critically, and rationally, between the merits of the arguments made by himself and his opponents in the mayoral race.

In the second attempt to persuade the voters to adopt a new charter, Phelan and his allies learned from the failure of the first, included more interest groups in their coalition, further radicalized the document, and won voter approval in the election of 1898.

---

[115]   The results of this analysis are not reported because each regression coefficient was insignificant. The model adjusted R^2 was .076, $p = .303$.

Breaking his silence about the first new charter on the evening of the 1896 general election, Phelan called for a second attempt, but determined that the slighted interest groups should be brought into the process on the second try: "We must be careful to elect free-holders who will do their duty to the whole city and to all the people," Phelan wrote.[116] One of the directors of the Merchants' Association agreed, admitting that "we have begun at the wrong end and tried to make a charter for the people without first finding out what they wanted."[117] One of Phelan's first acts as mayor was to appoint a "Committee of 100," which now included labor leaders Walter Macarthur of the *Coast Seaman's Journal* and P. H. McCarthy of the newly created Building Trades Council, as well as his reform ally Franklin K. Lane, who would serve at the first city attorney under the new charter when it went into effect in 1899. William Issel has shown that this Committee of 100 was far more inclusive than the freeholders elected in 1894 had been. One hundred percent of the 1896 Citizen's Charter Association and 86 percent of the 1894 freeholders could be found in the elite *San Francisco Blue Book*, but only 43 percent of Phelan's Committee of 100 could be so identified.[118]

Phelan's Committee of 100 drafted a charter that not only made it much easier to acquire and run utilities, but "hereby declared [it] be the purpose and intention of the people of the City and County that its public utilities shall be gradually acquired and ultimately owned by the City and County."[119] The new charter compromised with a minority of labor delegates, who desired an eighteen-member Board of Supervisors who were elected from the wards, and adopted an eighteen-member board elected at large. But here we have evidence that the advice of the Stanford intellectuals was not heeded.

There was a considerable weight of expert opinion in the 1890s in favor of strong legislative councils and weak mayors. Albert Shaw remarked that "there is nothing in British organization or experience to sustain the proposition of many American municipal re-

---

116   *Examiner*, 4 November 1896.
117   Quoted in Issel, "Class and Ethnic Conflict," 350.
118   San Francisco Board of Freeholders, *Charter* (1895); Issel, "Class and Ethnic Conflict," 342; Issel and Cherny, *San Francisco*, 141; McDonald, *Parameters of Urban Fiscal Policy*, 196–8.
119   San Francisco Board of Freeholders, *Charter for the City and County of San Francisco* (San Francisco: Woodward & Co., 1898), 124.

formers that good city government can be secured only by making the mayor a dictator."[120] Stanford economist E. Dana Durand was also sharply critical of the strong mayor plan.[121] And the outspoken Edward A. Ross agreed with Durand, Shaw, and Frank Goodnow, favoring a strong council. In 1895 he invited the British urban reformer J. H. Stallard to give a series of lectures at Stanford. Stallard, who had also lectured in San Francisco during the first charter campaign of 1895–6, made a strong case for restoring democracy in the cities by increasing the responsibilities of the legislative branch.[122] The "'Boss Mayor' idea," Ross declared, "is unsound. The plan of getting your city government further away from the people simply gets it nearer the 'machine' and the political 'boss.' Periodical dictatorship is undemocratic."[123]

Phelan had already made up his mind about the virtues of a strong mayoral office. "I think, with the experience of Brooklyn and Philadelphia before us," he wrote in his kickoff for the second charter campaign, "that the powers of the mayor should be largely yet prudently increased."[124] The key to a democratic charter, Ross countered, was to limit the power of the mayor and the council by providing a mechanism to circumvent them both with the initiative and referendum. The Board of Supervisors, Ross claimed, had "forfeited the public confidence. With a fraction of the Council possessing the power to bring the measures of a corrupt majority . . . to the test of a popular vote, the people of San Francisco would have the whip-hand. Boodlers would not sit in the seat of the scornful." Labor leaders, in helping to defeat the first new charter, had complained that it did not include the initiative and referendum. In fact, the second Board of Freeholders did include the initiative and referendum in the new charter, but not one that gave the "people" the "whip hand." Franchise grants were now required to go before

---

[120]   Shaw, *Municipal Government in Great Britain*, 78

[121]   "In Brooklyn the first election under its famous 'model charter'," Durand writes, "brought Mr. Low to the mayor's chair, but for eight years after he left office 'mayors were elected, and appointments were made by them, on party grounds.'" E. Dana Durand, *Council Government Versus Mayor Government* (Boston: Athenaeum Press, 1900), 435 (reprinted from *Political Science Quarterly*, vol. 15, nos. 3 and 4).

[122]   J. H. Stallard, "The Municipal Government of San Francisco," *Overland Monthly* 2d Ser. 29 (January–June 1897): 44–51, 135–44, 278–89, 386–91, 491–8.

[123]   E. A. Ross, "Charter for the People," *The Star* [November 7 1897] [letter to editor], clipping in Edward A. Ross Papers.

[124]   *Examiner*, 4 November 1896.

the voters in referendum, but there was no provision for repeal of supervisorial ordinances.[125]

The second Board of Freeholders also removed the offending provision on teacher training, and Father Yorke certified the second new charter as "entirely free of bigotry and prejudice."[126] The *Voice of Labor*, although recognizing criticism that the majority of the Committee of 100 had underrepresented labor, dropped its opposition to the second charter. Phelan and McCarthy, representing business and labor interest groups in league under Irish Catholic leadership, stumped together for the new charter in the special election of 1898. The second new charter was even printed under a union label, whereas the first had appeared without one.

William Randolph Hearst's *Examiner* had by 1894 commercialized melodramatic political communication and turned political parties, the Southern Pacific, and the public utility franchises into the means of journalistic production. In that year a quarrel between Hearst and his editorialist, Arthur McKewen, reveals the utter break Hearst had made with the institutions of the party system – or of any system, for that matter. "I would prefer somewhat fewer editorials," Hearst told McKewen: "Be careful not to be drawn into too many fights. We are now after the Democrats and the Republicans, the lawyers and the businessmen, with occasional sideswipes at the people."[127] Hearst's institutional independence helped to define what would have to be an ideological contest within a structure of communicative action that privileged the satisfaction of group "needs." The *Examiner* worked its most impressive influence by framing the charter debate in terms that Hearst, McKewen, and Chamberlain had created in the previous ten years of media reconstruction. Issue after issue of the *Examiner* featured cartoons of huge pigs, labeled "S.P. Ry. Co," feeding at the trough labeled "San

125 Issel and Cherny, *San Francisco*, 143; Chapter 1, sec. 20 of the 1898 charter enabled ordinances to be submitted directly to the voters with a petition from 15% of the votes cast at the last preceding State or City and County election. The supervisors were given the power to submit a referendum for the repeal of any ordinance enacted by popular referendum, but the voters could not start a referendum to repeal ordinances other than franchise grants and large sales of lands. San Francisco Board of Freeholders, *Charter*, (1898), 8.

126 Quoted in Issel, "Class and Ethnic Conflict," 355.

127 W. A. Swanberg, *Citizen Hearst: A Biography of William Randolph Hearst* (New York: Charles Scribner's Sons, 1961), 73.

Francisco," or of Collis P. Huntington whipping the anticharter ticket into line, the SP pig at his side. Stories exposing the horrible service provided by the utilities were a daily staple of the *Examiner*'s political coverage: "MANGLED UNDER PILOT BOARD," one of the *Examiner*'s many stories about streetcar accidents began. "WHEELS OF AN ELECTRIC STREETCAR GRIND OVER ANOTHER BREADWINNER," ran the caption to the illustration, showing Patrick Welsh, who had "a wife and seven children dependent on him," going under the wheels of the streetcar.[128]

Who opposed the second new charter? There can be little doubt that the Southern Pacific and the remaining organizational politicians felt deeply threatened by it. The provisions for municipal ownership threatened the former, whereas the civil service provisions and at-large elections threatened the latter. More immediately, Phelan threatened a "shifting of tax burdens" in his first address to the Board of Supervisors, by raising the assessments on the Spring Valley Water Company, the San Francisco Gaslight Company, and the Market Street Cable Railway Company.[129] The *Examiner* poured abuse on the SP-controlled franchises: "Take the Market-street system of street railways, for instance," the *Examiner* explained in an article entitled "Why the Allied Infamies are Opposed to an honest Board of Freeholders": For the utilities "use of the public streets the taxpayers get no return, except to be knocked down and run over by criminally fenderless cars."[130] Fremont Older, editor of the *Bulletin*, later reported that the Southern Pacific's W. H. Mills, "who handled the newspapers ... for the railroad company," increased the *Bulletin*'s monthly subsidy from $150 to $250 in return for going "light" on the new charter. Older reports that "I killed several articles that had been prepared by the editorial writer favoring the charter" on account of this bribery. For their part, the organizational politicians of both major parties banded together to compose a "Fusion" freeholders ticket to retain the central features of the old charter. The Southern Pacific then backed the Fusion Ticket, while the *Examiner*, the *Chronicle*, and the Merchants' Association backed the "Non-Partisan" freeholders ticket, which was selected by and

[128] *Examiner*, 23, 24, 25 December 1897.
[129] Phelan, "Address to the Board of Supervisors."
[130] *Examiner*, 23 December 1897.

Table 8.2. *Multiple linear regression analysis of voting on
the 1898 city charter*

Predictor variables	Regression coefficient (β)	P-value
Working Class	.3	.83
Suburban	.7	.03ᵃ
Irish Stock	.8	.51
U.S. Stock	2.9	.04ᵃ

ᵃ = Significant Relationship

Notes: $N = 18$ assembly districts; model adjusted $R^2 = .563$ ($p = .004$). Voting returns from San Francisco Board of Supervisors, *Municipal Reports*, vol. 1898–9. For population data, 1900 U.S. Census sample described in the Appendix.

from the Committee of 100 to propose the charter that the committee had just drafted in the freeholders' election of 1897.[131]

Table 8.2, presenting the results of a multiple linear regression analysis, shows that patterns of voting on the new charter in the 1898 election contrasts sharply with the patterns of the 1896 voting results.

After Father Yorke certified the second charter in 1898 as "entirely free of bigotry and prejudice," the Irish-stock opposition to the charter disappeared completely; that variable had no effect whatever on the vote two years after the first charter. Whereas the Irish-stock voters were highly mobilized in the 1896 campaign but not in the 1898 charter campaigns, the reverse was true among the U.S.-stock voters. The percentage of U.S.-stock voters in each assembly district had no relationship to the patterns in the 1896 election, but a moderate positive relationship to the vote for the 1898 charter. It was only *after* the Irish Catholic representation among the authors of the charter had been increased and the favor of the Irish Catholic interest-group leaders positively identified with the new charter that the U.S.-stock voters showed a strong inclination toward the new charter. This result attests to the genuine bridge-building capabilities of the Irish Catholic mayor, James Duval Phelan. But it also indicates a degree of ethnic-group mobilization. Once the new charter had been revised to more clearly present a choice between machine and reform politics, U.S.-stock voters may

131 Thus, a vote for the Nonpartisan Freeholders ticket was a vote for the Phelan-led progressive reform charter. This ticket won. *Examiner*, 24 December 1897.

have identified more strongly with reform in part because political machines had, in the national press, been associated with the Irish Catholics. The effect of living in a suburban ward had a slight positive influence on the vote for the new city charter of 1898, as we would expect from Phelan's mobilization of that group's interest since the early 1890s.

The reformed charter of 1898, which went into effect in 1899 and established the outline for the urban polity during the twentieth century, then, was a popular achievement among the mobilized interest groups of the 1890s. It shows the pivotal role of the public sphere as the site of contestation and persuasion, in which the capitalist class could rule only by convincing other classes and groups to go along with it.

THE WOMAN SUFFRAGE AMENDMENT

Following their kickoff of the California suffrage campaign at the end of the 1895 San Francisco Woman's Congress, National American Woman Suffrage Association President Susan B. Anthony and Vice-President Dr. Anna Howard Shaw relocated to the state for seven months in 1896, campaigning tirelessly alongside the state and local organizations. Anthony's biographer, Ida Husted Harper, called it "the longest and hardest campaign ever made for a woman suffrage amendment."[132] Woman suffrage amendment campaigns present another defining moment in the history of urban reform. In stark contrast to the success of other kinds of reform, like revised city charters, voters rejected woman suffrage by huge margins prior to the First World War in the great cities. Paula Baker has suggested that the Progressive Era marked the "domestication of politics," as male progressive leaders adopted social welfare reforms devised by women in their nineteenth-century voluntary associations. But the influx of women into public life in the 1890s proved the strongest challenge to the masculine-defined "public" of the nineteenth century.

The failed campaign for the woman suffrage amendment in the 1896 general election presents a stark contrast to both the 1896 and 1898 charter campaigns and reveals the deep divisions in the changing political community along gender lines. The intensive mobilization of women in the two years prior to that general election

---

[132]   Susan B. Anthony and Ida Husted Harper eds., *History of Woman Suffrage* (New York, 1920), 4:487.

may in fact have mobilized men more than did the agitation for a new charter. Voter turnout on the suffrage amendment (49,710) was far higher than on the charter measure (33,857), although not as high as the presidential and mayoral turnout (each about 62,000 votes cast). And the vote in San Francisco against granting women the ballot in 1896 was overwhelming: 36,741 to 12,969 (74% against). The 1896 charter, by contrast, was defeated by a few thousand votes (53% against).[133] The suffrage vote, then, does not seem to align at all with urban progressivism in other policy domains. The same voters who provided a victory for the strongest representative of progressivism, James Duval Phelan, also assured that women would not share in the progressive reconstruction of urban political life.

The big vote against woman suffrage in the midst of urban progressivism is especially significant because the National American Woman Suffrage Association (NAWSA) had targeted California as a crucial test. California was the largest state in the West, the region where the only victories for woman suffrage had yet been won. Led by Anthony and Shaw, suffrage activists organized San Francisco not only by its eighteen assembly districts but by precinct as well.[134] Some suffrage leaders saw the liquor and saloon interests as their main opponents. Indeed, the WCTU played a prominent role in the campaign, and the San Francisco Liquor Dealers' Association claimed that suffrage would lead to prohibition.[135] Given that San Francisco had perhaps the highest per capita density of saloons of any major city (one for every 218 persons), such a charge must have been an important argument against the amendment.[136] Other suffrage leaders attempted to decouple the suffrage and prohibition issue, arguing that woman suffrage was a fundamental right as well as an avenue to achieving a host of social justice goals outlined in the Woman's Congresses. The Woman's Congress of 1896, in fact, chose as its theme "Woman and Government," the most

---

[133] San Francisco Board of Supervisors, *Municipal Reports*, vol. 1895–6 1006–10.

[134] Anthony and Harper, *History of Woman Suffrage*, 4:490. The precinct method of suffrage organization is usually credited to the Woman Suffrage party of New York (for example, see Buhle and Buhle, *Concise History of Woman Suffrage*, 34), but Eleanor Flexner remarks that the practice was, by 1907, "so axiomatic in suffrage as well as all political organizations that its origins are forgotten." *Century of Struggle* 2d ed., 261.

[135] Flexner, *Century of Struggle*, 230, 263–5.

[136] In 1915 New York City had one saloon for every 515 persons, Chicago one for every 335 residents. Jon Kingsdale, "'The Poor-Man's Club': Social Functions of the Urban Working-Class Saloon," *American Quarterly* 25 (October 1973): 472–3.

provocative theme to date.[137] Mary McHenry Keith, by this time one of the leaders of the San Francisco suffrage movement, argued that suffrage went beyond any specific issue or group identity:

If Catholic women are seen talking to the A.P.A.'s, and if A.P.A women speak before Catholic organizations, and hob-nob with Father Yorke, its all on the bill of fare, and when the saloon men are besieged and button-holed, we're only trying to show them that prohibition and woman suffrage are two distinct propositions."[138]

Multiple linear regression analysis of the pattern of voting on the 1896 woman suffrage amendment indicates that voting against the woman suffrage amendment bore no relationship either to the pattern of voting on the 1896 charter or in the 1896 presidential contest. Neither class, ethnicity, nor suburban residence had any relationship to the patterns in the suffrage vote; women managed to mobilize male voters across the social spectrum against their campaign.[139] Woman suffrage may have posed a fundamental threat to the gender axis of public political identity. As Keith's strategy of advocating suffrage to all interest groups indicates, it seems to have been an issue decided by each male voter on the basis of his own personal feelings about women taking a large share in the political authority of the urban public sphere. Taking stock after the 1896 defeat, the veteran suffragist and political strategist Ellen Sargent disagreed with the theory that the saloons and their immigrant patrons had defeated suffrage. She roughly averaged the favorable votes in several neighborhoods of the city and observed that "the so-called best people" voted against woman suffrage in greater proportions than voters in those districts containing, as she put it facetiously, "the ignorant, vicious, and the foreign-born."[140] The highly

[137]   "It is our desire that the treatment of this subject shall be exhaustive and thorough, beginning with an analysis of Government as a social function and tracing its birth, growth, and latest development, with some indication of the main lines of governmental excesses and abuses." Minna V. Gaden to E. A. Ross, 20 January 1896, Ross Papers.

[138]   Mary McHenry Keith, typescript, [untitled speech, 1896], Keith-Pond Family Papers, Bancroft Library.

[139]   As in the case of the analysis of the vote for Phelan in 1896, the results of this analysis are not reported because each regression coefficient was insignificant. The model adjusted R^2 was $-.034$, $p = .513$.

[140]   Anthony and Harper, *History of Woman Suffrage*, 4:493–4. I attribute this statement to Sargent because she submitted the California chapter to Anthony and Harper for that volume of the *History*. It could just as easily have been written by Ida Husted Harper, however. Harper was in charge of press relations for the campaign.

articulated woman's consciousness, as expressed at the Woman's Congresses, threatened to conflate the state with the home. Here men were confronted as men first, and as members of their other group identities secondarily. How they decided on this issue depended, most probably, on the perceived validity of the argumentative claims made in the discursive forums of the urban public sphere. That was, after all, what the women activists were doing best: joining others (men and women) in a critical-rational debate of the public sphere over the governing relations of the state and civil society. But they did not convince the men nor persuade them to share the power of the masculine progressive project. The story of the failed woman suffrage fight of 1896 suggests that the enfranchisement of women was an issue apart from the other major reform issues of the Progressive Era, and it does not at all support the argument made by some historians that progressivism marked a friendly convergence of women's political culture and male reform leaders in the origins of the social welfare state.

CONCLUSIONS

We return to the question posed at the beginning of Chapter 7. Why did so many changes in the American polity take place during this intense period of political and social upheaval? To recapitulate very briefly, I have argued that progressivism arose from the contradictions of the organizational party system of the 1880s. That system flourished because of the institutional strengths of the two major parties during a decade in which local elections were tied to national ones. That system also flourished because under it municipal governments avoided redistribution of taxpayer resources by relying on corporation patronage and franchises. But that system was also vulnerable to infiltration. First labor and then business lobbies with interest-group agendas achieved footholds within the parties. That system was also deeply vulnerable to delegitimation by the sensational, mass media introduced by William Randolph Hearst. Hearst forced the city's political discourse toward melodramatic portrayals of political villains who steal money, which eclipsed completely the earlier discourse about political tyrants who steal liberty. Hearst also played a central role in recasting political discourse to revolve around the new keywords: "progressive" and "needs." "There has been a decided change in Pacific Coast journalism within the last year," Hearst wrote in 1888, "but there has also been a change in the character of the people and their needs."[141]

In 1891, the infiltrators, in league with the Hearst-reoriented press, undermined the organizational regime with the achievement of the Reform Ballot Act, which opened the political system to a decade of voter independence. Once the major parties were dislodged from their positions of institutional advantage, the electoral market became competitive again, and the ideas and groups that had organized in the late 1880s and early 1890s could be aggregated by political entrepreneurs in the public sphere. The mobilization of group identities and the advancement of reform projects now took place in a public sphere restructured by a mass press that had partially repositioned the citizen in the role of a consumer. The reification of groups in concert with the media and political mobilization generated a politics of "needs." In the marketplace of ideas, however, some people had the ideas and others had the market. Charlotte Gilman orchestrated a crystallization of women's political consciousness in the Woman's Congress forums, and the Stanford intellectuals formulated sociology as a study of the conditions of urban modernity. But the political entrepreneurs remade the structure of urban government through the new charter of 1898 largely without the help of the intellectuals, and in opposition to the participation by women, with their agenda of widening the home to widen the authority of women. The analysis of voting in elections from 1896 through 1900 suggests that social-group identities were plastic and that voters were persuaded to oppose or support urban reform by arguments made in the public-sphere debates over those reforms. It also suggests that social-group identities did not count at all in many cases, as in the voting for James Duval Phelan and the woman suffrage amendment.

What, then, does the San Francisco experience add to our understanding of the origins of progressivism? First, we have seen that in San Francisco the reformers were led, since the late 1880s, by Irish Catholics. It simply does not make sense to identify progressivism in San Francisco with Protestant evangelicalism, as some have tried to do for the nation as a whole.[142] Perhaps the reason why different

---

[141]   William Randolph Hearst, "Pacific Coast Journalism," *Overland Monthly* 2d ser. 11 (April 1888): 403.

[142]   Richard Hofstadter, *The Age of Reform: From Bryan to F.D.R.* (New York: Alfred A. Knopf, 1955); Robert M. Crunden, *Ministers of Reform: The Progressives' Achievement in American Civilization, 1889–1920* (Urban: University of Illinois Press, 1984).

groups acted differently in different cities is, again, that progressivism remade the American polity so that all social-group configurations could become possible. What at first glance here might seem to be the peculiarities of San Francisco may in fact be a window on the most basic features of the altered political culture across the nation. San Francisco under the new charter, which went into effect in 1899–1900, illustrates some of these possibilities.

James Duval Phelan served three terms as Mayor of San Francisco. Reelected in 1898, he was elected again as the first mayor under the new charter, in 1899. Phelan had constructed a winning coalition of interest groups to achieve the new charter and, by mobilizing voters and constituents, had played a leading role in legitimating the politics of interests and needs. But he had, after all, done so from his barely obscured position as a merchant prince, a millionaire, a banker. Although willing to deal with labor as labor, he was, as his reaction to the Pullman strike showed, anxious about "class rule." By Phelan's third term in office, San Francisco's well-placed labor leaders had recuperated their memberships in the prosperity that accompanied the Spanish-American War. From a nadir of forty-one hundred members in 1897, union memberships reached an astonishing forty-five thousand in 1902.[143] In 1904 Ray Stannard Baker would label San Francisco "the city where unionism holds undisputed sway."[144] Phelan, fostering labor as the junior partner in his reform drive while unions were at their weakest, was not prepared to deal with unions on an equal basis. In the bloody waterfront strike of 1901, he decided in favor of the Employer's Association, called out the police to protect strikebreakers, and met sudden defeat at the polls as his price. The Union Labor party came to power, with the musician Eugene Schmitz replacing Phelan.[145]

Labor's role in the creation of progressivism, as detailed in this chapter, and the triumph of class-conscious politics in the 1901 elections, a story that lies beyond this study, again put to rest the idea that progressivism was, as Hofstadter, Mowry, Wiebe, and others have argued, quintessentially middle class. These developments

---

[143] Cross, *History of the Labor Movement in California*, 337.

[144] Ray Stannard Baker, "A Corner in Labor: What Is Happening in San Francisco Where Unionism Holds Undisputed Sway," *McLure's* 22 (February 1904): 366–78.

[145] Walton Bean, *Boss Ruef's San Francisco* (Berkeley: University of California Press, 1972); Jules Tygiel, "Workingmen in San Francisco, 1880–1901" (Ph.D. diss., University of California, Los Angeles, 1975).

also illustrate the unintended consequences of urban reform in the Progressive Era. The fundamental achievements and breakthroughs had been process reforms: the Reform Ballot Act of 1891 and the new charter of 1898. The authors of these reforms identified misgovernment with party-controlled elections, with weak mayors and fragmented authority, and so on. But the centralization of authority in the mayor, and the creation of an eighteen-member Board of Supervisors elected at large could not in themselves end organizational politics. Indeed, the second period of organizational party government in San Francisco began, ironically, with the Union Labor party, which, under Abe Ruef, operated the extensive patronage and kickback schemes exposed by the dramatic graft prosecutions of 1907, that in turn launched the career of Hiram Johnson and the state-level phase of Progressive Era policy and constitutional innovation. The climax of that phase was the year 1911, in which voters adopted twenty-three amendments embodying the essential features of the social welfare state: workers' compensation, powerful regulatory commissions, government inspection of merchandise and commodities, nonpartisan local elections, the initiative, referendum, and recall, and woman suffrage (although San Franciscans voted overwhelmingly against woman suffrage again). Only in that phase of the policy innovations of the Progressive Era were the settlement- and university-trained social-justice progressives empowered in positions of administrative authority.[146]

As the last two chapters should have made clear, however, those state-level reforms in the political system (leading the way in the making of weak-party, issue-oriented, interest-group, media-driven campaigns) were predicated on the transformed political culture of San Francisco in the 1890s. Richard L. McCormick, then, is right to argue that progressivism had political, not social origins. He has traced state- and national-level progressivism to a "discovery that business corrupts politics" in the first decade of the twentieth century. This study would suggest, however, that the "discovery" about business corrupting politics could not have been new to the Progressive Era. Instead, the entire meaning of "corruption" was changed by the mass media of the 1890s. Once the antithesis of

---

[146] For the history of the juvenile court system in California, for example, see Mary E. Odem, "Delinquent Daughters: The Sexual Regulation of Female Minors in the United States, 1880– 1920," (Ph.D. diss., University of California, Berkeley, 1989).

"virtue," corruption was now a crime to be exposed, just as lurid reports of rapes and murders were exposed, to attract readers. "Virtue," in fact, had entirely disappeared from the public discourse of the 1890s.

Another interpretation of progressivism holds that the distinctive features of the early-twentieth-century political reforms – nonpartisan elections, social-justice policies, social-control agendas, and efficiency programs – arose in response to social crises attendant upon industrialization – overcrowding, governmental waste, immigration, poverty – that were essentially urban in nature. These problems, however, could conceivably have been addressed within the organizational politics of the pre-1890s period. Instead, progressive reformers like Phelan insisted upon altering the framework of government before attempting to engage in a politics of social needs. Here we can recognize that which was *not* new in the Progressive Era transformation of urban political culture. As Morton Keller has argued, many Progressive Era policy innovations in fact look very traditional on close inspection. We must question, for example, Martin Scheisl's conclusion that an ethics of efficiency that was central to the progressive political discourse at the turn of the century was "a new conception of politics."[147] From the Vigilante movement of the 1850s through the 1890s, no ideological goal had been more consistently stated than the desire to put municipal politics on a "business basis." The San Francisco reformers of the 1890s seem to have learned as much or more from their own political traditions as they did from intellectuals or the reform plans being circulated at the National Municipal League (NML) conventions. Indeed, it is a curious fact that delegates from San Francisco did not attend the NML conventions of the 1890s, but rather sent papers and had them read. "It is a long time since the Vigilance Committee," Isaac Milliken's paper to the 1895 NML convention read, "but there is no city in the union with a quarter of a million people ... which would not be the better for a little judicious hanging."[148]

The account in the preceding two chapters of women participants

---

[147] Martin J. Scheisl, *The Politics of Efficiency: Municipal Administration and Reform in America, 1880–1920* (Berkeley: University of California Press, 1977), 6.

[148] Isaac J. Milliken, "Municipal Conditions in San Francisco," in National Municipal League, *Proceedings, 1895* (Philadelphia, 1895): 449–52. Quotation from p. 452.

in the San Francisco political public sphere does not support Paula Baker's influential thesis, that progressivism was built in large part from the contributions of women. We have seen that politically active women met massive resistance to their attempt to participate, from James Duval Phelan himself down to the majority of voters who defeated the suffrage amendment to the state constitution. We have also seen why this should have been so. Both men and women politicized the home in its relation to the state, and both engaged in an open discourse about the virtues of "patriarchy." This overt debate about male versus female political authority arose in a public sphere segregated deeply along gender lines, among a people who participated in a massive network of single-sex voluntary organizations. Ironically, women, by attempting to join men in the public sphere the latter had created, seem to have raised men's consciousness of the masculine nature of that sphere, formerly mystified as having universal access. Women political activists met male reform activists in collision not collusion.

Finally, this study concluded with an analysis of voter participation and preferences in the last half of the 1890s. Although this analysis is not conducted as a time series comparable to the national- and state-level analyses of other scholars, it is possible to offer a few suggestions about changes in political participation. The analysis in the previous chapter does not support the idea that voter participation in urban politics dropped suddenly in the 1890s. Instead, there was a continuation of the trend, identified in earlier chapters and by McDonald, of low turnout in municipal-only elections and issues. As indicated in earlier chapters, this differential in turnout levels between low local and high national turnouts is attributable largely to the occupation, stability, and household status of the potential voters. But, as discussed earlier, there was an overall, long-term drop-off in all kinds of elections, from the 1880s through the first decade of the twentieth century.[149]

Progressivism emphatically did not constitute the triumph of a social group, nor did it embody the goals or aspirations of a social group. It represented the practical triumph of the social-group con-

---

[149] Such early beginnings to the decline in voter participation, also established by John Reynolds for New Jersey, cast doubt on the possibility that structural, electoral reforms, were the cause. John F. Reynolds, *Testing Democracy: Electoral Behavior and Progressive Reform in New Jersey, 1880–1920* (Chapel Hill: University of North Carolina Press, 1988).

ception of political contestation. The triumph of urban progressivism was the triumph of a social understanding of politics in the political culture of San Francisco. That understanding finally and irretrievably replaced the political conception of society that had so marked the political culture of the city in its first years of United States rule before the Civil War.

Conclusion

We must recognize the fact that, aside from their general interest as citizens, special groups of citizens have special interests.
                                        – Theodore Roosevelt[1]

It is the business of government to organize the common interest against the special interests.
                                        – Woodrow Wilson[2]

By the first decades of the twentieth century, the social conception
of politics – embodied in the interest-group paradigm – had won
the field of political discourse and set the agenda of the public
sphere. Within this new discourse, which I have designated as pluralist liberalism, social groups had been reified as the building blocks
and the stumbling blocks of political action. Political conflict would
be understood for most of the twentieth century as the natural outcome of social-group conflict. The terms of debate now turned on
the question of the proper relation between these groups, and on
the question of their access to political power. A look backward
through three moments in San Francisco's history will illustrate the
depth of the transformation over the course of a half century. In the
San Francisco mayoral campaign of 1901, following the bitter waterfront strike of that year, Union Labor party candidate Eugene
Schmitz explained the campaign as "a fight for the representation
of the workingman in government of this city."[3] A quarter of a cen-

---

[1] Quoted in Richard L. McCormick, *The Party Period and Public Policy: American Politics from the Age of Jackson to the Progressive Era* (New York: Oxford University Press, 1986), 303.

[2] Quoted in Richard Hofstadter, *The American Political Tradition and the Men Who Made It* (New York: Vintage, 1973), 330.

[3] Quoted in Terrence J. McDonald, *The Parameters of Urban Fiscal Policy: Socioeconomic Change and Political Culture in San Francisco, 1860–1906* (Berkeley: University of California Press, 1986), 229.

tury earlier, Denis Kearney, at the head of the Workingmen's Party of California, had not claimed as much. Working within an already outmoded republican-liberal idiom, with its assumption of a unitary public good, Kearney claimed that "the people" were all workingmen. Those who supported the WPC, whether journalists or capitalists, were workingmen; those who opposed it were not. For Kearney and the WPC, social identity still hinged on ethical criteria established as authoritative and legitimate in the public sphere of political debate. Ironically, Kearney was forced to use the label "workingman" rather than the less socioeconomic "citizen" because mainstream party politicians had begun to mobilize class identities in the aftermath of the Civil War. Another quarter century earlier, the movement culture generated by the two vigilance committees in the 1850s had effectively stratified society between the virtuous and the corrupt. To be a "respectable" citizen in the 1850s had little or nothing to do with what we would call socioeconomic factors. Laborers and merchant capitalists alike could belong to the fraternity of citizens whose loyalty could be relied upon to keep taxes and expenditures low and to enforce the laws against criminals – civil and political. In that republican-liberal political culture, the universal struggle was to maintain justice in a liberal marketplace, where every economic actor understood the fairness of the market to be a function of sterling virtue in the character of the political leaders in control of law and its execution.

The story of this transformation is the story of the urban public sphere, where leaders mobilized followers within institutional confines and in doing so, gradually altered the scripts recognized as legitimate among the members of the political community. The bulk of historical scholarship on nineteenth-century urban political development has lost sight of the public dimension of social change. The triumph of a social-group conception of politics had been carried out in a public realm that had constructed the meaning of civil society. Ironically, however, that very triumph covered up the tracks leading to our twentieth-century political culture of interest groups and their needs.[4] With the social conception of politics legitimated

---

[4] On the politics of needs, see Daniel Bell, "The Public Household: On 'Fiscal Sociology' and the Liberal Society," *The Public Interest* 37 (Fall 1974): 29–68; and Nancy Fraser, "Struggle over Needs: Outline of a Socialist-Feminist Critical Theory of Late Capitalist Political Culture," in *Unruly Practices: Power, Discourse, and Gender in Contemporary Social Theory* (Minneapolis: University of Minnesota Press, 1989).

in everyday practice and in the universities as a branch of economic science, scholars and the popular press interpreted American political development as the story of interest groups competing for political power. The "Progressive" historians, especially Charles Beard and Frederick Jackson Turner, argued that ideologies were fig leaves for underlying economic interests. Decades later, "Consensus" historians, especially Richard Hofstadter and Louis Hartz, argued that social groups all had the same underlying liberal ideology. More recently, "New Left" scholars revived the Beardian perspective to argue that different social groups promoted contested ideologies, which grew from their experience as workers, as bourgeois, or in ethnic and racial communities. All, however, have agreed that social groups worked in history through the evolution of civil society. Public discourse, ideology, and language either mystified, stitched together, or reflected the experience of groups as such. In various formulations, successive schools of American historical scholarship have struggled to connect the state with society without paying attention to the sphere of action that is the very intersection of the political and the social: the public sphere.

Through an analytical narrative covering fifty years of urban history, this book has sought to demonstrate the autonomous historical role of the public sphere. The public sphere was no mere platform for the expression of interests or attitudes acquired in the experience of groups in the world of social labor. The nineteenth-century public sphere was the stage of history itself where the worlds of social labor and of government were disputed, legitimated, constructed, and reconstructed. Political power was a function of both public authority and institutional exclusion. That is, in order for men, and later women, to lead, they had to convince citizens to follow their definition of the public, and later plural, good. But to participate in this process, one needed to meet the qualifications set down in law by the already empowered European ("white") male political community. Exclusion by biological criteria – race and sex – was accomplished at the state constitutional level. These elemental social-group markers gave some actors in the economy privileges over others. To so designate some adults as ineligible for the privileges and immunities of the law was a political act guided by political ideologies. To free African Americans from the ancient status of slavery required a titanic civil war, in which radical liberals briefly won the field of legislation and constitutional change. European-descended males could behave as though only virtue distinguished correct from incorrect policy, while race and gender remained categories of uncontested exclusion. Once the Civil War threw these exclusions into doubt, mobilization would increasingly turn on citizens' group identities. The emancipation of slaves proved to be the paradigmatic case for exclusion and empowerment. The story of urban social and political development had sources in the national political conflicts of the Civil War. The origins of the Chinese exclusion movement was in the politics of Reconstruction. Europeans and Africans even united in the ostracism of Chinese as ineligible for participation or citizenship. Women took up where blacks left off, wielding natural rights radicalism against the hierarchical assumptions at the base of republicanism. The working class found its first clear advocates in the voices of the mainstream party politicians attempting to create order out of the chaotic electoral market of the 1870s. Mainstream party leaders, seeing a market, sold class identities for a temporary profit but also unleashed the monster of the Workingmen's Party of California. At each successive stage of this process of mobilization, the social groups identified by law (and therefore constructed from above, as it were) became more and more "real" to the leaders and followers alike. The origins of "progressivism" were found in the institutionalization and creative use of these identities by political entrepreneurs who changed the rules of the public sphere in the 1890s.

I have tried in this book to restore to the history of a city its public dimension. The "public city" was that site of contestation where leaders sought followers: from David C. Broderick, William Tell Coleman, and Edward D. Baker of the antebellum and Civil War city; Henry Huntley Haight, Laura de Force Gordon, Henry George, and Denis Kearney of the postwar and Gilded Age city; and William Randolph Hearst, Charlotte Perkins Gilman, and James Duval Phelan of the emergent Progressive Era city. In this political narrative about a single city during the second half of the nineteenth century, I have sought to reconstruct the press and political parties in a way contemporaries would have found familiar: as institutions of the public sphere. The public sphere stood between the social formations of civil society and the policies of the state. Studies of American political development need to account not only for leaders and institutions, but also for the changing behavior of the mass of ordinary participants. To win power leaders had to sell their justifications for power in a highly competitive public marketplace. Historians relying so heavily on the social-group paradigm have gradually diminished the creative autonomy of the ordinary participants in American political life.

Another important finding of this book, however, is that "the public" of the public city was itself a constantly reconstructed sphere of action. As the discussion of the concept of the public sphere in the Introduction made clear, the "public" was in effect a sociopolitical institution; it was not simply the space out of doors where parades were held and speeches were made. Indeed, its location in the print media was more important than its location in a physical public space, like the Plaza. As a political institution, the public sphere mediated access to the state (at the federal, state, and municipal levels); as a social institution, the public sphere constructed the boundary of private life and profoundly shaped the gender identities of urban residents. To participate politically in self-government, individuals needed to attain a voice in the debates of the public city. Blacks and women during the Civil War and Reconstruction founded newspapers to place their voices in the political realm. But the increasing number of group voices, including that of the working class, and the steady willingness by party leaders to recognize those group voices, fundamentally transformed the shape and function of the urban public sphere. The political mobilization of women, under the leadership of Charlotte Gilman in the 1890s, seriously blurred the once-rigid boundaries of the public sphere by opening it not only to both genders but also to debate about the domestic household. The print media also underwent a fundamental transformation in the postwar years, with the rise of sensational commercial journalism. Hearst contributed to the erosion of the boundaries between public and private by converting policy questions like streetcar safety regulation into melodrama that could be consumed domestically.

The public sphere was altered fundamentally by its journey from the Romantic, republican-liberal struggle for honor, virtue, and the right to represent an indivisible "public good" in the antebellum years, to the pluralist-liberal struggle among men and women to represent interest groups and social needs in the Progressive Era. But the city remained a "public city" in fundamental ways as well. Social-group identities, so clearly experienced by residents at the turn of the century, were still protean and overlapping. Political leaders, as we saw in the case of the charter reform and woman suffrage struggles of the 1890s, sometimes activated voters along one axis of social-group identification, and sometimes mobilized them along others. What this means is that politicians and journalists still needed to persuade voters and media consumers. The arrival of group identities and the social-group conception of politics did not mean that people would henceforth behave predictably; both leaders and followers remained relatively rational decision makers.

By making the public sphere the central focus of this book I have also highlighted the role women and gender played in political development. The social-group paradigm privileges race, class, and ethnicity as the fundamental factors in political development, but only, as we have seen, by skipping over the institutional site where society meets the polity. The public sphere was intrinsically gendered, predicated as it was on the maintenance of a female "private" sphere, in a fascinating mixture of bourgeois liberal and ancient republican theory. The gender axis of political change ran perpendicular to the socioeconomic and race-ethic axes so familiar to scholars. Its operation in urban political history is so little understood that only a beginning has been made in this book to recover its visibility and operation. At the very least it should be apparent that women activists, by transforming the public sphere, were critical agents in the origins of pluralist liberalism. When women like Laura de Force Gordon in the 1870s and 1880s confronted the patriarchal boundaries of a political culture in transition from republicanism to pluralist liberalism, they stressed their humanity, citizenship, and natural rights. Once political discourse had definitively left the political conception of society behind, however, and the interest-group paradigm had taken hold, the insurgent project of woman suffragists was represented in Mary McHenry Keith's explanation that "Women, as a sex, have special rights to protect, special wrongs to remedy, and special interests to promote."[5]

The triumph of an interest-group discourse within a public sphere

---

5 Mary McHenry Keith, "Doubling the Vote," *The People's Forum,* [clipping, n.d.], Keith-Pond Papers, Bancroft Library, Berkeley; On the role of women activists in the creation of interest-group politics, see also Naucy F. Cott, *The Grounding of Modern Feminism* (New Haven: Yale University Press, 1987), 1–50.

reconstituted to contain politically active yet disfranchised women worked to the creation of a theory of government oriented toward interest groups and their "needs," and with it a new meaning attached to the word "people." When the organizer of San Francisco's first reform coalition, Mayor James Duval Phelan, explained that municipal government should "care for the health, the comfort, the education, the property, and the general well-being of the people," he was articulating the twentieth-century's most familiar understanding of the state. Government of a polity of interest groups is today understood in the terms articulated by Frances Willard in 1898 that "government is only housekeeping on the broadest scale," or by Jane Addams, who called in 1907 for women to participate in "city housekeeping," and by Gunnar Myrdal, who later called modern government an exercise in "collective housekeeping."[6]

Once the political practice of the late nineteenth century shattered the republican myth of a single public good, the attendant theory of the state died as well. Politicians had no longer to practice some form of philosophical or constitutional search for universally good policies. Gone forever was Lincoln's belief, even at Gettysburg, that "the people" constituted *all* the nation, and that policies should benefit all equally. Eugene Schmitz's Union Labor party candidacy in 1901 accorded with a very powerful base of voting union workers. In 1901 the card-carrying membership of the San Francisco Labor Council and the Building Trades Council combined totaled at least forty thousand, and thousands more unorganized workers undoubtedly wished to be organized and cast their lot with the ULP. These unions had achieved a virtually closed-shop city in San Francisco. It was, as the horrified Ray Stannard Baker put it, "the city where unionism holds undisputed sway."[7]

What Baker, Roosevelt, Wilson, and San Francisco progressives like James Duval Phelan wanted was, of course, to achieve some "common" or "public" *interest*. But their pluralist-liberal assumptions guaranteed that such an interest would be the sum of group

---

[6] Willard and Addams quoted in Aileen Kraditor, *The Ideas of the Woman Suffrage Movement 1890–1920* (New York: Columbia University Press, 1980), 68n., 70; Gunnar Myrdal, *The Political Element in the Development of Economic Theory* (1953), xl, cited in Hannah Arendt, *Human Condition* (Chicago, 1958), 29.

[7] Michael Kazin, *Barons of Labor: The San Francisco Building Trades and Union Power in the Progressive Era* (Urbana: University of Illinois Press, 1987), 13, 51.

parts. The crucial development across the long haul of the nineteenth century was the legitimation of policy goals intended to benefit less than the whole people. From Madison through Lincoln
interest groups were recognized as incipient in a liberal constitutional polity but rejected ethically. From Lincoln's death through
the end of the century, mobilization of interests and the disintegration of antebellum Romantic republicanism simultaneously
transformed political contestation and the public presentation of
segments of civil society. The idea that interest groups were the key
players in politics had passed to the level of semiconscious assumption. The project for political activists now became one of proving
that one represented a legitimate interest group and that exclusion
of one's interest group from ruling coalitions would seriously hurt
the "common interest." Accordingly, the progressive mayor of San
Francisco James Rolph Jr. (1912–32) liked to be called "the mayor
of all the people." By the time of his first year in office, his slogan
was meant in the coalitional sense. Now that the polity was organized by groups whose interests were made known through their
leaders, the task of city government had become a technical one.
Rolph appropriately established a "Bureau of Efficiency," to fine-
tune the governance of a city of interests.[8]

These deep, and gradually constructed, changes in the urban
public sphere made possible the great drama of the "Progressive
Era" itself. On 26 May 1898 the voters of San Francisco voted to
adopt a city charter appropriate to the new political culture. The
reform charter, drafted by a Board of Freeholders that included
not only representatives of the Merchant's Association but P. H.
McCarthy of the Building Trades Council, strengthened the
mayor's office, set a goal of municipal ownership of utilities, expanded the city's capacity to raise funds, put the Board of Supervisors on a citywide basis, and centralized the school system.[9] On 10
October 1911 the voters of California went to the polls for a special
election, called to decide the fate of twenty-three state constitutional
amendments drafted by Hiram Johnson's progressive state legislature. The result was perhaps the most sweeping victory for progres-

---

[8]   William Issel and Robert W. Cherny, *San Francisco, 1865–1932: Politics, Power, and Urban
       Development* (Berkeley: University of California Press, 1986), 165–6.
[9]   William Issel, "Class and Ethnic Conflict in San Francisco Political History: The Reform
       Charter of 1898," *Labor History* 18 (1977): 341–59; Issel and Cherny, *San Francisco*, 136–52;
       McDonald, *Parameters of Urban Fiscal Policy*, 205–15.

sive measures the nation had seen. In one stroke, voters ratified the initiative, referendum, and recall, provided for government inspection of merchandise and commodities and for workers' compensation insurance, and established a powerful railroad regulatory commission.[10] The drama that took place between these two dates, 1898 and 1911, a span of years defining the most dynamic phase of San Francisco's Progressive Era, was only possible because of the transformation of the political culture of the city that took place prior to 1898. That story began, as we have seen, with the operation of the republican political discourse in its last phase of full operation, from 1850 through the end of the Civil War. It ended with the operation of the pluralist-liberal discourse in the first phase of its full operation, in the campaign for the new city charter in the late 1890s.

Given the radical differences between the political culture found at the beginning of this study, one characterized by a political conception of society, and the one identified at the end of this study, one characterized by a social conception of politics, it is difficult to draw a final judgment about the quality of democratic participation over that fifty-year period. One might even conclude that political participation was a glass half empty in the 1850s, and still a glass half empty in the 1890s. Statistical measures of political participation have shown throughout these chapters that there was no sudden decline in voter turnout at the end of the century, with the arrival of Progressive Era reforms. Turnout in municipal-only elections was always low since the 1850s. The emphasis on the public sphere gives us a different way to judge the extent to which achievement of the democratic ideal of full participation has improved or declined. Following a long line of thinkers attentive to the necessity of creativity to democracy, including John Dewey, Theodor Adorno, and Jürgen Habermas, I would argue that political participation is more democratic when participants have a direct, creative role in their self-government, not solely when more people or more groups

---

[10] San Francisco *Chronicle*, 12 October 1911; George E. Mowry, *The California Progressives* (Berkeley: University of California Press, 1951); Spencer C. Olin, Jr., *California's Prodigal Sons: Hiram Johnson and the Progressives, 1911–1917* (Berkeley: University of California Press, 1968); Walton Bean and James J. Rawls, *California: An Interpretive History*, 5th ed. (New York: McGraw Hill, 1988), 239–65.

can be said to have voted.[11] By this measure, the white, masculine, bourgeois-oriented public sphere of the antebellum years was the most democratic. Leaders struggled in critical-rational debate to gain followers, who would desert them days later when another man persuaded them more effectively. That public sphere, however, was severely restrictive. A polity is also less democratic when whole groups of people are excluded from effective citizenship. It excluded women, people of color, and, because they were not geographically permanent, the transient working class. The political culture of the last decades of the nineteenth century gained in access but lost in the creativity of its participants. Blacks (but not yet the Chinese, who were barred from citizenship), women, and the working class all gained an institutional voice in the political proceedings of the public sphere. But, as they did so, the press, which remained the central institution of that sphere, altered the role of the voter from that of a citizen that of a consumer. The reconstruction of the public city to enable a politics of groups and their needs also enabled the institutionalization of group identities in the form of lobbies and the manipulation of group behavior by an emergent culture industry that made persuasion into a science of marketing. In short, this study does not tell a story of decline, nor does it romanticize some golden age of American politics destroyed by the arrival of modernity.

Instead, I have tried to trace the genealogy of American political culture as it appeared at the beginning of the twentieth century. I have also tried to suggest how that emergent political culture established elaborate conceptual barriers that thwarted scholars of the twentieth century, working within a social conception of politics, from fully understanding the political conception of society that preceded it. And I have tried to do this simply by narrating a story about voters, leaders, private and public persons, movements, and

---

[11] For the importance of creative participation to John Dewey and his social-democratic contemporaries, see especially James T. Kloppenberg, *Uncertain Victory: Social Democracy and Progressivism in European and American Thought, 1870–1920* (New York: Oxford University Press, 1986); and Robert B. Westbrook, *John Dewey and American Democracy* (Ithaca, N.Y.: Cornell University Press, 1991). On Adorno, see Martin Jay, *The Dialectical Imagination: A History of the Frankfurt School and the Institute of Social Research, 1923–1950* (Boston: Little, Brown, 1973); Max Horkheimer and Theodor W. Adorno, *Dialectic of Enlightenment* (1944; New York: Continuum, 1969); Jürgen Habermas, *The Structural Transformation of the Public Sphere: An Inquiry into a Category of Bourgeois Society*, trans. Thomas Burger (Cambridge, Mass.: MIT Press, 1989). See also discussion of the public sphere in Introduction.

events. I have embedded this narrative in social-scientific methods of analysis, hoping to do some justice to the excitement felt by participants in the political development of San Francisco. Literally thousands of men and women devoted their whole adult lives – and many lost their lives – to the struggle for justice in the city of San Francisco. Their achievements were mixed. They created new forms of equality and inequality, new understandings of state and society, new contexts for the creation of power and wealth in an American city. Those historical actors, through achievement and failure, would have best understood their role as having been played out on the dramatic stage of the public city.

Statistical sources, methods and supplementary tables

OVERVIEW

The foundation on which the statistical analyses in this book rests is a population of about ten thousand individuals collected as "observations" and assembled into "samples." The quantitative analysis performed in this investigation is built upon systematic samples of adult males drawn from the manuscript schedules of the 1852 California Census and the 1860, 1870, 1880, and 1900 U.S. Censuses of San Francisco. To study rates of political participation I have analyzed two sets of data: election returns and voter registration lists. For election returns I assembled my data set from the tabular returns in the city's newspapers from 1849 through 1900. A key source for this study is the California Great Registers. Beginning in 1866, the California state legislature established the most extensive system of voter registration in the United States. The Great Registers, updated regularly, give the name, age, occupation, place of birth, address, and naturalization information for each citizen qualified to vote. I have drawn extensive samples from these registers to determine, with individual-level data, the precise social composition of the electorate. Summations of these data are also available in many volumes of San Francisco Board of Supervisors, *Municipal Reports* (San Francisco, 1867–1901). I have supplemented these principal sources of quantitative data with several other sources as well, especially samples drawn from the city directories. The one "comprehensive" sample taken in this study is the data drawn from the twenty-three hundred membership applications to the 1856 committee held at the Huntington Library in San Marino, California. Because it was practical to collect data from every surviving membership application, and because this is such an interesting source, I took the ideal "sample" in this case, which ensures the highest level of significance.

SAMPLING METHODS

To ensure statistical significance in my analysis of the several sources of quantifiable data used for this study, I have drawn systematic and random samples from census manuscripts, voter registers, and other sources. Systematic samples are drawn by observing every nth person from the total population. The method of drawing systematic samples in this study was to calculate the interval required in order to obtain a sample of greater than 300 observations evenly from the beginning to the end of the source. The larger the sample, the more useful it is, because subgroup analyses can be more reliably performed. When possible, therefore, I collected larger samples. Thus, my sample of the 1852 California manuscript census totals 479 observations. These were taken at every 25th adult male in the census. My sample sizes range from about 300 to more than 2,000, as in the case with the applications to the San Francisco Committee of Vigilance of 1856.[1] The 1890 manuscript census was destroyed in an archival fire in the 1940s, so no sample for 1890 is used in this study. The sample drawn from the 1900 U.S. Census manuscript differs from the others. I began with a core of 423 observations drawn from the "United States Census Data, 1900: Public Use Sample" made available by the Inter-university Consortium for Political and Social Research, Ann Arbor (ICSPR 7825). These data were originally collected by the Center for Studies in Demography and Ecology, University of Washington. Neither the original collector nor the consortium bears any responsibility for the analyses or interpretations presented here. Using the same random sampling methods as the original researchers, I augmented this sample by collecting 981 additional observations, for a total of 1,406 individuals. Although all other samples used in this study are of adult males, the 1900 sample is composed of all persons.[2]

The size of these samples are more than sufficient to test the relationships of interest, such as between occupational or ethnic group membership and political participation. For example, in the comparison of groups by occupation in Table 2.1, the combined sample

---

[1]   Charles M. Dollar and Richard J. Jensen, *Historian's Guide to Statistics* (New York: Holt, Rinehart and Winston, 1971); Konrad H. Jarausch and Kenneth A. Hardy, *Quantitative Methods for Historians: A Guide to Research, Data, and Statistics* (Chapel Hill: University of North Carolina Press, 1991).

[2]   W. G. Cochran, *Sampling Techniques*, 2d ed. (New York: John Wiley, 1963).

size of 810 persons, accepting an error rate of .05 provides 88% power to detect even as weak a correlation of 0.1 between group membership and political participation, and virtually 100% power for finding a correlation of 0.2 or greater.[3] An example of a sample-size calculation designed to estimate the proportion of native-born males in the 1900 U.S. Census for San Francisco (known to be 57% of all males, see Table A.2) with a margin of error of .05 and a 95% confidence interval requires an approximate sample size of 390 subjects. Therefore, the actual sample size of 440 males used in this study is of a sufficient size.[4]

ELECTORAL DATA

Newspaper reports of vote totals were primarily used to determine voter turnout and election outcomes. Census reports were used to determine the number of eligible voters used in the denominator of voter turnout rate calculations. Following general practice, I have used the number of white males twenty-one years and older as the determinant of eligible electors. Ideally, one would like to use the number of male citizens twenty-one years or older for this figure, but citizenship is not consistently reported in the censuses. Fortunately, using all adult white males is a conservative approach, due to the verified high rates of census underreporting, especially for aliens.[5]

CODING

Data were coded according to occupation, nativity, residential status, ward, and other variables. In the text I indicate important facts pertaining to variable definition. For instance, I consistently use the five-tier scheme of classifying occupations familiar to most American social historians, with minor adjustments imposed by the nature of the local economy. I have stayed as close as possible to the standards set by Stephan Thernstrom, and a refinement of Thernstrom's

---

[3] Jacob Cohen, *Statistical Power Analysis for the Behavioral Sciences* 2d ed. (New Jersey: Lawrence Erlbaum Associates, 1988), 75–84.

[4] Jarausch and Hardy, *Quantitative Methods for Historians*, 63–81.

[5] Ray M. Shortridge, "Estimating Voter Participation," in *Analyzing Electoral History: A Guide to the Study of American Voter Behavior*, edited by Jerome M. Clubb, William H. Flanigan, and Nancy H. Zingale (Beverly Hills: Sage Publications, 1981), 137–52; Howard W. Allen and Kay Warren Allen, "Vote Fraud and Data Validity," in *Analyzing Electoral History*, 153–94.

methods by Theodore Hershberg et al.[6] All of the occupations appearing in the samples used follow, organized by the category in which they were coded.

Occupational codes

I.   *High White-Collar*
     A.   *Professional*
          Clergy, Gentleman, Lawyer, Physician.
     B.   *Major Proprietors*
          Broker, Commission Merchant, Contractor, Merchant, Manufacturer.
     C.   *Major Officials*
          (e.g., Mayor, Judge)
II. *Low White-Collar*
     A.   *Petty Proprietors and Managers*
          Agent, Broker (some), Builder, Captain (ship), Chemist, Dealer, Dentist, Druggist, Dry/Fancy Goods, Farmer, Foreman, Grocer, Hotel Keeper, Innkeeper, Jeweler, Liquor Dealer, Master Mariner, Pilot (harbor), Sales Agent, Storekeeper, Tavern Keeper, Tobacconist, Victualer.
     B.   *Clerks and Sales*
          Bookkeeper, Clerk, Copyist, Salesman, Scrivener, Solicitor.
     C.   *Semiprofessionals*
          Artist, Musician, Student, Teacher.
     D.   *Minor Officials*
          (e.g., City Supervisor, Customs House Worker)
III. *Skilled*
          Baker, Barber, Blacksmith, Boilermaker, Bookbinder, Brewer, Bricklayer, Brickmason, Butcher, Carpenter, Carriage Maker, Cigar Maker, Conductor, Confectioner, Cooper, Cordwainer, Dyer, Engineer, Fisherman, Gas Fitter, Glass Blower, Hatter, Joiner, Locksmith, Machinist, Mason, Moulder, Operator, Painter, Paper Hanger, Pattern Maker, Peddler, Piano Maker, Plasterer, Plumber, Policeman, Printer, Puddler, Saddlemaker,

[6] Stephan Thernstrom, "On the Socioeconomic Ranking of Occupations," in *The Other Bostonians* (Cambridge, Mass., 1975); 289–302; Theodore Hershberg, Michael Katz, Stuart Blumin, Laurence Glasco, and Clyde Griffen, "Occupation and Ethnicity in Five Nineteenth-Century Cities: A Collaborative Inquiry," *Historical Methods Newsletter* 7 (1974): 174–216.

Saddler, Ship Carpenter, Shipwright, Shoemaker, Stonecutter, Stonemason, Tailor, Tanner, Tinsmith, Turner, Typesetter, Upholsterer, Weaver, Wheelwright.

Note: For some tests, skilled workers were further broken down by "Independent" and "employee" categories. For most tests this information was not known.

IV. *Semiskilled*

Bartender, Boatman, Carman, Cartman, Coachman, Drayman, Driver, Expressman, Extraman, Furnaceman, Gardener, Hostler, Mariner, Porter, Sailor, Seaman, Servant, Special Policeman, Teamster, Waiter, Watchman.

V. *Unskilled*

Carrier (coal, wood, etc.), Hand (farm, etc.), Laborer, Waterman, Worker (factory, etc.)

STATISTICAL ANALYSIS

The use of quantitative data and analyses make generalizations reliable and verifiable. To test whether some groups were more likely to participate than others I used a Chi-square test. In Chapters 6 and 8 I used the *multiple linear regression* analysis to assess the voting behavior of various groups in the electorate while controlling for potentially confounding characteristics. It is not possible to provide a full or even adequate explanation of the statistical tests used in this study.[7] It might be helpful, however, to provide a thumbnail definition of the key terms and tests I have used. The Chi-square test is a comparison of proportions within two samples, to determine whether the proportions within those two samples are different. (e.g., the proportions of occupations within the U.S. Census samples and those within the Great Register sample). We also must know whether the differences observed are *significantly* different, meaning that there is less than a 5% probability that the observed differences could have occurred by chance alone. *Significance* in the Chi-square and all other tests is estimated by the "*p-value*," which is the probability of concluding that there is a difference between

---

[7] See for example, Dollar and Jensen, *Historian's Guide to Statistics*; Michael S. Lewis-Beck, *Applied Regression: An Introduction* (Beverly Hills: Sage Publications, 1980); J. Morgan Kousser, "Ecological Regression and the Analysis of Past Politics," *Journal of Interdisciplinary History* 4:2 (Autumn 1973): 237–62; Laura Irwin Langbein and Allan J. Lichtman, *Ecological Inference* (Beverly Hills: Sage Publications, 1978).

two groups when in fact a difference does not exist. A p-value of .05 or less is the standard level of statistical significance for a two-tailed test.

The "relative risk" is the ratio of the risk of an outcome, such as membership in the Vigilance Committee of 1856, experienced by persons with a particular group characteristic, such as occupation, to those without that characteristic. It is calculated by dividing the rate of the outcome (in this case vigilante membership) among subjects with the designated characteristic (for instance, low white-collar occupation) by the rate among the subjects who are of a low white-collar occupation.

The *confidence interval* is a range of values about the sample mean or proportion. The confidence interval is essentially a measure of precision of the sample estimate. I have set the level of confidence in this study at 95%, which is the standard among social scientists.[8]

Linear regression analyses were used to develop models containing multiple predictors of continuous outcomes. These models, such as: "the vote for the Democratic candidate for mayor is explained by the proportion of working-class voters plus the proportion of native-born voters in each ward," estimate the amount of variance in the outcome variable (in this case the vote for the Democratic candidate) that is "explained," or accounted for, by each independent variable (in this case the proportions of working-class and native-born voters in each ward), and by the composite of those predictor variables. The great strength of multiple linear regression is that it controls for the effect of each independent predictor variable simultaneously. I have used the least-squares solution to calculate these linear regressions. The "R^2" is the percent of the variance explained by the model divided by the total variance present in the model. All statistical analysis was performed with SAS/PC version 6.03 software.[9]

SUPPLEMENTARY TABLES

The following tables provide basic statistical breakdowns and analyses which are referred to throughout this book.

---

[8] Jarausch and Hardy, *Quantitative Methods for Historians*, 68–81.

[9] All tests performed in this study are fully explained in SAS/STAT User's Guide, Release 6.03 Edition (Cary, North Carolina: SAS Institute, 1988).

Table A.1. *Population and rates of increase: San Francisco, 1848–1900*

Year	Total Population	Rate of Increase
1848	1,000	
1852	36,151	3,600%
1860	56,802	57%
1870	149,473	163%
1880	233,959	57%
1890	298,997	28%
1900	342,782	15%

Sources: For the year 1848, Roger Lotchin, *San Francisco*, 8; Manuscript schedule of the California Census of 1852, "Recapitulation," 812; U.S. Bureau of the Census, *Eighth Census* (Washington, D.C., 1864), 1:31; *Ninth Census*, 3 vols. (Washington, D.C., 1872), 1:91; *Tenth Census*, 22 vols. (Washington, D.C., 1883–8), 1:671; *Eleventh Census*, 15 vols. (Washington, D.C., 1892–7), 1:9; *Twelfth Census*, 10 vols. (Washington, D.C., 1901–2), 1:lxix.

Table A.2. *Percentages of population by sex and nativity in San Francisco, 1852–1900 (All ages, percentages read horizontally)*

	Male	Female	Totals
1852			
Native Born	14,088 (82.3)	2,760 (17.7)	17,118
Foreign Born	16,537 (86.9)	2,766 (13.1)	19,033
City total	30,625 (84.7)	5,526 (15.3)	36,151
1860			
Native Born	16,610 (58.6)	11,738 (41.4)	28,348
Foreign Born	18,166 (63.8)	10,288 (36.2)	28,454
City total	34,776 (61.2)	20,026 (38.8)	56,802
1890			
Native Born	88,285 (51.3)	83,901 (48.7)	172,186
Foreign Born	81,515 (64.3)	45,296 (35.7)	126,811
City Total	169,800 (56.8)	129,197 (43.2)	298,997
1900			
Native Born	107,771 (49.6)	109,381 (50.4)	217,152
Foreign Born	80,211 (63.9)	45,384 (36.1)	125,595
City total	187,982 (54.8)	154,765 (45.2)	342,782

Sources: Manuscript schedule of the California Census of 1852, "Recapitulation," 812; U.S. Bureau of the Census, *Eighth Census*, vol. 1, 33; *Ninth Census*, 3 vols. (Washington, D.C., 1872), 1:91 *Tenth Census*, 22 vols. (Washington, D.C., 1883–8), 1:671; *Eleventh Census* (Washington, D.C., 1897), vol. 2, pp. 668–9. The figures in the cells for 1900 are based on the sample of the 1900 U.S. Census manuscript described earlier.

Table A.3. *Native origins of eligible voters in San Francisco, 1860–1900.*
Broken down by countries (Excludes Chinese, who were nearly all
ineligible for citizenship)

Year	U.S.	Ireland	Germany	Britain	Scandinavia	Other
1860	37.8	18.9	18.0	9.9	6.0	3.3
1870	44.1	25.5	18.5	5.8	2.7	3.3
1880	38.1	22.8	16.8	12.4	2.3	6.9
1900	60.9	13.8	11.3	4.3	3.8	5.9

Sources: Manuscript schedules of the 1852 California Census and the 1860, 1870, 1880, and 1900 U.S. Censuses. The figures in the cells for 1900 are based on the sample of the 1900 U.S. Census manuscript described earlier.

Table A.4. *Occupations of eligible voters in San Francisco, 1852–1900*
(Percent)

Category	1852	1860	1870	1880	1900
High White-Collar	11%	9%	10%	6%	10%
Low White-Collar	20	21	28	32	32
Skilled	32	31	26	25	26
Semiskilled	21	25	22	25	22
Unskilled	16	14	15	9	10
Sample $N=$	536	334	330	435	440

Sources: Manuscript schedules of the 1852 California Census and the 1860, 1870, 1880, and 1900 U.S. Censuses. The figures in the cells for 1900 are based on the sample of the 1900 U.S. Census manuscript described earlier.

Bibliography

PART I: PRIMARY SOURCES

Manuscripts

Berkeley, California. Bancroft Library, University of California:
Phineus Underwood Blunt Papers.
Andrew Jackson Bryant. Dictation for H. H. Bancroft.
Martin J. Burke. Dictation for H. H. Bancroft. [1884].
Henry Perin Coon. "Annals of San Francisco." Dictation for H. H. Bancroft.
Michael H. de Young. Dictation for H. H. Bancroft. [1875].
Clancey J. Dempster. Dictation for H. H. Bancroft.
John L. Durkee. Dictation for H. H. Bancroft.
Thomas Fitch Papers.
Laura de Force Gordon Papers.
Haight Family Papers.
Theodore H. Hittell Papers.
Keith-Pond Family Papers.
LaMotte Family Letters.
McCracken Family Letters.
James Duval Phelan Papers.
Loring Pickering. Dictation for H. H. Bancroft.
Gerritt W. Ryckman. Dictation for H. H. Bancroft.
San Francisco Committee of Vigilance, 1856. Papers.
William A. Scott Papers.
Adolph Heinrich Sutro Papers.
Cambridge, Massachusetts. Schlesinger Library of Radcliffe College. Charlotte P. Gilman Papers.
Madison, Wisconsin. State Historical Society of Wisconsin. Edward A. Ross Papers (microfilm, 1986).
San Francisco, California. California Historical Society Library. Henry H. Ellis Papers.
San Francisco, California. San Francisco City Archives, City Hall. "Poll List, 12th Ward, 7th Precinct." 1878.

San Marino, California. Huntington Library. San Francisco Committee of Vigilance Papers.
Santa Rosa, California. Private Collection of Winifred H. Medin. Duane Family Papers.

Newspapers and periodicals

Chronicle, 1865–1911. San Francisco.
Daily Alta California, 1849–1891. San Francisco.
Daily California Chronicle, 1856. San Francisco.
Daily Herald, 1856–1858. San Francisco.
Evening Bulletin, 1855–1901. San Francisco.
Examiner, 1865–1911. San Francisco.
Mercantile Gazette and Shipping Register, 1851–1858. San Francisco.
Morning Call, 1865–1882. San Francisco.
Times, 1871–1878. New York.
Union, 1859–1900. Sacramento.

Government documents

California Constitution of 1850. In *The Codes and Statutes of the State of California*. Edited by Theodore H. Hittell. 2 vols. San Francisco: A. L. Bancroft and Company, 1876. 1:39–68.
California Constitution of 1879. In James Bryce, *The American Commonwealth*. 2 vols. London: Macmillan and Co., 1888. 1:709–50.
California Great Registers. 1866–1880. Microfilm. Sacramento. California State Library.
Clarke, Alfred. *A Compilation of Laws Relating to Elections, Now in Force in the State of California*. San Francisco: A. L. Bancroft and Co., Printers and Lithographers, 1875.
Congressional Globe. Washington, D.C. 35th Congress, 1st Session. Appendix.
Debates and Proceedings of the Constitutional Convention of the State of California, convened at the City of Sacramento, Saturday, September 28, 1878. 3 vols. Sacramento: State Office, J. D. Young, Sup't., 1880–1881.
Kaplan, Louis. *Extracts from the United States Statutes, the Constitution of the State of California, and the Political and Penal Codes, Relating to the Elective Franchise, Registration of Citizens, and Elections*. San Francisco: Board of Election Commissioners, 1878.
North, S. N. D. "The Newspaper and Periodical Press," in U.S. Department of the Interior, *Tenth Census of the United States*. Vol. 8. Washington, D.C.: Government Printing Office, 1884.
Statutes of California. Sacramento. 1861–1878.
San Francisco Board of Freeholders, *Charter for the City and County of San Francisco*. San Francisco: Geo. Spaulding and Co., 1895.
San Francisco Board of Freeholders, *Charter for the City and County of San Francisco*. San Francisco: Woodward & Co., 1898.

San Francisco Board of Supervisors. *Municipal Reports.* San Francisco. 1860–1880.

U.S. Bureau of the Census. *Eighth Census.* Washington, D.C. 1864
Ninth Census. 3 vols. Washington, D.C. 1872.
Tenth Census. 22 vols. Washington, D.C. 1883–1888.
Eleventh Census. 15 vols. Washington, D.C. 1892–1897.
Twelfth Census. 10 vols. Washington, D.C. 1901–1902.
Report on Statistics of Churches in the Eleventh Census. Washington, D.C.: Government Printing Office, 1894.

U.S. National Archives and Records Service. General Services Administration. *Federal Population Census Schedules.* 1860–1900. Washington, D.C.: National Archives and Records Service. Microfilm.

U.S. Work Projects Administration. *History of San Francisco Journalism.* Vol. 4, Emerson L. Daggett, Supervisor, *Trends in Size, Circulation, News and Advertising in San Francisco Journalism, 1870–1938.* San Francisco, 1940. [Mimeograph]. Harvard College Library.

U.S. Work Projects Administration. *History of San Francisco Journalism.* Vol. 6, Charles Holmes and Isom Shepard, *History of the Physical Growth and Technological Advance of the San Francisco Press.* San Francisco, 1940. [Mimeograph]. Harvard College Library.

Pamphlets and rare materials

Brierly, Rev. Benjamin. *Thoughts for the Crisis: A Discourse Delivered in the Washington St. Baptist Church. San Francisco, Cal., On the Sabbath Following the Assassination of James King of William By James P. Casey.* San Francisco: Eureka Book and Job Office, 1856. San Marino, California. Huntington Library.

Broadside. "The Revolution of the People." [n.d.]. San Francisco Committee of Vigilance Papers. San Marino, California. Huntington Library.

Broadside. "To the People of California." [n.d.]. San Francisco Committee of Vigilance Papers. San Marino, California. Huntington Library.

Broadside. [May 1856]. San Francisco Committee of Vigilance Papers. San Marino, California. Huntington Library.

Chit-Chat Club of San Francisco. "Eighteenth Annual Meeting, San Francisco, Nov. 7 1892." San Francisco, 1892. [Pamphlet]. Widener Library, Harvard College.

Frear, Rev'd Walter. *A Sermon on the Death of Jas. King of William, Preached at Iowa Hill, on Sunday. May 25, 1856.* Iowa Hill [Calif.]: Miller and Olmstead, 1856. San Marino, California. Huntington Library.

[Gilman], Charlotte Perkins Stetson. *The Labor Movement: A Prize Essay read before the Trades and Labor Unions of Alameda County, Sepember 5, 1892.* Oakland: Alameda County Federation of Trades, 1893. [Pamphlet]. Schlesinger Library, Radcliffe College.

Gutsch, Gustav. *A Comparison of the Consolidation Act with the New Charter.* San Francisco: Citizen's Charter Association, 1896. [Pamphlet]. Stanford University Library.

Haight, H. H. "The Currency Question." Argument for Appellant. "In the Supreme Court of the State of California, James Lick, Apellant, vs., William Faulkner, et al., Respondents." San Francisco: B. F. Sterett, Printer, 533 Clay St. [1864]. Berkeley. Bancroft Library.

[Haynes, Fred]. "The San Francisco Settlement Association." *Prospect Union Review* 1:15 (January 1895): 3–4. Widener Library, Harvard College.

Kennedy, Kate. *Doctor Paley's Foolish Pigeons, and Short Sermons to Working-Men.* San Francisco: Cubery and Co., 1906. [Pamphlet]. Berkeley. Bancroft Library.

The Labor Agitators; Or the Battle for Bread: The Party of the Future: The Workingmen's Party of California. Its Birth and Organization – Its Leaders and Its Purposes: Corruption in Our Local and State Governments: Venality of the Press. San Francisco: George W. Greene, Publisher, [February 1878]. Berkeley. Bancroft Library.

Leland Stanford Junior University. *Register.* Vols. 1891/2–1899/00.

McCoppin, Hon. Frank. "Address on the New Charter for the City and County of San Francisco." 8 November 1896. [Pamphlet]. Stanford University Library.

Morgan, A. W. *San Francisco City Directory, September 1852.* First Publication. San Francisco: F. A. Bonnard, 1852. San Francisco. California Historical Society Library.

[O'Meara, James]. *The Vigilance Committee of 1856: By a Pioneer Journalist.* San Francisco: James H. Barry, Publisher, 1890. Berkeley. Bancroft Library.

"Oration of Col. E. D. Baker, Over the Dead Body of Broderick." Berkeley. Bancroft Library.

A 'Pile' or a Glance at the Wealth of the Moneyed Men of San Francisco and Sacramento City. San Francisco, 1851. Berkeley. Bancroft Library.

"Remarks, Delivered in the Senate and the House of Representatives of the United States, on the Announcement of the Death of Hon. David C. Broderick, of California, Late a Member of the Senate of the United States in the Thirty-Fifth Congress. In the Senate of the United States, February 13, 1860." Berkeley. Bancroft Library.

The San Francisco Directory for the Year 1852–53. First Publication. San Francisco: James M. Parker, 1852. San Francisco. California Historical Society Library.

Scott, Rev. Dr. Wm. A. Scott. *A Discourse for the Times: Delivered in Calvary Church, Sunday. July 27. 1856.* San Francisco, 1856. San Marino, California. Huntington Library.

"Speech of Hon. John S. Hager, of San Francisco, In the Senate of California, January 28, 1870, on Senator Hager's Joint Resolution to Reject the Fifteenth Amendment to the Constitution of the United States." Berkeley. Bancroft Library.

"Speech of H. H. Haight, Democratic Candidate for Governor, Delivered at the Great Democratic Mass Meeting at Union Hall, Tuesday Evening, July 9th, 1867." Berkeley. Bancroft Library.

Speeches of Dennis [sic] Kearney, Labor Champion. New York: Jesse Haney & Co., 1878. [Pamphlet]. Stanford, California. Stanford Library. Special Collections.

Stedman, J. C., and Leonard, R. A. *The Workingmen's Party of California: An Epitome of its Rise and Progress.* San Francisco: Bacon & Company, Book and Job Printers, 1878. [Pamphlet]. Berkeley. Bancroft Library.

Truesdell, Dr. A. P. "Mob-Law, with Violence vs. Peaceful Revolution, By Ballot: A Speech Delivered at 'The Sand Lot,' April 14th, 1878." In Truesdell, *The People's Champion: The Voice of the People Must Be Heard!* San Francisco: A. L. Bancroft & Co., Printer, 1878. Berkeley. Bancroft Library.

PART II: SECONDARY SOURCES

Dissertations and unpublished studies

Burke, Martin J. "The Conundrum of Class: Public Discourse on the Social Order in America." Ph.D. diss. University of Michigan, 1987.

Chandler, Robert Joseph. "The Press and Civil Liberties in California during the Civil War, 1861–1865." Ph.D. diss. University of California, Riverside, 1978.

Erie, Steven P. "The Development of Class and Ethnic Politics in San Francisco, 1870–1910: A Critique of the Pluralist Interpretation." Ph.D. diss. University of California, Los Angeles, 1975.

Ethington, Philip J. "The Dual Urban Political Universe: Structures of Political Participation in San Francisco, 1860–1880." Paper given at the annual conference of the Pacific Coast Branch of the American Historical Association in San Francisco, 13 August 1988.

Fels, Anthony. "The Square and the Compass: San Francisco's Freemasons and American Religion, 1870–1900." Ph.D. diss. Stanford University, 1987. 2 vols.

Ingels, Helen H. "The History of the Workingmen's Party of California." Master's thesis, University of California, Berkeley, 1919.

McKinney, Mary Frances. "Denis Kearney, Organizer of the Workingmen's Party of California." Master's thesis, University of California, Berkeley, 1939.

Petersen, Eric Falk. "Prelude to Progressivism: California Election Reform, 1870–1909." Ph.D. diss. University of California, Los Angeles, 1969.

Sawislak, Karen Lynn. "Smoldering City: Class, Ethnicity, and Politics in

Chicago at the Time of the Great Fire, 1867–1873." Ph.D. diss. Yale University, 1990.

Tygiel, Jules. "Workingmen in San Francisco, 1870–1901." Ph.D. diss. University of California, Los Angeles, 1977.

Varcados, Peter. "Labor and Politics in San Francisco, 1880–1892." Ph.D. diss. University of California, Berkeley, 1968.

Yung, Judy. "Unbinding the Feet, Unbinding Their Lives: Social Change for Women in San Francisco, 1902–1945." Ph.D. Dissertation, University of California, Berkeley, 1990.

Published books and articles

Addams, Jane. *Democracy and Social Ethics.* New York: Macmillan, 1902.
Twenty Years at Hull-House. New York: Macmillan, 1936.

Alcorn, Richard S. "Leadership and Stability in Mid-Nineteenth Century America: A Case Study of an Illinois Town." *Journal of American History* 61 (December 1974): 685–702.

Allen, Howard W., and Allen, Kay Warren. "Vote Fraud and Data Validity." In *Analyzing Electoral History: A Guide to the Study of American Voter Behavior,* edited by Jerome M. Clubb, William H. Flanigan, and Nancy H. Zingale. Beverly Hills, California: Sage, 1981, 153–94.

Allswang, John M. *Bosses, Machines, and Urban Voters: An American Symbiosis.* Port Washington, N.Y, 1977.

Almond, Gabriel, and Verba, Sidney. *The Civic Culture: Political Attitudes and Democracy in Five Nations.* Princeton, N.J., 1963.

Anthony, Susan B., and Harper, Ida Husted, eds. *History of Woman Suffrage.* Vol. 4. New York: Susan B. Anthony, 1902.

Appleby, Joyce. "Republicanism and Ideology." *American Quarterly* 37:4 (Fall 1985): 461–73.
"Republicanism in Old and New Contexts." *William and Mary Quarterly* 43 (January 1986): 20–34.

Arendt, Hannah. *The Human Condition.* Chicago: University of Chicago Press, 1958.
On Revolution. New York: Viking Press, 1965.
On Violence. New York: Harcourt, Brace, and World, 1970.

Babcock, Barbara Allen. "Clara Shortridge Foltz: Constitution-Maker," *Indiana Law Journal* 66:4 (Fall 1991): 849–940.
"Clara Shortridge Foltz: First Woman." *Arizona Law Review* 30:4 (1988): 673–717.

Babcock, Barbara, Freedman, Ann E., Norton, Eleanor Holmes, and Ross, Susan C., eds. *Sex Discrimination and the Law: Causes and Remedies.* Boston: Little, Brown, 1975.

Bailyn, Bernard. *The Ideological Origins of the American Revolution.* Cambridge, Mass.: Belknap Press, 1967.

Baker, Jean H. *Affairs of Party: The Political Culture of Northern Democrats in the Mid-Nineteenth Century.* Ithaca, N.Y.: Cornell University Press, 1983.

——. "The Ceremonies of Politics: Nineteenth-Century Rituals of National Affirmation." In *A Master's Due: Essays in Honor of David Herbert Donald,* edited by William J. Cooper, Michael F. Holt, and John McCordell, 169–71. Baton Rouge: Louisiana State University Press, 1985.

——. "Deconstructing America." *Reviews in American History* 15:4 (December 1987): 603–608.

Baker, Keith M., ed. *The Political Culture of the Old Regime.* Vol. 1 of *The French Revolution and the Creation of Modern Political Culture.* Oxford: Pergamon Press, 1987.

Baker, Paula. "The Domestication of Politics: Women and American Political Society, 1780–1920." *American Historical Review* 89:3 (June 1984): 620–47.

Bancroft, Hubert Howe [et al.]. *History of California.* 7 vols. San Francisco: History Co. Publishers, 1884–90.

——. *History of the Life of William T. Coleman: A Character Study.* San Francisco: History Co. Publishers, 1891.

——. *Popular Tribunals.* 2 vols. San Francisco: History Co. Publishers, 1887.

Banning, Lance. "Some Second Thoughts on Virtue and the Course of Revolutionary Thinking." In *Conceptual Change and the Constitution,* edited by Terrence Ball and J. G. A Pocock, 194–203. Lawrence: University Press of Kansas, 1988.

Barnhart, Jacqueline Baker. *The Fair but Frail: Prostitution in San Francisco, 1849–1900.* Reno: University of Nevada Press, 1986.

Beale, Howard K. *The Critical Year: A Study of Andrew Johnson and Reconstruction.* New York: Frederick Ungar, 1930.

Bean, Walton. *Boss Ruef's San Francisco: The Story of the Union Labor Party, Big Business, and the Graft Prosecution.* Berkeley: University of California Press, 1952.

Bean, Walton, and Rawls, James J. *California: An Interpretive History.* New York: McGraw-Hill, Book Co. 1988.

Benedict, Michael Les. *A Compromise of Principle: Congressional Republicans and Reconstruction, 1863–1869.* New York: W. W. Norton, 1974.

——. "Preserving the Constitution: The Conservative Basis of Radical Reconstruction." *Journal of American History* 61(1974): 65–90.

Bennion, Sherilyn Cox. "The Pioneer: The First Voice for Women's Suffrage in the West." *Pacific Historian* 25:4 (Winter 1981): 15–21.

Berthoff, Rowland. "Independence and Attachment, Virtue and Interest: From Republican Citizen to Free Enterpriser, 1787–1837." In *Uprooted Americans: Essays to Honor Oscar Handlin,* Boston: Little, Brown, edited by Richard Bushman et al. 1979.

Blassingame, John W. *Black New Orleans, 1860–1880.* Chicago: University of Chicago Press, 1973.

Blau, Joseph L., ed. *Social Theories of Jacksonian Democracy*. Indianapolis: Bobbs-Merrill, 1954.

Blumin, Stuart M. *The Emergence of the Middle Class: Social Experience in the American City, 1760–1900*. New York: Cambridge University Press, 1989.

Boorstin, Daniel. *The Image: A Guide to Pseudo-Events in America*. New York: Atheneum, 1987.

Boyer, M. Christine. *Dreaming the Rational City: The Myth of American City Planning*. Cambridge, Mass.: MIT Press, 1983.

Bridges, Amy. "Becoming American: The Working Classes in the United States before the Civil War." In *Working-Class Formation: Nineteenth-Century Patterns in Western Europe and the United States*, edited by Ira Katznelson and Aristide Zolberg. Princeton, N.J.: Princeton University Press, 1986, 157–96.

A City in the Republic: Antebellum New York and the Origins of Machine Politics. Cambridge: Cambridge University Press, 1984.

Brown, M. Craig, and Halaby, Charles N. "Machine Politics in America, 1870–1945." *Journal of Interdisciplinary History* 17:3 (Winter 1987): 587–612.

Brown, Richard Maxwell. *Strain of Violence: Historical Studies of American Violence and Vigilantism*. New York: Oxford University Press, 1975.

Bryce, James *The American Commonwealth*. 2 vols. London: Macmillan, 1889.

Buckley, Christopher. "The Reminiscences of Christopher Buckley," edited by James H. Wilkins. San Francisco *Bulletin*, 31 August–9 October 1918, 23 December 1918–5 February 1919.

Buechler, Stephen M. *The Transformation of the Woman Suffrage Movement: The Case of Illinois, 1850–1920*. New Brunswick, N.J.: Rutgers University Press, 1986.

Buenker, John D. "Sovereign Individuals and Organic Networks: Political Cultures in Conflict during the Progressive Era." *American Quarterly* 40:2 (June 1988): 187–204.

Buhle, Mari Jo, and Buhle, Paul. *The Concise History of Woman Suffrage*. Urbana: University of Illinois Press, 1978.

Bullough, William R. *The Blind Boss and His City: Christopher Augustine Buckley and Nineteenth-Century San Francisco*. Berkeley: University of California Press, 1979.

Bulmer, Martin. *The Chicago School of Sociology: Institutionalization, Diversity, and the Rise of Sociological Research*. Chicago: University of Chicago Press, 1984.

Burchell, Robert A. *The San Francisco Irish, 1848–1880*. Berkeley: University of California Press, 1980.

Burnham, Walter Dean. "The Changing Shape of the American Political Universe." *American Political Science Review* 54 (March 1965): 7–28.

Critical Elections and the Mainsprings of American Politics. New York: W. W. Norton, 1970.

Presidential Ballots, 1836–1892. New York: Arno Press, 1976.

"The System of 1896: An Analysis." In *The Evolution of American Electoral Systems*, edited by Paul Kleppner, Walter D. Burnham, Ronald P. Formisano, Samuel P. Hays, Richard Jensen, and William G. Shade, 47–202. Westport, Conn. 1981.

Calhoun, Craig, ed., *Habermas and the Public Sphere*. Cambridge, Mass.: MIT Press, 1992.

Callow, Alexander B., Jr. "San Francisco's Blind Boss." *Pacific Historical Review* 25 (August 1956): 261–79.

The Tweed Ring. New York: Oxford University Press, 1966.

Camarillo, Albert. *Chicanos in California*. San Francisco: Boyd and Fraser, 1984.

Campbell, Angus. "Surge and Decline: A Study of Electoral Change." In *Elections and the Political Order*, edited by Angus Campbell, Philip E. Converse, Warlen E. Miller, and Donald E. Stokes, 42–3. New York: John Wiley and Sons, 1966.

Carlyle, Thomas. *On Heroes, Hero Worship, and the Heroic in History*. London: Chapman and Hall, 1872.

Carnes, Mark C. "Middle-Class Men and the Solace of Fraternal Ritual." In *Meanings for Manhood: Constructions of Masculinity in Victorian America*, edited by Mark C. Carnes and Clyde Griffen, 37–52. Chicago: University of Chicago Press, 1990.

Caughey, John Walton. *California*. 2 ed. Englewood Cliffs, N.J.: Prentice-Hall, 1953.

Ceplair, Larry, ed. *Charlotte Perkins Gilman: A Nonfiction Reader*. New York: Columbia University Press, 1991.

Chan, Sucheng. *Asian Americans: An Interpretive History*. Boston: Twayne Publishers, 1991.

Chandler, Robert J. "'Anti-Coolie Rabies': The Chinese Issue in California Politics in the 1860s." *The Pacific Historian* (Spring 1984): 29–42.

"Friends in Time of Need: Republicans and Black Civil Rights in California during the Civil War." *Arizona and the West* 24 (Winter 1982): 320–7.

Chinn, Thomas W., ed. *A History of the Chinese in California: A Syllabus*. San Francisco: Chinese Historical Society of America, 1969.

Clark, John Bates. "How to Deal with Communism." *New Englander* 37 (July 1878): 533–42.

Clubb, Jerome M., Flanigan, William H., and Zingale, Nancy H. *Analyzing Electoral History: A Guide to the Study of American Voter Behavior*. Beverly Hills: Sage Publications, 1981.

Partisan Realignment: Voters, Parties, and Government in American History. Beverly Hills: Sage Publications, 1980.

Cmiel, Kenneth. *Democratic Eloquence: The Fight over Popular Speech in Nineteenth-Century America*. New York: William Morrow and Co., 1990.

Coleman, William T. "San Francisco Vigilance Committees: By the

Chairman of the Committees of 1851, 1856, and 1877." *Century Magazine* 43 (November, 1891): 133–50.

[Coleman, William T.]. "The Vigilantes of '56: William T. Coleman's Record of the Early Days, The Secret Archives of a Moral Earthquake ... " San Francisco *Morning Call*, 20 April 1884.

Coman, Katherine. "The South Park Settlement, San Francisco." *The Commons* 8 (August 1903): 7–9.

Cott, Nancy. *The Bonds of Womanhood: 'Woman's Sphere' in New England, 1780–1835*. New Haven: Yale University Press, 1977.

⎯⎯⎯ *The Grounding of Modern Feminism*. New Haven: Yale University Press, 1987.

Coville, Samuel. *San Francisco City Directory for the Year Commencing October, 1856*. San Francisco: Commercial Steam Press, 1856.

Cronin, Bernard Cornelius. "Father Yorke and the Labor Movement in San Francisco, 1900–1910." *The Catholic University of America Studies in Economics*. Vol. 12. Washington, D.C.: Catholic University of America Press, 1943.

Cross, Ira B. *Financing an Empire: History of Banking in California*. 2 vols. Chicago and San Francisco: S. J. Clarke Publishing Company, 1927.

⎯⎯⎯ *A History of the Labor Movement in California*. Berkeley: University of California Press, 1935.

Crunden, Robert M. *Ministers of Reform: The Progressives' Achievement in American Civilization, 1889–1920*. Urbana: University of Illinois Press, 1984.

Dahl, Robert. *Who Governs?: Democracy and Power in an American City*. New Haven: Yale University Press, 1961.

Dancis, Bruce. "Social Mobility and Class Consciousness: San Francisco's International Workingmen's Association in the 1880s." *Journal of Social History* 11:1 (Fall 1977): 75–98.

Daniels, Roger. *Asian America: Chinese and Japanese in the United States since 1850*. Seattle: University of Washington Press, 1991.

Darnton, Robert. *The Great Cat Massacre and Other Episodes in French Cultural History*. New York: Basic Books, 1984.

Darnton, Robert, and Roche, Daniel, eds. *Revolution in Print: The Press in France, 1775–1800*. (Berkeley: University of California Press in collaboration with the New York Public Library, New York, 1989.

Davis, Allen F. *American Heroine: The Life and Legend of Jane Addams*. New York: Oxford University Press, 1973.

Davis, David Brion. *The Slave Power Conspiracy and the Paranoid Style*. Baton Rouge: Louisiana State University Press, 1969.

Davis, David Brion, ed. *The Fear of Conspiracy: Images of Un-American Subversion from the Revolution to the Present*. Ithaca, N.Y.: Cornell University Press, 1971.

Davis, Winfield J. *History of Political Conventions in California, 1849–1892*. Sacramento: Publications of the California State Library, 1893.

Dawley, Alan. *Class and Community: The Industrial Revolution in Lynn*. Cambridge, Mass.: Harvard University Press, 1976.

Decker, Peter R. *Fortunes and Failures: White Collar Mobility in Nineteenth Century San Francisco.* Cambridge, Mass.: Harvard University Press, 1978.

Deegan, Mary Jo. *Jane Addams and the Men of the Chicago School, 1892–1918* New Brunswick, N.J.: Transaction Books, 1988.

Deegan, Mary Jo, and Burger, John S. "W. I. Thomas and Social Reform: His Work and Writings." *Journal of the Behavioral Sciences* 17 (1981): 114–25.

Degler, Carl N. "American Political Parties and the Rise of the City: An Interpretation." *Journal of American History* 51 (June 1964): 41–59.

At Odds: Women and the Family in America from the Revolution to the Present. New York: Oxford University Press, 1980.

Delmatier, Royce D., McIntosh, Clarence F., and Waters, Earl G. *The Rumble of California Politics: 1848–1970.* New York: John Wiley & Sons, 1970.

D'Emilio, John, and Freedman, Estelle B. *Intimate Matters: A History of Sexuality in America.* New York: Harper and Row, 1988.

Diggins, John Patrick. "Comrades and Citizens: New Mythologies in American Historiography." *American Historical Review* 90 (June 1985): 614–38.

The Lost Soul of American Politics: Virtue, Self-Interest, and the Foundations of Liberalism. New York: Basic Books, 1984.

"The Misuses of Gramsci." *Journal of American History* 75:1 (June 1988): 141–5.

Dilts, Bryan Lee, ed. *1860 California Census Index.* Salt Lake City: Index Publishers, 1984.

Diner, Steven J. *A City and Its Universities: Public Policy in Chicago, 1892–1919.* Chapel Hill: University of North Carolina Press, 1980.

Donovan, Josephine *Feminist Theory: The Intellectual Traditions of American Feminism.* New York: Frederick Ungar Publishing Co., 1985.

Dreyfus, Hubert L., and Rabinow, Paul. *Michel Foucault: Beyond Structuralism and Hermeneutics.* 2d ed. Chicago: University of Chicago Press, 1982.

DuBois, Ellen Carol. *Feminism and Suffrage: The Emergence of an Independent Women's Movement in America, 1848–1869.* Ithaca N.Y.: Cornell University Press, 1978.

"Outgrowing the Compact of the Fathers: Equal Rights, Woman Suffrage, and the United States Constitution, 1820–1878." *Journal of American History* 74:3 (December 1987): 836–62.

Durand, E. Dana. *Council Government versus Mayor Government.* Boston: Athenaeum Press, 1900. (Reprinted from *Political Science Quarterly* 15:3 and 4.)

Duverger, Maurice. *Political Parties: Their Organization and Activity in the Modern State.* Translated by Barbara North and Robert North. New York: Science Editions, 1963.

Eaves, Lucile. *A History of California Labor Legislation with an Introductory Sketch of the San Francisco Labor Movement.* Berkeley: University of California Press, 1910.

Einhorn, Robin L. "The Civil War and Municipal Government in Chicago." In *Toward a Social History of the American Civil War: Exploratory Essays*, edited by Maris A. Vinovskis, 117–38. New York: Cambridge University Press, 1990.

  Property Rules: Political Economy in Chicago, 1833–1872. Chicago: University of Chicago Press, 1991.

Ely, Geoff, and Nield, Keith. "Why Does Social History Ignore Politics?" *Social History* 5:2 (May, 1980): 249–71.

Emerson, R. W. *Representative Men: Seven Lectures*. Boston: Phillips, Sampson, and Co., 1850.

Engerman, Stanley. "Up or Out: Social and Geographic Mobility in the United States." *Journal of Interdisciplinary History* 3 (Winter 1975): 469–89.

Ethington, Philip J. "Hypotheses from Habermas: Notes on Reconstructing American Political and Social History, 1890–1920." *Intellectual History Newsletter* 16 (1992): 21–40.

  "Recasting Urban Political History: Gender, the Public, the Household, and Political Participation in Boston and San Francisco during the Progressive Era." *Social Science History* 16:2 (Summer 1992): 301–333.

  "Vigilantes and the Police: The Creation of a Professional Police Bureaucracy in San Francisco, 1847–1900." *Journal of Social History* 21:2 (Winter 1987): 197–228.

Faragher, John Mack. *Sugar Creek: Life on the Illinois Prarie*. New Haven and London: Yale University Press, 1986.

Fehrenbacher, Don E. "The Origins and Purpose of Lincoln's 'House-Divided' Speech." *Mississippi Valley Historical Review* 46:4 (March 1960): 615–43.

  Slavery, Law, and Politics: The Dred Scott Case in Historical Perspective. Oxford: Oxford University Press, 1981.

Fields, Barbara J. "Ideology and Race in American History." In *Region, Race, and Reconstruction: Essays in Honor of C. Vann Woodward*, edited by J. Morgan Kousser and James M. McPherson, 143–77. New York: Oxford University Press, 1982.

Fink, Leon. The New Labor History and the Powers of Historical Pessimism: Consensus, Hegemony, and the Case of the Knights of Labor." *Journal of American History* 75:1 (June 1988): 115–136.

  "Politics as Social History: A Case Study of Class Conflict and Political Development in Nineteenth-Century New England." *Social History* 7:1 (January 1982): 57–8.

  Workingmen's Democracy: The Knights of Labor and American Politics. Urbana: University of Illinois Press, 1983.

Finley, M. I. *Politics in the Ancient World*. Cambridge: Cambridge University Press, 1983.

Flexner, Eleanor. *Century of Struggle: The Woman's Rights Movement in the United States*. Cambridge, Mass: Belknap Press, 1976.

Foner, Eric. *Free Labor, Free Soil, Free Men: The Ideology of the Republican Party Before the Civil War.* New York: Oxford University Press, 1970.

Reconstruction: America's Unfinished Revolution, 1863–1877. New York: Harper and Row, 1988.

Foner, Philip S. *History of the Labor Movement in the United States.* Vol. 1. New York: International Publishers, 1947.

Formisano, Ronald P. "Federalists and Republicans: Parties, Yes – System, No." In *The Evolution of American Electoral Systems*, edited by Paul Kleppner et al. Westport, Conn., 1981.

The Transformation of Political Culture: Massachusetts Parties, 1790–1840's. New York: Oxford University Press, 1983.

Foucault, Michel. *Discipline and Punish: The Birth of the Prison.* Translated by Alan Sheridan. New York: Vintage Books, 1979.

The Order of Things: An Archaeology of the Human Sciences. New York: Vintage Books, 1970.

Fredrickson, George M. *The Black Image in the White Mind: The Debate on Afro-American Character and Destiny, 1817–1914.* New York: Harper Torchbooks, 1971.

The Inner Civil War: Northern Intellectuals and the Crisis of the Union. New York: Harper and Row, 1965.

Frisch, Michael H. *Town into City: Springfield, Massachusetts and the Meaning of Community, 1840–1880.* Cambridge, Mass.: Harvard University Press, 1972.

"Urban Theorists, Urban Reform, and American Political Culture in the Progressive Period." *Political Science Quarterly* 97:1 (Spring, 1982): 295–315.

Frisch, Michael H., and Walkowitz, Daniel J., eds, *Working-Class America: Essays on Labor, Community, and American Society.* Urbana: University of Illinois Press, 1983.

Fritz, Christian G. "Politics and the Courts: The Struggle over Land in San Francisco 1846–1866." *Santa Clara Law Review* 26:1 (Winter 1986): 127–64.

Fritzsche, Bruno. "San Francisco 1846–1848: The Coming of the Land Speculator." *California Historical Quarterly* 51:1 (Spring 1972): 17–34.

Gallman, J. Matthew. *Mastering Wartime: A Social History of Philadelphia during the Civil War.* New York: Cambridge University Press, 1990.

Geertz, Clifford. *The Interpretation of Cultures.* New York: Basic Books, 1973.

Genovese, Eugene D. *Roll, Jordan, Roll: The World the Slaves Made.* New York: Vintage, 1972.

Genovese, Eugene, and Fox-Genovese, Elizabeth. "The Political Crisis of Social History: A Marxian Perspective." *Journal of Social History* 10 (Winter 1976): 205–20.

George, Henry. "The Kearney Agitation in California." *Popular Science Monthly* 107 (August 1880), pp. 433–53.

Giddens, Anthony. *The Constitution of Society: Outline of the Theory of Structuration.* Berkeley: University of California Press, 1984.

"Structuralism, Post-structuralism, and the Production of Culture." In *Social Theory and Modern Sociology*, edited by Anthony Giddens, 73–108. Stanford, Calif.: Stanford University Press, 1987.

Gienapp, William E. "'Politics Seem to Enter into Everything': Political Culture in the North, 1840–1860." In *Essays on American Antebellum Politics, 1840–1860*, edited by Stephen E. Maizlish and John J. Kushma, 15–69. College Station: Texas A & M University Press, 1982.

Gilkeson, John S., Jr. *Middle-Class Providence, 1820–1940.* Princeton, N.J.: Princeton University Press, 1986.

[Gilman], Charlotte Perkins Stetson. *In This Our World.* Oakland, Calif.: McCombs and Vaughn, 1893.

Gilmore, Michael T. *American Romanticism and the Marketplace.* Chicago: University of Chicago Press, 1985.

Glaab, Charles N., and Brown, A. Theodore, eds. *A History of Urban America.* 3d ed. New York: Macmillan Publishing Co., 1983.

Gonnaud, Maurice. *An Uneasy Solitude: Individual and Society in the Work of Ralph Waldo Emerson.* Translated by Lawrence Rosenwald. 1964; Princeton, N.J.: Princeton University Press, 1987.

Goodnow, Frank J. *Municipal Home Rule: A Study in Administration.* New York: Macmillan, 1895.

Goodwyn, Lawrence. *The Populist Moment: A Short History of the Agrarian Revolt in America.* New York: Oxford University Press, 1978.

Gordan, John D., III. *Authorized By No Law: The San Francisco Committee of Vigilance and the United States Circuit Court for the Districts of California.* Pasadena: Ninth Judicial Court Historical Society, 1987.

Graybar, Lloyd J. *Albert Shaw of the* Review of Reviews: *An Intellectual Biography.* Lexington: University Press of Kentucky, 1974.

Greenberg, Kenneth S. *Masters and Statesmen: The Political Culture of American Slavery.* Baltimore: Johns Hopkins University Press, 1985.

"The Nose, the Lie, and the Duel in the Antebellum South." *American Historical Review* 95:1 (February 1990): 57–74.

Grivas, Theodore. "Alcalde Rule: The Nature of Local Government in Spanish and Mexican California." *California Historical Society Quarterly* 40:1 (March 1961):11–32.

Gutman, Herbert. "Trouble on the Railroads in 1873–1874: Prelude to the 1877 Crisis?" In Gutman, *Work, Culture and Society in Industrializing America*, 295–320.

Work, Culture and Society in Industrializing America: Essays in American Working-Class and Social History. Oxford: Basil Blackwell, 1977.

Habermas, Jürgen. "Hannah Arendt's Communications Concept of Power." *Social Research* 44 (Spring 1977): 3–24.

"The Public Sphere." *New German Critique* 1:3 (Fall 1974): 49–55.

The Structural Transformation of the Public Sphere: An Inquiry into a Category of Bourgeois Society. Translated by Thomas Burger. Cambridge, Mass.: MIT Press, 1989.

The Theory of Communicative Action. 2 vols. Cambridge: Polity Press, 1985–6.

Hahn, Steven. *Roots of Southern Populism: Yeomen Farmers and the Transformation of the Georgia Upcountry, 1850–1890.* New York: Oxford University Press, 1983.

Hammack, David. *Power and Society: Greater New York at the Turn of the Century.* New York: Columbia University Press, 1987.

Hammond, Bray. "The North's Empty Purse, 1861–1862." *American Historical Review* 68 (October 1961): pp. 1–18.

Hanagan, Michael. "Response to Sean Wilentz, 'Against Exceptionalism: Class Consciousness and the American Labor Movement, 1790–1920.'" *International Labor and Working Class History* 26 (Fall 1984): 31–6.

Handlin, Oscar. *Boston's Immigrants.* Rev. and enl. Cambridge, Mass.: Belknap Press of Harvard University Press, 1979.

"The Modern City as Field of Historical Study." In *American Urban History*, edited by Alexander B. Callow, Jr., 7–25. New York: Oxford University Press, 1969.

Harris, Joseph P. *Election Administration in the United States.* Washington, D.C.: The Brookings Institution, 1934.

Registration of Voters in the United States. Washington, D.C.: The Brookings Institution, 1929.

Hawkes, Terence. *Structuralism and Semiotics.* Berkeley and Los Angeles: University of California Press, 1977.

Hay, John. *The Bread-Winners: A Social Study.* New York: Harper and Bros., 1884.

Hayden, Dolores. *The Grand Domestic Revolution: A History of Feminist Designs for American Homes, Neighborhoods, and Cities.* Cambridge, Mass.: MIT Press, 1981.

Hayne, James Henry. "Socialistic and Other Assassinations." *Atlantic Monthly* 46 (October 1880): 466–75.

Hays, Samuel P. "The Changing Political Structure of the City in Industrial America." *Journal of Urban History* 1:1 (November. 1974): 6–38.

"The Politics of Reform in Municipal Government in the Progressive Era." *Pacific Northwest Quarterly* 55 (1964): 157–69.

City at the Point: Essays on the Social History of Pittsburgh. Pittsburgh: University of Pittsburgh Press, 1989.

Hearst, William Randolph. "Pacific Coast Journalism." *Overland Monthly* 2 ser., vol. 2 (April 1888): 402–403.

Heizer, Robert F., and Almquist, Alan J. *The Other Californians: Prejudice and Discrimination under Spain, Mexico, and the United States to 1920.* Berkeley: University of California Press, 1971.

Herlihy, David Joseph. "Battle against Bigotry: Father Peter C. Yorke and the American Protective Association, 1893–1897." *Record of the American Catholic Historical Society of Philadelphia* 62:2 (June 1951): 95–120.

Hill, Mary A. *Charlotte Perkins Gilman: The Making of a Radical Feminist, 1860–1896*. Philadelphia; Temple University Press, 1980.

Hittell, John S. *A History of the City of San Francisco and Incidentally of the State of California*. San Francisco: A. L. Bancroft and Co., 1878.

Hittell, Theodore H. *Codes and Statutes of California*. 2 vols. San Francisco: A. L. Bancroft and Co., 1876.

———. *History of California*. 4 vols. San Francisco, 1885–1897.

Hofstadter, Richard. *Age of Reform: From Bryan to FDR*. New York: Vintage, 1955.

———. *The Idea of a Party System: The Rise of Legitimate Opposition in the United States, 1780–1840*. Berkeley: University of California Press, 1969.

Holt, Michael F. "The Antimasonic and Know Nothing Parties." In *History of United States Political Parties*, edited by Arthur M. Schlesinger, Jr., 2 vols., vol. 1, 575–620. New York: Chelsea House Publishers, 1973.

———. *Political Crisis of the 1850's*. New York: John Wiley and Sons, 1978.

———. "The Politics of Impatience: The Origins of Know-Nothingism." *Journal of American History* 60 (1973): 309–31.

Hopkins, Ernest Jerome, comp. and ed. *The Ambrose Bierce Satanic Reader: Selections from the Invective Journalism of the Great Satarist*. Garden City, N.Y.: Doubleday & Co., 1968.

Howe, Daniel Walker. *The Political Culture of the American Whigs*. Chicago: University of Chicago Press, 1979.

———. ed., *The American Whigs: An Anthology*. New York: John Wiley & Sons, 1973.

Hurt, Peyton. "The Rise and Fall of the Know Nothing Order in California." *California Historical Society Quarterly* [two parts] 9:1 (March 1930): 16–48 and 9:2 (June 1930): 99–128.

Issel, William. "'Citizens Outside Government': Business and Urban Policy in San Francisco and Los Angeles, 1890–1932." *Pacific Historical Review* 58 (May 1988): 117–46.

———. "Class and Ethnic Conflict in San Francisco Political History: The Reform Charter of 1898." *Labor History* 18 (1977): 341–59.

Issel, William, and Cherny, Robert W. *San Francisco, 1865–1932: Politics, Power, and Urban Development*. Berkeley: University of California Press, 1986.

James, Henry Ammon. *Communism in America*. New York: Henry Holt and Co., 1879.

James, William *Pragmatism and the Meaning of Truth*. Cambridge, Mass.: Harvard University Press, 1975.

Jensen, Richard. *The Winning of the Midwest: Social and Political Conflict, 1888–1896*. Chicago, 1971.

Johnson, David A. "Vigilance and the Law: The Moral Authority of Popular Justice in the Far West." *American Quarterly* 33:5 (Winter 1981): 558–86.

Joll, James. *The Anarchists.* New York: Grosset & Dunlap, 1964.

Jones, Gareth Stedman. *Languages of Class: English Working Class History, 1832–1982.* Cambridge: Cambridge University Press, 1983.

Kahn, Judd. *Imperial San Francisco: Politics and Planning in an American City, 1897–1906.* Lincoln: University of Nebraska Press, 1979.

Katz, Michael, Doucet, Michael, and Stern, Mark. *The Social Organization of Early Industrial Capitalism.* Cambridge, Mass., 1982.

Katznelson, Ira. *City Trenches: Urban Politics and the Patterning of Class in the United States.* Chicago: Univerity of Chicago Press, 1981.

Katznelson, Ira, and Weir, Margaret. *Schooling for All: Class, Race and the Decline of the Democratic Ideal.* New York: Basic Books, 1985.

Kauer, Ralph. "The Workingmen's Party of California." *Pacific Historical Quarterly* 13 (1944): 278–91.

Kazin, Michael. *Barons of Labor: The San Francisco Building Trades and Union Power in the Progressive Era.* Urbana: University of Illinois Press, 1987.

"The Great Exception Revisited: Organized Labor and Politics in San Francisco and Los Angeles, 1870–1940." *Pacific Historical Review* 55:3 (August 1986): 371–402.

"Prelude to Kearneyism: The July Days in San Francisco, 1877." *New Labor Review* 3 (June 1980): 5–47.

"Struggling with Class Struggle: Marxism and the Search for a Synthesis of US Labor History." *Labor History* 28:4 (Fall 1987): 497–514.

Keller, Morton. *Affairs of State: Public Life in Late Nineteenth-Century America.* Cambridge, Mass.: Harvard Univsersity Press, 1977.

Kelly, Martin. "Martin Kelly's Story." San Francisco *Bulletin*, 1 September to 26 November 1917.

Kerber, Linda. *Women of the Republic: Intellect and Ideology in Revolutionary America.* Chapel Hill: University of North Carolina Press, 1980.

Kingsdale, Jon. "'The Poor-Man's Club': Social Functions of the Urban Working-Class Saloon." *American Quarterly* 25 (October 1973): 472–3.

Kleppner, Paul. "Politics without Parties: The Western States, 1900–1984." In *The Twentieth-Century West; Historical Interpretations* edited by Gerald Nash and Richard Etulian. Albuquerque: University of New Mexico Press, 1989, 295–338.

The Third Electoral System, 1853–1892: Parties, Voters, and Political Cultures. Chapel Hill, N.C., 1979.

"Voters and Parties in the Western States, 1876–1900." *Western Historical Quarterly* 14 (January 1983): 49–68.

Who Voted?: The Dynamics of Electoral Turnout, 1870–1900. New York: Praeger, 1982.

Kloppenberg, James T. *Uncertain Victory: Social Democracy and Progressivism in European and American Thought, 1870–1920.* New York: Oxford University Press, 1986.

"The Virtues of Liberalism: Christianity, Republicanism, and Ethics in Early American Political Discourse." *Journal of American History* 74:1 (June 1987): 9–33.

Knapp, Adeline. "San Francisco and the Civic Awakening." *Arena* 12 (March–May 1895): 241–9.

Kolko, Gabriel. *Wealth and Power in America: An Analysis of Social Class and Income Distribution.* New York: Praeger, 1962.

Kousser, J. Morgan. *The Shaping of Southern Politics: Suffrage Restriction and the Establishment of the One-Party South, 1880–1910.* New Haven and London: Yale University Press, 1974.

Kraditor, Aileen. *The Ideas of the Woman Suffrage Movement, 1890–1920.* New York: Columbia University Press, 1965.

Kurzweil, Edith. *The Age of Structuralism: Levi-Strauss to Foucault.* New York: Columbia University Press, 1980.

Lane, Anne Wintermute, and Wall, Louis Herrick, eds. *The Letters of Franklin K. Lane: Personal and Political.* Boston and New York: Houghton Mifflin Co., 1922.

Lane, Roger. *Violent Death in the City: Suicide, Accident, and Murder in Nineteenth-Century Philadelphia.* Cambridge, Mass.: Harvard University Press, 1979.

Langley, Henry G. *San Francisco Directory.* San Francisco: Henry G. Langley, Publisher, 1860–80.

Lasch, Christopher. *The New Radicalism in America, 1889–1963: The Intellectual as a Social Type.* New York: Alfred A. Knopf, 1965.

——— ed. *The Social Thought of Jane Addams.* Indianapolis: Bobbs Merrill, 1965.

Laurie, Bruce. *Working People of Philadelphia, 1800–1850.* Philadelphia: Temple University Press, 1980.

Lazarow, Jama. "'The Workingmen's Hour': The 1886 Labor Uprising in Boston." *Labor History* 21:2 (Spring 1980): 207–208.

Lee, Eugene C., and Keith, Bruce E. *California Votes, 1960–1972: A Review and Analysis of Registration and Voting.* Berkeley: Institute of Government Studies, University of California, 1974.

Levine, Lawrence W. *Highbrow / Lowbrow: The Emergence of Cultural Hierarchy in America.* Cambridge, Mass: Harvard University Press, 1988.

Levine, Susan. "Labor's True Woman: Domesticity and Equal Rights in the Knights of Labor." *Journal of American History* 70 (September 1983): 323–39.

Littlefield, Roy Everett, III. *William Randolph Hearst: His Role in American Journalism.* Lanham, Md.: University Press of America, 1980.

Lotchin, Roger. *San Francisco, 1846–1856: From Hamlet to City.* New York: Oxford University Press, 1974.

Lothrop, Gloria Ricci, and Jensen, Joan M. *California Women: A History.* San Francisco: Boyd and Fraser, 1987.

Lowi, Theodore J. "American Business, Public Policy, Case-Studies, and Political Theory." *World Politics* 16:4 (July 1964): 677–715.

Luckingham, Bradford. "Immigrant Life in Emergent San Francisco." *Journal of the West* 12:4 (October 1973): 600–17.

Lundberg, Ferdinand. *Imperial Hearst: A Social Biography*. With a preface by Dr. Charles A. Beard. New York: Equinox Press, 1936.

Maier, Pauline. *The Old Revolutionaries: Political Lives in the Age of Samuel Adams*. New York: Knopf, 1980.

Marberry, M. M. *The Golden Voice: A Biography of Isaac Kalloch*. New York: Farrar, Straus and Co., 1947.

March, James G., and Olsen, Johan P. "The New Institutionalism: Organizational Factors in Political Life." *American Political Science Review* 78 (1984): 734–49.

Marx, Karl. *Surveys from Exile*. Edited by David Fernbach. New York: Vintage Books, 1974.

Marx, Karl, and Engels, Frederick. *Letters to Americans, 1848–1895: A Selection*. Edited by Alexander Tractenberg. Translated by Leonard E. Mins. New York: International Publishers, 1953.

Masur, Louis P. *Rites of Execution: Capital Punishment and the Transformation of American Culture, 1776–1865*. New York: Oxford University Press, 1989.

Matthews, Glenna. *The Rise of Public Woman: Woman's Power and Place in the United States, 1630–1970*. New York: Oxford University Press, 1992.

Mayer, Arno J. "The Lower Middle Class as Historical Problem." *Journal of Modern History* 47 (1975): 409–36.

McCormick, John. "Emerson's Theory of Human Greatness." *New England Quarterly* 26 (September 1953): 290–314.

McCormick, Richard L. *From Realignment to Reform: Political Change in New York State, 1893–1910*. Ithaca, N.Y.: Cornell University Press, 1981.

The Party Period and Public Policy: American Politics from the Age of Jackson to the Progressive Era. New York: Oxford University Press, 1986.

"The Realignment Synthesis in American History." *Journal of Interdisciplinary History* 13:1 (Summer 1982): 85–105.

"Restoring Politics to Political History." *Journal of Interdisciplinary History* 12:4 (Spring 1982): 569–95.

"The Social Analysis of American Political History – After Twenty Years." In McCormick, *The Party Period and Public Policy*, 137–38.

"Walter Dean Burnham and 'The System of 1896'" *Social Science History* 10:3 (Fall 1986): 245–62.

McCoy, Drew R. *The Elusive Republic: Political Economy in Jeffersonian America*. Chapel Hill: University of New Carolina Press, 1980.

McCrary, George W. *A Treatise on the American Law of Elections*. 4th ed. Edited by Henry L. McCune. Chicago: Callaghan & Co., 1897.

McDonald, Terrence J. *The Parameters of Urban Fiscal Policy: Socioeconomic Change and Political Culture in San Francisco, 1860–1906*. Berkeley: University of California Press, 1986.

"The Problem of the Political in Recent American Urban History:

Liberal Pluralism and the Rise of Functionalism." *Social History* 10:3 (October 1985): 323–45.

McDonald, Terrence J., and Ward, Sally K., eds., *The Politics of Urban Fiscal Policy*. Beverly Hills: Sage Publications, 1984.

McGerr, Michael E. *The Decline of Popular Politics: The American North, 1865–1928*. New York: Oxford University Press, 1986.

McGowan, Edward. *Narrative of Edward McGowan: Including a Full Account of the Author's Adventures and Perils, While Being Persecuted by the San Francisco Vigilance Committee of 1856*. San Francisco: Published by the Author, 1857.

McKitrick, Eric L. *Andrew Johnson and Reconstruction*. Chicago: University of Chicago Press, 1960.

McLean, Fannie W. "South Park Settlement: Characteristic Work in a San Francisco Neighborhood." *The Commons* 14 (June 1897): 1–3.

McWilliams, Carey. *Southern California: An Island on the Land*. 1946; Salt Lake City: Peregrine Smith Books, 1973.

Melville, Herman. *Moby-Dick: Or, The Whale*. Berkeley: University of California Press, 1979.

Merriam, C. Edward. *Primary Elections: A Study of the History and Tendencies of Primary Election Legislation*. Chicago: University of Chicago Press, 1908.

Merton, Robert K. "The Latent Functions of the Machine." In *Social Theory and Social Structure*, rev. and enl., 71–82. New York: Free Press, 1957.

Mills, C. Wright. *White Collar: The American Middle Classes*. New York: Oxford University Press, 1956.

Mollenkopf, John H. *The Contested City*. Princeton, N. J.: Princeton University Press, 1982.

Monkkonen, Eric. *America Becomes Urban: The Development of Cities and Towns, 1780–1980*. Berkeley: University of California Press, 1988.

Montgomery, David. *Beyond Equality: Labor and the Radical Republicans, 1862–1872*. New York: Knopf, 1972.

———. *The Fall of the House of Labor: The Workplace, the State, and American Labor Activism, 1865–1925*. Cambridge, U.K. and N.Y.: Cambridge University Press, 1987.

———. "Gutman's Nineteenth-Century America." *Labor History* 19 (1978): 416–29.

———. "Labor and the Republic in Industrial America: 1860–1920." *Le mouvement social* no. 111 (avril-juin, 1980): 201–15.

Moore, Barrington, Jr. *Injustice*. White Plains, N.Y.: M. E. Sharpe, 1978.

Morgan, J. Graham. "Courses and Texts in Sociology." *Journal of the History of Sociology* 5 (Spring 1983): 42–65.

———. "Women in American Sociology in the Nineteenth Century." *Journal of the History of Sociology* 2:2 (Spring 1980): 1–34.

Moses, Bernard. "The Establishment of Municipal Government in San Francisco." In *Johns Hopkins Studies in Historical and Political Science*, edited by Herbert Baxter Adams, 7 ser., vols. 1–2 Baltimore, 1889.

Mott, Frank Luther. *American Journalism: A History of Newspapers in the United States Through 260 Years: 1690 to 1950*. Rev. New York: Macmillan Co., 1950.

Mowry, George E. "The California Progressive and His Rationale: A Study in Middle Class Politics." *Mississippi Valley Historical Review* 36 (September 1949): 239–50.

The California Progressives. Chicago: Quadrangle Books, 1963.

Mullen, Kevin J. *Let Justice Be Done: Crime and Politics in Early San Francisco*. Reno: University of Nevada Press, 1989.

Nichols, Roy F., and Berwanger, Eugene H. *The Stakes of Power, 1845–1877*. Rev. New York: Hill and Wang, 1982.

Nicholson, Linda J. *Gender and History: The Limits of Social Theory in the Age of the Family*. New York: Columbia University Press, 1986.

Nord, David Paul. "The Public Community: The Urbanization of Journalism in Chicago." *Journal of Urban History* 11:4 (August 1985): 411–42.

Norton, Anne. *Alternative Americas: A Reading of Antebellum Political Culture*. Chicago: University of Chicago Press, 1986.

Norton, Mary Beth *Liberty's Daughters: The Revolutionary Experience of American Women, 1750–1800*. Boston, 1980.

O'Connor, Richard. *Ambrose Bierce: A Biography*. Boston: Little, Brown and Co., 1967.

Oestreicher, Richard. "Urban Working-Class Political Behavior and Theories of American Electoral Politics, 1870–1940." *Journal of American History* 74:4 (March 1988): 1257–86.

O'Meara, James. *Broderick and Gwin. The Most Extraordinary Contest for a Seat in the Senate of the United States Ever Known: A Brief History of Early Politics in California*. San Francisco: Bacon & Co., 1881.

O'Neill, William L. *Everyone Was Brave: The Rise and Fall of Feminism in America*. Chicago, 1969.

Okin, Susan Moller. *Women in Western Political Thought*. Princeton, N.J.: Princeton University Press, 1979.

Older, Fremont. *My Own Story*. San Francisco: Call Publishing Co., 1919.

Pateman, Carole. *The Sexual Contract*. Stanford, Calif.: Stanford University Press, 1988.

Pateman, Carole. "The Civic Culture: A Philosophic Critique." In *The Civic Culture Revisited: An Analytic Study*, edited by Gabriel A. Almond and Sidney Verba, 57–102. Boston: Little, Brown, 1980.

Peterson, J. A. "The City Beautiful Movement: Forgotten Origins and Lost Meanings." *Journal of Urban History* 2 (August 1976): 415–34.

Piaget, Jean. *Structuralism*. Translated and edited by Chaninah Maschler. New York: Basic Books, 1970.

Pinkerton, Allan. *Strikers, Communists, Tramps, and Detectives*. New York: G. W. Carleton & Co., Publishers, 1878.

Pitt, Leonard. *The Decline of the Californios: A Social History of the Spanish-Speaking Californians, 1846–1890*. Berkeley: University of California Press, 1966.

Pitt-Rivers, Julian. "Honor." In *International Encyclopedia of the Social Sciences*. 18 vols. Edited by David L. Sills, 6:505. New York: MacMillan Co., 1968.

"Honour and Social Status." In *Honour and Shame: The Values of Mediterranean Society*, edited by J. G. Peristiany, 503–10. Chicago: University of Chicago Press, 1966.

Piven, Frances Fox, and Cloward, Richard A. *Why Americans Don't Vote*. New York: Pantheon, 1989.

Pocock, J. G. A. *The Machiavellian Moment: Florentine Political Thought and the Atlantic Republican Tradition*. Princeton, N.J.: Princeton University Press, 1975.

"Virtue, Rights, and Manners: A Model for Historians of Political Thought." In *Virtue, Commerce, and History: Essays on Political Thought and History, Chiefly in the Eighteenth Century*, by J. G. A. Pocock, 37–50. Cambridge: Cambridge University Press, 1985.

Pole, J. R. *American Individualism and the Promise of Progress*. Oxford: Clarendon Press, 1980.

Posner, Russell M. "The Lord and the Drayman: James Bryce vs. Denis Kearney." *The California Historical Society Quarterly* 50:3 (September 1971): 277–84.

Potter, David M. *The Impending Crisis, 1848–1861*. Completed and edited by Don E. Fehrenbacher. New York: Harper and Row, 1976.

Przybyszewski, Linda C. A. "Judge Lorenzo Sawyer and the Chinese: Civil Rights Decisions in the Ninth Circuit." *Western Legal History* 1:1 (Winter/Spring 1988): 23–56.

Ralph, Julian. "California's Great Grievance." *Harper's Weekly* 39 (2 March 1895): 204–7.

"Reform in San Francisco." *Harper's Weekly* 39 (9 March 1895): 230–1.

Richardson, James F. *The New York Police: Colonial Times to 1901*. New York, 1970.

Righter, Robert W. "Washington Bartlett: Mayor of San Francisco, 1883–1887." *Journal of the West* 3:1 (January 1964): 102–13.

Riordan, William L. *Plunkitt of Tammany Hall*. New York: E. P. Dutton, 1963.

Rodecape, Lois Foster. "Tom Maguire, Napoleon of the Stage." [two parts] *California Historical Society Quarterly* 20 (December 1941): 289–96; 21 (September 1942): 239–75.

Rogin, Michael Paul. *The Intellectuals and McCarthy: The Radical Specter*. Cambridge, Mass.: M.I.T. Press, 1967.

Subversive Genealogy: The Politics and Art of Herman Melville. Berkeley: University of California Press, 1985.

Rogin, Michael Paul, and Shover, John L. *Political Change in California: Critical Elections and Social Movements, 1890–1966*. Westport, Conn.: Greenwood Publishing Co., 1970.

Roney, Frank. *Frank Roney: Irish Rebel and California Labor Leader: An Autobio-*

graphy. Edited by Ira B. Cross. Berkeley: University of California Press, 1931.

Ross, Edward A. *Social Control: A Study in the Foundations of Order.* New York: Macmillan, 1901.

Ross, Steven J. "The Politicization of the Working Class: Production, Ideology, Culture and Politics in Late Nineteenth-Century Cincinnati." *Social History*: 2 (May 1986): 171–95.

Workers on the Edge: Work, Leisure, and Politics in Industrializing Cincinnati: 1788–1890. New York: Columbia University Press, 1985.

Royce, Josiah. *California, from the Conquest in 1846 to the Second Vigilance Committee in San Francisco.* Boston: Houghton Miffin Co., 1886; Santa Barbara, Calif.: Peregrine Publishers, Inc., 1970.

Ruef, Abraham. "The Road I Traveled." San Francisco *Bulletin*, 6 April–15 September 1912.

Rusk, Jerrold G. "The American Electoral Universe: Speculation and Evidence." *American Political Science Review* 68 (1974): 1028–49.

"The Effect of the Australian Ballot Reform on Split-Ticket Voting: 1876–1908." *American Political Science Review* 64 (December, 1970): 1220–38.

Ryan, Mary P. *Cradle of the Middle Class: The Family in Oneida County, New York, 1790–1865.* New York: Cambridge University Press, 1981.

Women in Public: Between Banners and Ballots, 1825–1880. Baltimore: Johns Hopkins University Press, 1990.

Salvatore, Nick. *Eugene V. Debs: Citizen and Socialist.* Urbana and Chicago: University of Illinois Press, 1982.

Saxton, Alexander. "George Wilkes: The Transformation of a Radical Ideology." *American Quarterly* 33:4 (Fall 1981): 437–58.

Indispensible Enemy: Labor and the Anti-Chinese Movement in California. Berkeley: University of California Press, 1971.

"San Francisco Labor and the Populist and Progressive Insurgencies." *Pacific Historical Review* 34 (November 1965): 421–38.

Schlesinger, Arthur M. "The City in American Civilization." In Schlesinger, *Paths to the Present*, 210–33. New York: MacMillan, 1949.

Schlesinger, Arthur M., Jr. *The Age of Jackson.* Boston: Little, Brown, and Co., 1945.

Schudson, Michael. *Discovering the News: A Social History of American Newspapers.* New York: Basic Books, 1978.

Schwantes, Carlos A. "The Concept of a Wageworker's Frontier: A Framework for Future Research." *Western Historical Quarterly* 18:1 (January 1987): 39–56.

Scoby, David. "Boycotting the Politics Factory: Labor Radicalism and the New York City Mayoral Election of 1884." *Radical History Review* 28–30 (1984): 280–325.

Scott, Thomas A. "The Recent Strikes." *North American Review* 125 (1877): 351–62.

Senkewicz, Robert M., S.J. "Religion and Non-Partisan Politics in Gold Rush San Francisco." *Southern California Quarterly* 61:4 (Winter 1979): 351–78.

Vigilantes in Gold Rush San Francisco. Stanford, Calif.: Stanford University Press, 1985.

Shalhope, Robert E. "Republicanism and Early American Historiography." *William and Mary Quarterly* 39 (1982): 334–356.

"Toward a Republican Synthesis: The Emergence of an Understanding of Republicanism in American Historiography." *William and Mary Quarterly* 29:1 (January 1972): 49–80.

Sharkey, Robert P. *Money, Class, and Party: An Economic Study of the Civil War and Reconstruction.* Baltimore, 1959.

Shefter, Martin. "Trade Unions and Political Machines: The Organization and Disorganization of the Working Class in the Late Nineteenth Century." In *Working-Class Formation: Nineteenth-Century Patterns in Western Europe and the United States,* edited by Ira Katznelson and Aristide R. Zolberg, 197–276. Princeton, N.J.: Princeton University Press, 1986.

Sherman, William T. "Sherman and the San Francisco Vigilantes: Unpublished Letters of General W. T. Sherman." *Century Magazine* 43 (December 1891): 296–309.

Shinn, Charles Howard. *Mining Camps: A Study in American Frontier Government.* New York: Charles Scribner's Sons, 1885; New York: Alfred L. Knopf, 1948.

Shinn, M[ilicent] W. "Women on School Boards." *Overland Monthly,* n.s. 12 (November 1888): 547–54.

Shortridge, Ray M. "Estimating Voter Participation." In *Analyzing Electoral History: A Guide to the Study of American Voter Behavior,* edited by Jerome M. Clubb, William H. Flanigan, and Nancy H. Zingale, 137–52. Beverly Hills: Sage Publications, 1981.

Shumsky, Neil L. "San Francisco's Workingmen Respond to the Modern City." *California Historical Quarterly* 55:1 (Spring 1976): 46–57.

Silbey, Joel H. *A Respectable Minority: The Democratic Party in the Civil War Era, 1860–1868.* New York: W. W. Norton and Co., 1977.

Skocpol, Theda. "Bringing the State Back In: Strategies of Analysis in Current Research." In *Bringing the State Back In,* edited by Peter B. Evans, Dietrich Reuschemeyer, and Theda Skocpol, New York: Cambridge University Press, 1985.

Skowronek, Stephen. *Building a New American State: The Expansion of National Administrative Capacities, 1877–1920.* Cambridge: Cambridge University Press, 1982.

Smail, John. "New Languages for Labour and Capital: The Transformation of Discourse in the Early Years of the Industrial Revolution." *Social History* 12:1 (January 1987): 49–71.

Small, Albion W., and Vincent, George E. *An Introduction to the Study of Society.* New York: American Book Co., 1894.

Smith-Rosenberg, Carroll. *Disorderly Conduct: Visions of Gender in Victorian America.* New York: Oxford University Press, 1985.

Sombart, Werner. *Why is There No Socialism in the United States?* Translated by Patricia M. Hocking and C. T. Husbands. 1906; London: Macmillan, 1976.

Soulé, Frank, Gihon, John H., and Nisbet, James. *The Annals of San Francisco; Containing a Summary of the History of the First Discovery, Settlement, Progress, and Present Condition of California, and a Complete History of all the Important Events Connected with Its Great City: to which are added, Biographical Memoirs of Some Prominent Citizens.* New York: D. Appleton & Co., 1855.

Spaulding, J. L. "Are We in Danger of Revolution?" *The Forum* 1 (July 1886): 405–15.

Stallard, J. H.. "The Municipal Government of San Francisco." *Overland Monthly,* 2d. ser. 29 (January–June 1897): 44–51; 135–44; 278–89; 386–91; 491–8.

Stambaugh, John E. *The Ancient Roman City.* Baltimore: Johns Hopkins University Press, 1988.

Stanley, Gerald. "Civil War Politics in California." *Southern California Quarterly* 64 (Summer 1982): 115–32.

"Racism and the Early Republican Party: The 1856 Presidential Election in California." *Pacific Historical Review* 43:2 (May 1974): 178.

"Slavery and the Origins of the Republican Party in California." *Southern California Quarterly* 40:1 (Spring 1978): 1–16.

Stanton, Elizabeth Cady, Anthony, Susan B., Gage, Matilda Joslyn, and Harper, Ida Husted eds. *History of Women Suffrage.* 6 vols. New York: [publisher varies], 1881–1922.

Stephenson, Charles. "A Gathering of Strangers? Mobility, Social Structure, and Political Participation in the Formation of Nineteenth-Century American Workingclass Culture." In *American Workingclass Culture: Explorations in American Labor and Social History,* edited by Milton Cantor, 31–60. Westport, Conn.: Greenwood Press, 1979.

Stewart, Robert E., and Stewart, Mary F. *Adolph Sutro: A Biography.* Berkeley, 1962.

Swanberg, W. A. *Citizen Hearst: A Biography of William Randolph Hearst.* New York: Charles Scribner's Sons, 1961.

Swisher, Carl Brent. *Motivation and Technique in the California Constitutional Convention 1878–1879.* Claremont, Calif.: Pomona College, 1930.

Teaford, Jon. "*Finis* for Tweed and Steffens: Rewriting the History of Urban Rule." *Reviews in American History* 10 (1982): 133–49.

The Unhearalded Triumph: City Government in America, 1870–1920. Baltimore: Johns Hopkins University Press, 1984.

Thelen, David P. *The New Citizenship: Origins of Progressivism in Wisconsin.* Columbia: University of Missouri Press, 1972.

"Urban Politics: Beyond Bosses and Reformers." *Reviews in American History* 7: (1979): 406–12.

Thernstrom, Stephan. *The Other Bostonians: Poverty and Progress in the American Metropolis, 1880–1970.* Cambridge, Mass.: Harvard University Press, 1973.

——. *Poverty and Progress: Social Mobility in a Nineteenth Century City.* New York: Atheneum, 1964.

Thornton, J. Mills, III. "Fiscal Policy and the Failure of Radical Reconstruction in the Lower South." In *Region, Race, and Reconstruction: Essays in Honor of C. Vann Woodward,* edited by J. Morgan Kousser and James M. McPherson, 349–94. New York: Oxford University Press, 1982.

——. *Politics and Power in a Slave Society: Alabama, 1800–1860.* Baton Rouge: Louisiana State University Press, 1978.

Tilly, Charles. *The Contentious French.* Cambridge, Mass.: Harvard University Press, 1986.

Tocqueville, Alexis de. *Democracy in America: The Henry Reeve Text as Revised by Francis Bowen and Further Corrected by Phillips Bradley.* Abridged with an Introduction by Thomas Bender. New York: Modern Library, 1981.

Towne, Marian K. "Charlotte Gilman in California." *Pacific Historian* 28:1 (1984): 4–17.

Trachtenberg, Alan. *The Incorporation of America; Culture and Society in the Gilded Age.* New York: Hill and Wang, 1982.

Tygiel, Jules. "'Where Unionism Holds Undisputed Sway': A Reappraisal of San Francisco's Union Labor Party." *California History* 62 (Fall 1983): 196–215.

Verba, Sidney. "Comparative Political Culture." In *Political Culture and Political Development,* edited by Lucian Pye and Sidney Verba, 512–60. Princeton, N.J.: Princeton University Press, 1965.

Walker, Francis Amasa. "The Socialists." *The Forum* 3 (May 1887): 230–42.

Walsh, James P. "Abe Ruef Was No Boss: Machine Politics, Reform, and San Francisco." *California Historical Quarterly* 51:1 (Spring 1872): 3–16.

Warner, Amos G. *American Charities: A Study in Philanthropy and Economics.* New York: Thomas Y. Crowell and Co., 1894.

Warner, Sam Bass, Jr., *The Private City: Philadelphia in Three Periods of Growth.* Philadelphia: University of Pennsylvania Press, 1968.

Weinberg, Julius. *Edward Alsworth Ross and the Sociology of Progressivism.* Madison: State Historical Society of Wisconsin, 1972.

Wiebe, Robert. *The Search for Order, 1877–1920.* New York: Hill and Wang, 1967.

Welter, Barbara. "The Cult of True Womanhood." *American Quarterly* 18 (Summer 1966): 151–74.

White, Hayden. *Tropics of Discourse: Essays in Cultural Criticism.* Johns Hopkins University Press, 1978.

White, Lawrence H., ed., *Democratick Editorials: Essays in Jacksonian Political Economy by William Leggett.* Indianapolis: Liberty Press, 1984.

Wilentz, Sean. "Against Exceptionalism: Class Consciousness and the American Labor Movement, 1790–1920." *International Labor and Working Class History* 26 (Fall 1984): 1–24.

Chants Democratic: New York City and the Rise of the American Working Class, 1788–1850. New York, Oxford University Press, 1984.

Williams, David A. *David C. Broderick: A Political Portrait.* San Marino, Calif.: The Huntington Library, 1969.

Williams, Mary F. *History of the San Francisco Committee of Vigilance of 1851: A Study of Social Control on the California Frontier in the Days of the Gold Rush.* Berkeley: University of California Press, 1921.

Williams, Mary F., ed. *Papers of the San Francisco Committee of Vigilance.* Vol. 3. Berkeley: University of California Press, 1919.

Williams, R. Hal. *The Democratic Party and California Politics 1880–1896.* Stanford, Calif.: Stanford University Press, 1973.

Wilson, William H. "The Ideology, Aesthetics, and Politics of the City Beautiful Movement." In *The Rise of Modern Urban Planning: 1800–1914,* edited by Anthony Sutcliffe, 165–98. London: Mansell, 1980.

Winchell, Alexander. "Communism in the United States." *North American Review* 136 (May 1883): 454–66.

Winkle, Kenneth J. *The Politics of Community: Migration and Politics in Antebellum Ohio.* Cambridge: Cambridge University Press, 1988.

"A Social Analysis of Voter Turnout in Ohio, 1850–1860." *Journal of Interdisciplinary History* 13:3 (Winter 1983): 411–35.

Winkler, John K. *W. R. Hearst: An American Phenomenon.* New York: Simon and Shuster, 1928.

Wood, Gordon. *The Creation of the American Republic, 1776–1787.* New York: W. W. Norton, 1969.

Woodbridge, Sally B., and Waldhorn, Judith Lynch. *Victoria's Legacy.* San Francisco: 101 Productions, 1978.

Woolsey, Ronald C. "Disunion or Dissent?: A New Look at an Old Problem in Southern California Attitudes Toward the Civil War." *Southern California Quarterly.* 66 (Fall 1984): 185–205.

Wright, Doris Marion. "The Making of Cosmopolitan California: An Analysis of Immigration, 1848–1870." [two parts] *California Historical Society Quarterly* 19:4 (December 1940): 323–43 20:1 (March 1941): 65–79.

Wuthnow, Robert, Hunter, James Davidson, Bergeson, Albert, and Kurzweil, Edith. *Cultural Analysis: The Work of Peter L. Berger, Mary Douglas, Michel Foucault, and Jürgen Habermas.* Boston: Routledge and Kegan Paul, 1984.

Wyatt-Brown, Bertram. *Southern Honor: Ethics and Behavior in the Old South.* New York: Oxford University Press, 1982.

Yearley, Clifton K. *The Money Machines: The Breakdown and Reform of Party Finance in the North, 1860–1920.* Albany: State University of New York Press, 1972.

Young, John P. *History of Journalism in San Francisco.* San Francisco: Chronicle Publishing Co. 1915.

Index

Abbott, Grace, 349
abortion, 332
Addams, Jane, 11, 13, 289, 349, 352, 414
African Americans, 29, 31–2; against Chinese, 188; and public sphere, 185–6, 237, 410–1; and civil rights movement during Civil War, 186–8; *see also* newspapers
age, of population, 48–9
agora, 21, 78
Allswang, John, 289
American Protective Association (APA), 324–5, 390, 400
American Railway Union (ARU), 370
American Charities (1894), by Amos G. Warner, 349–50
Anderson, Jerome, 389
Anthony, Susan B., 327, 360, 363, 398
Anti-Boss Club (ABC), 294
Anti-Coolie clubs, 202, 322
APA, *see* American Protective Association
Appleby, Joyce, 247
Archy Lee case, 186–7
Arendt, Hannah, on public and private spheres, 15–6; on authority, 77; on power, 105
ARU, *see* American Railway Union
Australian (secret) ballot, *see* ballots
authority, and agonal struggle among men, 77; and gender, 364; and heroism, 80; and duelling, 81–3; and Vigilance Committee of 1851, 105–6; and Vigilance Committee of 1856, 143–5, 157

Babcock, Barbara Allen, 212
Baker, Ray Stannard, 403
Baker, Paula, 398, 406
Baker, Edward D., pleads for Archy Lee, 187; opposes Vigilance Committee, 137–8; hero to women's rights leaders, 212; founder of California Republican party, 172; funeral oration for Broderick, 178–9;

oratory of, 180–1; dies at Ball's Bluff, 181; racial liberalism of, 184–5
ballot box, significance of for republicanism 117–8; as vaginal symbol, 118; as icon of Vigilante movement, 122, 156; false-bottom, 122; discovery of false-bottom ballot box, by Vigilantes, 134, 140; glass, 219–20; purity of, 225; Australian or "secret", 228, 339–41, 370; law to regulat appearance, 228
ballots, counting, 76; splitting, 76; *see also* election law
Bancroft, Hubert Howe, 28, 90, 93, 105, 154 188
Bank of California, 228–9
Barbour, Judge William T., 196
Bartlett, Washington, 339
Beard, Charles, 410
Belasco, David, 44
Bellamy, Edward (Nationalist Clubs), 355
Bennett, James Gordon, 312, 314
Bentley, Arthur F., 10
Berdue, Thomas, 106–9
bicycle clubs, 366
Bierce, Ambrose, 275, 277, 309, 314, 317
Black, Winifred Sweet "Annie Laurie", 316, 360
Blumin, Stuart, 252
Blunt, Phineus Underwood, 43
Bluxome, Isaac, Jr., 88
Board of Police Commissioners, 376
Board of Election Commissioners, 376
Board of Education, 333
Board of Freeholders, 388–90, 392–4
Bohemian Club, 378
Boorstin, Daniel, 316
Booth, Junius Brutus, 59, 64, 207
Booth, Newton, 257
Booth, Edwin, 59
Booth, John Wilkes, 207
bosses, *see* machines, political

Boston, 26
Bowles, Ada C., 362
boycotts, *see* strikes and boycotts
Brannan, Samuel, 88, 106, 108
Breckinridge, Sophonisba, 349
Bridges, Amy, 249
Brisbane, Arthur "Brainy", 314–15
Brisbane, Albert, 314
Broderick, David C., introduced, 43–4; and
class identity, 57–8; and party organiza-
tion, 67, 116, 119–20, 188; and duelling,
81–2; compared to Cataline, 120; opposi-
tion to Vigilantes, 137–8, 158–9; party
leadership during sectional crisis, 173–7;
on "Slave Power," 174, 177–8; as martyr to
freedom, 183
Broom Rangers, 196
Brown, Richard Maxwell, 90–1
Brown, M. Craig, 27
Bryant, Andrew Jackson, 66–7
Bryant, Colonel J. J., 68–9
Bryce, Lord James, 26, 379
BTC, *see* Building Trades Council
Buckley, Christopher Augustine, 289, 290,
296, 339, 342–3, 373
Budd, Governor James, 376
Building Trades Council (BTC), 215, 365,
415
Bureau of Labor Statistics, 302
Burke, Martin J. (historian), 252
Burke, Dr. Martin J., 128; police chief dur-
ing Civil War, 193; introduces riot control
techniques, 197;
Burnham, Daniel, 381

California State Woman Suffrage Associa-
tion (CWSA), 327, 331–2, 335
Californios, 1; as small part of electorate, 31
n79
Campbell, Helen Stuart, 356, 359, 360
Casey, execution (lynching) of, 131
Casey, James P., 82, 89, 120–1, 139
Cataline (Lucius Sergius Catalina), 86, 110,
120, 148
Central Pacific Railroad, 205; *see also* South-
ern Pacific Railroad (SP), 395
Chamberlain, Sam S., 314
character, 247, 272
Charters, Municipal, Consolidation Act,
1856, 141, 224, 388; of 1896, 387–92; of
1898, 346, 392–8; voting on, 390–2, 415
Chi-square, 423
Chicago, 27, 249, 359, 381
Child Labor bill of 1889, 307

Chinese, and civil rights during Civil War,
187–8; exclusion from citizenship and
public sphere, 31–2, 411; place in
analytical narrative, 36–7; origins of
anti-Chinese movement during Civil
War, 201–5; and political heirarchy, 78;
harrassment ordinances, 255–6; and
C. C. O'Donnell, 322; Chinese Exclusion
Act renewed, 1892, 370
Chit-Chat Club, 378
Cicero, Marcus Tullius, 62, 77, 86–7, 110,
148
Citizen's Charter Association, 389, 393
Citizen's Defense Association, 377
Citizen's Non-Partisan party, 373
city housekeeping, 414
City Hall, 17–18
Civic Federation, 389
civil rights, 32
Civil War, unleashes social revolution, 170;
see also Chivalry Democrats; Douglas
(Free-Soil or Anti-Lecompton) Democrats
class legislation, 306
class, socioeconomic, *see* social class
clergy, and Vigilance Committee of 1856,
152; and Civil War, 190–1; and public
sphere, 240; and American Protective Association, 324–5; and progressivism, 341;
see also Kalloch, Isaac; Scott, William A.;
Yorke, Father Peter C.
Cleveland, Grover, 341, 342
Cmiel, Kenneth, 62
Coast Seamen's Union (CSU), 306, 322, 326
n102, 388
coding, quantitative, 421–3
Coleman, William Tell, introduced, 49; and
Vigilance Committee of 1851, 106–8; hon-
ors David C. Broderick, 127; supports
Broderick's Anti-Lecompton Democrats,
177; leading member of Executive Com-
mittee, 128, 135, 144–5, 166; as McClellan
Democrat in 1864, 195; and reform of
Democratic party in 1890, 343, 373
Colton Letters, 257
community kitchens, 360
confidence interval, 424
Conness, John, 222
Constitution, California, 218; constitutional
convention of 1878–9, 279–81
Coolidge, *see* Smith, Mary Roberts
Cora, Charles, 62; defense of, by Edward D.
Baker, 179; execution (lynching) of, 131
corporate liberalism, 12
corruption, 273; meaning of, 404–5

Cotter, John, 81
crime, rates of, 98; and punishment, 98–9; and vengeance, 104; political 120–4
Crimmins, Phil, 289
Crocker, Charles, 172, as early racial liberal, 184; Central Pacific Railroad magnate, 253
Crunden, Robert, 337, 341
CSU, *see* Coast Seamen's Union
currency and inflation, 193–4
CWSA, *see* California State Woman Suffrage Association

Dashaway Hall, 18
Davis, Jefferson, 190
Dawley, Alan, 264
Day, John G., 267, 280
Day, Benjamin, 312
de Young Charles, 82, 237, murdered, 282
de Young, Michael, 228, 237, 344
de Force, Laura, *see* Gordon, Laura de Force
Decker, Peter R., 90, 92
Democratic party, original organization of, 68; Chivalry wing of Democratic party, 45, 171; Douglas (Free-Soil or Anti-Lecompton) Democrats, 171–2, 173, 188; and George Hearst, 313; reform of, 339, 373
Dempster, Clancy, 142, 152, 155
Dewey, John, 349
Dibble, Henry, 344
Dollar Limit on taxation, 296
domesticity and domestic sphere, 154, 336
Douglas, Stepen A., 173
dual urban political universe, defined, 34–5; and Vigilante-People's regime, 169, 221; and postwar political community, 235–6
Duane, Charles P., 139, 158, 160
duelling, and political authority, 81–3; Broderick-Terry duel, 177–8
DuPuy, John J. R., 72
Durand, E. Dana, 350
Duverger, Maurice, 70–1

Eating House Keepers Association, 306
Eaves, Lucile, 305
eight-hour day, 256, 282–3, 300
Einhorn, Robin, 26–7, 365
El Dorado, 17
election law, in timing of elections, 198, 221, 291; regulation of voting, 220–3; Registry Act of 1866, 223–7; Piece Club act, 229–30, 291; Purity of Elections, 376
elections, 1850s, 166–7; 1859–60, 182–3; 1864–7, 196; 1867–82, 261–4; 1882–90, 292; 1892, 373; 1896, 380; charters of 1896 and 1898, 391–8; on 1896 woman suffrage amendment, 398–401
elective franchise, and citizenship, 225; extent of, 30; and women, 214; constitutional law of, 217–18; and race, 226
electoral fraud, 74–5; as metaphoric rape, 118; in origins of Vigilance Committee of 1856, 117–21
electorate, and Chinese, 31–2; and Mexicans, 31 n79; and women, 32
Ellert, Levi, 323, 373
Ellon, Florence, 385
Ely, Richard T., 356
Emancipation Proclamation, 222
Emerson, Ralph Waldo, 80
Employer's Association, 403
Engineers' and Iron Founders' Association, 306
Enos, John S., 302
equal opportunity clause of constitution, 307
Equal Rights party, or National Equal Rights Party, 328–9
ethnic conflict, in Know-Nothing party, 113–14; in charter reform, 390–8
ethnicity, 33, 49; of membership in Vigilance Committees, 93, 96–7; 319; and Irish Catholics, 324–6; *see also* social groups; Irish Catholics; participation
executions, in penal reform, 99–105; *see also* violence

family, political dimension of, 153, 164–5, 361–2, 369
Federated Trades Council (FTC), 304, 322, 339, 344, 353
Federation of Improvement Clubs, 366, 377
feminism, 356–8; *see also* Gilman, Charlotte Perkins
Fergusen, William, 82
Fetter, Frank, 350, 352
Fields, Barbara J., 201
Fifteenth Amendment, 219
fiscal policy, 165, 296, 365–6
Fitch, George K., 305
Foltz, Clara Shortridge, 212; and "women's lawyer's bill," 216; and Constitutional Convention of 1878–9, 299
Foltz, Clara Shortridge, 326, 327, 331
Forni, José, execution of, 102–3
Forrest, Edwin, plays *Macbeth*, 206–7
Foucault, Michel, 99, 104
Fourteenth Amendment, 253
Fox-Genovese, Elizabeth, 78
franchise, *see* electoral franchise

fraternal societies, 368–9
Fredrickson, George M. 200–1
Freedman's Bureau Bill, 205
Freemasons, 146–7, 321, 368
Frémont, John C. 172, 180, 190
Freud, J. Richard, 371
Friedman, Lawrence M., 99
FTC, see Federated Trades Council

Gallagher, Martin 135
gender, population imbalance of, 47; and
    shape of public sphere, 32, 47, 59–62, 84,
    406, 412; identity, 367–9, 401; in pro-
    gressivism, 385–6, 398; see also feminism,
    masculinity, patriarchy, women
Genovese, Eugene, 78
George, Henry, 254–5, 260, 303, 317, 333; on
    Kearneyism, 284; on machine politics,
    296
Gibbs, John S., 307
Gienapp, William E., 112–13
Gilman, Charlotte Perkins Stetson, 336, 345,
    346, 354–60, 362, 363, 402
Godkin, E. L., on press, 21; on social class,
    282
Gold Rush, 2–6
Golden Gate Park, 364
good, common or public, 6–9; Lincoln on,
    12; and plural, 9 n21; and Romantic re-
    publicanism, 79; single and plural, 84, 410,
    412
Goodnow, Frank, 348, 354
Gordon, Laura de Force, 326–9, 331, 358,
    385; as trance medium, 209–10; and
    "women's lawyer's bill," 216; in Constitu-
    tional Convention of 1878–9, 299; and
    Equal Rights party, 329;
Gordon, George W., 187
gothic genre, 277, 283
Graft Prosecutions, 377, 404
Great Upheaval, 242
groups, see social groups
Gunst, "Mose," 376
Gwin, William M., and party organization,
    67

Habermas, Jürgen, on public sphere, 15–16,
    59
Hager, George, 219
Haight, Henry Huntley, and Chinese, 255;
    on civil liberties, 193–4; free-soil back-
    ground in Missouri, 189; free labor ideol-
    ogy, 190; Legal Tender Acts, 191–2; rejects
    Republican Party, 191–4; Republican
    party leaderhship, 188–9; republicanism

of, 192–4; against Fifteenth Amendment,
    219
Halaby, Charles N. 27
Hallidie, Andrew S., 307
Haltunnen, Karen, 252
Hammack, David, 249
Hanagan, Michael, 26
Handlin, Oscar, 13, 289
Harper, Ida Husted, 350, 398
Harrington, James 6, 55
Hartz, Louis, 410
Haskell, Burnette G., 304, 321, 322
Hastings College of the Law, 341, 361
Hawes, Horace, 224–5
Haxton, H.R., 316
Hay, John, 236
Haynes, Fred E., 353
Hays, Colonel Jack, 68–70
Hays, Samuel P., 289, 295, 336; "Hays
    thesis," 371
health and sanitation, 338
Hearst, William Randolph, 120, 308–9, 312–
    17, 319, 342, 343, 346, 353, 354, 386, 401;
    strategies during new charter campaign,
    395–6, on needs, 402
Hearst, Phoebe Apperson, 353
Hearst, George, 313, 343
Hichborn, Franklin, 350, 354
Higgins, William T. "Bill," 289, 302
Hofstadter, Richard, 289, 410; on pro-
    gressivism, 336
Holt, Michael, 113
home, see household
home ownership, rates of, 365
honor, 77–83, 157–9, see also authority,
    shame
Hoover, Herbert, 350
Hough, Eugene, 356, 370
Hounds (gang), 88
household status, 153, 367
household, political dimension of, 360, 362–
    7, 412
Howard, William D. M., 45
Howe, Frederic, 380
Huntington, Collis P., 172, 375, 396

iconography, see Vigilance Committee of
    1856
immigration, sources of, to San Francicso,
    45–6
individualism, 7; in progressive thought,
    350
infrastructure, 298
institutions, in theory and method, 25
intellectuals, 347–8

International Workingmen's Association (IWA), 304, 321–2

Irish Catholics, and origins of Vigilance Committee, 125–7, 125 n122; exclusion from Vigilante–People's regime, 129, 167; and party realignment of 1859–60, 183; and school reform, 334; and voter registration, 226; and Father Peter C. Yorke, 324–36, 390–1; and James Duval Phelan, 382; and municipal charters of 1896 and 1898, 391–8, 402

Issel, William, 388

IWA, *see* International Workingmen's Association

James, William, 313

Jansen, C. J., 106

Jenkins, John, 88, 108

Jenny Lind Theatre, 18, 59; *see also* Tom Maguire

Johns Hopkins Seminary of History and Politics, 349, 380

Johnson, J. Neely (Governor), 135, 137

Johnson, Hiram, 345, 346, 404

Johnston, George Pen, 82

Joint Committee on Labor Organization, 268–72

Kalloch, Isaac, 19, 237–40, 263; as Workingmen's Party of California mayoral candidate, 281–2

Kansas-Nebraska Act, 171

Kearney, Denis, 265; conception of workingmen, 271–3; class chameleonism of, 274–6; 409; *see also* language

Keith, Mary McHenry, 216–17, 327–8, 361, 378, 385

Keller, Morton, 299

Kelly, Martin, 289, 290

Kelly, Florence, 349

Kennedy, Kate, 333–5

King, James (James King of William), 81–2, 89, 131

King, Thomas Starr, 190

Kloppenberg, James, 13

Knapp, Adeline, 355, 377

Knight, Henry L., 267

Knights of Labor, 242, 304, 322, 329

Know-Nothing (American) party, 112–17

La Follette, Robert, 383

labor unions, *see* trade unions

labor republicanism, 243–4

Labor party, 340

Lake, Delos, 228

LaMotte, Robert S., 66

Lane, Franklin K., 317, 324, 340–1, 345–6, 393

language, Kearney on, 277–8, 315; and violence, 278; and sensational newspapers, 315; multilingual schools, 333

languages, of class and politics, 245–8, 265–6

Lasch, Christopher, 347

Latham, Milton S., 171

Lathrop, Julia, 349

Laurie, Annie, *see* Black, Winifred Sweet

Law and Order Party, leadership of, 137–8

League of the Cross Cadets, 324

Lecompton constitution for Kansas, 173, 175

liberal pluralism, 9–10, 10 n22

liberalism, 5–8; and women's rights, 209–15; *see also* republican liberalism; pluralist liberalism; liberal pluralism; republicanism; natural rights; patriarchy

Lincoln, Abraham, 63, 173, 207, 415

literacy, 19

lobbies, origins and significance of, 301–2

Lockwood, Belva, 328–9

Loco-Foco wing of New York Democratic party, 44

Long Hairs, 196–7, 224

Los Angeles, 381

Lotchin, Roger, 29, 90

Low, Frederick, 197

machines, political, 26–8

McAllister, Hall, 88

Macarthur, Walter, 393

McCabe, James, 61

McClellan, George B., 188

McComas, Charles, 363

McCormick, Richard, 11, 25, 249, 404

McCready, Irene, 61

McDonald, Terrence, 26–7, 30, 379, 406

McGowan, Frank, 363

McGowan, Edward "Ned," 143, 158, 160

McHenry, Mary, *see* Keith, Mary McHenry

Mackay, John W., 314

McKewen, Arthur, 314–15, 386, 395

Madison, James, 11–12, 415

Maguire, James G., 307, 340, 341, 370, 378

Maguire, Tom, 18, introduced, 59; and Shakespearian public sphere, 63–4; and Vigilance Committee of 1856, 159

Maine, Sir Henry, 361

Manufacturers' Association of California, 306–7

marital status, 367

Market Street Railway Company, 298, 396

Markham, Edwin, 355, 356

Markham, Governor Henry H., 376
Martin, Ann, 350
Marx, Karl, 5, 242
masculinity, 210, 368–9, 386, 398
Masur, Louis, 99
matriarchy, *see* patriarchy
mayor, office of, debate on, 393–5
Mead, George Herbert, 349
Mechanic's Pavilion, 19
Mechanic's Assembly, 338
Melville, Herman, 80
Merchant's Association, 371–2, 377, 388, 415
Merton, Robert K., 289
Metropolitan Temple, 376
Mexican-Americans, *see* Californios
Miller, Joaquin, 356
Milliken, Isaac, 405
Mills, W. H., 396
Mission Dolores, 1, 125–6
mobility, geographic, 34–5, 47–8
Moby-Dick, as model of authority, 80
Mollenkopf, John, 338
Montesquieu, Baron de, 6, 55
Montgomery, John, 1, 17
motherhood, 358
Mowry, George, 336
Mulligan, Billy, 135, 139
Muncy, Robin, 13
municipal ownership, 338
Municipal Reform League, 340
Municipal Government, loss of legitimacy of, 141–2
Murray, Hugh C., 32 n81, 49
mutualism, *see* republicanism
Myrdal, Gunnar, 414

Nahl, Charles, 155
Napoleon, Louis, 118
National Household Economics Association, 356 n23
National American Woman Suffrage Association (NAWSA), 399
National Municipal League (NML), 387–8, 405–6
National Woman Suffrage Association (NWSA), 328
natural rights, 212
NAWSA, *see* National Woman Suffrage Association
needs, politics of, 347, 366, 409; in social scientific thought, 348; in new charter of 1898, 395; in journalistic discourse, 402
neighborhood improvement clubs, 365–6
neighborhoods, 297–8, 310, 334–5, 364–5
neoclassicism, 13, 246; and city planning,

381; and Roman practice of banishment, 110–11; in funeral orations, 178–80; 193; of Adolph Sutro, 374; in women's rights movement, 217, 327;
New Left scholarship, 410
New York, 26, 181, 200
newspapers, *Alta California*, 22, 22–3 n59, 317; *Chronicle*, 22, 236–8, 310, 312; *Argonaut*, 275; *Call*, and Woman's Column, 330–1; *Coast Seamen's Journal*, 388, 393; *Democratic Press*, 198; *Echo du Pacifique*, 198; *Elevator* (African American), 186, 188; *Evening Bulletin*, 23, 119–20; *Examiner*, 22–3, 236–8, 310–17; *Franco-Americaine*, 198; *Herald*, 121, 137, 183–4, 202; *Impress* (organ of Pacific Coast Women's Press Association), 356, 362; *Le Matin* (Paris); *Mirror of the Times* (African American), 186; *Monitor* (Catholic), 198, 325, 390; *News-Letter*, 198; *Occidental*, 198; *Pacific Appeal* (African American), 186; *The Pioneer* (women's rights), 211–13; *The Revolution* (women's rights), 211; *Truth*, 322; *Voice of Labor*, 388, 395; *World* (New York), 313–15; *see also* William Randolph Hearst, Charles and Michael de Young, Emily Pitts
newspapers (general), circulation, 20, 310, 319; consumer orientation of reader, 310–13, 316; early development of, 19–20; as enterprises, 23–4; partisanship of, 22; rise of mass commerical journalism, 309–12; sensationalism, 309, 312; and reconstruction of public sphere, 309; and language, 315; muckraking, 309; in new charter campaign, 395–6; *see also* language
NML, *see* National Municipal League
Non-Partisan party, 323
Non-Partisan freeholder ticket, 396
Nord, David Paul, 240–1
Nugent, John, 81, 121, 137, 184

O'Donnell, C.C., 322–4, 334, 373
Older, Fremont, 377, 396
Order of the Star-Spangled Banner, *see* Know Nothing or American party

Pacific Coast Women's Press Association, 355, 359, 385
Palace Hotel, 259
Palóu, Father Francisco, 1
parades, political, May Day, 1854, 118; Vigilante disbandment, 1856, 130–1; during Civil War, 198; eight-hour day, 1867, 250; Denis Kearney leads Thanksgiving Day

Parade, 1877; first Labor Day parade, 1886, 305
Park, Robert, 240–1
participation, political, John Dewey and, 416; long-term patterns in, 33–5; and ethnicity, 233–4; and geographic mobility 30, 34–5; and household status, 367; exclusion and, 417; Habermas and, 416; and social groups, 33–5, 231–3, 390–2, 403; vis-à-vis policy outputs, 38; in Vigilance Committees, 105–11, 140; and working-class, 232–4
parties, political, and Australian ballot, 341–2; disintegration of, in 1855–6, 116–17; contradictions of, in 1880s, 296–9; early organization, 65–7; legitimation crises, 119; and participation, 70–1; realignment (1859–60), 182; as "private" associations, 290; need for money by, 296–8; suspicion of, 66, 168; survival of, in Great Upheaval, 284–6; see also party loyalty; in office, 67; organizational or "machine," sources of power described, 289–90, 294–5; see also primaries, People's party, third party system, 234; independent labor, 249; proliferation of, 250; see also Democratic, Equal Rights, Republican, Workingmen's Party of California, Non-Partisan, People's
party, disloyalty of voters, 66–7, 70, 250
patriarchy, 208, 328, 361–3, 369
patronage, party, 296
People's (Populist) party, 375
People's party (Vigilante-People's), 196–7, 339, 388, course of, 163–7; formation of, 161–2; secret nomination of candidates, 163; legacy of, in policies of progressive era, 388
Peyton, Bailie, 143
Phelan, James Duval, 324, 340, 343, 345, 346, 354, 377; on functions of government, 380–1; misogyny of, 384–6; in new charter campaigns, 390–7; as mayor, 403
Pickering, Loring, 275, 305
Piece Clubs, defined, 229–30
Pierce, Bessie Louise, 249
Pierce, Franklin, 136
Piercy, Charles W., 83
Pingree, Hazen, 375
Pitts, Emily A., 211, 328
Pixley, Frank, 275
Plaza, the (Portsmouth Square), 17–18
pluralist liberalism, 8–9, 14, 39, 317, 346, 408–9, 413
police, established by Vigilante-People's regime, 168–9

political culture, as "script," 15
political public sphere, defined, 17; see public sphere
political entrepreneurship, defined, 338
political community, defined, 29–31; and geographic mobility, 34–5
Pond, E. B., 323, 329
population, growth of, 2, 251
Porter Primary Law of 1866, 290
Portsmouth Square, see Plaza, the
press, central role in public sphere, 19–24; see also newspapers
primary elections, 71–72; laws to regulate, 223; source of power for organizational party leaders, 292–4
print media, see newspapers
privacy, see private sphere
private sphere, 16, 25, 32; lack of, in antebellum San Francisco, 60–1; boundaries of, 62; see also public sphere
progress, as keyword, 209, 366
progressive, as political label, 371–2; as political adjective, 378–9; see also silurian
Progressive Era (1890–1920), 41, 287; interpretations of, 287–8, 336–7; 403–4
progressivism, 41; as discourse, 345–6; misogyny in, 384–6
prostitutes, as surrogate wives and "ladies," 61
public sphere, definition of, 15–17; and communication, 15; exclusion from, 32; and executions, 98; institutions of, 33; and press, 17–24; race and, 84; and space, indoor and outdoor, 17–19; and social settlements, 353–4; theatricality of, 59–60; and women, 16, 211–12; 330, 398–9; reconstruction after Civil War, 241; transformation of, by progressivism, 408–10, 412–16; summary of, 410–11, 412–16; see also, gender, newspapers, press, private sphere,
public city, concept of, 24
public schools, 333–4
public relief, 33
Pulitzer, Joseph, 309, 312, 346
Pullman company, 370

race, 171, 184, 185; and political mobilization, 200, 202–5, 207, 264; and social-group formation, 200–2
racism, 184–5; anti-Chinese, 244; and Workingmen's Party of California, 285; imperial, 382–3
Ralph, Julian, 288

Ralston, William C., 228; disgrace and suicide of, 257–9
Reform Ballot Act (1891), 344, 345, 402
Reform Charter Association, 377
Registry Act of 1866, *see* election law
regression, linear, 424
relative risk estimate, explained, 94, 424
reproduction, relations of, 358–9
republican liberalism, 7–8, 14, 39, 208, 412; and social class, 55; and changes in political understanding, 409
Republican party, organization of, in 1856, 172; support for, 183; and race, 184; ideologies of, 190; in 1880s, 295
republicanism, 6–9, 55–6; as companion of liberalism, 56; and character, 57; death of, 283–4; gothic, 283; as political language, 57, 246–8; and Vigilante ideology, 129; and labor, 194; and mutualism, 156–7; and Workingmen's Party of California, 268–9, 276; *see also* labor republicanism
rhetoric, and public sphere, 62; and class stratification, 63
Richardson, W. H. (U.S. Marshal), 62, 179
Richmond district, 298
Richmond District Improvement Association, 376
Riordan, Archbishop, 324–5
riots, following assassination of Lincoln, 198–9; New York City Draft Riots, 200; anti-Chinese, 244
Rogin, Michael Paul, 277
Rolph, James, Jr., 415
Roman Republic, 13, 77–8, 87, 207
Romantic republicanism, 79; and Civil War, 206; and public executions, 105; and slavery, 174, 180, 184; and race, 184; *see also* republican liberalism, republicanism.
Romanticism, 77–80, 206
Roney, Frank, 280, 286, 302–3, 305, 338
Roosevelt, Theodore, 345, 383, 408
Rosecrans, William, 294
Ross, Reverend Donald, 325–6
Ross, Steven J., 283
Ross, Edward Alsworth, 345–7, 349, 350–2, 354
Royce, Josiah, 61, 90, 154, 313
Royce, Sarah, 61
Ruef, Abraham, 292, 404
Ryan, Arabella, 62
Ryan, Mary, 61, 252
Ryckman, Gerritt, 154, 158

San Francisco Female Hospital, 332

San Francisco Settlement, 352–3; and public sphere, 354
San Francisco Labor Council, 353, 388, 390
San Francisco Liquor Dealers' Association, 399
San Francisco Gaslight Company, 396
San Francisco, founding and U.S. conquest, early development, 1; as site for study of American developments, 14; scholarship on, 28–9
San Francisco Trades Assembly, 302
San Francicso Benevolent Association, 332
Sargent, Ellen Clark, 215, 328, 385, 400
Sargent, Aaron, A. 215, 328
Saxton, Alexander, 201–2
Scheisl, Martin, 405
Schell, Rodney, 187
Schmitz, Eugene, 403, 408
school reform, 334–5
Scott, William A., and Vigilantes, 153; and Civil War, 190–1
Seneca Falls, 209
Senkewicz, Robert, 90
settlement houses, *see* San Francisco Settlement
Shakespeare, William, and rhetoric, 63; on liberty and corruption 65; and theatricality of public sphere, 64–5; *Henry VIII*, 148; *Richard III*, 64–5; *Macbeth*, 64, 206–7; *Julius Caesar*, 65, 180
shame, as political-cultural weapon, 157–61
Shattuck, Judge D. O., 107
Shaw, Dr. Anna Howard, 360, 361, 363, 398
Shaw, Albert, 379, 393
Sherman, William Tecumseh, 5, 122–3, 207; defeated by Vigilance Committee and resigns as Major-General of State Militia, 135–6
Shinn, M. W., 334, 335
Shinn, Charles Howard, 87
Ship Owner's Association, 306
Short Hairs, 196–7
Showalter, Daniel, 83
significance, statistical, 423
silurian, as political label, 372
Skocpol, Theda, 13
Skowronek, Stephen, 340
slavery, 171; Republican and Douglas Democratic positions on, 172; and republicanism, 184; *see also* race and racism
Sloat, John D., 1
Small, Albion, 349, 352
Smith, Caleb B., 81
Smith, Mary Roberts, 350, 362

social class, categorizations of, 55; in Vigilance Committee of 1856, 94–6; in third party system, 230–6; and registered voters, 426

social class, formation, and working class, 50–1, 222, 251–2; and middle class, 51–2; and capitalist or upper class, 52–3, 308, 378; and Gold Rush migration, 53–5; and identities, 54, 167; and language, 55; and privilege, 78; and party realignment of 1859–60, 182–3; and republicanism, 55–8; thwarted by ideology of mutualism, 129; and political discourse, 58, 282–6; in Vigilance Committees, 94–6, 167; and mass communication, 236–7; and working–class voting bloc, 253, 260–3, 383; and women, 358–9

Social Control (1901), by E. A. Ross, 350–1

social groups, and consciousness, 320; theory of, 10; as source of political action, 11; formation of, 14; methods of analyzing, 33, 36–7; and political mobilization, 84, 321, 390–1; and political discourse, 246; institutionalization of identities, 299, 319–26; as combination of institutional resources, 320; and newspapers, 319; and political entrepreneurship, 338; and progressivism, 406–7; *see also* social-group paradigm, social class, ethnicity, gender

social-group paradigm, defined, 13; and American scholarship, 25; and Progressive Era, 288; and social scientists, 348–9; and the state, 351

social settlements, *see* San Francisco Settlement

socialism, 357, 359

sociology, of state and society, 349–52

Solomons, Selina, 361, 362

South Park Settlement, *see* San Francisco Settlement

Southern Pacific Railroad (SP), 288, 297, 300, 350, 356, 370–1, 373–4, 375, 395–6

SP, *see* Southern Pacific Railroad

Spanish-American War, 382

special assessments, 365

Spreckels, Claus, 307, 317

Spring Valley Water Company, 257, 274, 375, 396

Spritualism, and women in the public sphere, 209–13

St. Ignatius College, 378

Stanford, Leland, 172, 187, 253

Stanford University, courses and instruction at, 351–2

state, in theory and method, 25–6

statistical methods, 419–21, 423–4

status, *see* social class

Stead, William, 375

Stetson, Charlotte Perkins, *see* Gilman, Charlotte Perkins Stetson

Story, C. R., 323

Stowe, Marietta B., 328, 329, 331

strikes and boycotts, assessments 304; Typographical Union, 304–5; streetcarmen, 305–6, 334; American Railway Union, 1894, 370, 375; waterfront, 1901, 403; *see also* trade unions

Stuart, James, 106; confession of, 109–11

suburbs, 297, 374, 381, 398

suffrage, *see* elective franchise, woman suffrage

Sullivan, James "Yankee," 89; confession and suicide of, 123–5

Sullivan, William, 325

Sunderson, G., 323

Sunset district, 298

Supervisors, mode of election, 389

Sutro Gardens and Baths, 374

Sutro, Adolph, 323, 363, 370, 373–7

Taylor, Graham, 349

teaching and teachers, 332–6 *see also* Kate Kennedy

Teaford, Jon, 26

terror, and crime, 98, 101–4

Terry, David S., introduced, 44–5; opponent of Vigilantes, 135, 136–7, 157; leader of Chivalry Democrats and duel with Broderick, 177–8; in Archy Lee case, 186–7

Thernstrom, Stephan, 34, 48

Thomas, W. I., 349

Tocqueville, Alexis de, on interests and individualism, 7–8; on public sphere, 16–17

trade unions, during Civil War, 198–9; Eight-Hour movement, 198; Industrial League, 200; postwar, 215; white label (anti-Chinese) movement, 304; women in, 329–30; lose strength in 1890s, 371; and Union Labor party, 403–5; *see also* Federated Trades Council, Building Trades Council, San Francisco Labor Assembly

Trades Assembly, 303

Turner, Frederick Jackson, 78, 87, 410

Typographical Union, 304

Union Square, 382

Union Labor party (ULP), 403–4, 408, 414

unions, labor, *see* trade unions
United Labor party, 334
utilities, 298, 393, 396

Vigilance Committee of 1851, introduced, 88; social composition of, 92–3; interpretations of, 90–2
Vigilance Committee of 1856, introduced, 88–9; age and, 96; applications to membership in, 94; course of, 130–7; disbandment of, 161–2; enrollment patterns, 132–5, 157; ethnic conflict and, 97; families, 150–2; iconography of, 145–8; Irish and, 97; masculinity, 150; social composition of, 92–7; interpretations of, 90–2; legitimacy of, 131, 138; legacy of in Progressive Era, 405; *see also* ballot box, violence, terror; People's party
Vigilante-People's regime, 128, *see also* People's party
Vincent, George, 352
violence, as communication, 98–9, 104–5; in strikes, 305, 370; *see also* duelling, terror, riots, executions
virtue, civic, 6–8; and Romantic republicanism, 79; and honor, 81; and legitimacy, 85; in discourse of Workingmen's Party of California, 270–1; meaning of, in Progressive Era, 404–5
voluntary associations, women's, 332; men's 367–8
voting, experience of, 73–7; levels of turnout, 30, 231, 399; violence of, 75; *see also* electorate; electoral fraud; election law

Walker, William, 80
Ward, Lester Frank, 351
Warner, Sam Bass, Jr., 24
Warner, Amos G., 349, 350, 352
Washburn, Charles A., 81
Washington, Benjamin F., 81
WCTU, *see* Women's Christian Temperence Union
Weinstein, James, 12
Welles, Orson, 313
Wellock, William, 267, 271, 277
Westbrook, Robert, 13

Whig party, original organization of in San Francisco, 68
Whitaker, S., 109–11
Wiebe, Robert, 336
Wigmore, John Henry, 324, 340, 378
Wilkes, George, 63
Willard, Frances, 331, 414
Williams, R. Hal, 300
Williams, Mary F., 90
Williams, T. T., 372
Wilson, Woodrow, 345, 383
Winkle, Kenneth J., 34
woman suffrage, 346, 398–401, 404
Woman's Congresses, 357, 359–62, 399–400, 402
women's rights movement, early, 209–14; and suffrage expansion, 214
Women's Christian Temperance Union (WCTU), 331, 399
women, as vestal virgins in party politics, 61; and Vigilance Committee of 1856, 154; politicization of, 209–15, 327–9; working-class, 329, 358; Woman's Column, in *Call*, 330–1
Woodhull, Victoria, 215
Woods, Robert, 289
Woodworth, F. A., 166
working class, *see* social class, formation
workingman, term defined, 270
Workingmen's Party of California, organization of, 267–8; and labor reublicanism, 242–4; leadership, background of, 273 n81; aftermath of 321; and social identity, 409
Workingmen's Trade and Labor Union, 264
Workingmen's Party of the United States (WPUS), 267
WPC, *see* Workingmen's Party of California

Yearly, Clifton, 297
Yorke, Father Peter C., 324–6, 390–2, 395, 397
Young Men's Democratic League, 340, 343, 370
Young America movement, 49, 174

Zueblin, Charles, 349

Learning Resources
Centre